Ōoku

⊕ THE INNER CHAMBERS

by **Fumi Yoshinaga**

VOL. **15**

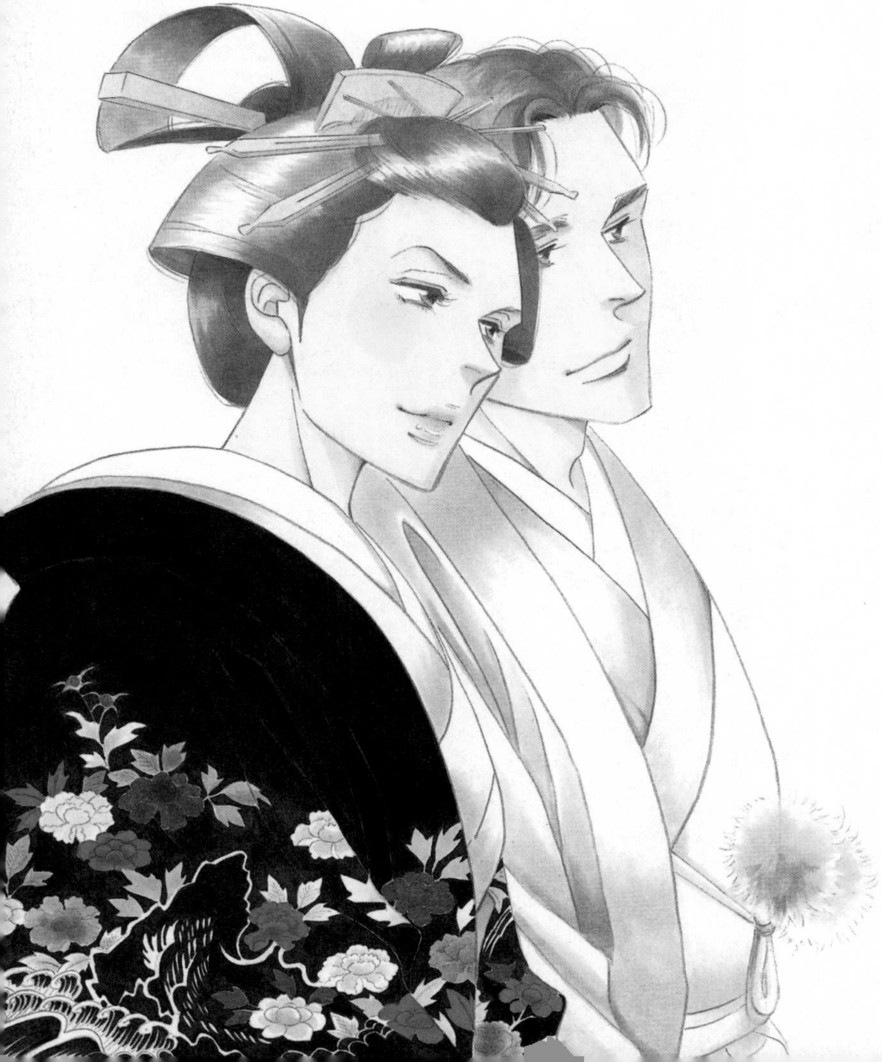

TABLE *of* CONTENTS

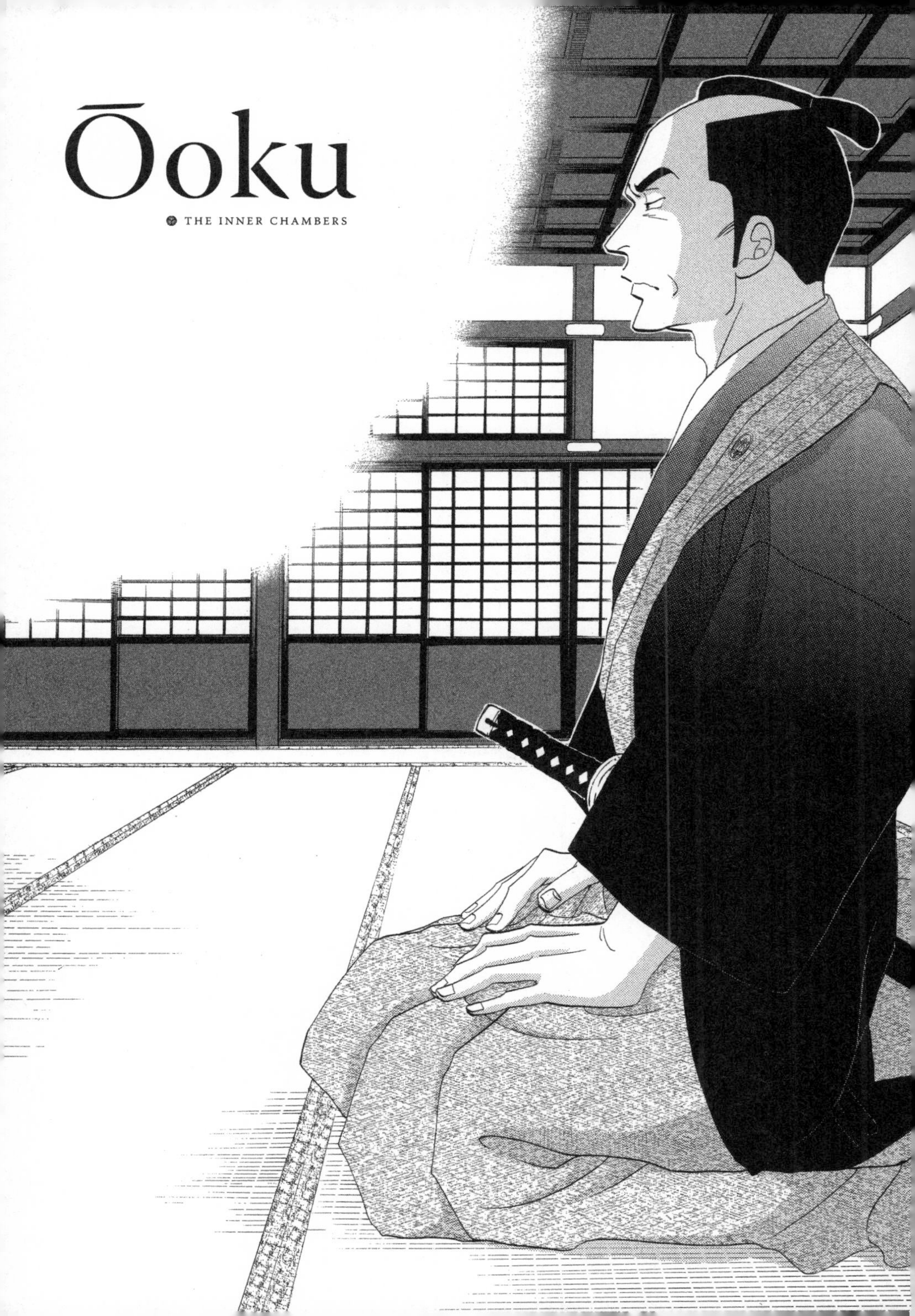
Ōoku
THE INNER CHAMBERS

THE INNER CHAMBERS

CAST *of* CHARACTERS

From the birth of the "inverse Inner Chambers" to its zenith, to eradicating the Redface Pox, and now to the end of Tokugawa rule...?

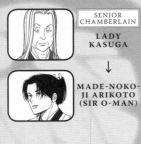

SENIOR CHAMBERLAIN

LADY KASUGA

↓

MADE-NOKOJI ARIKOTO (SIR O-MAN)

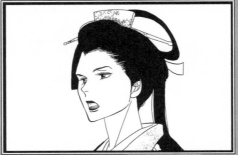

TOKUGAWA IEMITSU (III)

Impersonated her father, Iemitsu, at Lady Kasuga's urging after he died of the Redface Pox. Later became the first female shogun.

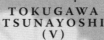

TOKUGAWA TSUNAYOSHI (V)

TOKUGAWA TSUNASHIGE

TOKUGAWA IETSUNA (IV)

SENIOR CHAMBERLAIN

EMONNOSUKE

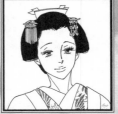

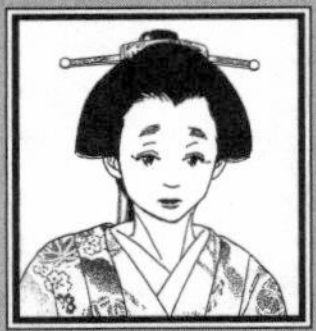

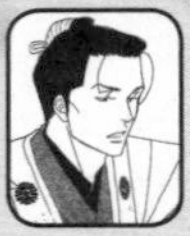

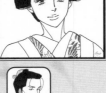

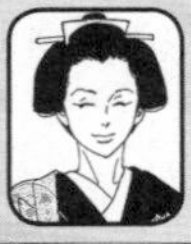

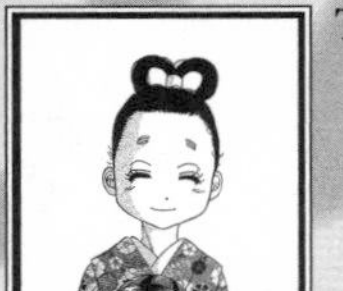

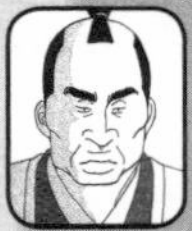

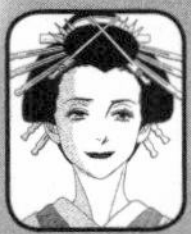

PRIVY COUNCILLOR

YANAGISAWA YOSHIYASU

TOKUGAWA IENOBU (VI)

TOKUGAWA IETSUGU (VII)

SENIOR CHAMBERLAIN

EJIMA

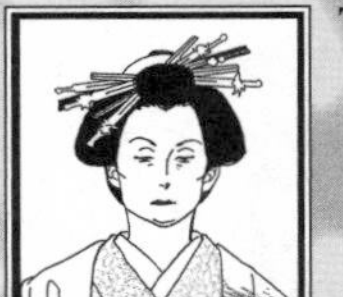

PRIVY COUNCILLOR

MANABE AKIFUSA

PRIVY COUNCILLOR

KANO HISAMICHI

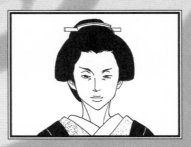

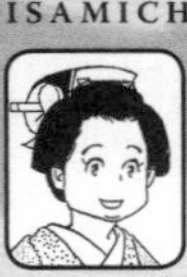

TOKUGAWA YOSHIMUNE (VIII)

Third daughter of Mitsusada, the second head of the Kii branch of the Tokugawa family. Acceded to domain lord and then, upon the death of Ietsugu, to shogun. Imposed and lived by a strict policy of austerity, dismissing large numbers of Inner Chambers courtiers and pursuing policies designed to increase income to the treasury.

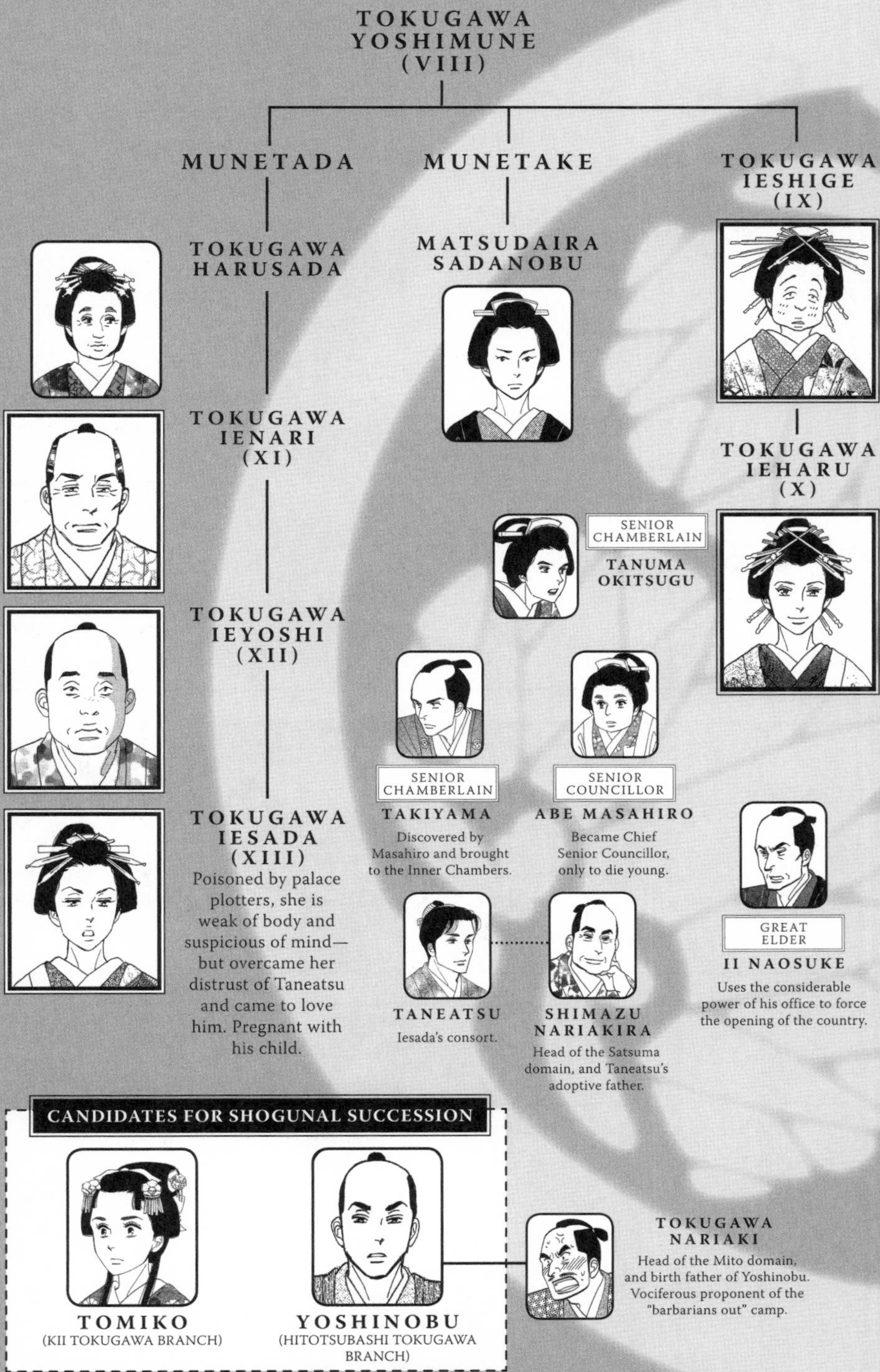
TOKUGAWA YOSHIMUNE (VIII)
MUNETADA
MUNETAKE
TOKUGAWA IESHIGE (IX)
TOKUGAWA HARUSADA
MATSUDAIRA SADANOBU
TOKUGAWA IENARI (XI)
TOKUGAWA IEHARU (X)
SENIOR CHAMBERLAIN
TANUMA OKITSUGU
TOKUGAWA IEYOSHI (XII)
SENIOR CHAMBERLAIN
TAKIYAMA
Discovered by Masahiro and brought to the Inner Chambers.
SENIOR COUNCILLOR
ABE MASAHIRO
Became Chief Senior Councillor, only to die young.
TOKUGAWA IESADA (XIII)
Poisoned by palace plotters, she is weak of body and suspicious of mind—but overcame her distrust of Taneatsu and came to love him. Pregnant with his child.
GREAT ELDER
II NAOSUKE
Uses the considerable power of his office to force the opening of the country.
TANEATSU
Iesada's consort.
SHIMAZU NARIAKIRA
Head of the Satsuma domain, and Taneatsu's adoptive father.
CANDIDATES FOR SHOGUNAL SUCCESSION
TOMIKO
(KII TOKUGAWA BRANCH)
YOSHINOBU
(HITOTSUBASHI TOKUGAWA BRANCH)
TOKUGAWA NARIAKI
Head of the Mito domain, and birth father of Yoshinobu. Vociferous proponent of the "barbarians out" camp.

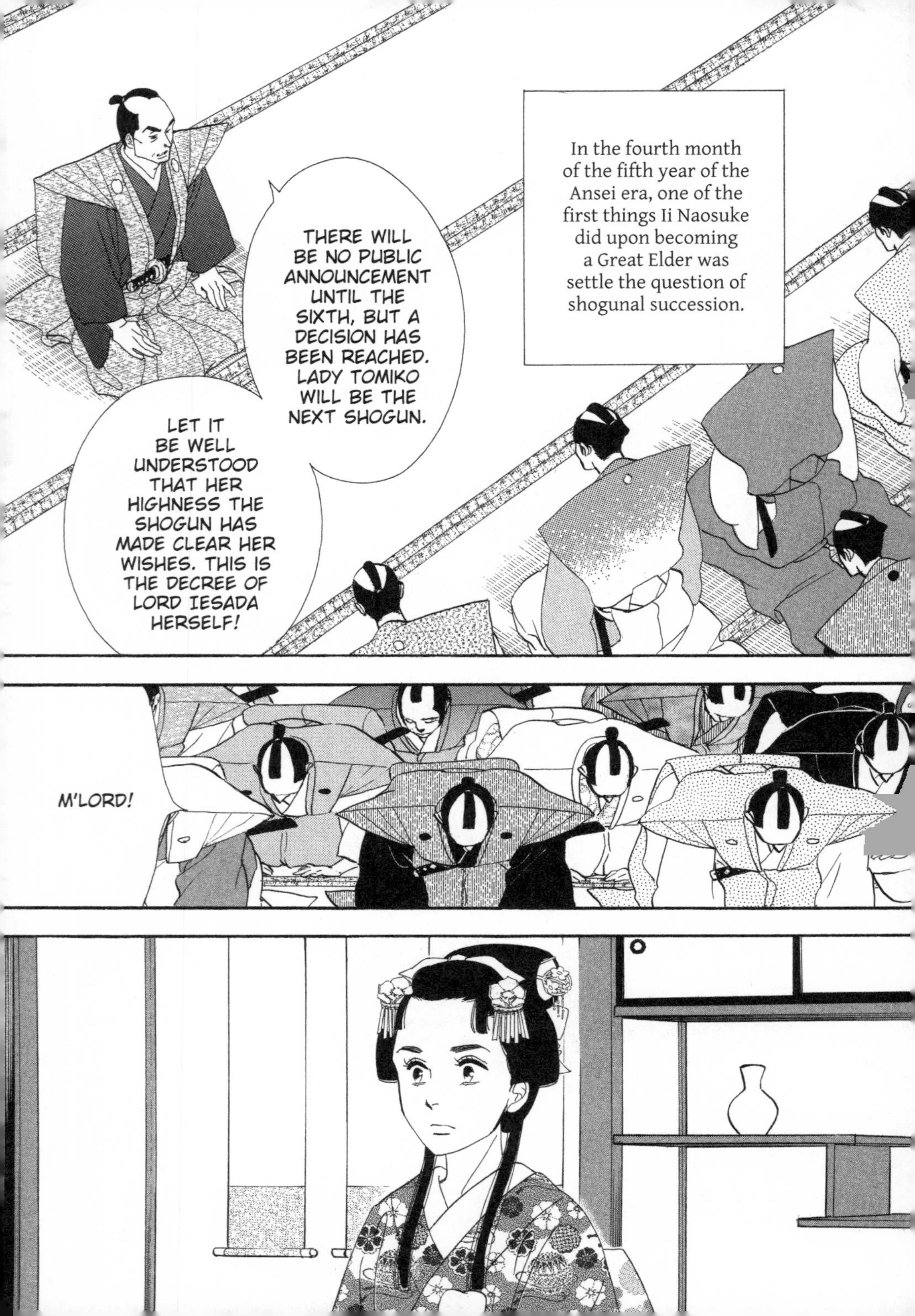
In the fourth month of the fifth year of the Ansei era, one of the first things Ii Naosuke did upon becoming a Great Elder was settle the question of shogunal succession.
THERE WILL BE NO PUBLIC ANNOUNCEMENT UNTIL THE SIXTH, BUT A DECISION HAS BEEN REACHED. LADY TOMIKO WILL BE THE NEXT SHOGUN.
LET IT BE WELL UNDERSTOOD THAT HER HIGHNESS THE SHOGUN HAS MADE CLEAR HER WISHES. THIS IS THE DECREE OF LORD IESADA HERSELF!
M'LORD!

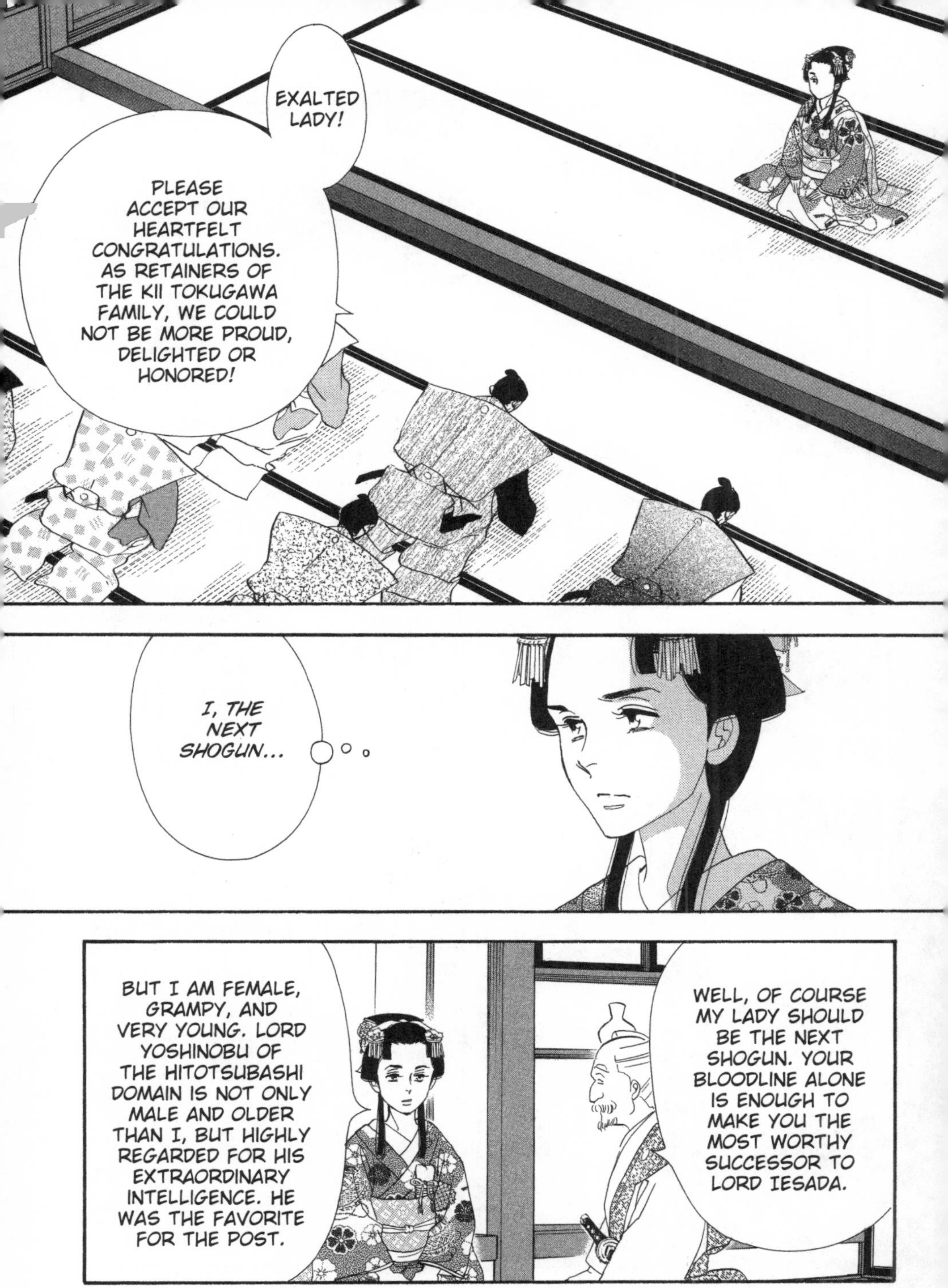
EXALTED LADY!
PLEASE ACCEPT OUR HEARTFELT CONGRATULATIONS. AS RETAINERS OF THE KII TOKUGAWA FAMILY, WE COULD NOT BE MORE PROUD, DELIGHTED OR HONORED!
I, THE NEXT SHOGUN...
WELL, OF COURSE MY LADY SHOULD BE THE NEXT SHOGUN. YOUR BLOODLINE ALONE IS ENOUGH TO MAKE YOU THE MOST WORTHY SUCCESSOR TO LORD IESADA.
BUT I AM FEMALE, GRAMPY, AND VERY YOUNG. LORD YOSHINOBU OF THE HITOTSUBASHI DOMAIN IS NOT ONLY MALE AND OLDER THAN I, BUT HIGHLY REGARDED FOR HIS EXTRAORDINARY INTELLIGENCE. HE WAS THE FAVORITE FOR THE POST.

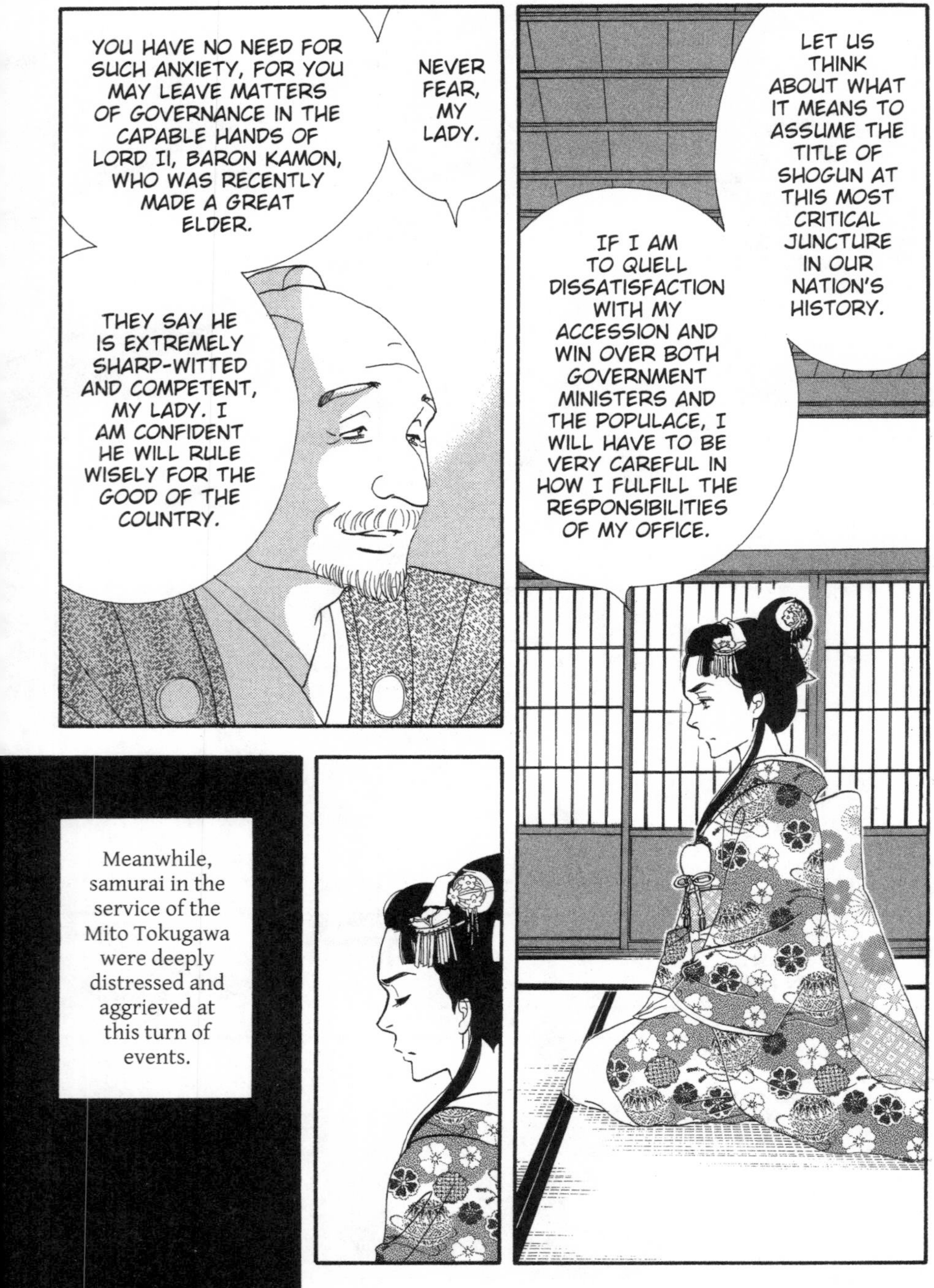
LET US THINK ABOUT WHAT IT MEANS TO ASSUME THE TITLE OF SHOGUN AT THIS MOST CRITICAL JUNCTURE IN OUR NATION'S HISTORY.
IF I AM TO QUELL DISSATISFACTION WITH MY ACCESSION AND WIN OVER BOTH GOVERNMENT MINISTERS AND THE POPULACE, I WILL HAVE TO BE VERY CAREFUL IN HOW I FULFILL THE RESPONSIBILITIES OF MY OFFICE.
NEVER FEAR, MY LADY.
YOU HAVE NO NEED FOR SUCH ANXIETY, FOR YOU MAY LEAVE MATTERS OF GOVERNANCE IN THE CAPABLE HANDS OF LORD II, BARON KAMON, WHO WAS RECENTLY MADE A GREAT ELDER.
THEY SAY HE IS EXTREMELY SHARP-WITTED AND COMPETENT, MY LADY. I AM CONFIDENT HE WILL RULE WISELY FOR THE GOOD OF THE COUNTRY.
Meanwhile, samurai in the service of the Mito Tokugawa were deeply distressed and aggrieved at this turn of events.

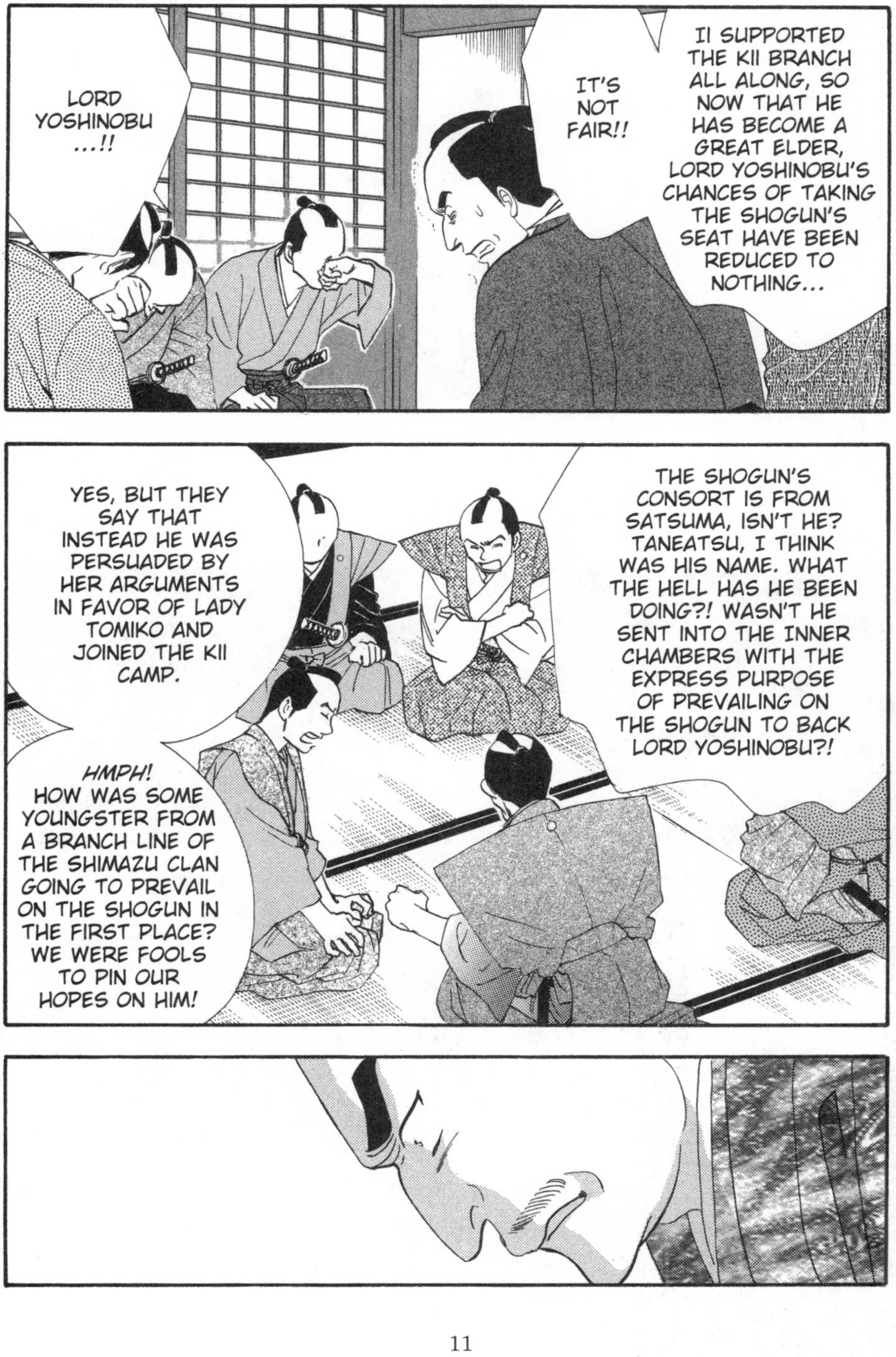
II SUPPORTED THE KII BRANCH ALL ALONG, SO NOW THAT HE HAS BECOME A GREAT ELDER, LORD YOSHINOBU'S CHANCES OF TAKING THE SHOGUN'S SEAT HAVE BEEN REDUCED TO NOTHING...
IT'S NOT FAIR!!
LORD YOSHINOBU ...!!
THE SHOGUN'S CONSORT IS FROM SATSUMA, ISN'T HE? TANEATSU, I THINK WAS HIS NAME. WHAT THE HELL HAS HE BEEN DOING?! WASN'T HE SENT INTO THE INNER CHAMBERS WITH THE EXPRESS PURPOSE OF PREVAILING ON THE SHOGUN TO BACK LORD YOSHINOBU?!
YES, BUT THEY SAY THAT INSTEAD HE WAS PERSUADED BY HER ARGUMENTS IN FAVOR OF LADY TOMIKO AND JOINED THE KII CAMP.
HMPH! HOW WAS SOME YOUNGSTER FROM A BRANCH LINE OF THE SHIMAZU CLAN GOING TO PREVAIL ON THE SHOGUN IN THE FIRST PLACE? WE WERE FOOLS TO PIN OUR HOPES ON HIM!

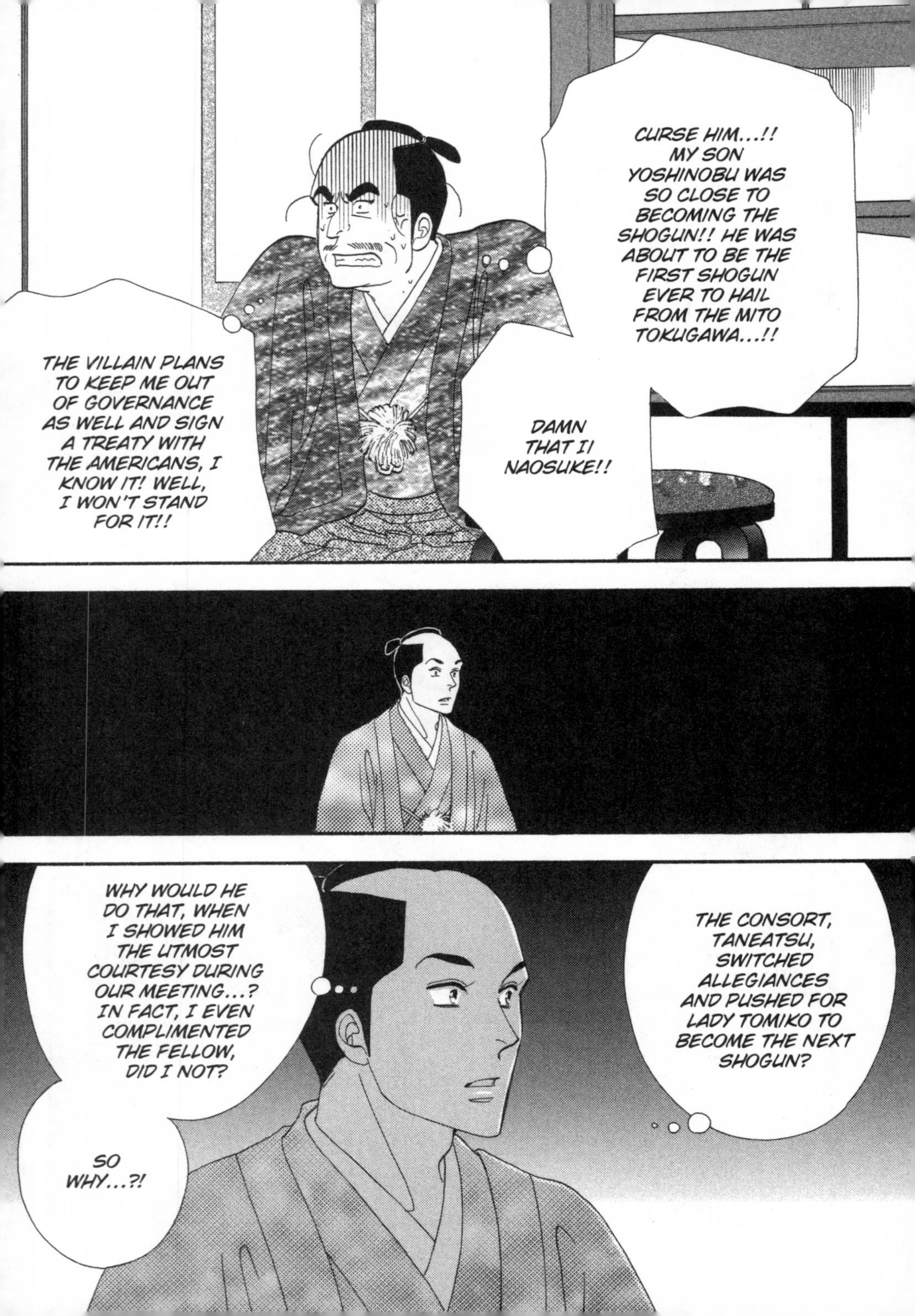
CURSE HIM...!! MY SON YOSHINOBU WAS SO CLOSE TO BECOMING THE SHOGUN!! HE WAS ABOUT TO BE THE FIRST SHOGUN EVER TO HAIL FROM THE MITO TOKUGAWA...!!
DAMN THAT II NAOSUKE!!
THE VILLAIN PLANS TO KEEP ME OUT OF GOVERNANCE AS WELL AND SIGN A TREATY WITH THE AMERICANS, I KNOW IT! WELL, I WON'T STAND FOR IT!!
THE CONSORT, TANEATSU, SWITCHED ALLEGIANCES AND PUSHED FOR LADY TOMIKO TO BECOME THE NEXT SHOGUN?
WHY WOULD HE DO THAT, WHEN I SHOWED HIM THE UTMOST COURTESY DURING OUR MEETING...? IN FACT, I EVEN COMPLIMENTED THE FELLOW, DID I NOT?
SO WHY...?!

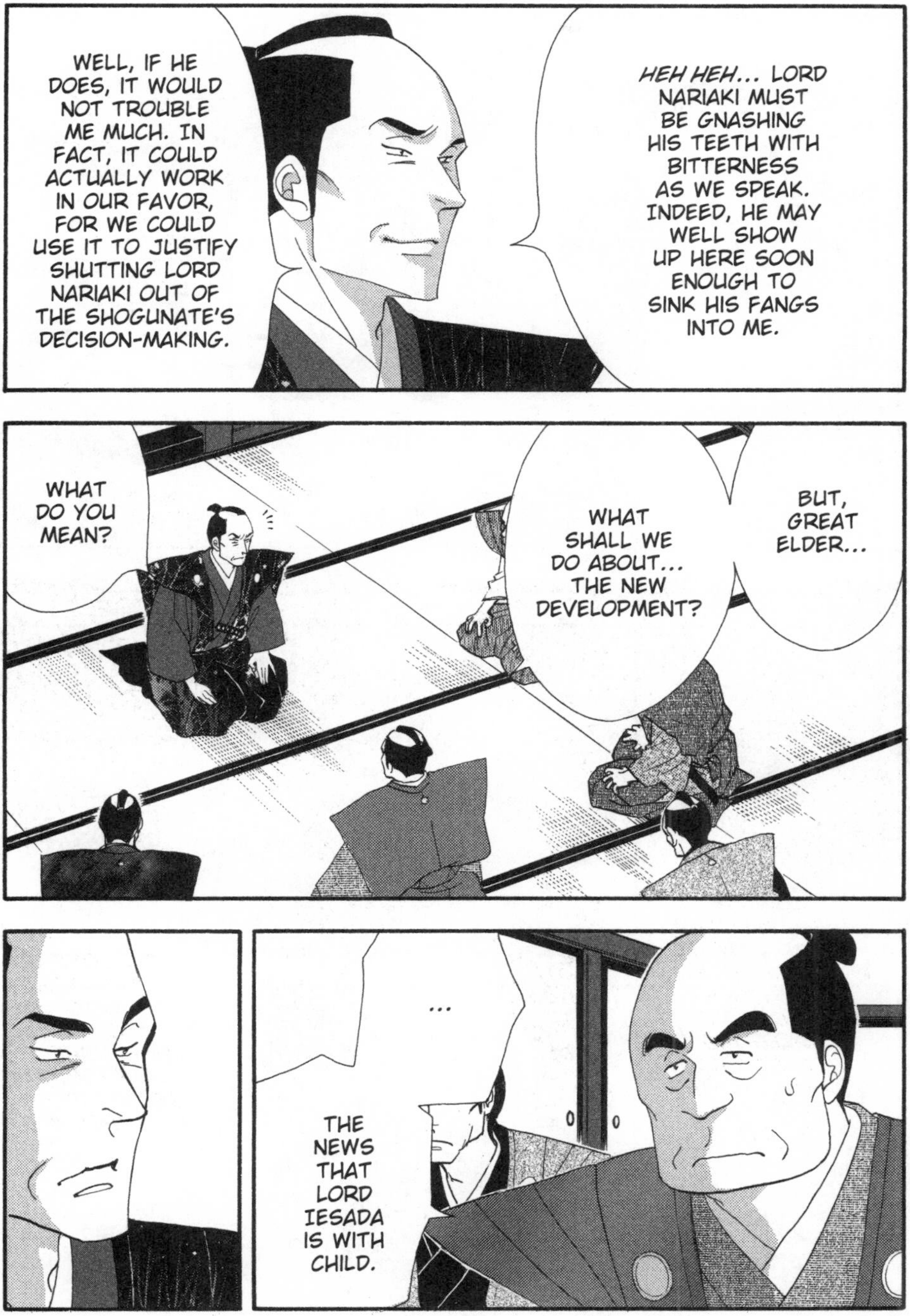
HEH HEH... LORD NARIAKI MUST BE GNASHING HIS TEETH WITH BITTERNESS AS WE SPEAK. INDEED, HE MAY WELL SHOW UP HERE SOON ENOUGH TO SINK HIS FANGS INTO ME.
WELL, IF HE DOES, IT WOULD NOT TROUBLE ME MUCH. IN FACT, IT COULD ACTUALLY WORK IN OUR FAVOR, FOR WE COULD USE IT TO JUSTIFY SHUTTING LORD NARIAKI OUT OF THE SHOGUNATE'S DECISION-MAKING.
BUT, GREAT ELDER...
WHAT SHALL WE DO ABOUT... THE NEW DEVELOPMENT?
WHAT DO YOU MEAN?
...
THE NEWS THAT LORD IESADA IS WITH CHILD.

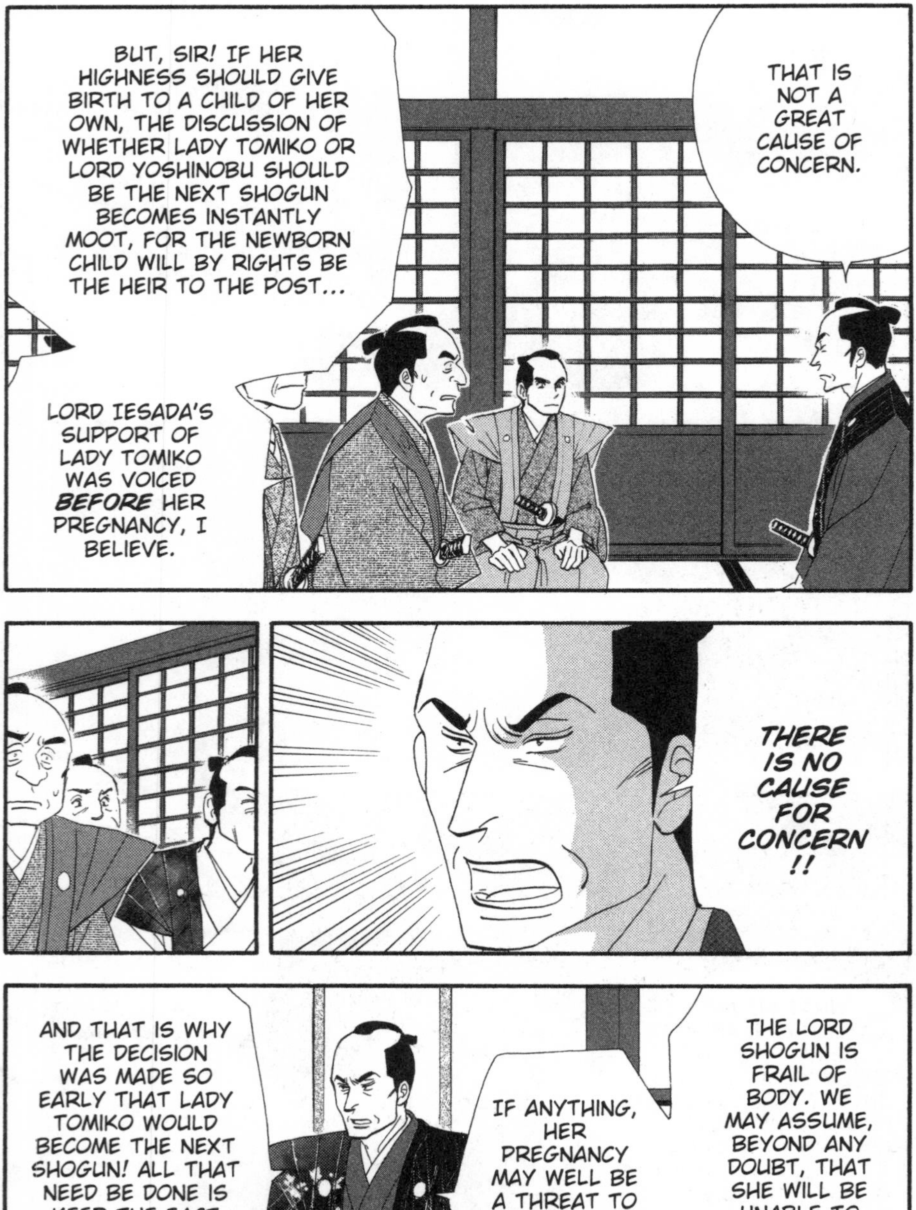
THAT IS NOT A GREAT CAUSE OF CONCERN.
BUT, SIR! IF HER HIGHNESS SHOULD GIVE BIRTH TO A CHILD OF HER OWN, THE DISCUSSION OF WHETHER LADY TOMIKO OR LORD YOSHINOBU SHOULD BE THE NEXT SHOGUN BECOMES INSTANTLY MOOT, FOR THE NEWBORN CHILD WILL BY RIGHTS BE THE HEIR TO THE POST...
LORD IESADA'S SUPPORT OF LADY TOMIKO WAS VOICED **BEFORE** HER PREGNANCY, I BELIEVE.
THERE IS NO CAUSE FOR CONCERN!!
THE LORD SHOGUN IS FRAIL OF BODY. WE MAY ASSUME, BEYOND ANY DOUBT, THAT SHE WILL BE UNABLE TO GIVE BIRTH TO A HEALTHY CHILD!
IF ANYTHING, HER PREGNANCY MAY WELL BE A THREAT TO HER HEALTH, INDEED TO HER VERY LIFE.
AND THAT IS WHY THE DECISION WAS MADE SO EARLY THAT LADY TOMIKO WOULD BECOME THE NEXT SHOGUN! ALL THAT NEED BE DONE IS KEEP THE FACT OF LORD IESADA'S PREGNANCY A SECRET!

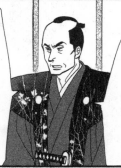

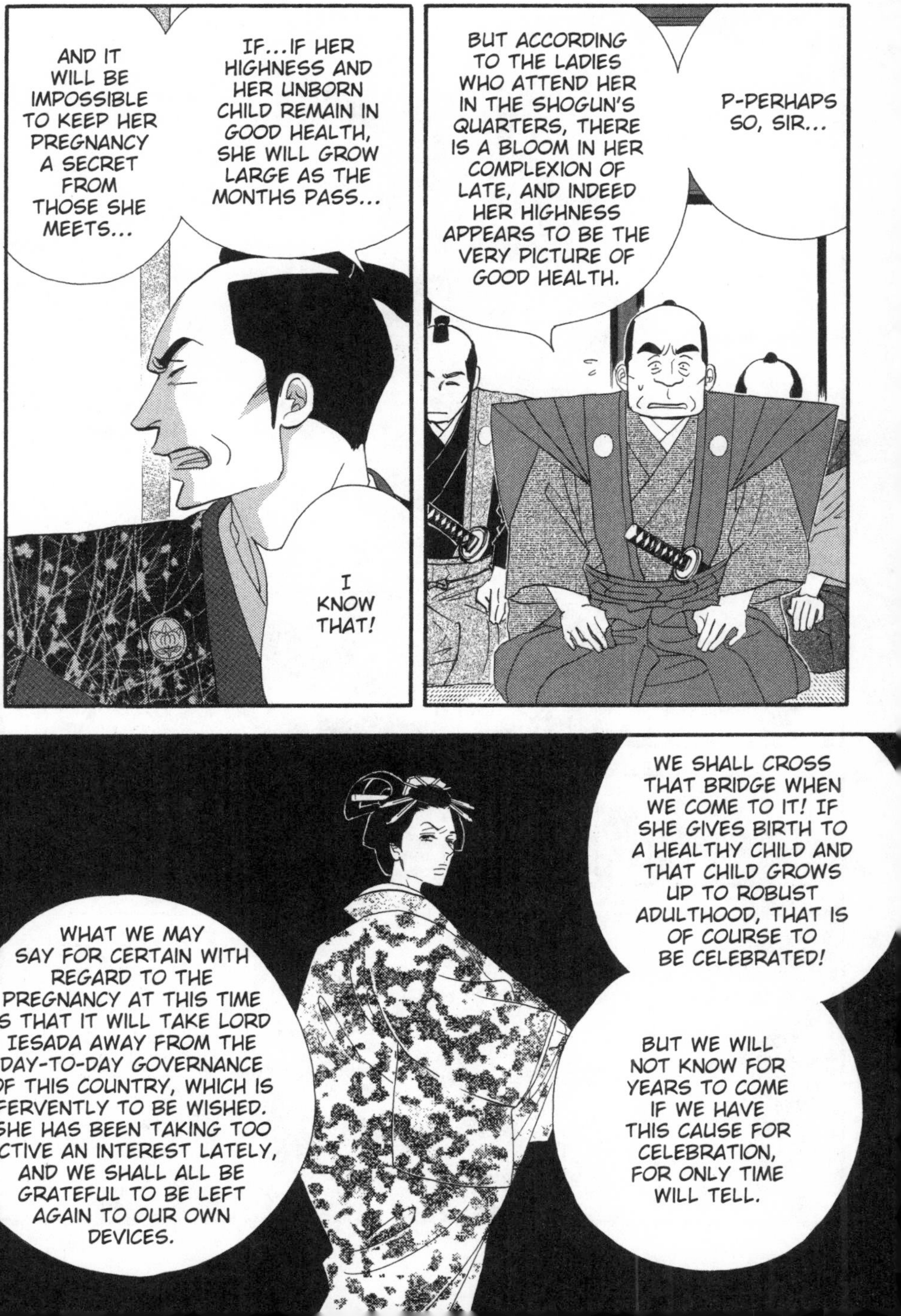
BUT ACCORDING TO THE LADIES WHO ATTEND HER IN THE SHOGUN'S QUARTERS, THERE IS A BLOOM IN HER COMPLEXION OF LATE, AND INDEED HER HIGHNESS APPEARS TO BE THE VERY PICTURE OF GOOD HEALTH.
P-PERHAPS SO, SIR...
IF...IF HER HIGHNESS AND HER UNBORN CHILD REMAIN IN GOOD HEALTH, SHE WILL GROW LARGE AS THE MONTHS PASS...
AND IT WILL BE IMPOSSIBLE TO KEEP HER PREGNANCY A SECRET FROM THOSE SHE MEETS...
I KNOW THAT!
WE SHALL CROSS THAT BRIDGE WHEN WE COME TO IT! IF SHE GIVES BIRTH TO A HEALTHY CHILD AND THAT CHILD GROWS UP TO ROBUST ADULTHOOD, THAT IS OF COURSE TO BE CELEBRATED!
BUT WE WILL NOT KNOW FOR YEARS TO COME IF WE HAVE THIS CAUSE FOR CELEBRATION, FOR ONLY TIME WILL TELL.
WHAT WE MAY SAY FOR CERTAIN WITH REGARD TO THE PREGNANCY AT THIS TIME IS THAT IT WILL TAKE LORD IESADA AWAY FROM THE DAY-TO-DAY GOVERNANCE OF THIS COUNTRY, WHICH IS FERVENTLY TO BE WISHED. SHE HAS BEEN TAKING TOO ACTIVE AN INTEREST LATELY, AND WE SHALL ALL BE GRATEFUL TO BE LEFT AGAIN TO OUR OWN DEVICES.

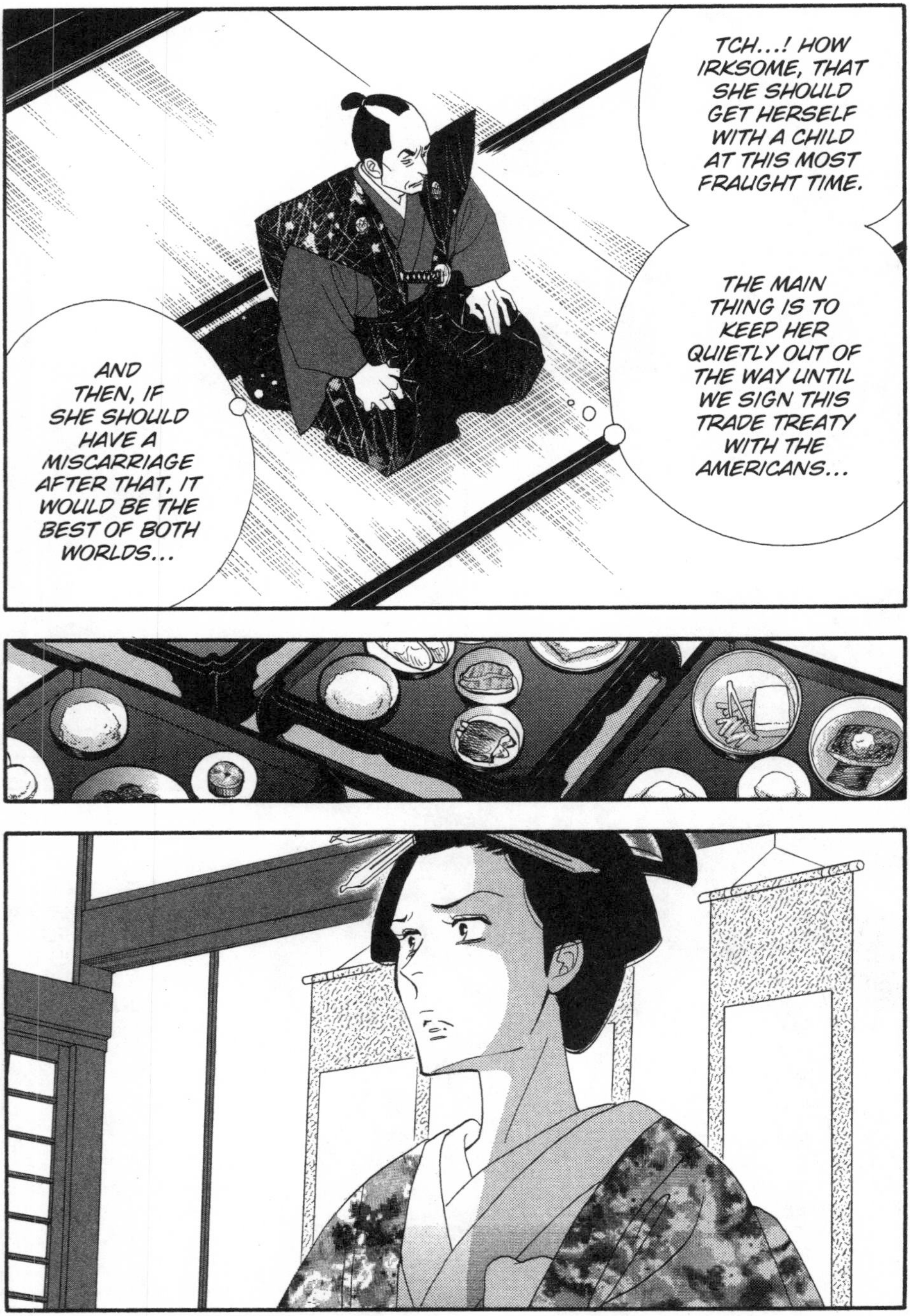
TCH...! HOW IRKSOME, THAT SHE SHOULD GET HERSELF WITH A CHILD AT THIS MOST FRAUGHT TIME.
THE MAIN THING IS TO KEEP HER QUIETLY OUT OF THE WAY UNTIL WE SIGN THIS TRADE TREATY WITH THE AMERICANS...
AND THEN, IF SHE SHOULD HAVE A MISCARRIAGE AFTER THAT, IT WOULD BE THE BEST OF BOTH WORLDS...

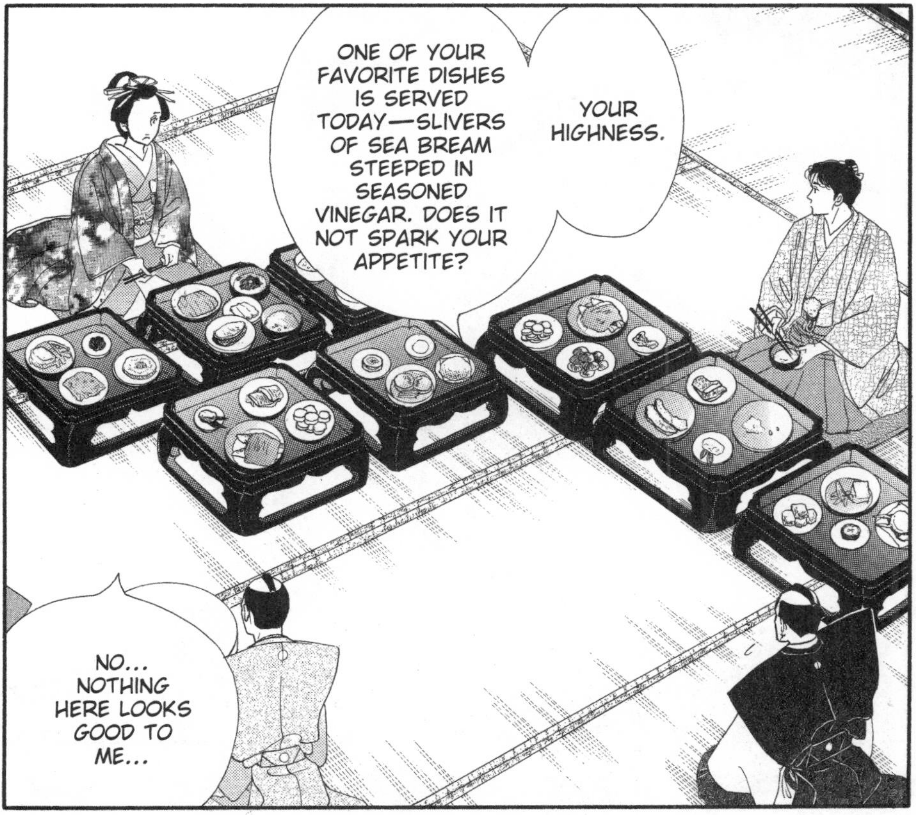
YOUR HIGHNESS.
ONE OF YOUR FAVORITE DISHES IS SERVED TODAY—SLIVERS OF SEA BREAM STEEPED IN SEASONED VINEGAR. DOES IT NOT SPARK YOUR APPETITE?
NO... NOTHING HERE LOOKS GOOD TO ME...

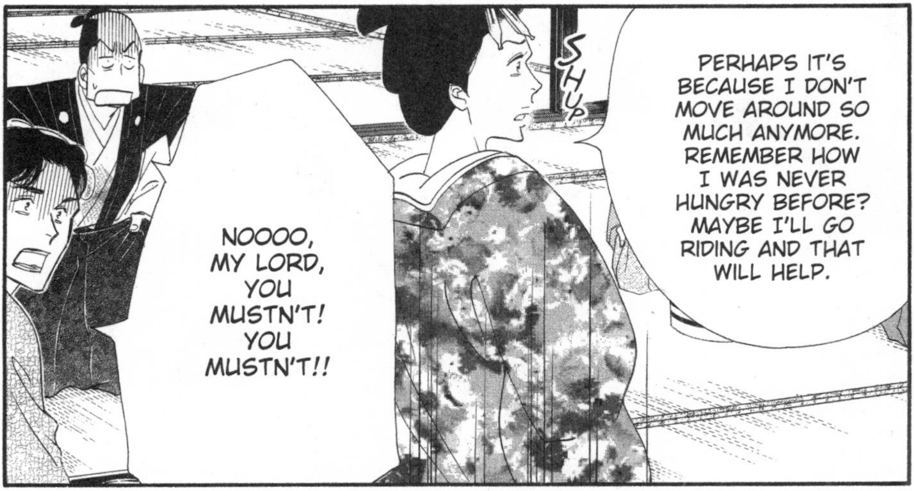
PERHAPS IT'S BECAUSE I DON'T MOVE AROUND SO MUCH ANYMORE. REMEMBER HOW I WAS NEVER HUNGRY BEFORE? MAYBE I'LL GO RIDING AND THAT WILL HELP.
SHUP
NOOOO, MY LORD, YOU MUSTN'T! YOU MUSTN'T!!

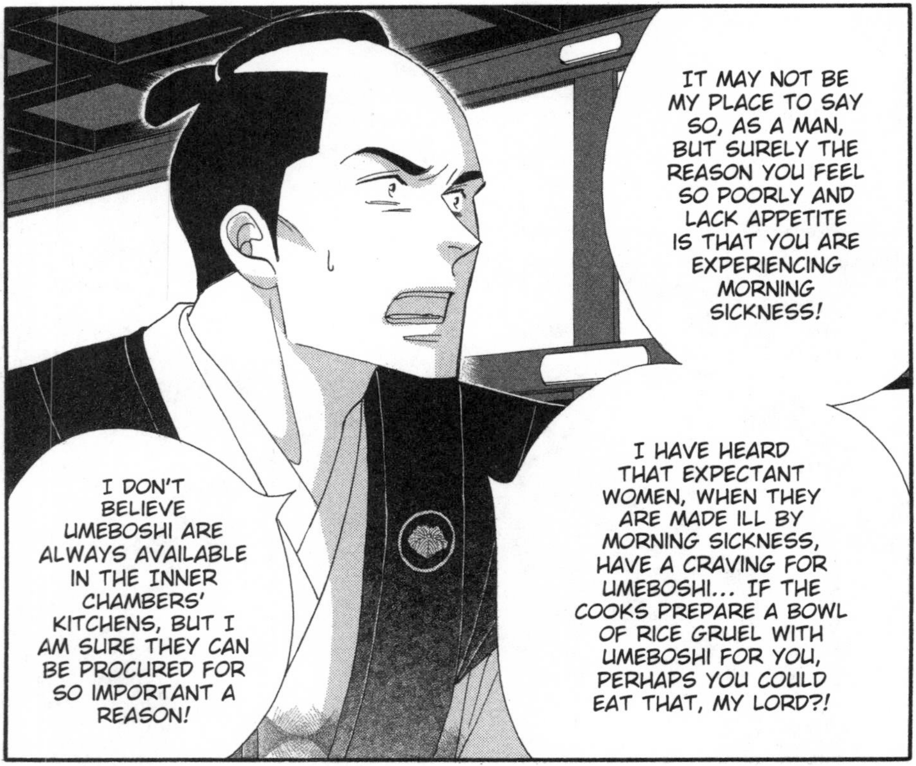
IT MAY NOT BE MY PLACE TO SAY SO, AS A MAN, BUT SURELY THE REASON YOU FEEL SO POORLY AND LACK APPETITE IS THAT YOU ARE EXPERIENCING MORNING SICKNESS!
I HAVE HEARD THAT EXPECTANT WOMEN, WHEN THEY ARE MADE ILL BY MORNING SICKNESS, HAVE A CRAVING FOR UMEBOSHI... IF THE COOKS PREPARE A BOWL OF RICE GRUEL WITH UMEBOSHI FOR YOU, PERHAPS YOU COULD EAT THAT, MY LORD?!
I DON'T BELIEVE UMEBOSHI ARE ALWAYS AVAILABLE IN THE INNER CHAMBERS' KITCHENS, BUT I AM SURE THEY CAN BE PROCURED FOR SO IMPORTANT A REASON!
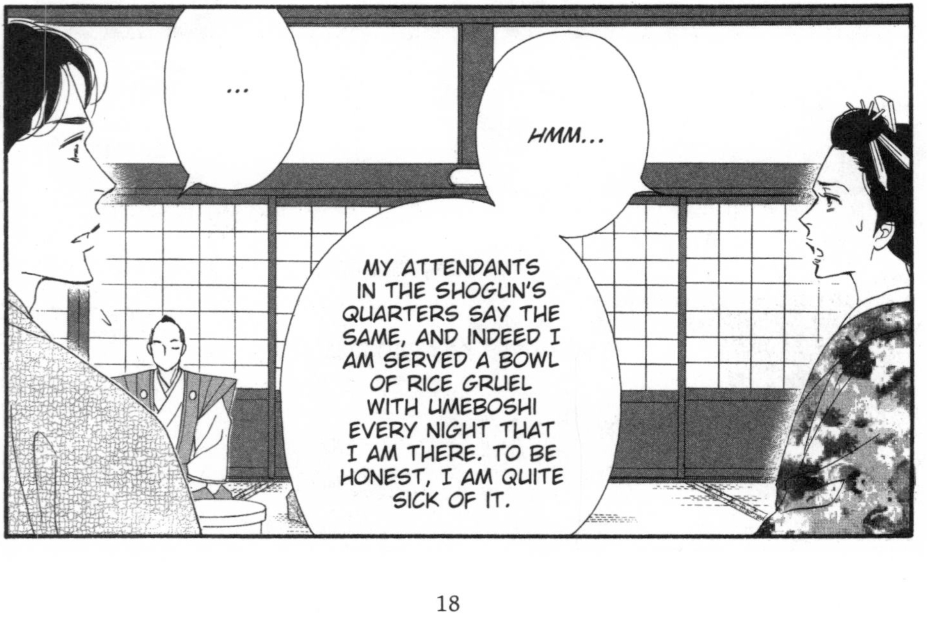
HMM...
MY ATTENDANTS IN THE SHOGUN'S QUARTERS SAY THE SAME, AND INDEED I AM SERVED A BOWL OF RICE GRUEL WITH UMEBOSHI EVERY NIGHT THAT I AM THERE. TO BE HONEST, I AM QUITE SICK OF IT.
...

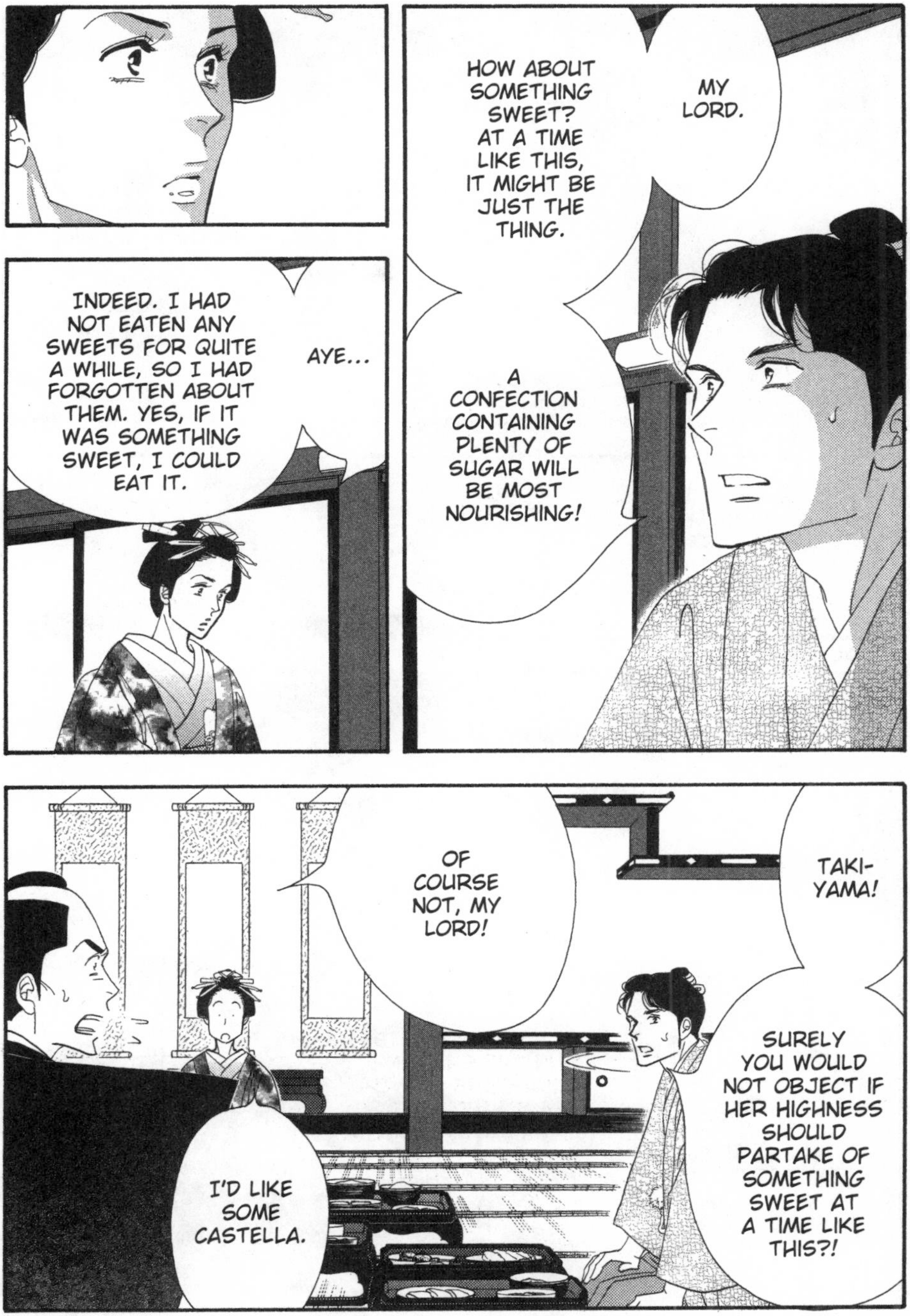
MY LORD.
HOW ABOUT SOMETHING SWEET? AT A TIME LIKE THIS, IT MIGHT BE JUST THE THING.
A CONFECTION CONTAINING PLENTY OF SUGAR WILL BE MOST NOURISHING!
AYE...
INDEED. I HAD NOT EATEN ANY SWEETS FOR QUITE A WHILE, SO I HAD FORGOTTEN ABOUT THEM. YES, IF IT WAS SOMETHING SWEET, I COULD EAT IT.
TAKI-YAMA!
SURELY YOU WOULD NOT OBJECT IF HER HIGHNESS SHOULD PARTAKE OF SOMETHING SWEET AT A TIME LIKE THIS?!
OF COURSE NOT, MY LORD!
I'D LIKE SOME CASTELLA.

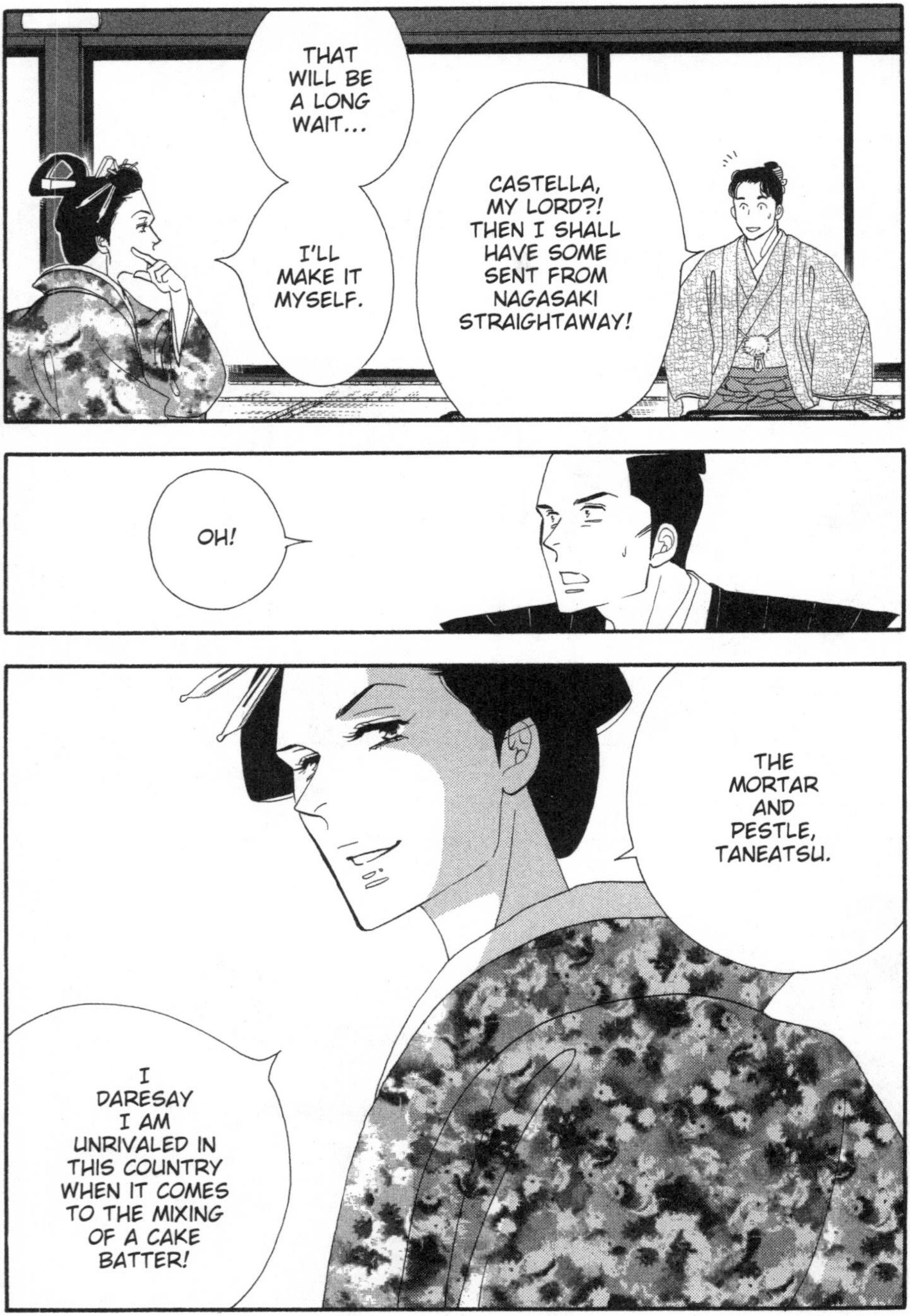
CASTELLA, MY LORD?! THEN I SHALL HAVE SOME SENT FROM NAGASAKI STRAIGHTAWAY!
THAT WILL BE A LONG WAIT...
I'LL MAKE IT MYSELF.
OH!
THE MORTAR AND PESTLE, TANEATSU.
I DARESAY I AM UNRIVALED IN THIS COUNTRY WHEN IT COMES TO THE MIXING OF A CAKE BATTER!

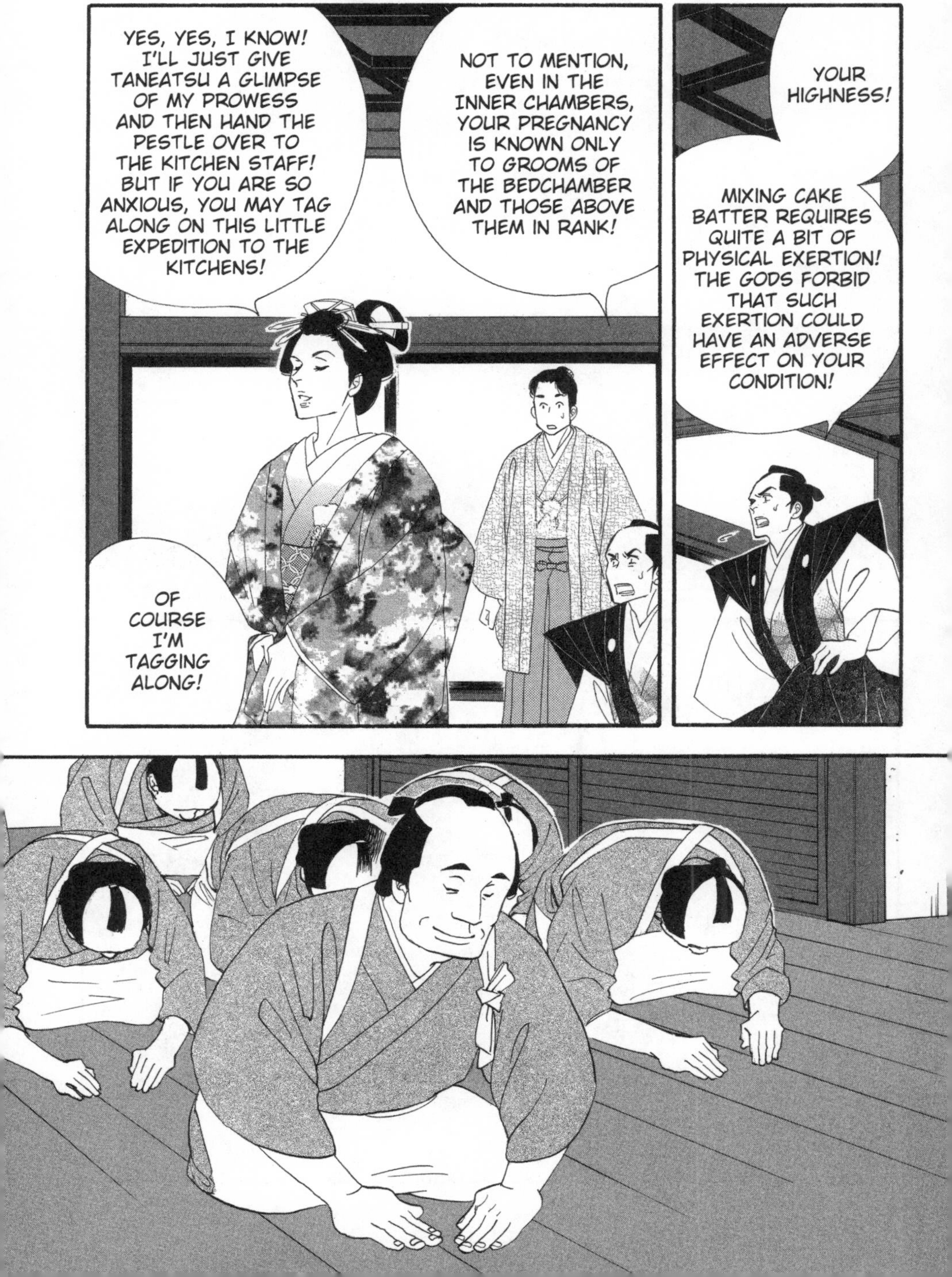
YOUR HIGHNESS!
MIXING CAKE BATTER REQUIRES QUITE A BIT OF PHYSICAL EXERTION! THE GODS FORBID THAT SUCH EXERTION COULD HAVE AN ADVERSE EFFECT ON YOUR CONDITION!
NOT TO MENTION, EVEN IN THE INNER CHAMBERS, YOUR PREGNANCY IS KNOWN ONLY TO GROOMS OF THE BEDCHAMBER AND THOSE ABOVE THEM IN RANK!
YES, YES, I KNOW! I'LL JUST GIVE TANEATSU A GLIMPSE OF MY PROWESS AND THEN HAND THE PESTLE OVER TO THE KITCHEN STAFF! BUT IF YOU ARE SO ANXIOUS, YOU MAY TAG ALONG ON THIS LITTLE EXPEDITION TO THE KITCHENS!
OF COURSE I'M TAGGING ALONG!

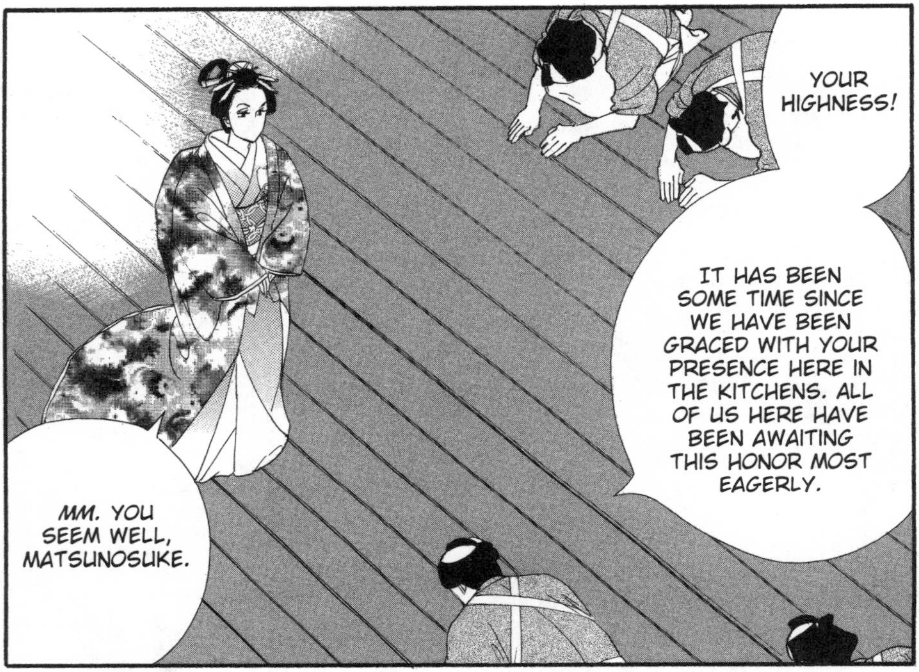
YOUR HIGHNESS!
IT HAS BEEN SOME TIME SINCE WE HAVE BEEN GRACED WITH YOUR PRESENCE HERE IN THE KITCHENS. ALL OF US HERE HAVE BEEN AWAITING THIS HONOR MOST EAGERLY.
MM. YOU SEEM WELL, MATSUNOSUKE.

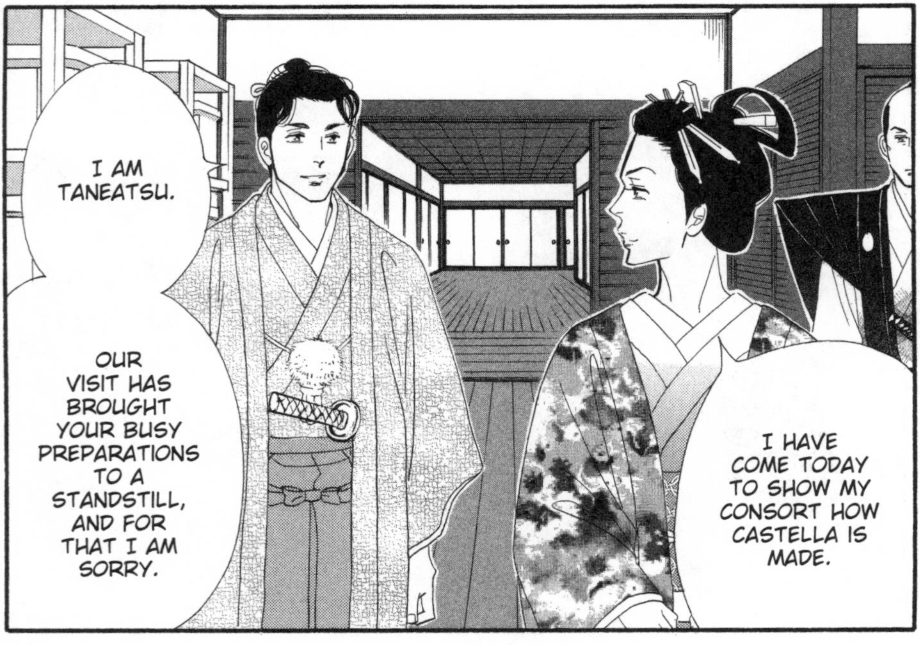
I HAVE COME TODAY TO SHOW MY CONSORT HOW CASTELLA IS MADE.
I AM TANEATSU.
OUR VISIT HAS BROUGHT YOUR BUSY PREPARATIONS TO A STANDSTILL, AND FOR THAT I AM SORRY.

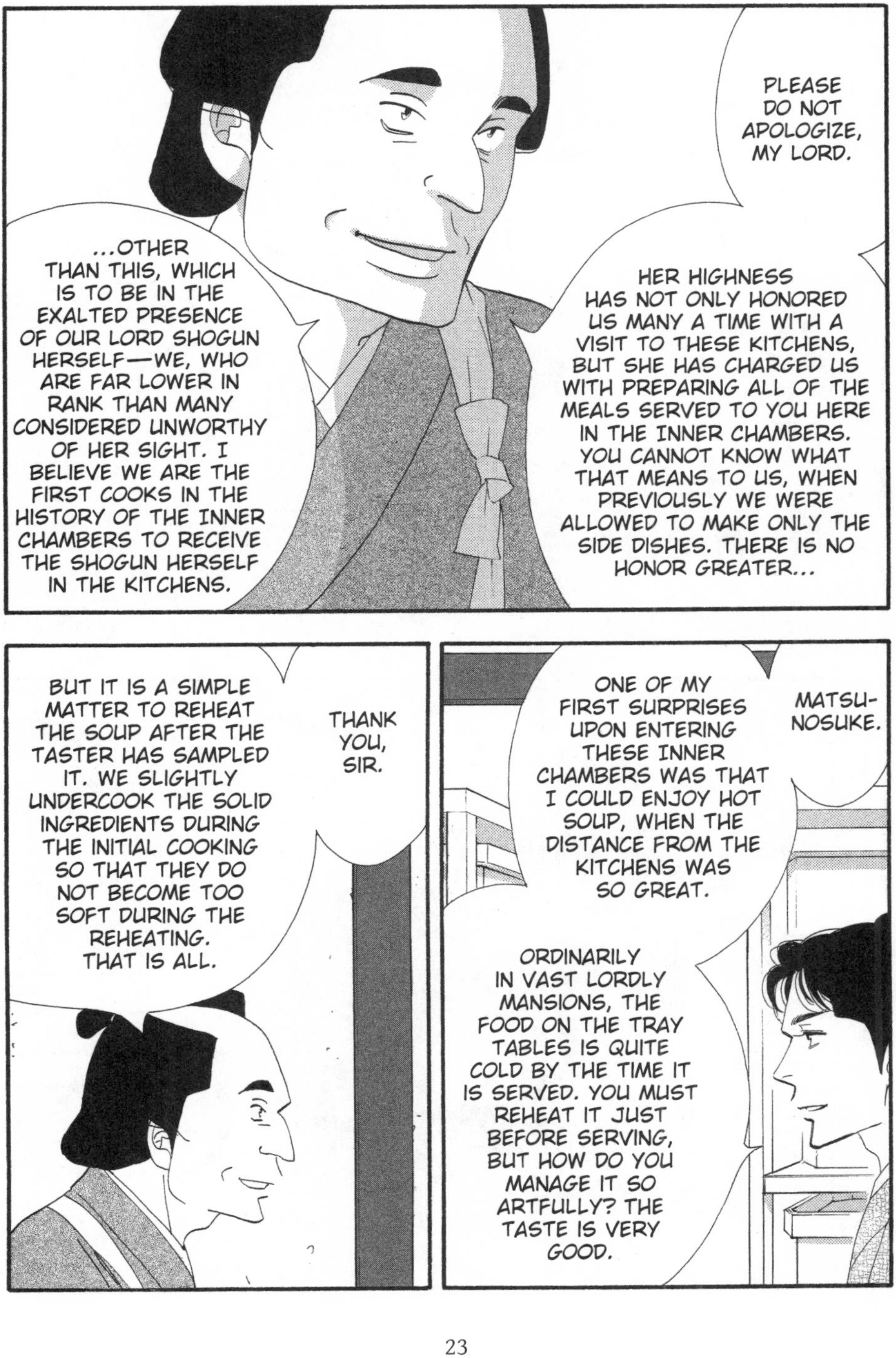
PLEASE DO NOT APOLOGIZE, MY LORD.
HER HIGHNESS HAS NOT ONLY HONORED US MANY A TIME WITH A VISIT TO THESE KITCHENS, BUT SHE HAS CHARGED US WITH PREPARING ALL OF THE MEALS SERVED TO YOU HERE IN THE INNER CHAMBERS. YOU CANNOT KNOW WHAT THAT MEANS TO US, WHEN PREVIOUSLY WE WERE ALLOWED TO MAKE ONLY THE SIDE DISHES. THERE IS NO HONOR GREATER...
...OTHER THAN THIS, WHICH IS TO BE IN THE EXALTED PRESENCE OF OUR LORD SHOGUN HERSELF—WE, WHO ARE FAR LOWER IN RANK THAN MANY CONSIDERED UNWORTHY OF HER SIGHT. I BELIEVE WE ARE THE FIRST COOKS IN THE HISTORY OF THE INNER CHAMBERS TO RECEIVE THE SHOGUN HERSELF IN THE KITCHENS.
MATSU-NOSUKE.
ONE OF MY FIRST SURPRISES UPON ENTERING THESE INNER CHAMBERS WAS THAT I COULD ENJOY HOT SOUP, WHEN THE DISTANCE FROM THE KITCHENS WAS SO GREAT.
ORDINARILY IN VAST LORDLY MANSIONS, THE FOOD ON THE TRAY TABLES IS QUITE COLD BY THE TIME IT IS SERVED. YOU MUST REHEAT IT JUST BEFORE SERVING, BUT HOW DO YOU MANAGE IT SO ARTFULLY? THE TASTE IS VERY GOOD.
THANK YOU, SIR.
BUT IT IS A SIMPLE MATTER TO REHEAT THE SOUP AFTER THE TASTER HAS SAMPLED IT. WE SLIGHTLY UNDERCOOK THE SOLID INGREDIENTS DURING THE INITIAL COOKING SO THAT THEY DO NOT BECOME TOO SOFT DURING THE REHEATING. THAT IS ALL.

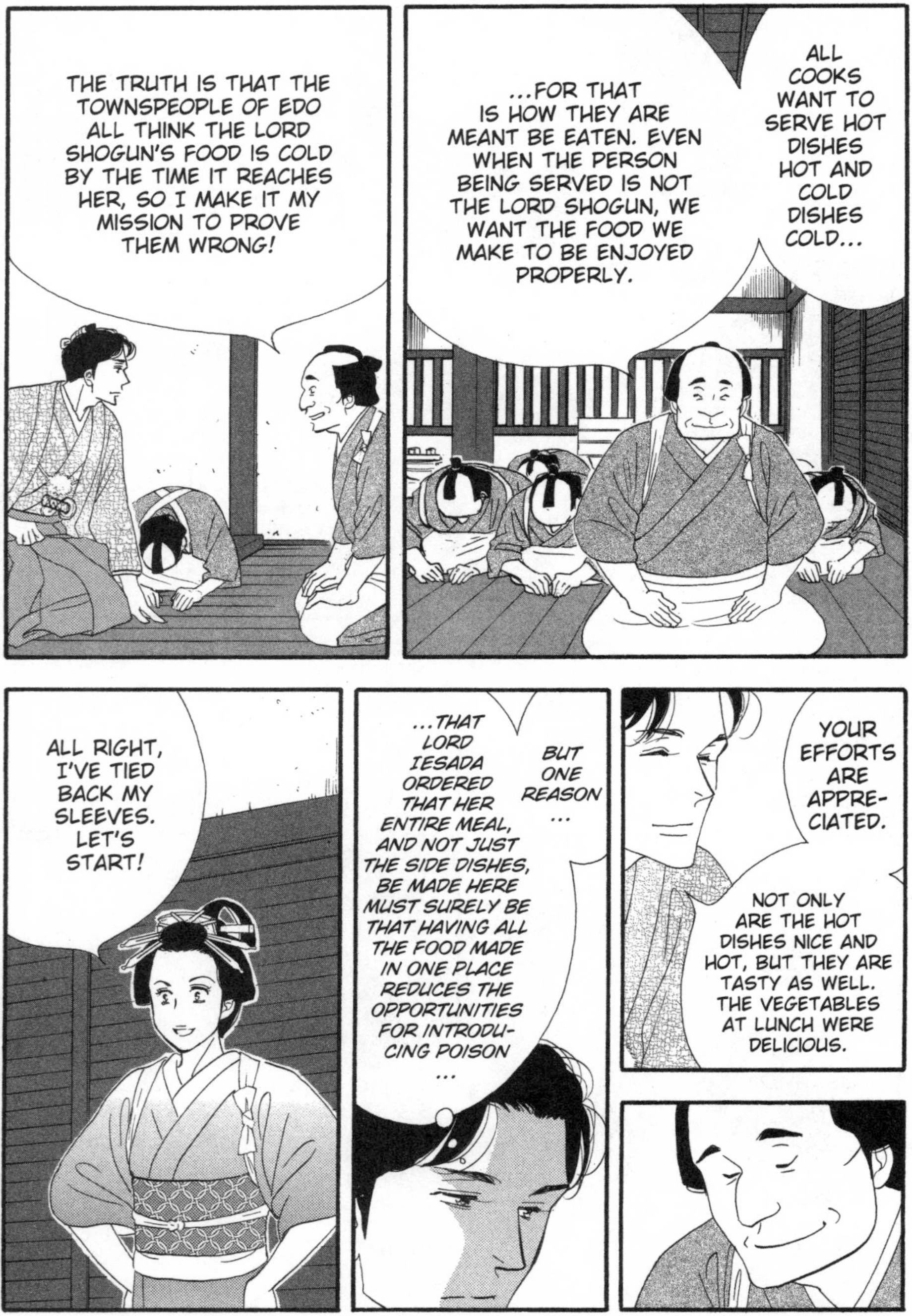
ALL COOKS WANT TO SERVE HOT DISHES HOT AND COLD DISHES COLD...
...FOR THAT IS HOW THEY ARE MEANT BE EATEN. EVEN WHEN THE PERSON BEING SERVED IS NOT THE LORD SHOGUN, WE WANT THE FOOD WE MAKE TO BE ENJOYED PROPERLY.
THE TRUTH IS THAT THE TOWNSPEOPLE OF EDO ALL THINK THE LORD SHOGUN'S FOOD IS COLD BY THE TIME IT REACHES HER, SO I MAKE IT MY MISSION TO PROVE THEM WRONG!
YOUR EFFORTS ARE APPRE-CIATED.
NOT ONLY ARE THE HOT DISHES NICE AND HOT, BUT THEY ARE TASTY AS WELL. THE VEGETABLES AT LUNCH WERE DELICIOUS.
BUT ONE REASON ...
...THAT LORD IESADA ORDERED THAT HER ENTIRE MEAL, AND NOT JUST THE SIDE DISHES, BE MADE HERE MUST SURELY BE THAT HAVING ALL THE FOOD MADE IN ONE PLACE REDUCES THE OPPORTUNITIES FOR INTRODU-CING POISON ...
ALL RIGHT, I'VE TIED BACK MY SLEEVES. LET'S START!

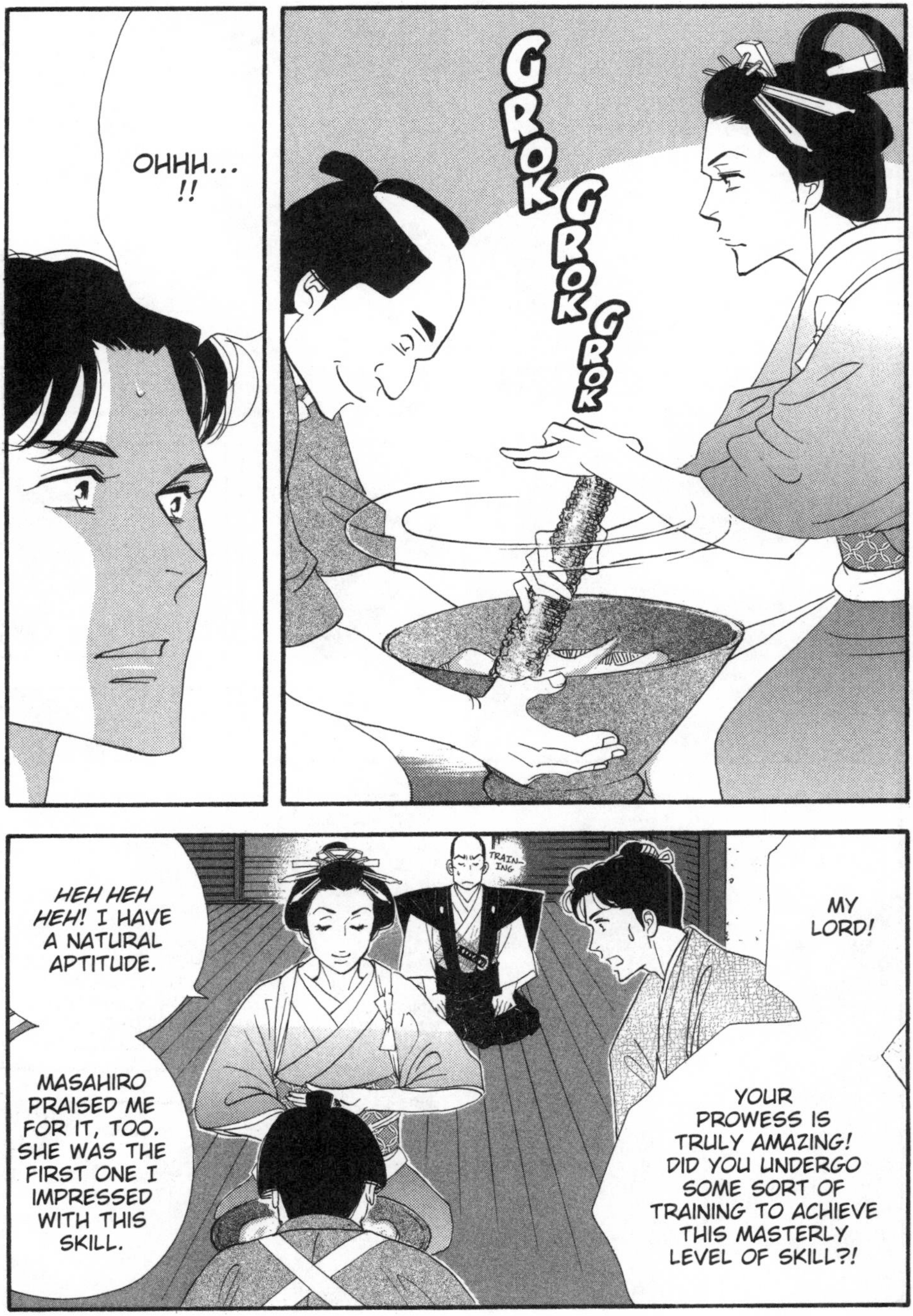
GROK GROK GROK
OHHH... !!
MY LORD!
TRAIN-ING
HEH HEH HEH! I HAVE A NATURAL APTITUDE.
YOUR PROWESS IS TRULY AMAZING! DID YOU UNDERGO SOME SORT OF TRAINING TO ACHIEVE THIS MASTERLY LEVEL OF SKILL?!
MASAHIRO PRAISED ME FOR IT, TOO. SHE WAS THE FIRST ONE I IMPRESSED WITH THIS SKILL.

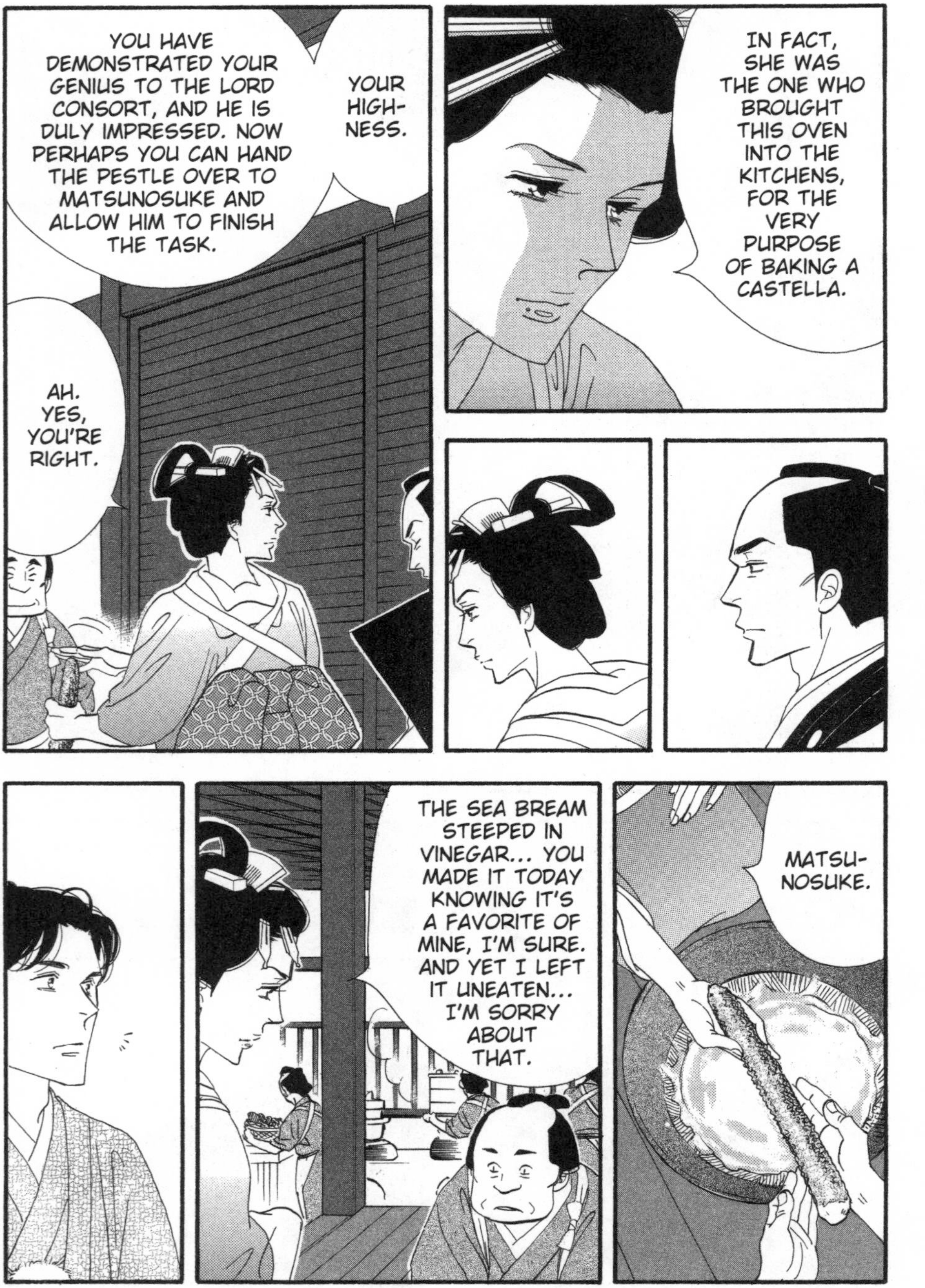
IN FACT, SHE WAS THE ONE WHO BROUGHT THIS OVEN INTO THE KITCHENS, FOR THE VERY PURPOSE OF BAKING A CASTELLA.
YOUR HIGHNESS.
YOU HAVE DEMONSTRATED YOUR GENIUS TO THE LORD CONSORT, AND HE IS DULY IMPRESSED. NOW PERHAPS YOU CAN HAND THE PESTLE OVER TO MATSUNOSUKE AND ALLOW HIM TO FINISH THE TASK.
AH. YES, YOU'RE RIGHT.
MATSU-NOSUKE.
THE SEA BREAM STEEPED IN VINEGAR... YOU MADE IT TODAY KNOWING IT'S A FAVORITE OF MINE, I'M SURE. AND YET I LEFT IT UNEATEN... I'M SORRY ABOUT THAT.

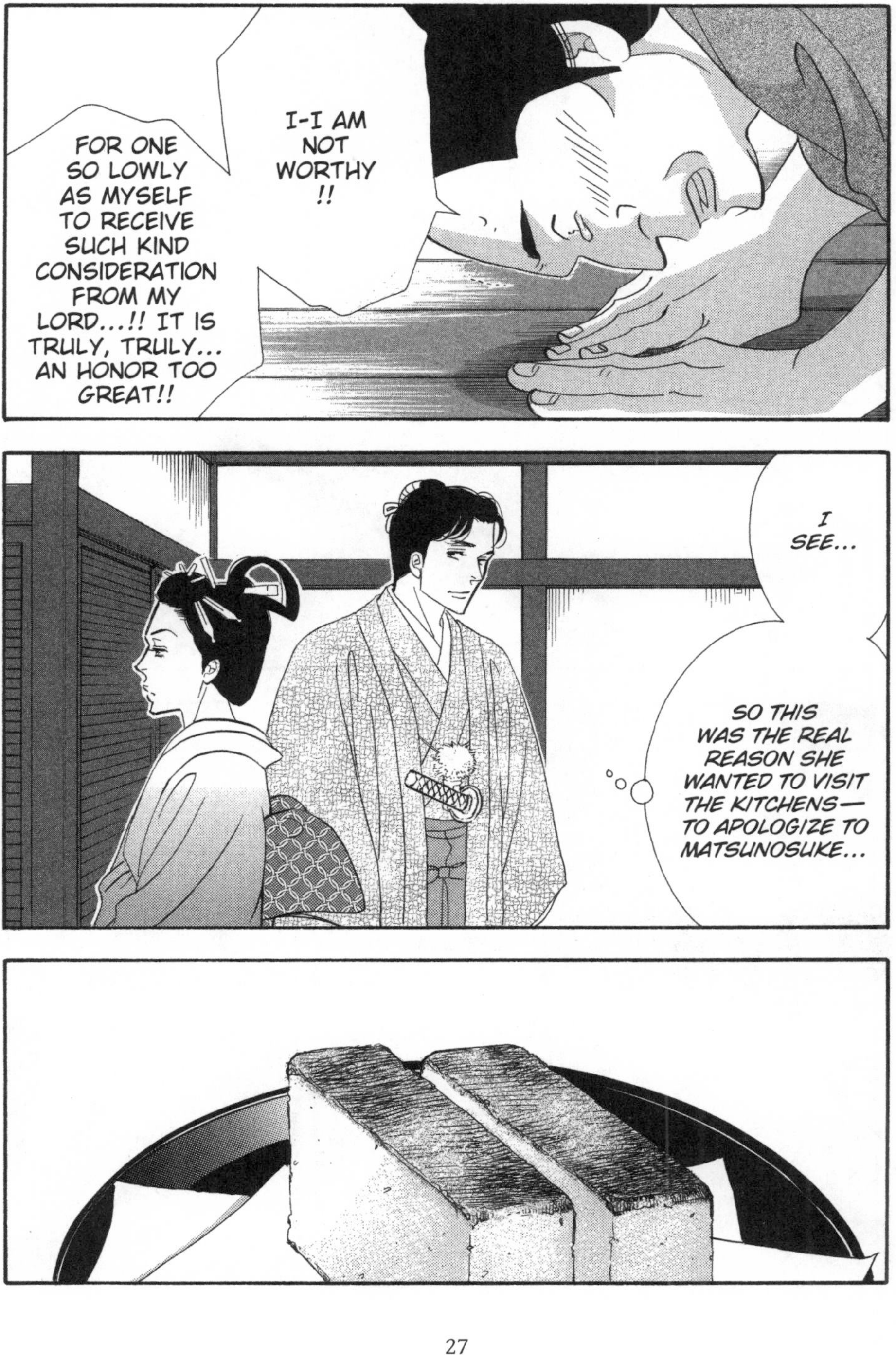
I-I AM NOT WORTHY !!
FOR ONE SO LOWLY AS MYSELF TO RECEIVE SUCH KIND CONSIDERATION FROM MY LORD...!! IT IS TRULY, TRULY... AN HONOR TOO GREAT!!
I SEE...
SO THIS WAS THE REAL REASON SHE WANTED TO VISIT THE KITCHENS— TO APOLOGIZE TO MATSUNOSUKE...

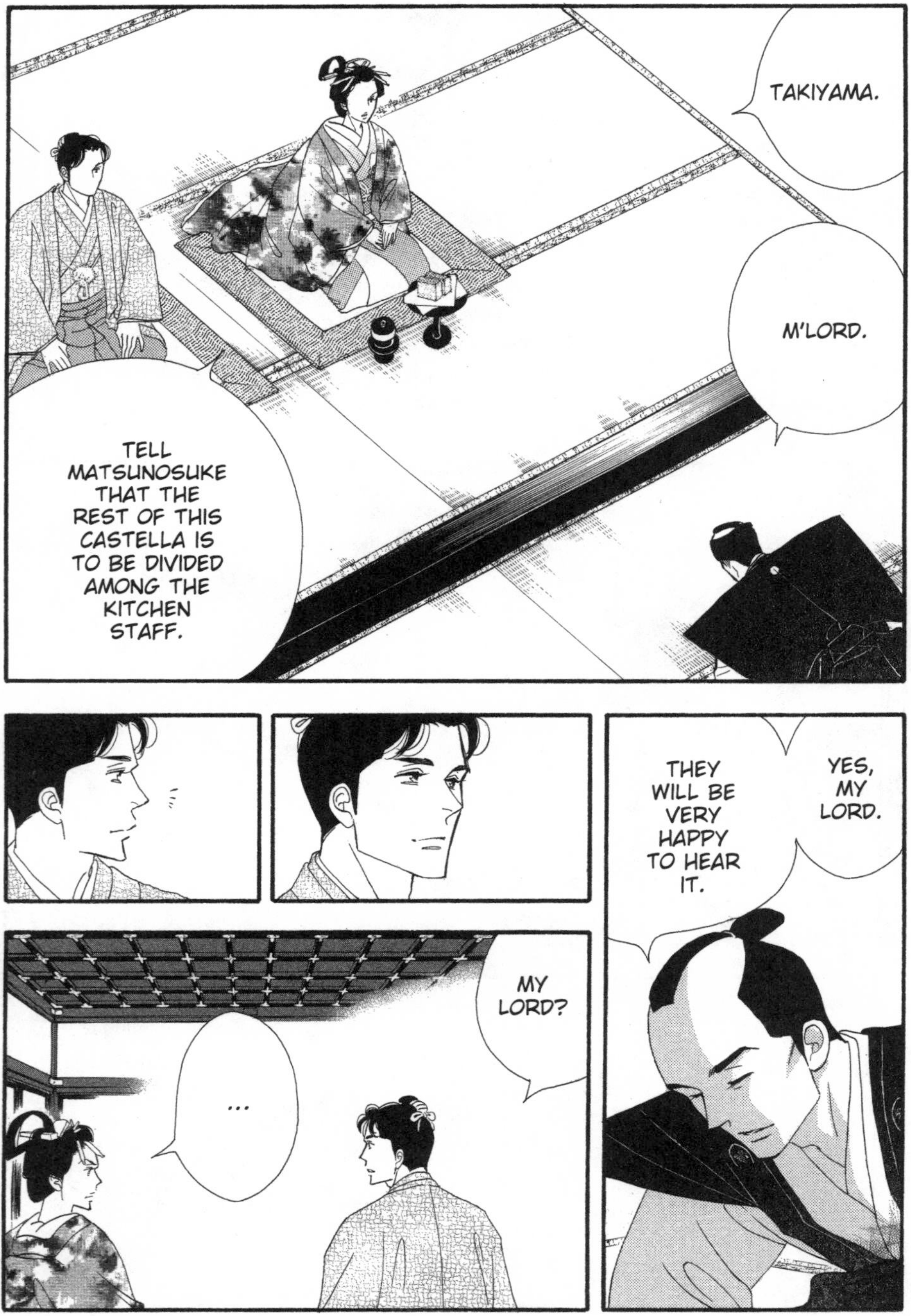
TAKIYAMA.
M'LORD.
TELL MATSUNOSUKE THAT THE REST OF THIS CASTELLA IS TO BE DIVIDED AMONG THE KITCHEN STAFF.
YES, MY LORD.
THEY WILL BE VERY HAPPY TO HEAR IT.
MY LORD?
...

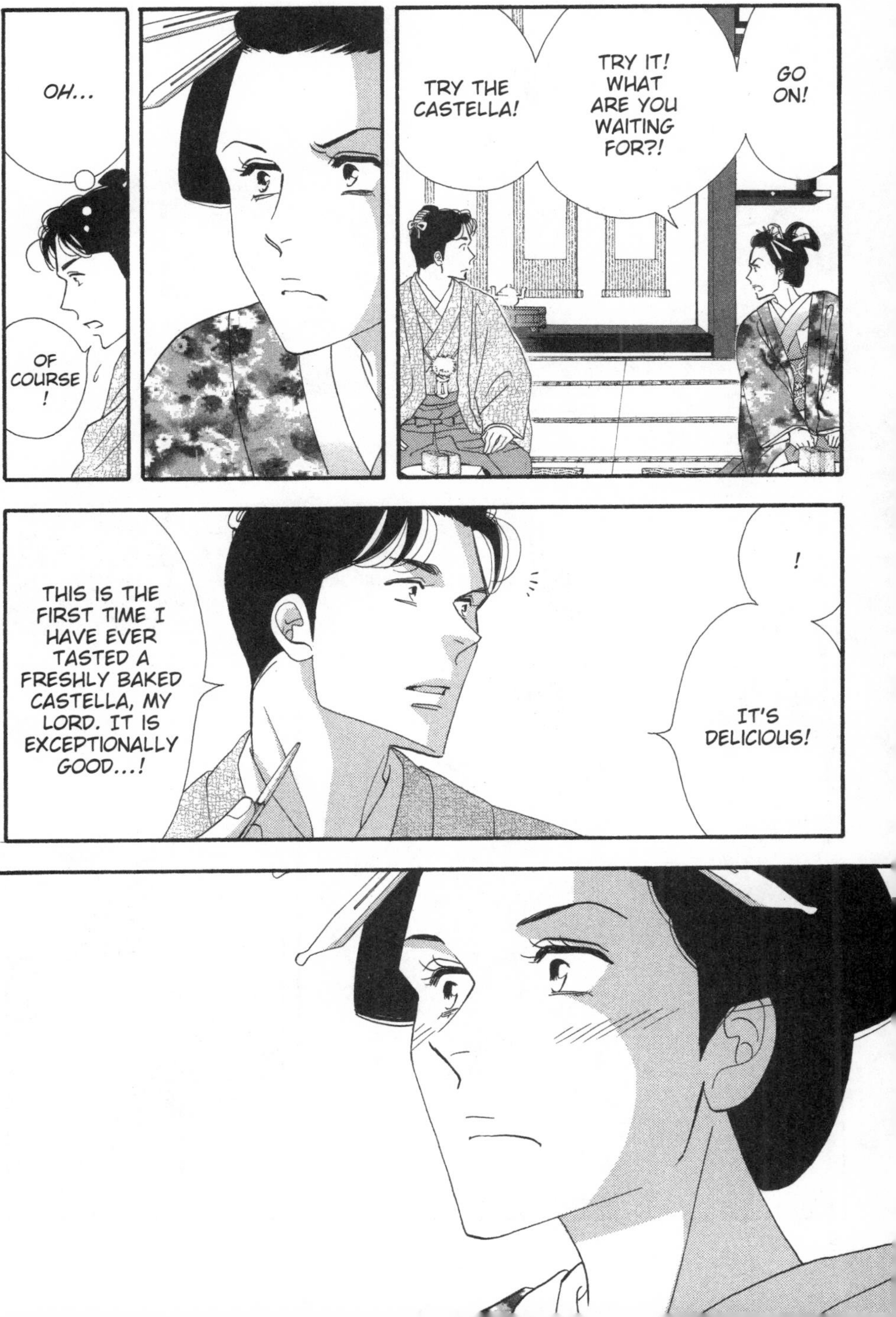
GO ON!
TRY IT! WHAT ARE YOU WAITING FOR?!
TRY THE CASTELLA!
OH...
OF COURSE!
!
IT'S DELICIOUS!
THIS IS THE FIRST TIME I HAVE EVER TASTED A FRESHLY BAKED CASTELLA, MY LORD. IT IS EXCEPTIONALLY GOOD...!

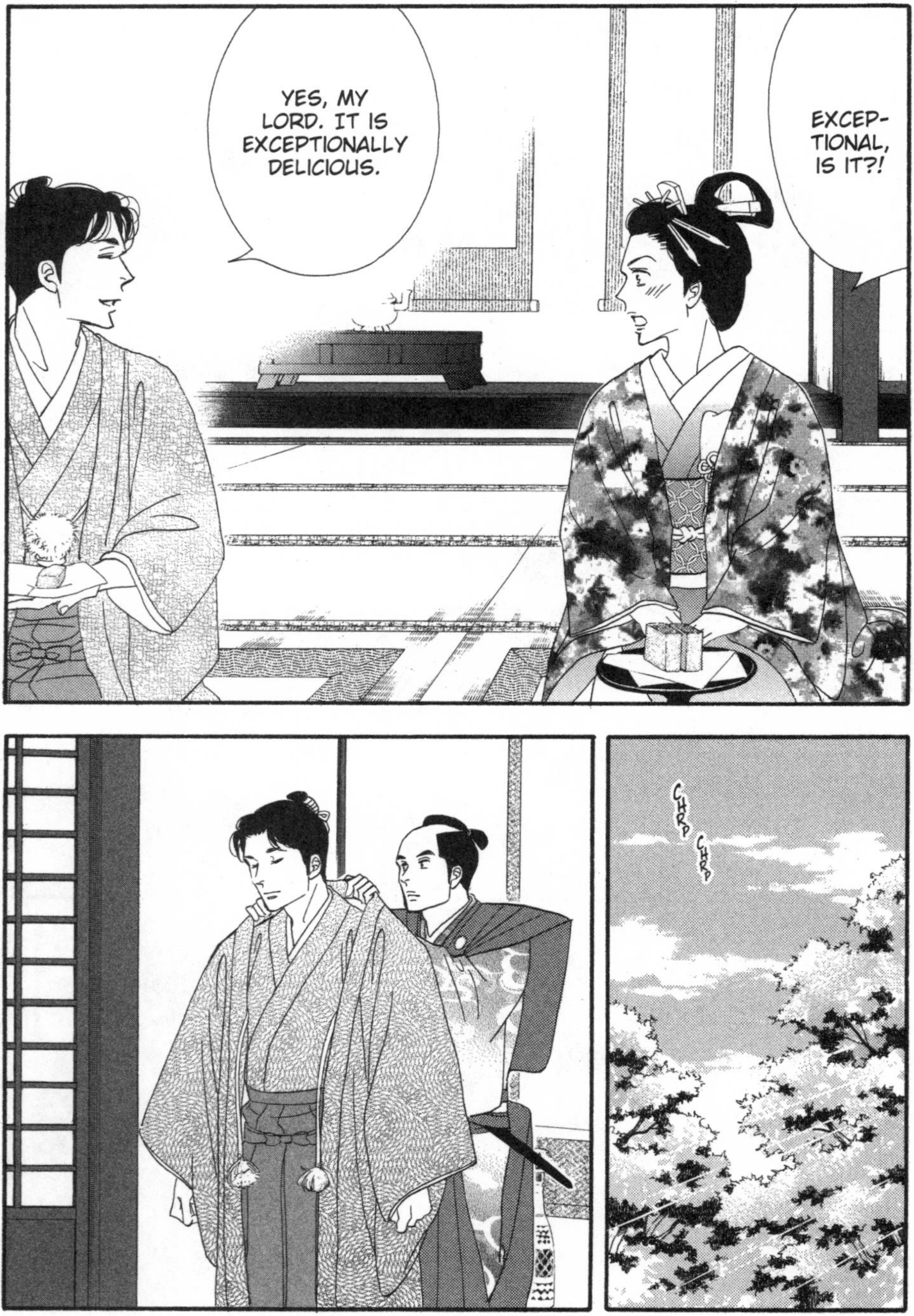
EXCEPTIONAL, IS IT?!
YES, MY LORD. IT IS EXCEPTIONALLY DELICIOUS.
CHRP CHRP

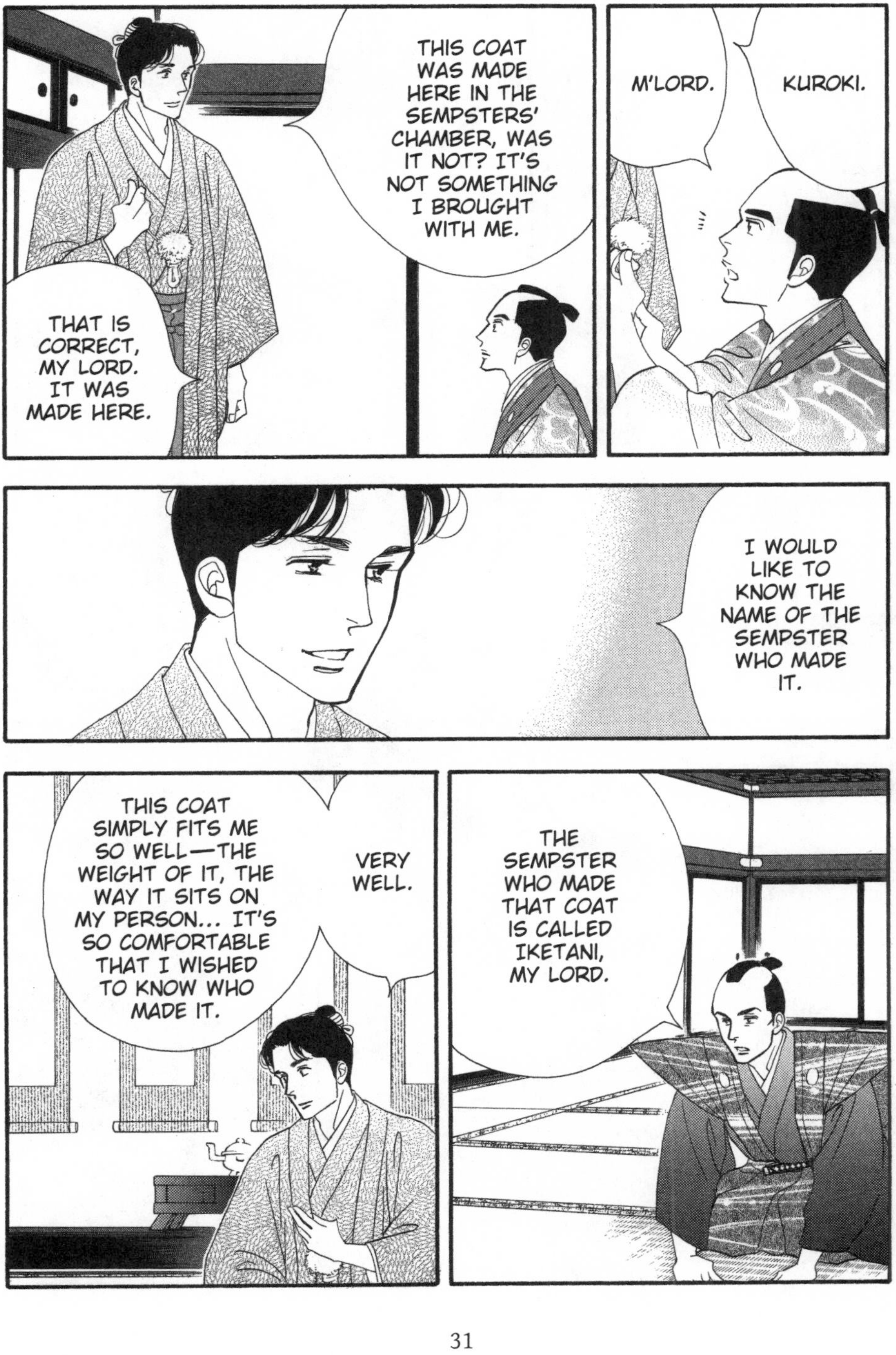
KUROKI.
M'LORD.
THIS COAT WAS MADE HERE IN THE SEMPSTERS' CHAMBER, WAS IT NOT? IT'S NOT SOMETHING I BROUGHT WITH ME.
THAT IS CORRECT, MY LORD. IT WAS MADE HERE.
I WOULD LIKE TO KNOW THE NAME OF THE SEMPSTER WHO MADE IT.
THE SEMPSTER WHO MADE THAT COAT IS CALLED IKETANI, MY LORD.
VERY WELL.
THIS COAT SIMPLY FITS ME SO WELL—THE WEIGHT OF IT, THE WAY IT SITS ON MY PERSON... IT'S SO COMFORTABLE THAT I WISHED TO KNOW WHO MADE IT.

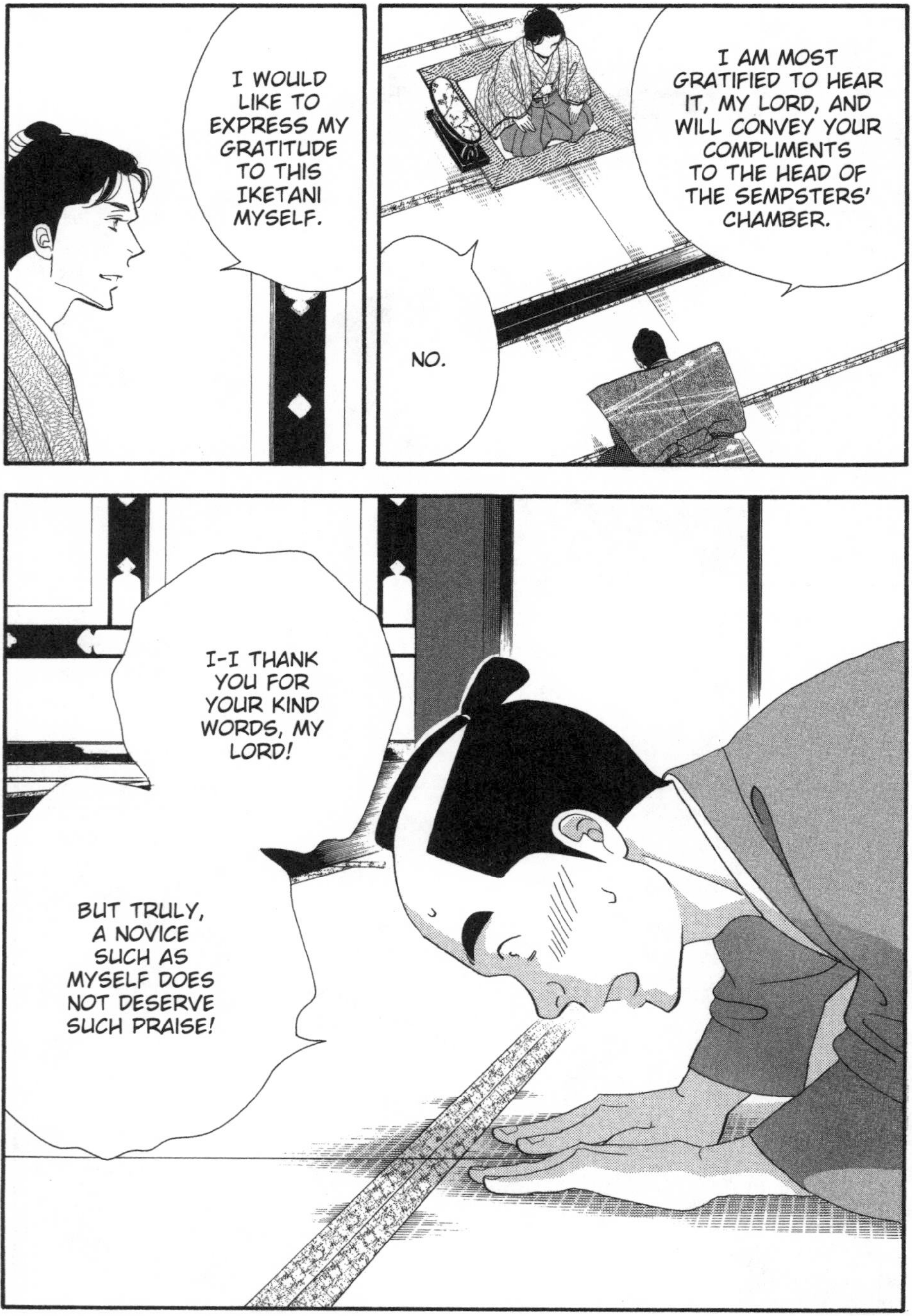
I AM MOST GRATIFIED TO HEAR IT, MY LORD, AND WILL CONVEY YOUR COMPLIMENTS TO THE HEAD OF THE SEMPSTERS' CHAMBER.
NO.
I WOULD LIKE TO EXPRESS MY GRATITUDE TO THIS IKETANI MYSELF.
I-I THANK YOU FOR YOUR KIND WORDS, MY LORD!
BUT TRULY, A NOVICE SUCH AS MYSELF DOES NOT DESERVE SUCH PRAISE!

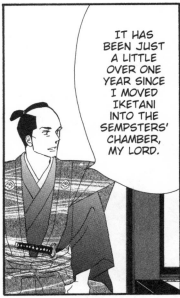

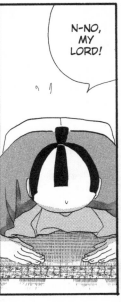

NOVICE? SO YOU HAVE NOT BEEN IN THE SEMPSTERS' CHAMBER FOR LONG?
N-NO, MY LORD!
IT HAS BEEN JUST A LITTLE OVER ONE YEAR SINCE I MOVED IKETANI INTO THE SEMPSTERS' CHAMBER, MY LORD.
IF YOU WERE ABLE TO MASTER SUCH SKILL WITH THE NEEDLE AS TO MAKE A COAT SO WELL-MADE AS THIS IN SO SHORT A TIME, THEN YOU QUITE CLEARLY HAVE A NATURAL GIFT.
OH NO, SIR! NOT AT ALL!
AS IT HAPPENS, MY MOTHER IS A KIMONO MAKER, AND BEFORE ENTERING INTO SERVICE HERE, I WOULD OFTEN HELP HER WITH HER WORK. I HAD A LITTLE BIT OF PREVIOUS EXPERIENCE, THAT IS ALL.

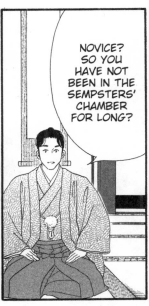

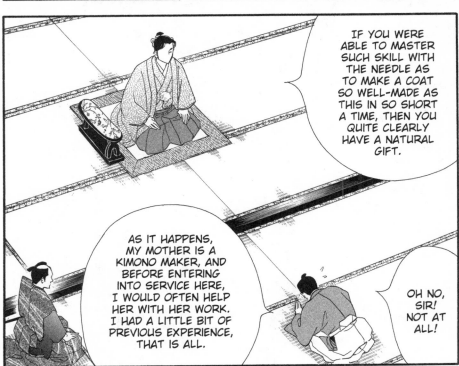

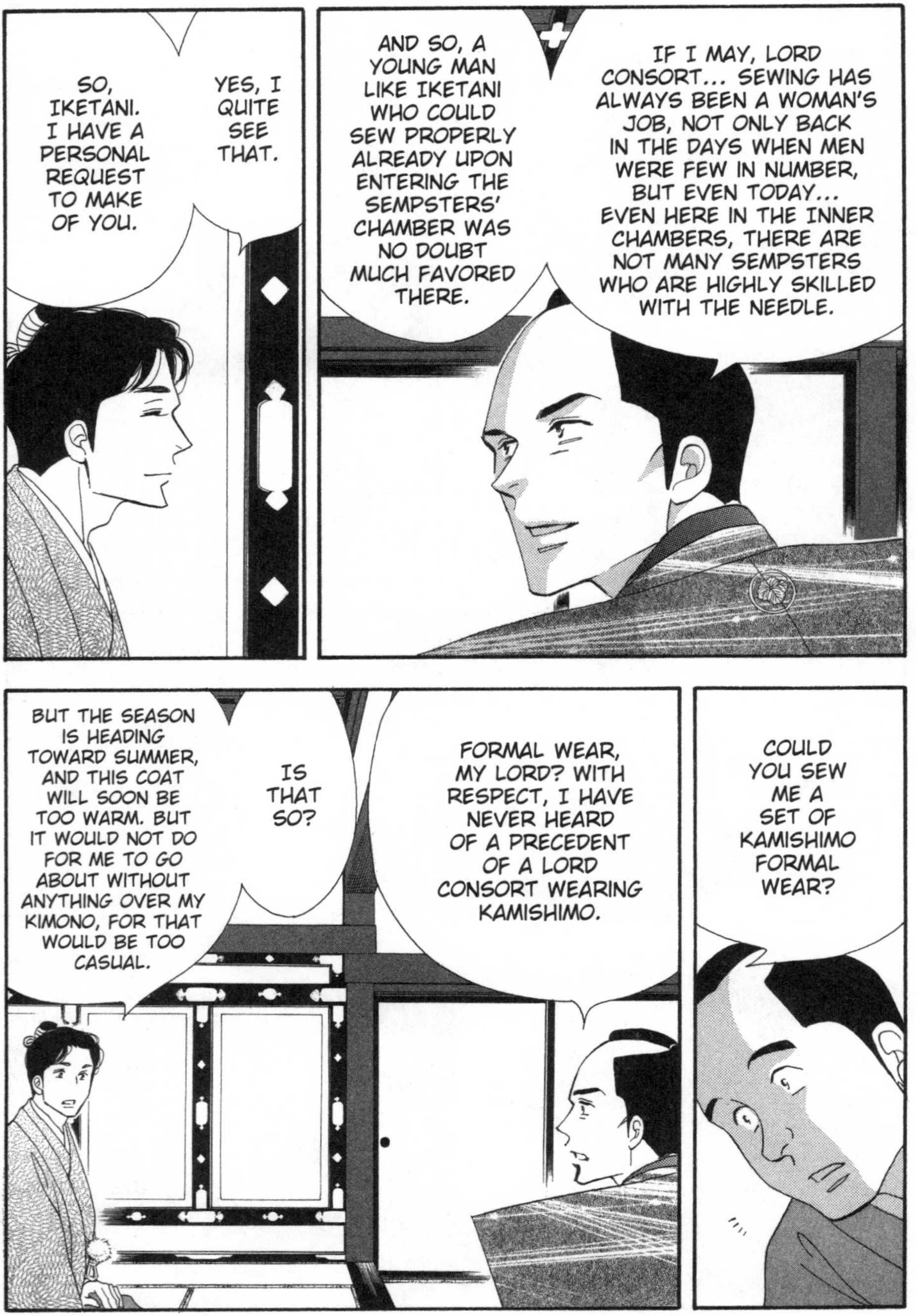
IF I MAY, LORD CONSORT... SEWING HAS ALWAYS BEEN A WOMAN'S JOB, NOT ONLY BACK IN THE DAYS WHEN MEN WERE FEW IN NUMBER, BUT EVEN TODAY... EVEN HERE IN THE INNER CHAMBERS, THERE ARE NOT MANY SEMPSTERS WHO ARE HIGHLY SKILLED WITH THE NEEDLE.
AND SO, A YOUNG MAN LIKE IKETANI WHO COULD SEW PROPERLY ALREADY UPON ENTERING THE SEMPSTERS' CHAMBER WAS NO DOUBT MUCH FAVORED THERE.
YES, I QUITE SEE THAT.
SO, IKETANI. I HAVE A PERSONAL REQUEST TO MAKE OF YOU.
COULD YOU SEW ME A SET OF KAMISHIMO FORMAL WEAR?
FORMAL WEAR, MY LORD? WITH RESPECT, I HAVE NEVER HEARD OF A PRECEDENT OF A LORD CONSORT WEARING KAMISHIMO.
IS THAT SO?
BUT THE SEASON IS HEADING TOWARD SUMMER, AND THIS COAT WILL SOON BE TOO WARM. BUT IT WOULD NOT DO FOR ME TO GO ABOUT WITHOUT ANYTHING OVER MY KIMONO, FOR THAT WOULD BE TOO CASUAL.

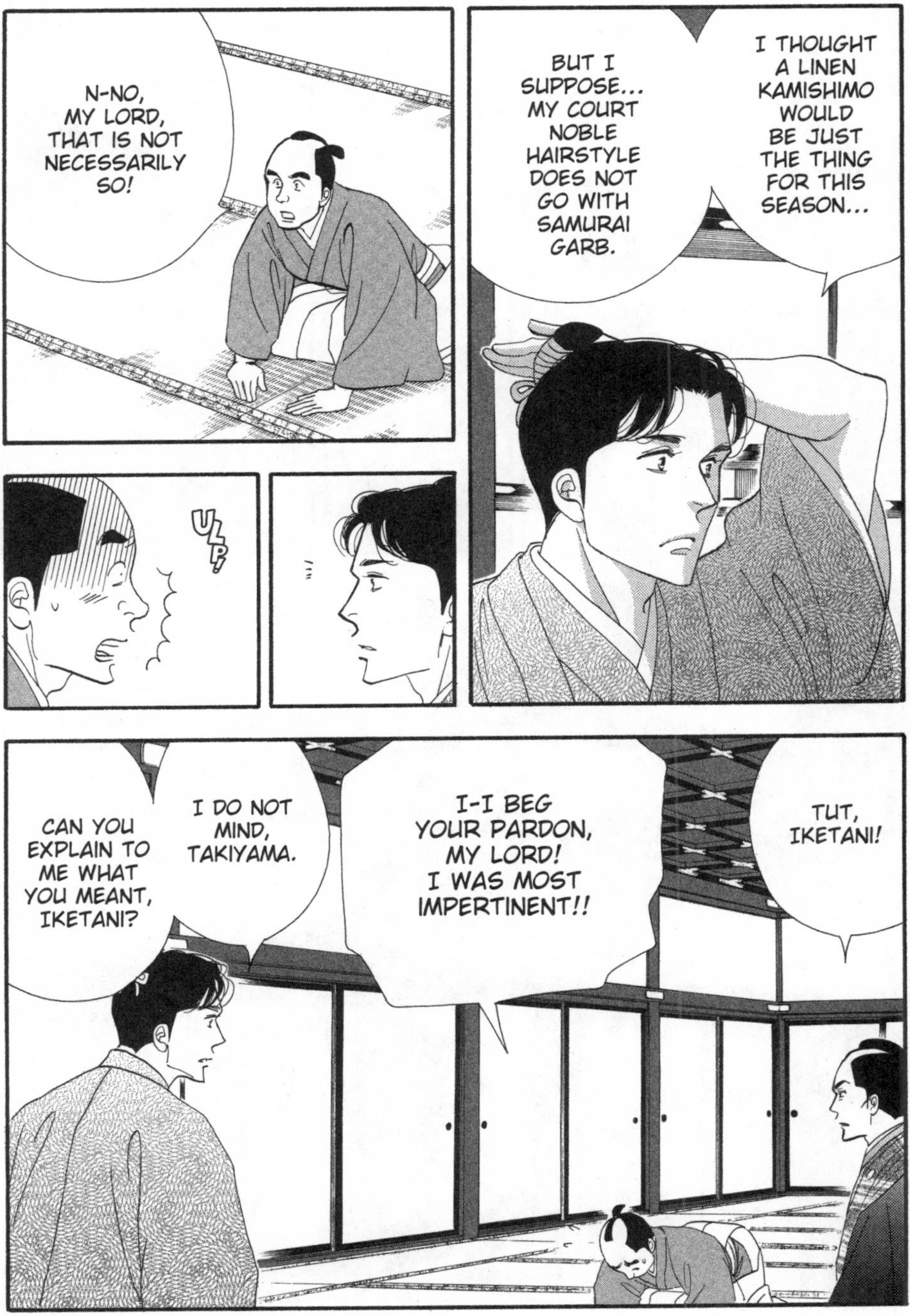
I THOUGHT A LINEN KAMISHIMO WOULD BE JUST THE THING FOR THIS SEASON...
BUT I SUPPOSE... MY COURT NOBLE HAIRSTYLE DOES NOT GO WITH SAMURAI GARB.
N-NO, MY LORD, THAT IS NOT NECESSARILY SO!
ULP!
TUT, IKETANI!
I-I BEG YOUR PARDON, MY LORD! I WAS MOST IMPERTINENT!!
I DO NOT MIND, TAKIYAMA.
CAN YOU EXPLAIN TO ME WHAT YOU MEANT, IKETANI?

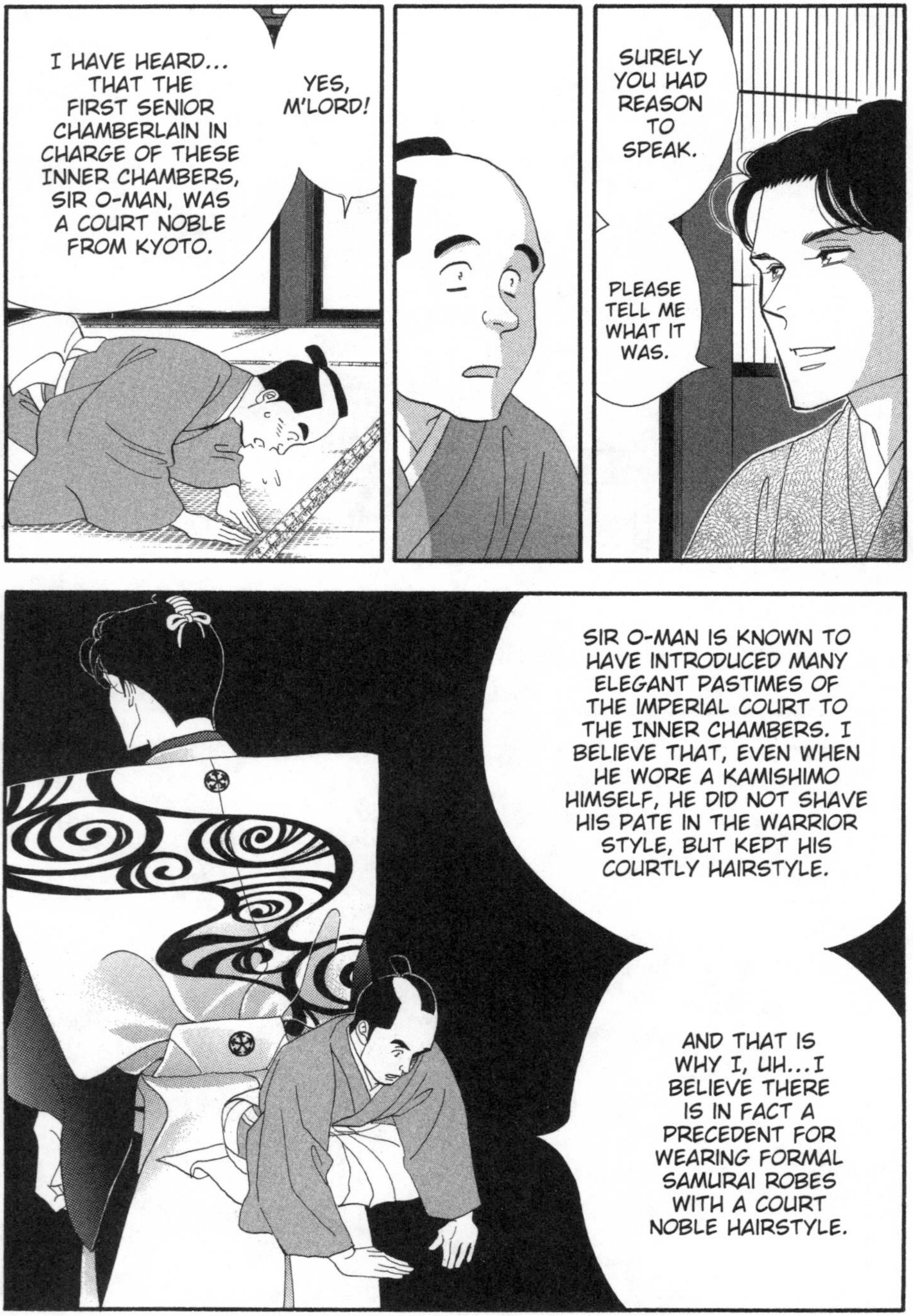
SURELY YOU HAD REASON TO SPEAK.
PLEASE TELL ME WHAT IT WAS.
YES, M'LORD!
I HAVE HEARD... THAT THE FIRST SENIOR CHAMBERLAIN IN CHARGE OF THESE INNER CHAMBERS, SIR O-MAN, WAS A COURT NOBLE FROM KYOTO.
SIR O-MAN IS KNOWN TO HAVE INTRODUCED MANY ELEGANT PASTIMES OF THE IMPERIAL COURT TO THE INNER CHAMBERS. I BELIEVE THAT, EVEN WHEN HE WORE A KAMISHIMO HIMSELF, HE DID NOT SHAVE HIS PATE IN THE WARRIOR STYLE, BUT KEPT HIS COURTLY HAIRSTYLE.
AND THAT IS WHY I, UH...I BELIEVE THERE IS IN FACT A PRECEDENT FOR WEARING FORMAL SAMURAI ROBES WITH A COURT NOBLE HAIRSTYLE.

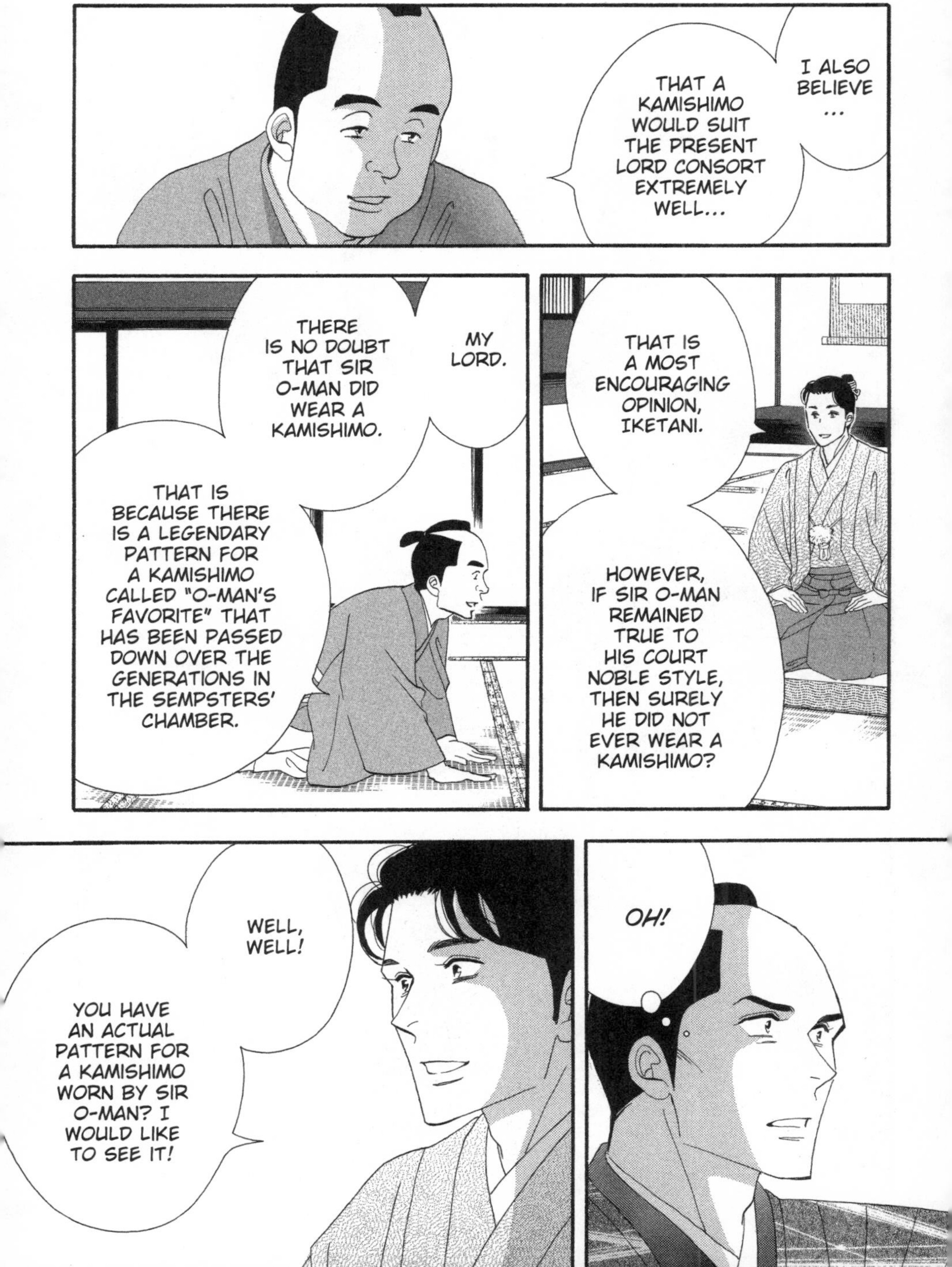
I ALSO BELIEVE ...
THAT A KAMISHIMO WOULD SUIT THE PRESENT LORD CONSORT EXTREMELY WELL...
THAT IS A MOST ENCOURAGING OPINION, IKETANI.
HOWEVER, IF SIR O-MAN REMAINED TRUE TO HIS COURT NOBLE STYLE, THEN SURELY HE DID NOT EVER WEAR A KAMISHIMO?
MY LORD.
THERE IS NO DOUBT THAT SIR O-MAN DID WEAR A KAMISHIMO.
THAT IS BECAUSE THERE IS A LEGENDARY PATTERN FOR A KAMISHIMO CALLED "O-MAN'S FAVORITE" THAT HAS BEEN PASSED DOWN OVER THE GENERATIONS IN THE SEMPSTERS' CHAMBER.
OH!
WELL, WELL!
YOU HAVE AN ACTUAL PATTERN FOR A KAMISHIMO WORN BY SIR O-MAN? I WOULD LIKE TO SEE IT!

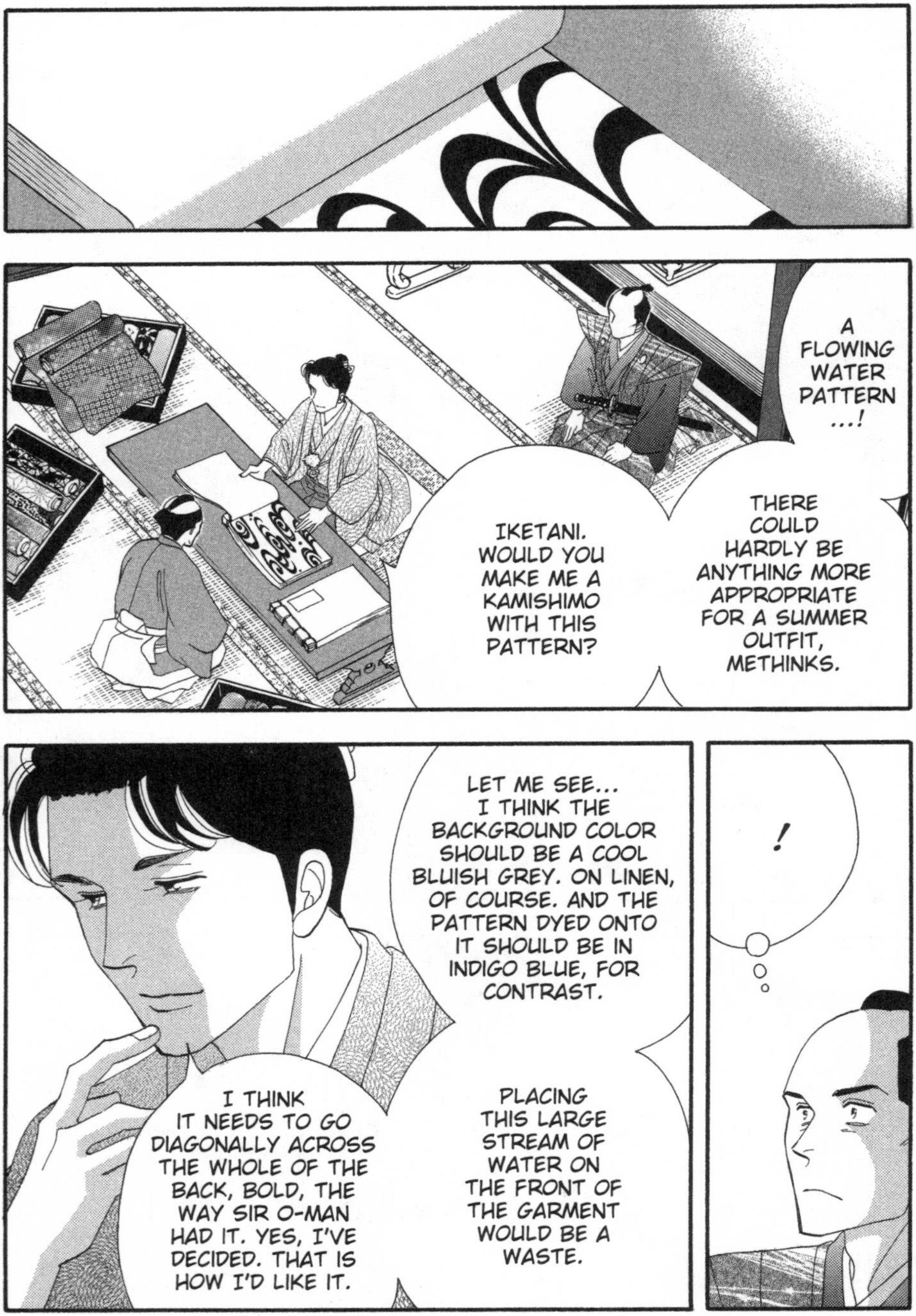
A FLOWING WATER PATTERN...!
THERE COULD HARDLY BE ANYTHING MORE APPROPRIATE FOR A SUMMER OUTFIT, METHINKS.
IKETANI. WOULD YOU MAKE ME A KAMISHIMO WITH THIS PATTERN?
!
LET ME SEE... I THINK THE BACKGROUND COLOR SHOULD BE A COOL BLUISH GREY. ON LINEN, OF COURSE. AND THE PATTERN DYED ONTO IT SHOULD BE IN INDIGO BLUE, FOR CONTRAST.
PLACING THIS LARGE STREAM OF WATER ON THE FRONT OF THE GARMENT WOULD BE A WASTE.
I THINK IT NEEDS TO GO DIAGONALLY ACROSS THE WHOLE OF THE BACK, BOLD, THE WAY SIR O-MAN HAD IT. YES, I'VE DECIDED. THAT IS HOW I'D LIKE IT.

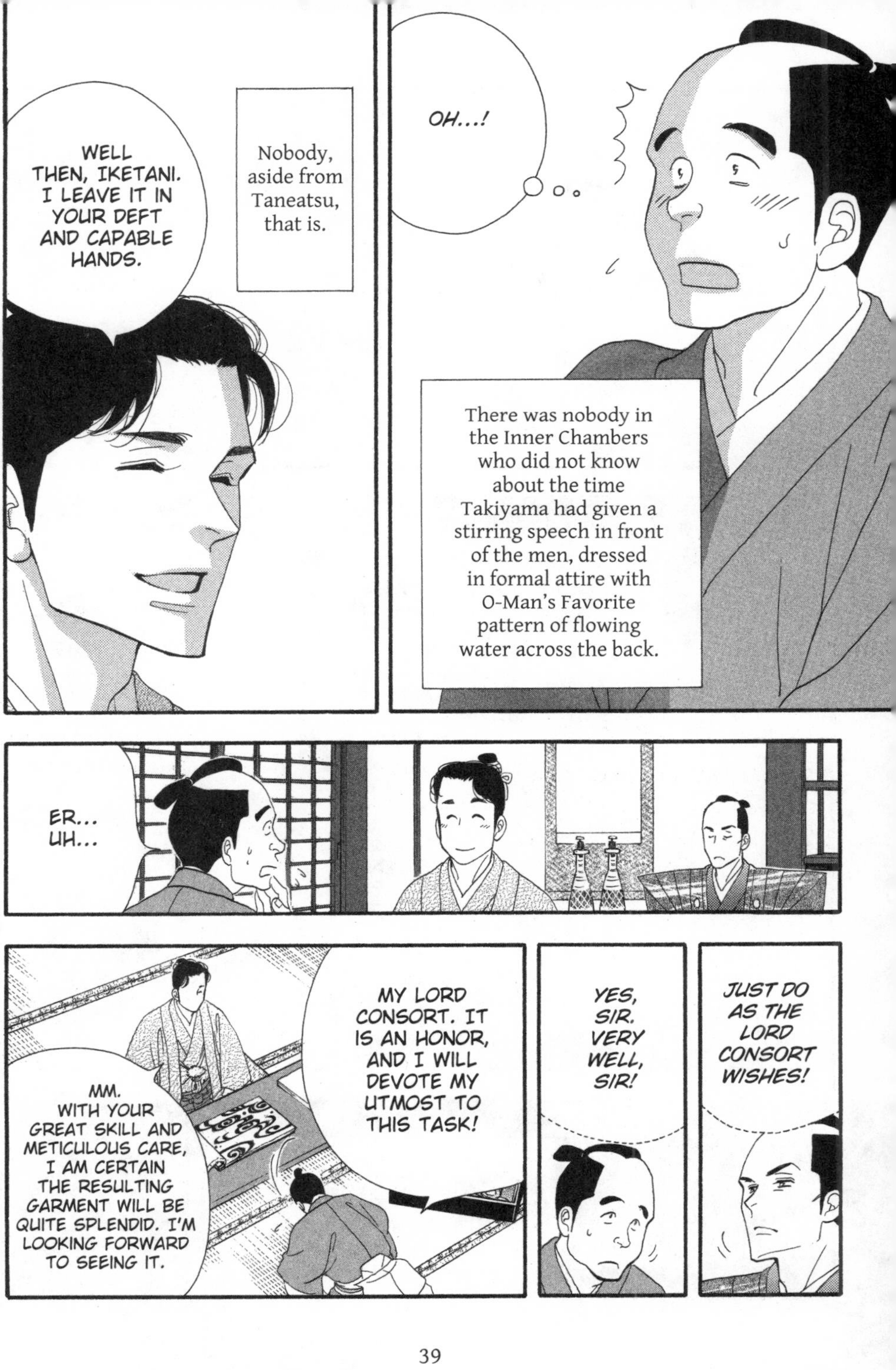
OH...!
There was nobody in the Inner Chambers who did not know about the time Takiyama had given a stirring speech in front of the men, dressed in formal attire with O-Man's Favorite pattern of flowing water across the back.
Nobody, aside from Taneatsu, that is.
WELL THEN, IKETANI. I LEAVE IT IN YOUR DEFT AND CAPABLE HANDS.
ER... UH...
JUST DO AS THE LORD CONSORT WISHES!
YES, SIR. VERY WELL, SIR!
MY LORD CONSORT. IT IS AN HONOR, AND I WILL DEVOTE MY UTMOST TO THIS TASK!
MM. WITH YOUR GREAT SKILL AND METICULOUS CARE, I AM CERTAIN THE RESULTING GARMENT WILL BE QUITE SPLENDID. I'M LOOKING FORWARD TO SEEING IT.

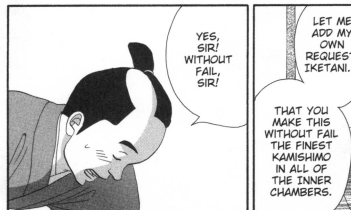

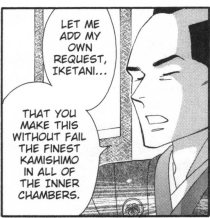

LET ME ADD MY OWN REQUEST, IKETANI...
THAT YOU MAKE THIS WITHOUT FAIL THE FINEST KAMISHIMO IN ALL OF THE INNER CHAMBERS.
YES, SIR! WITHOUT FAIL, SIR!
AAGH... THIS MEANS I SHALL NEVER AGAIN BE ABLE TO WEAR MY OWN KAMISHIMO WITH THE FLOWING WATER PATTERN ON IT.
TOO BAD... IT WAS ONE OF MY FAVORITES...

Iesada's morning sickness had finally subsided, and for the first time in quite a while she and Taneatsu were going to enjoy a stroll in the gardens together.

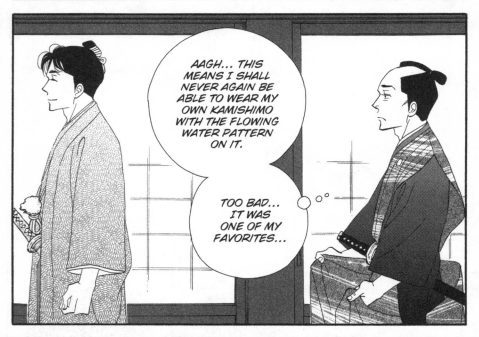

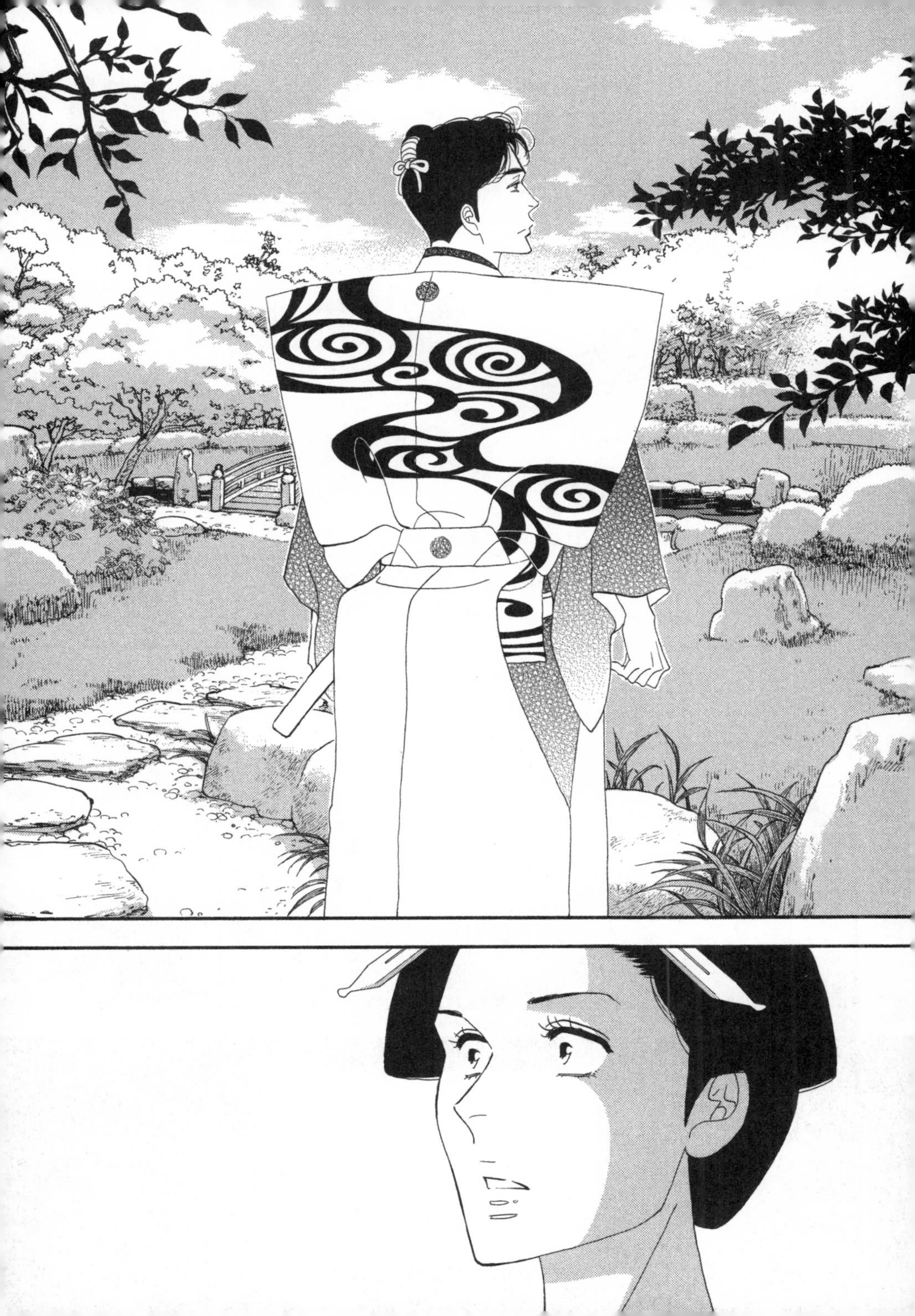

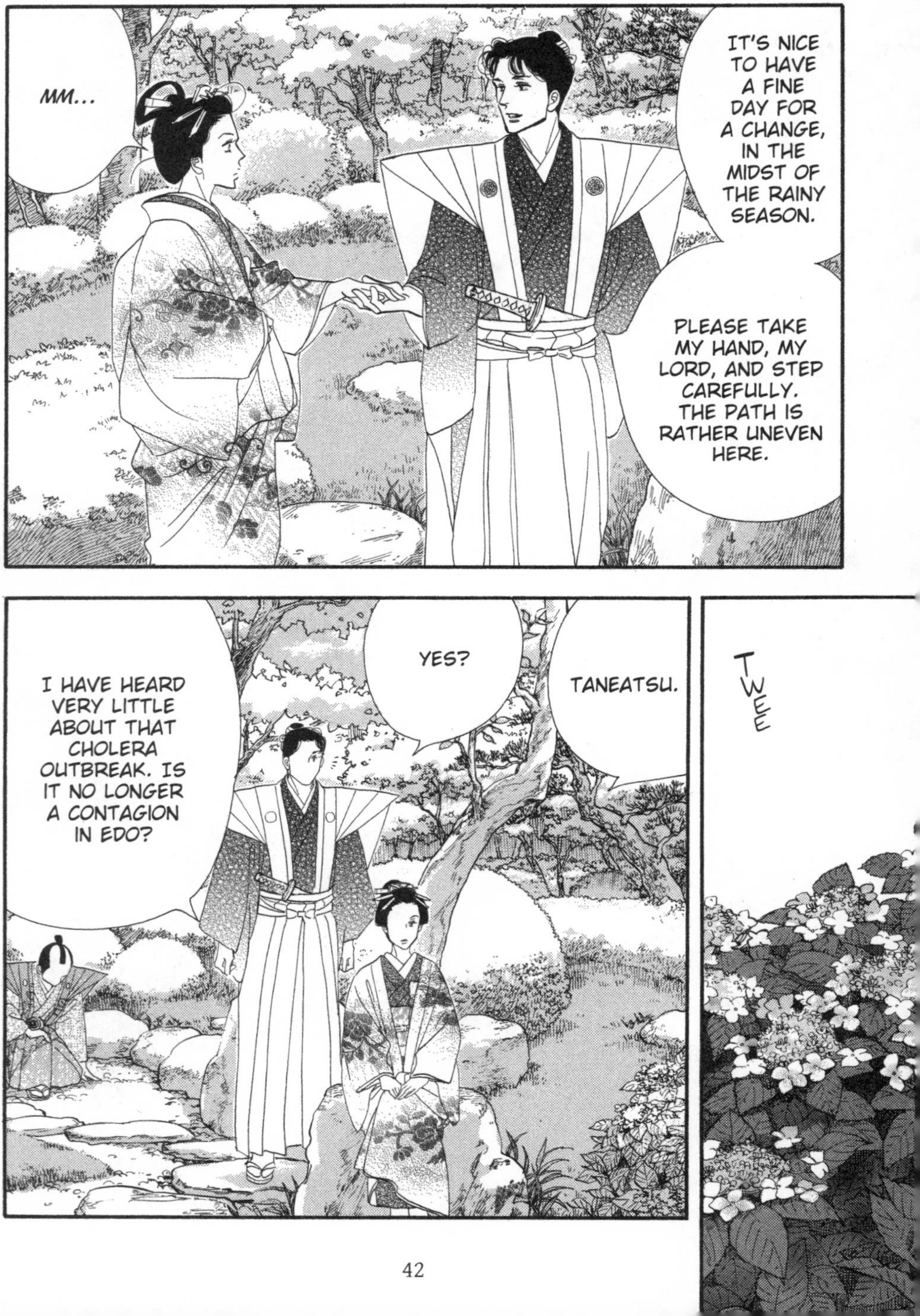
IT'S NICE TO HAVE A FINE DAY FOR A CHANGE, IN THE MIDST OF THE RAINY SEASON.
PLEASE TAKE MY HAND, MY LORD, AND STEP CAREFULLY. THE PATH IS RATHER UNEVEN HERE.
MM...
TWEE
TANEATSU.
YES?
I HAVE HEARD VERY LITTLE ABOUT THAT CHOLERA OUTBREAK. IS IT NO LONGER A CONTAGION IN EDO?

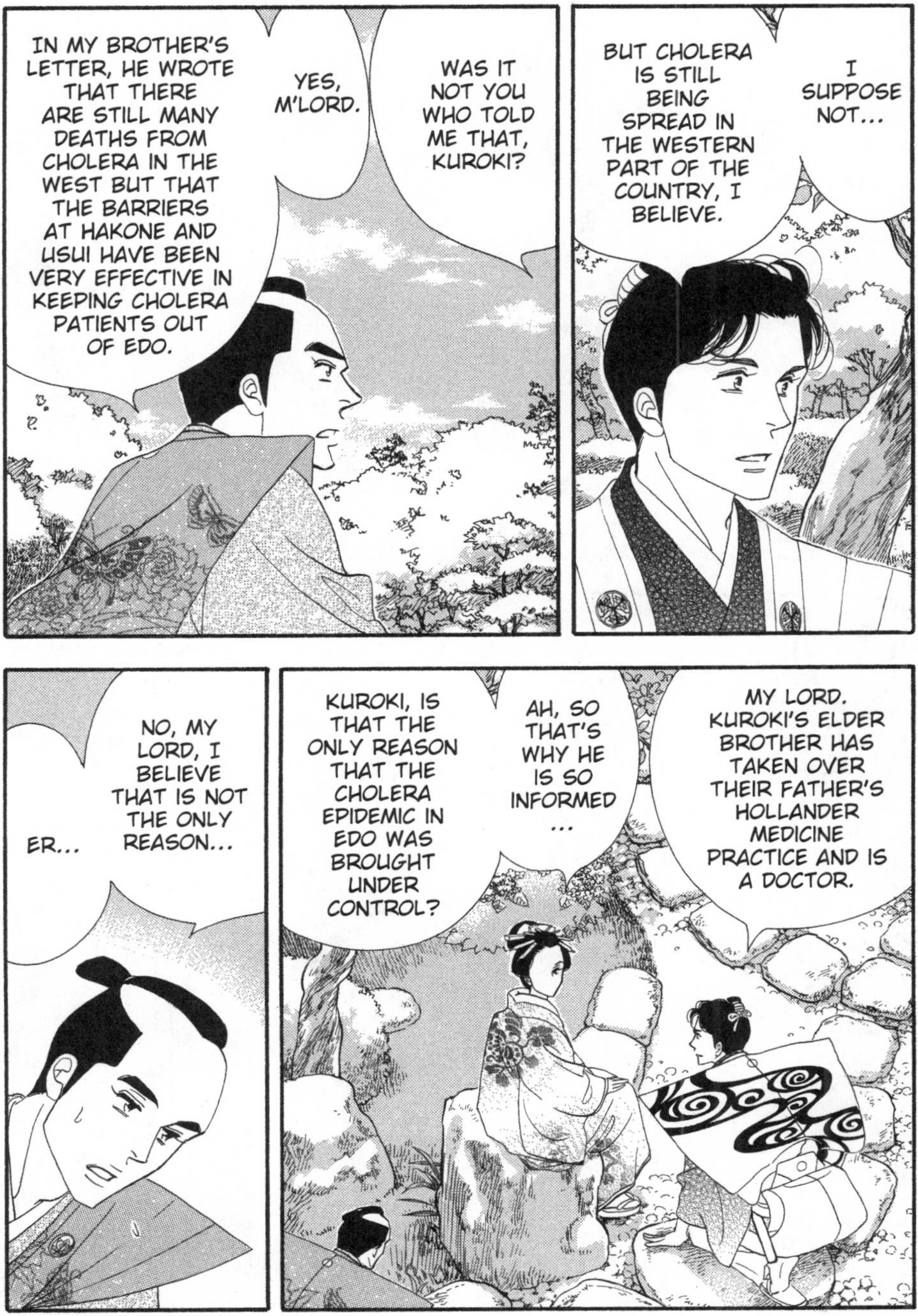
I SUPPOSE NOT...
BUT CHOLERA IS STILL BEING SPREAD IN THE WESTERN PART OF THE COUNTRY, I BELIEVE.
WAS IT NOT YOU WHO TOLD ME THAT, KUROKI?
YES, M'LORD.
IN MY BROTHER'S LETTER, HE WROTE THAT THERE ARE STILL MANY DEATHS FROM CHOLERA IN THE WEST BUT THAT THE BARRIERS AT HAKONE AND USUI HAVE BEEN VERY EFFECTIVE IN KEEPING CHOLERA PATIENTS OUT OF EDO.
MY LORD. KUROKI'S ELDER BROTHER HAS TAKEN OVER THEIR FATHER'S HOLLANDER MEDICINE PRACTICE AND IS A DOCTOR.
AH, SO THAT'S WHY HE IS SO INFORMED ...
KUROKI, IS THAT THE ONLY REASON THAT THE CHOLERA EPIDEMIC IN EDO WAS BROUGHT UNDER CONTROL?
NO, MY LORD, I BELIEVE THAT IS NOT THE ONLY REASON...
ER...

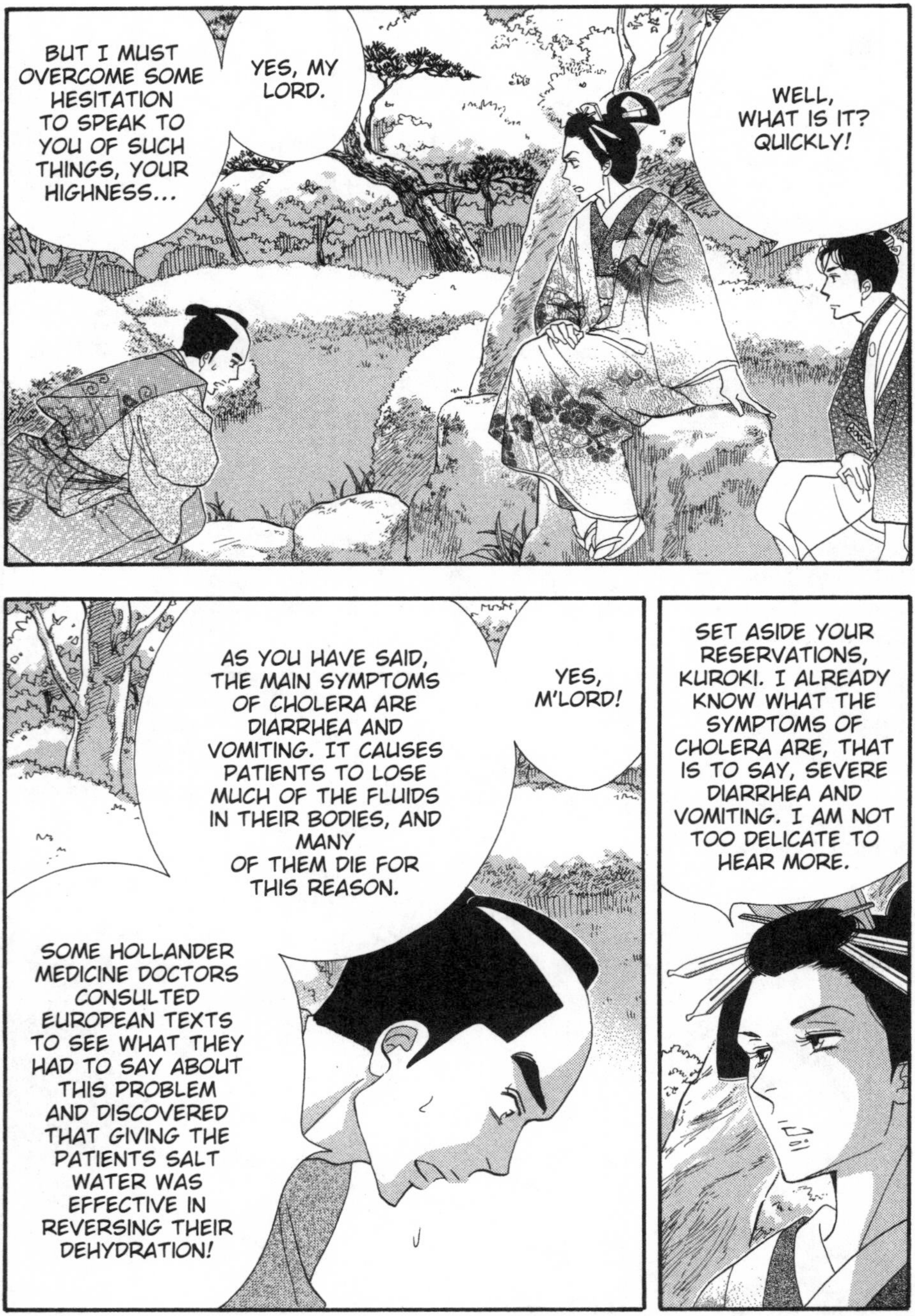
WELL, WHAT IS IT? QUICKLY!
YES, MY LORD.
BUT I MUST OVERCOME SOME HESITATION TO SPEAK TO YOU OF SUCH THINGS, YOUR HIGHNESS...
SET ASIDE YOUR RESERVATIONS, KUROKI. I ALREADY KNOW WHAT THE SYMPTOMS OF CHOLERA ARE, THAT IS TO SAY, SEVERE DIARRHEA AND VOMITING. I AM NOT TOO DELICATE TO HEAR MORE.
YES, M'LORD!
AS YOU HAVE SAID, THE MAIN SYMPTOMS OF CHOLERA ARE DIARRHEA AND VOMITING. IT CAUSES PATIENTS TO LOSE MUCH OF THE FLUIDS IN THEIR BODIES, AND MANY OF THEM DIE FOR THIS REASON.
SOME HOLLANDER MEDICINE DOCTORS CONSULTED EUROPEAN TEXTS TO SEE WHAT THEY HAD TO SAY ABOUT THIS PROBLEM AND DISCOVERED THAT GIVING THE PATIENTS SALT WATER WAS EFFECTIVE IN REVERSING THEIR DEHYDRATION!

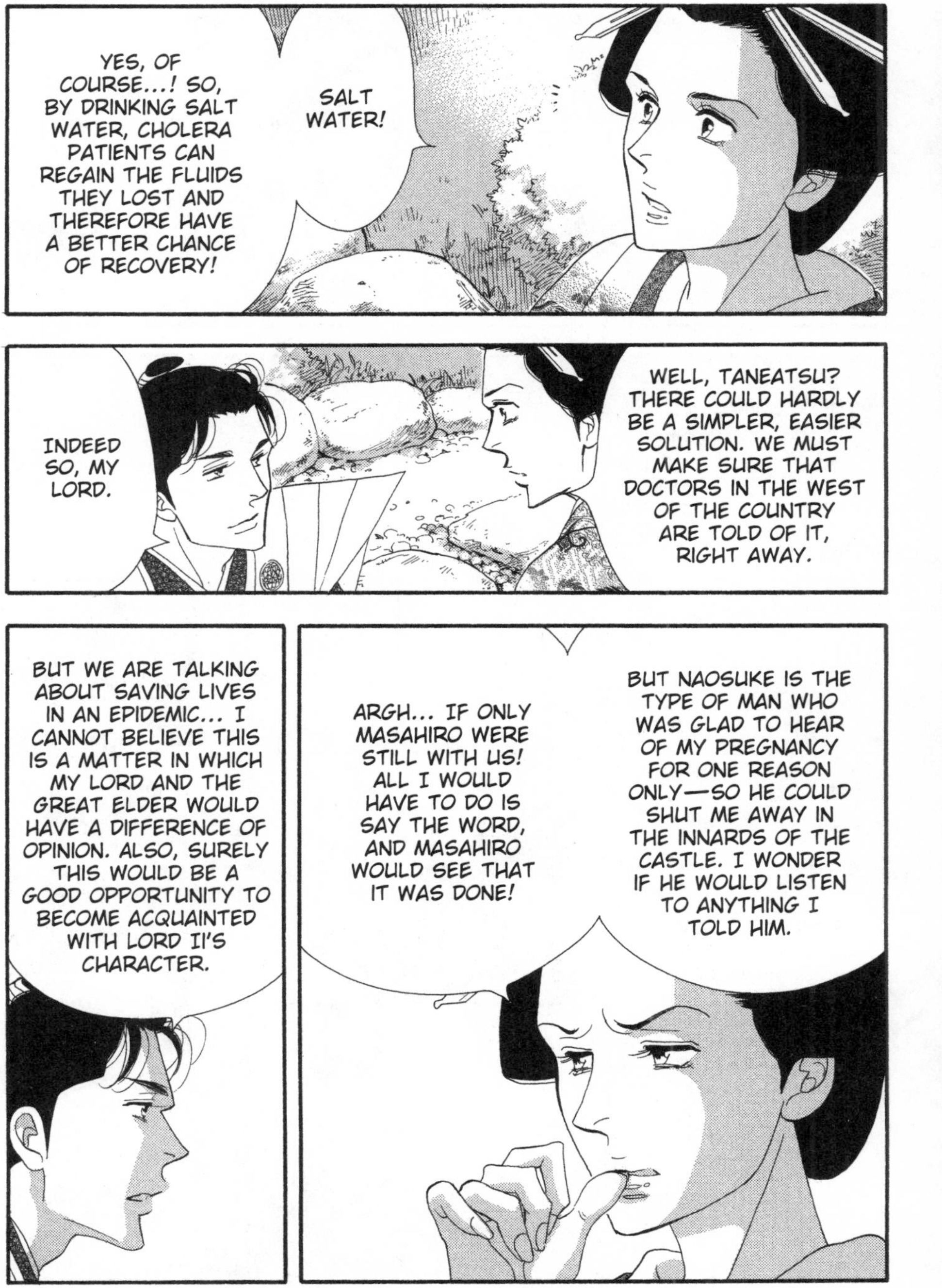
SALT WATER!
YES, OF COURSE...! SO, BY DRINKING SALT WATER, CHOLERA PATIENTS CAN REGAIN THE FLUIDS THEY LOST AND THEREFORE HAVE A BETTER CHANCE OF RECOVERY!
WELL, TANEATSU? THERE COULD HARDLY BE A SIMPLER, EASIER SOLUTION. WE MUST MAKE SURE THAT DOCTORS IN THE WEST OF THE COUNTRY ARE TOLD OF IT, RIGHT AWAY.
INDEED SO, MY LORD.
BUT NAOSUKE IS THE TYPE OF MAN WHO WAS GLAD TO HEAR OF MY PREGNANCY FOR ONE REASON ONLY—SO HE COULD SHUT ME AWAY IN THE INNARDS OF THE CASTLE. I WONDER IF HE WOULD LISTEN TO ANYTHING I TOLD HIM.
ARGH... IF ONLY MASAHIRO WERE STILL WITH US! ALL I WOULD HAVE TO DO IS SAY THE WORD, AND MASAHIRO WOULD SEE THAT IT WAS DONE!
BUT WE ARE TALKING ABOUT SAVING LIVES IN AN EPIDEMIC... I CANNOT BELIEVE THIS IS A MATTER IN WHICH MY LORD AND THE GREAT ELDER WOULD HAVE A DIFFERENCE OF OPINION. ALSO, SURELY THIS WOULD BE A GOOD OPPORTUNITY TO BECOME ACQUAINTED WITH LORD II'S CHARACTER.

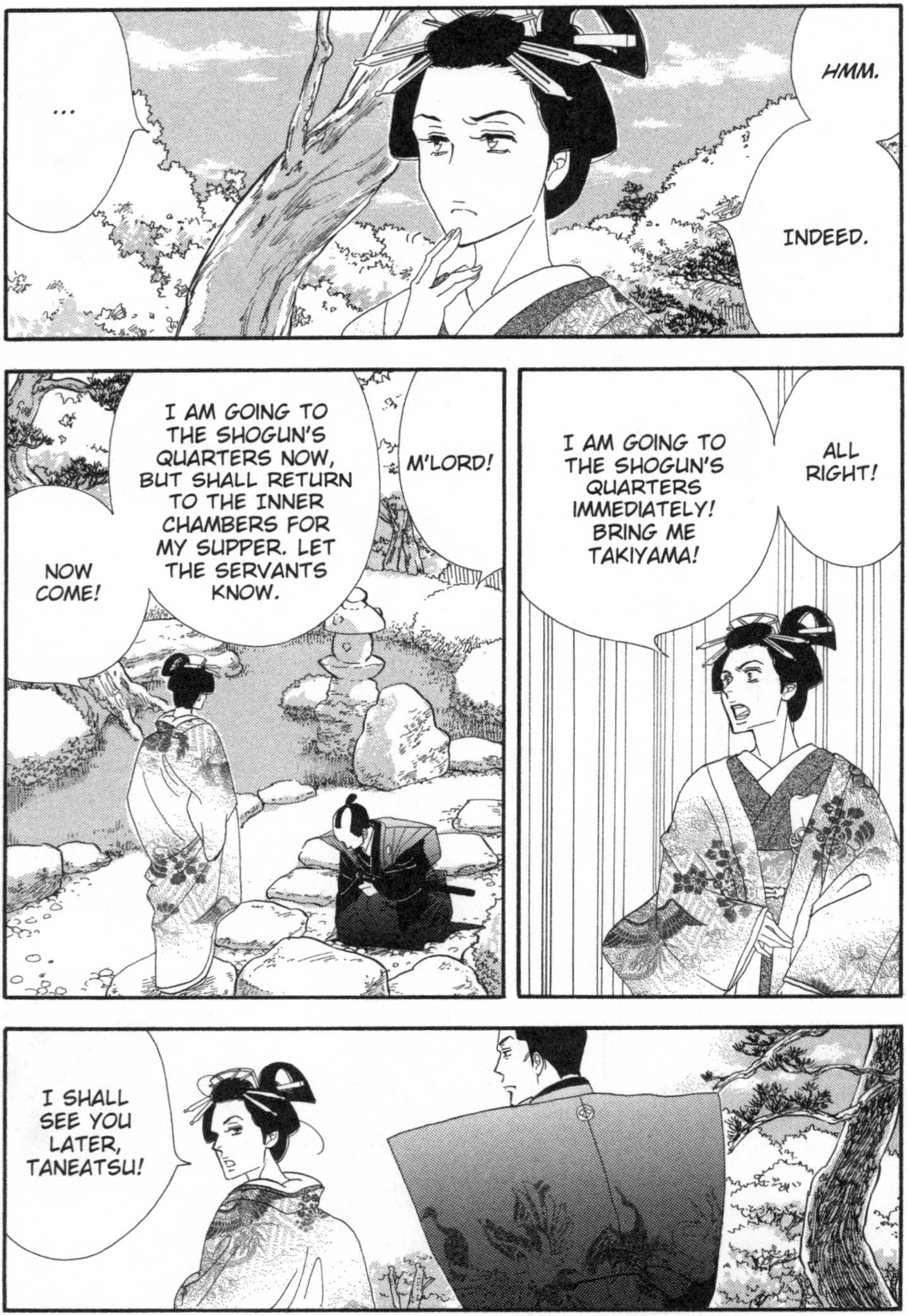
HMM.
INDEED.
...
ALL RIGHT!
I AM GOING TO THE SHOGUN'S QUARTERS IMMEDIATELY! BRING ME TAKIYAMA!
M'LORD!
I AM GOING TO THE SHOGUN'S QUARTERS NOW, BUT SHALL RETURN TO THE INNER CHAMBERS FOR MY SUPPER. LET THE SERVANTS KNOW.
NOW COME!
I SHALL SEE YOU LATER, TANEATSU!

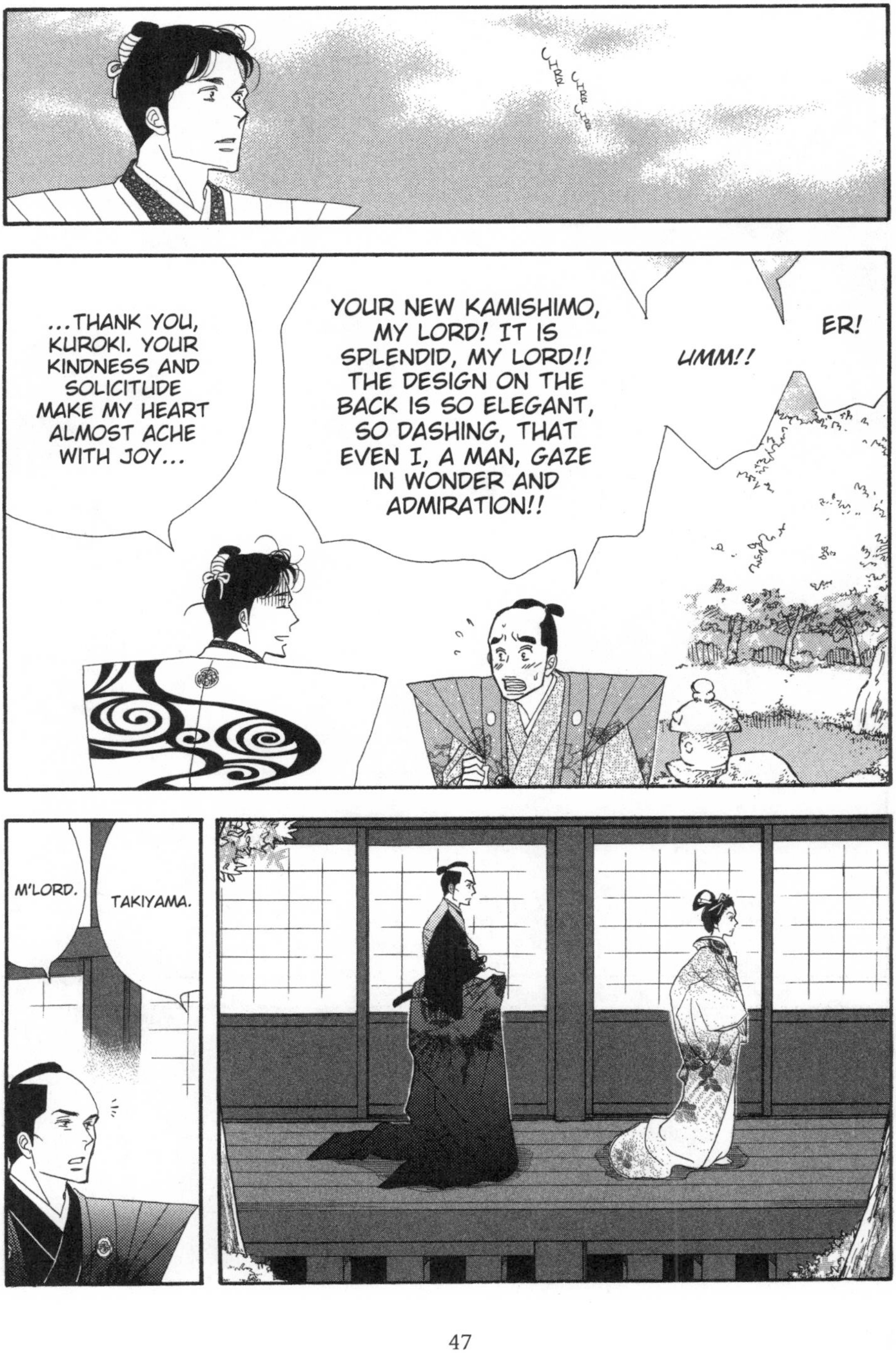
CHRR CHRR CHRR
ER!
UMM!!
YOUR NEW KAMISHIMO, MY LORD! IT IS SPLENDID, MY LORD!! THE DESIGN ON THE BACK IS SO ELEGANT, SO DASHING, THAT EVEN I, A MAN, GAZE IN WONDER AND ADMIRATION!!
...THANK YOU, KUROKI. YOUR KINDNESS AND SOLICITUDE MAKE MY HEART ALMOST ACHE WITH JOY...
TAKIYAMA.
M'LORD.

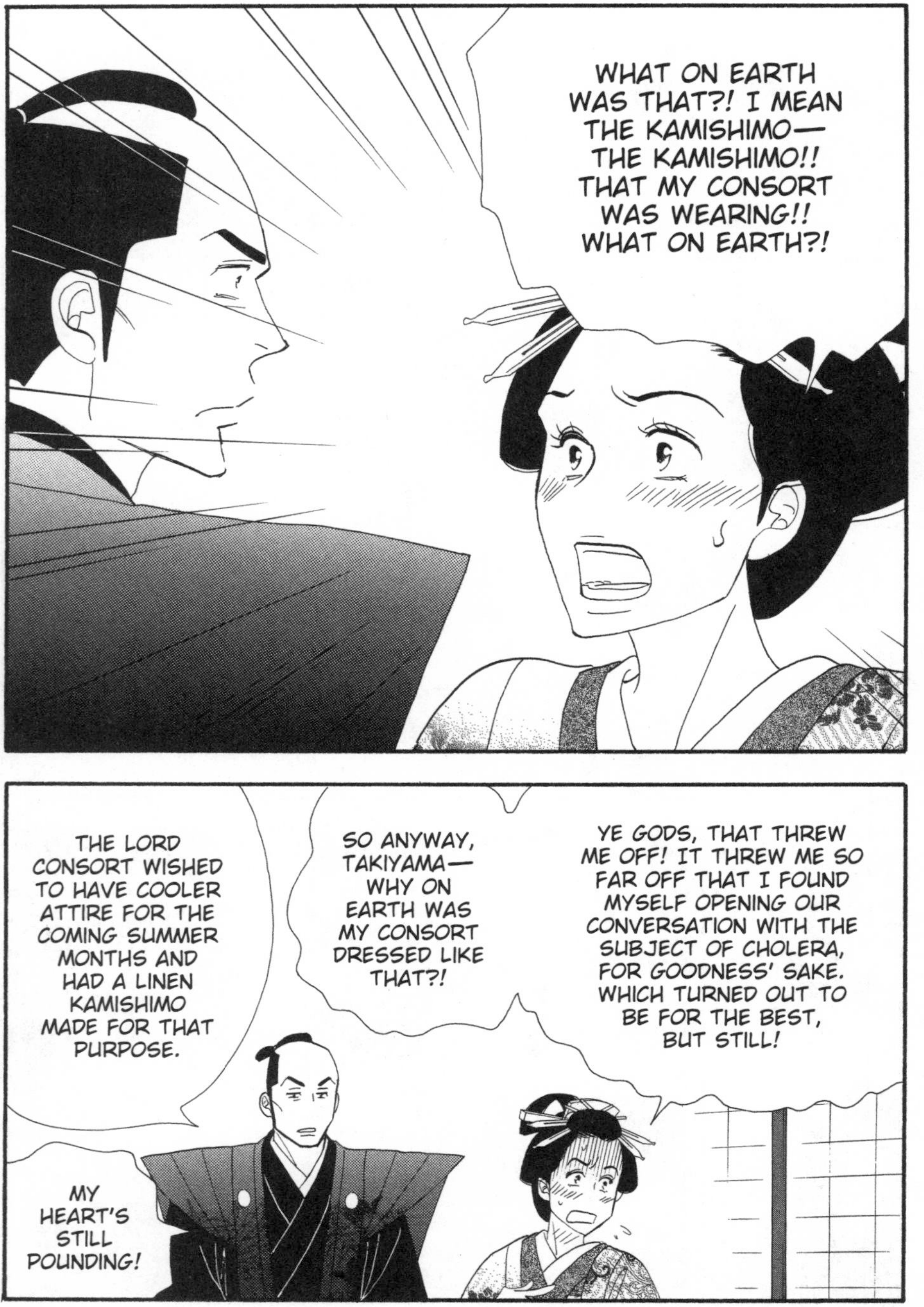
WHAT ON EARTH WAS THAT?! I MEAN THE KAMISHIMO— THE KAMISHIMO!! THAT MY CONSORT WAS WEARING!! WHAT ON EARTH?!
YE GODS, THAT THREW ME OFF! IT THREW ME SO FAR OFF THAT I FOUND MYSELF OPENING OUR CONVERSATION WITH THE SUBJECT OF CHOLERA, FOR GOODNESS' SAKE. WHICH TURNED OUT TO BE FOR THE BEST, BUT STILL!
SO ANYWAY, TAKIYAMA— WHY ON EARTH WAS MY CONSORT DRESSED LIKE THAT?!
THE LORD CONSORT WISHED TO HAVE COOLER ATTIRE FOR THE COMING SUMMER MONTHS AND HAD A LINEN KAMISHIMO MADE FOR THAT PURPOSE.
MY HEART'S STILL POUNDING!

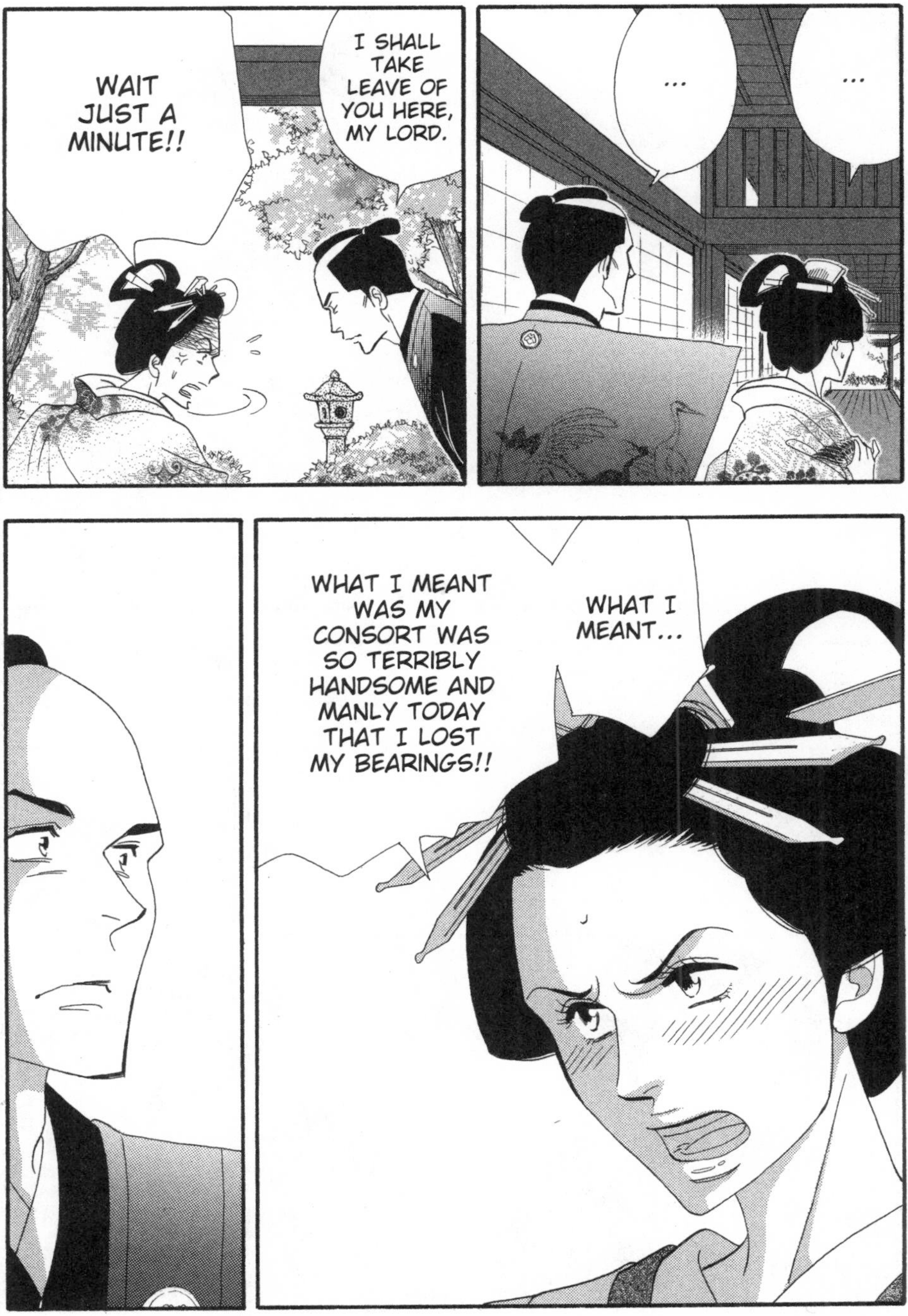
...
...
I SHALL TAKE LEAVE OF YOU HERE, MY LORD.
WAIT JUST A MINUTE!!
WHAT I MEANT...
WHAT I MEANT WAS MY CONSORT WAS SO TERRIBLY HANDSOME AND MANLY TODAY THAT I LOST MY BEARINGS!!

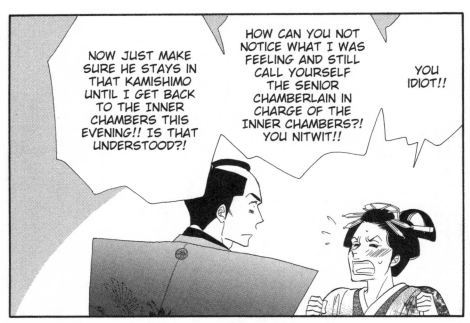

YOU IDIOT!!
HOW CAN YOU NOT NOTICE WHAT I WAS FEELING AND STILL CALL YOURSELF THE SENIOR CHAMBERLAIN IN CHARGE OF THE INNER CHAMBERS?! YOU NITWIT!!
NOW JUST MAKE SURE HE STAYS IN THAT KAMISHIMO UNTIL I GET BACK TO THE INNER CHAMBERS THIS EVENING!! IS THAT UNDERSTOOD?!
HMPH!
MY LORD SO COMMAND-ED?

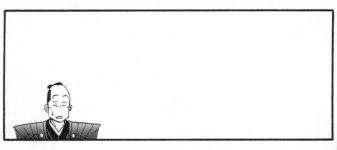

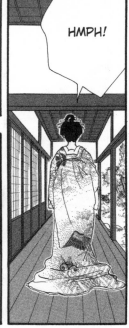

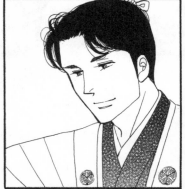

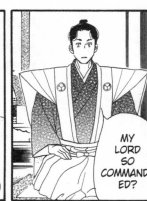

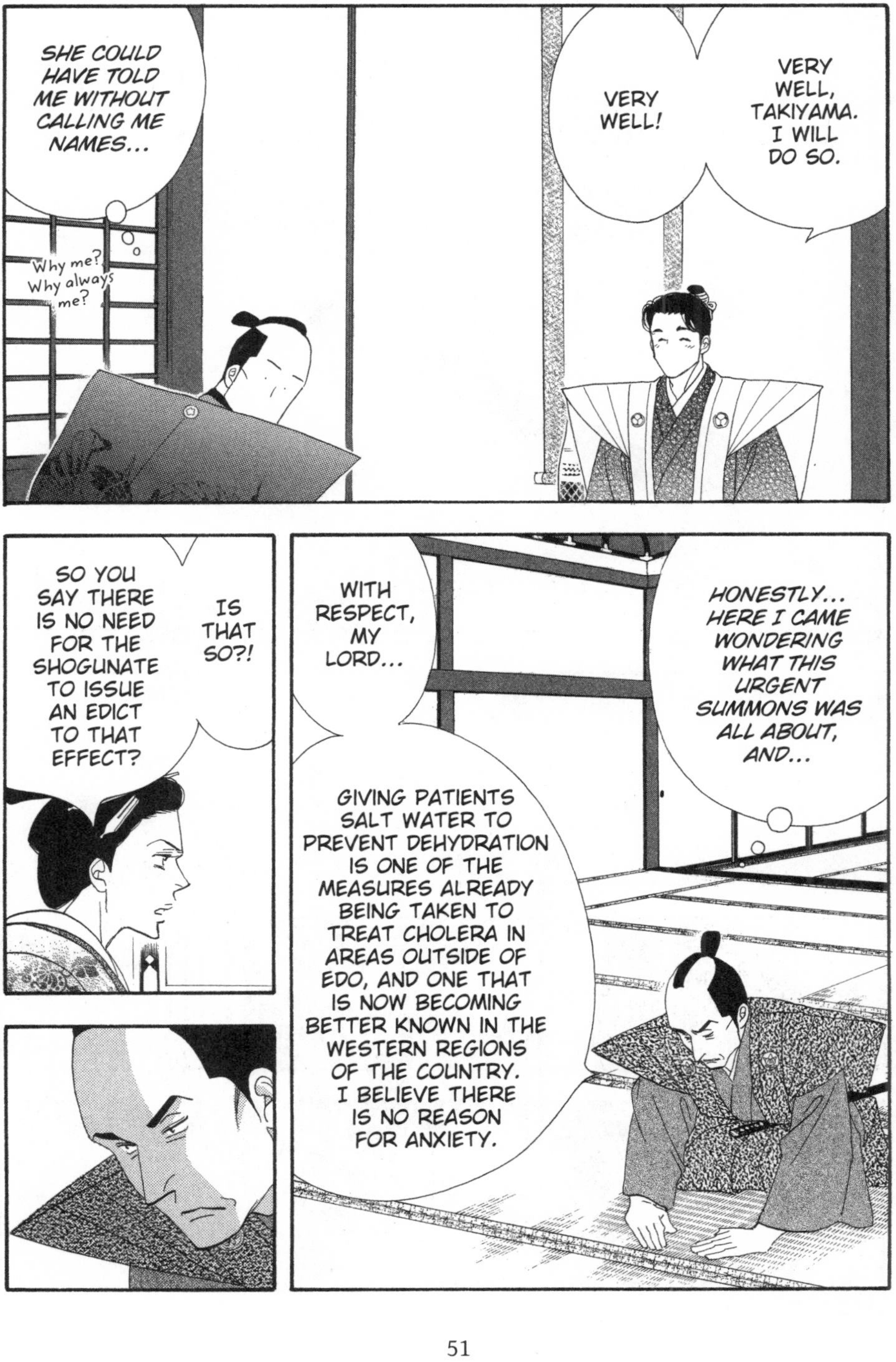
VERY WELL, TAKIYAMA. I WILL DO SO.
VERY WELL!
SHE COULD HAVE TOLD ME WITHOUT CALLING ME NAMES...
Why me? Why always me?
HONESTLY... HERE I CAME WONDERING WHAT THIS URGENT SUMMONS WAS ALL ABOUT, AND...
WITH RESPECT, MY LORD...
GIVING PATIENTS SALT WATER TO PREVENT DEHYDRATION IS ONE OF THE MEASURES ALREADY BEING TAKEN TO TREAT CHOLERA IN AREAS OUTSIDE OF EDO, AND ONE THAT IS NOW BECOMING BETTER KNOWN IN THE WESTERN REGIONS OF THE COUNTRY. I BELIEVE THERE IS NO REASON FOR ANXIETY.
IS THAT SO?!
SO YOU SAY THERE IS NO NEED FOR THE SHOGUNATE TO ISSUE AN EDICT TO THAT EFFECT?

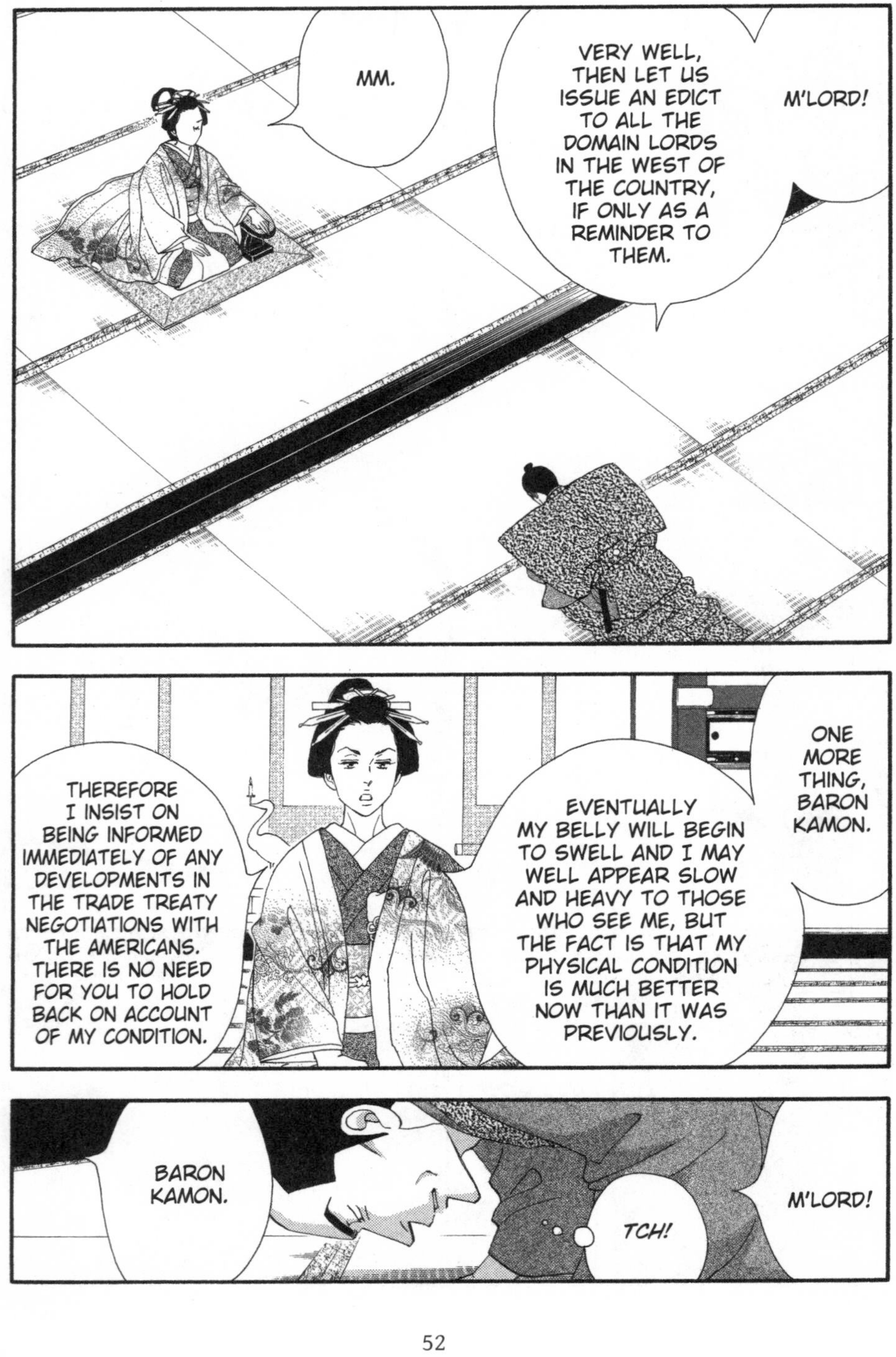
M'LORD!
VERY WELL, THEN LET US ISSUE AN EDICT TO ALL THE DOMAIN LORDS IN THE WEST OF THE COUNTRY, IF ONLY AS A REMINDER TO THEM.
MM.
ONE MORE THING, BARON KAMON.
EVENTUALLY MY BELLY WILL BEGIN TO SWELL AND I MAY WELL APPEAR SLOW AND HEAVY TO THOSE WHO SEE ME, BUT THE FACT IS THAT MY PHYSICAL CONDITION IS MUCH BETTER NOW THAN IT WAS PREVIOUSLY.
THEREFORE I INSIST ON BEING INFORMED IMMEDIATELY OF ANY DEVELOPMENTS IN THE TRADE TREATY NEGOTIATIONS WITH THE AMERICANS. THERE IS NO NEED FOR YOU TO HOLD BACK ON ACCOUNT OF MY CONDITION.
M'LORD!
TCH!
BARON KAMON.

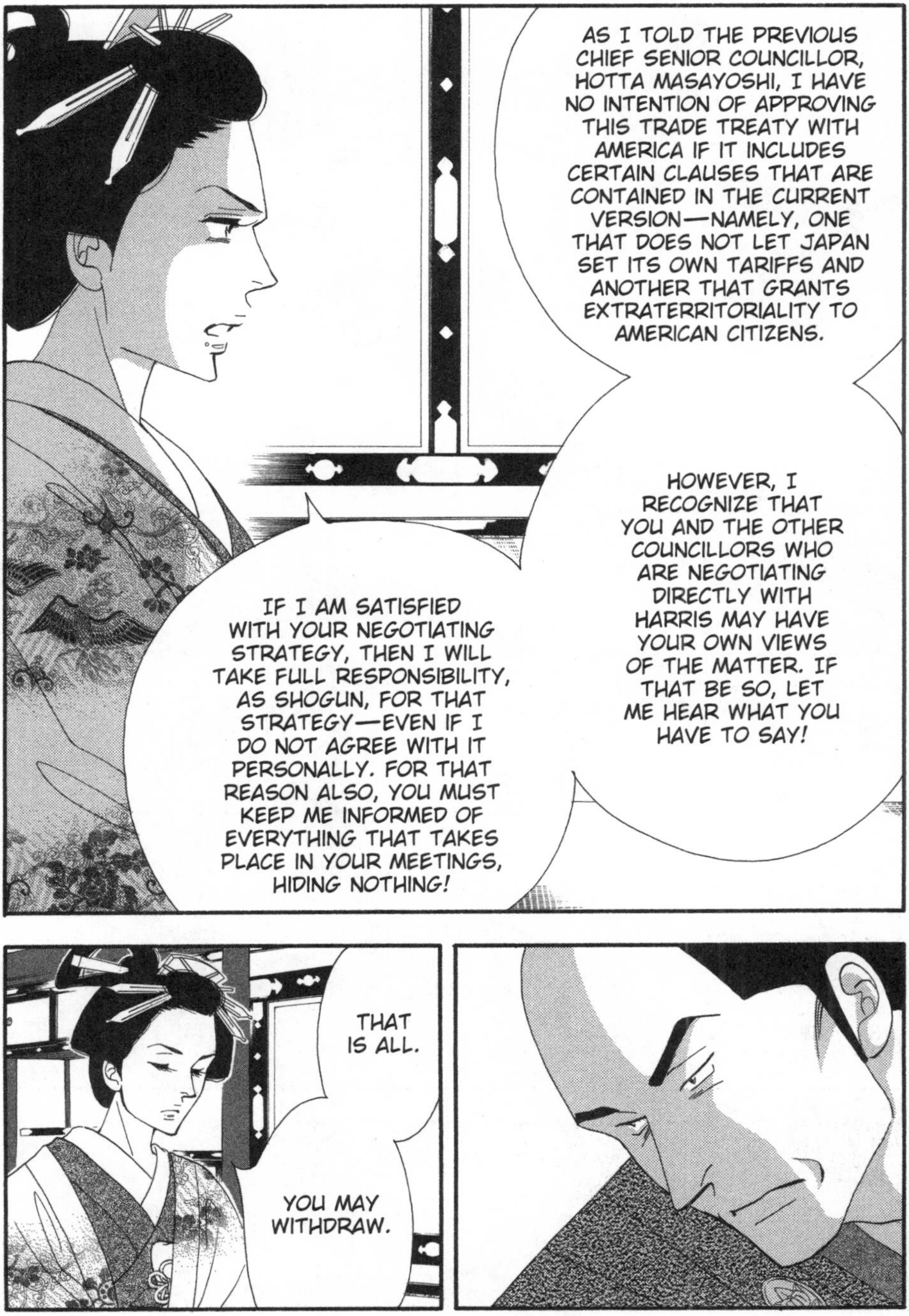
AS I TOLD THE PREVIOUS CHIEF SENIOR COUNCILLOR, HOTTA MASAYOSHI, I HAVE NO INTENTION OF APPROVING THIS TRADE TREATY WITH AMERICA IF IT INCLUDES CERTAIN CLAUSES THAT ARE CONTAINED IN THE CURRENT VERSION—NAMELY, ONE THAT DOES NOT LET JAPAN SET ITS OWN TARIFFS AND ANOTHER THAT GRANTS EXTRATERRITORIALITY TO AMERICAN CITIZENS.
HOWEVER, I RECOGNIZE THAT YOU AND THE OTHER COUNCILLORS WHO ARE NEGOTIATING DIRECTLY WITH HARRIS MAY HAVE YOUR OWN VIEWS OF THE MATTER. IF THAT BE SO, LET ME HEAR WHAT YOU HAVE TO SAY!
IF I AM SATISFIED WITH YOUR NEGOTIATING STRATEGY, THEN I WILL TAKE FULL RESPONSIBILITY, AS SHOGUN, FOR THAT STRATEGY—EVEN IF I DO NOT AGREE WITH IT PERSONALLY. FOR THAT REASON ALSO, YOU MUST KEEP ME INFORMED OF EVERYTHING THAT TAKES PLACE IN YOUR MEETINGS, HIDING NOTHING!
THAT IS ALL.
YOU MAY WITHDRAW.

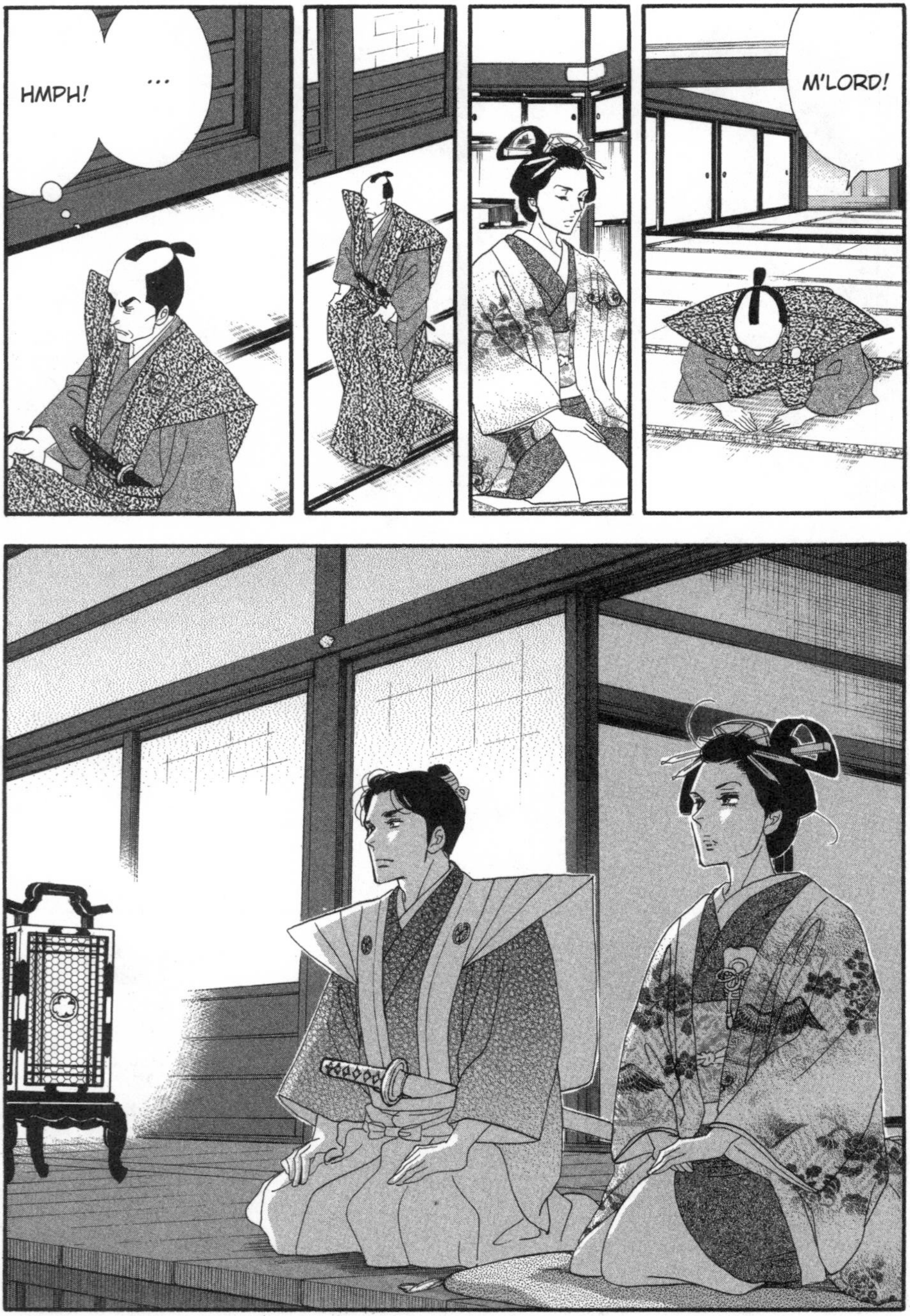
M'LORD!
...
HMPH!

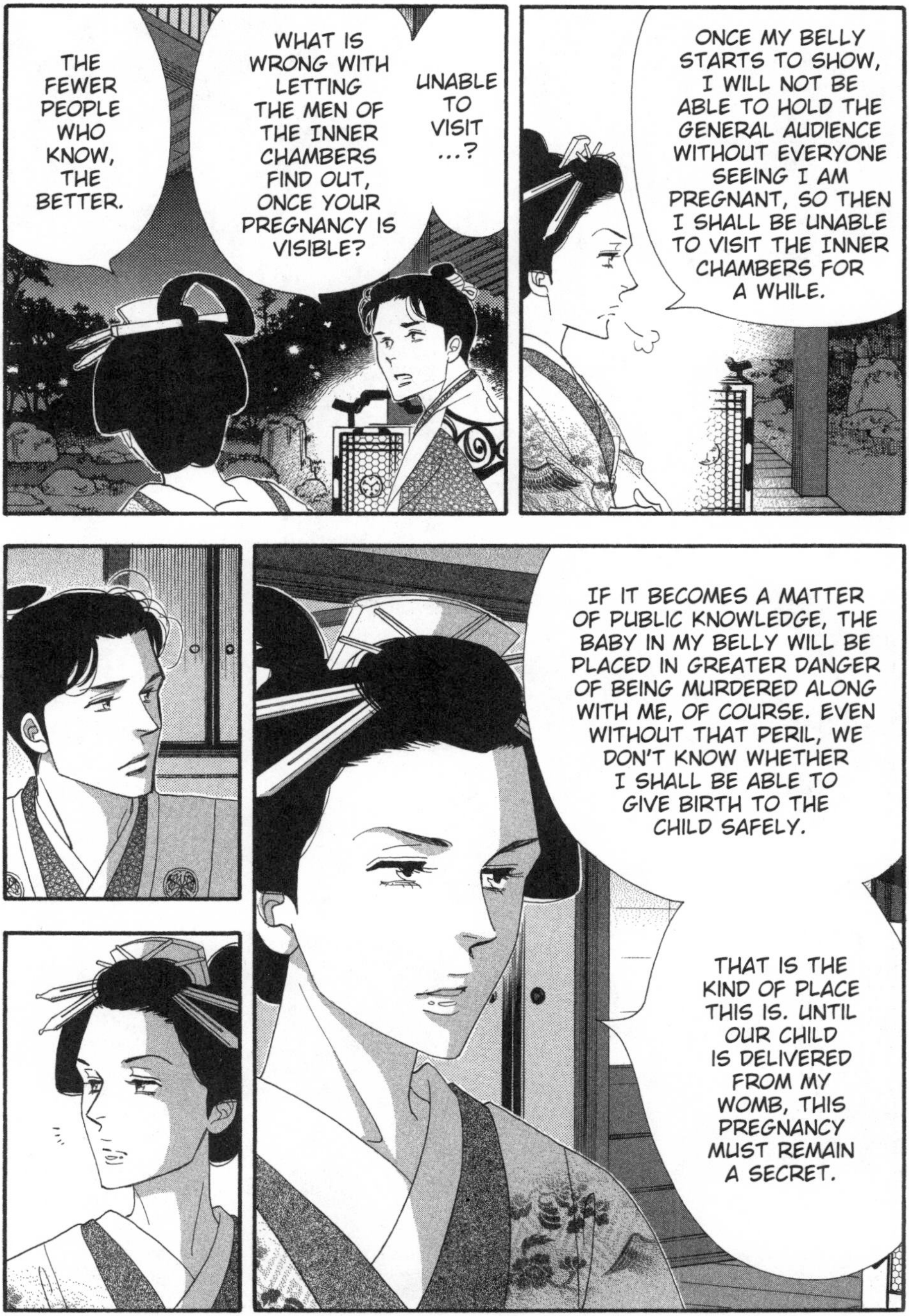
ONCE MY BELLY STARTS TO SHOW, I WILL NOT BE ABLE TO HOLD THE GENERAL AUDIENCE WITHOUT EVERYONE SEEING I AM PREGNANT, SO THEN I SHALL BE UNABLE TO VISIT THE INNER CHAMBERS FOR A WHILE.
UNABLE TO VISIT ...?
WHAT IS WRONG WITH LETTING THE MEN OF THE INNER CHAMBERS FIND OUT, ONCE YOUR PREGNANCY IS VISIBLE?
THE FEWER PEOPLE WHO KNOW, THE BETTER.
IF IT BECOMES A MATTER OF PUBLIC KNOWLEDGE, THE BABY IN MY BELLY WILL BE PLACED IN GREATER DANGER OF BEING MURDERED ALONG WITH ME, OF COURSE. EVEN WITHOUT THAT PERIL, WE DON'T KNOW WHETHER I SHALL BE ABLE TO GIVE BIRTH TO THE CHILD SAFELY.
THAT IS THE KIND OF PLACE THIS IS. UNTIL OUR CHILD IS DELIVERED FROM MY WOMB, THIS PREGNANCY MUST REMAIN A SECRET.

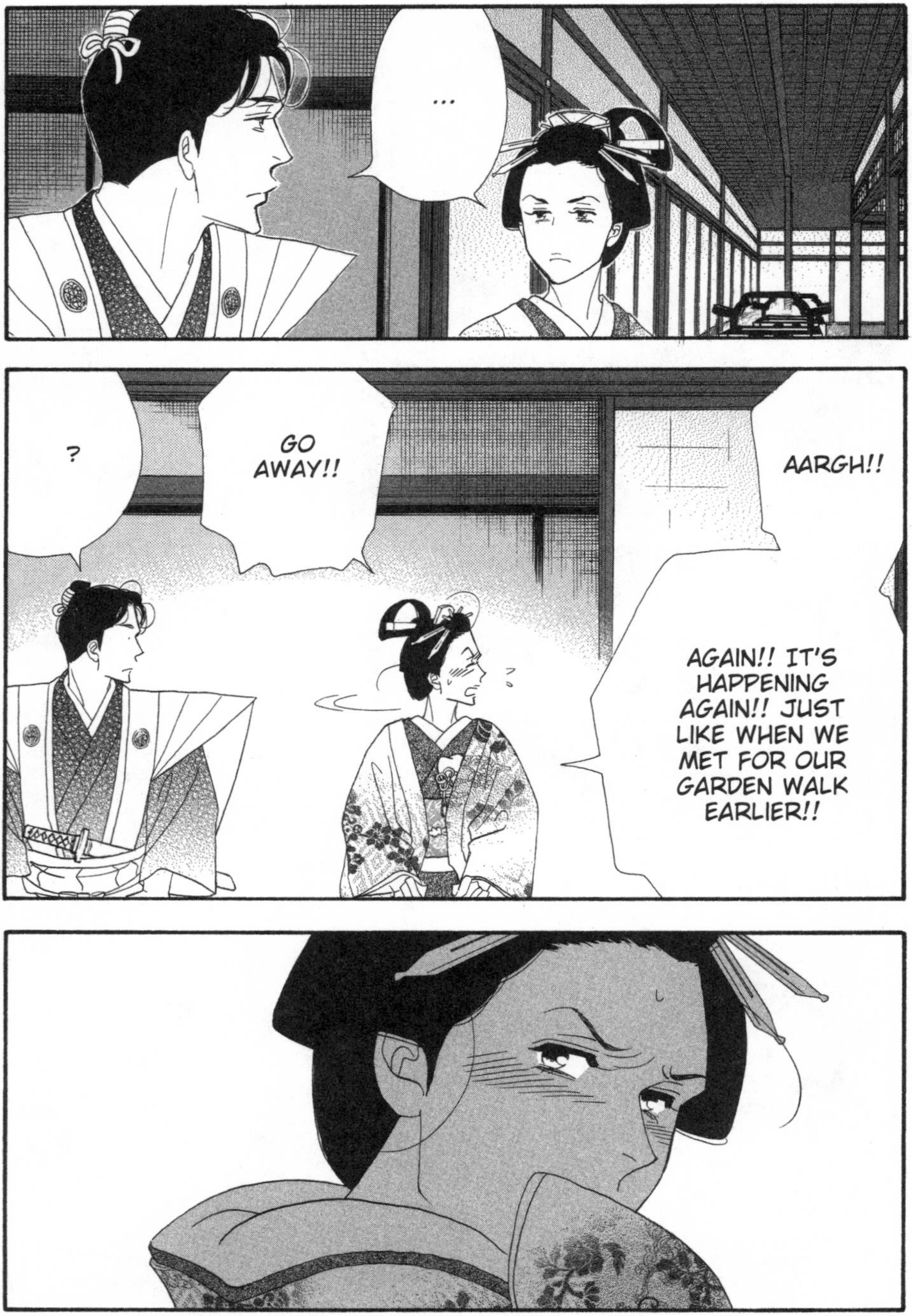
...
AARGH!!
GO AWAY!!
?
AGAIN!! IT'S HAPPENING AGAIN!! JUST LIKE WHEN WE MET FOR OUR GARDEN WALK EARLIER!!

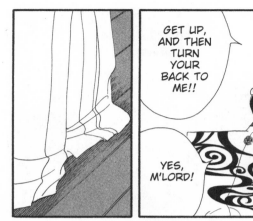

GET UP, AND THEN TURN YOUR BACK TO ME!!

UH...

KOFF

GET UP!

YES, M'LORD!

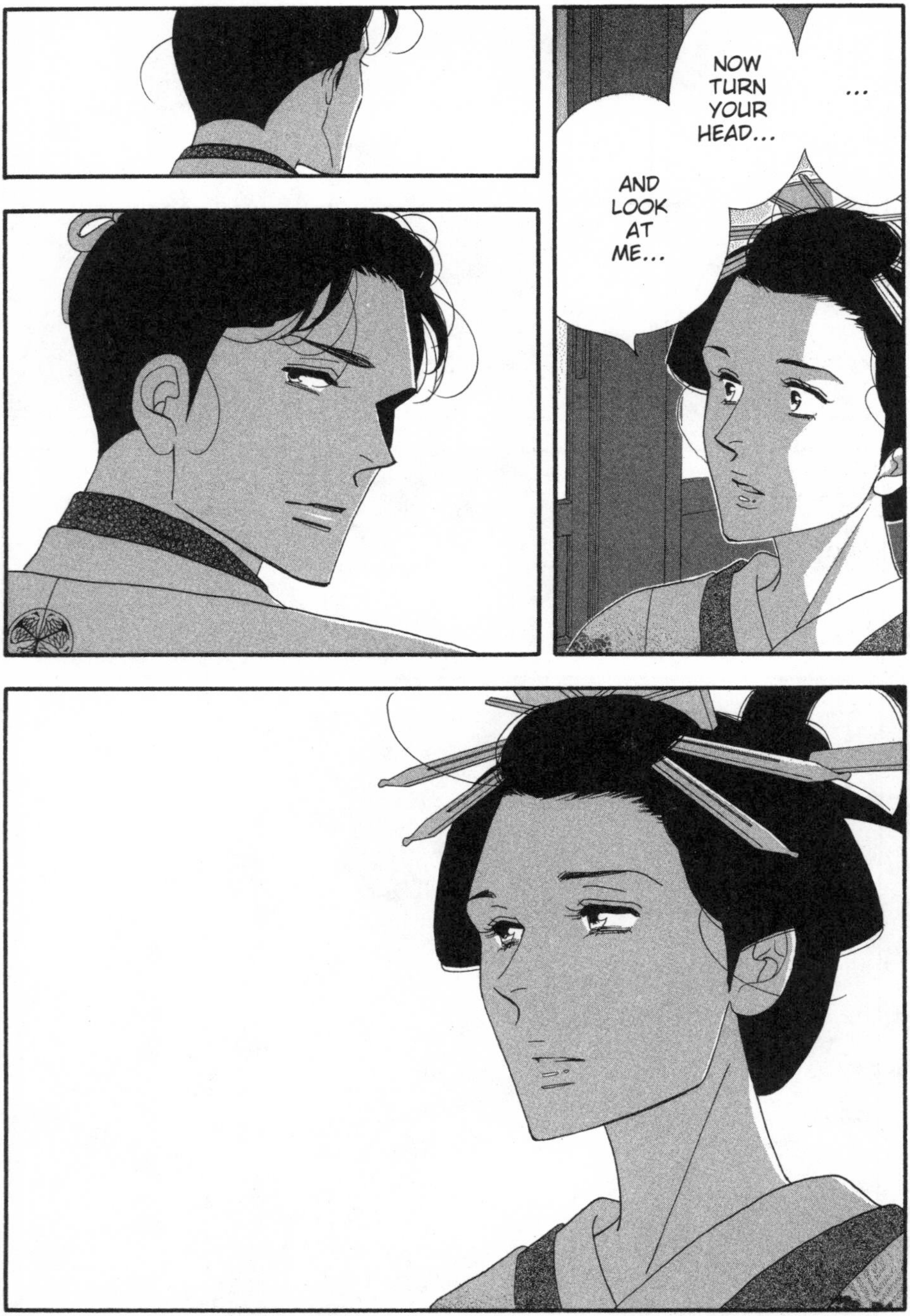
...
NOW TURN YOUR HEAD...
AND LOOK AT ME...

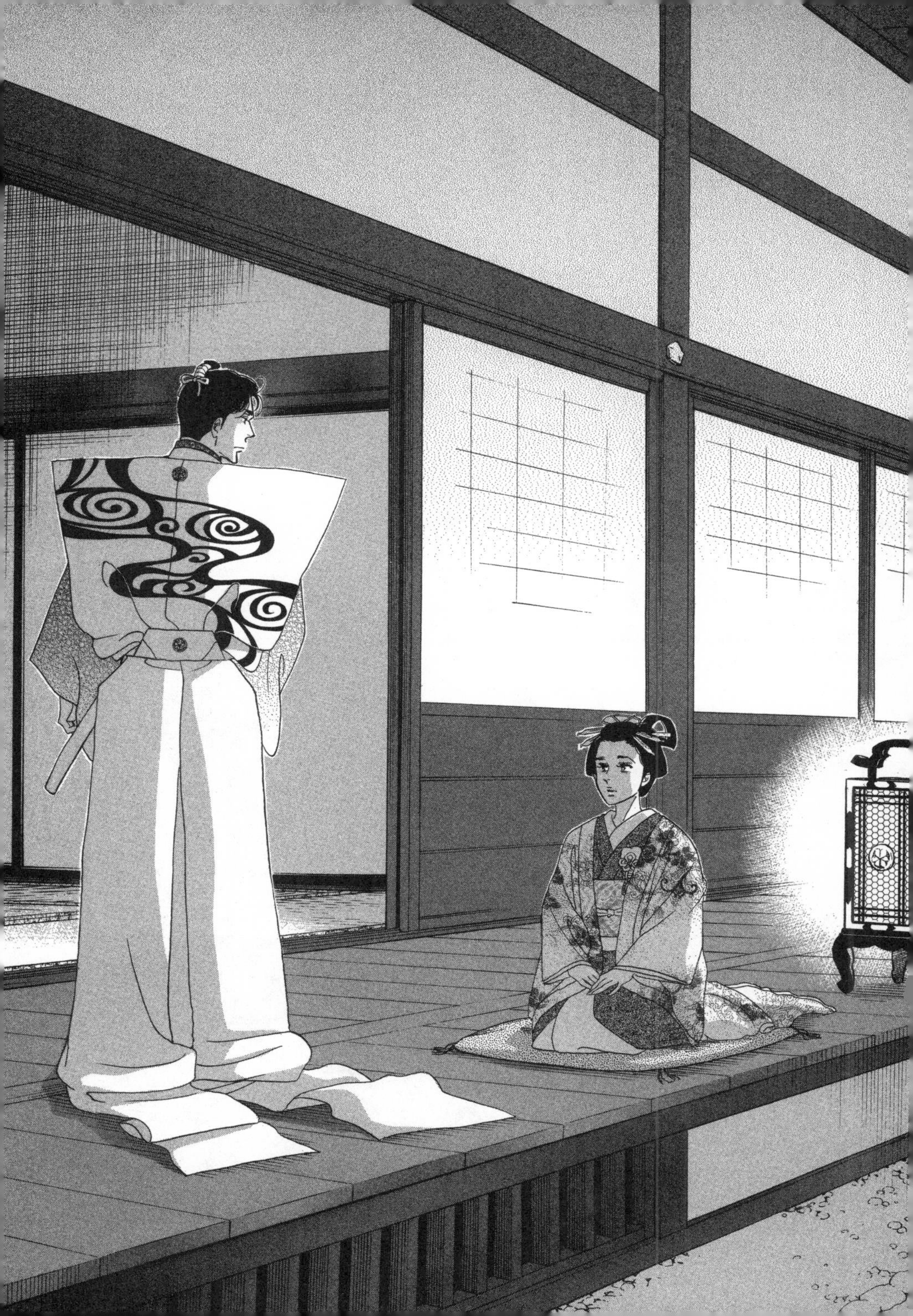

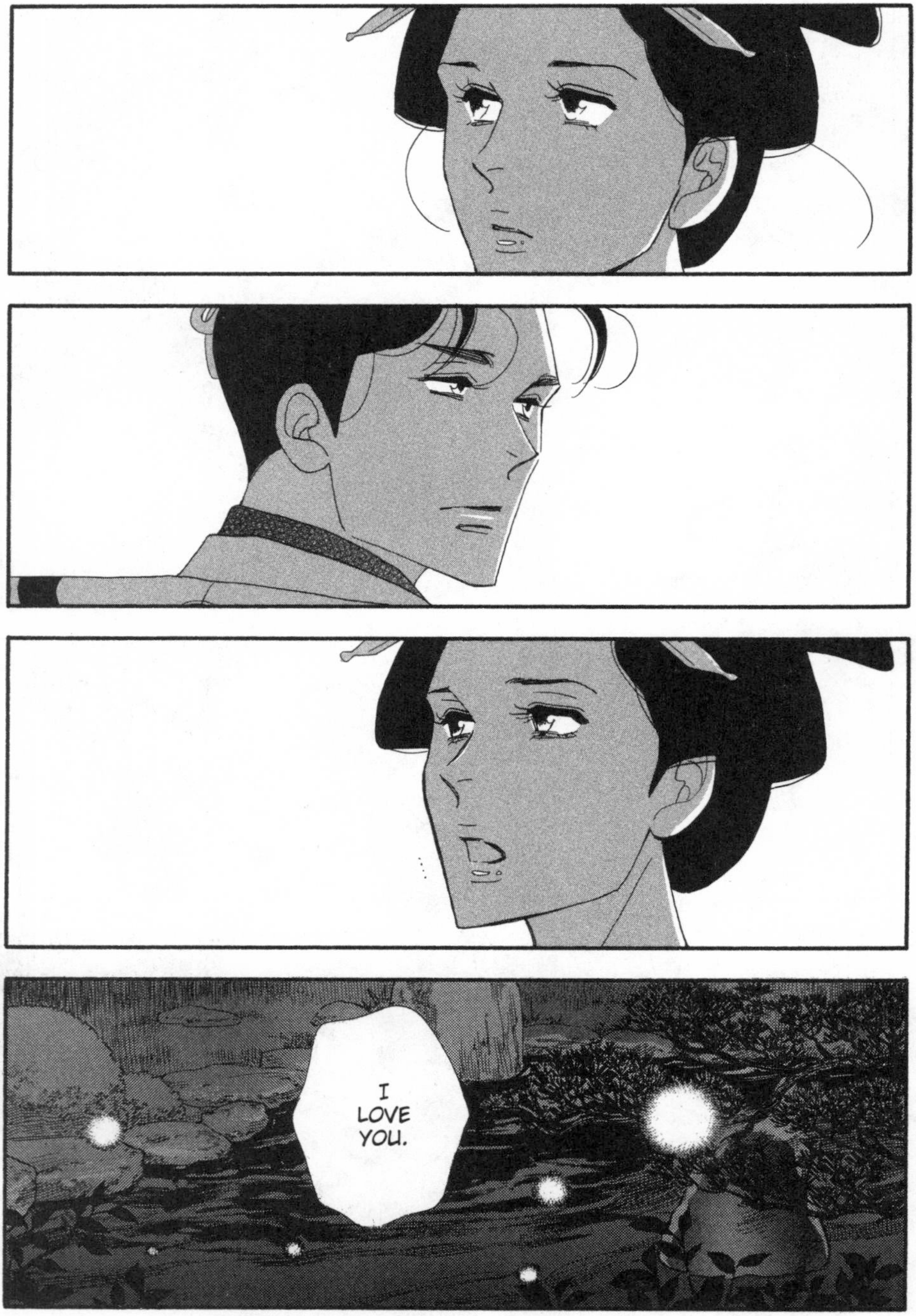
I LOVE YOU.

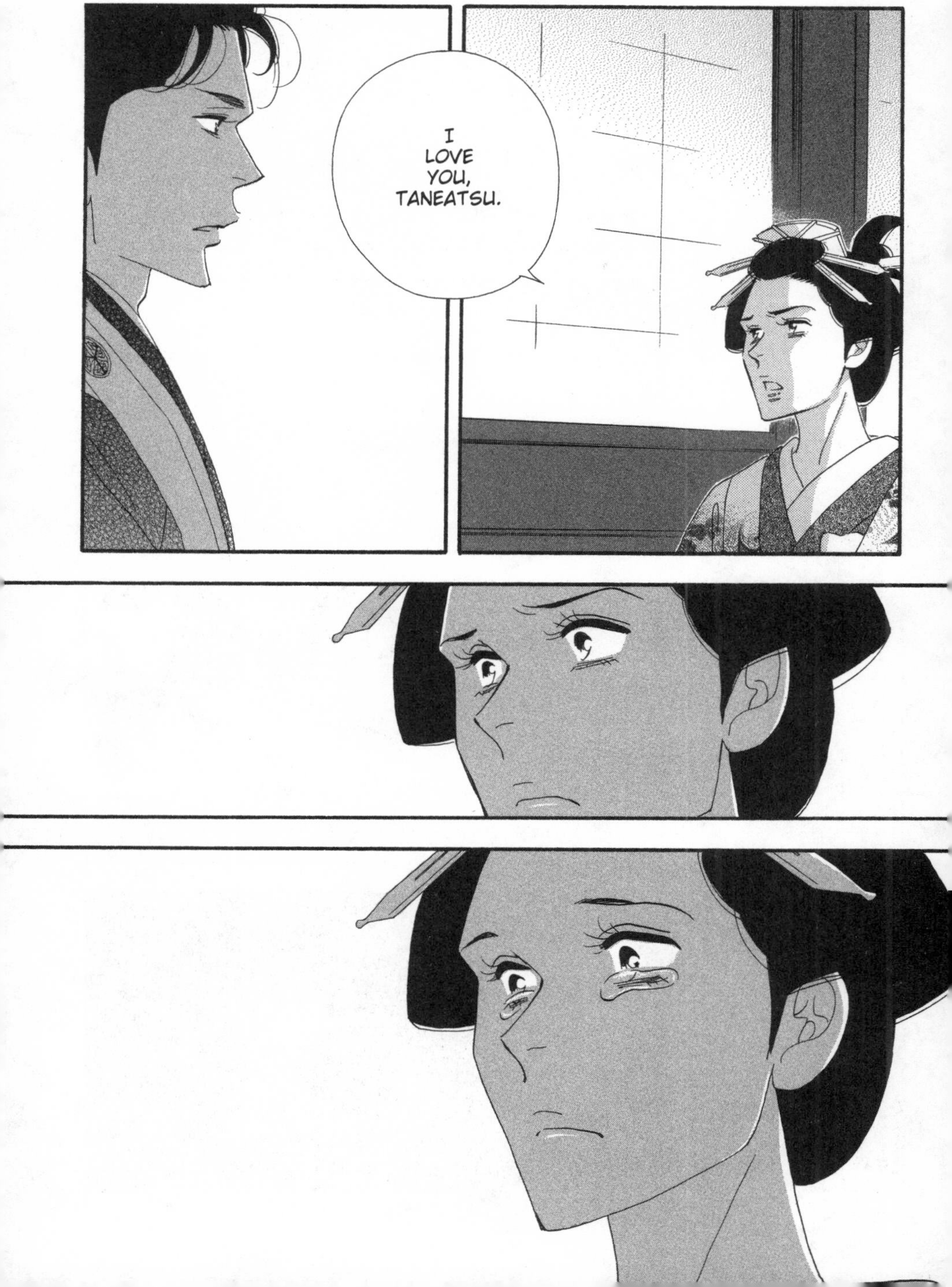
I LOVE YOU, TANEATSU.

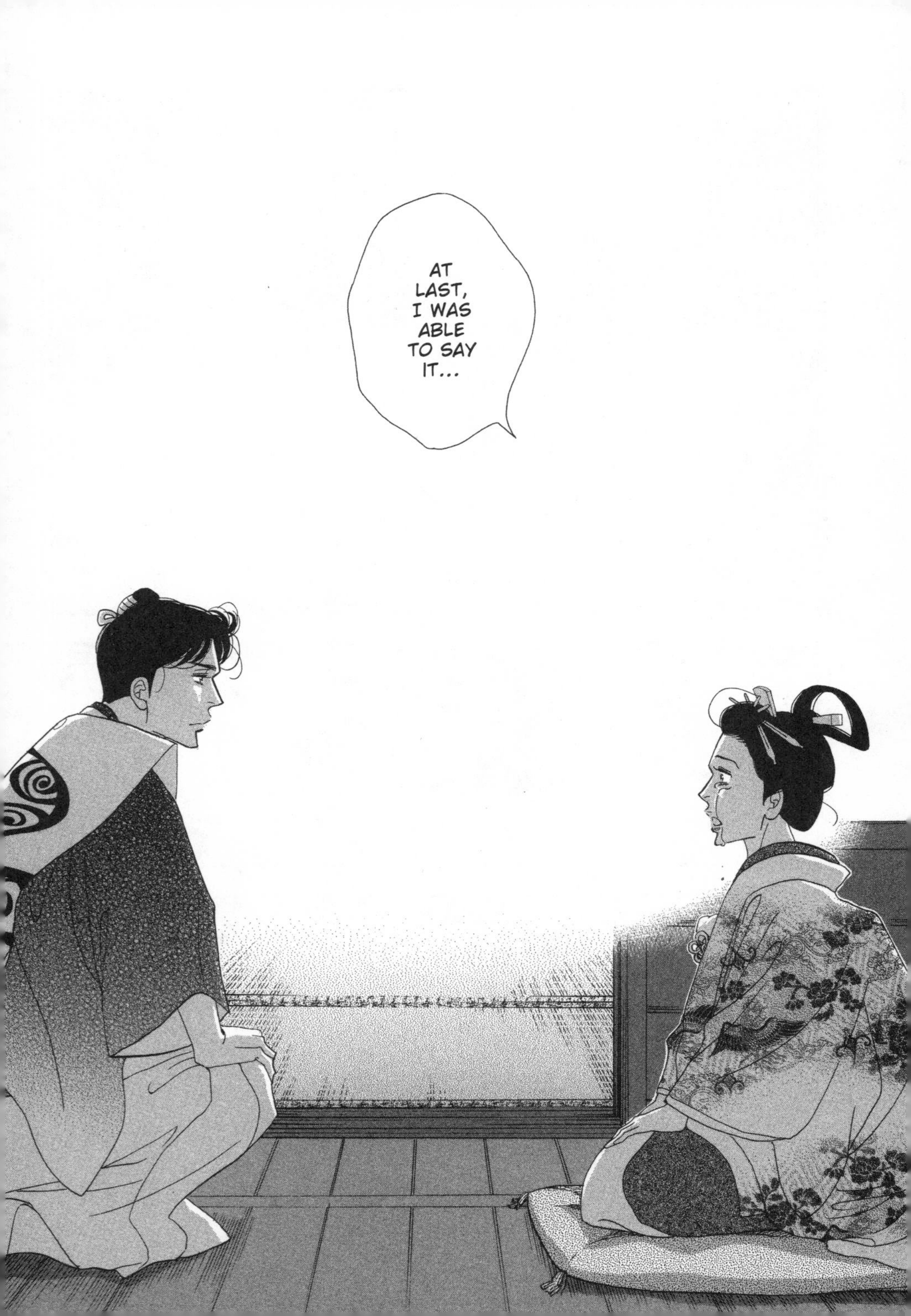
AT LAST, I WAS ABLE TO SAY IT...

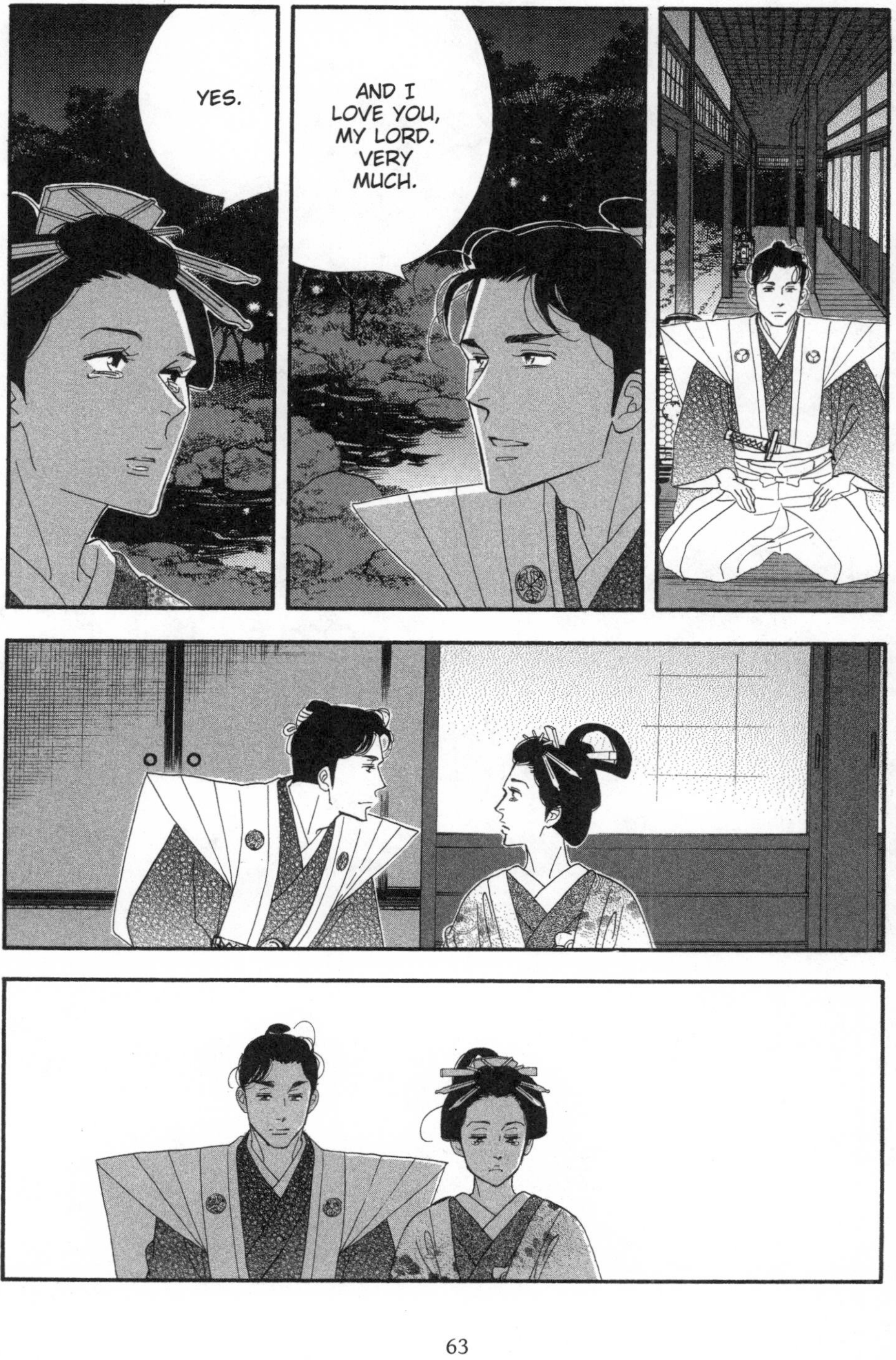
AND I LOVE YOU, MY LORD. VERY MUCH.
YES.

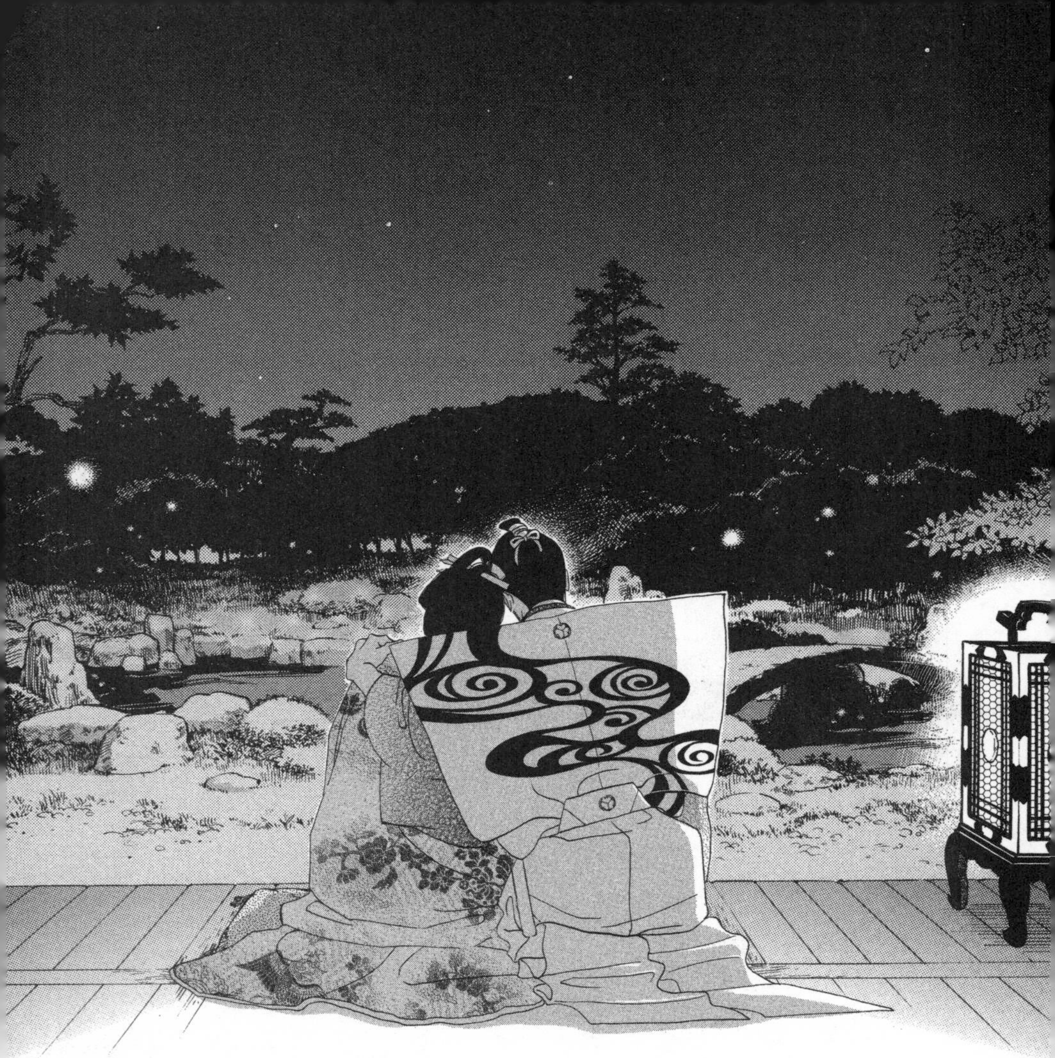

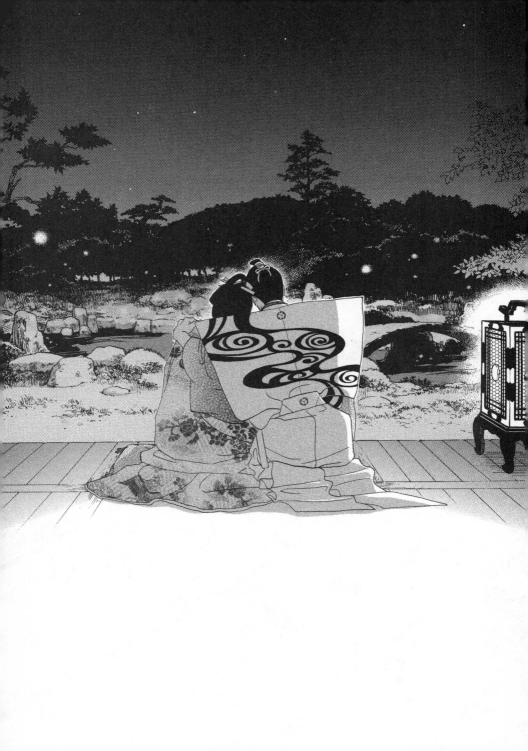

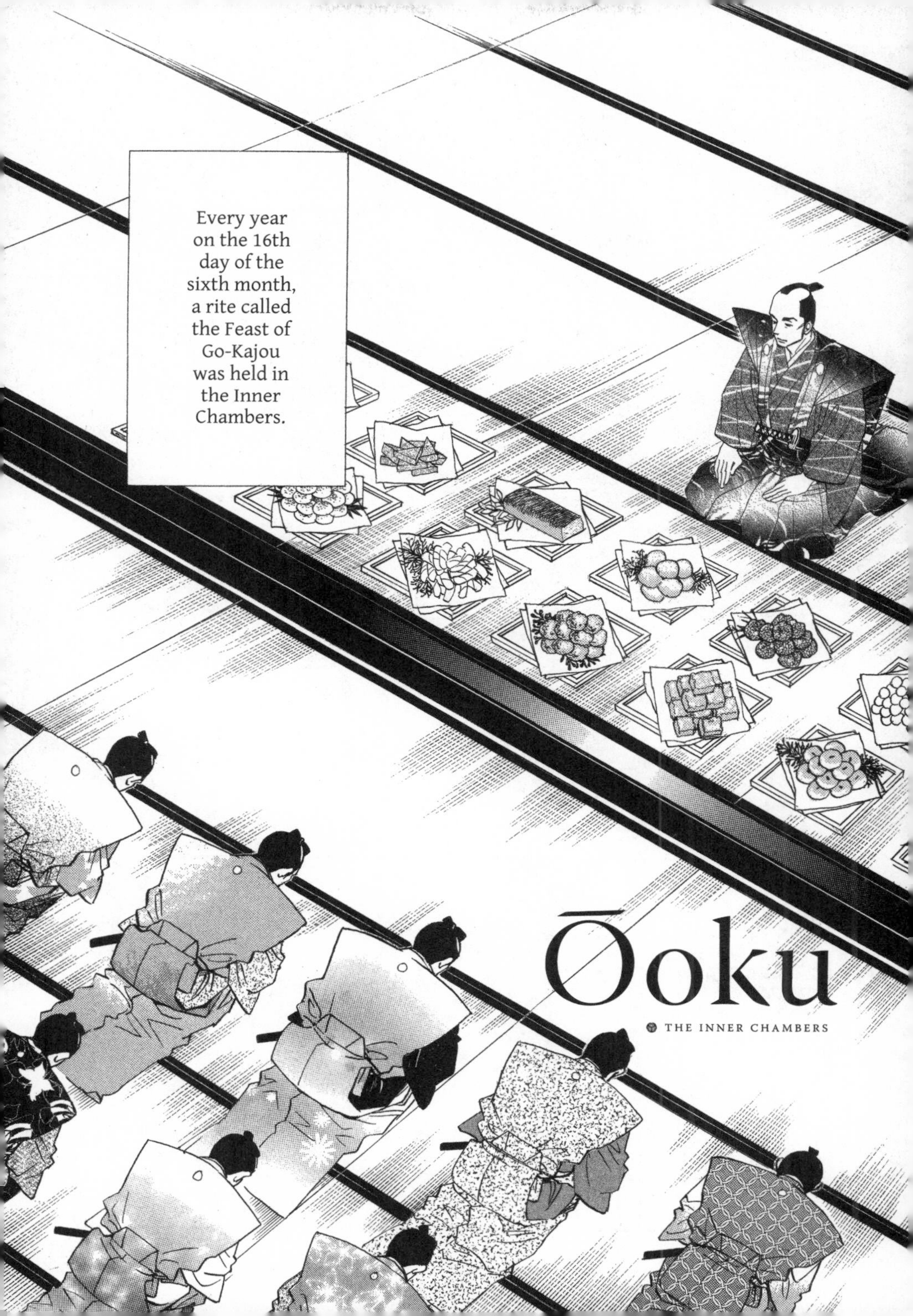
Every year on the 16th day of the sixth month, a rite called the Feast of Go-Kajou was held in the Inner Chambers.
Ōoku
THE INNER CHAMBERS

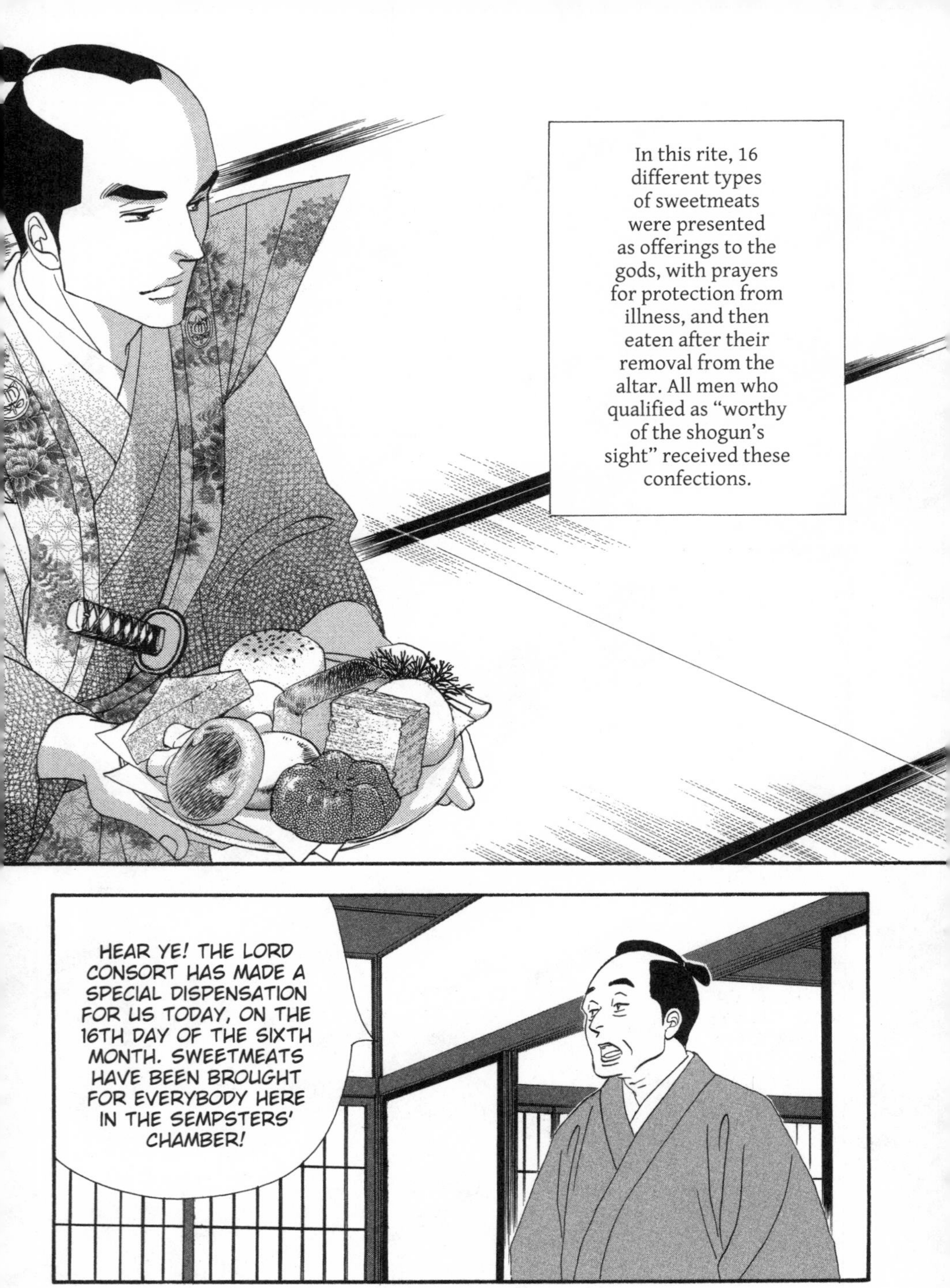
In this rite, 16 different types of sweetmeats were presented as offerings to the gods, with prayers for protection from illness, and then eaten after their removal from the altar. All men who qualified as “worthy of the shogun’s sight” received these confections.
HEAR YE! THE LORD CONSORT HAS MADE A SPECIAL DISPENSATION FOR US TODAY, ON THE 16TH DAY OF THE SIXTH MONTH. SWEETMEATS HAVE BEEN BROUGHT FOR EVERYBODY HERE IN THE SEMPSTERS' CHAMBER!

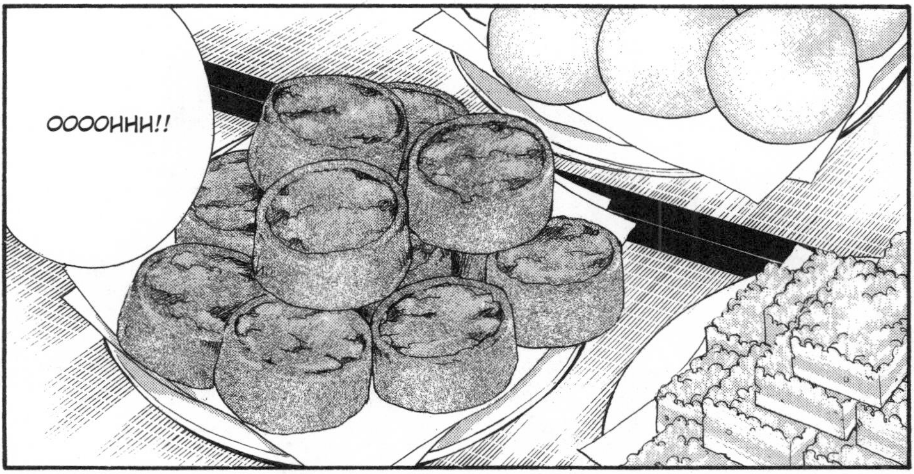
OOOOHHH!!

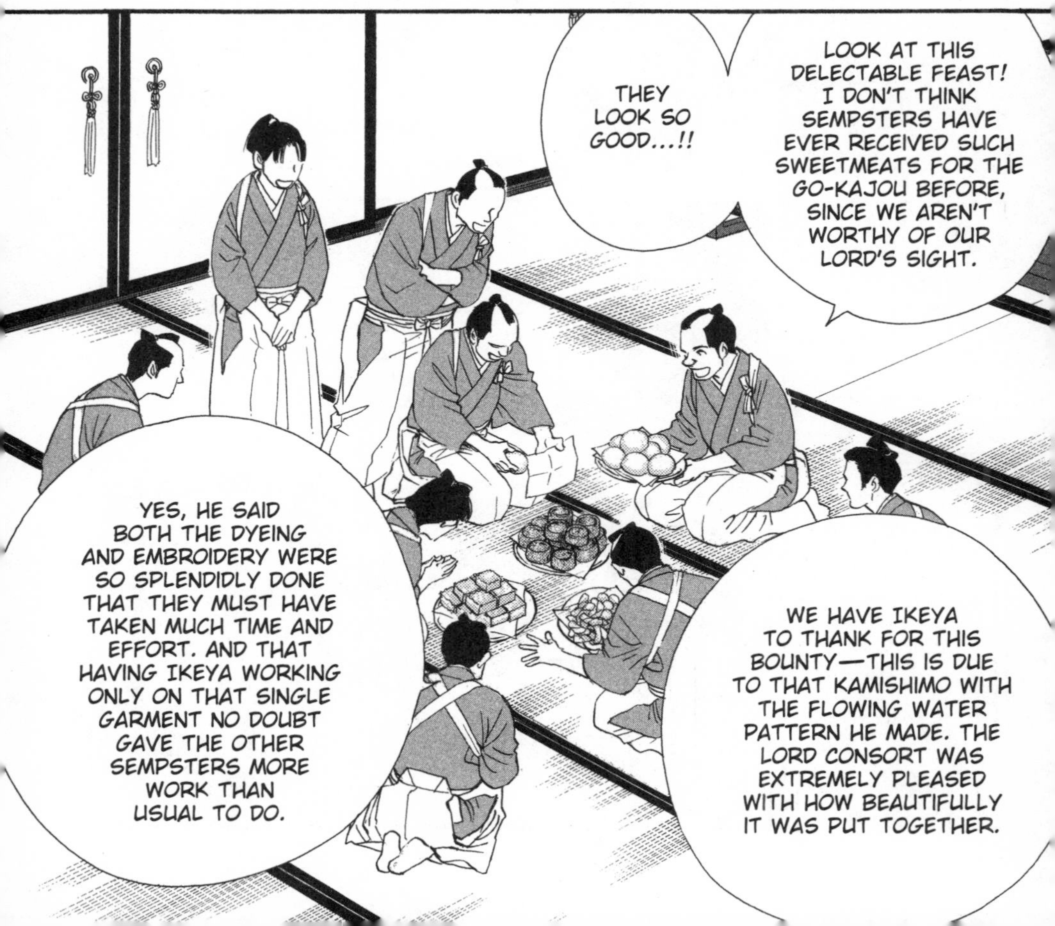
LOOK AT THIS DELECTABLE FEAST! I DON'T THINK SEMPSTERS HAVE EVER RECEIVED SUCH SWEETMEATS FOR THE GO-KAJOU BEFORE, SINCE WE AREN'T WORTHY OF OUR LORD'S SIGHT.
THEY LOOK SO GOOD...!!
WE HAVE IKEYA TO THANK FOR THIS BOUNTY—THIS IS DUE TO THAT KAMISHIMO WITH THE FLOWING WATER PATTERN HE MADE. THE LORD CONSORT WAS EXTREMELY PLEASED WITH HOW BEAUTIFULLY IT WAS PUT TOGETHER.
YES, HE SAID BOTH THE DYEING AND EMBROIDERY WERE SO SPLENDIDLY DONE THAT THEY MUST HAVE TAKEN MUCH TIME AND EFFORT. AND THAT HAVING IKEYA WORKING ONLY ON THAT SINGLE GARMENT NO DOUBT GAVE THE OTHER SEMPSTERS MORE WORK THAN USUAL TO DO.

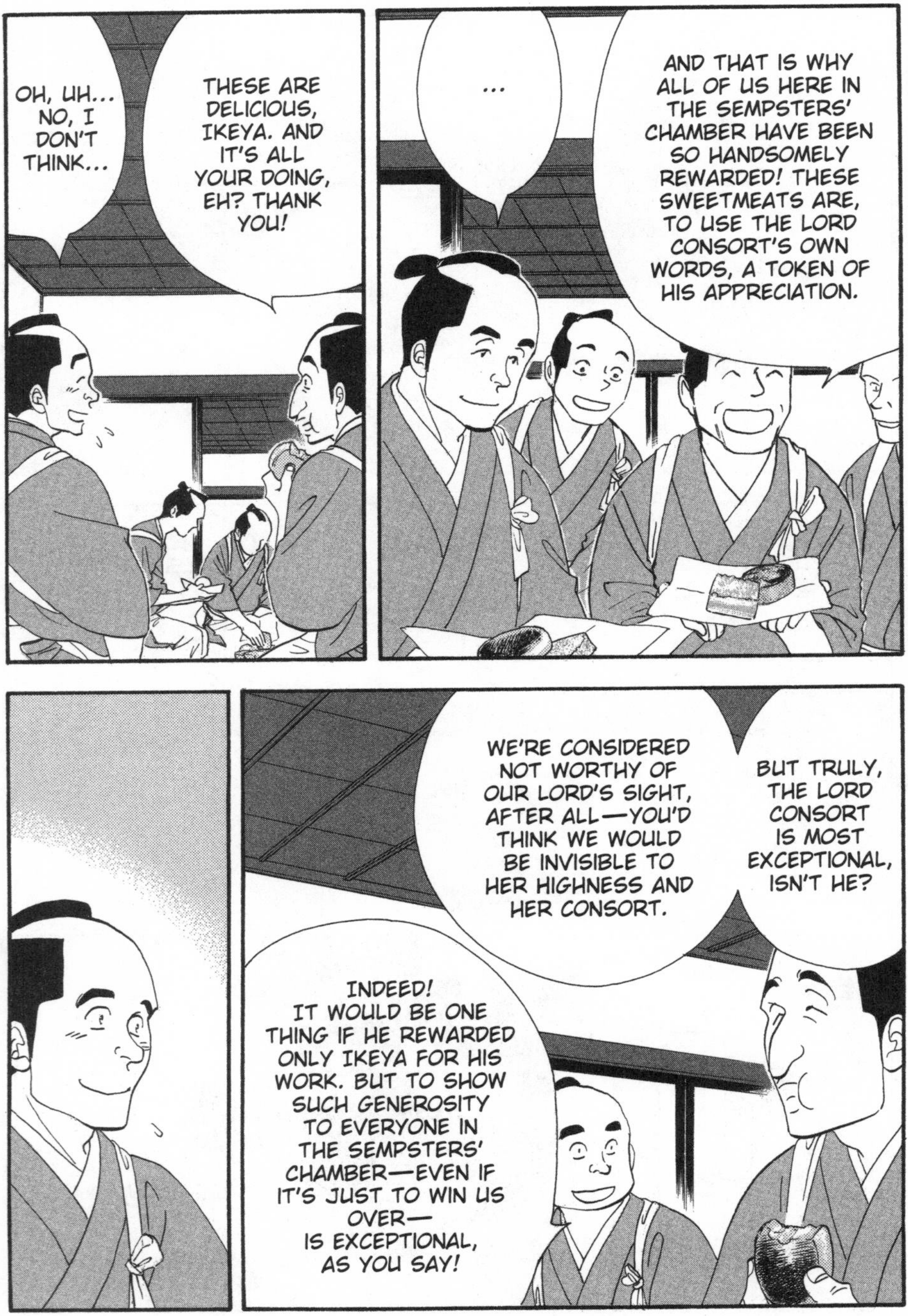
AND THAT IS WHY ALL OF US HERE IN THE SEMPSTERS' CHAMBER HAVE BEEN SO HANDSOMELY REWARDED! THESE SWEETMEATS ARE, TO USE THE LORD CONSORT'S OWN WORDS, A TOKEN OF HIS APPRECIATION.
...
THESE ARE DELICIOUS, IKEYA. AND IT'S ALL YOUR DOING, EH? THANK YOU!
OH, UH... NO, I DON'T THINK...
BUT TRULY, THE LORD CONSORT IS MOST EXCEPTIONAL, ISN'T HE?
WE'RE CONSIDERED NOT WORTHY OF OUR LORD'S SIGHT, AFTER ALL—YOU'D THINK WE WOULD BE INVISIBLE TO HER HIGHNESS AND HER CONSORT.
INDEED! IT WOULD BE ONE THING IF HE REWARDED ONLY IKEYA FOR HIS WORK. BUT TO SHOW SUCH GENEROSITY TO EVERYONE IN THE SEMPSTERS' CHAMBER—EVEN IF IT'S JUST TO WIN US OVER— IS EXCEPTIONAL, AS YOU SAY!

JUST BETWEEN YOU AND ME, THOUGH, IKEYA... WHAT DO YOU THINK ABOUT THOSE RUMORS THAT THE LORD CONSORT POISONED LADY TOMIKO OF KII IN ORDER TO MAKE LORD YOSHINOBU THE NEXT SHOGUN...?
IT'S OUT OF THE QUESTION!
PEOPLE CAN BELIEVE WHAT THEY WANT TO BELIEVE, BUT FROM WHAT I HAVE SEEN, THE LORD CONSORT WOULD NEVER DO SOMETHING LIKE THAT!
BUT EVEN IF, JUST FOR THE SAKE OF ARGUMENT, HE WERE THE KIND OF SHREWD, CALCULATING PERSON YOU INSINUATE HE IS—GIVING US THESE SWEETS JUST TO WIN US OVER AND SO ON—HE WOULD NEVER GIVE LADY TOMIKO POISON, WOULD HE, BECAUSE HE WOULD BE THE VERY FIRST ONE TO BE SUSPECTED OF IT!!
OH...
THAT'S TRUE...
I'M SORRY TO INTERRUPT YOU AT A TIME LIKE THIS.
BUT I'VE GOT A FAVOR TO ASK OF YOU ALL.

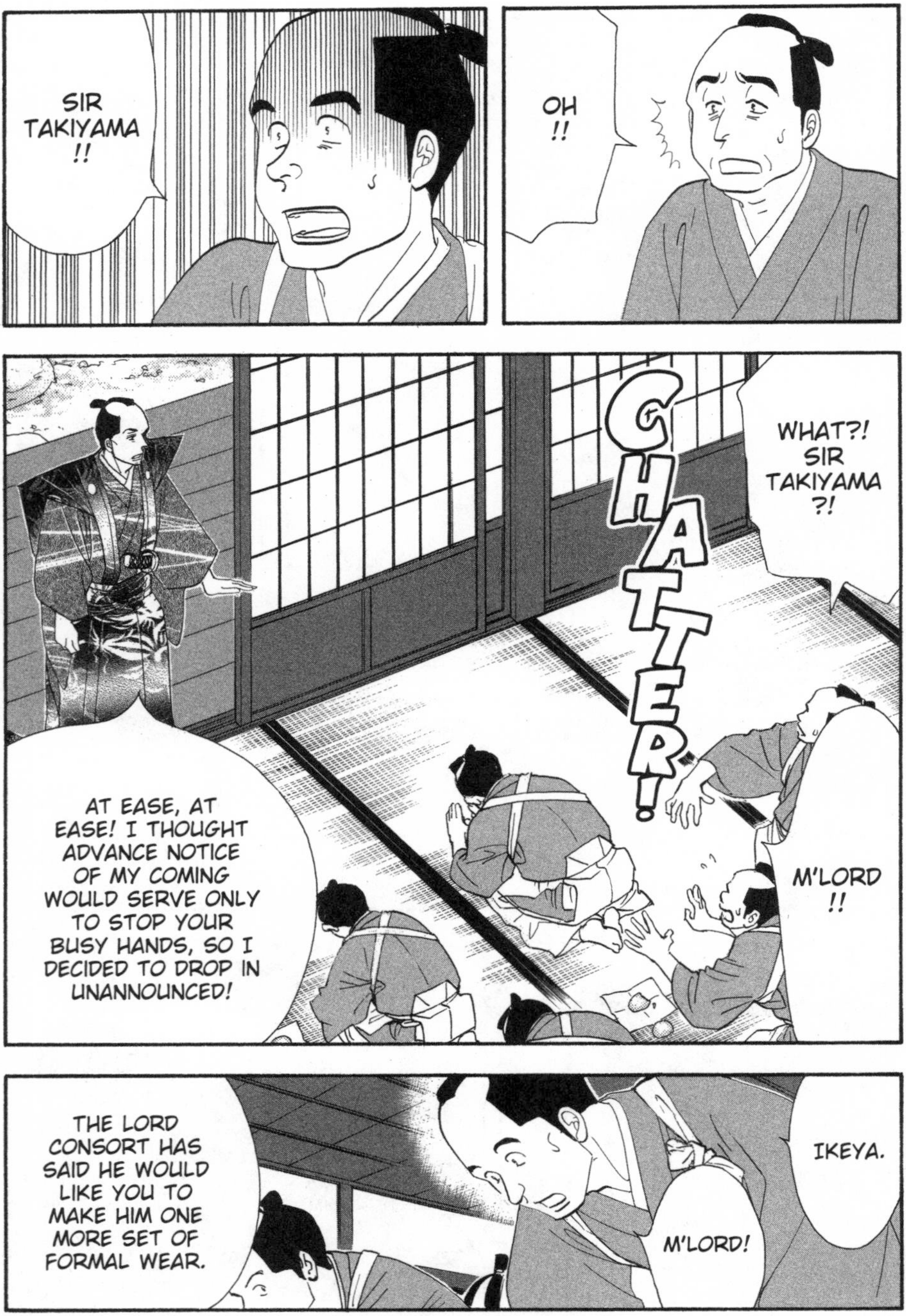
OH !!
SIR TAKIYAMA !!
WHAT?! SIR TAKIYAMA ?!
CHATTER!
M'LORD !!
AT EASE, AT EASE! I THOUGHT ADVANCE NOTICE OF MY COMING WOULD SERVE ONLY TO STOP YOUR BUSY HANDS, SO I DECIDED TO DROP IN UNANNOUNCED!
IKEYA.
M'LORD!
THE LORD CONSORT HAS SAID HE WOULD LIKE YOU TO MAKE HIM ONE MORE SET OF FORMAL WEAR.

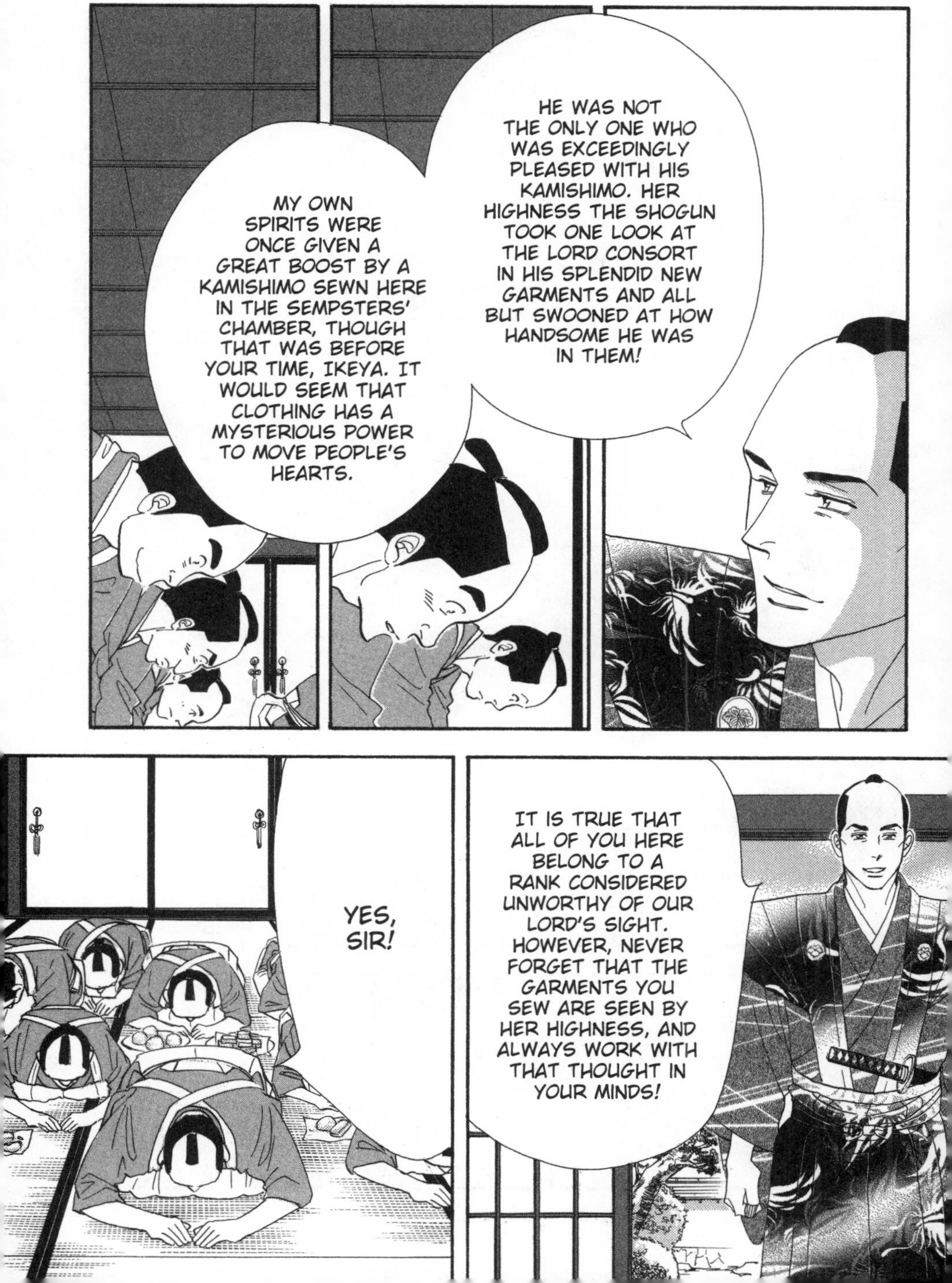
HE WAS NOT THE ONLY ONE WHO WAS EXCEEDINGLY PLEASED WITH HIS KAMISHIMO. HER HIGHNESS THE SHOGUN TOOK ONE LOOK AT THE LORD CONSORT IN HIS SPLENDID NEW GARMENTS AND ALL BUT SWOONED AT HOW HANDSOME HE WAS IN THEM!
MY OWN SPIRITS WERE ONCE GIVEN A GREAT BOOST BY A KAMISHIMO SEWN HERE IN THE SEMPSTERS' CHAMBER, THOUGH THAT WAS BEFORE YOUR TIME, IKEYA. IT WOULD SEEM THAT CLOTHING HAS A MYSTERIOUS POWER TO MOVE PEOPLE'S HEARTS.
IT IS TRUE THAT ALL OF YOU HERE BELONG TO A RANK CONSIDERED UNWORTHY OF OUR LORD'S SIGHT. HOWEVER, NEVER FORGET THAT THE GARMENTS YOU SEW ARE SEEN BY HER HIGHNESS, AND ALWAYS WORK WITH THAT THOUGHT IN YOUR MINDS!
YES, SIR!

M'LORD.

I'M GLAD TO HEAR IKEYA IS DOING WELL.

THANK YOU, TAKIYAMA.

NO, M'LORD...

ONE MORE THING. WILL MY LORD NOT BE COMING HERE TOMORROW EITHER?

YES...

HOWEVER, THERE IS STILL TIME UNTIL THE DAY SHE WILL DON THE MATERNITY BELT. I AM CERTAIN HER HIGHNESS SHALL COME TO THE INNER CHAMBERS AGAIN BEFORE THAT DAY, MY LORD.

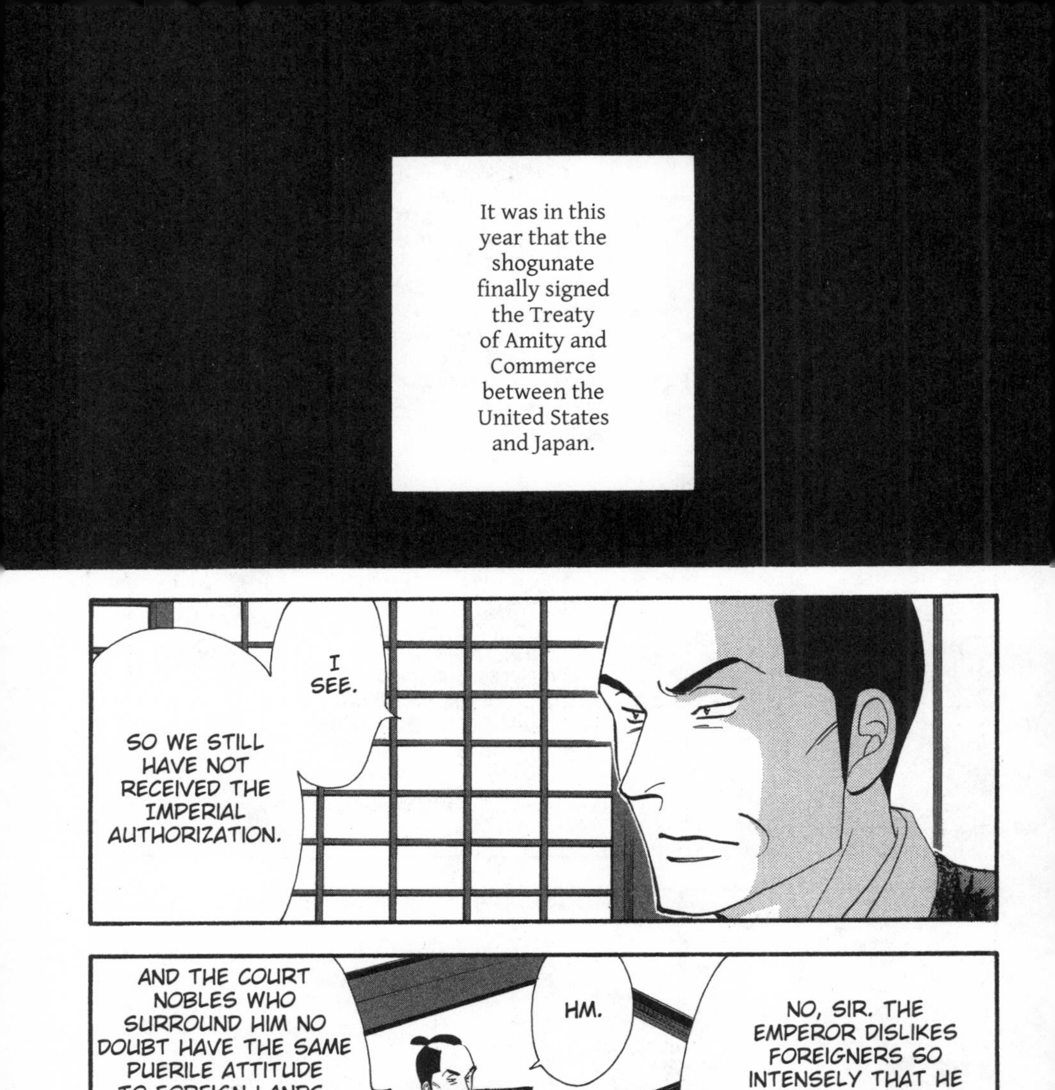
It was in this year that the shogunate finally signed the Treaty of Amity and Commerce between the United States and Japan.
I SEE.
SO WE STILL HAVE NOT RECEIVED THE IMPERIAL AUTHORIZATION.
NO, SIR. THE EMPEROR DISLIKES FOREIGNERS SO INTENSELY THAT HE REFERS TO THEM AS "BEASTS." I THINK IT IS HOPELESS TO EXPECT THAT HE WOULD EVER GRANT PERMISSION TO SIGN THIS TREATY.
HM.
AND THE COURT NOBLES WHO SURROUND HIM NO DOUBT HAVE THE SAME PUERILE ATTITUDE TO FOREIGN LANDS. SO THOSE OUTSIDE LORDS FROM SATSUMA AND CHOSHU GO TO KYOTO AND INGRATIATE THEMSELVES WITH THE COURT BY PRETENDING TO SHARE THOSE VIEWS.

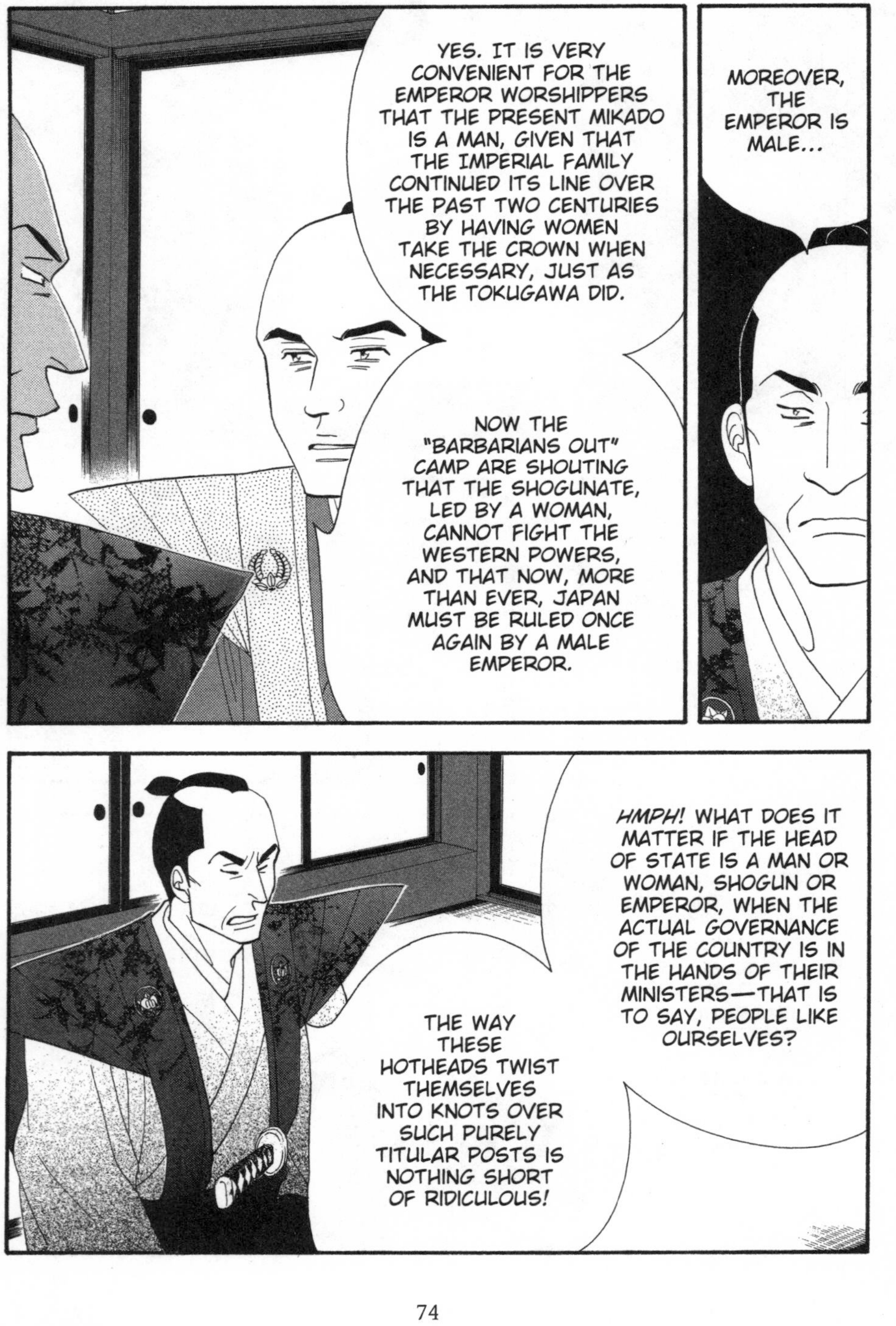
MOREOVER, THE EMPEROR IS MALE...
YES. IT IS VERY CONVENIENT FOR THE EMPEROR WORSHIPPERS THAT THE PRESENT MIKADO IS A MAN, GIVEN THAT THE IMPERIAL FAMILY CONTINUED ITS LINE OVER THE PAST TWO CENTURIES BY HAVING WOMEN TAKE THE CROWN WHEN NECESSARY, JUST AS THE TOKUGAWA DID.
NOW THE "BARBARIANS OUT" CAMP ARE SHOUTING THAT THE SHOGUNATE, LED BY A WOMAN, CANNOT FIGHT THE WESTERN POWERS, AND THAT NOW, MORE THAN EVER, JAPAN MUST BE RULED ONCE AGAIN BY A MALE EMPEROR.
HMPH! WHAT DOES IT MATTER IF THE HEAD OF STATE IS A MAN OR WOMAN, SHOGUN OR EMPEROR, WHEN THE ACTUAL GOVERNANCE OF THE COUNTRY IS IN THE HANDS OF THEIR MINISTERS—THAT IS TO SAY, PEOPLE LIKE OURSELVES?
THE WAY THESE HOTHEADS TWIST THEMSELVES INTO KNOTS OVER SUCH PURELY TITULAR POSTS IS NOTHING SHORT OF RIDICULOUS!

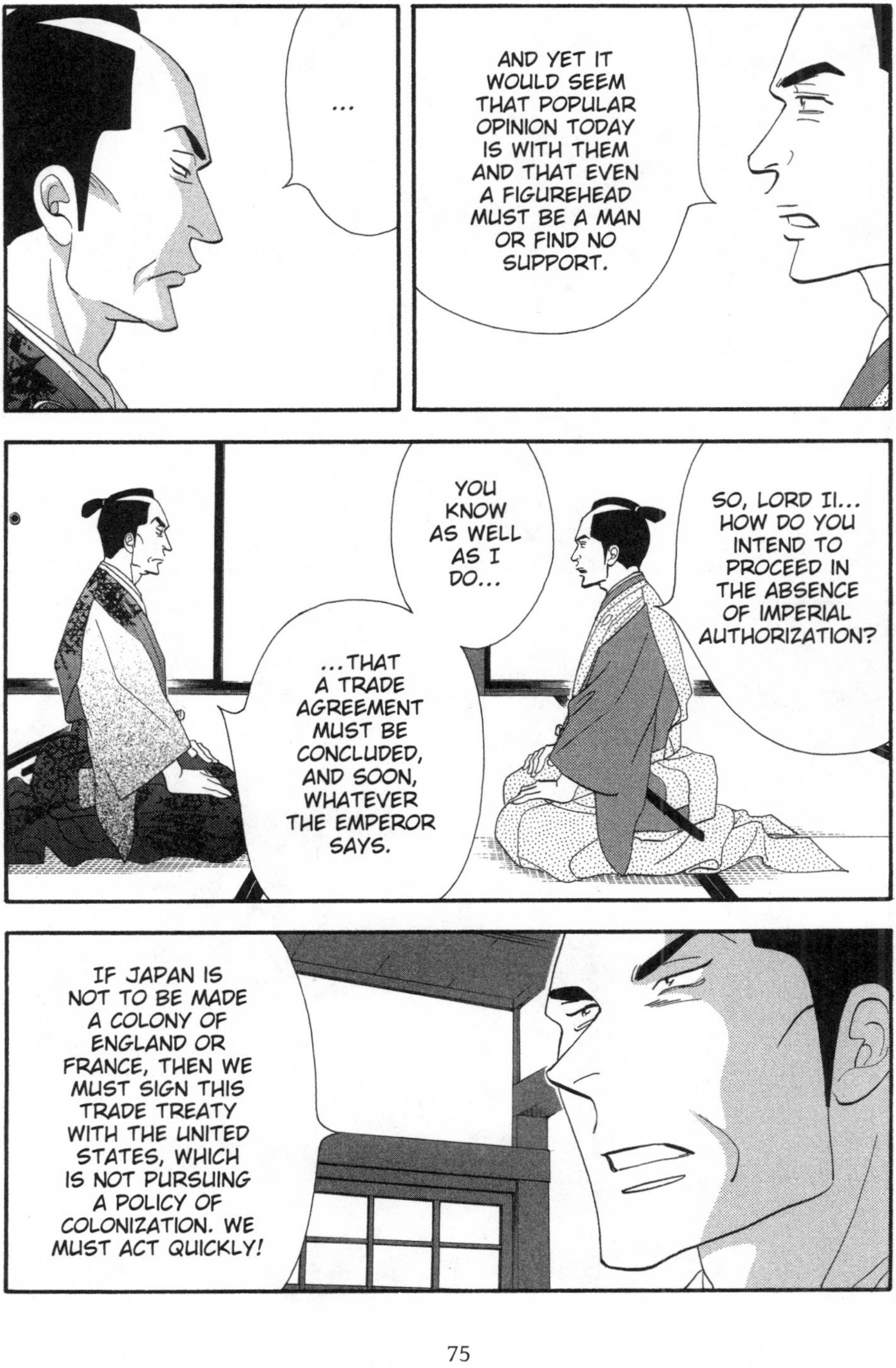
AND YET IT WOULD SEEM THAT POPULAR OPINION TODAY IS WITH THEM AND THAT EVEN A FIGUREHEAD MUST BE A MAN OR FIND NO SUPPORT.
...
SO, LORD II... HOW DO YOU INTEND TO PROCEED IN THE ABSENCE OF IMPERIAL AUTHORIZATION?
YOU KNOW AS WELL AS I DO...
...THAT A TRADE AGREEMENT MUST BE CONCLUDED, AND SOON, WHATEVER THE EMPEROR SAYS.
IF JAPAN IS NOT TO BE MADE A COLONY OF ENGLAND OR FRANCE, THEN WE MUST SIGN THIS TRADE TREATY WITH THE UNITED STATES, WHICH IS NOT PURSUING A POLICY OF COLONIZATION. WE MUST ACT QUICKLY!

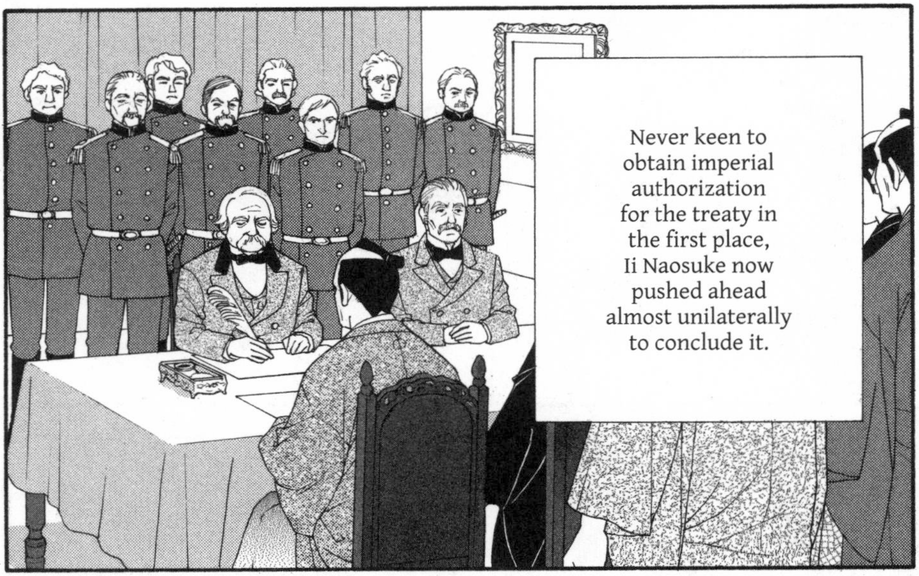
Never keen to obtain imperial authorization for the treaty in the first place, Ii Naosuke now pushed ahead almost unilaterally to conclude it.
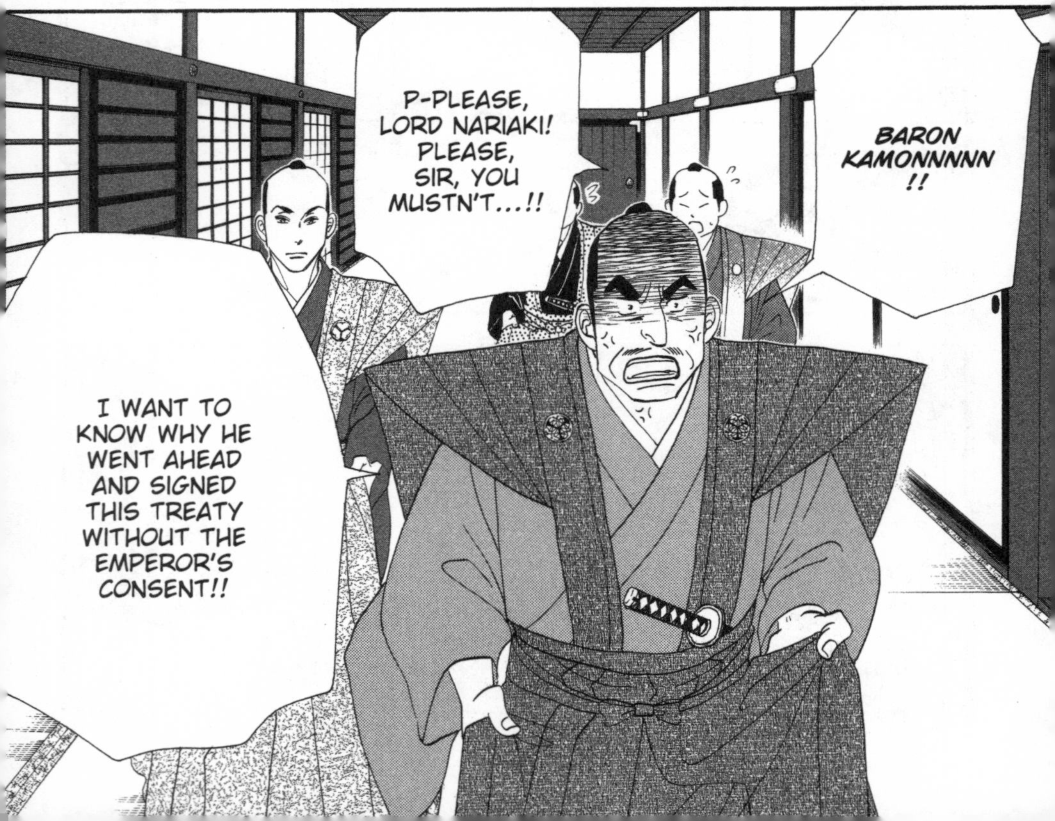
BARON KAMONNNNN!!
P-PLEASE, LORD NARIAKI! PLEASE, SIR, YOU MUSTN'T...!!
I WANT TO KNOW WHY HE WENT AHEAD AND SIGNED THIS TREATY WITHOUT THE EMPEROR'S CONSENT!!

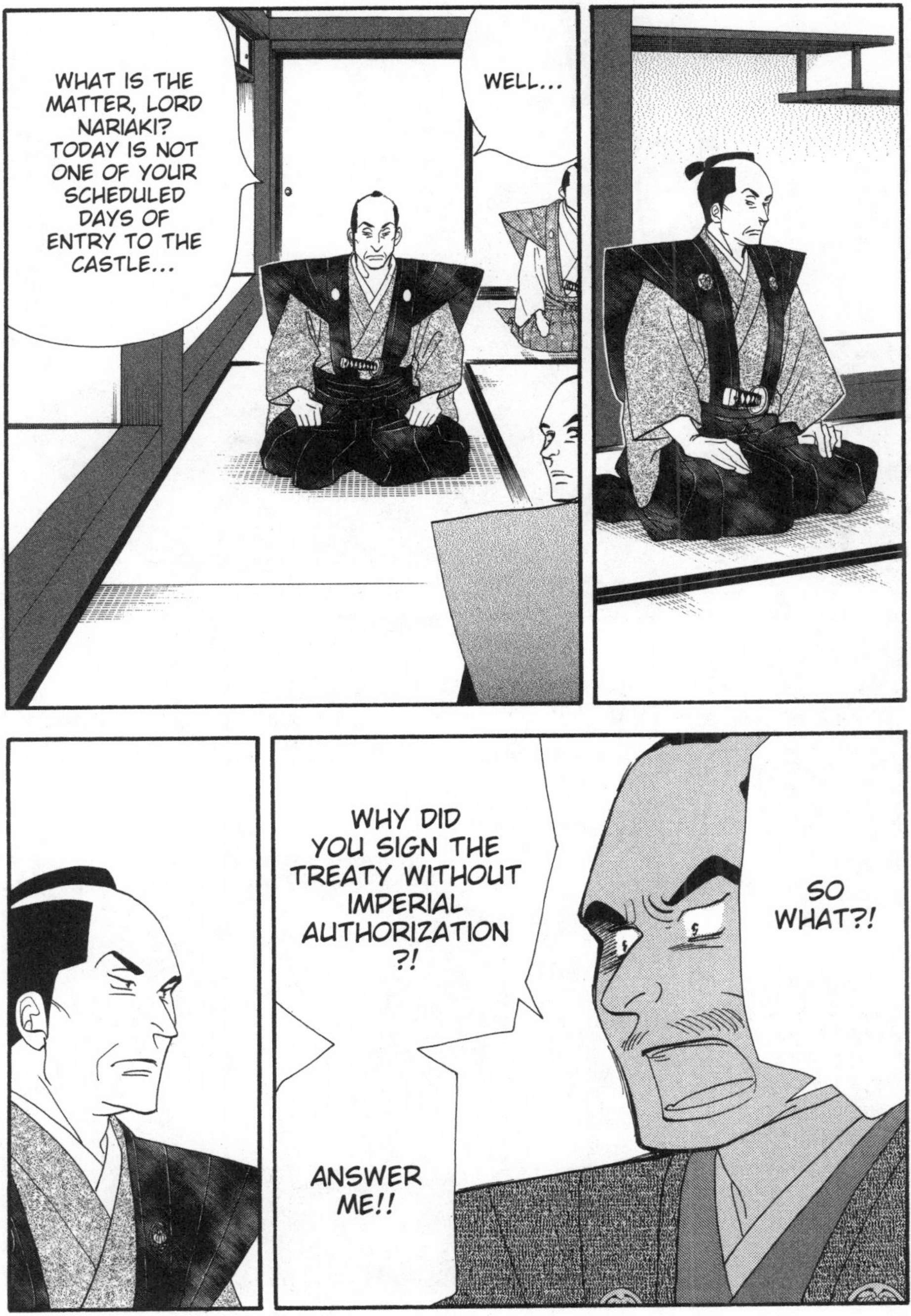

WELL...
WHAT IS THE MATTER, LORD NARIAKI? TODAY IS NOT ONE OF YOUR SCHEDULED DAYS OF ENTRY TO THE CASTLE...
SO WHAT?!
WHY DID YOU SIGN THE TREATY WITHOUT IMPERIAL AUTHORIZATION ?!
ANSWER ME!!

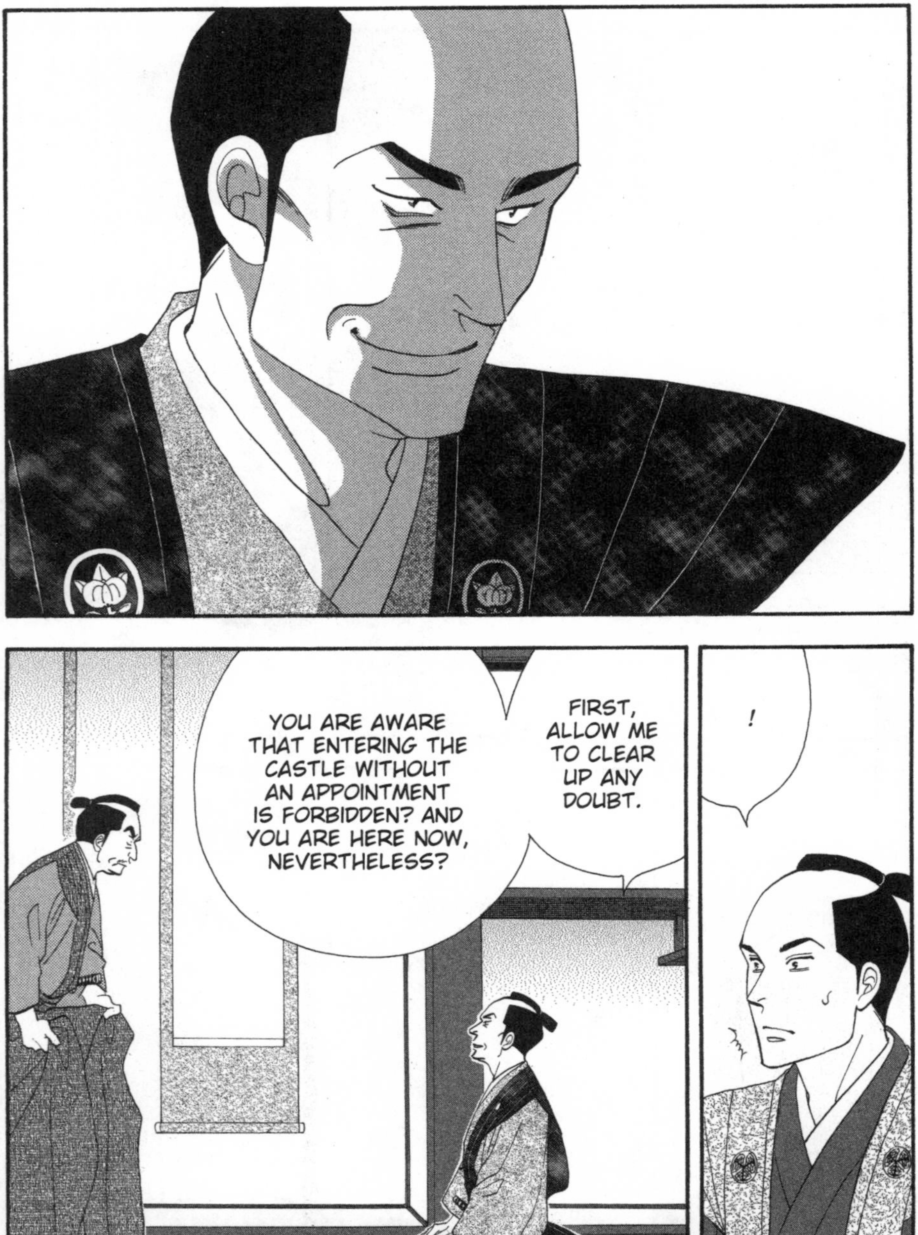
!
FIRST, ALLOW ME TO CLEAR UP ANY DOUBT.
YOU ARE AWARE THAT ENTERING THE CASTLE WITHOUT AN APPOINTMENT IS FORBIDDEN? AND YOU ARE HERE NOW, NEVERTHELESS?

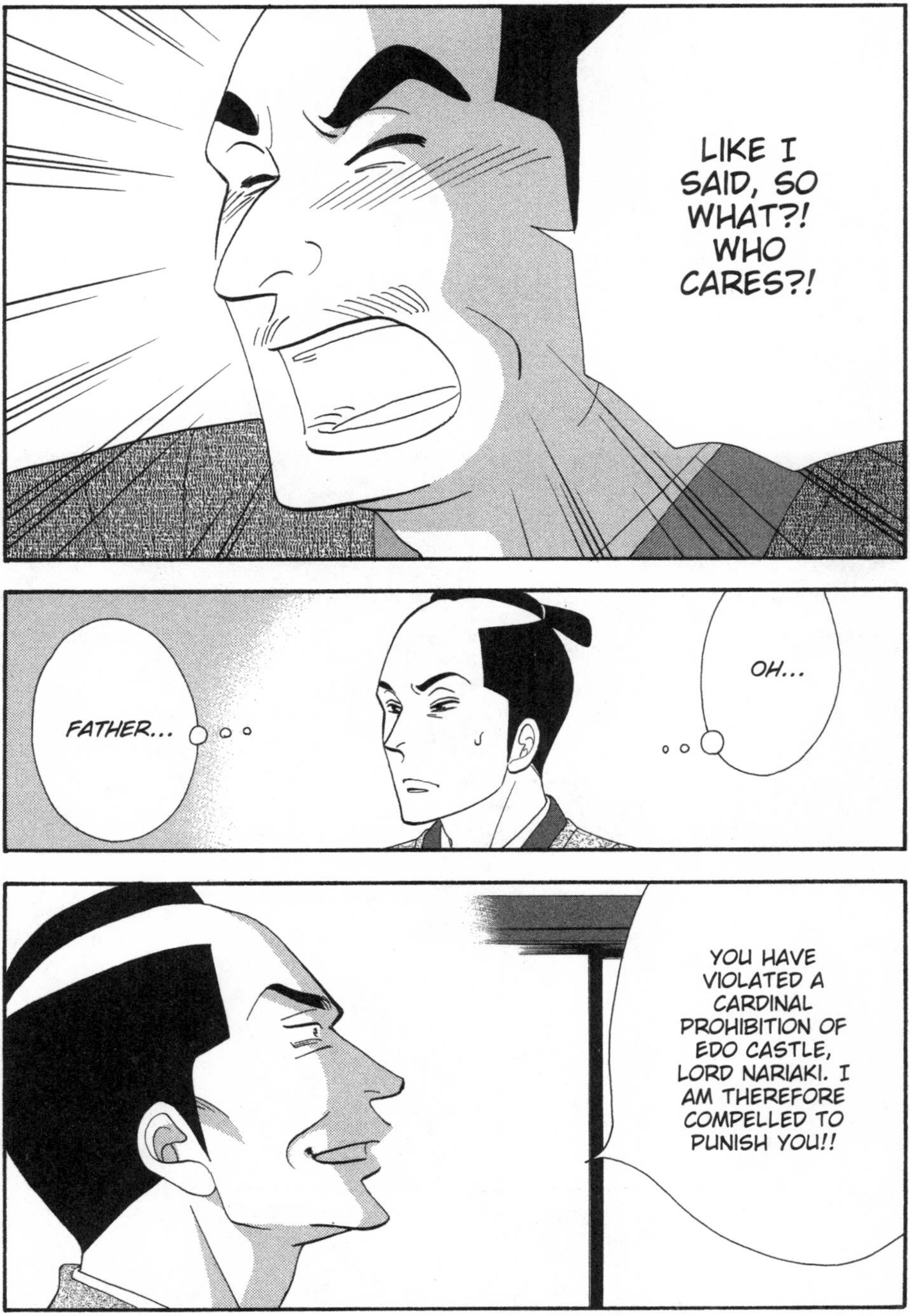
LIKE I SAID, SO WHAT?! WHO CARES?!
OH...
FATHER...
YOU HAVE VIOLATED A CARDINAL PROHIBITION OF EDO CASTLE, LORD NARIAKI. I AM THEREFORE COMPELLED TO PUNISH YOU!!

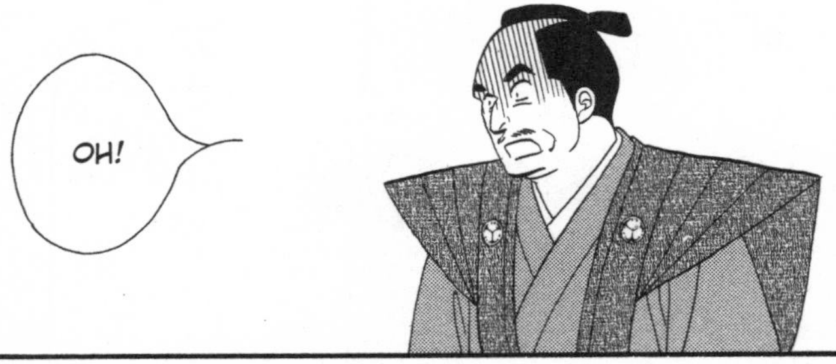
OH!

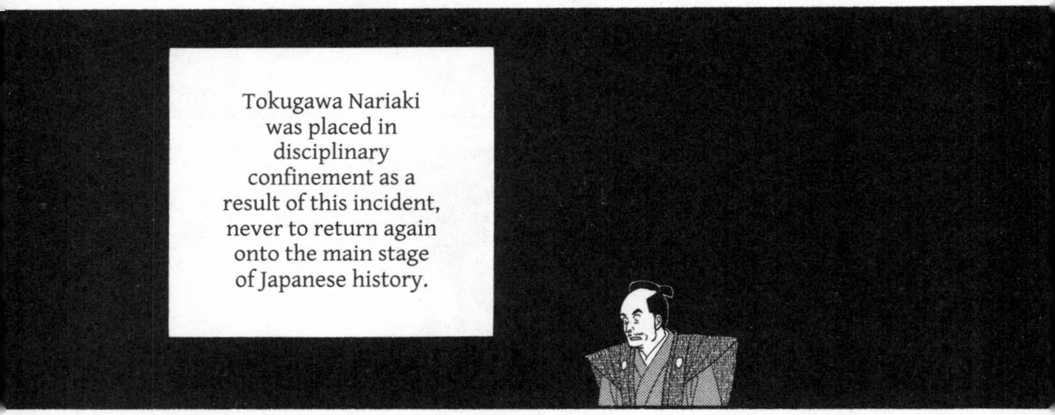
Tokugawa Nariaki was placed in disciplinary confinement as a result of this incident, never to return again onto the main stage of Japanese history.

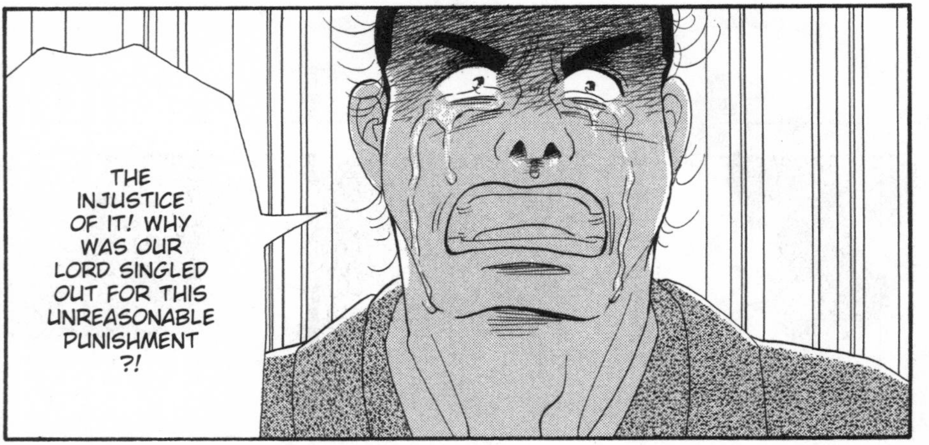
THE INJUSTICE OF IT! WHY WAS OUR LORD SINGLED OUT FOR THIS UNREASONABLE PUNISHMENT ?!

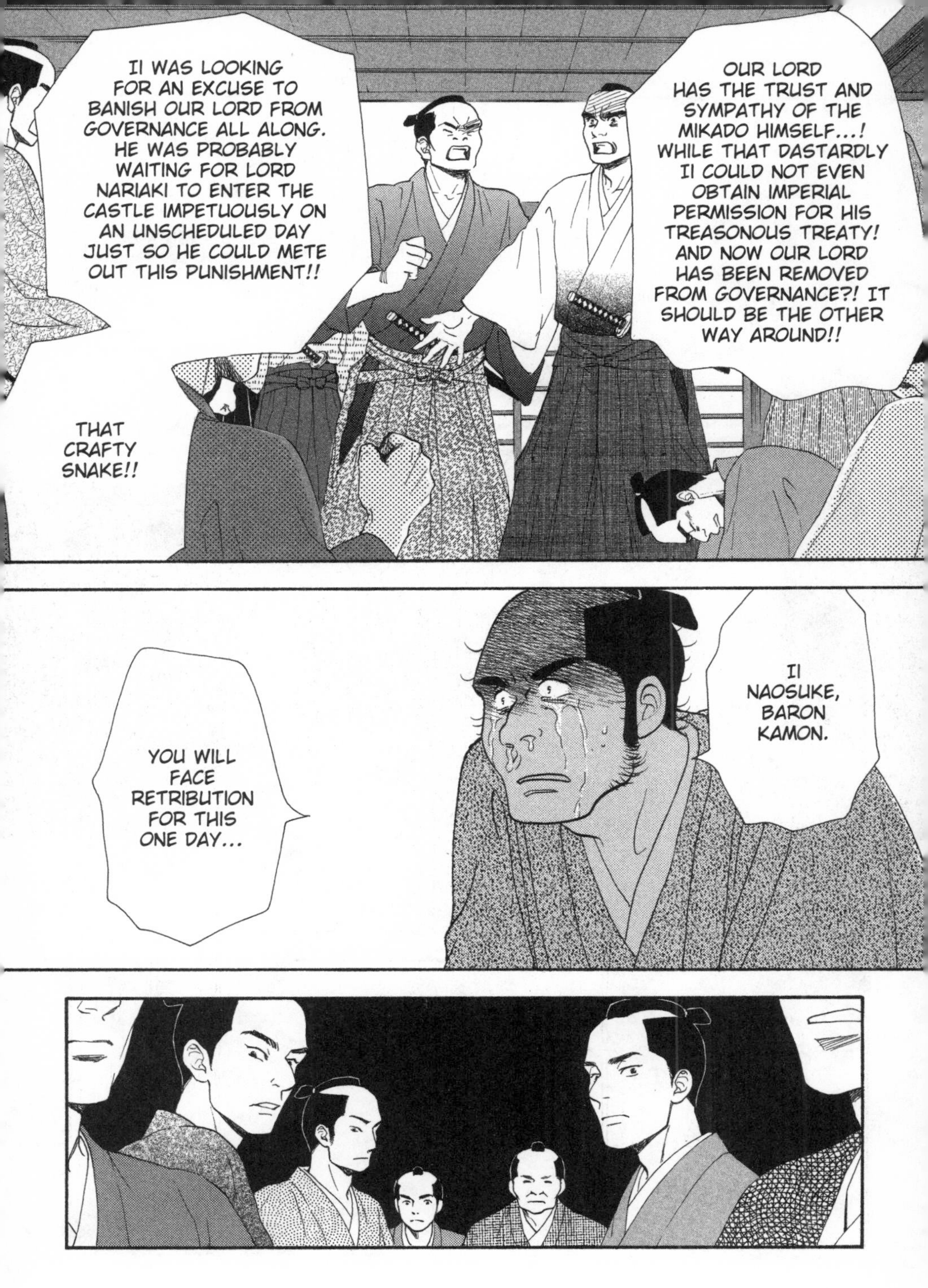
OUR LORD HAS THE TRUST AND SYMPATHY OF THE MIKADO HIMSELF...! WHILE THAT DASTARDLY II COULD NOT EVEN OBTAIN IMPERIAL PERMISSION FOR HIS TREASONOUS TREATY! AND NOW OUR LORD HAS BEEN REMOVED FROM GOVERNANCE?! IT SHOULD BE THE OTHER WAY AROUND!!
II WAS LOOKING FOR AN EXCUSE TO BANISH OUR LORD FROM GOVERNANCE ALL ALONG. HE WAS PROBABLY WAITING FOR LORD NARIAKI TO ENTER THE CASTLE IMPETUOUSLY ON AN UNSCHEDULED DAY JUST SO HE COULD METE OUT THIS PUNISHMENT!!
THAT CRAFTY SNAKE!!
II NAOSUKE, BARON KAMON.
YOU WILL FACE RETRIBUTION FOR THIS ONE DAY...

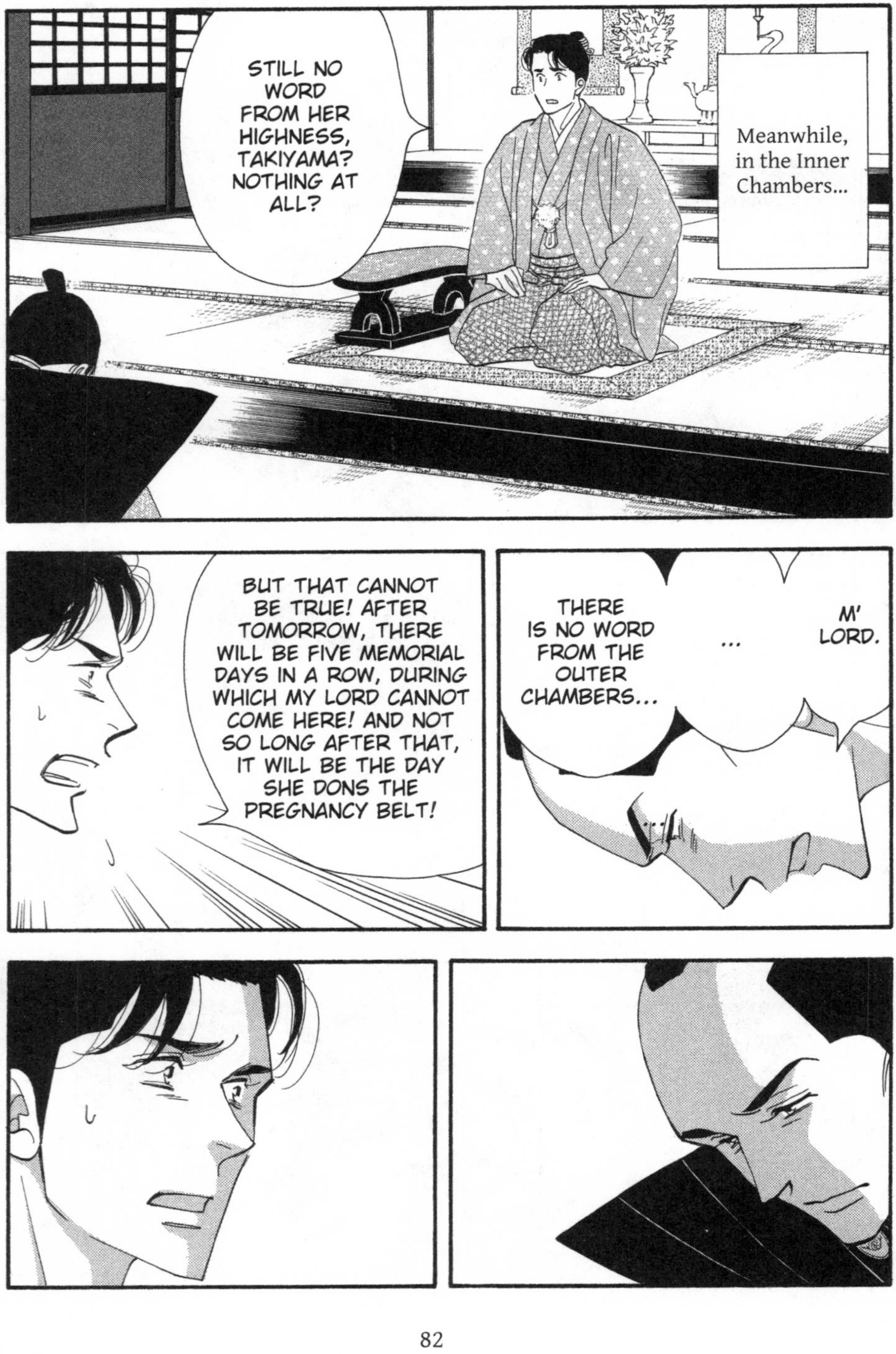
Meanwhile, in the Inner Chambers...
STILL NO WORD FROM HER HIGHNESS, TAKIYAMA? NOTHING AT ALL?
M' LORD.
...
THERE IS NO WORD FROM THE OUTER CHAMBERS...
BUT THAT CANNOT BE TRUE! AFTER TOMORROW, THERE WILL BE FIVE MEMORIAL DAYS IN A ROW, DURING WHICH MY LORD CANNOT COME HERE! AND NOT SO LONG AFTER THAT, IT WILL BE THE DAY SHE DONS THE PREGNANCY BELT!

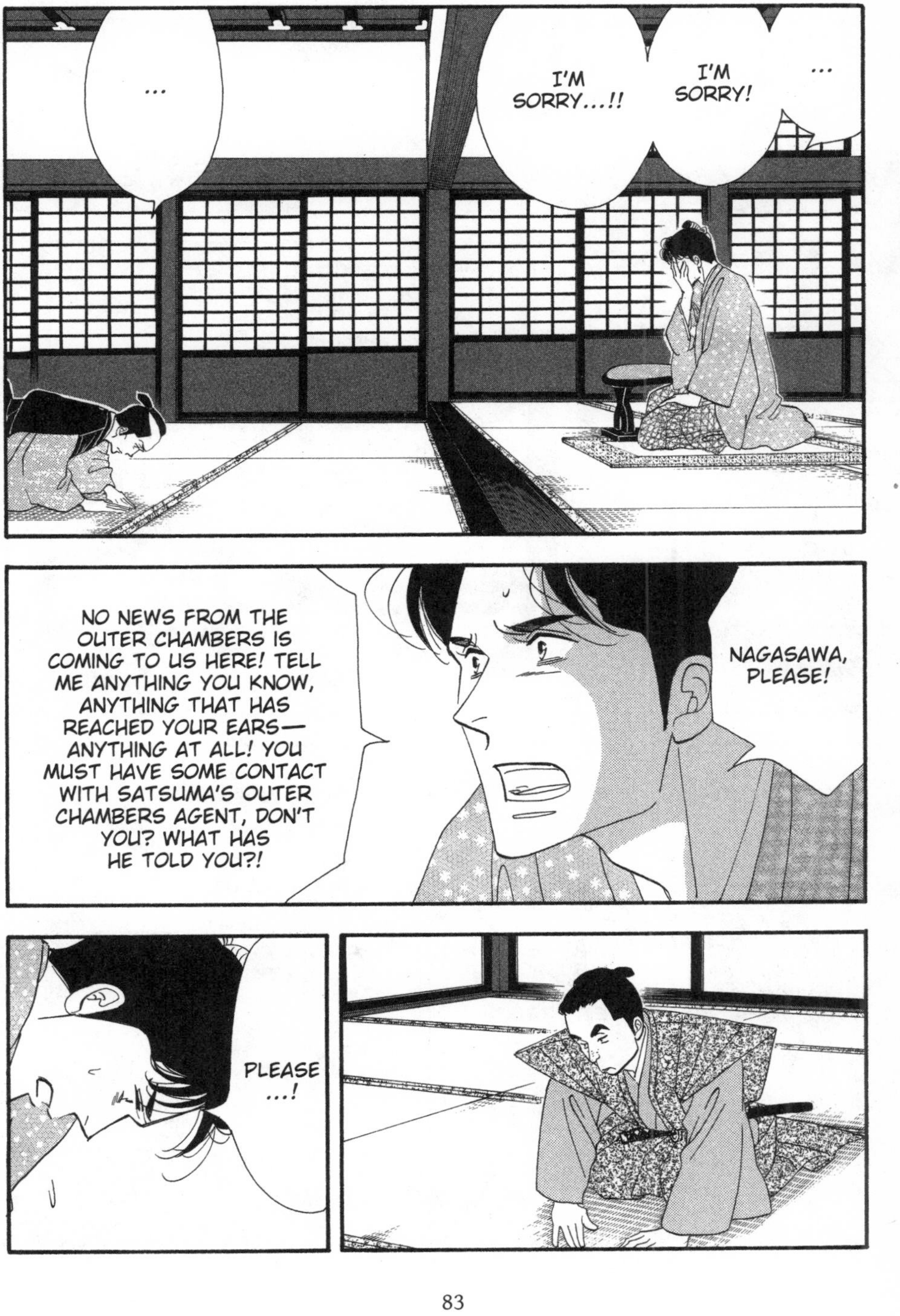
...
I'M SORRY!
I'M SORRY...!!
...
NAGASAWA, PLEASE!
NO NEWS FROM THE OUTER CHAMBERS IS COMING TO US HERE! TELL ME ANYTHING YOU KNOW, ANYTHING THAT HAS REACHED YOUR EARS—ANYTHING AT ALL! YOU MUST HAVE SOME CONTACT WITH SATSUMA'S OUTER CHAMBERS AGENT, DON'T YOU? WHAT HAS HE TOLD YOU?!
PLEASE ...!

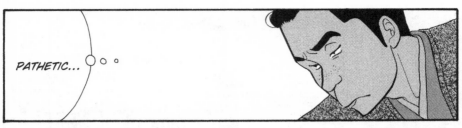

PATHETIC...
WELL, SIR, THERE WAS THE NEWS JUST THE OTHER DAY THAT HER HIGHNESS THE SHOGUN HAS ISSUED AN ORDER TO EMPLOY A DOCTOR OF HOLLANDER MEDICINE TO SERVE THE SHOGUN'S QUARTERS AND INNER CHAMBERS. UNTIL NOW, ONLY DOCTORS OF CHINESE MEDICINE WERE PERMITTED. HAD YOU HEARD THAT NEWS?
YES! I DID KNOW ABOUT THAT!
THAT WAS THE FIRST ORDER MY LORD ISSUED HERSELF SINCE THE DEATH OF BARON ABE OF ISE.
THERE IS SO MUCH I WANT TO DISCUSS WITH HER ON THAT SUBJECT, IF ONLY I COULD MEET HER FACE-TO-FACE.
THE RUMOR ON EVERYONE'S LIPS IS THAT THE REASON SHE ISSUED THIS ORDER WAS THAT SHE HERSELF IS NOT IN GOOD HEALTH AND RUSHED THE ORDER OUT IN DESPERATION.
!

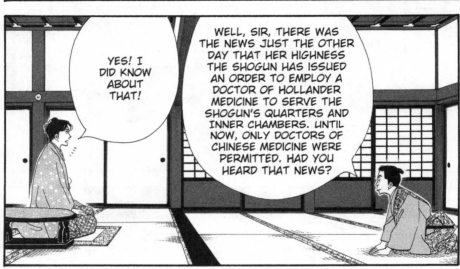

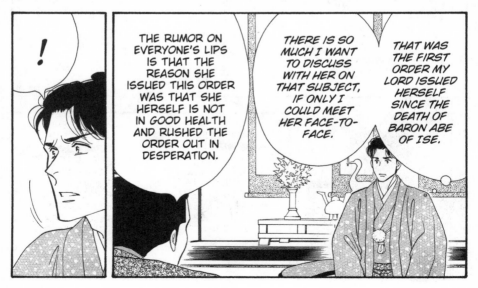

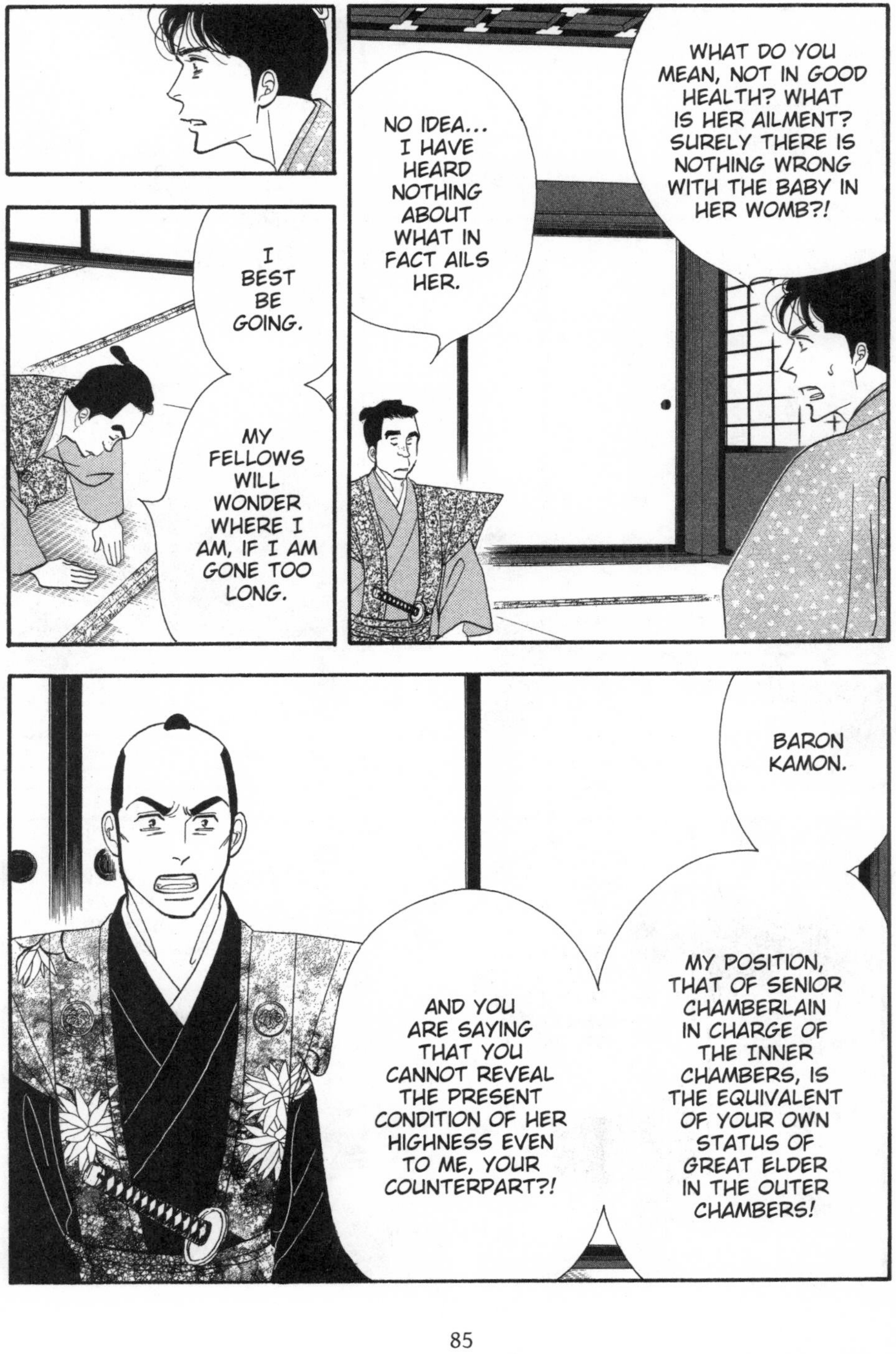
WHAT DO YOU MEAN, NOT IN GOOD HEALTH? WHAT IS HER AILMENT? SURELY THERE IS NOTHING WRONG WITH THE BABY IN HER WOMB?!
NO IDEA... I HAVE HEARD NOTHING ABOUT WHAT IN FACT AILS HER.
I BEST BE GOING.
MY FELLOWS WILL WONDER WHERE I AM, IF I AM GONE TOO LONG.
BARON KAMON.
MY POSITION, THAT OF SENIOR CHAMBERLAIN IN CHARGE OF THE INNER CHAMBERS, IS THE EQUIVALENT OF YOUR OWN STATUS OF GREAT ELDER IN THE OUTER CHAMBERS!
AND YOU ARE SAYING THAT YOU CANNOT REVEAL THE PRESENT CONDITION OF HER HIGHNESS EVEN TO ME, YOUR COUNTERPART?!

I DON'T KNOW WHAT TO SAY...
...OTHER THAN WHAT I HAVE BEEN TELLING YOU—NAMELY, THAT THERE IS NO CHANGE IN OUR LORD SHOGUN'S CONDITION. SHE IS THE SAME AS ALWAYS.
BUT THAT CANNOT BE! HER HIGHNESS IS WITH CHILD, AND THAT CHILD IN HER BELLY IS GROWING LARGER BY THE DAY! SURELY YOU CAN DIVULGE SOMETHING THAT I MAY REPORT TO THE LORD CONSORT—SOMETHING THE PHYSICIAN SAID AFTER EXAMINING HER, FOR EXAMPLE?!
AS YOU SAY, HER HIGHNESS IS PREGNANT! CONSEQUENTLY, SHE SPENDS HER DAYS ALMOST ENTIRELY IN THE SHOGUN'S QUARTERS WITH HER LADIES ATTENDING TO HER.
THAT BEING SO, EVEN I AS GREAT ELDER HAVE RARELY HAD OCCASION TO MEET HER IN RECENT DAYS.

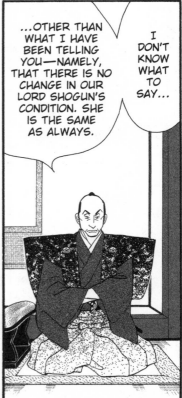

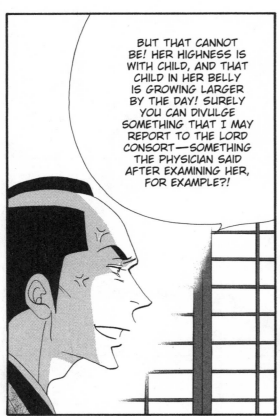

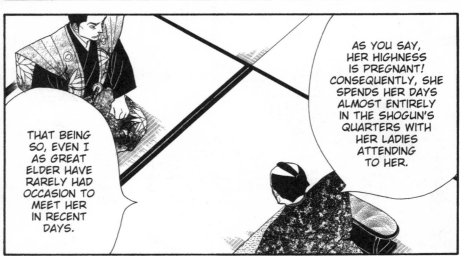

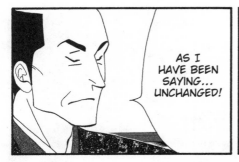

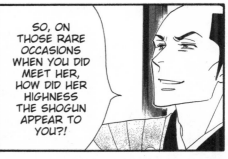

SO, ON THOSE RARE OCCASIONS WHEN YOU DID MEET HER, HOW DID HER HIGHNESS THE SHOGUN APPEAR TO YOU?!
AS I HAVE BEEN SAYING... UNCHANGED!
WELL THEN, I HAD BETTER GO... UNLIKE THE INNER CHAMBERS, WHERE HER HIGHNESS IS ABSENT, THE OUTER CHAMBERS ARE NOW HECTIC WITH PREPARATIONS FOR THE HASSAKU FESTIVAL.
IT IS THE MOST IMPORTANT OF ALL THE RITES OBSERVED AT EDO CASTLE, FOR AN ICON OF THE VERY FOUNDER OF THE TOKUGAWA SHOGUNATE WILL BE BROUGHT HERE FOR IT! THIS IS MY FIRST HASSAKU SINCE MY APPOINTMENT AS GREAT ELDER, AND I MUST SEE TO IT THAT THERE ARE NO MISTAKES.
SO, SIR TAKIYAMA, I SHALL TAKE MY LEAVE.

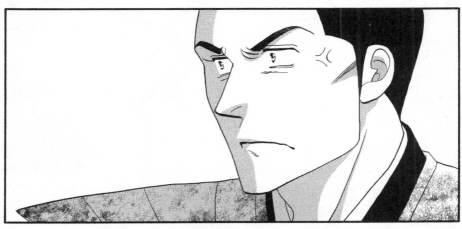

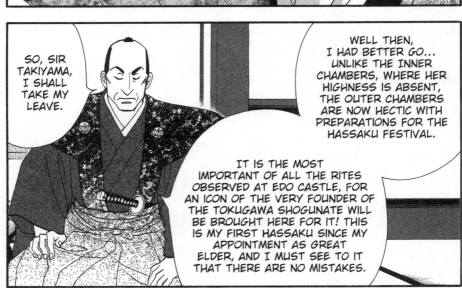

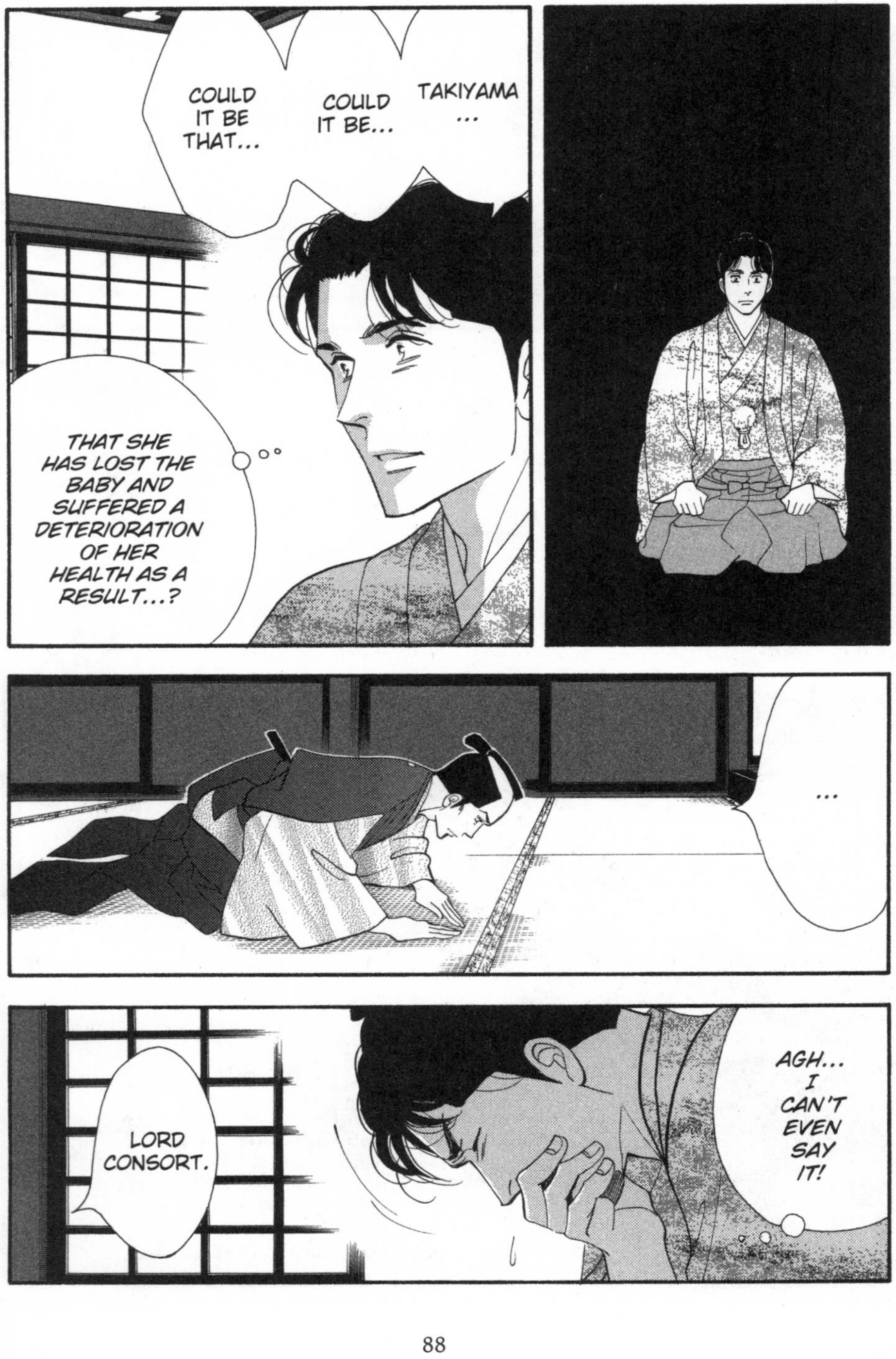
TAKIYAMA ...
COULD IT BE...
COULD IT BE THAT...
THAT SHE HAS LOST THE BABY AND SUFFERED A DETERIORATION OF HER HEALTH AS A RESULT...?
...
AGH... I CAN'T EVEN SAY IT!
LORD CONSORT.

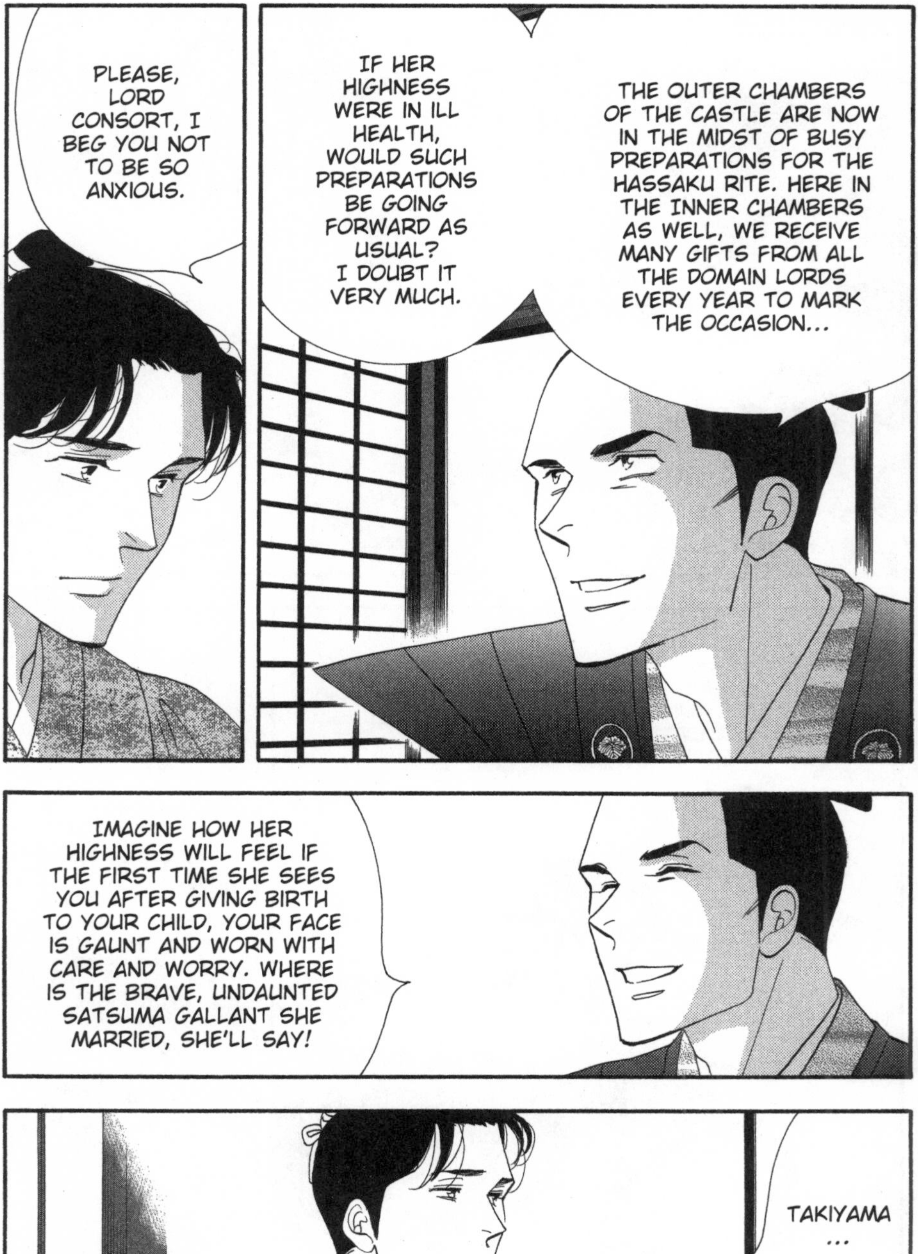
THE OUTER CHAMBERS OF THE CASTLE ARE NOW IN THE MIDST OF BUSY PREPARATIONS FOR THE HASSAKU RITE. HERE IN THE INNER CHAMBERS AS WELL, WE RECEIVE MANY GIFTS FROM ALL THE DOMAIN LORDS EVERY YEAR TO MARK THE OCCASION...
IF HER HIGHNESS WERE IN ILL HEALTH, WOULD SUCH PREPARATIONS BE GOING FORWARD AS USUAL? I DOUBT IT VERY MUCH.
PLEASE, LORD CONSORT, I BEG YOU NOT TO BE SO ANXIOUS.
IMAGINE HOW HER HIGHNESS WILL FEEL IF THE FIRST TIME SHE SEES YOU AFTER GIVING BIRTH TO YOUR CHILD, YOUR FACE IS GAUNT AND WORN WITH CARE AND WORRY. WHERE IS THE BRAVE, UNDAUNTED SATSUMA GALLANT SHE MARRIED, SHE'LL SAY!
TAKIYAMA ...

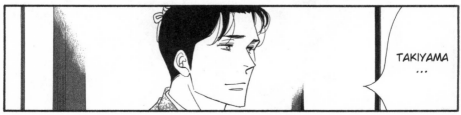

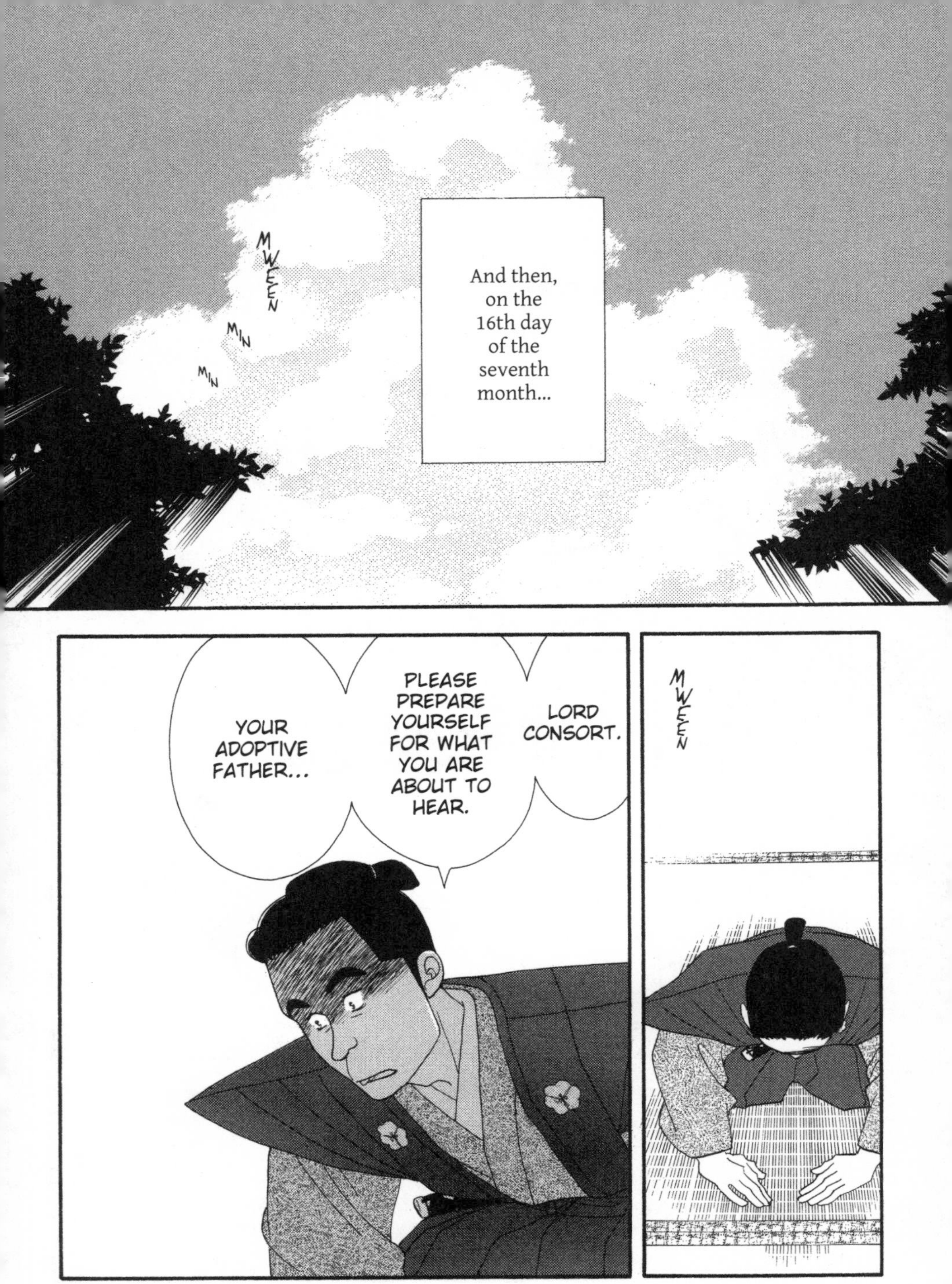
And then, on the 16th day of the seventh month...
MWEEN
MIN
MIN
MWEEN
LORD CONSORT.
PLEASE PREPARE YOURSELF FOR WHAT YOU ARE ABOUT TO HEAR.
YOUR ADOPTIVE FATHER...

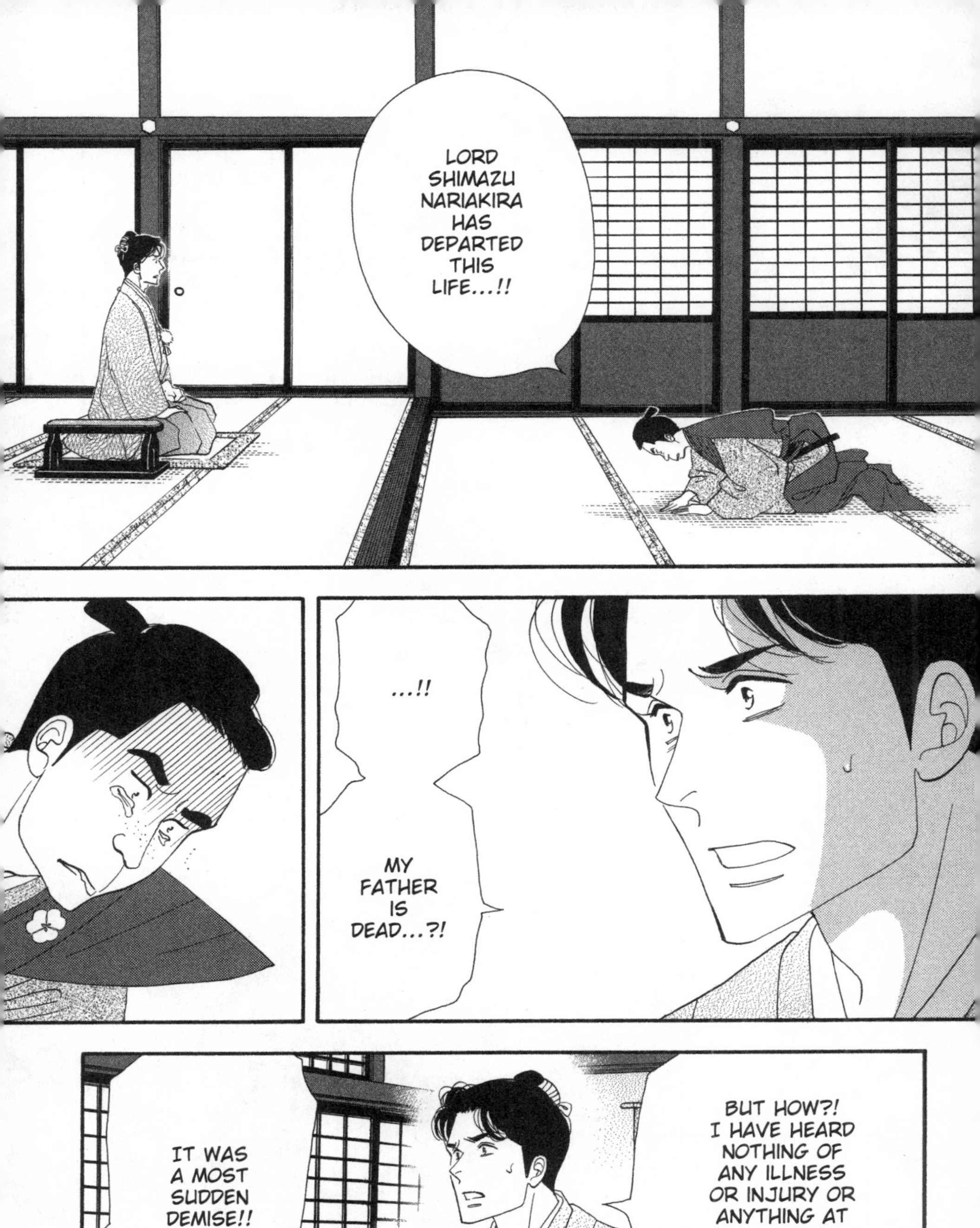
LORD SHIMAZU NARIAKIRA HAS DEPARTED THIS LIFE...!!
...!!
MY FATHER IS DEAD...?!
BUT HOW?! I HAVE HEARD NOTHING OF ANY ILLNESS OR INJURY OR ANYTHING AT ALL. HOW CAN IT BE...?!
IT WAS A MOST SUDDEN DEMISE!!

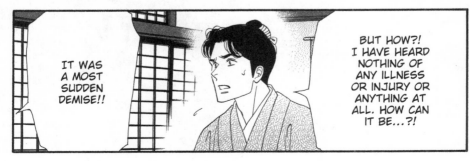

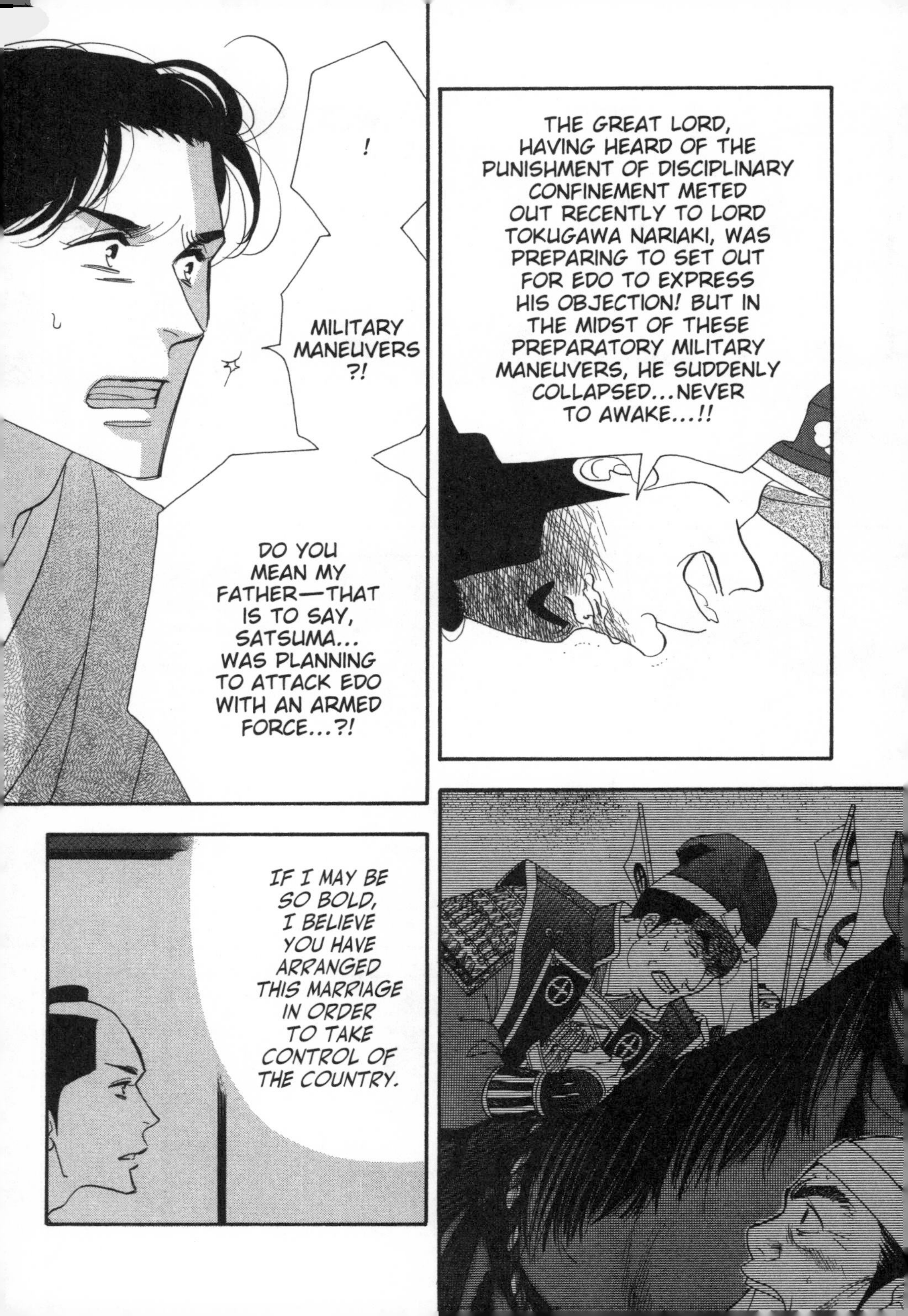
THE GREAT LORD, HAVING HEARD OF THE PUNISHMENT OF DISCIPLINARY CONFINEMENT METED OUT RECENTLY TO LORD TOKUGAWA NARIAKI, WAS PREPARING TO SET OUT FOR EDO TO EXPRESS HIS OBJECTION! BUT IN THE MIDST OF THESE PREPARATORY MILITARY MANEUVERS, HE SUDDENLY COLLAPSED...NEVER TO AWAKE...!!
!
MILITARY MANEUVERS?!
DO YOU MEAN MY FATHER—THAT IS TO SAY, SATSUMA... WAS PLANNING TO ATTACK EDO WITH AN ARMED FORCE...?!
IF I MAY BE SO BOLD, I BELIEVE YOU HAVE ARRANGED THIS MARRIAGE IN ORDER TO TAKE CONTROL OF THE COUNTRY.

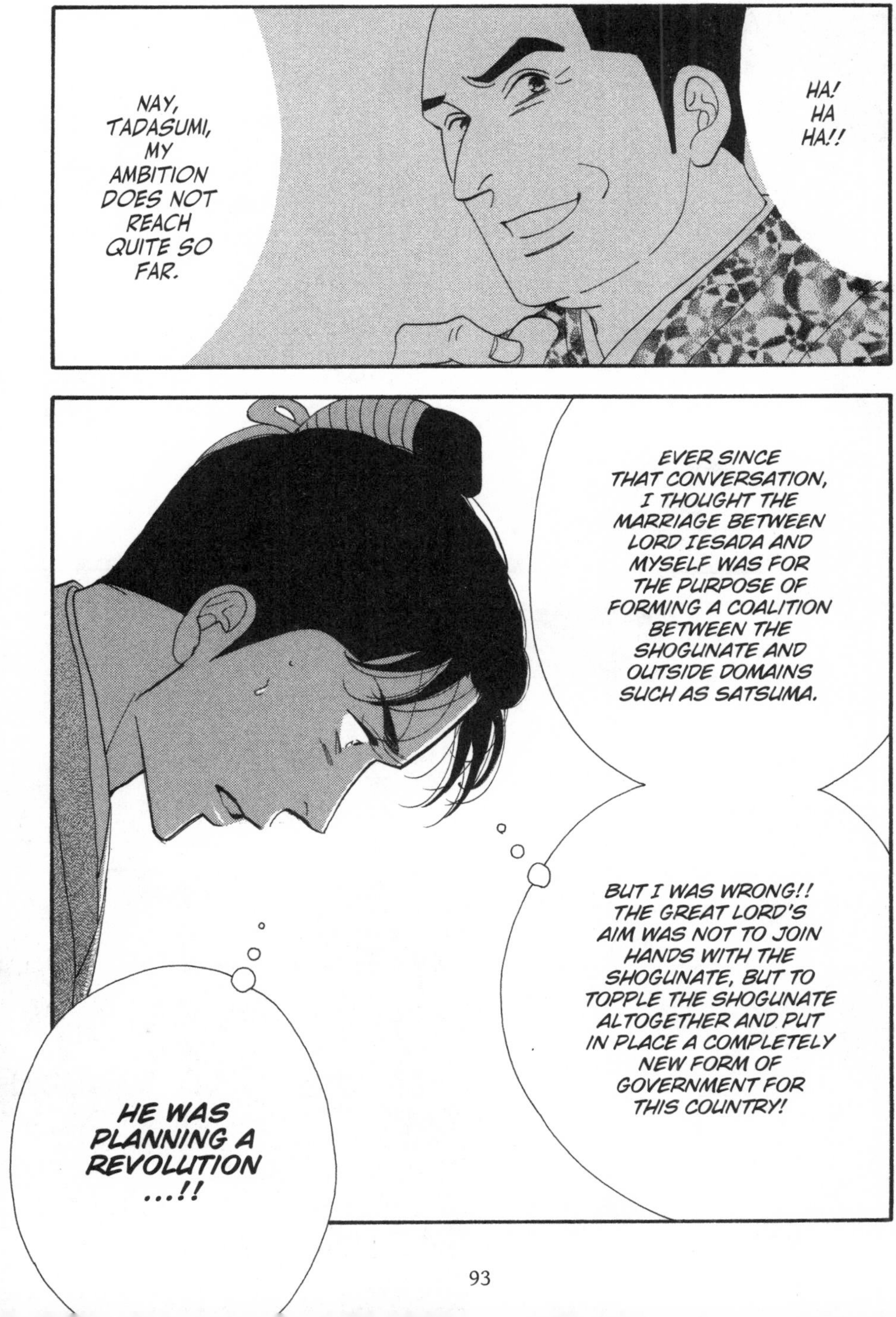
HA! HA HA!!
NAY, TADASUMI, MY AMBITION DOES NOT REACH QUITE SO FAR.
EVER SINCE THAT CONVERSATION, I THOUGHT THE MARRIAGE BETWEEN LORD IESADA AND MYSELF WAS FOR THE PURPOSE OF FORMING A COALITION BETWEEN THE SHOGUNATE AND OUTSIDE DOMAINS SUCH AS SATSUMA.
BUT I WAS WRONG!! THE GREAT LORD'S AIM WAS NOT TO JOIN HANDS WITH THE SHOGUNATE, BUT TO TOPPLE THE SHOGUNATE ALTOGETHER AND PUT IN PLACE A COMPLETELY NEW FORM OF GOVERNMENT FOR THIS COUNTRY!
HE WAS PLANNING A REVOLUTION ...!!

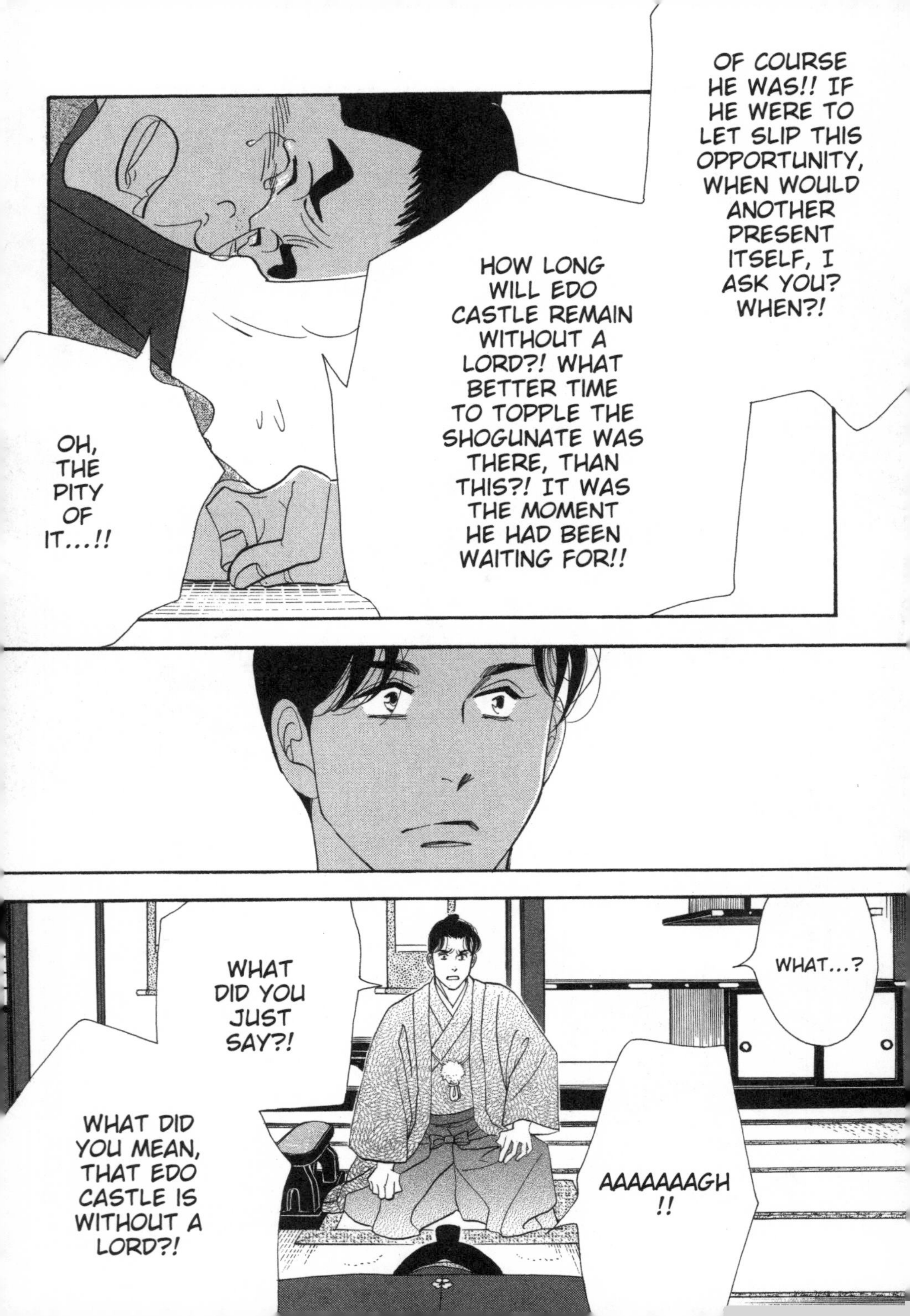
OF COURSE HE WAS!! IF HE WERE TO LET SLIP THIS OPPORTUNITY, WHEN WOULD ANOTHER PRESENT ITSELF, I ASK YOU? WHEN?!
HOW LONG WILL EDO CASTLE REMAIN WITHOUT A LORD?! WHAT BETTER TIME TO TOPPLE THE SHOGUNATE WAS THERE, THAN THIS?! IT WAS THE MOMENT HE HAD BEEN WAITING FOR!!
OH, THE PITY OF IT...!!
WHAT...?
WHAT DID YOU JUST SAY?!
AAAAAAAGH!!
WHAT DID YOU MEAN, THAT EDO CASTLE IS WITHOUT A LORD?!

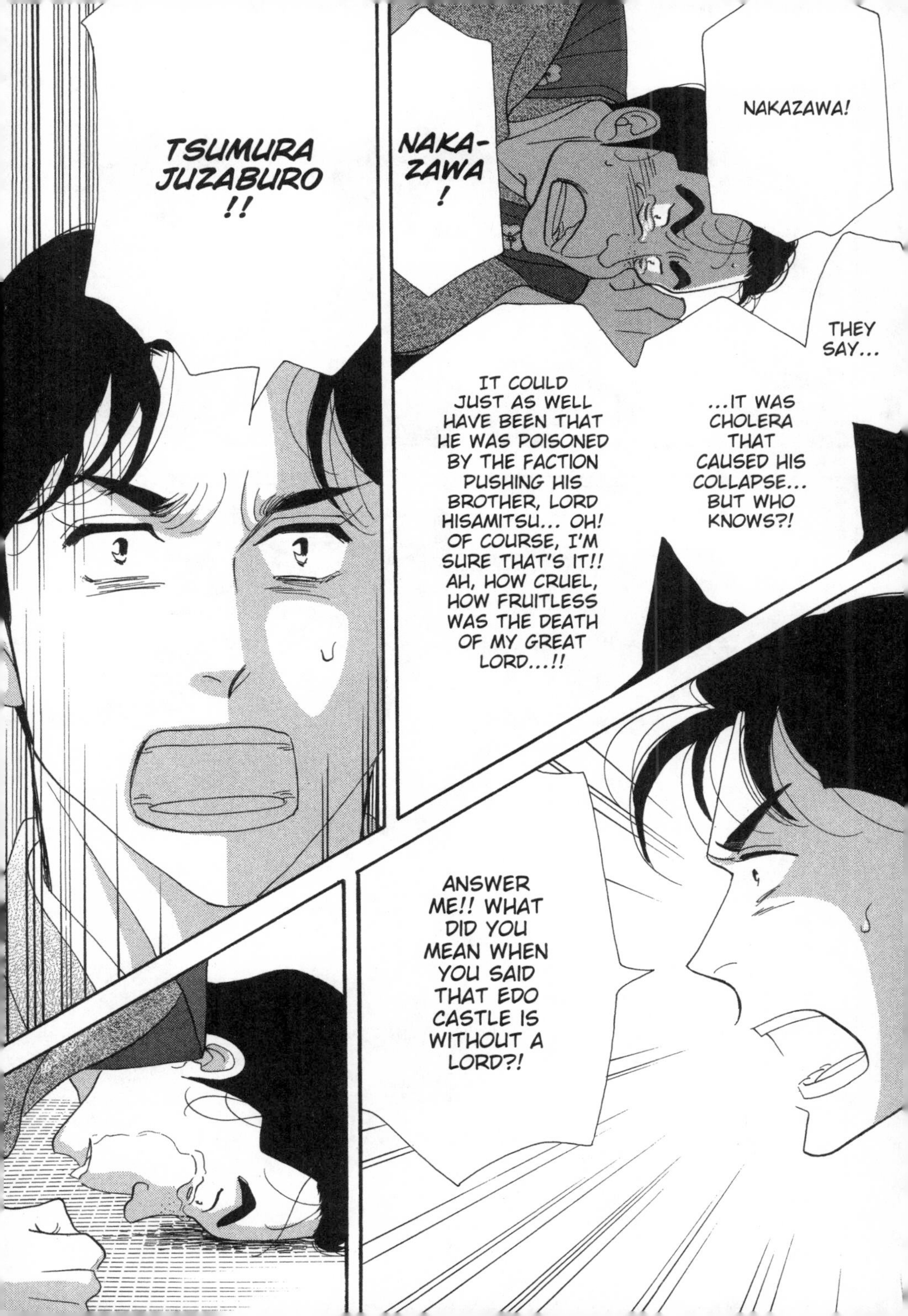
NAKAZAWA!
THEY SAY...
...IT WAS CHOLERA THAT CAUSED HIS COLLAPSE... BUT WHO KNOWS?!
IT COULD JUST AS WELL HAVE BEEN THAT HE WAS POISONED BY THE FACTION PUSHING HIS BROTHER, LORD HISAMITSU... OH! OF COURSE, I'M SURE THAT'S IT!! AH, HOW CRUEL, HOW FRUITLESS WAS THE DEATH OF MY GREAT LORD...!!
NAKA-ZAWA!
TSUMURA JUZABURO!!
ANSWER ME!! WHAT DID YOU MEAN WHEN YOU SAID THAT EDO CASTLE IS WITHOUT A LORD?!

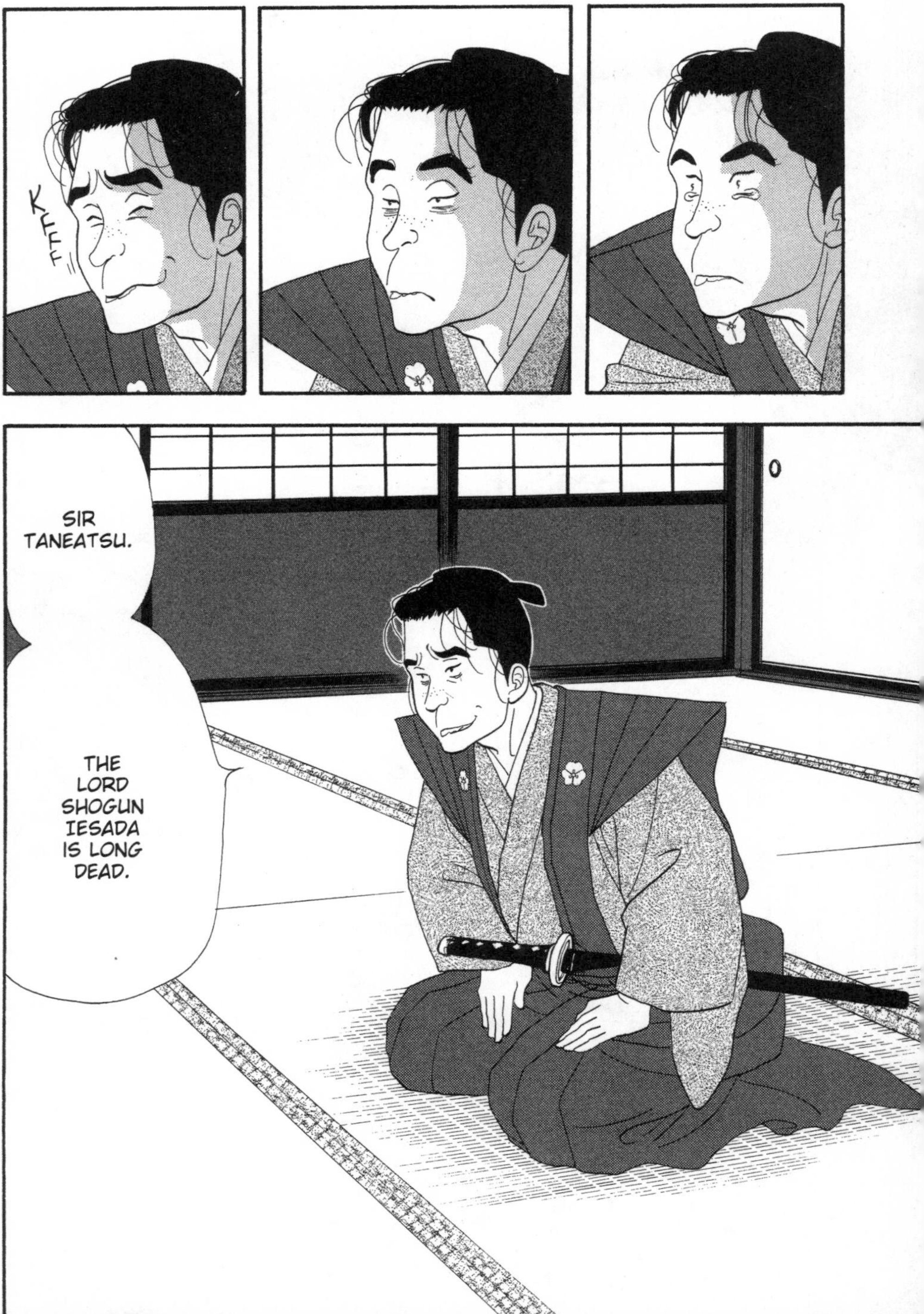
KFFF
SIR TANEATSU.
THE LORD SHOGUN IESADA IS LONG DEAD.

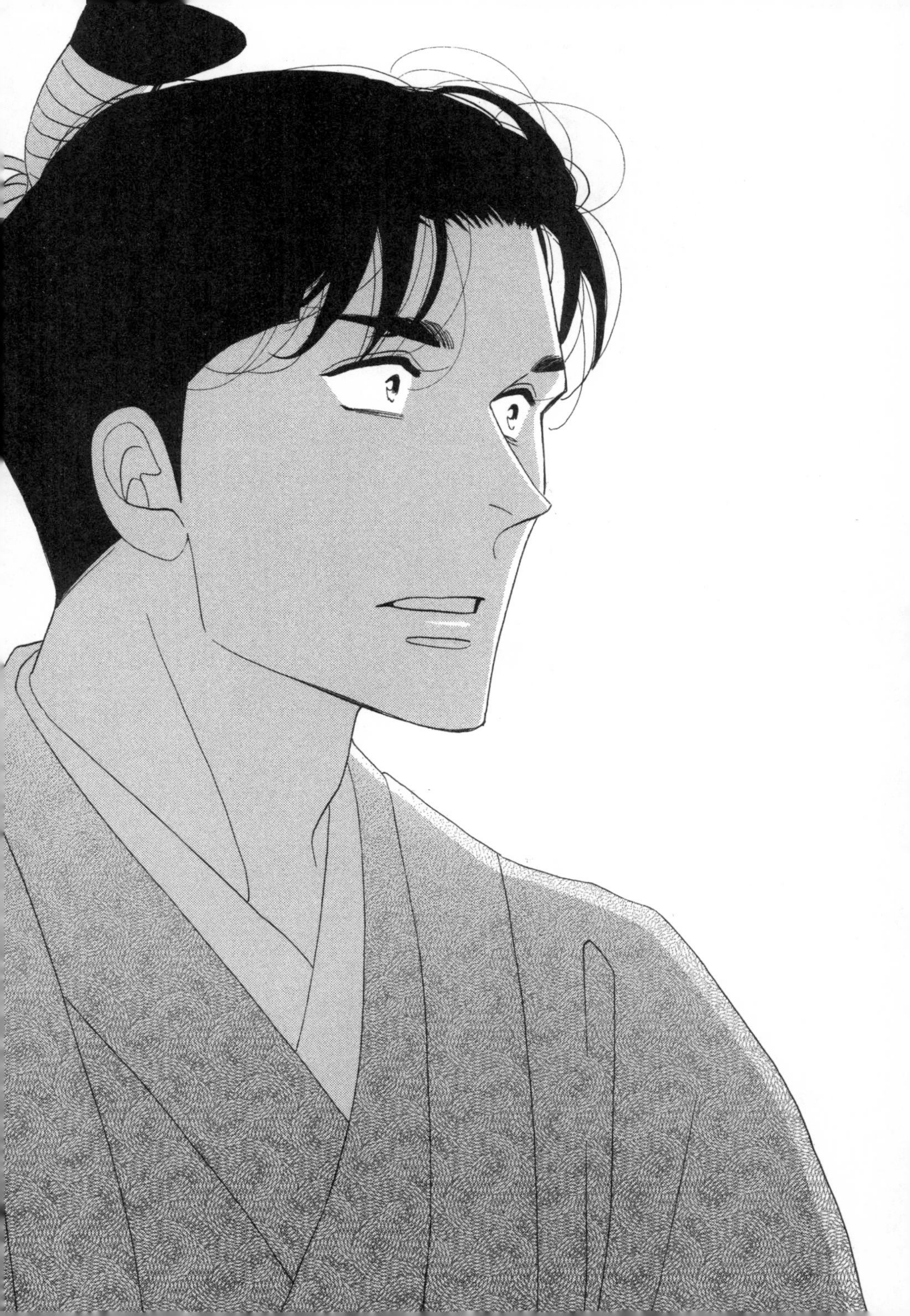

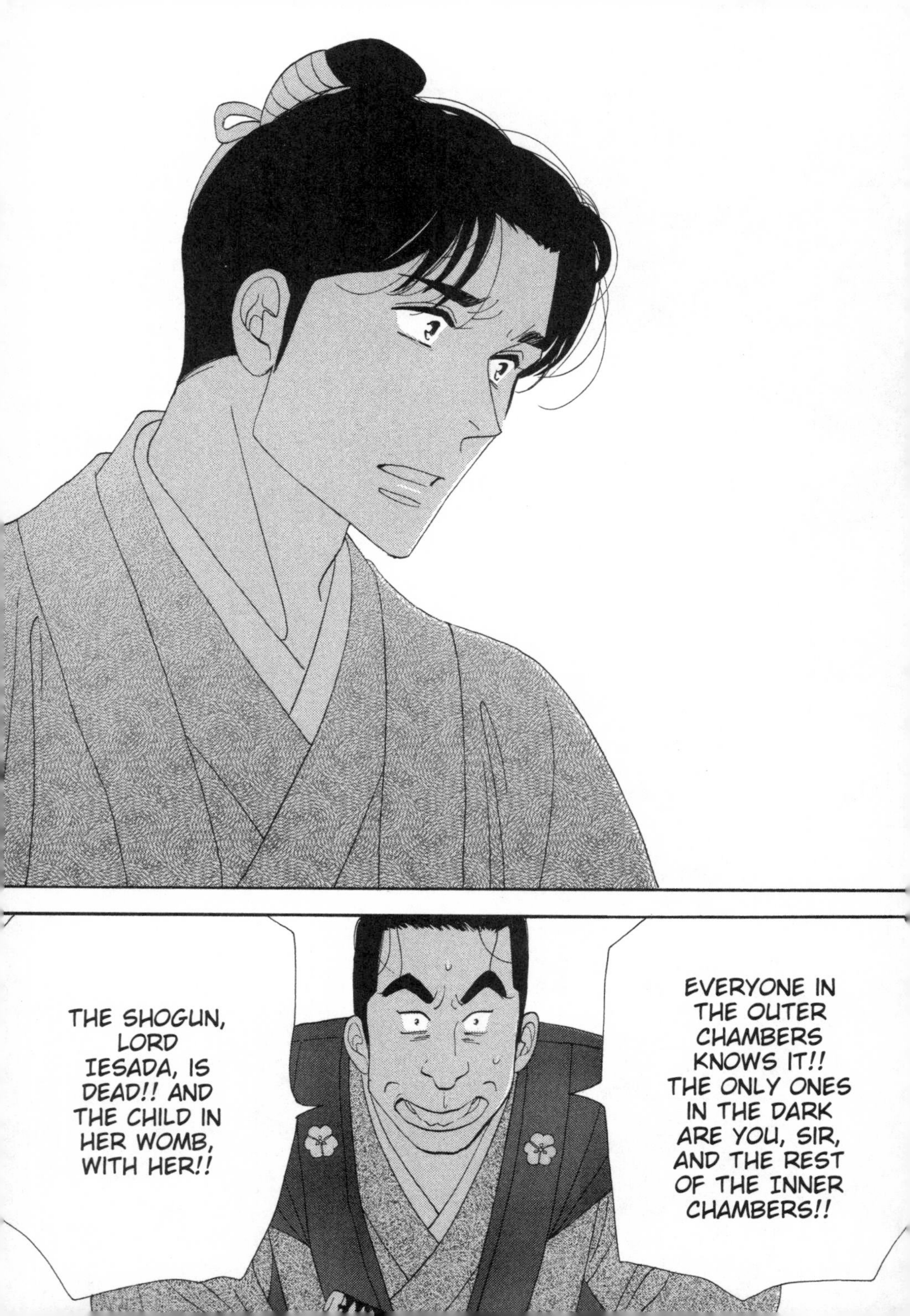
EVERYONE IN THE OUTER CHAMBERS KNOWS IT!! THE ONLY ONES IN THE DARK ARE YOU, SIR, AND THE REST OF THE INNER CHAMBERS!!
THE SHOGUN, LORD IESADA, IS DEAD!! AND THE CHILD IN HER WOMB, WITH HER!!

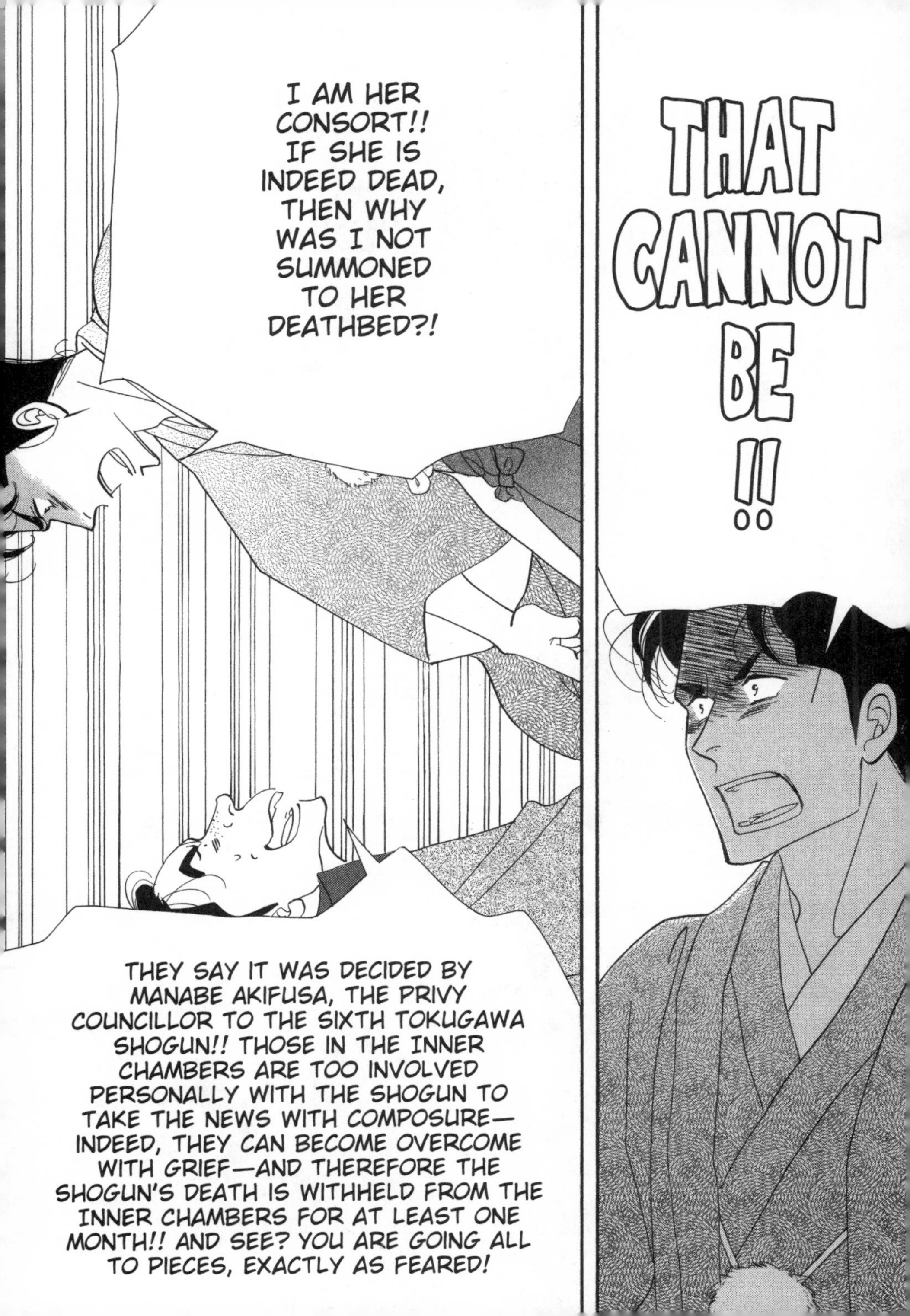
THAT CANNOT BE!!
I AM HER CONSORT!! IF SHE IS INDEED DEAD, THEN WHY WAS I NOT SUMMONED TO HER DEATHBED?!
THEY SAY IT WAS DECIDED BY MANABE AKIFUSA, THE PRIVY COUNCILLOR TO THE SIXTH TOKUGAWA SHOGUN!! THOSE IN THE INNER CHAMBERS ARE TOO INVOLVED PERSONALLY WITH THE SHOGUN TO TAKE THE NEWS WITH COMPOSURE—INDEED, THEY CAN BECOME OVERCOME WITH GRIEF—AND THEREFORE THE SHOGUN'S DEATH IS WITHHELD FROM THE INNER CHAMBERS FOR AT LEAST ONE MONTH!! AND SEE? YOU ARE GOING ALL TO PIECES, EXACTLY AS FEARED!

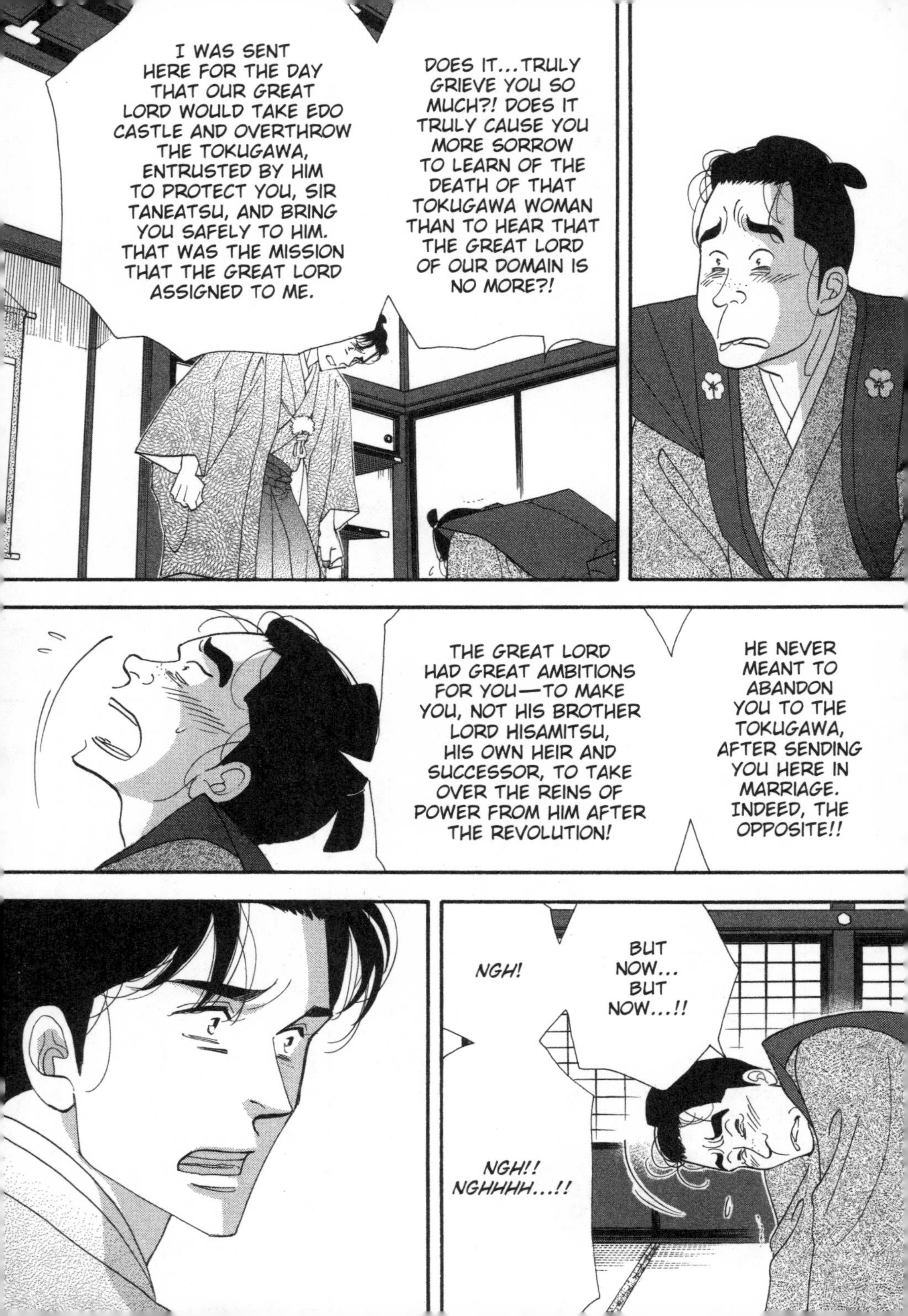
DOES IT...TRULY GRIEVE YOU SO MUCH?! DOES IT TRULY CAUSE YOU MORE SORROW TO LEARN OF THE DEATH OF THAT TOKUGAWA WOMAN THAN TO HEAR THAT THE GREAT LORD OF OUR DOMAIN IS NO MORE?!
I WAS SENT HERE FOR THE DAY THAT OUR GREAT LORD WOULD TAKE EDO CASTLE AND OVERTHROW THE TOKUGAWA, ENTRUSTED BY HIM TO PROTECT YOU, SIR TANEATSU, AND BRING YOU SAFELY TO HIM. THAT WAS THE MISSION THAT THE GREAT LORD ASSIGNED TO ME.
HE NEVER MEANT TO ABANDON YOU TO THE TOKUGAWA, AFTER SENDING YOU HERE IN MARRIAGE. INDEED, THE OPPOSITE!!
THE GREAT LORD HAD GREAT AMBITIONS FOR YOU—TO MAKE YOU, NOT HIS BROTHER LORD HISAMITSU, HIS OWN HEIR AND SUCCESSOR, TO TAKE OVER THE REINS OF POWER FROM HIM AFTER THE REVOLUTION!
BUT NOW... BUT NOW...!!
NGH!
NGH!! NGHHHH...!!

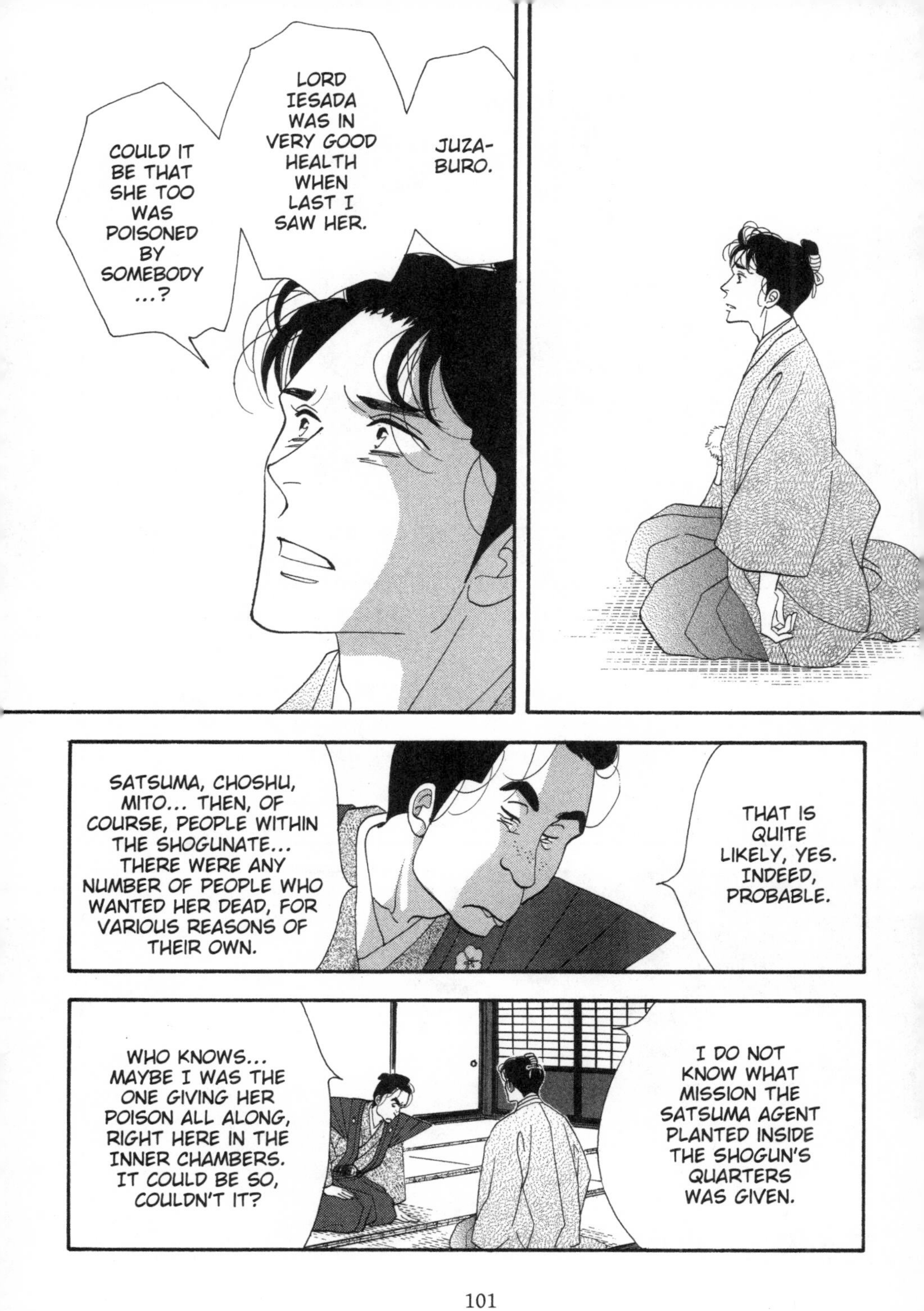
JUZA-BURO.
LORD IESADA WAS IN VERY GOOD HEALTH WHEN LAST I SAW HER.
COULD IT BE THAT SHE TOO WAS POISONED BY SOMEBODY ...?
THAT IS QUITE LIKELY, YES. INDEED, PROBABLE.
SATSUMA, CHOSHU, MITO... THEN, OF COURSE, PEOPLE WITHIN THE SHOGUNATE... THERE WERE ANY NUMBER OF PEOPLE WHO WANTED HER DEAD, FOR VARIOUS REASONS OF THEIR OWN.
I DO NOT KNOW WHAT MISSION THE SATSUMA AGENT PLANTED INSIDE THE SHOGUN'S QUARTERS WAS GIVEN.
WHO KNOWS... MAYBE I WAS THE ONE GIVING HER POISON ALL ALONG, RIGHT HERE IN THE INNER CHAMBERS. IT COULD BE SO, COULDN'T IT?

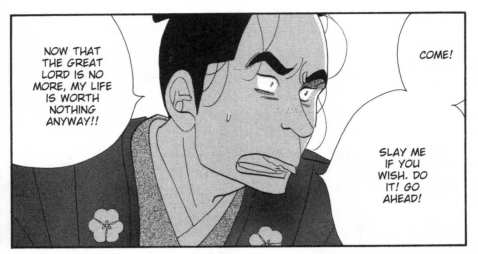

COME!
SLAY ME IF YOU WISH. DO IT! GO AHEAD!
NOW THAT THE GREAT LORD IS NO MORE, MY LIFE IS WORTH NOTHING ANYWAY!!
COME!!

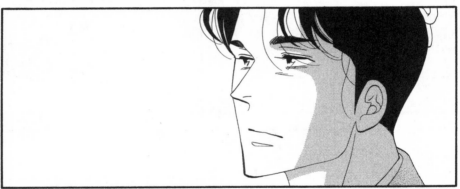

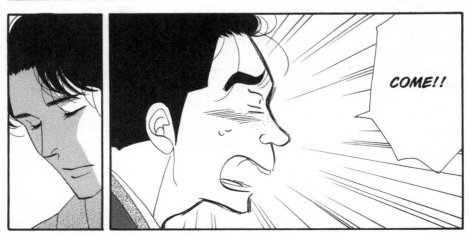

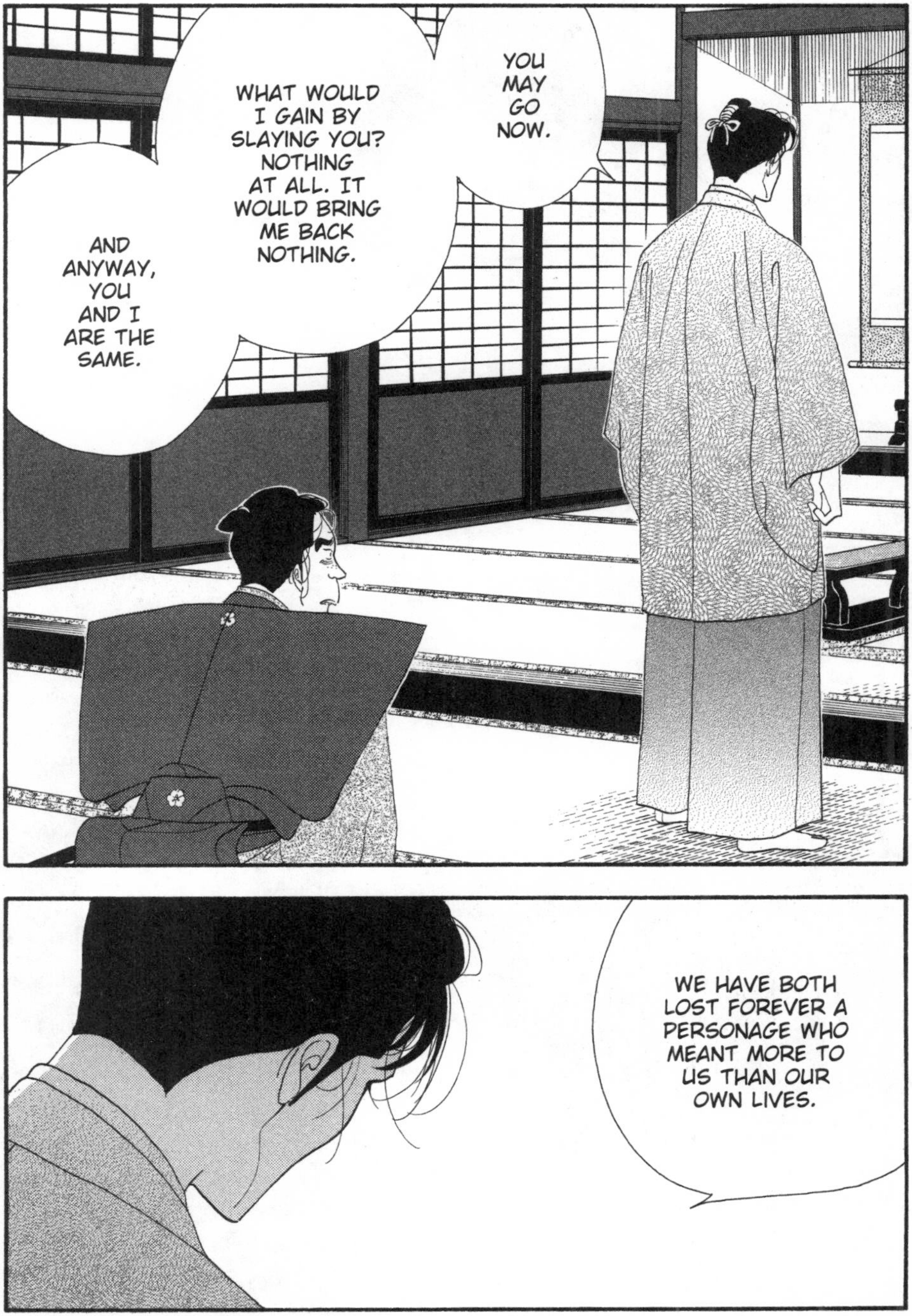
YOU MAY GO NOW.
WHAT WOULD I GAIN BY SLAYING YOU? NOTHING AT ALL. IT WOULD BRING ME BACK NOTHING.
AND ANYWAY, YOU AND I ARE THE SAME.
WE HAVE BOTH LOST FOREVER A PERSONAGE WHO MEANT MORE TO US THAN OUR OWN LIVES.

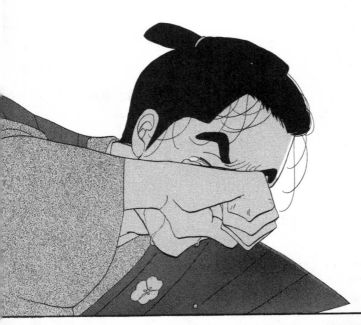

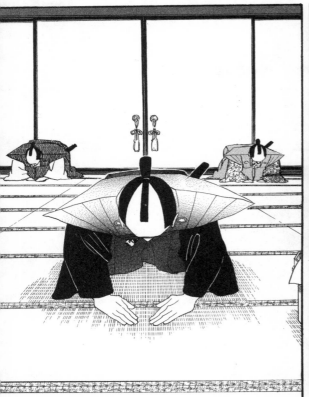

And then,
on the
eighth
day of the
eighth
month...

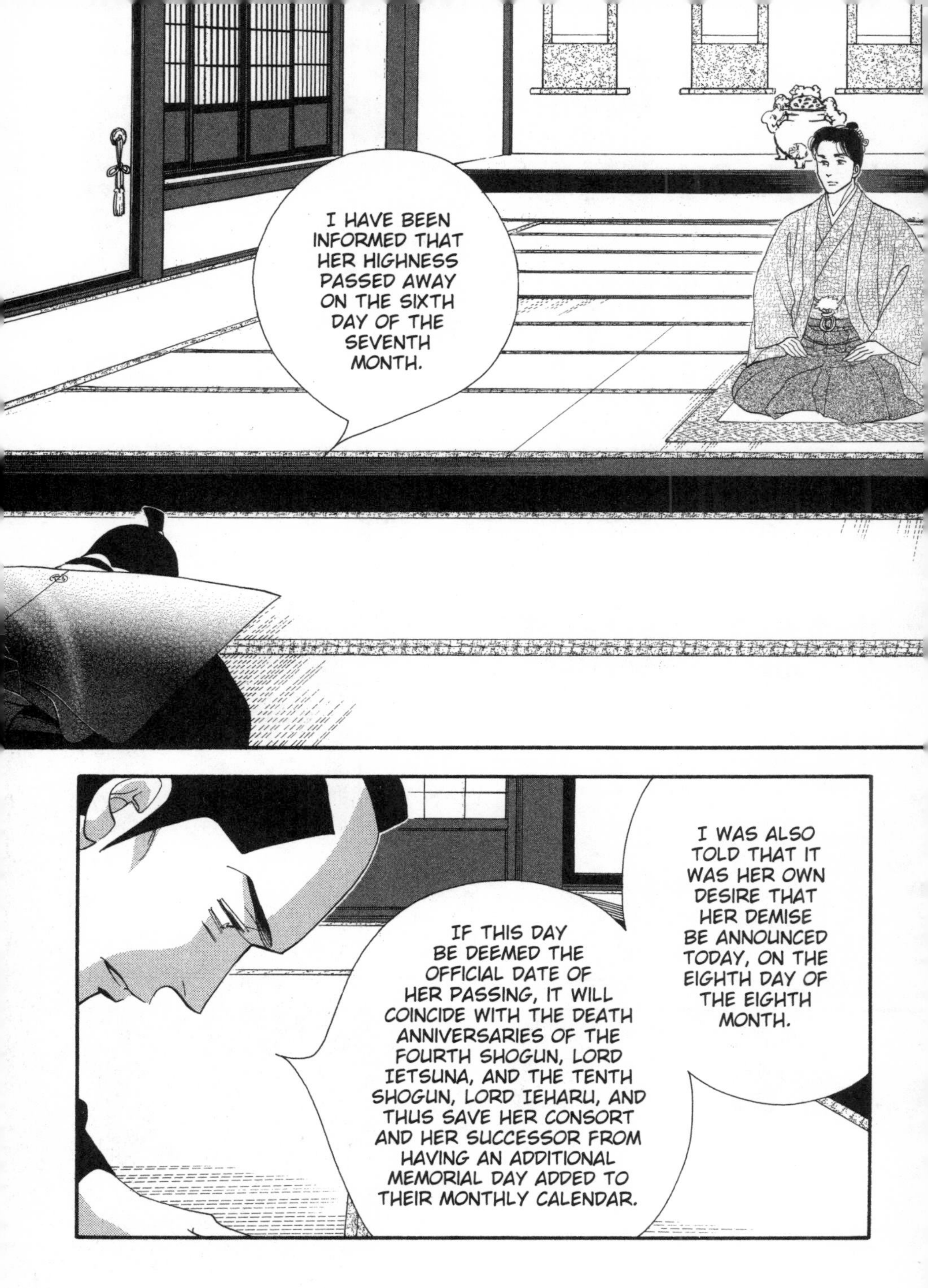
I HAVE BEEN INFORMED THAT HER HIGHNESS PASSED AWAY ON THE SIXTH DAY OF THE SEVENTH MONTH.
I WAS ALSO TOLD THAT IT WAS HER OWN DESIRE THAT HER DEMISE BE ANNOUNCED TODAY, ON THE EIGHTH DAY OF THE EIGHTH MONTH.
IF THIS DAY BE DEEMED THE OFFICIAL DATE OF HER PASSING, IT WILL COINCIDE WITH THE DEATH ANNIVERSARIES OF THE FOURTH SHOGUN, LORD IETSUNA, AND THE TENTH SHOGUN, LORD IEHARU, AND THUS SAVE HER CONSORT AND HER SUCCESSOR FROM HAVING AN ADDITIONAL MEMORIAL DAY ADDED TO THEIR MONTHLY CALENDAR.

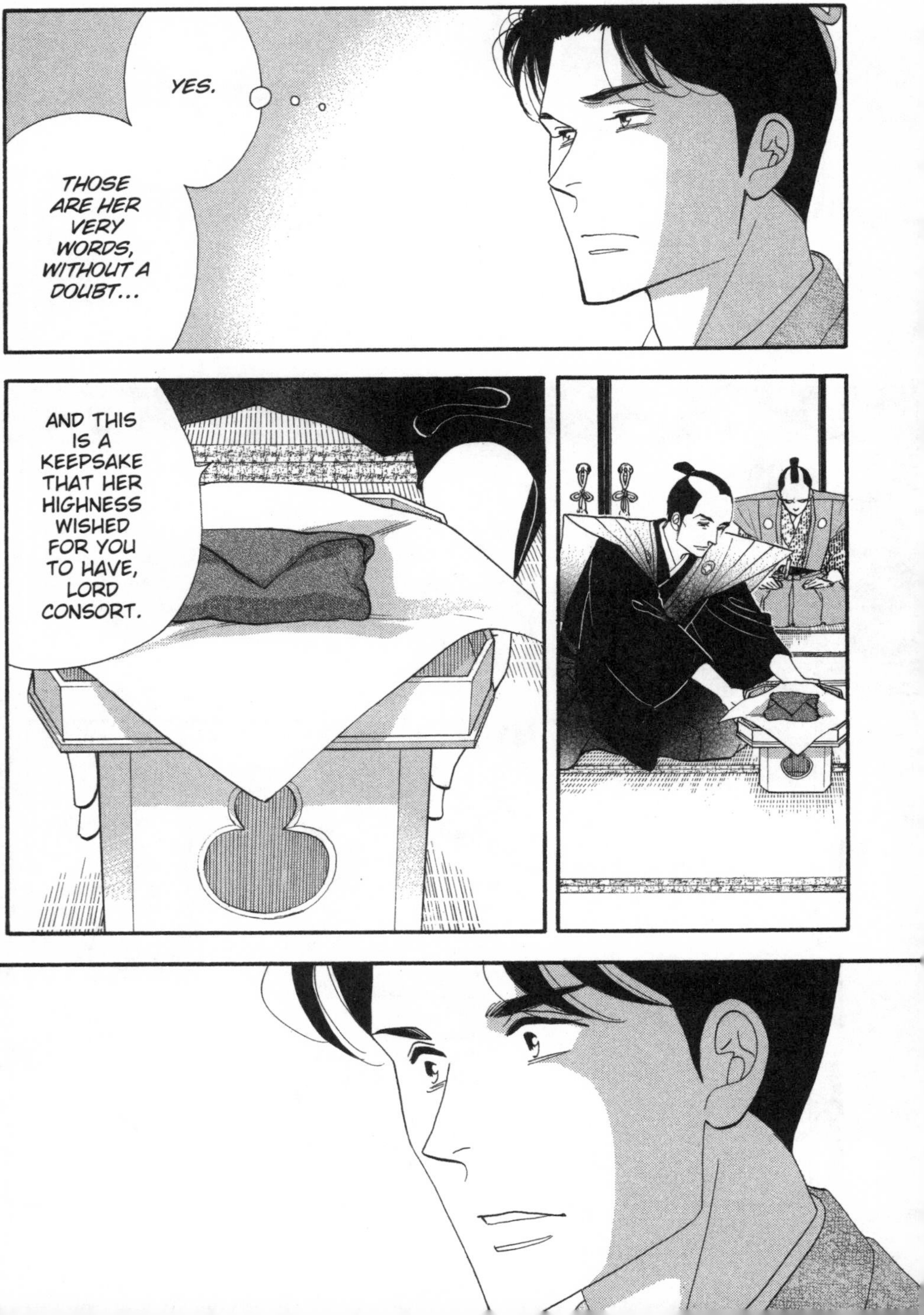
YES.
THOSE ARE HER VERY WORDS, WITHOUT A DOUBT...
AND THIS IS A KEEPSAKE THAT HER HIGHNESS WISHED FOR YOU TO HAVE, LORD CONSORT.

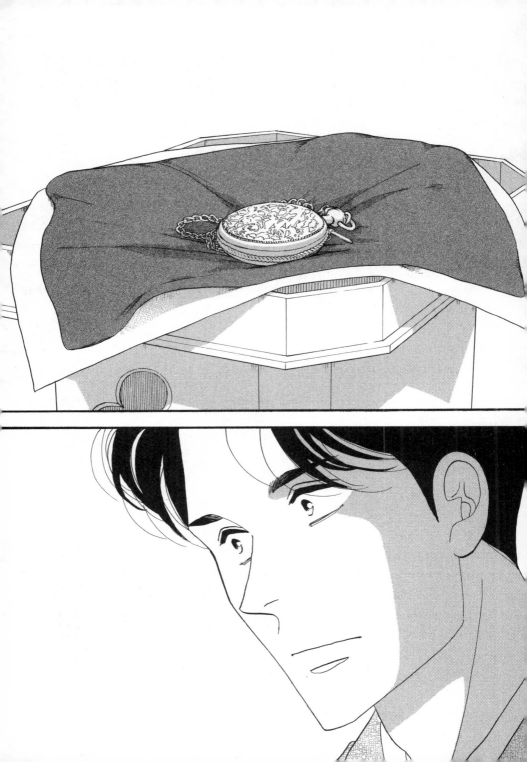

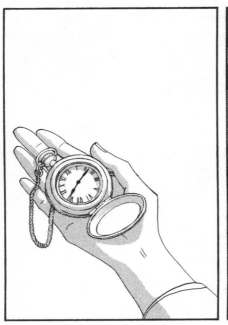

WE WILL BE SPENDING MUCH TIME APART FROM NOW ON, YOU IN THE SHOGUN'S QUARTERS AND I HERE. SO PLEASE, TAKE THIS...

MY LORD.

HM?

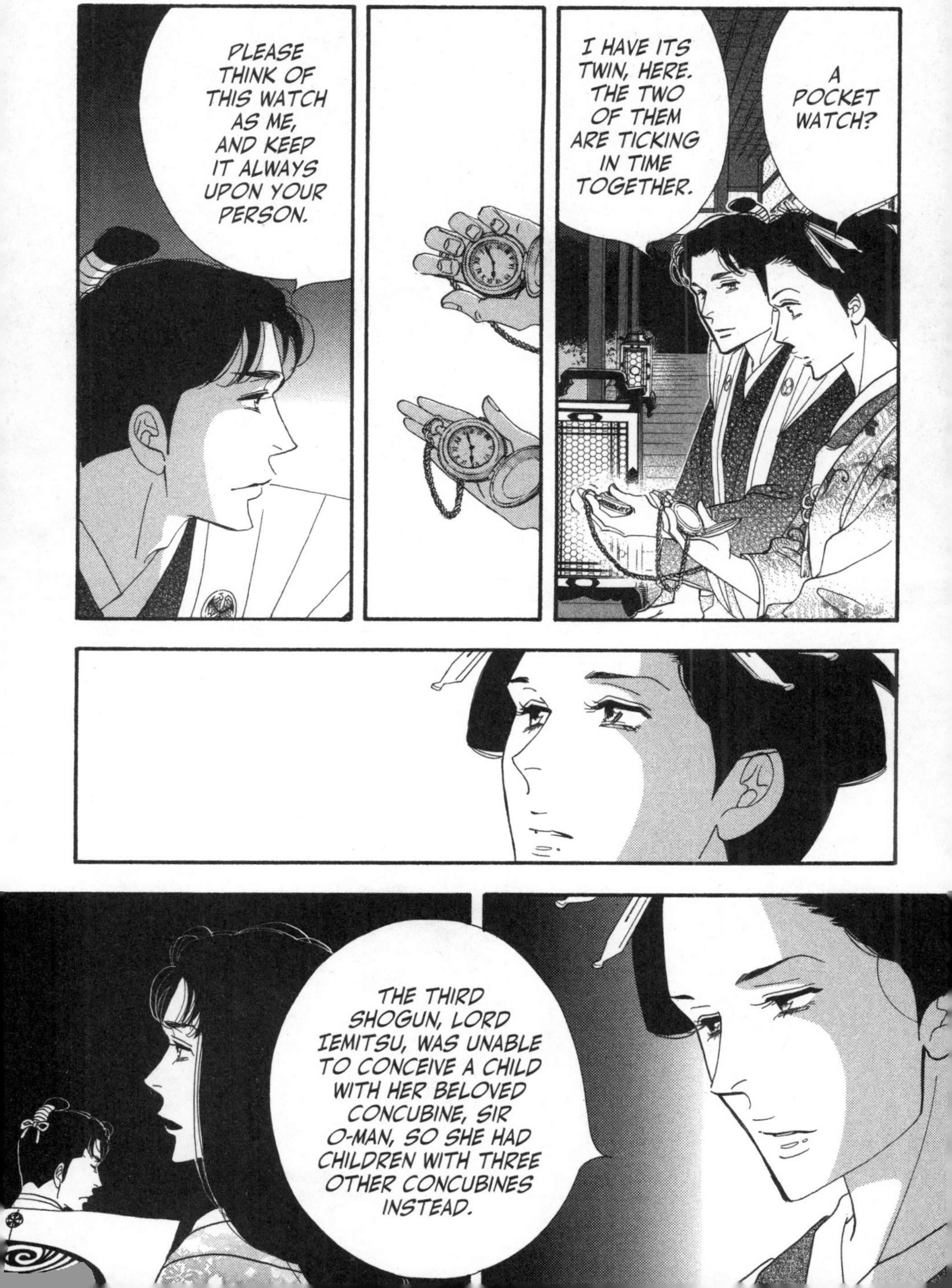
A POCKET WATCH?
I HAVE ITS TWIN, HERE. THE TWO OF THEM ARE TICKING IN TIME TOGETHER.
PLEASE THINK OF THIS WATCH AS ME, AND KEEP IT ALWAYS UPON YOUR PERSON.
THE THIRD SHOGUN, LORD IEMITSU, WAS UNABLE TO CONCEIVE A CHILD WITH HER BELOVED CONCUBINE, SIR O-MAN, SO SHE HAD CHILDREN WITH THREE OTHER CONCUBINES INSTEAD.

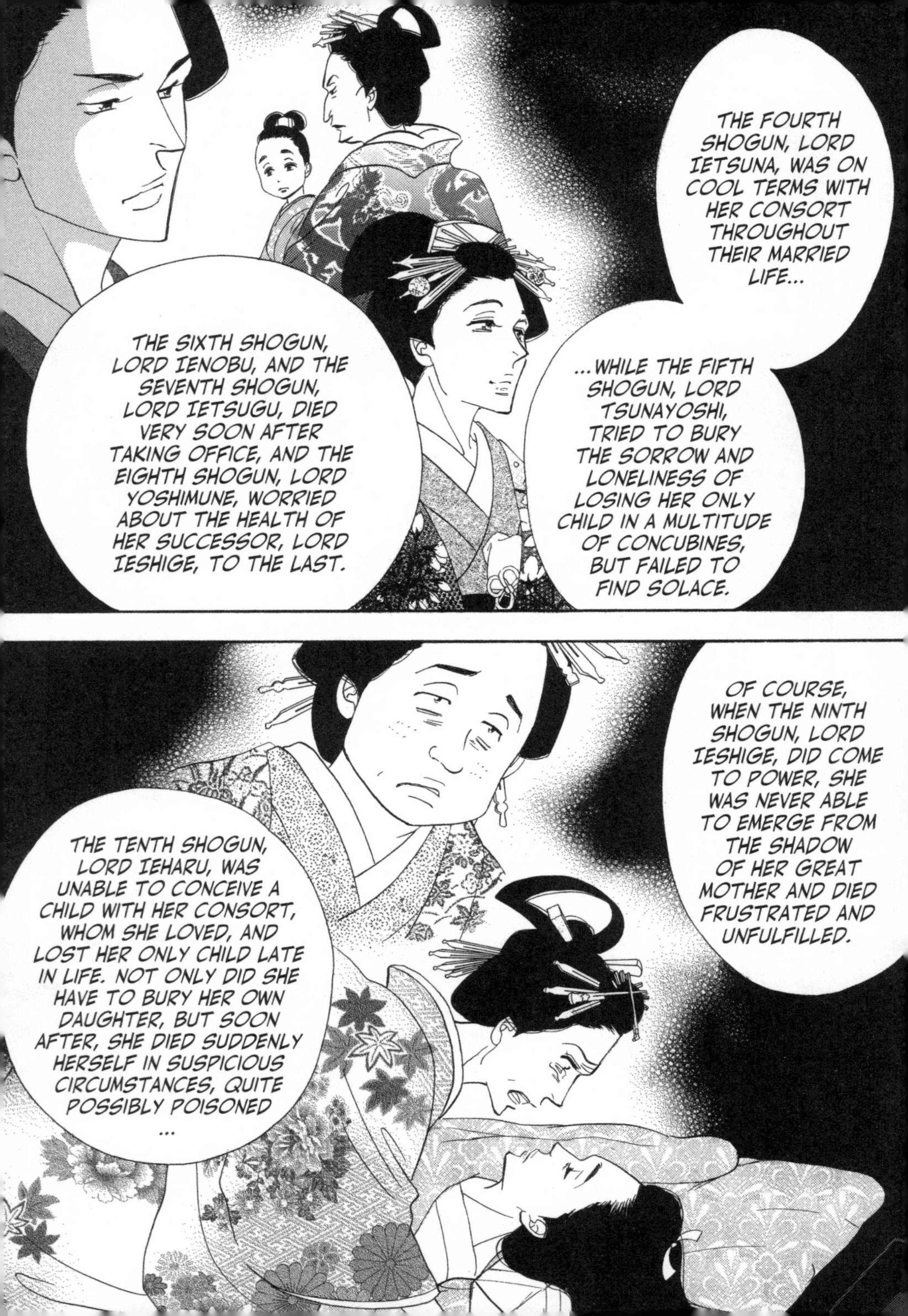
THE FOURTH SHOGUN, LORD IETSUNA, WAS ON COOL TERMS WITH HER CONSORT THROUGHOUT THEIR MARRIED LIFE...
...WHILE THE FIFTH SHOGUN, LORD TSUNAYOSHI, TRIED TO BURY THE SORROW AND LONELINESS OF LOSING HER ONLY CHILD IN A MULTITUDE OF CONCUBINES, BUT FAILED TO FIND SOLACE.
THE SIXTH SHOGUN, LORD IENOBU, AND THE SEVENTH SHOGUN, LORD IETSUGU, DIED VERY SOON AFTER TAKING OFFICE, AND THE EIGHTH SHOGUN, LORD YOSHIMUNE, WORRIED ABOUT THE HEALTH OF HER SUCCESSOR, LORD IESHIGE, TO THE LAST.
OF COURSE, WHEN THE NINTH SHOGUN, LORD IESHIGE, DID COME TO POWER, SHE WAS NEVER ABLE TO EMERGE FROM THE SHADOW OF HER GREAT MOTHER AND DIED FRUSTRATED AND UNFULFILLED.
THE TENTH SHOGUN, LORD IEHARU, WAS UNABLE TO CONCEIVE A CHILD WITH HER CONSORT, WHOM SHE LOVED, AND LOST HER ONLY CHILD LATE IN LIFE. NOT ONLY DID SHE HAVE TO BURY HER OWN DAUGHTER, BUT SOON AFTER, SHE DIED SUDDENLY HERSELF IN SUSPICIOUS CIRCUMSTANCES, QUITE POSSIBLY POISONED ...

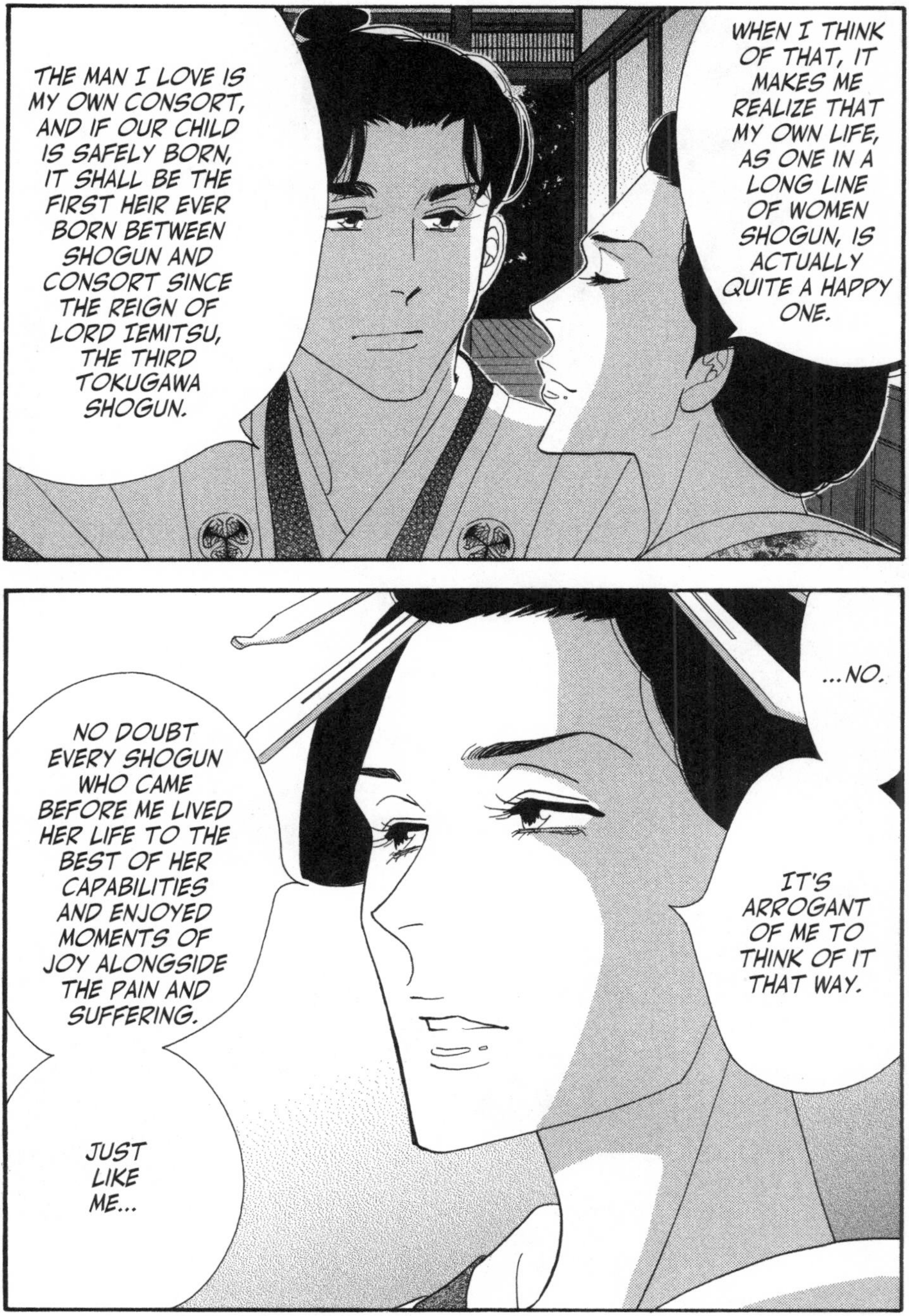
WHEN I THINK OF THAT, IT MAKES ME REALIZE THAT MY OWN LIFE, AS ONE IN A LONG LINE OF WOMEN SHOGUN, IS ACTUALLY QUITE A HAPPY ONE.
THE MAN I LOVE IS MY OWN CONSORT, AND IF OUR CHILD IS SAFELY BORN, IT SHALL BE THE FIRST HEIR EVER BORN BETWEEN SHOGUN AND CONSORT SINCE THE REIGN OF LORD IEMITSU, THE THIRD TOKUGAWA SHOGUN.
...NO.
IT'S ARROGANT OF ME TO THINK OF IT THAT WAY.
NO DOUBT EVERY SHOGUN WHO CAME BEFORE ME LIVED HER LIFE TO THE BEST OF HER CAPABILITIES AND ENJOYED MOMENTS OF JOY ALONGSIDE THE PAIN AND SUFFERING.
JUST LIKE ME...

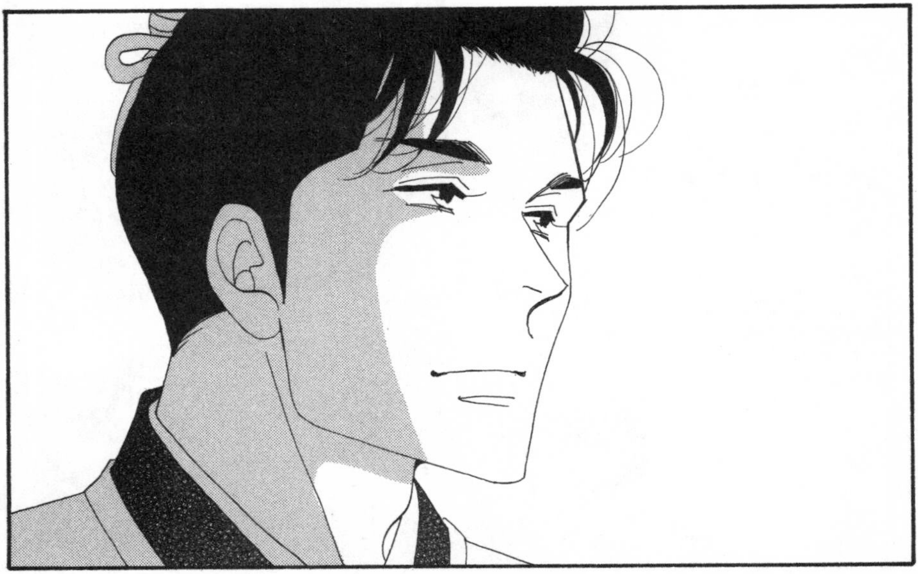

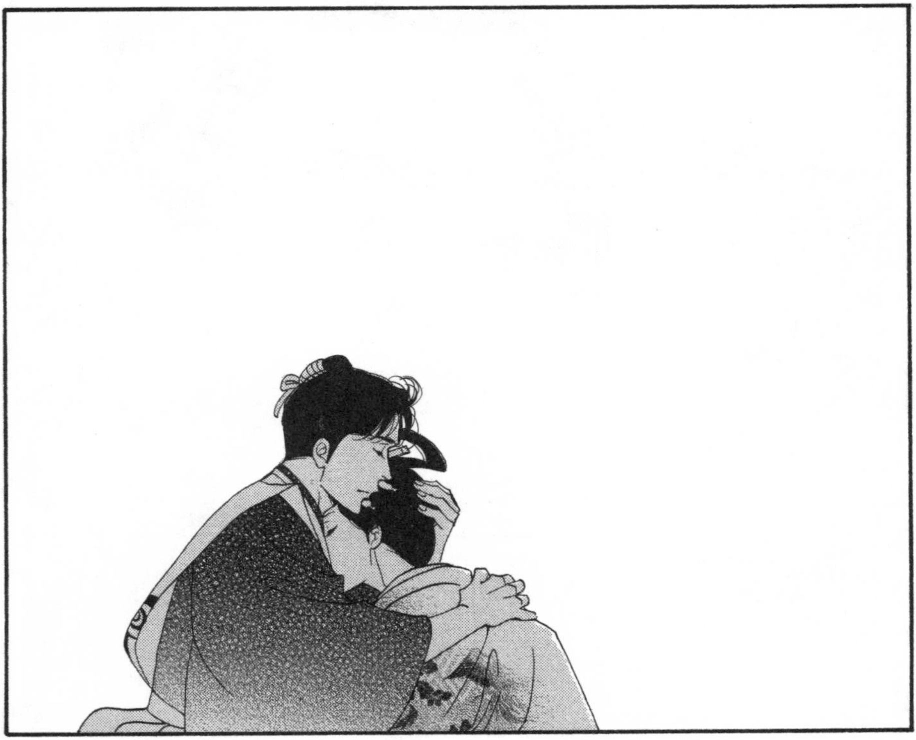

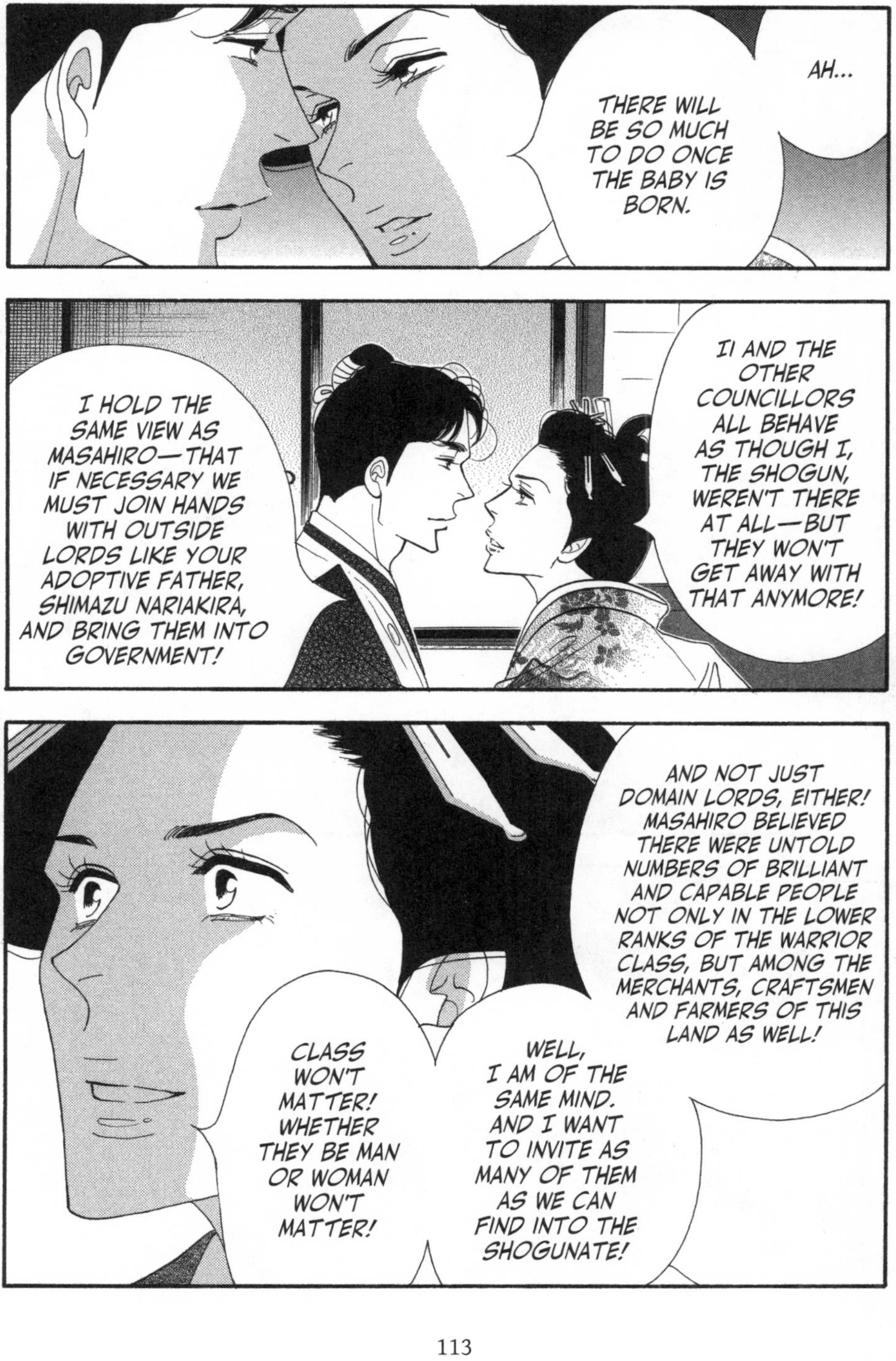
AH...
THERE WILL BE SO MUCH TO DO ONCE THE BABY IS BORN.
II AND THE OTHER COUNCILLORS ALL BEHAVE AS THOUGH I, THE SHOGUN, WEREN'T THERE AT ALL—BUT THEY WON'T GET AWAY WITH THAT ANYMORE!
I HOLD THE SAME VIEW AS MASAHIRO—THAT IF NECESSARY WE MUST JOIN HANDS WITH OUTSIDE LORDS LIKE YOUR ADOPTIVE FATHER, SHIMAZU NARIAKIRA, AND BRING THEM INTO GOVERNMENT!
AND NOT JUST DOMAIN LORDS, EITHER! MASAHIRO BELIEVED THERE WERE UNTOLD NUMBERS OF BRILLIANT AND CAPABLE PEOPLE NOT ONLY IN THE LOWER RANKS OF THE WARRIOR CLASS, BUT AMONG THE MERCHANTS, CRAFTSMEN AND FARMERS OF THIS LAND AS WELL!
WELL, I AM OF THE SAME MIND. AND I WANT TO INVITE AS MANY OF THEM AS WE CAN FIND INTO THE SHOGUNATE!
CLASS WON'T MATTER! WHETHER THEY BE MAN OR WOMAN WON'T MATTER!

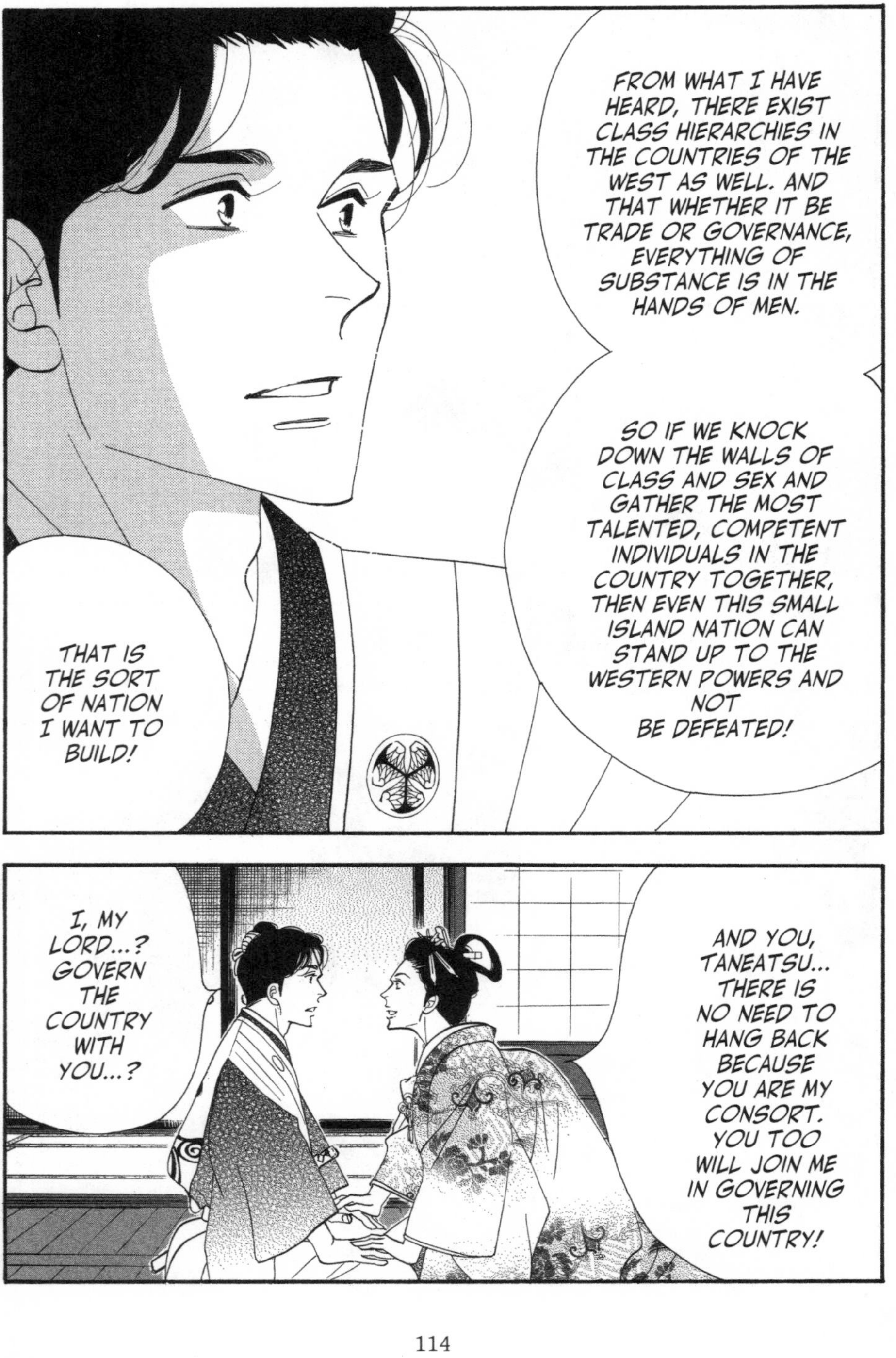
FROM WHAT I HAVE HEARD, THERE EXIST CLASS HIERARCHIES IN THE COUNTRIES OF THE WEST AS WELL. AND THAT WHETHER IT BE TRADE OR GOVERNANCE, EVERYTHING OF SUBSTANCE IS IN THE HANDS OF MEN.
SO IF WE KNOCK DOWN THE WALLS OF CLASS AND SEX AND GATHER THE MOST TALENTED, COMPETENT INDIVIDUALS IN THE COUNTRY TOGETHER, THEN EVEN THIS SMALL ISLAND NATION CAN STAND UP TO THE WESTERN POWERS AND NOT BE DEFEATED!
THAT IS THE SORT OF NATION I WANT TO BUILD!
AND YOU, TANEATSU... THERE IS NO NEED TO HANG BACK BECAUSE YOU ARE MY CONSORT. YOU TOO WILL JOIN ME IN GOVERNING THIS COUNTRY!
I, MY LORD...? GOVERN THE COUNTRY WITH YOU...?

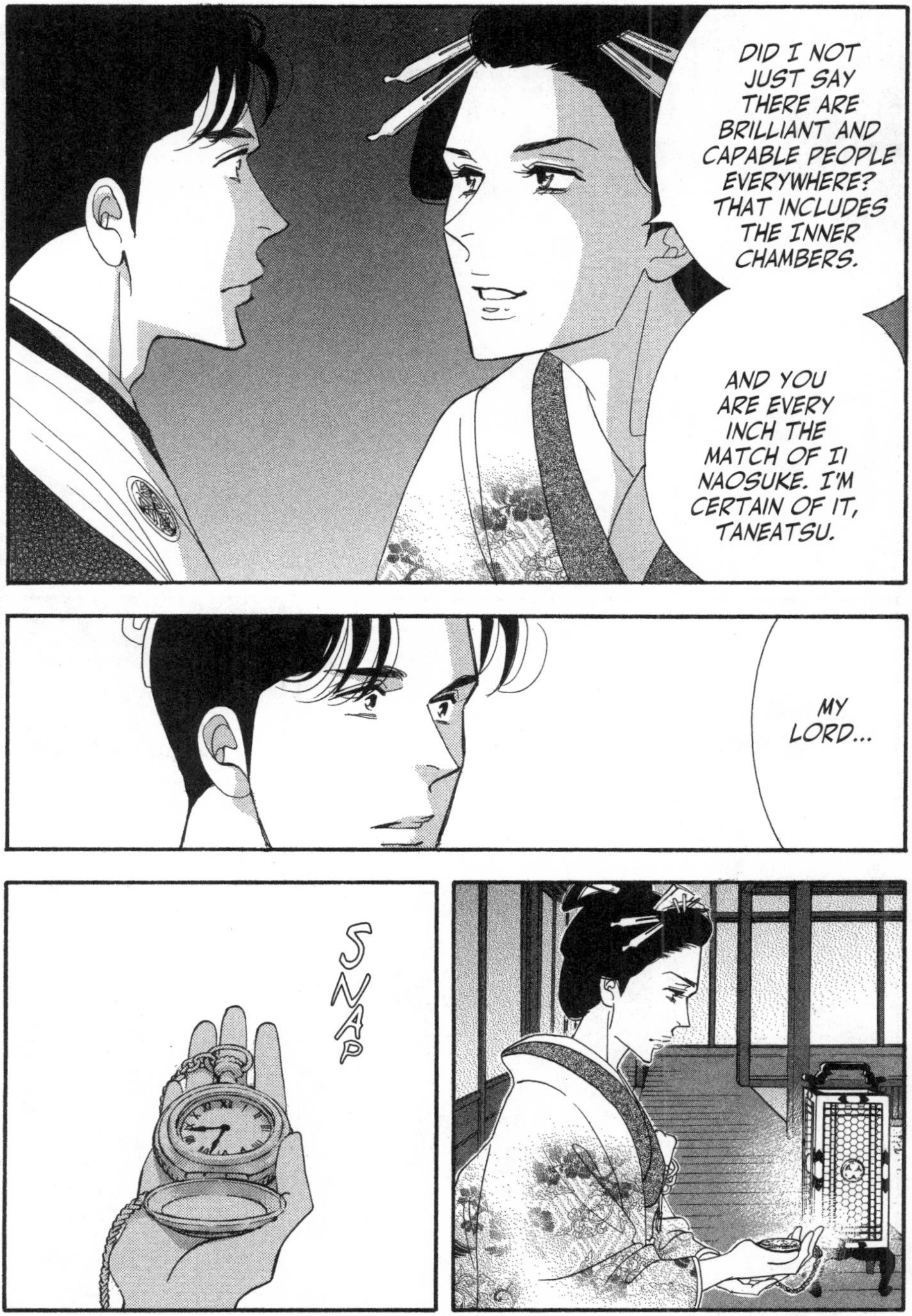
DID I NOT JUST SAY THERE ARE BRILLIANT AND CAPABLE PEOPLE EVERYWHERE? THAT INCLUDES THE INNER CHAMBERS.
AND YOU ARE EVERY INCH THE MATCH OF II NAOSUKE. I'M CERTAIN OF IT, TANEATSU.
MY LORD...
SNAP

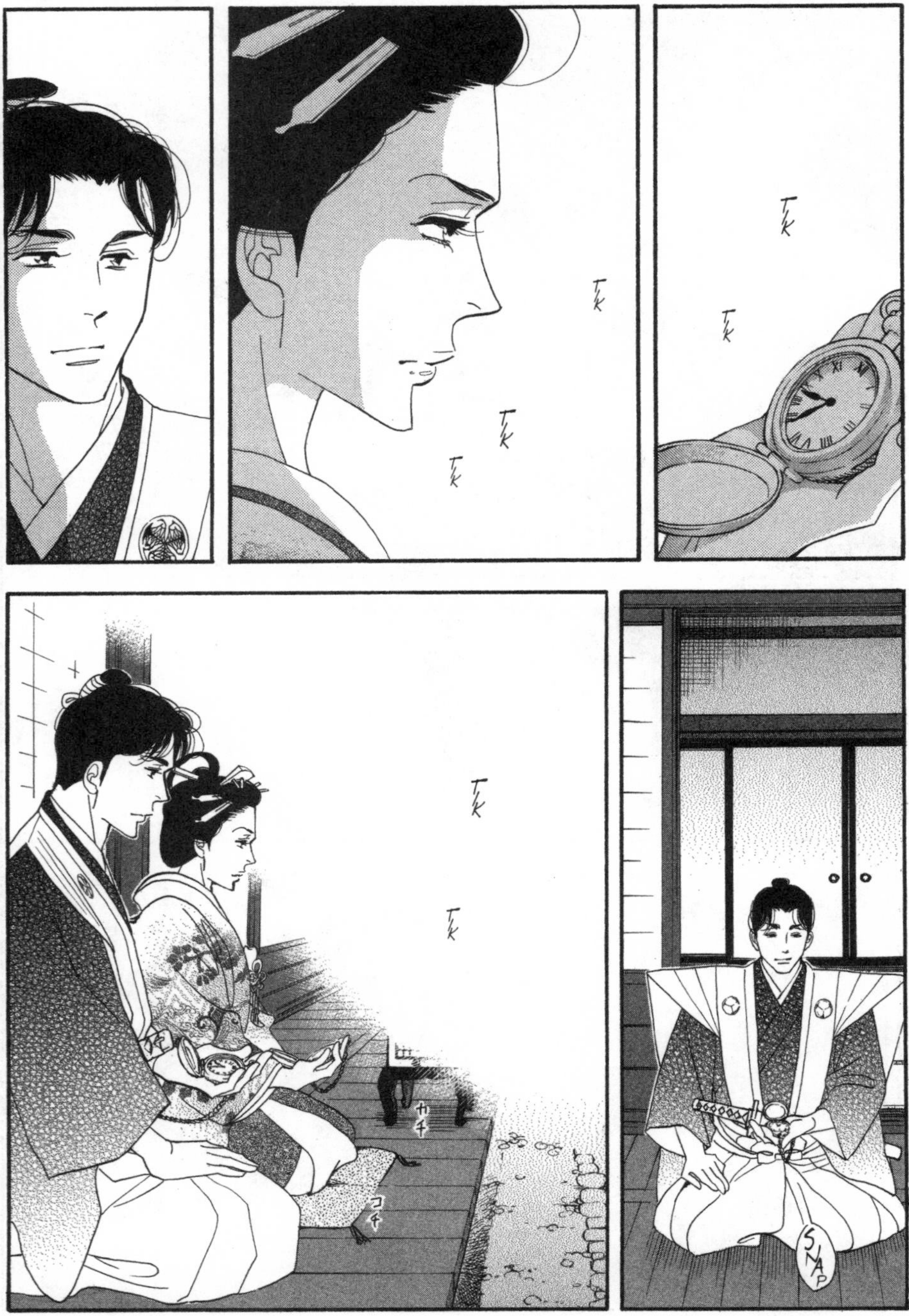
Tk
Tk
Tk
Tk
Tk
Tk
SNAP
Tk
Tk
カチ
コチ

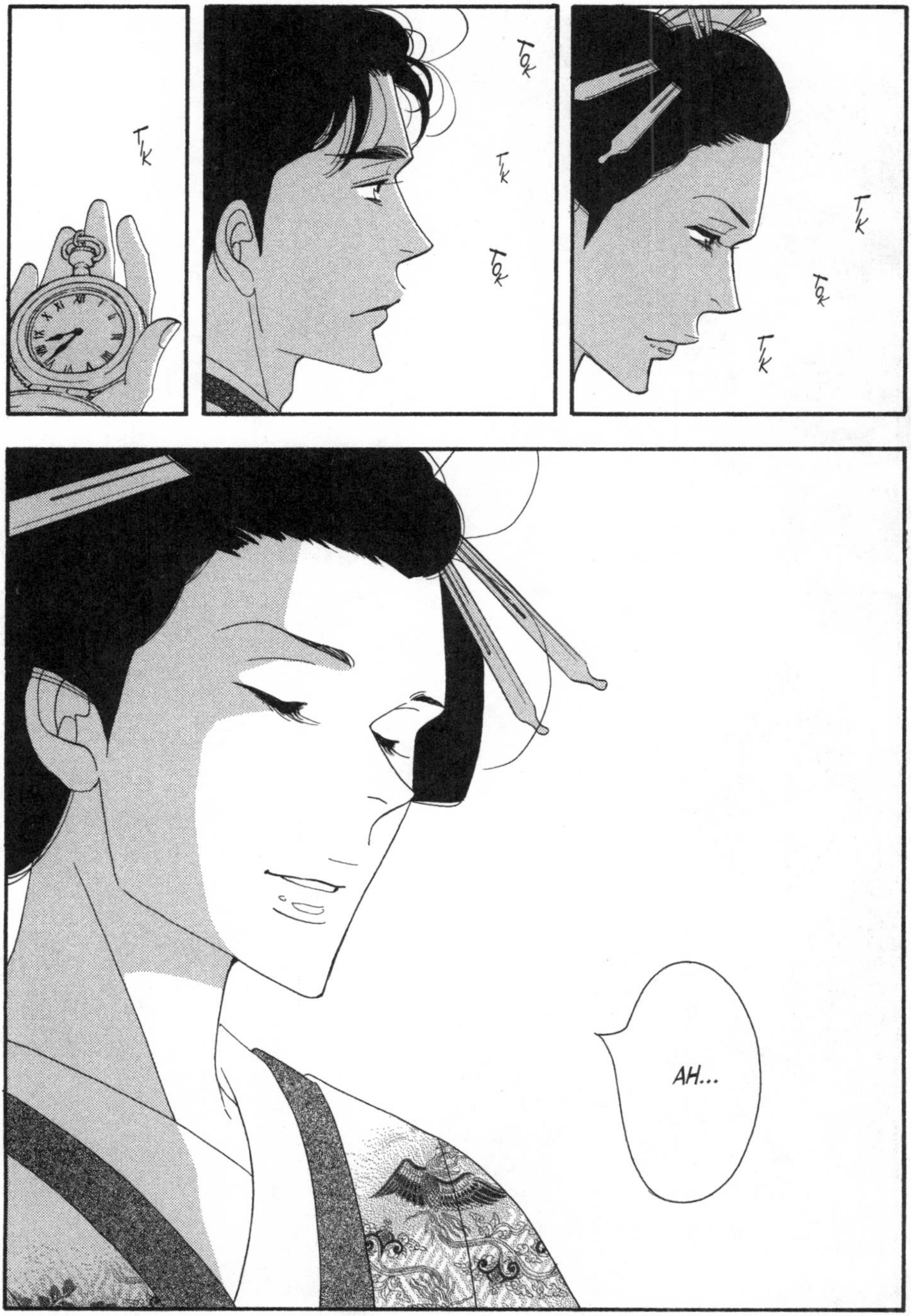
TK
TOK
TK
TOK
TK
TOK
TK
AH...

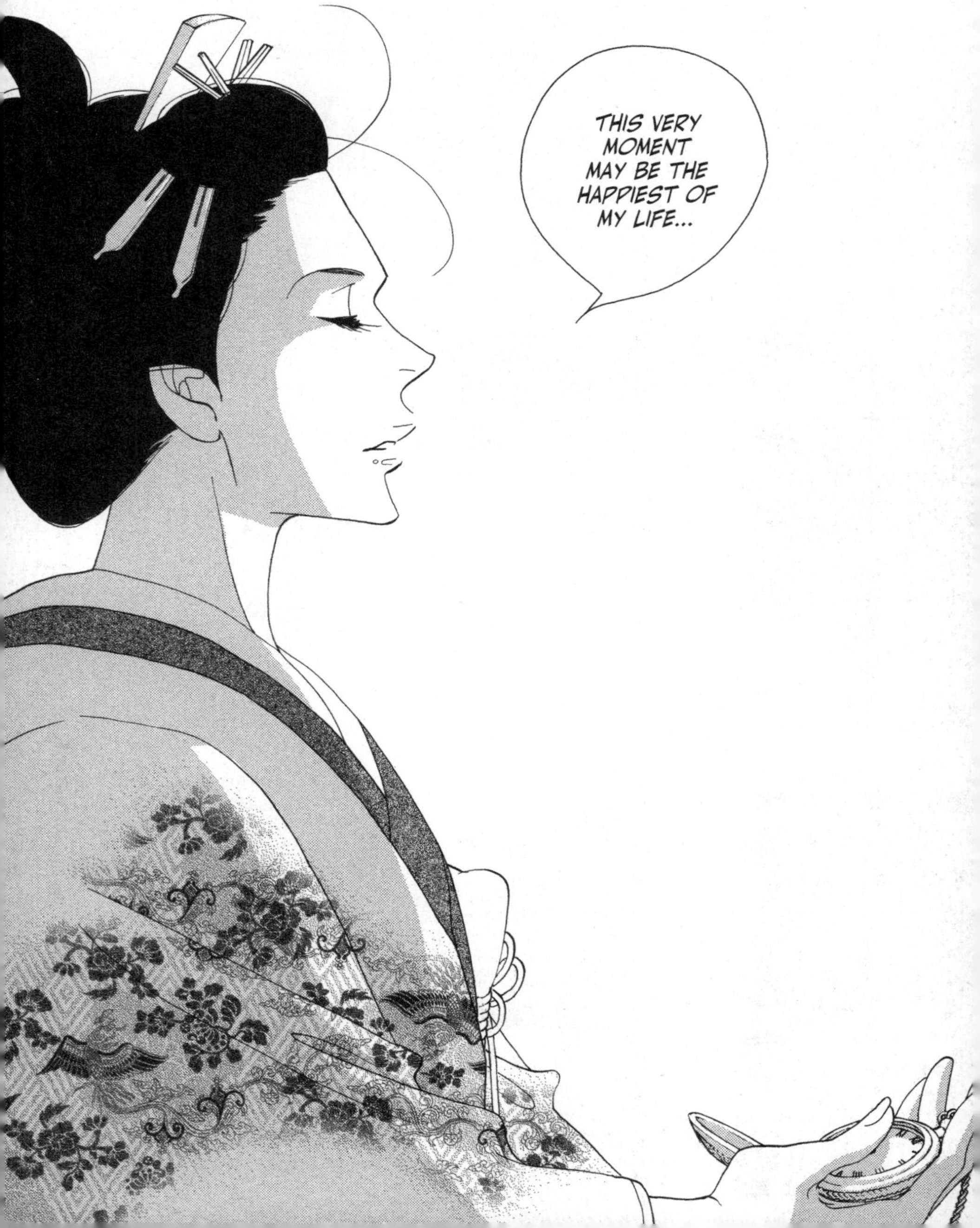
THIS VERY MOMENT MAY BE THE HAPPIEST OF MY LIFE...

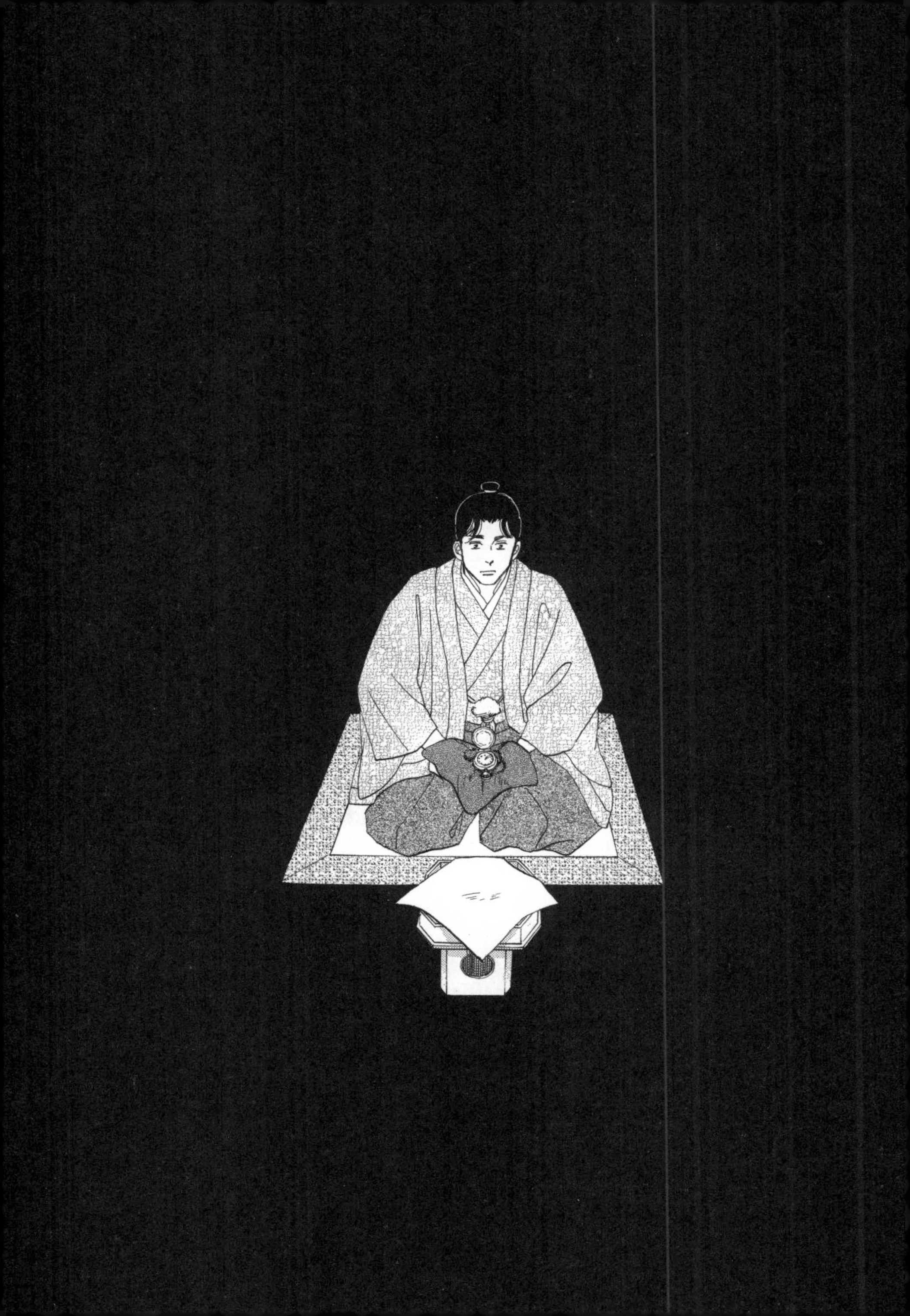

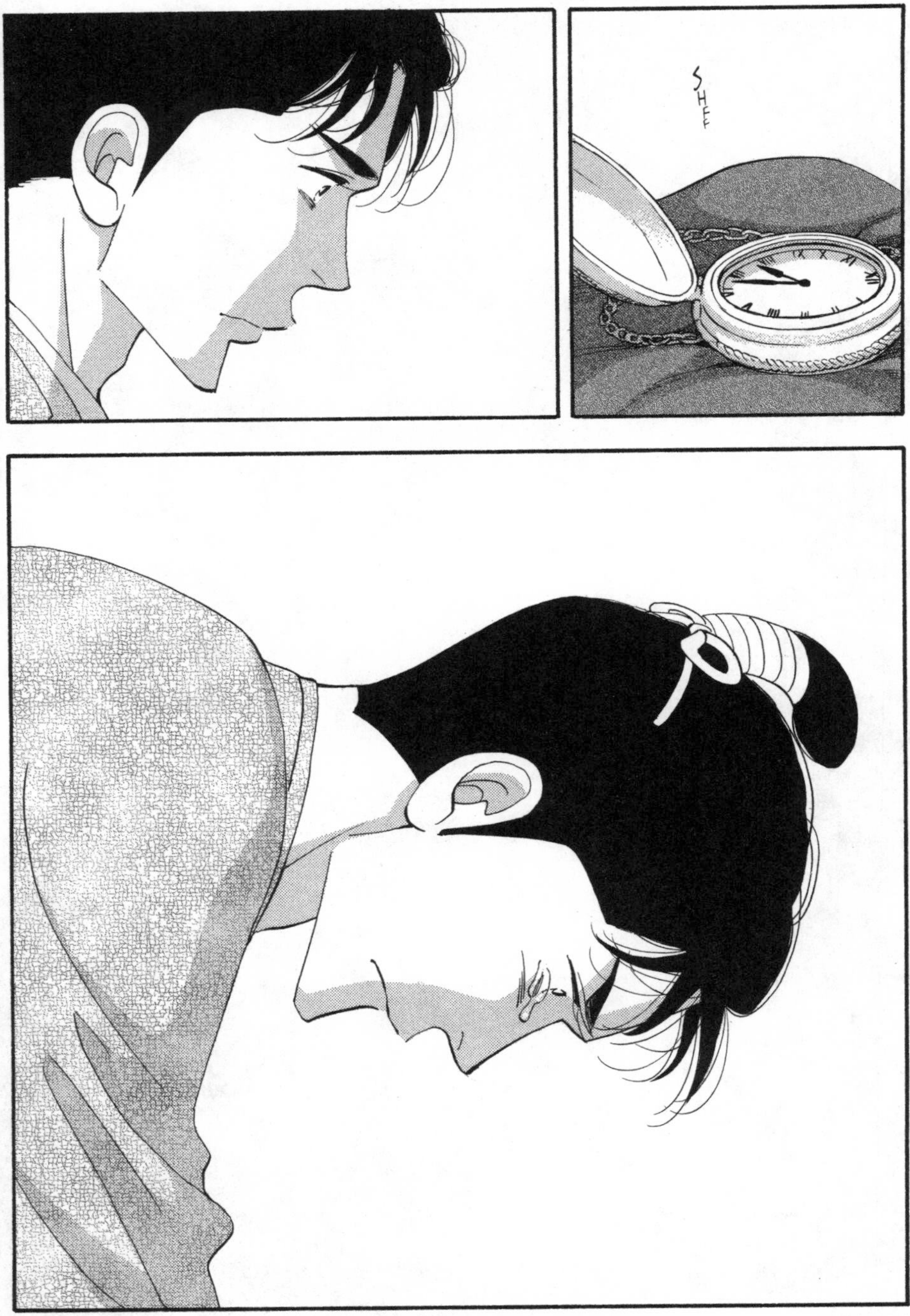
SHFF

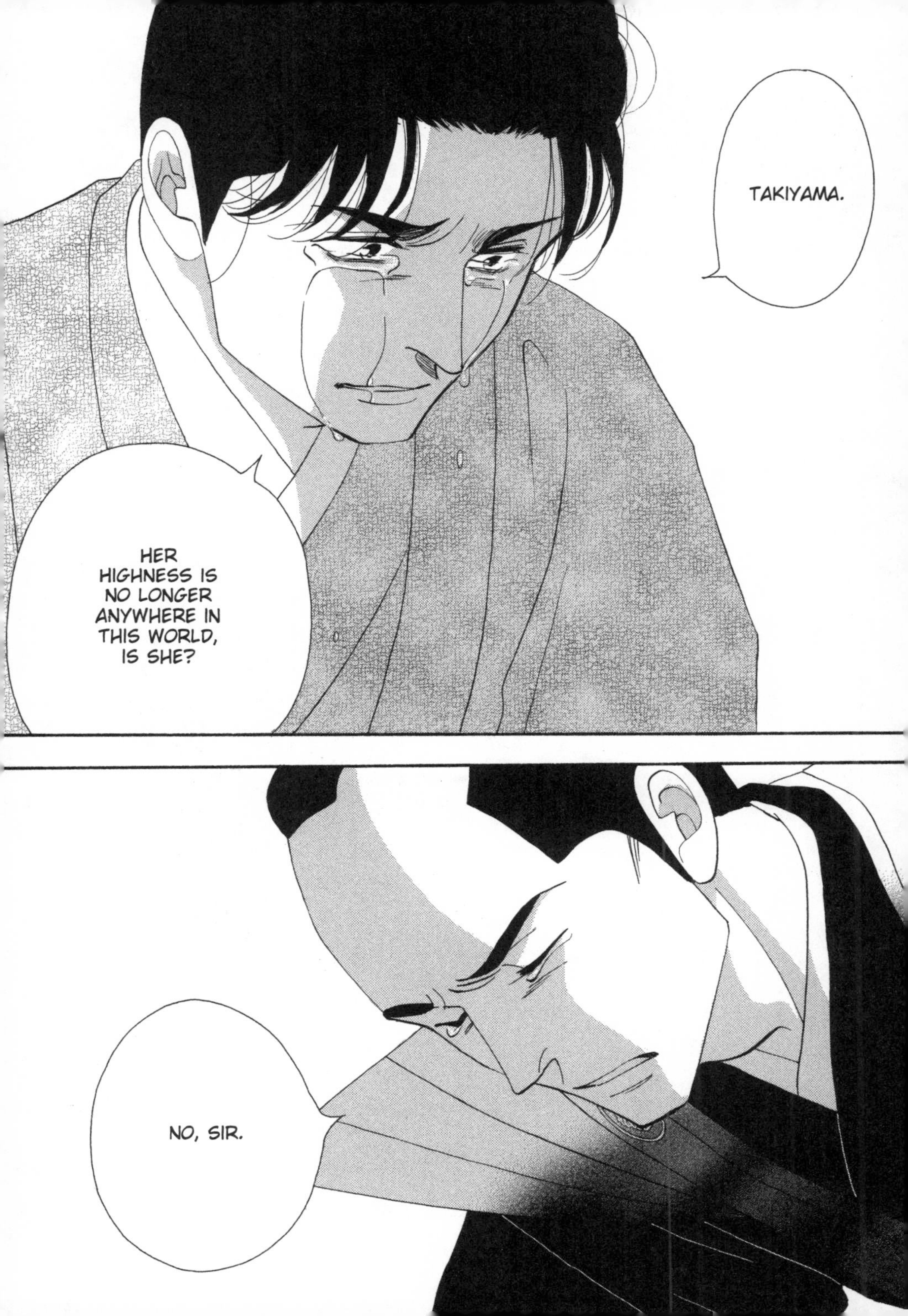
TAKIYAMA.
HER HIGHNESS IS NO LONGER ANYWHERE IN THIS WORLD, IS SHE?
NO, SIR.

"THIS VERY
MOMENT MAY BE
THE HAPPIEST
OF MY LIFE..."

Ōoku

THE INNER CHAMBERS

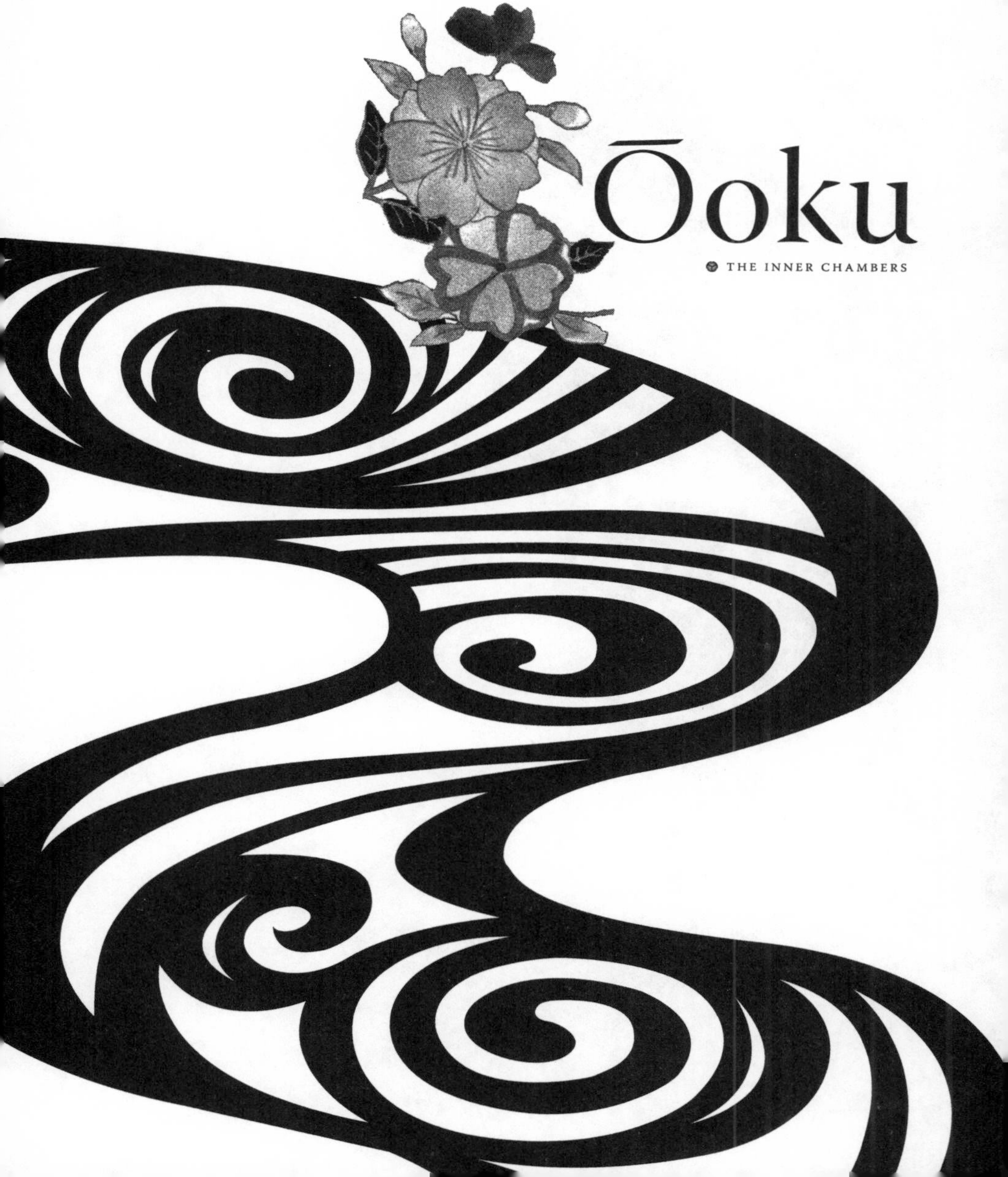

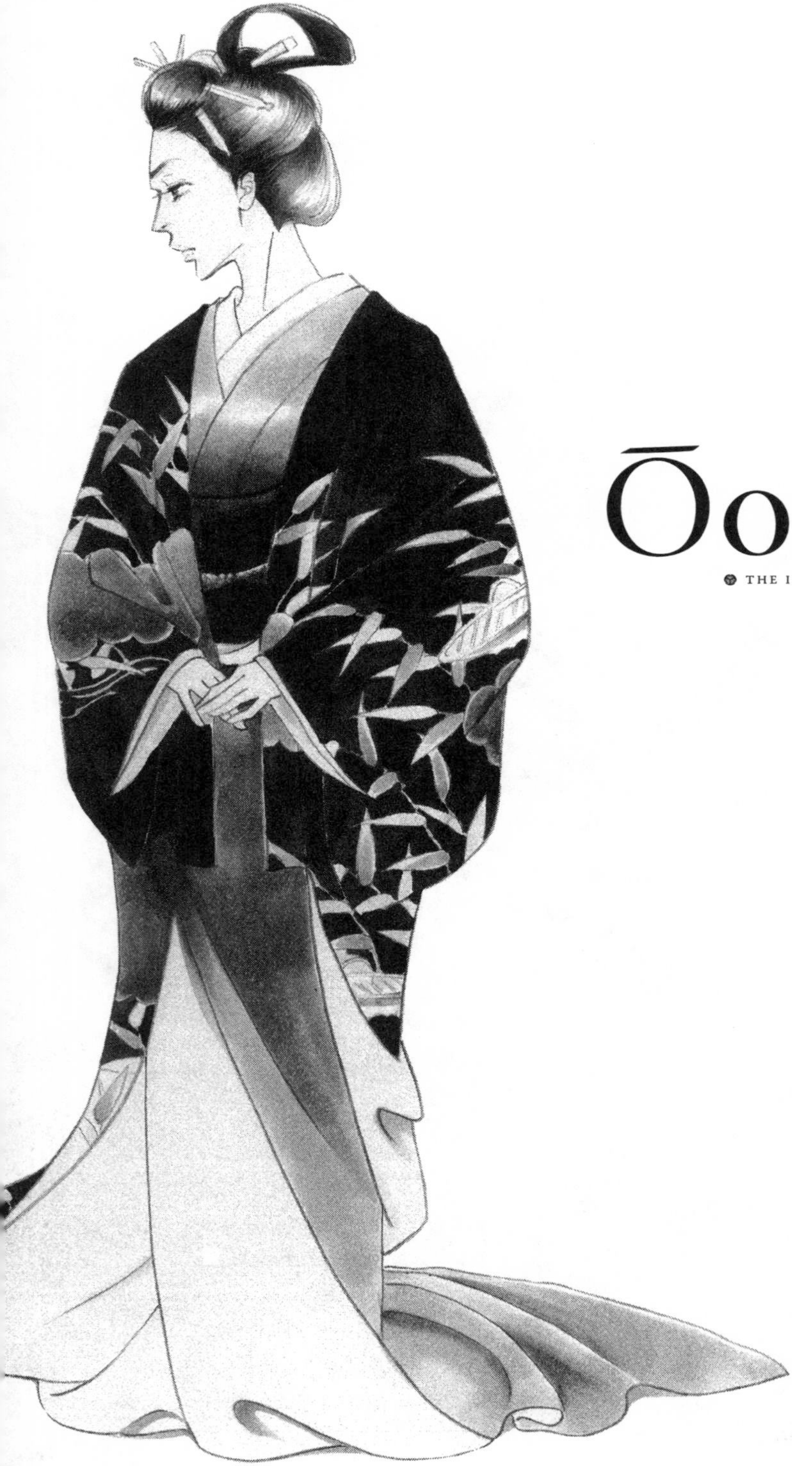

Ōoku

THE INNER CHAMBERS

Ōoku

THE INNER CHAMBERS

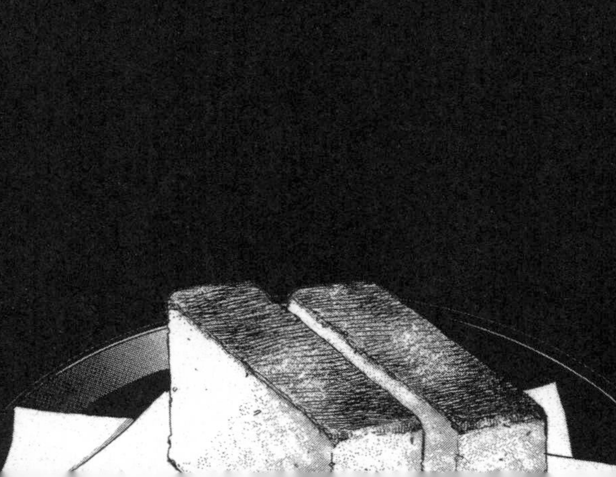

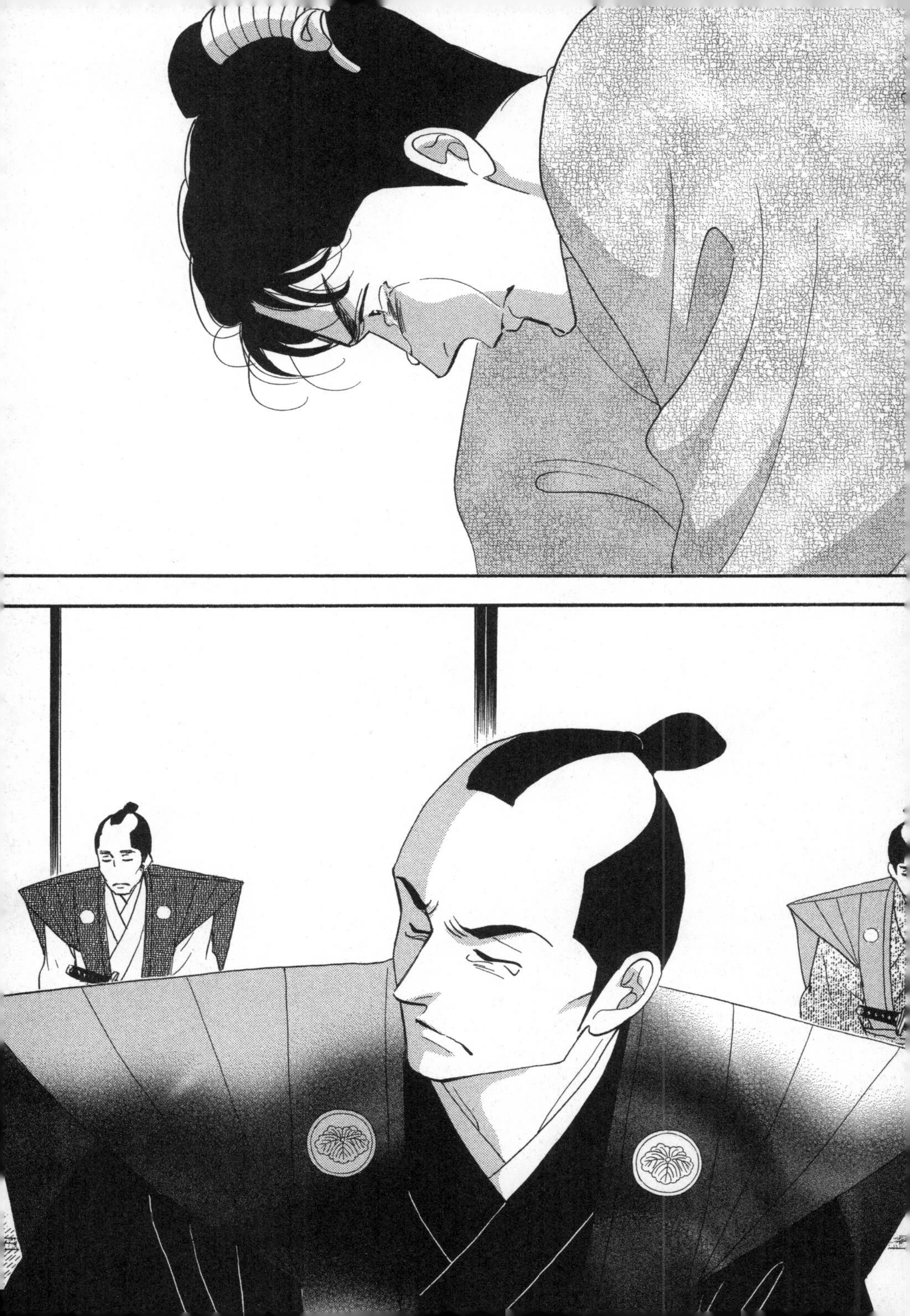

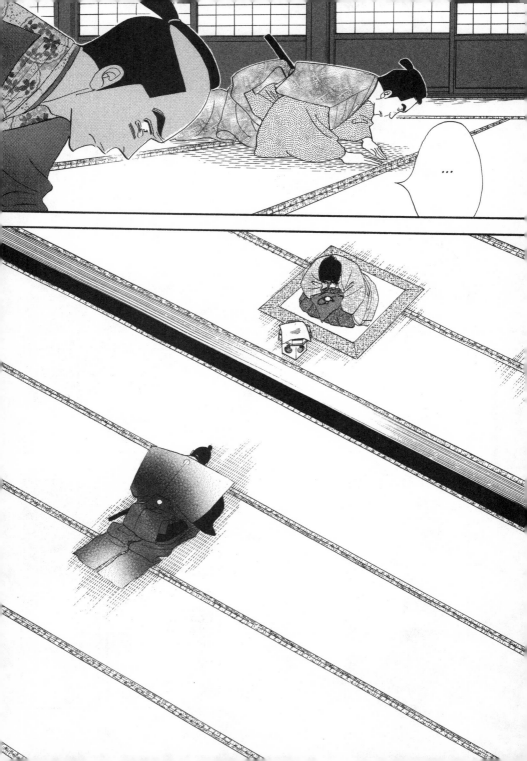

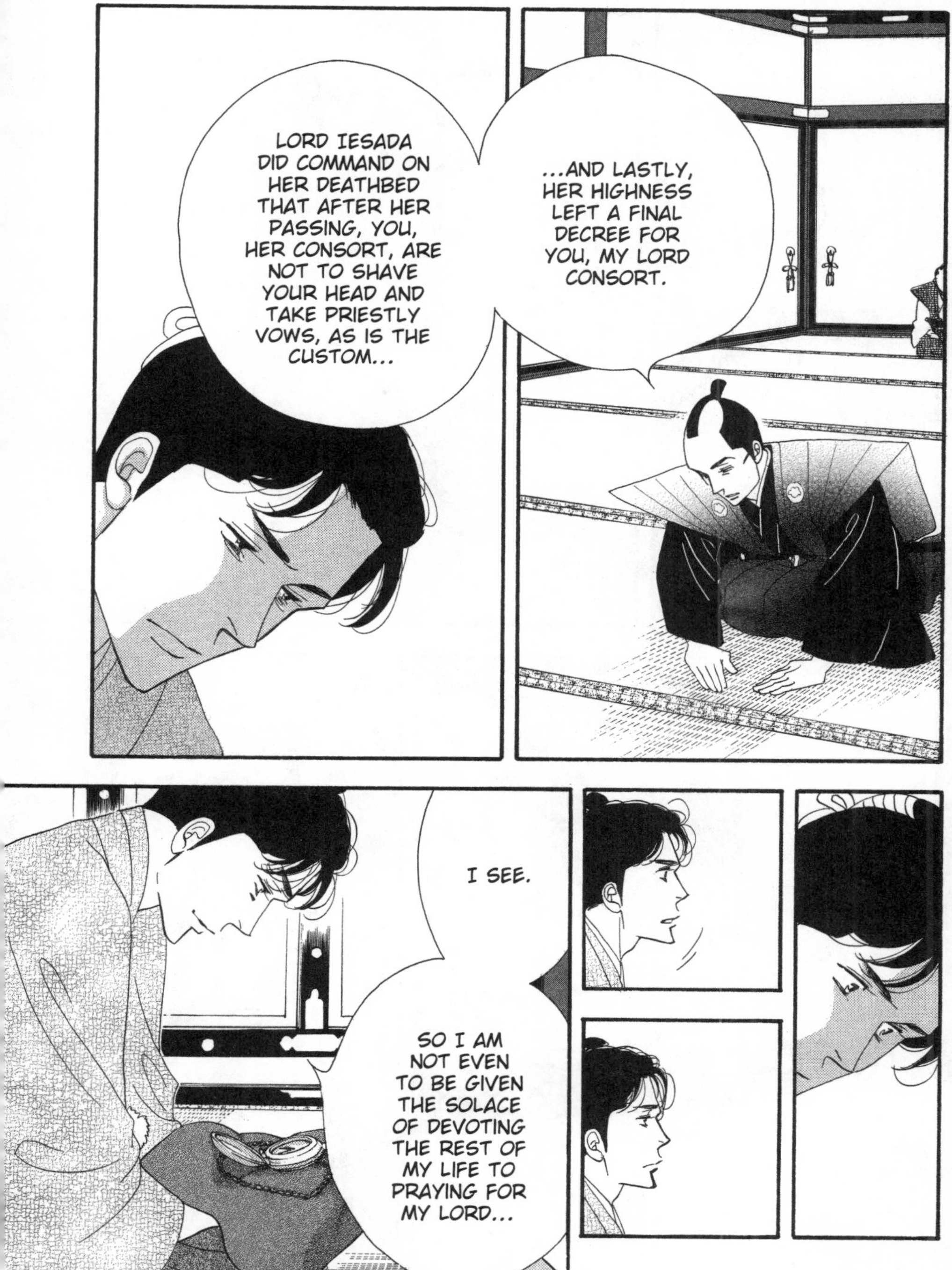
...AND LASTLY, HER HIGHNESS LEFT A FINAL DECREE FOR YOU, MY LORD CONSORT.
LORD IESADA DID COMMAND ON HER DEATHBED THAT AFTER HER PASSING, YOU, HER CONSORT, ARE NOT TO SHAVE YOUR HEAD AND TAKE PRIESTLY VOWS, AS IS THE CUSTOM...
I SEE.
SO I AM NOT EVEN TO BE GIVEN THE SOLACE OF DEVOTING THE REST OF MY LIFE TO PRAYING FOR MY LORD...

M'LORD!

WELL, THEN.

NOW PLEASE LEAVE ME ALONE WITH TAKIYAMA. EVERYONE ELSE MAY WITHDRAW.

AND THANK YOU.

SNAP

MM.

...

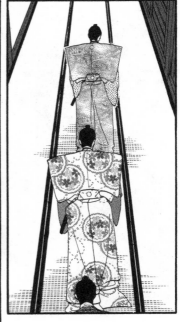

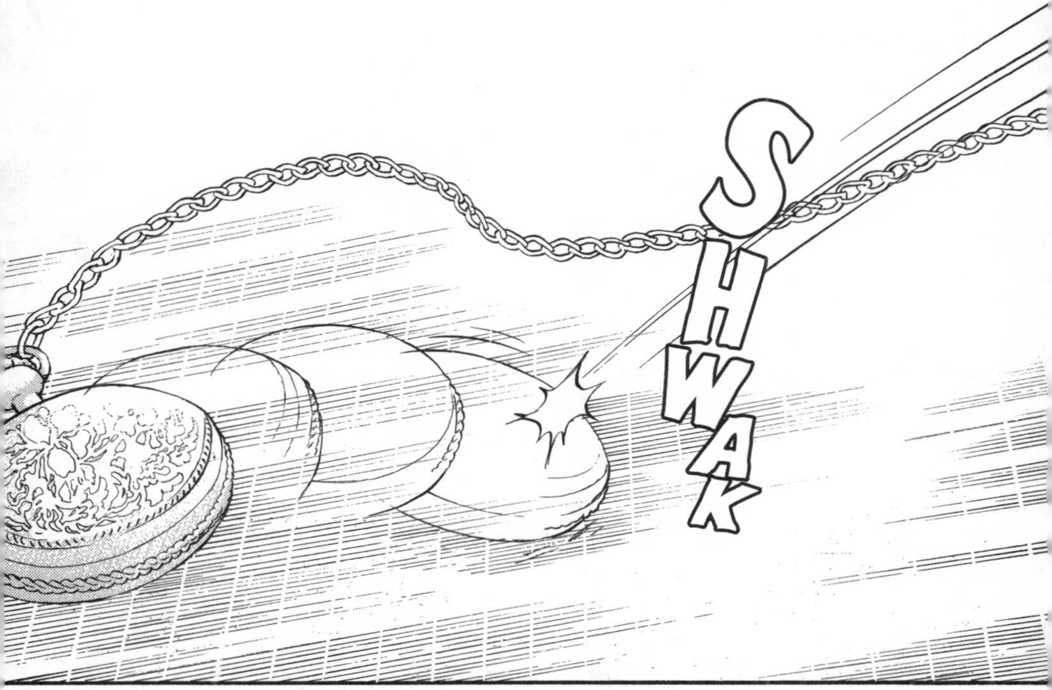
SHWAK
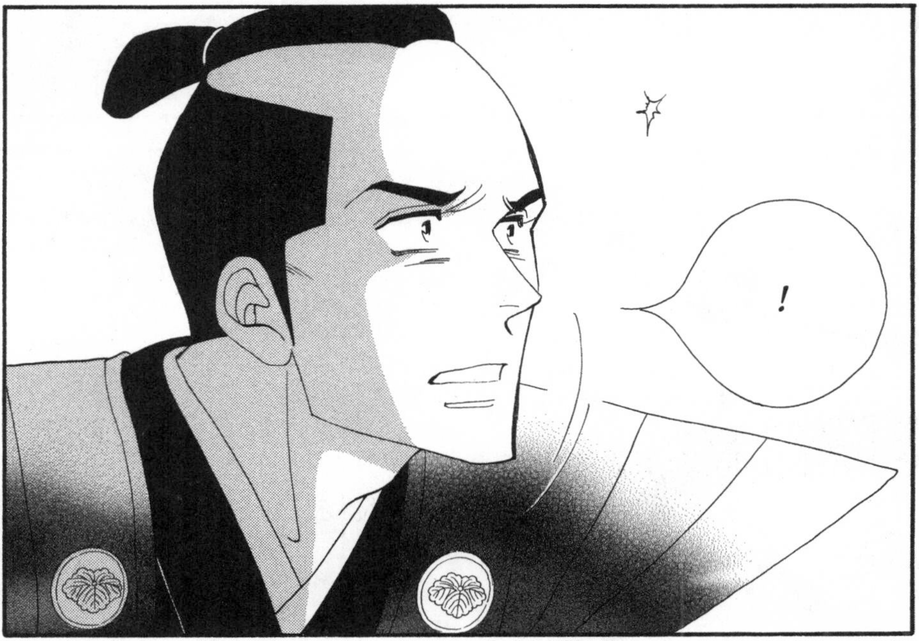
!

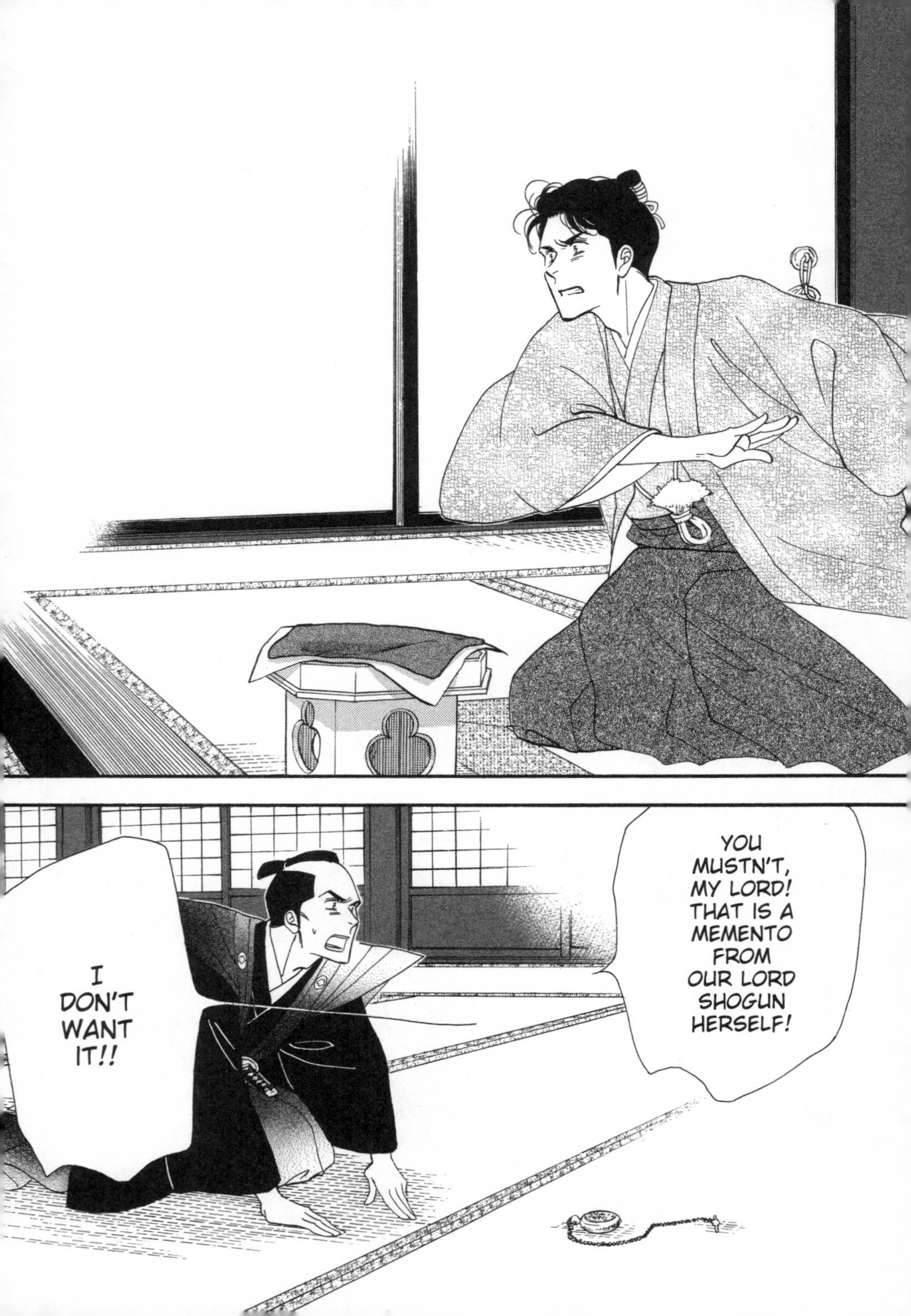
YOU MUSTN'T, MY LORD! THAT IS A MEMENTO FROM OUR LORD SHOGUN HERSELF!
I DON'T WANT IT!!

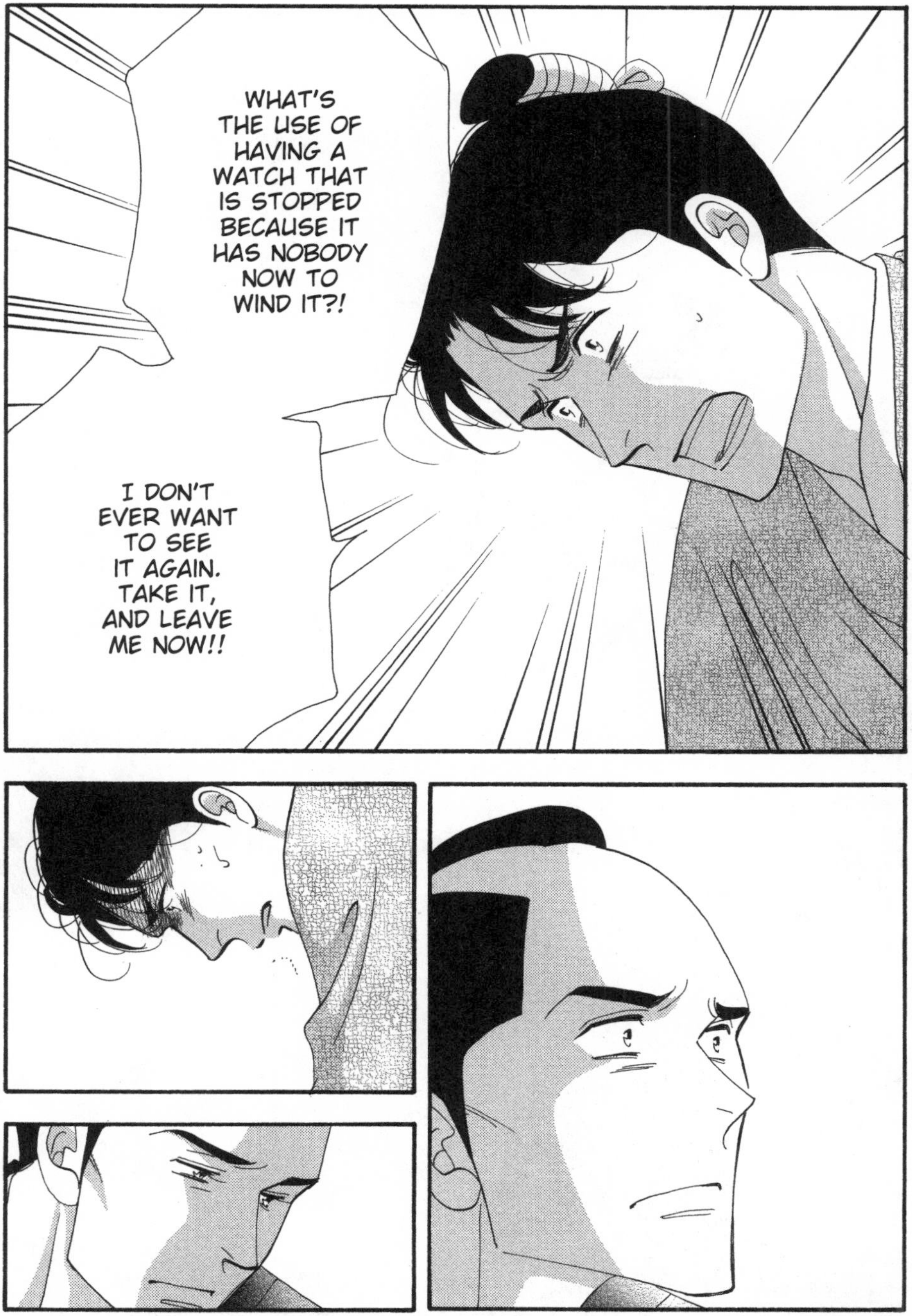
WHAT'S THE USE OF HAVING A WATCH THAT IS STOPPED BECAUSE IT HAS NOBODY NOW TO WIND IT?!
I DON'T EVER WANT TO SEE IT AGAIN. TAKE IT, AND LEAVE ME NOW!!

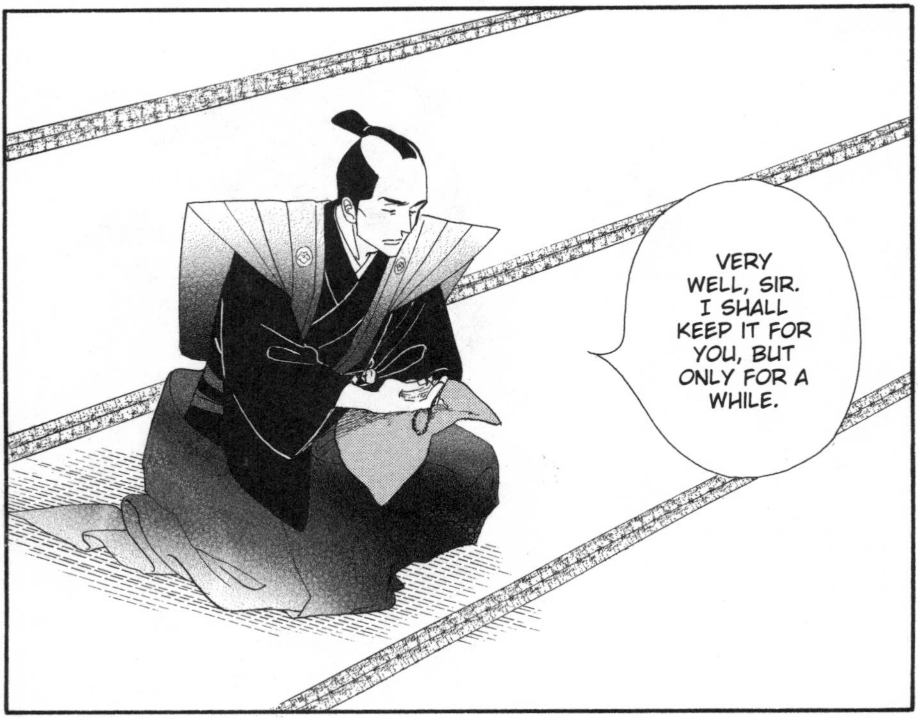
VERY WELL, SIR. I SHALL KEEP IT FOR YOU, BUT ONLY FOR A WHILE.

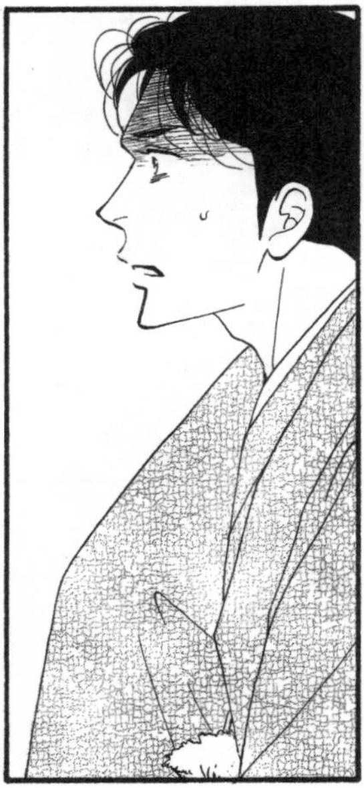

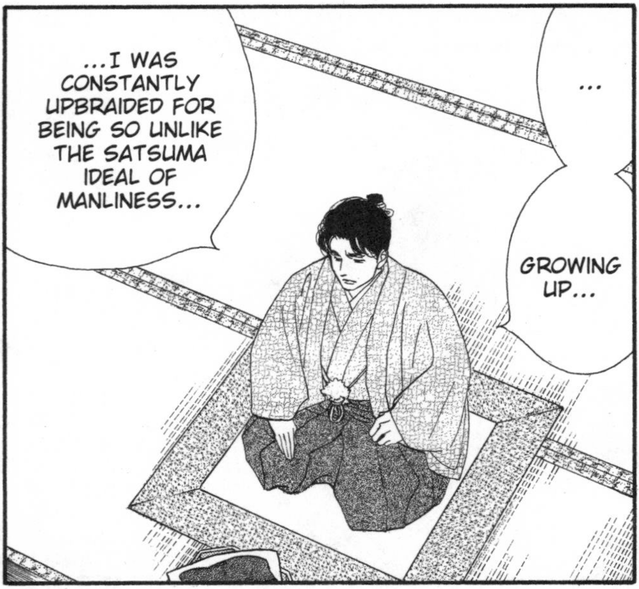
...
GROWING UP...
...I WAS CONSTANTLY UPBRAIDED FOR BEING SO UNLIKE THE SATSUMA IDEAL OF MANLINESS...

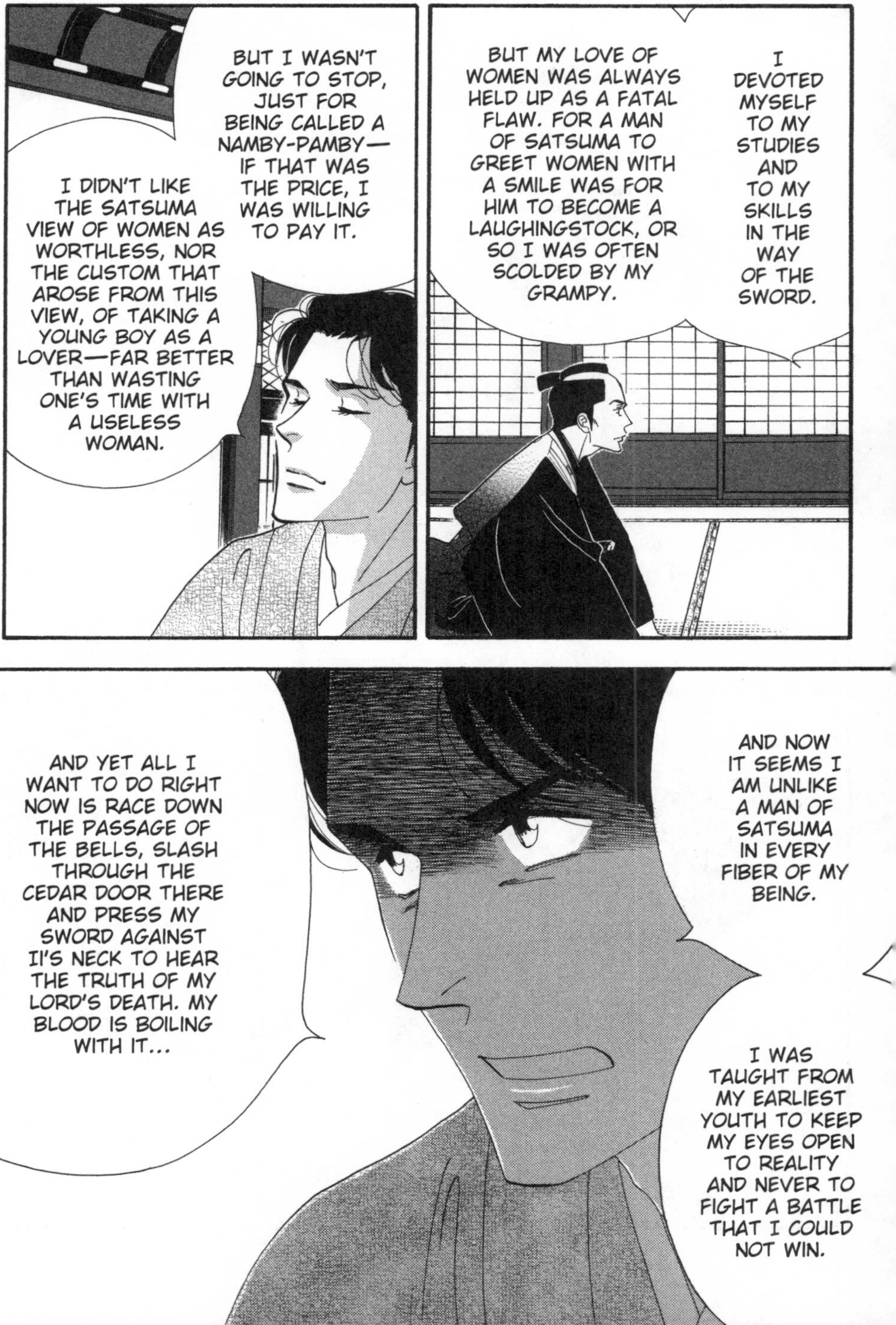
I DEVOTED MYSELF TO MY STUDIES AND TO MY SKILLS IN THE WAY OF THE SWORD.
BUT MY LOVE OF WOMEN WAS ALWAYS HELD UP AS A FATAL FLAW. FOR A MAN OF SATSUMA TO GREET WOMEN WITH A SMILE WAS FOR HIM TO BECOME A LAUGHINGSTOCK, OR SO I WAS OFTEN SCOLDED BY MY GRAMPY.
BUT I WASN'T GOING TO STOP, JUST FOR BEING CALLED A NAMBY-PAMBY—IF THAT WAS THE PRICE, I WAS WILLING TO PAY IT.
I DIDN'T LIKE THE SATSUMA VIEW OF WOMEN AS WORTHLESS, NOR THE CUSTOM THAT AROSE FROM THIS VIEW, OF TAKING A YOUNG BOY AS A LOVER—FAR BETTER THAN WASTING ONE'S TIME WITH A USELESS WOMAN.
AND NOW IT SEEMS I AM UNLIKE A MAN OF SATSUMA IN EVERY FIBER OF MY BEING.
AND YET ALL I WANT TO DO RIGHT NOW IS RACE DOWN THE PASSAGE OF THE BELLS, SLASH THROUGH THE CEDAR DOOR THERE AND PRESS MY SWORD AGAINST II'S NECK TO HEAR THE TRUTH OF MY LORD'S DEATH. MY BLOOD IS BOILING WITH IT...
I WAS TAUGHT FROM MY EARLIEST YOUTH TO KEEP MY EYES OPEN TO REALITY AND NEVER TO FIGHT A BATTLE THAT I COULD NOT WIN.

MY LORD CONSORT!!
I WON'T DO IT, OF COURSE.
I WON'T DO IT.
IT WOULD BE FUTILE.
BUT, MY LORD! YOUR DESIRE IS ENTIRELY JUSTIFIED!
WAITING TO INFORM THE INNER CHAMBERS OF THE LORD SHOGUN'S DEATH MAY INDEED BE A TIME-HONORED CUSTOM, BUT UNLESS HER CONDITION TOOK A DRASTIC AND SUDDEN TURN, IT IS ABSOLUTELY REASONABLE AND EXPECTED THAT YOU, HER LORD CONSORT, SHOULD HAVE BEEN ALLOWED TO VISIT HER IN THE SHOGUN'S QUARTERS.
I, TOO, AM STILL UNABLE TO COMPREHEND THIS TURN OF EVENTS!

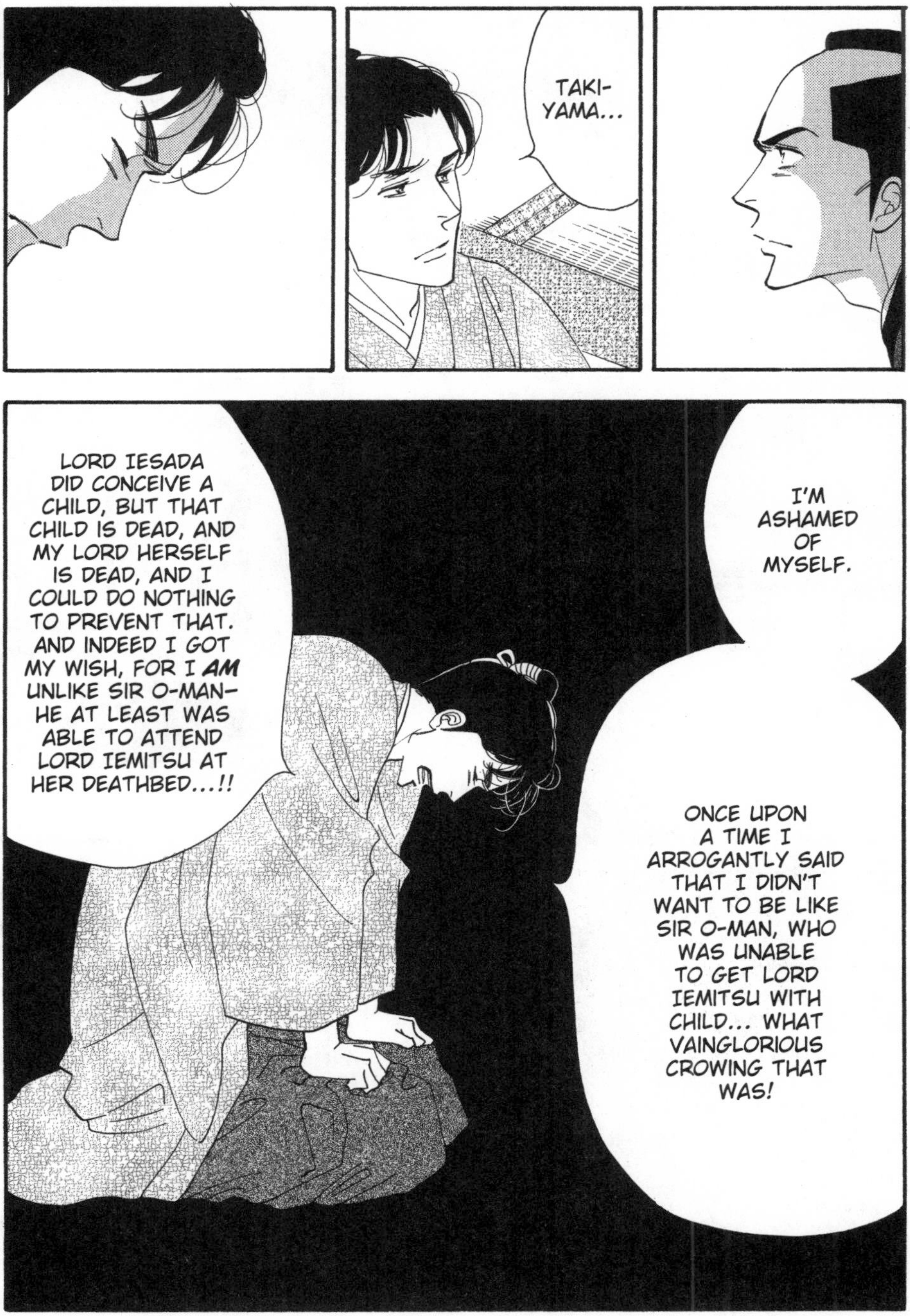
TAKI-YAMA...
I'M ASHAMED OF MYSELF.
ONCE UPON A TIME I ARROGANTLY SAID THAT I DIDN'T WANT TO BE LIKE SIR O-MAN, WHO WAS UNABLE TO GET LORD IEMITSU WITH CHILD... WHAT VAINGLORIOUS CROWING THAT WAS!
LORD IESADA DID CONCEIVE A CHILD, BUT THAT CHILD IS DEAD, AND MY LORD HERSELF IS DEAD, AND I COULD DO NOTHING TO PREVENT THAT. AND INDEED I GOT MY WISH, FOR I *AM* UNLIKE SIR O-MAN-HE AT LEAST WAS ABLE TO ATTEND LORD IEMITSU AT HER DEATHBED...!!

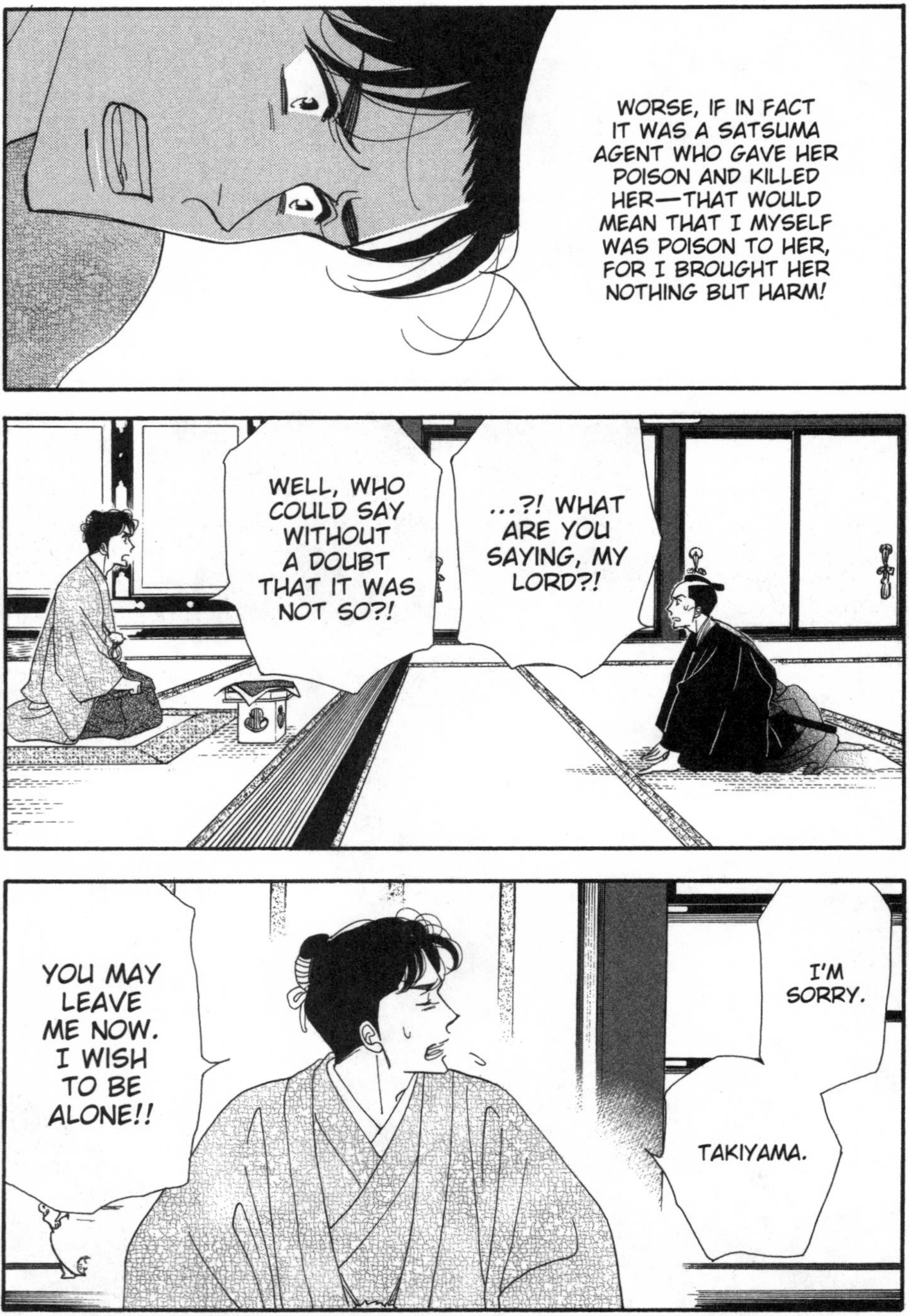
WORSE, IF IN FACT IT WAS A SATSUMA AGENT WHO GAVE HER POISON AND KILLED HER—THAT WOULD MEAN THAT I MYSELF WAS POISON TO HER, FOR I BROUGHT HER NOTHING BUT HARM!
...?! WHAT ARE YOU SAYING, MY LORD?!
WELL, WHO COULD SAY WITHOUT A DOUBT THAT IT WAS NOT SO?!
I'M SORRY.
TAKIYAMA.
YOU MAY LEAVE ME NOW. I WISH TO BE ALONE!!

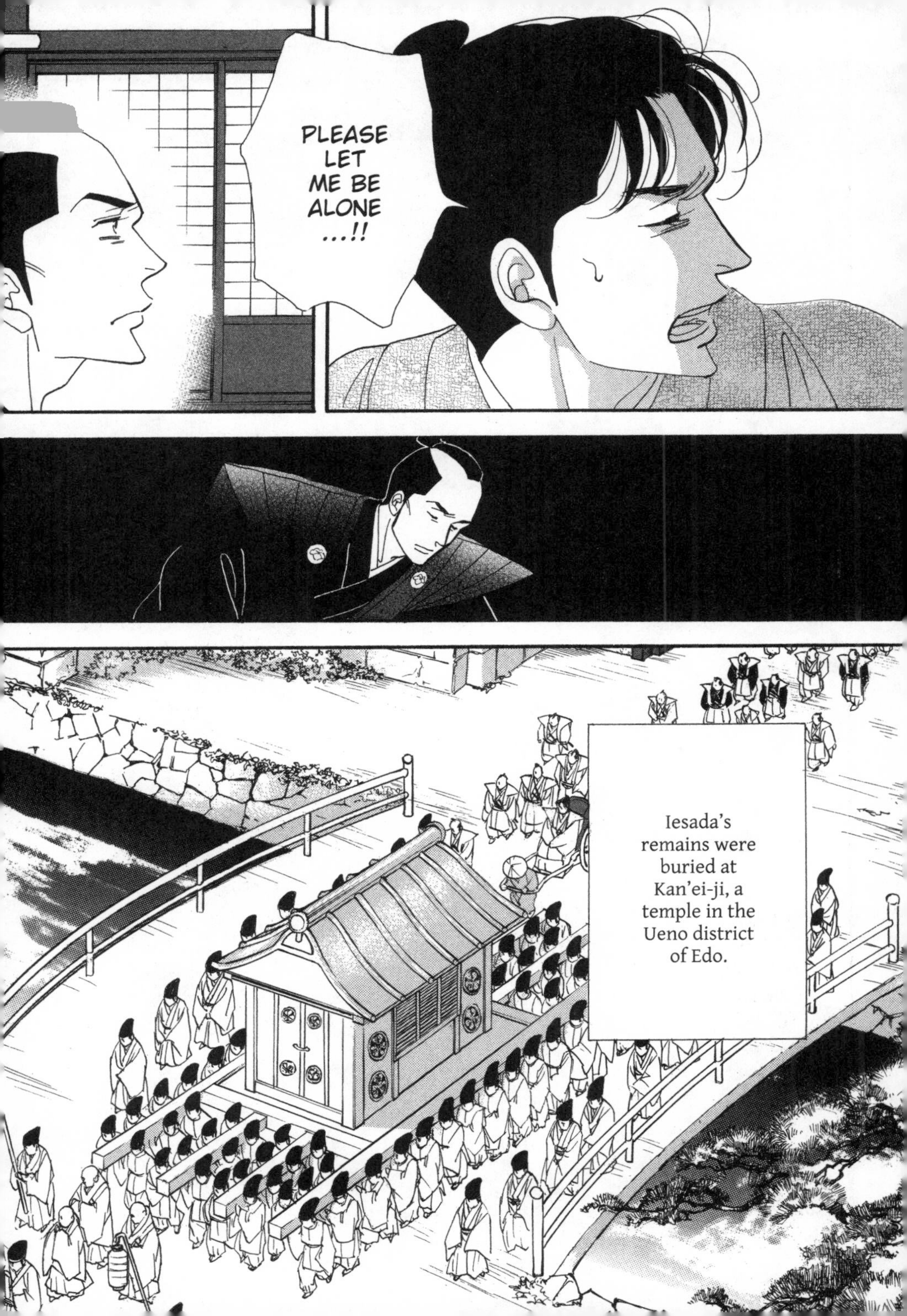
PLEASE LET ME BE ALONE ...!!
Iesada's remains were buried at Kan'ei-ji, a temple in the Ueno district of Edo.

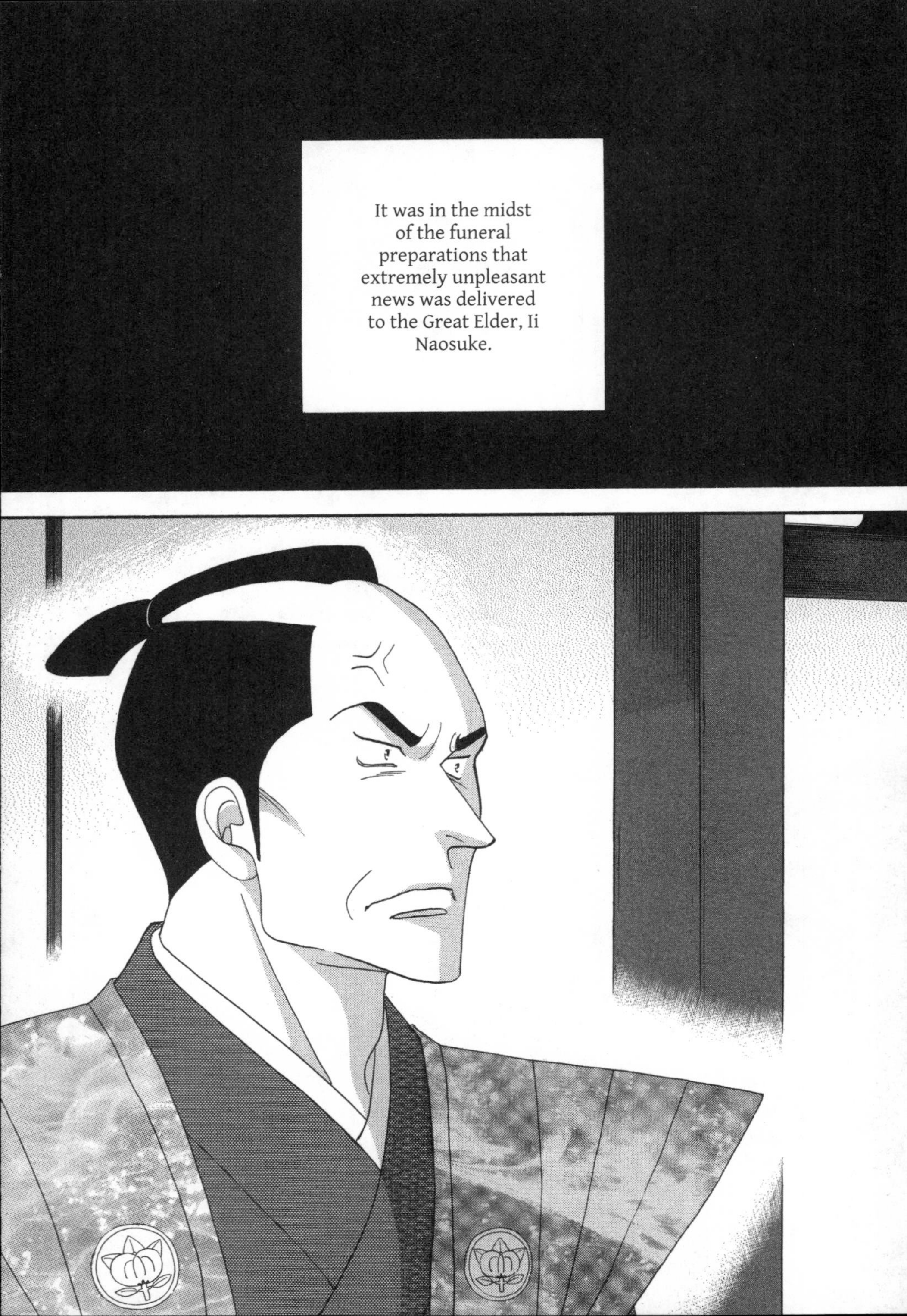
It was in the midst of the funeral preparations that extremely unpleasant news was delivered to the Great Elder, Ii Naosuke.

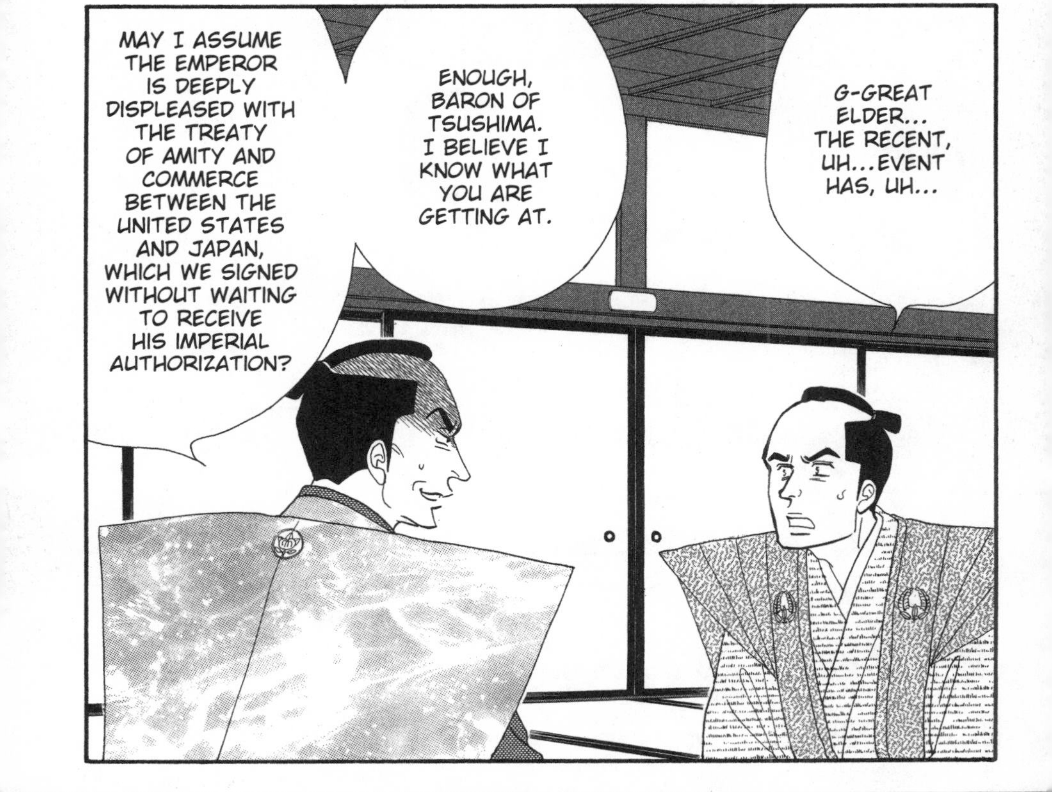
G-GREAT ELDER... THE RECENT, UH...EVENT HAS, UH...
ENOUGH, BARON OF TSUSHIMA. I BELIEVE I KNOW WHAT YOU ARE GETTING AT.
MAY I ASSUME THE EMPEROR IS DEEPLY DISPLEASED WITH THE TREATY OF AMITY AND COMMERCE BETWEEN THE UNITED STATES AND JAPAN, WHICH WE SIGNED WITHOUT WAITING TO RECEIVE HIS IMPERIAL AUTHORIZATION?

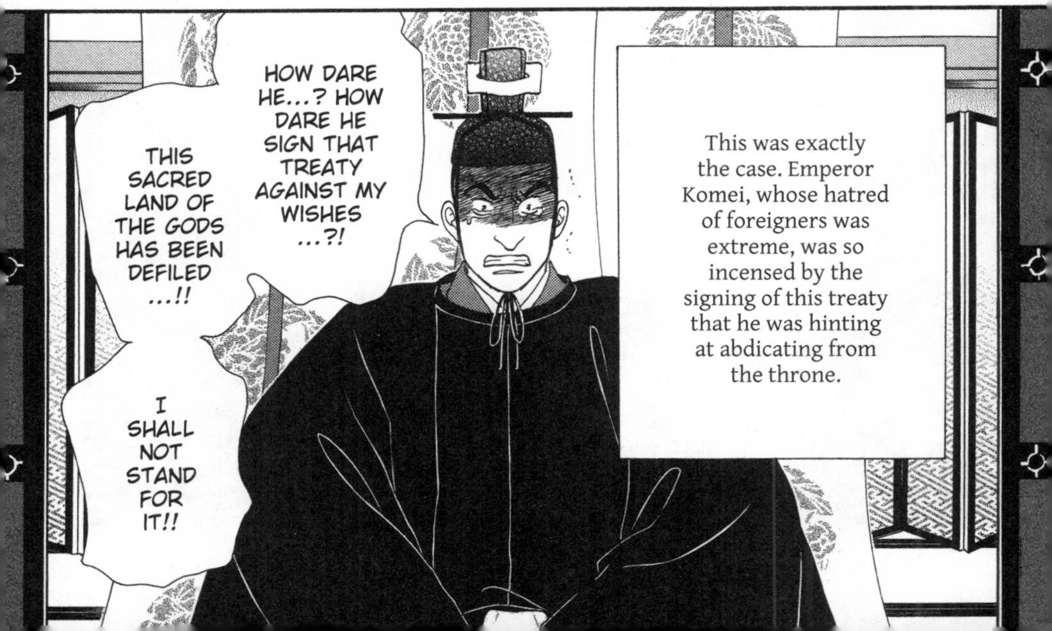
This was exactly the case. Emperor Komei, whose hatred of foreigners was extreme, was so incensed by the signing of this treaty that he was hinting at abdicating from the throne.
HOW DARE HE...? HOW DARE HE SIGN THAT TREATY AGAINST MY WISHES ...?!
THIS SACRED LAND OF THE GODS HAS BEEN DEFILED ...!!
I SHALL NOT STAND FOR IT!!

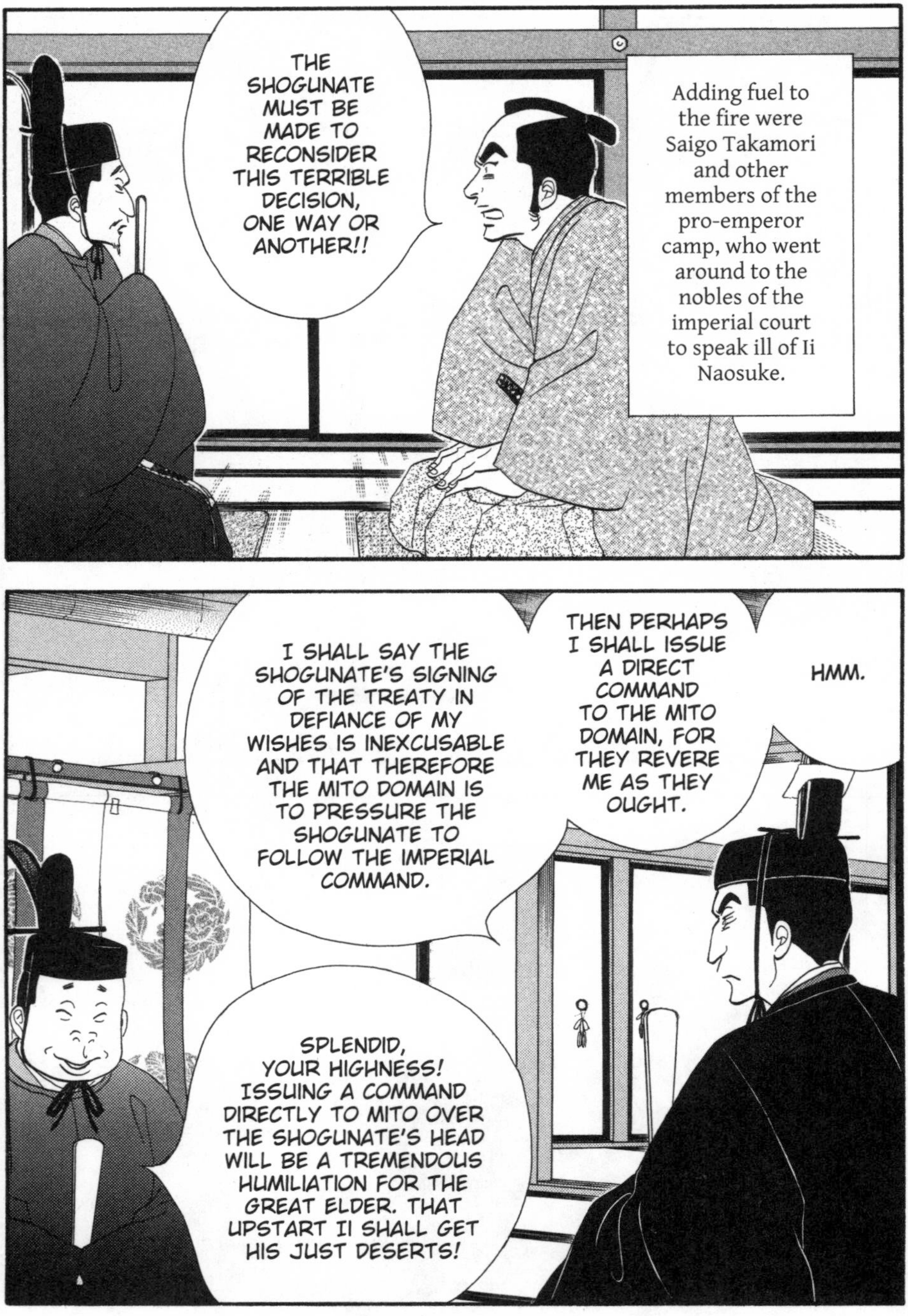
Adding fuel to the fire were Saigo Takamori and other members of the pro-emperor camp, who went around to the nobles of the imperial court to speak ill of Ii Naosuke.
THE SHOGUNATE MUST BE MADE TO RECONSIDER THIS TERRIBLE DECISION, ONE WAY OR ANOTHER!!
HMM.
THEN PERHAPS I SHALL ISSUE A DIRECT COMMAND TO THE MITO DOMAIN, FOR THEY REVERE ME AS THEY OUGHT.
I SHALL SAY THE SHOGUNATE'S SIGNING OF THE TREATY IN DEFIANCE OF MY WISHES IS INEXCUSABLE AND THAT THEREFORE THE MITO DOMAIN IS TO PRESSURE THE SHOGUNATE TO FOLLOW THE IMPERIAL COMMAND.
SPLENDID, YOUR HIGHNESS! ISSUING A COMMAND DIRECTLY TO MITO OVER THE SHOGUNATE'S HEAD WILL BE A TREMENDOUS HUMILIATION FOR THE GREAT ELDER. THAT UPSTART II SHALL GET HIS JUST DESERTS!

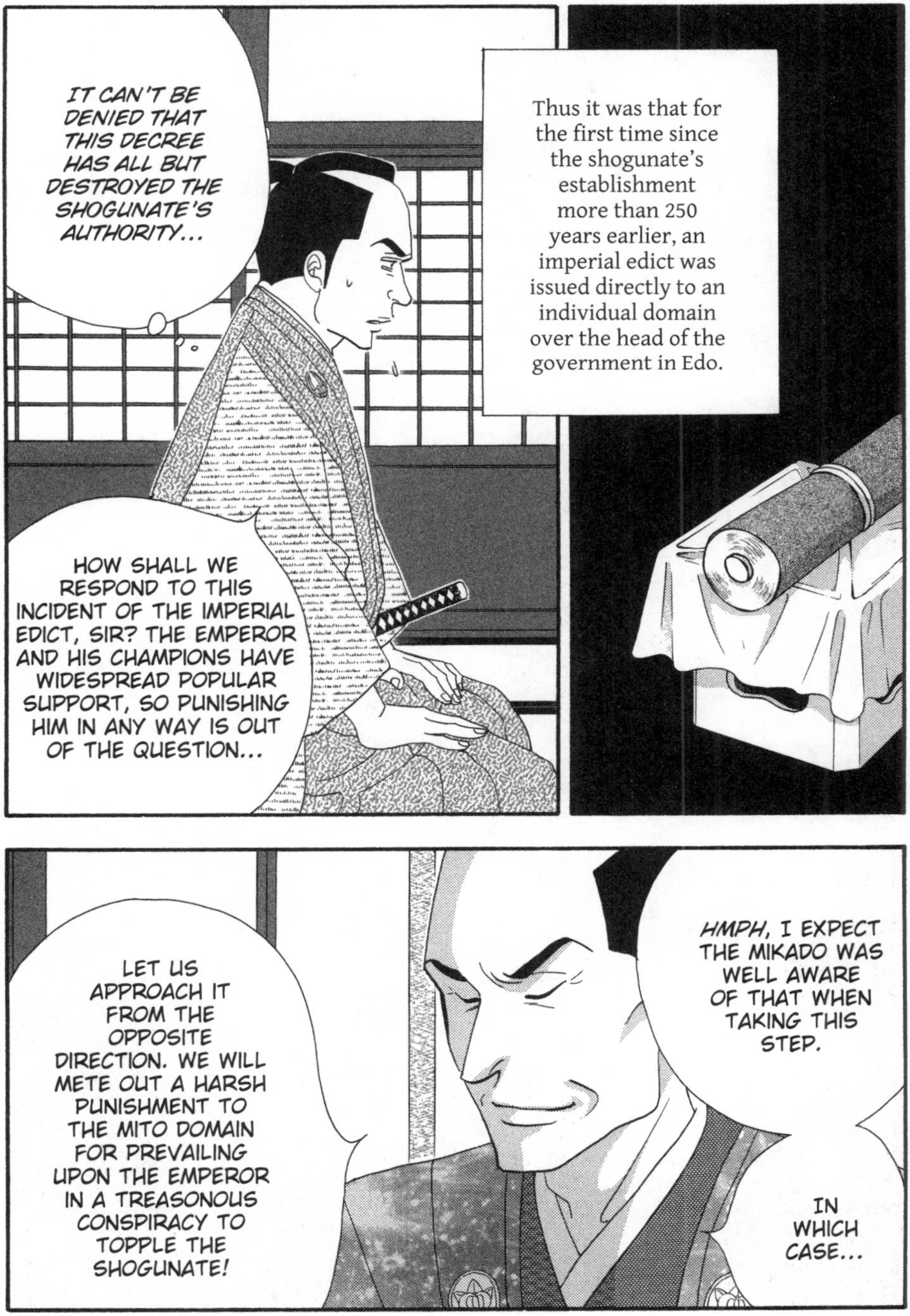
Thus it was that for the first time since the shogunate's establishment more than 250 years earlier, an imperial edict was issued directly to an individual domain over the head of the government in Edo.
IT CAN'T BE DENIED THAT THIS DECREE HAS ALL BUT DESTROYED THE SHOGUNATE'S AUTHORITY...
HOW SHALL WE RESPOND TO THIS INCIDENT OF THE IMPERIAL EDICT, SIR? THE EMPEROR AND HIS CHAMPIONS HAVE WIDESPREAD POPULAR SUPPORT, SO PUNISHING HIM IN ANY WAY IS OUT OF THE QUESTION...
HMPH, I EXPECT THE MIKADO WAS WELL AWARE OF THAT WHEN TAKING THIS STEP.
IN WHICH CASE...
LET US APPROACH IT FROM THE OPPOSITE DIRECTION. WE WILL METE OUT A HARSH PUNISHMENT TO THE MITO DOMAIN FOR PREVAILING UPON THE EMPEROR IN A TREASONOUS CONSPIRACY TO TOPPLE THE SHOGUNATE!

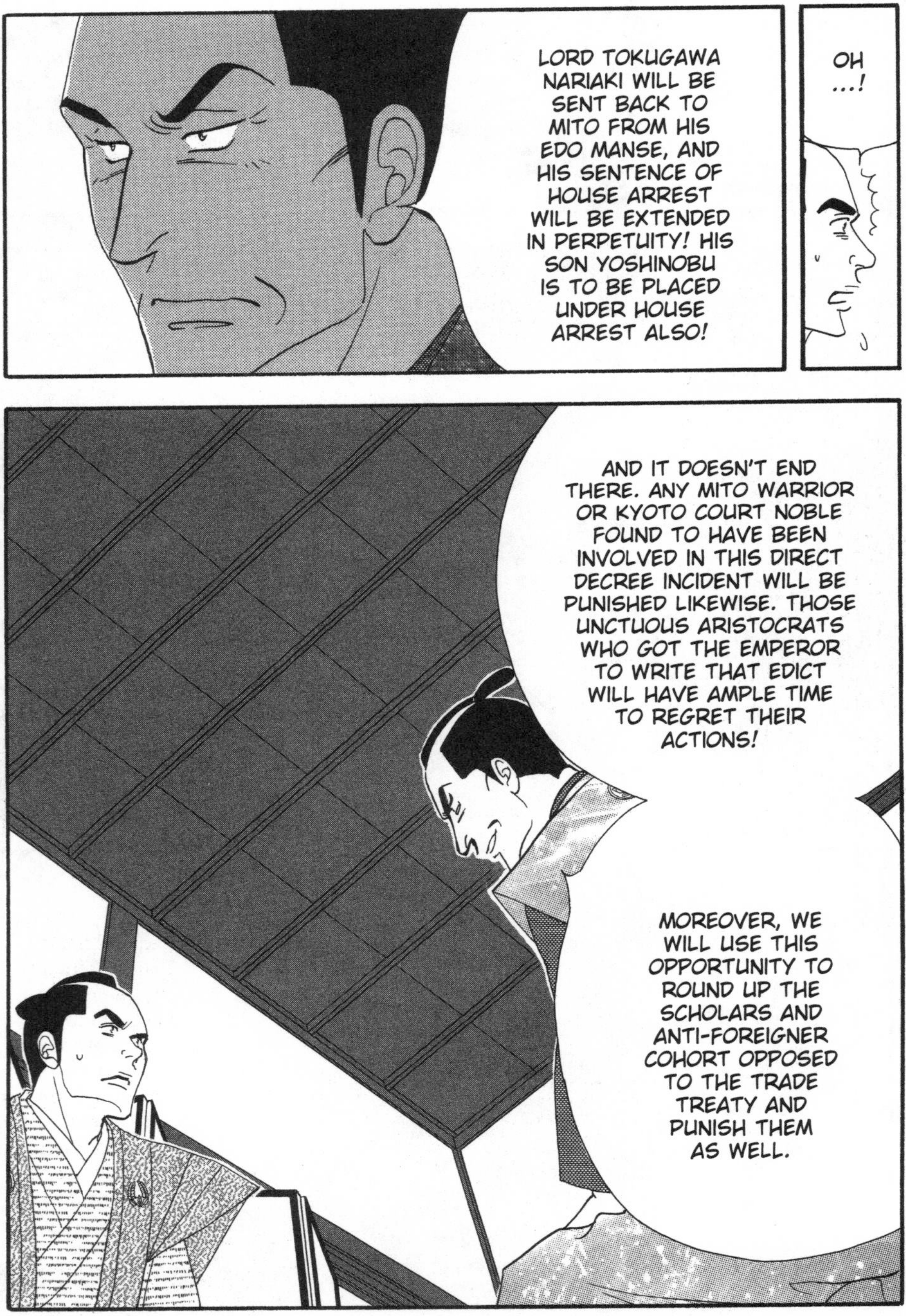
OH ...!
LORD TOKUGAWA NARIAKI WILL BE SENT BACK TO MITO FROM HIS EDO MANSE, AND HIS SENTENCE OF HOUSE ARREST WILL BE EXTENDED IN PERPETUITY! HIS SON YOSHINOBU IS TO BE PLACED UNDER HOUSE ARREST ALSO!
AND IT DOESN'T END THERE. ANY MITO WARRIOR OR KYOTO COURT NOBLE FOUND TO HAVE BEEN INVOLVED IN THIS DIRECT DECREE INCIDENT WILL BE PUNISHED LIKEWISE. THOSE UNCTUOUS ARISTOCRATS WHO GOT THE EMPEROR TO WRITE THAT EDICT WILL HAVE AMPLE TIME TO REGRET THEIR ACTIONS!
MOREOVER, WE WILL USE THIS OPPORTUNITY TO ROUND UP THE SCHOLARS AND ANTI-FOREIGNER COHORT OPPOSED TO THE TRADE TREATY AND PUNISH THEM AS WELL.

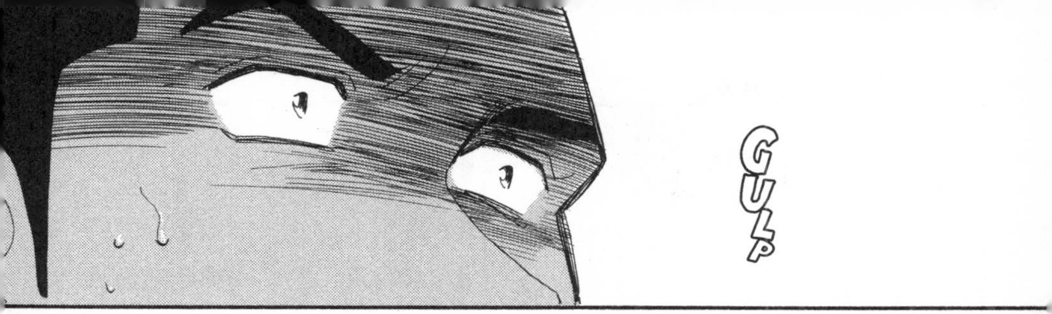
GULP

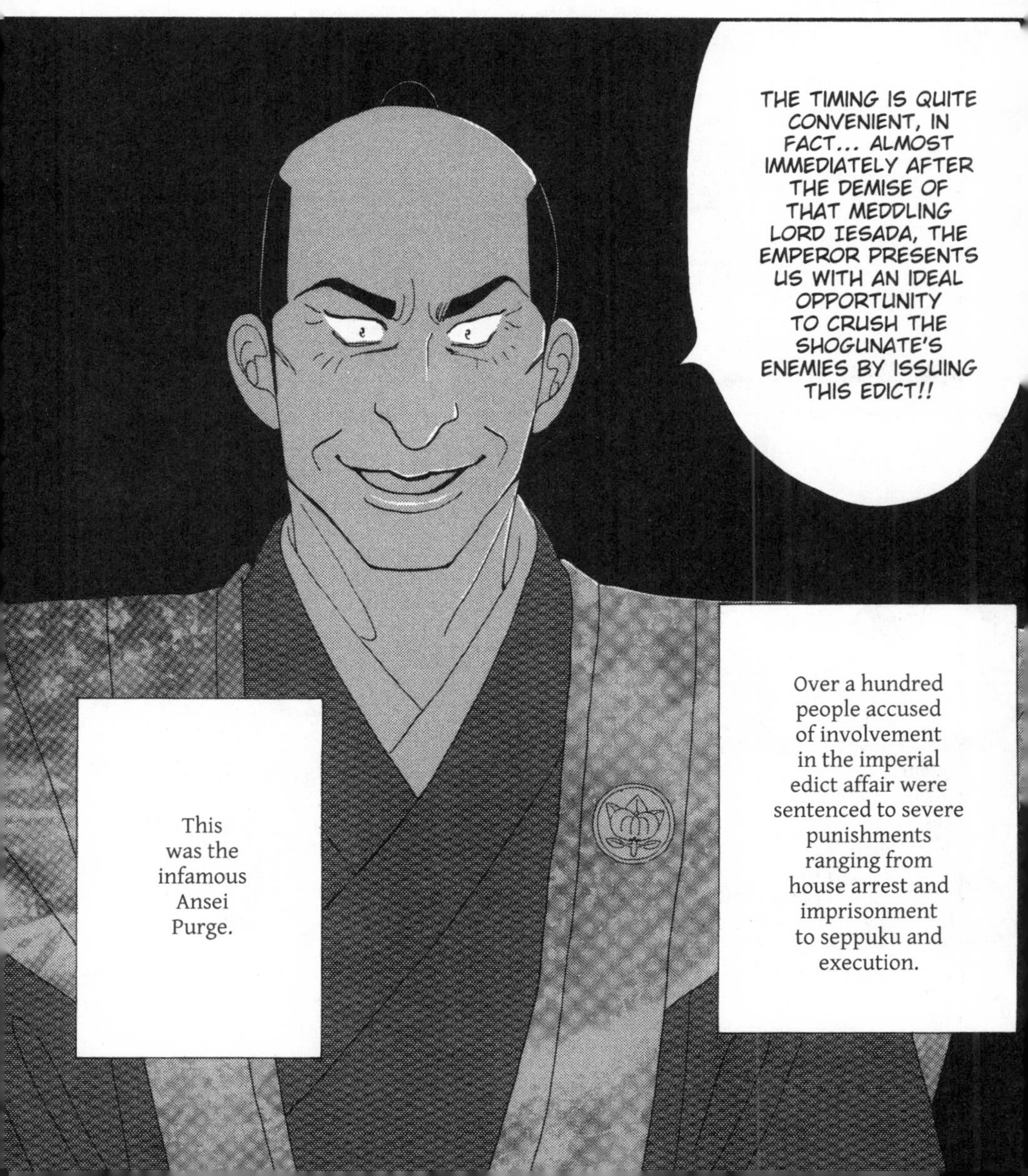
THE TIMING IS QUITE CONVENIENT, IN FACT... ALMOST IMMEDIATELY AFTER THE DEMISE OF THAT MEDDLING LORD IESADA, THE EMPEROR PRESENTS US WITH AN IDEAL OPPORTUNITY TO CRUSH THE SHOGUNATE'S ENEMIES BY ISSUING THIS EDICT!!
Over a hundred people accused of involvement in the imperial edict affair were sentenced to severe punishments ranging from house arrest and imprisonment to seppuku and execution.
This was the infamous Ansei Purge.

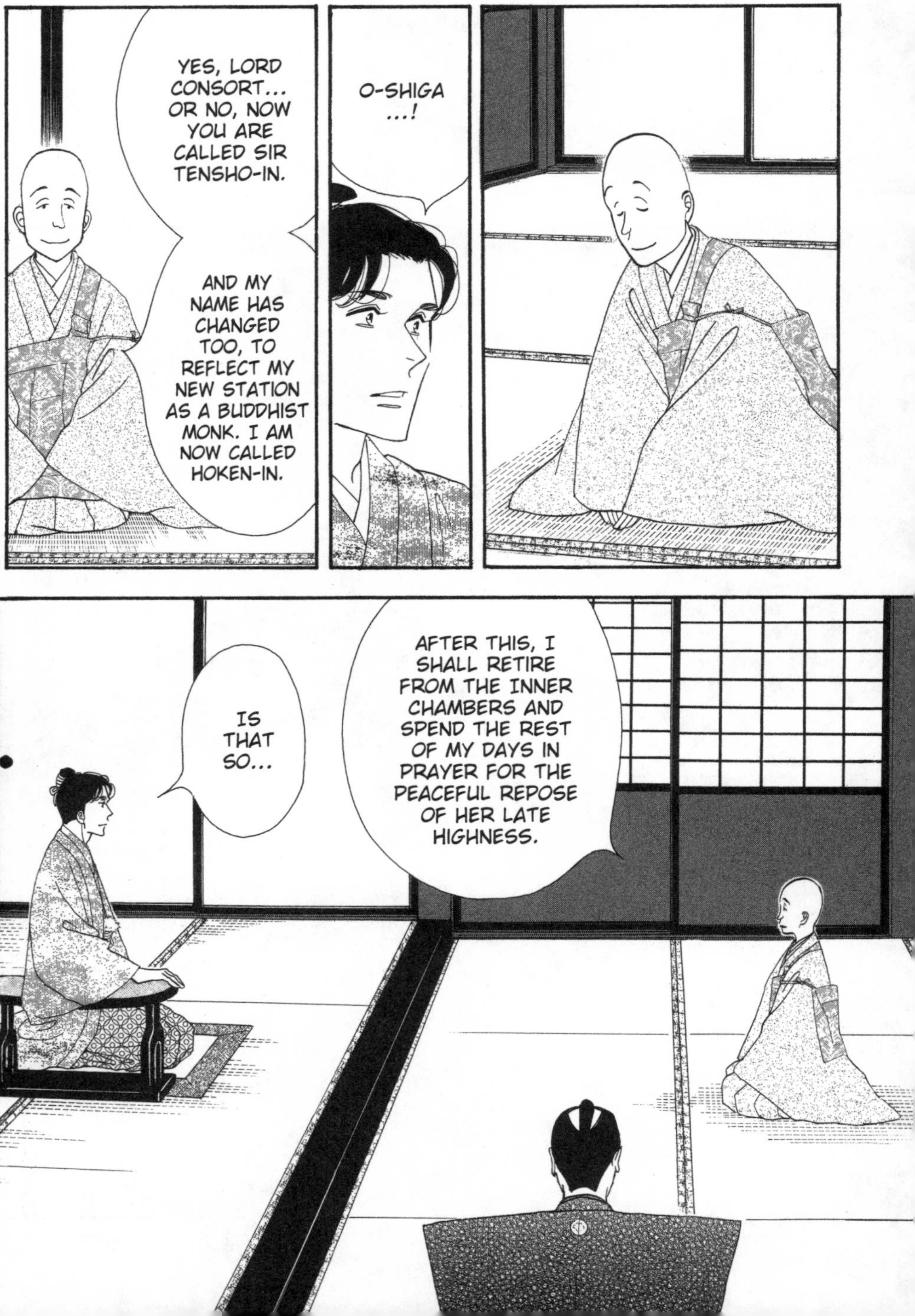
O-SHIGA ...!
YES, LORD CONSORT... OR NO, NOW YOU ARE CALLED SIR TENSHO-IN.
AND MY NAME HAS CHANGED TOO, TO REFLECT MY NEW STATION AS A BUDDHIST MONK. I AM NOW CALLED HOKEN-IN.
AFTER THIS, I SHALL RETIRE FROM THE INNER CHAMBERS AND SPEND THE REST OF MY DAYS IN PRAYER FOR THE PEACEFUL REPOSE OF HER LATE HIGHNESS.
IS THAT SO...

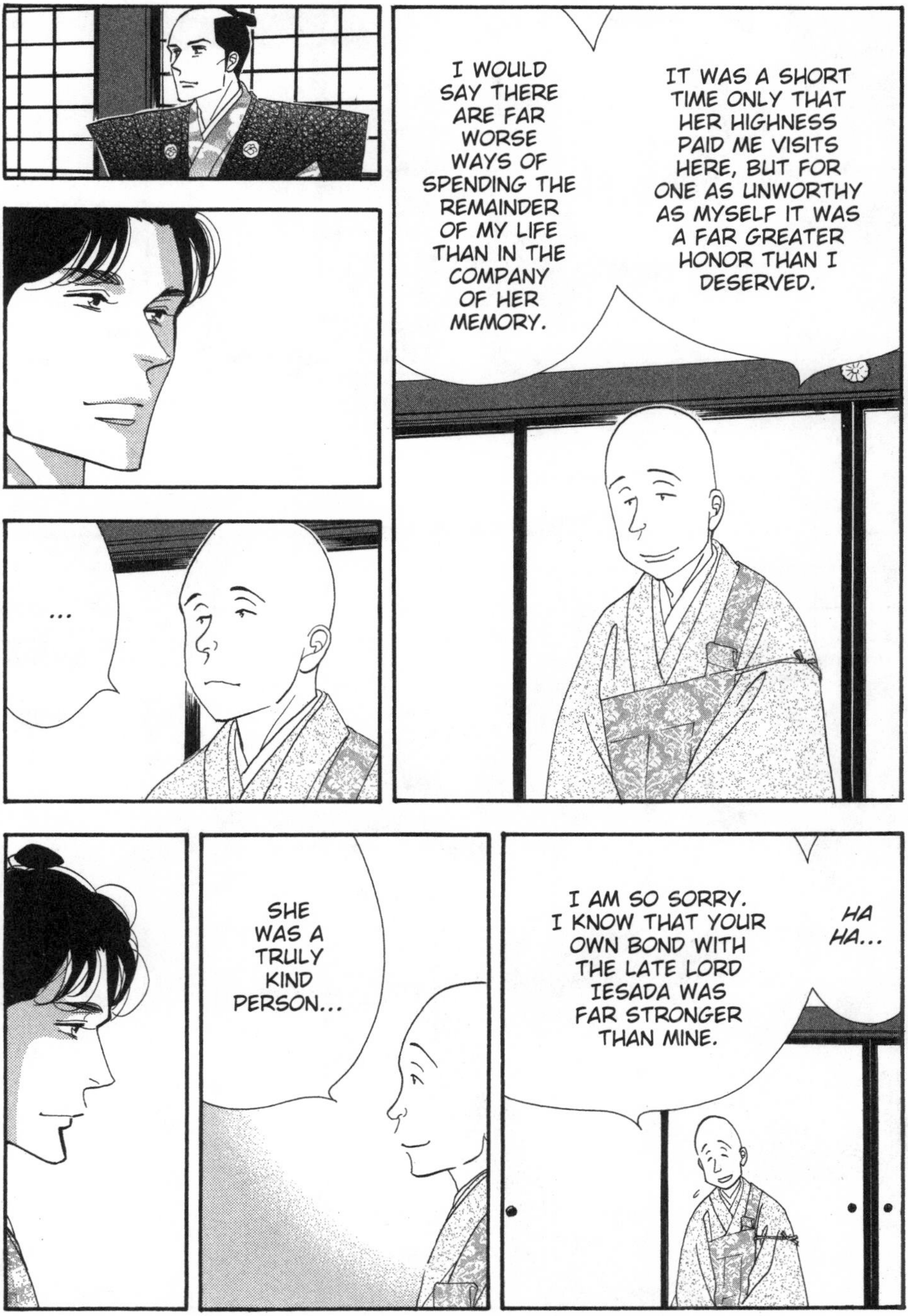
IT WAS A SHORT TIME ONLY THAT HER HIGHNESS PAID ME VISITS HERE, BUT FOR ONE AS UNWORTHY AS MYSELF IT WAS A FAR GREATER HONOR THAN I DESERVED.
I WOULD SAY THERE ARE FAR WORSE WAYS OF SPENDING THE REMAINDER OF MY LIFE THAN IN THE COMPANY OF HER MEMORY.
...
HA HA...
I AM SO SORRY. I KNOW THAT YOUR OWN BOND WITH THE LATE LORD IESADA WAS FAR STRONGER THAN MINE.
SHE WAS A TRULY KIND PERSON...

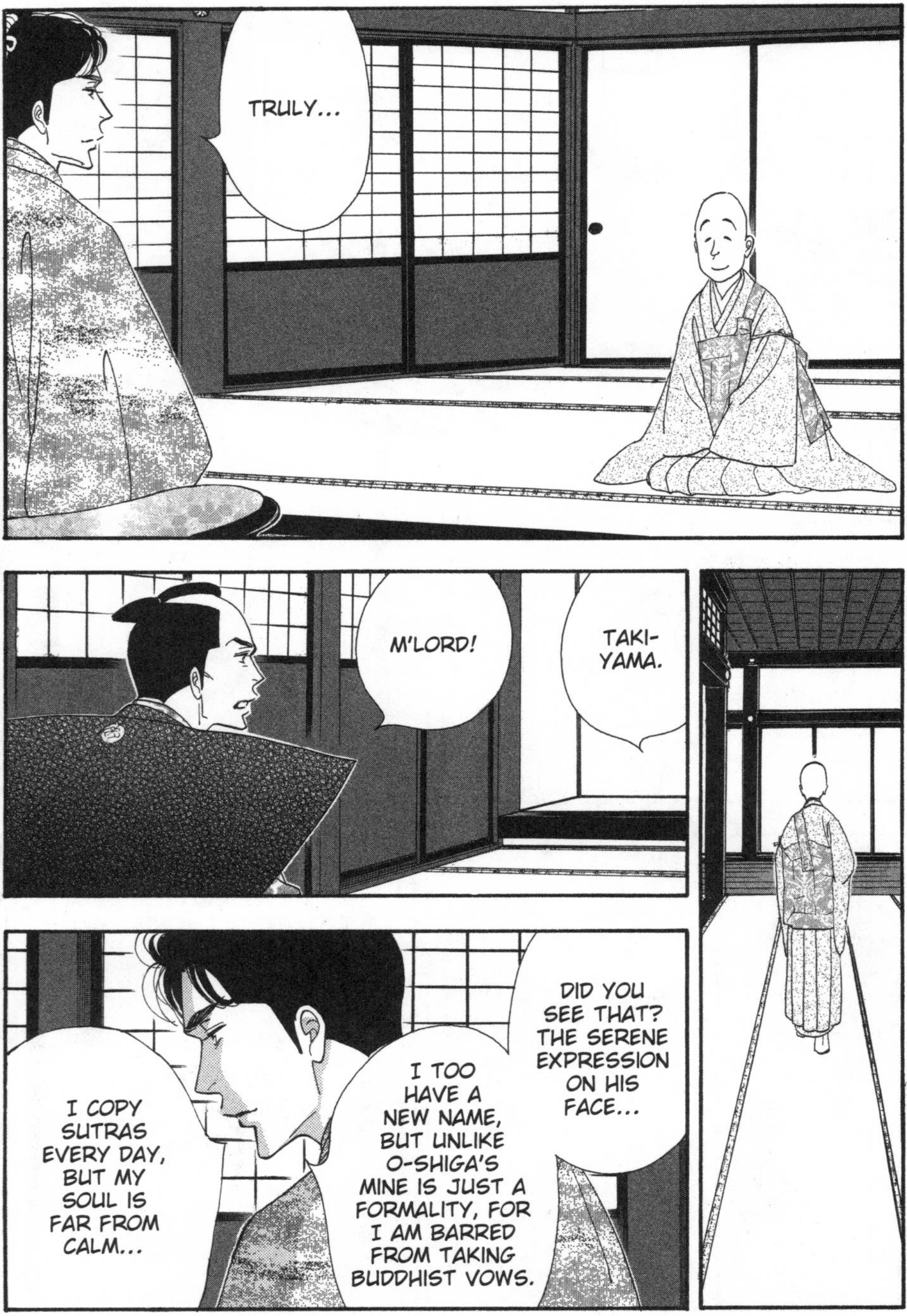
TRULY...
TAKI-YAMA.
M'LORD!
DID YOU SEE THAT? THE SERENE EXPRESSION ON HIS FACE...
I TOO HAVE A NEW NAME, BUT UNLIKE O-SHIGA'S MINE IS JUST A FORMALITY, FOR I AM BARRED FROM TAKING BUDDHIST VOWS.
I COPY SUTRAS EVERY DAY, BUT MY SOUL IS FAR FROM CALM...

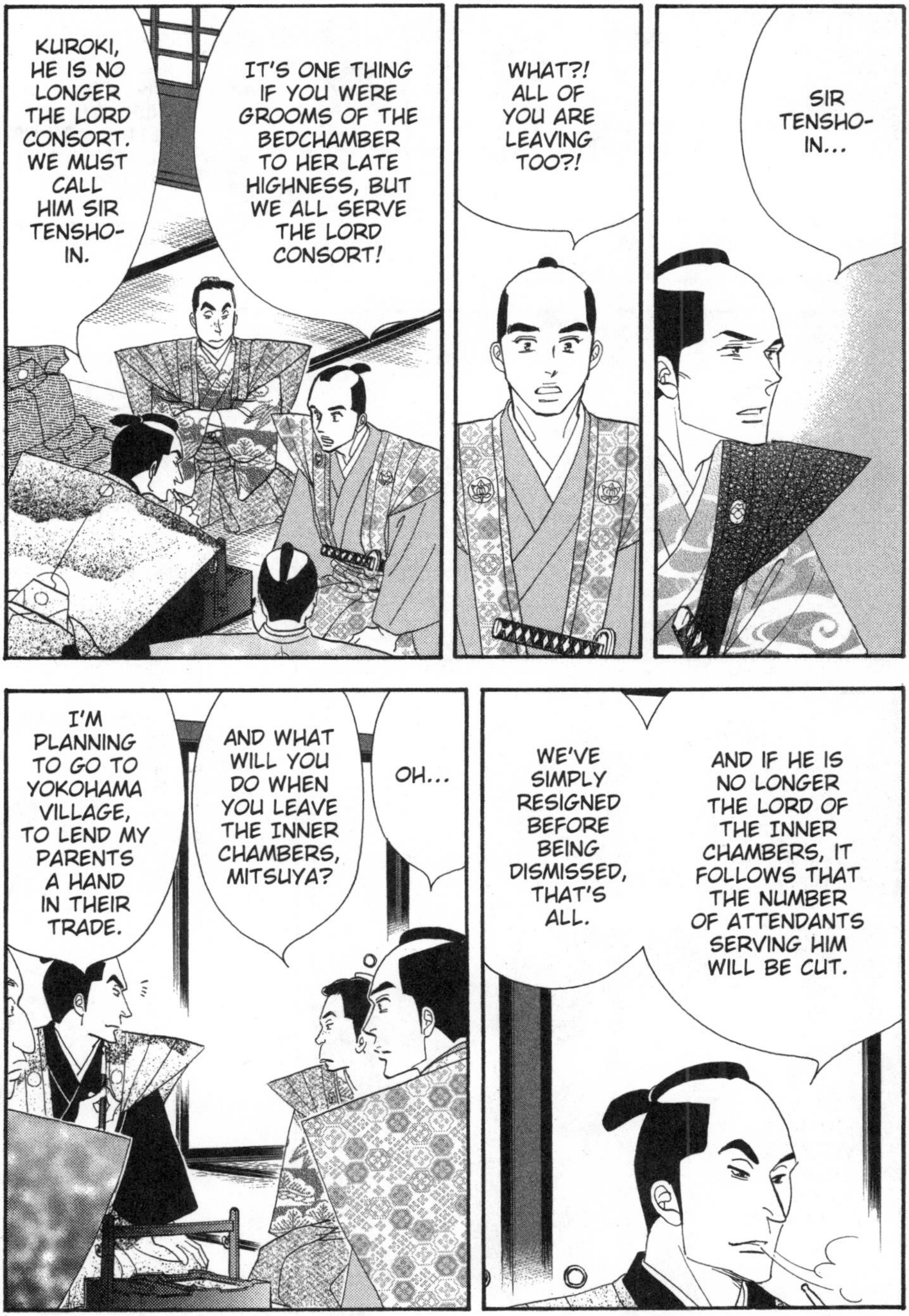
SIR TENSHO-IN...
WHAT?! ALL OF YOU ARE LEAVING TOO?!
IT'S ONE THING IF YOU WERE GROOMS OF THE BEDCHAMBER TO HER LATE HIGHNESS, BUT WE ALL SERVE THE LORD CONSORT!
KUROKI, HE IS NO LONGER THE LORD CONSORT. WE MUST CALL HIM SIR TENSHO-IN.
AND IF HE IS NO LONGER THE LORD OF THE INNER CHAMBERS, IT FOLLOWS THAT THE NUMBER OF ATTENDANTS SERVING HIM WILL BE CUT.
WE'VE SIMPLY RESIGNED BEFORE BEING DISMISSED, THAT'S ALL.
OH...
AND WHAT WILL YOU DO WHEN YOU LEAVE THE INNER CHAMBERS, MITSUYA?
I'M PLANNING TO GO TO YOKOHAMA VILLAGE, TO LEND MY PARENTS A HAND IN THEIR TRADE.

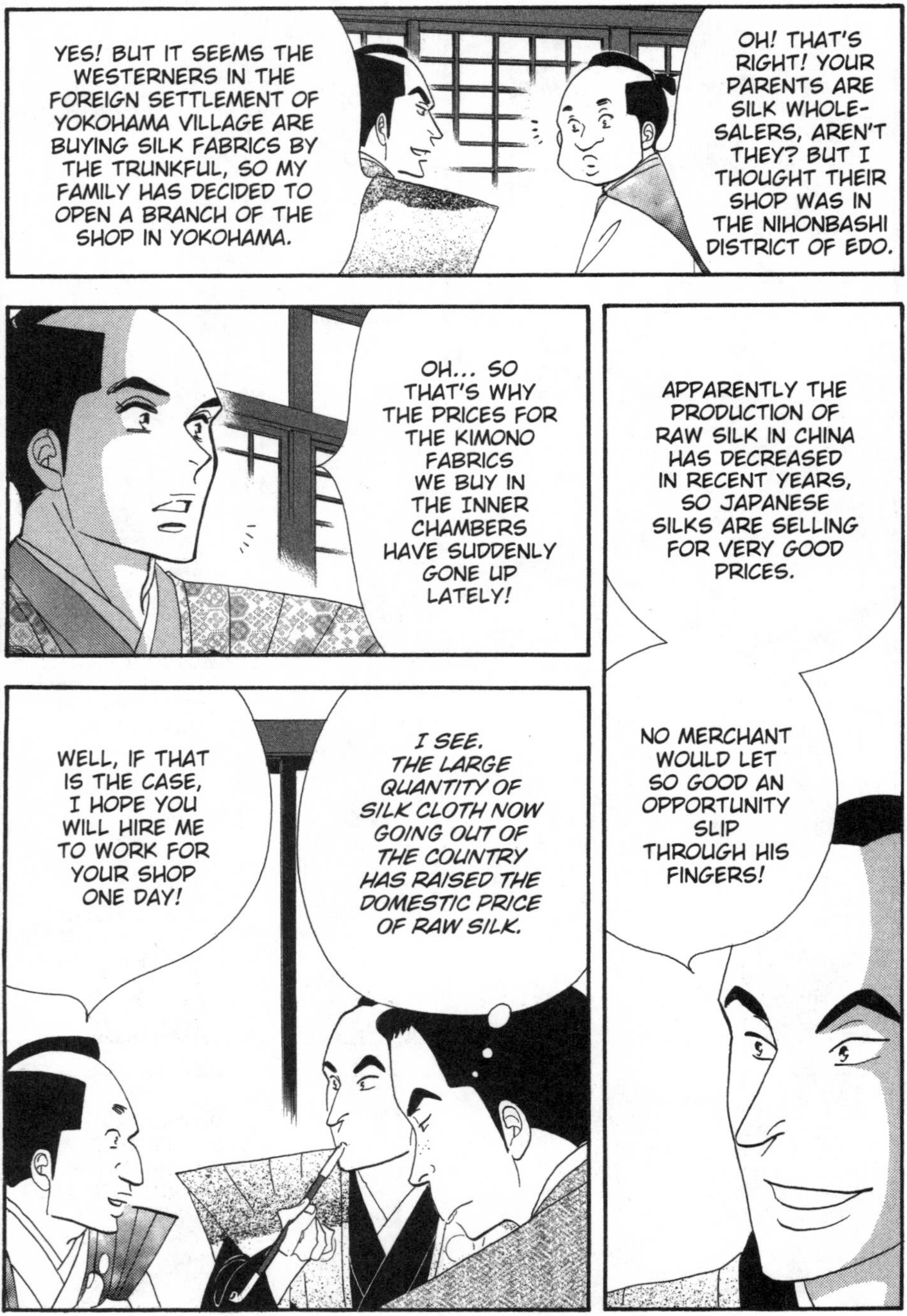
OH! THAT'S RIGHT! YOUR PARENTS ARE SILK WHOLE-SALERS, AREN'T THEY? BUT I THOUGHT THEIR SHOP WAS IN THE NIHONBASHI DISTRICT OF EDO.
YES! BUT IT SEEMS THE WESTERNERS IN THE FOREIGN SETTLEMENT OF YOKOHAMA VILLAGE ARE BUYING SILK FABRICS BY THE TRUNKFUL, SO MY FAMILY HAS DECIDED TO OPEN A BRANCH OF THE SHOP IN YOKOHAMA.
APPARENTLY THE PRODUCTION OF RAW SILK IN CHINA HAS DECREASED IN RECENT YEARS, SO JAPANESE SILKS ARE SELLING FOR VERY GOOD PRICES.
OH... SO THAT'S WHY THE PRICES FOR THE KIMONO FABRICS WE BUY IN THE INNER CHAMBERS HAVE SUDDENLY GONE UP LATELY!
NO MERCHANT WOULD LET SO GOOD AN OPPORTUNITY SLIP THROUGH HIS FINGERS!
I SEE. THE LARGE QUANTITY OF SILK CLOTH NOW GOING OUT OF THE COUNTRY HAS RAISED THE DOMESTIC PRICE OF RAW SILK.
WELL, IF THAT IS THE CASE, I HOPE YOU WILL HIRE ME TO WORK FOR YOUR SHOP ONE DAY!

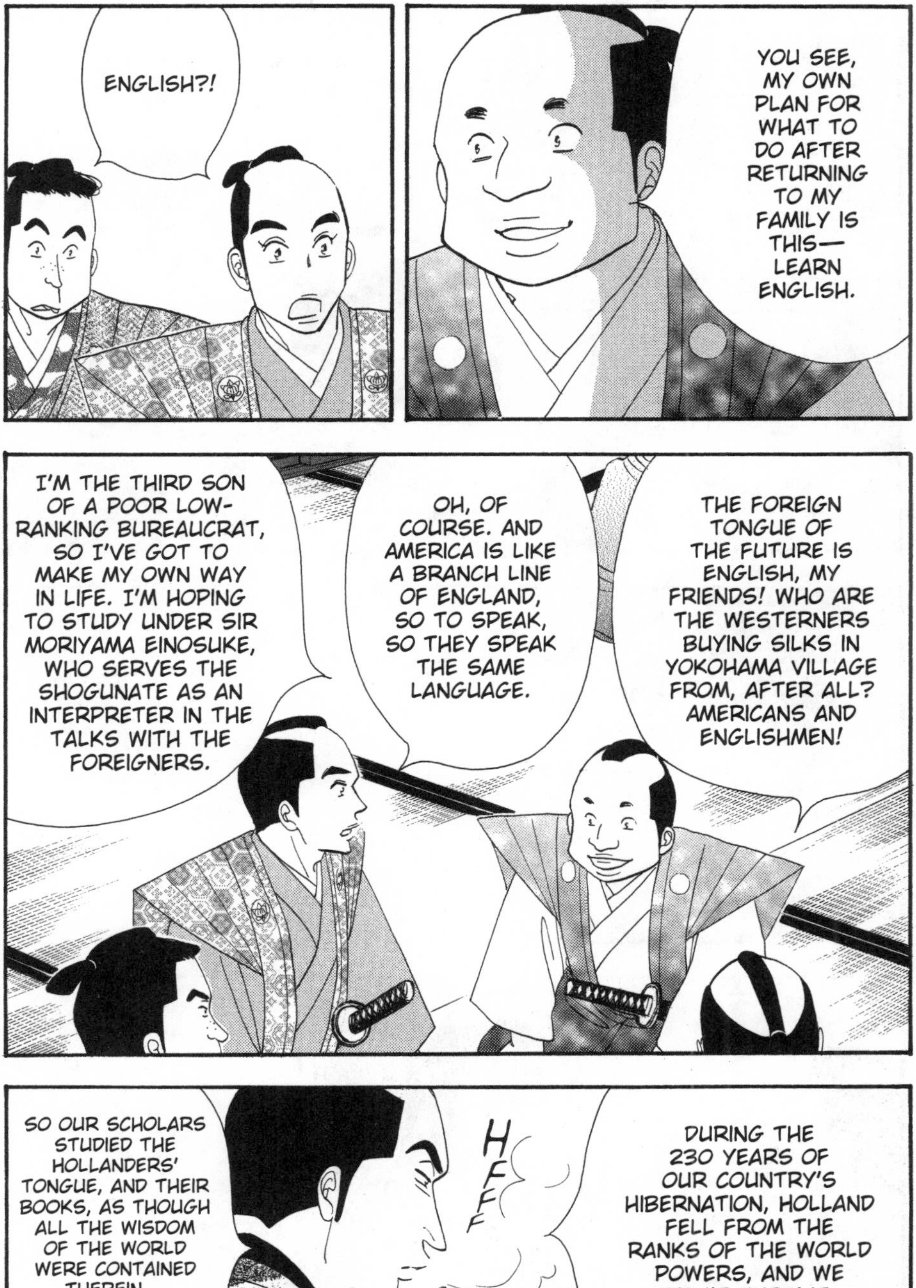
YOU SEE, MY OWN PLAN FOR WHAT TO DO AFTER RETURNING TO MY FAMILY IS THIS— LEARN ENGLISH.
ENGLISH?!
THE FOREIGN TONGUE OF THE FUTURE IS ENGLISH, MY FRIENDS! WHO ARE THE WESTERNERS BUYING SILKS IN YOKOHAMA VILLAGE FROM, AFTER ALL? AMERICANS AND ENGLISHMEN!
OH, OF COURSE. AND AMERICA IS LIKE A BRANCH LINE OF ENGLAND, SO TO SPEAK, SO THEY SPEAK THE SAME LANGUAGE.
I'M THE THIRD SON OF A POOR LOW-RANKING BUREAUCRAT, SO I'VE GOT TO MAKE MY OWN WAY IN LIFE. I'M HOPING TO STUDY UNDER SIR MORIYAMA EINOSUKE, WHO SERVES THE SHOGUNATE AS AN INTERPRETER IN THE TALKS WITH THE FOREIGNERS.
DURING THE 230 YEARS OF OUR COUNTRY'S HIBERNATION, HOLLAND FELL FROM THE RANKS OF THE WORLD POWERS, AND WE DIDN'T KNOW IT.
HFFF
SO OUR SCHOLARS STUDIED THE HOLLANDERS' TONGUE, AND THEIR BOOKS, AS THOUGH ALL THE WISDOM OF THE WORLD WERE CONTAINED THEREIN...

A-APOLOGIES!
YOUR FATHER AND BROTHERS ARE DOCTORS PRACTICING HOLLANDER MEDICINE, KUROKI!
NEVER MIND.
IT'S EXACTLY AS YOU SAY. I'M CERTAIN MY FATHER AND BROTHERS ARE REALIZING THE SAME THING NOW AND FEELING IT KEENLY.
WE MAY NEVER SEE EACH OTHER AGAIN. I WISH YOU BOTH WELL.
THANKS.
AND THE SAME TO YOU, KUROKI.

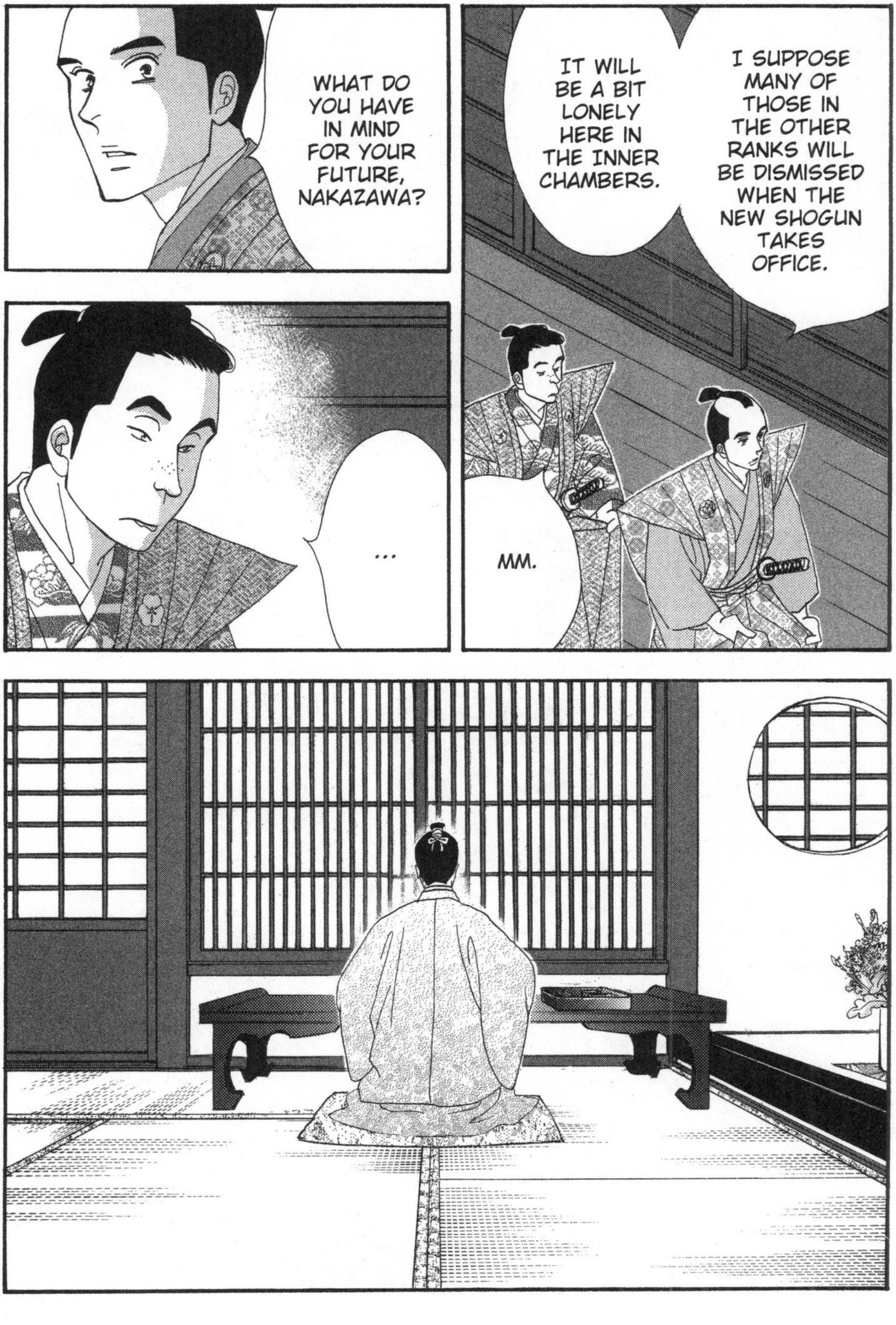
I SUPPOSE MANY OF THOSE IN THE OTHER RANKS WILL BE DISMISSED WHEN THE NEW SHOGUN TAKES OFFICE.
IT WILL BE A BIT LONELY HERE IN THE INNER CHAMBERS.
MM.
WHAT DO YOU HAVE IN MIND FOR YOUR FUTURE, NAKAZAWA?
...

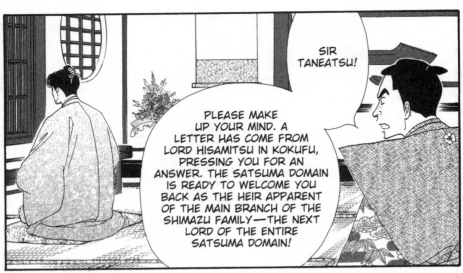

SIR TANEATSU!

PLEASE MAKE UP YOUR MIND. A LETTER HAS COME FROM LORD HISAMITSU IN KOKUFU, PRESSING YOU FOR AN ANSWER. THE SATSUMA DOMAIN IS READY TO WELCOME YOU BACK AS THE HEIR APPARENT OF THE MAIN BRANCH OF THE SHIMAZU FAMILY—THE NEXT LORD OF THE ENTIRE SATSUMA DOMAIN!

IT WAS ONLY A LITTLE MORE THAN A YEAR AGO THAT YOU MARRIED INTO THE TOKUGAWA CLAN... AND BESIDES, YOU ARE MUCH TOO YOUNG TO SPEND THE REST OF YOUR LIFE HERE IN THE INNER CHAMBERS OUT OF DUTY TO LORD IESADA!

MIGHT IT NOT BE THAT LORD IESADA HERSELF HAD YOUR RETURN TO SATSUMA IN MIND WHEN SHE MADE HER FINAL DECREE COMMANDING YOU NOT TO SHAVE YOUR PATE?! PERHAPS THAT IS WHAT SHE WISHED FOR YOU!

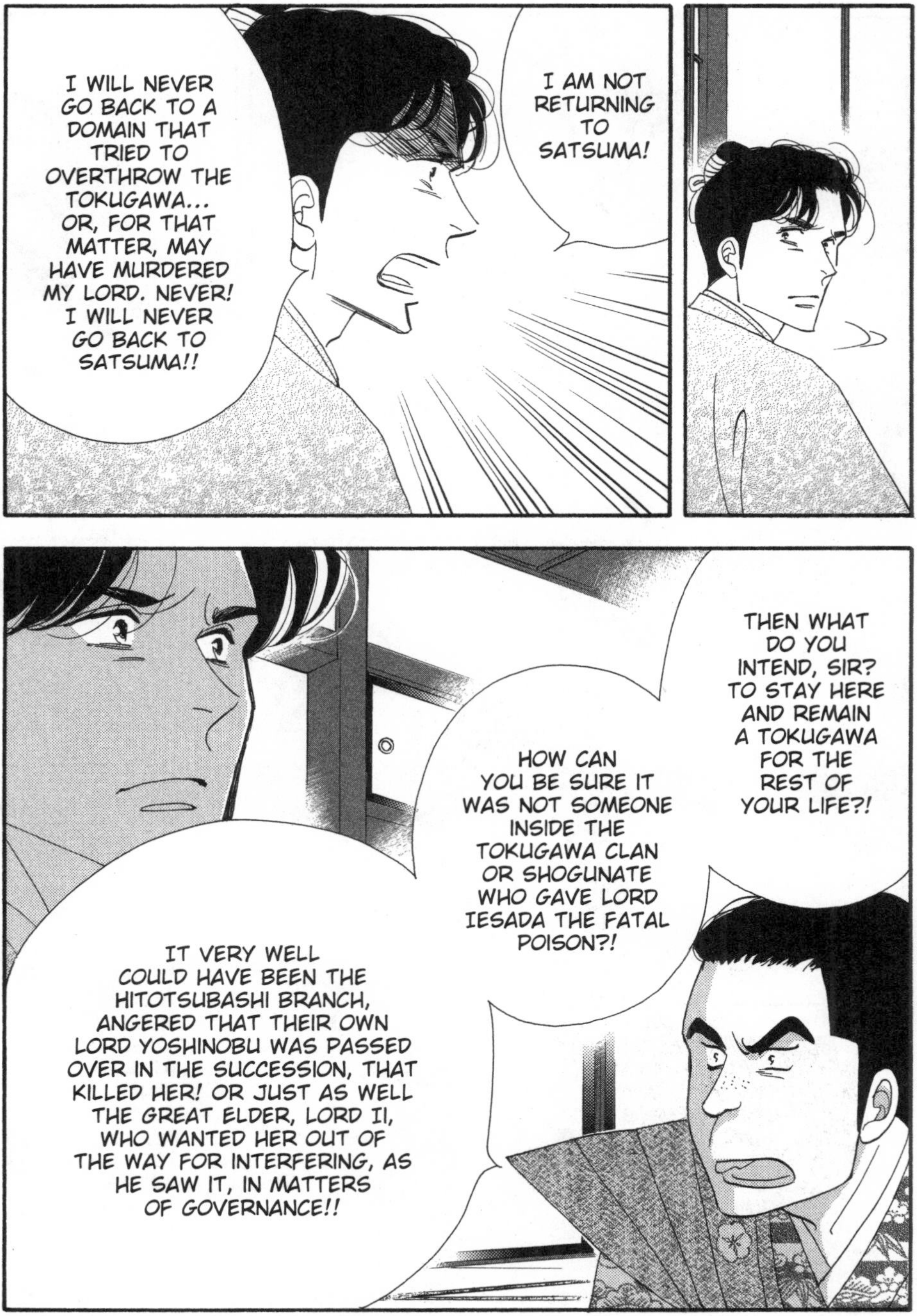
I AM NOT RETURNING TO SATSUMA!
I WILL NEVER GO BACK TO A DOMAIN THAT TRIED TO OVERTHROW THE TOKUGAWA... OR, FOR THAT MATTER, MAY HAVE MURDERED MY LORD. NEVER! I WILL NEVER GO BACK TO SATSUMA!!
THEN WHAT DO YOU INTEND, SIR? TO STAY HERE AND REMAIN A TOKUGAWA FOR THE REST OF YOUR LIFE?!
HOW CAN YOU BE SURE IT WAS NOT SOMEONE INSIDE THE TOKUGAWA CLAN OR SHOGUNATE WHO GAVE LORD IESADA THE FATAL POISON?!
IT VERY WELL COULD HAVE BEEN THE HITOTSUBASHI BRANCH, ANGERED THAT THEIR OWN LORD YOSHINOBU WAS PASSED OVER IN THE SUCCESSION, THAT KILLED HER! OR JUST AS WELL THE GREAT ELDER, LORD II, WHO WANTED HER OUT OF THE WAY FOR INTERFERING, AS HE SAW IT, IN MATTERS OF GOVERNANCE!!

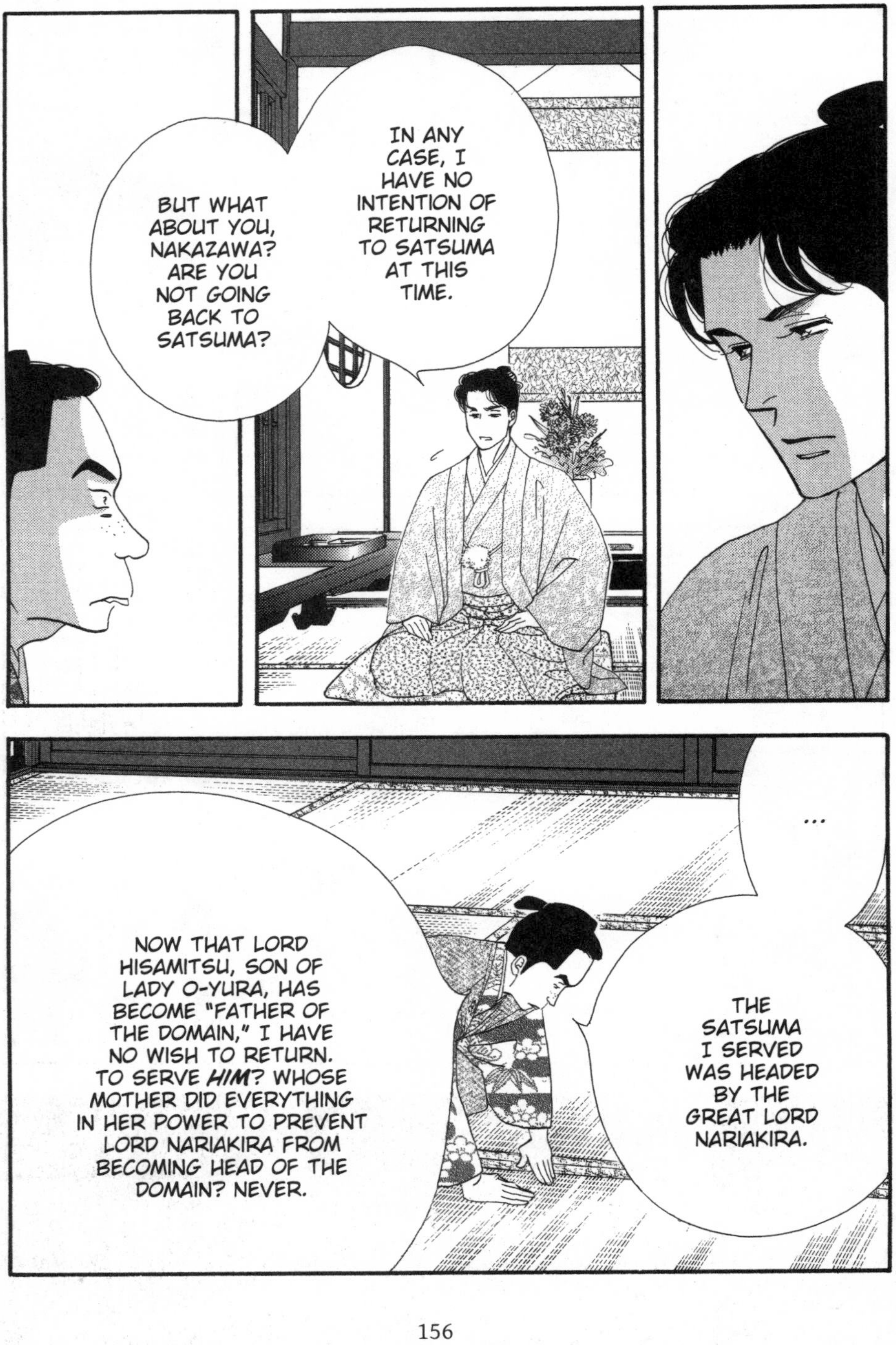
IN ANY CASE, I HAVE NO INTENTION OF RETURNING TO SATSUMA AT THIS TIME.
BUT WHAT ABOUT YOU, NAKAZAWA? ARE YOU NOT GOING BACK TO SATSUMA?
...
THE SATSUMA I SERVED WAS HEADED BY THE GREAT LORD NARIAKIRA.
NOW THAT LORD HISAMITSU, SON OF LADY O-YURA, HAS BECOME "FATHER OF THE DOMAIN," I HAVE NO WISH TO RETURN. TO SERVE *HIM*? WHOSE MOTHER DID EVERYTHING IN HER POWER TO PREVENT LORD NARIAKIRA FROM BECOMING HEAD OF THE DOMAIN? NEVER.

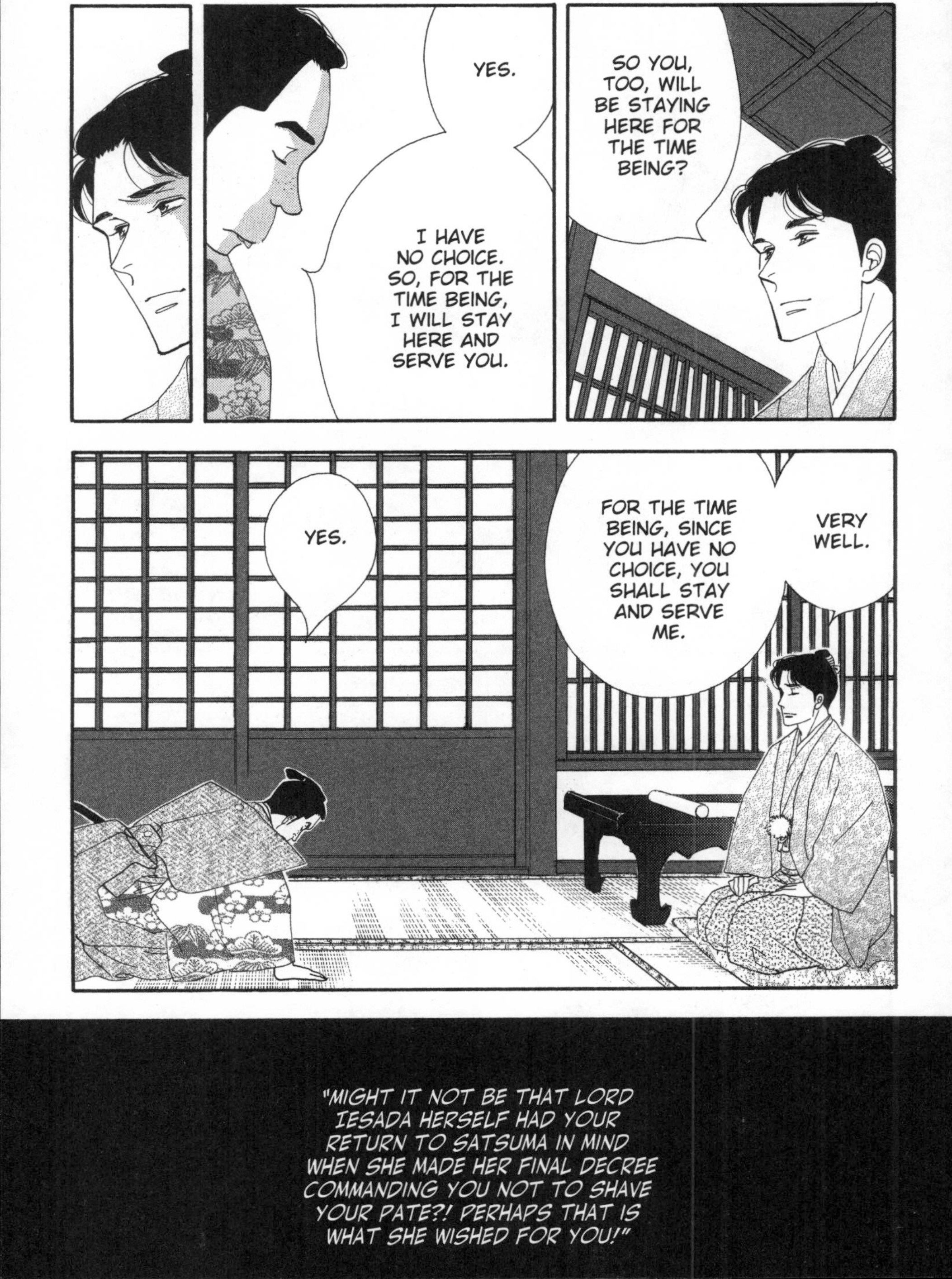
SO YOU, TOO, WILL BE STAYING HERE FOR THE TIME BEING?
YES.
I HAVE NO CHOICE. SO, FOR THE TIME BEING, I WILL STAY HERE AND SERVE YOU.
VERY WELL.
FOR THE TIME BEING, SINCE YOU HAVE NO CHOICE, YOU SHALL STAY AND SERVE ME.
YES.
"MIGHT IT NOT BE THAT LORD IESADA HERSELF HAD YOUR RETURN TO SATSUMA IN MIND WHEN SHE MADE HER FINAL DECREE COMMANDING YOU NOT TO SHAVE YOUR PATE?! PERHAPS THAT IS WHAT SHE WISHED FOR YOU!"

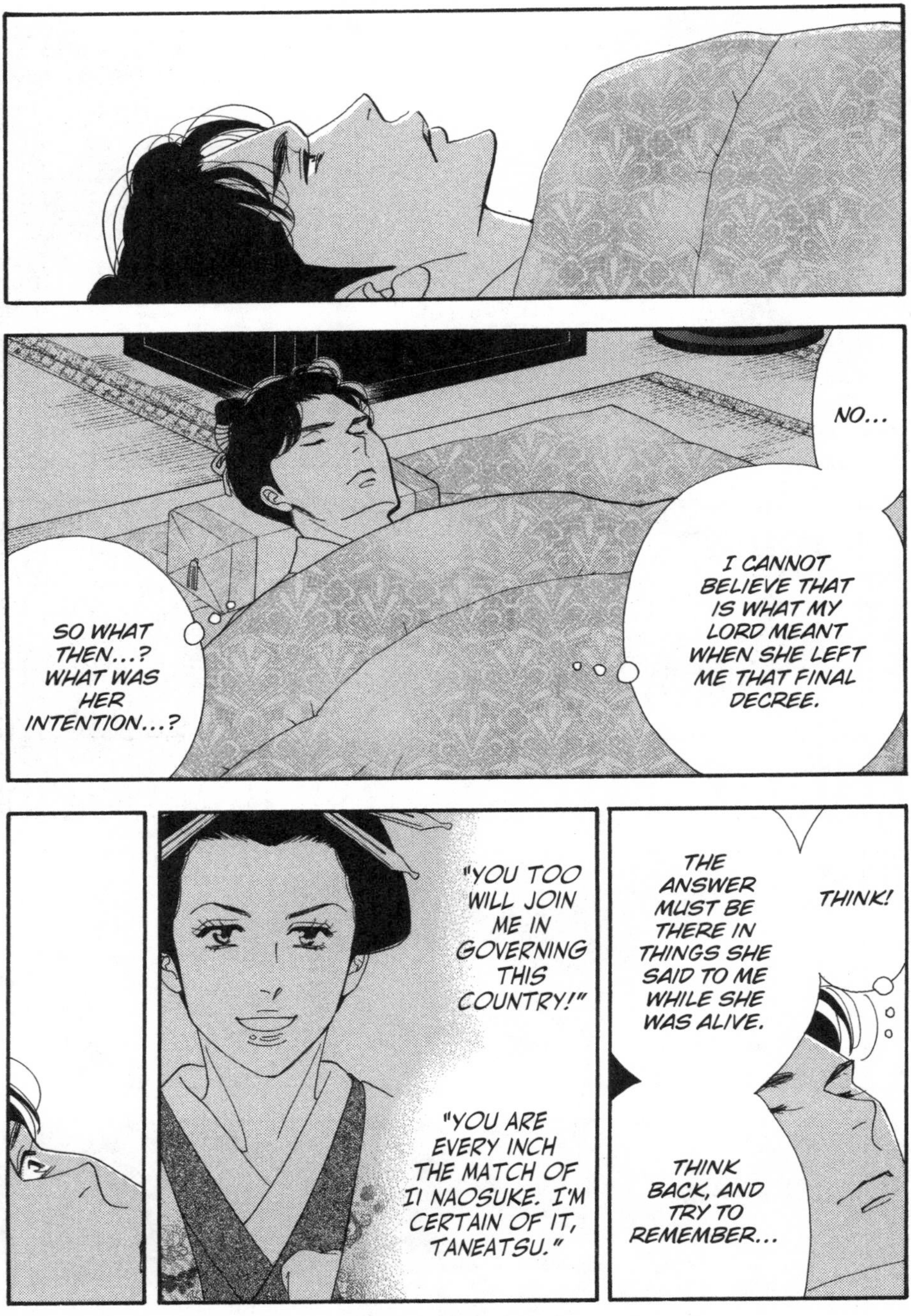
NO...
I CANNOT BELIEVE THAT IS WHAT MY LORD MEANT WHEN SHE LEFT ME THAT FINAL DECREE.
SO WHAT THEN...? WHAT WAS HER INTENTION...?
THINK!
THE ANSWER MUST BE THERE IN THINGS SHE SAID TO ME WHILE SHE WAS ALIVE.
THINK BACK, AND TRY TO REMEMBER...
"YOU TOO WILL JOIN ME IN GOVERNING THIS COUNTRY!"
"YOU ARE EVERY INCH THE MATCH OF II NAOSUKE. I'M CERTAIN OF IT, TANEATSU."

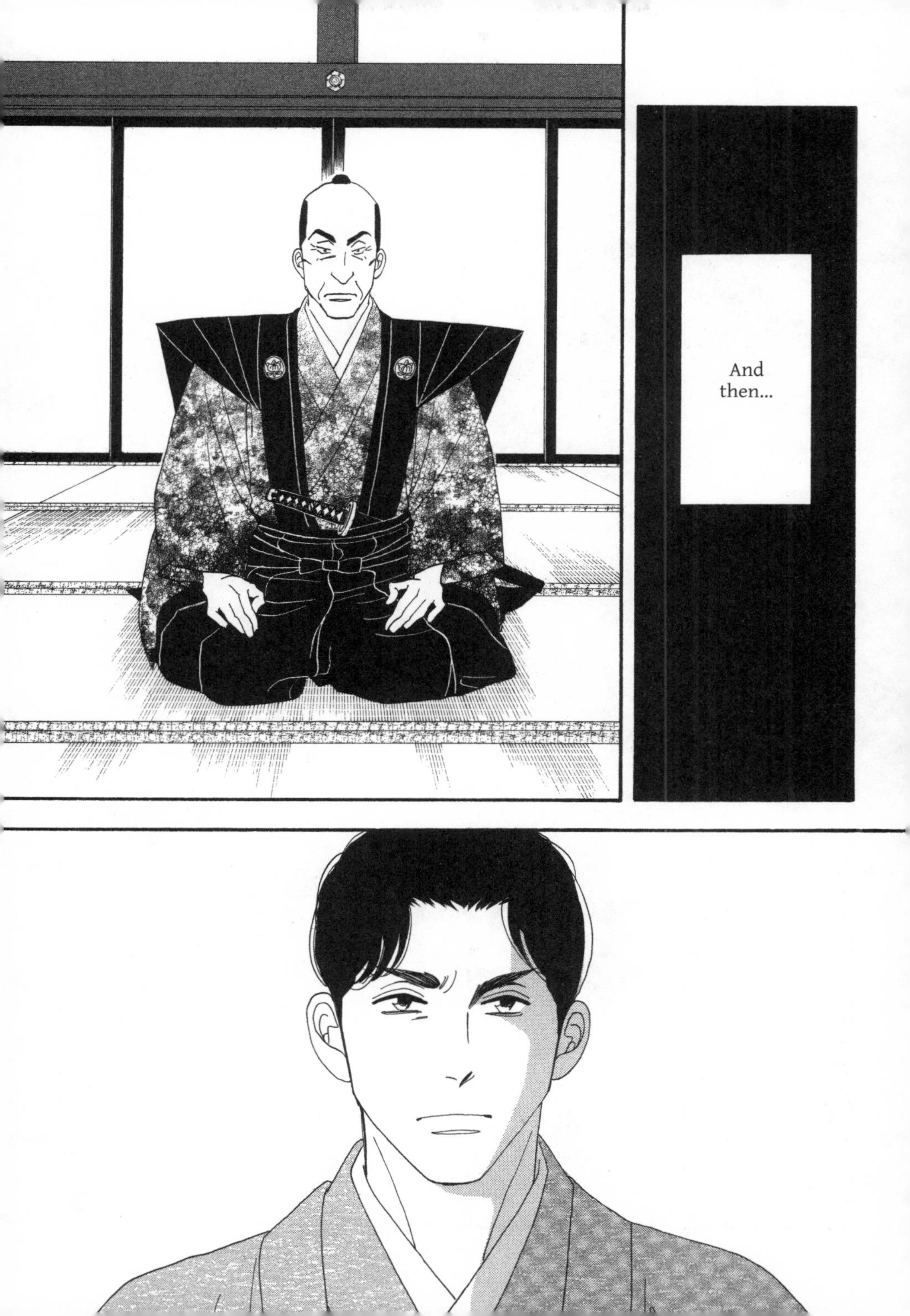
And then...

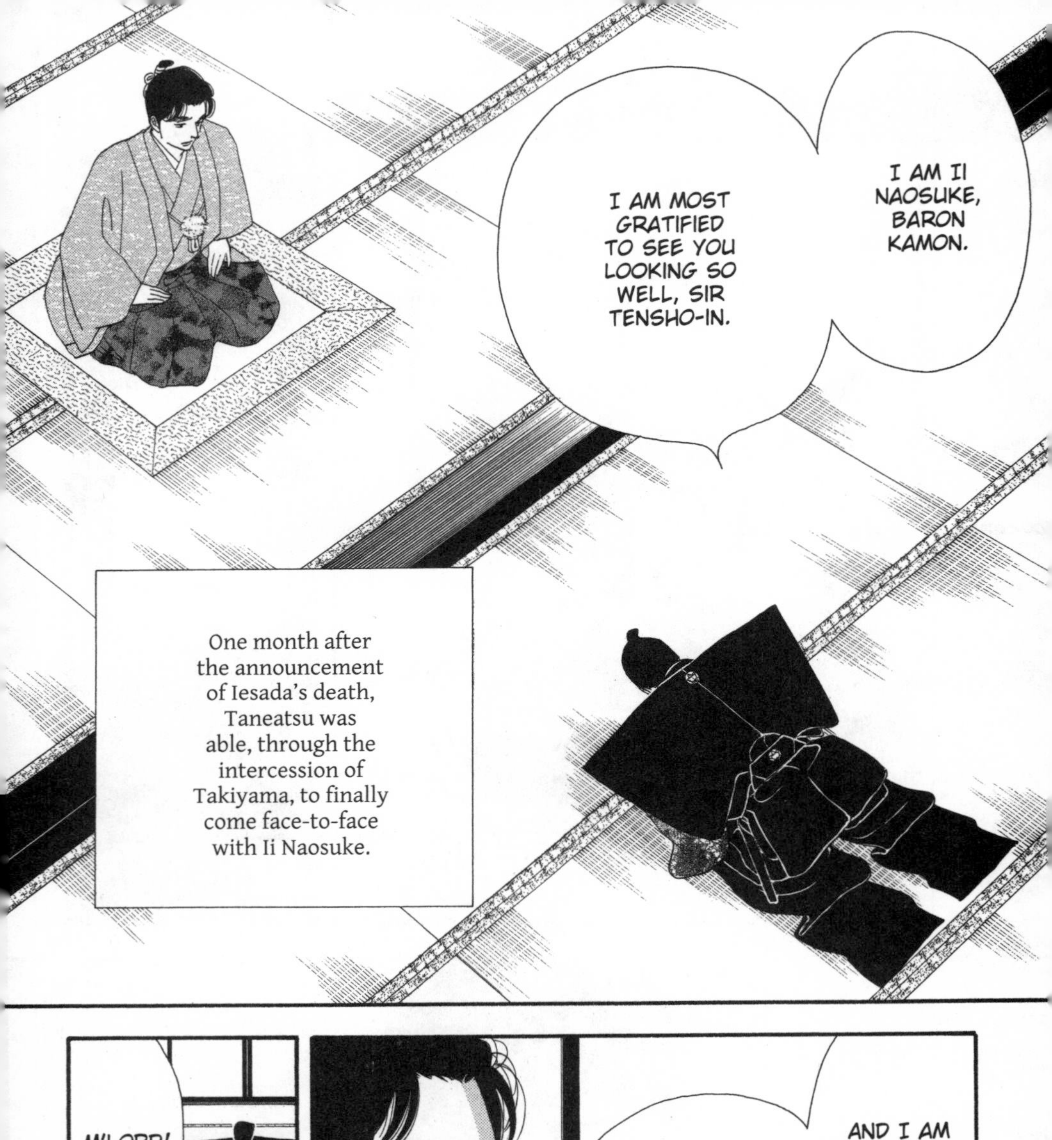
I AM II NAOSUKE, BARON KAMON.
I AM MOST GRATIFIED TO SEE YOU LOOKING SO WELL, SIR TENSHO-IN.
One month after the announcement of Iesada's death, Taneatsu was able, through the intercession of Takiyama, to finally come face-to-face with Ii Naosuke.
AND I AM TENSHO-IN TANEATSU.
I APPRECIATE YOUR EFFORTS IN MAKING LORD IESADA'S FUNERAL RITES PROCEED SMOOTHLY AND SATISFACTORILY.
M'LORD!

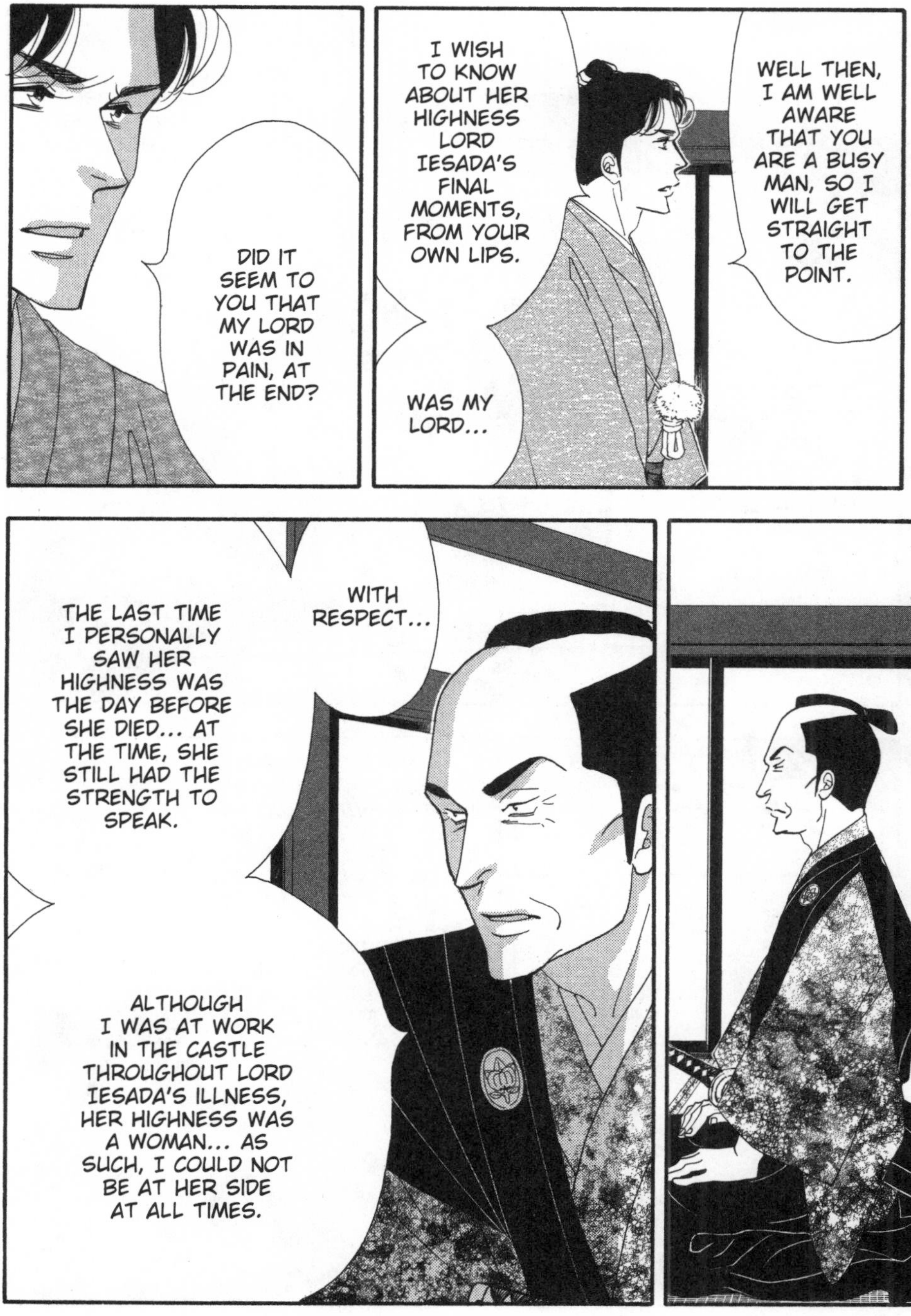
WELL THEN, I AM WELL AWARE THAT YOU ARE A BUSY MAN, SO I WILL GET STRAIGHT TO THE POINT.
I WISH TO KNOW ABOUT HER HIGHNESS LORD IESADA'S FINAL MOMENTS, FROM YOUR OWN LIPS.
WAS MY LORD...
DID IT SEEM TO YOU THAT MY LORD WAS IN PAIN, AT THE END?
WITH RESPECT...
THE LAST TIME I PERSONALLY SAW HER HIGHNESS WAS THE DAY BEFORE SHE DIED... AT THE TIME, SHE STILL HAD THE STRENGTH TO SPEAK.
ALTHOUGH I WAS AT WORK IN THE CASTLE THROUGHOUT LORD IESADA'S ILLNESS, HER HIGHNESS WAS A WOMAN... AS SUCH, I COULD NOT BE AT HER SIDE AT ALL TIMES.

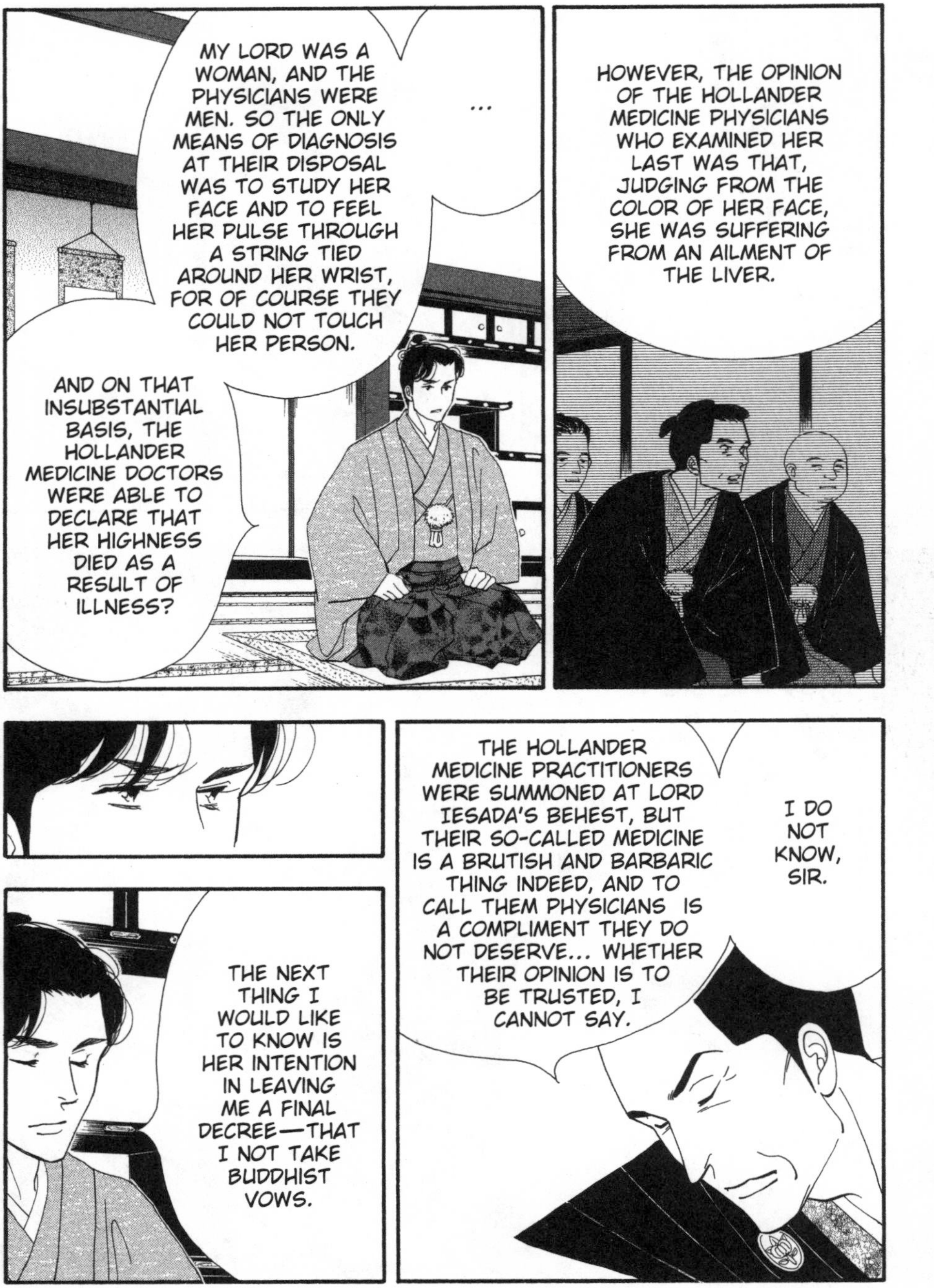

HOWEVER, THE OPINION OF THE HOLLANDER MEDICINE PHYSICIANS WHO EXAMINED HER LAST WAS THAT, JUDGING FROM THE COLOR OF HER FACE, SHE WAS SUFFERING FROM AN AILMENT OF THE LIVER.
...
MY LORD WAS A WOMAN, AND THE PHYSICIANS WERE MEN. SO THE ONLY MEANS OF DIAGNOSIS AT THEIR DISPOSAL WAS TO STUDY HER FACE AND TO FEEL HER PULSE THROUGH A STRING TIED AROUND HER WRIST, FOR OF COURSE THEY COULD NOT TOUCH HER PERSON.
AND ON THAT INSUBSTANTIAL BASIS, THE HOLLANDER MEDICINE DOCTORS WERE ABLE TO DECLARE THAT HER HIGHNESS DIED AS A RESULT OF ILLNESS?
I DO NOT KNOW, SIR.
THE HOLLANDER MEDICINE PRACTITIONERS WERE SUMMONED AT LORD IESADA'S BEHEST, BUT THEIR SO-CALLED MEDICINE IS A BRUTISH AND BARBARIC THING INDEED, AND TO CALL THEM PHYSICIANS IS A COMPLIMENT THEY DO NOT DESERVE... WHETHER THEIR OPINION IS TO BE TRUSTED, I CANNOT SAY.
THE NEXT THING I WOULD LIKE TO KNOW IS HER INTENTION IN LEAVING ME A FINAL DECREE—THAT I NOT TAKE BUDDHIST VOWS.

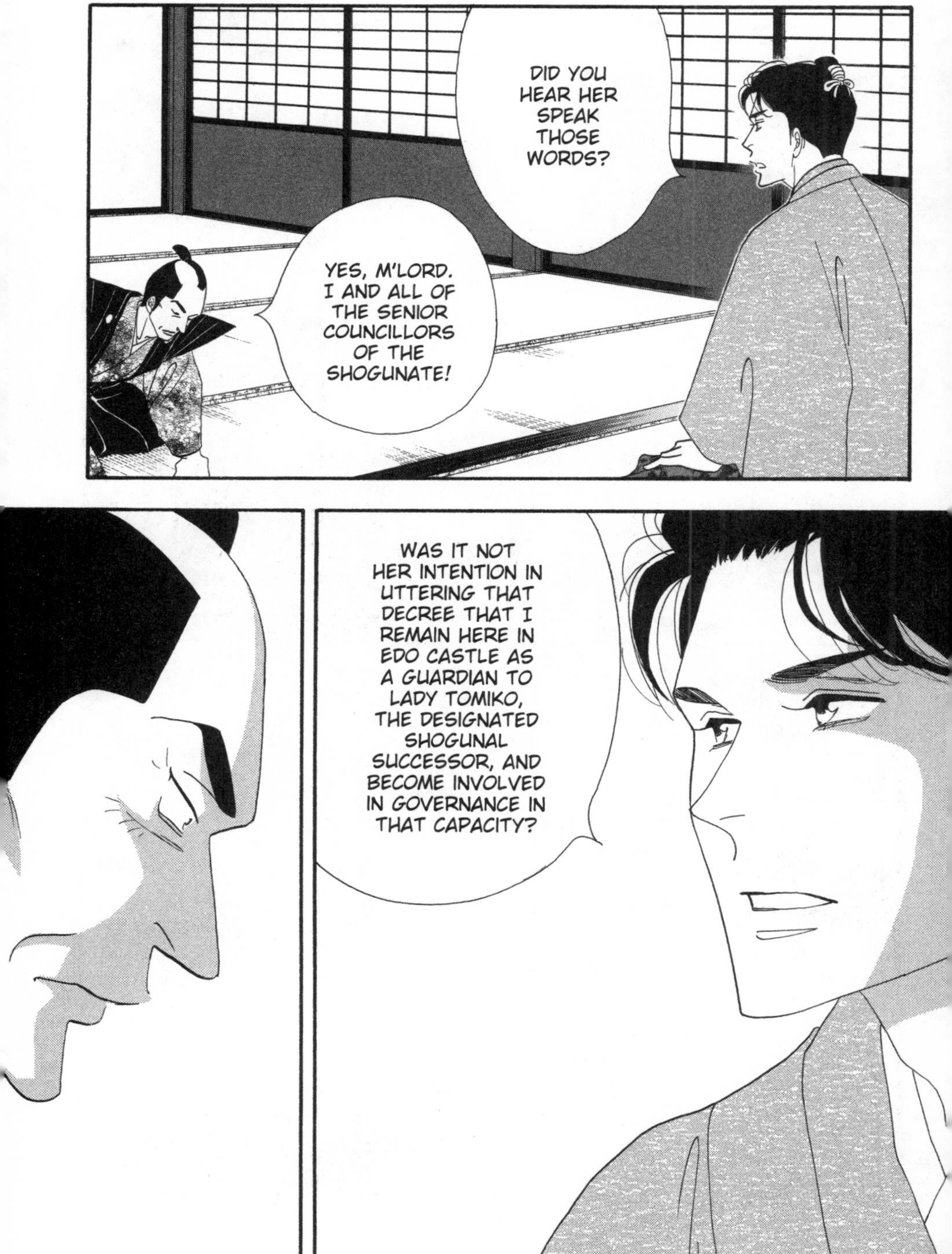
DID YOU HEAR HER SPEAK THOSE WORDS?
YES, M'LORD. I AND ALL OF THE SENIOR COUNCILLORS OF THE SHOGUNATE!
WAS IT NOT HER INTENTION IN UTTERING THAT DECREE THAT I REMAIN HERE IN EDO CASTLE AS A GUARDIAN TO LADY TOMIKO, THE DESIGNATED SHOGUNAL SUCCESSOR, AND BECOME INVOLVED IN GOVERNANCE IN THAT CAPACITY?

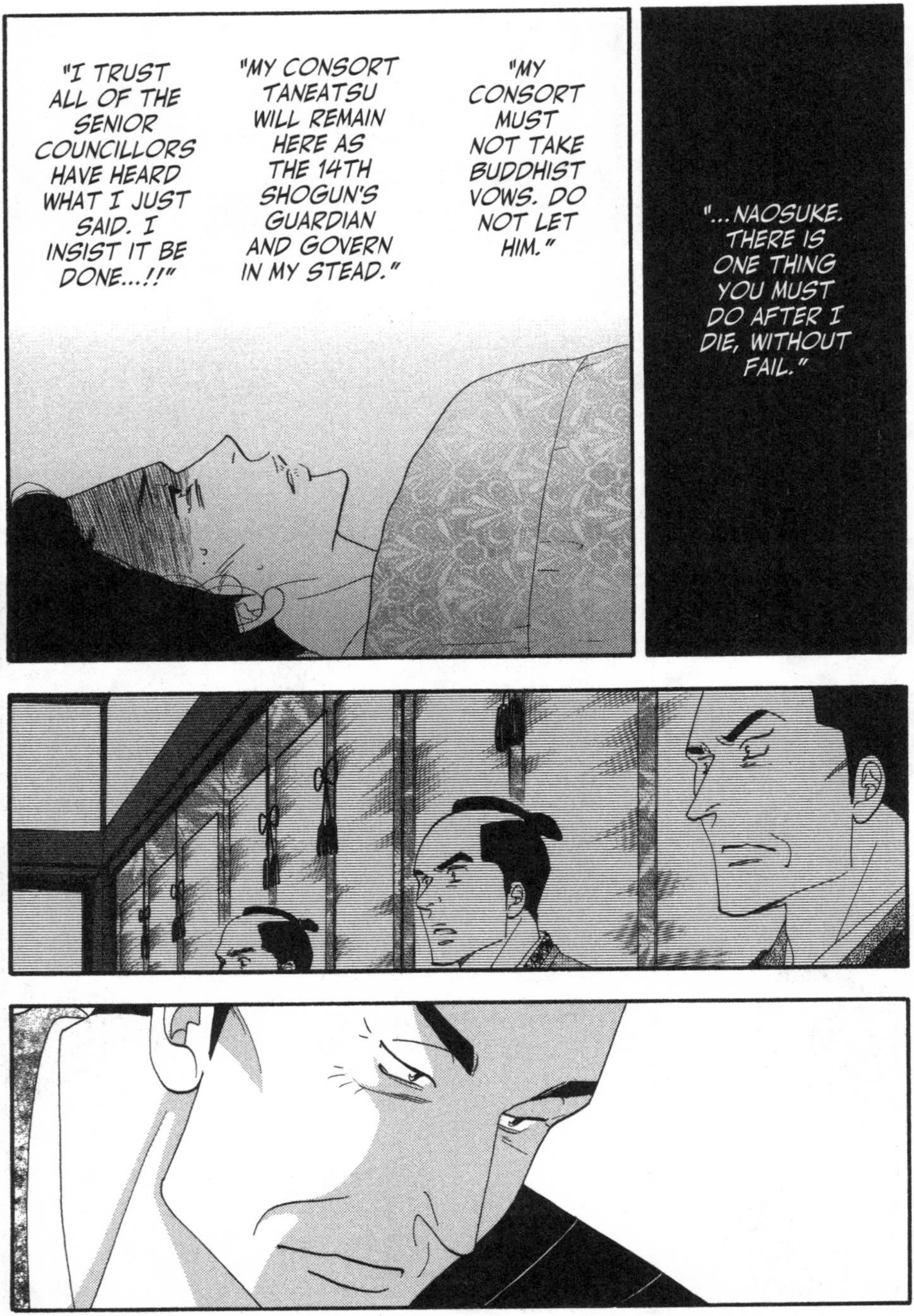
"...NAOSUKE. THERE IS ONE THING YOU MUST DO AFTER I DIE, WITHOUT FAIL."
"MY CONSORT MUST NOT TAKE BUDDHIST VOWS. DO NOT LET HIM."
"MY CONSORT TANEATSU WILL REMAIN HERE AS THE 14TH SHOGUN'S GUARDIAN AND GOVERN IN MY STEAD."
"I TRUST ALL OF THE SENIOR COUNCILLORS HAVE HEARD WHAT I JUST SAID. I INSIST IT BE DONE...!!"

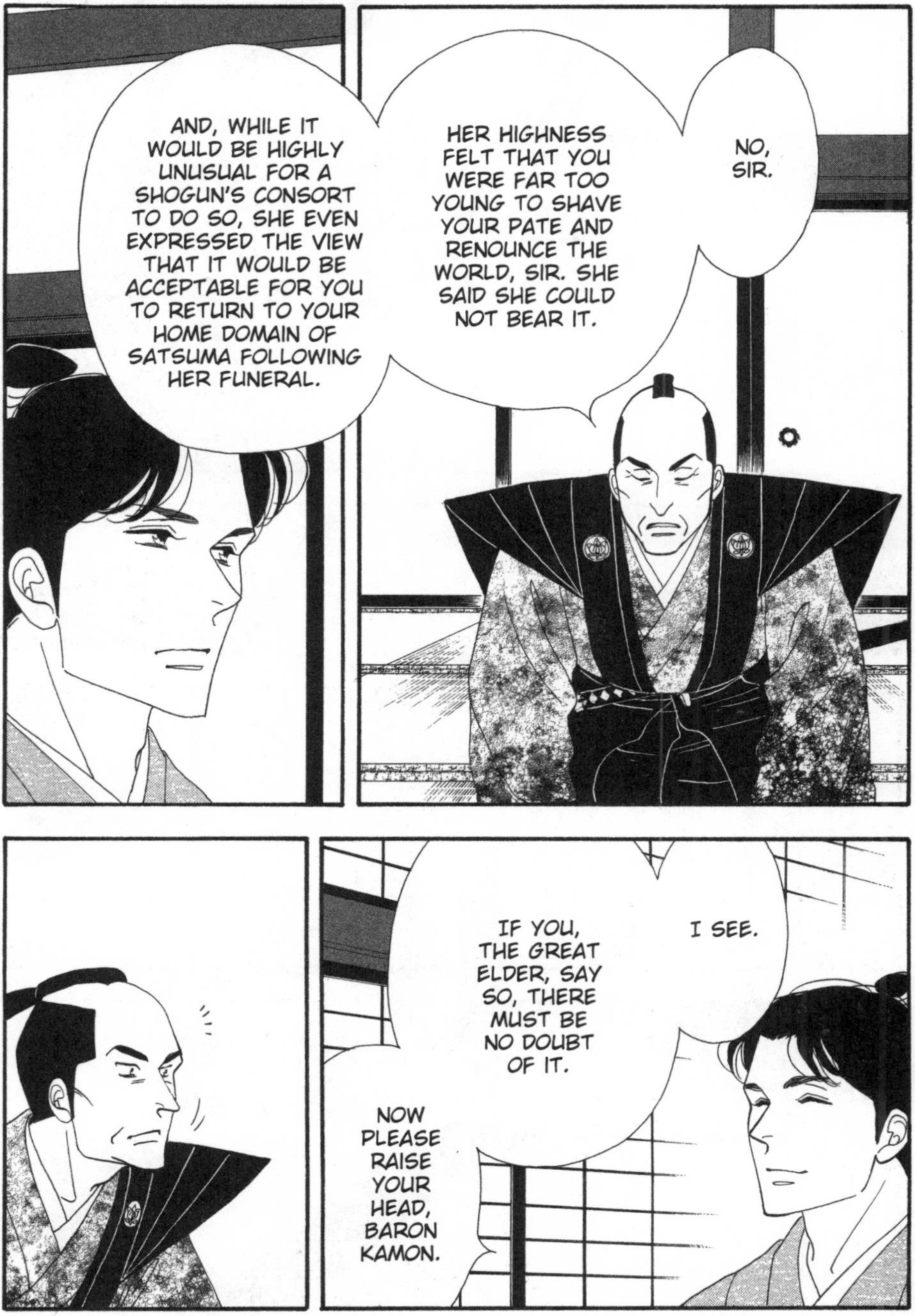
NO, SIR.
HER HIGHNESS FELT THAT YOU WERE FAR TOO YOUNG TO SHAVE YOUR PATE AND RENOUNCE THE WORLD, SIR. SHE SAID SHE COULD NOT BEAR IT.
AND, WHILE IT WOULD BE HIGHLY UNUSUAL FOR A SHOGUN'S CONSORT TO DO SO, SHE EVEN EXPRESSED THE VIEW THAT IT WOULD BE ACCEPTABLE FOR YOU TO RETURN TO YOUR HOME DOMAIN OF SATSUMA FOLLOWING HER FUNERAL.
I SEE.
IF YOU, THE GREAT ELDER, SAY SO, THERE MUST BE NO DOUBT OF IT.
NOW PLEASE RAISE YOUR HEAD, BARON KAMON.

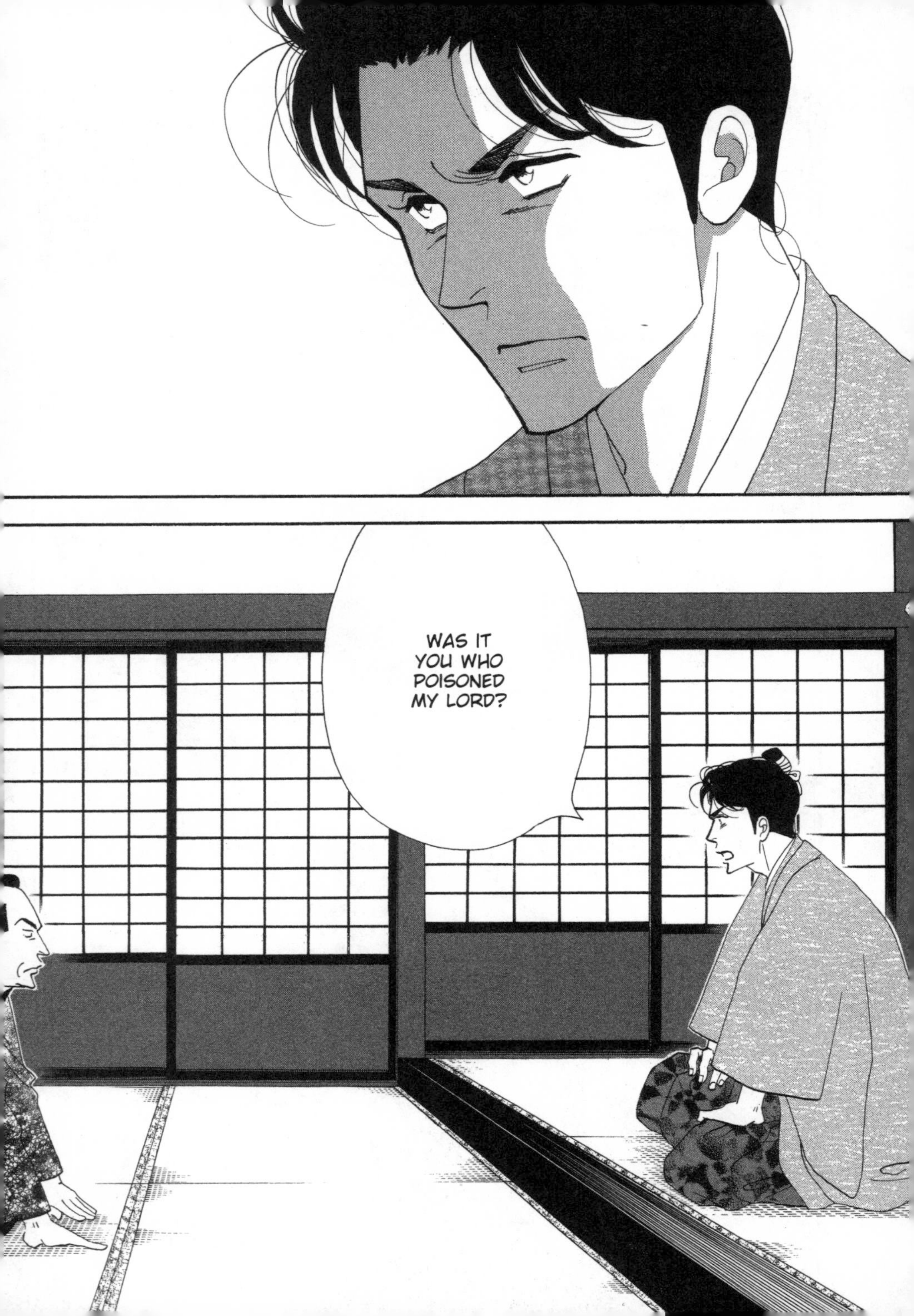
WAS IT YOU WHO POISONED MY LORD?

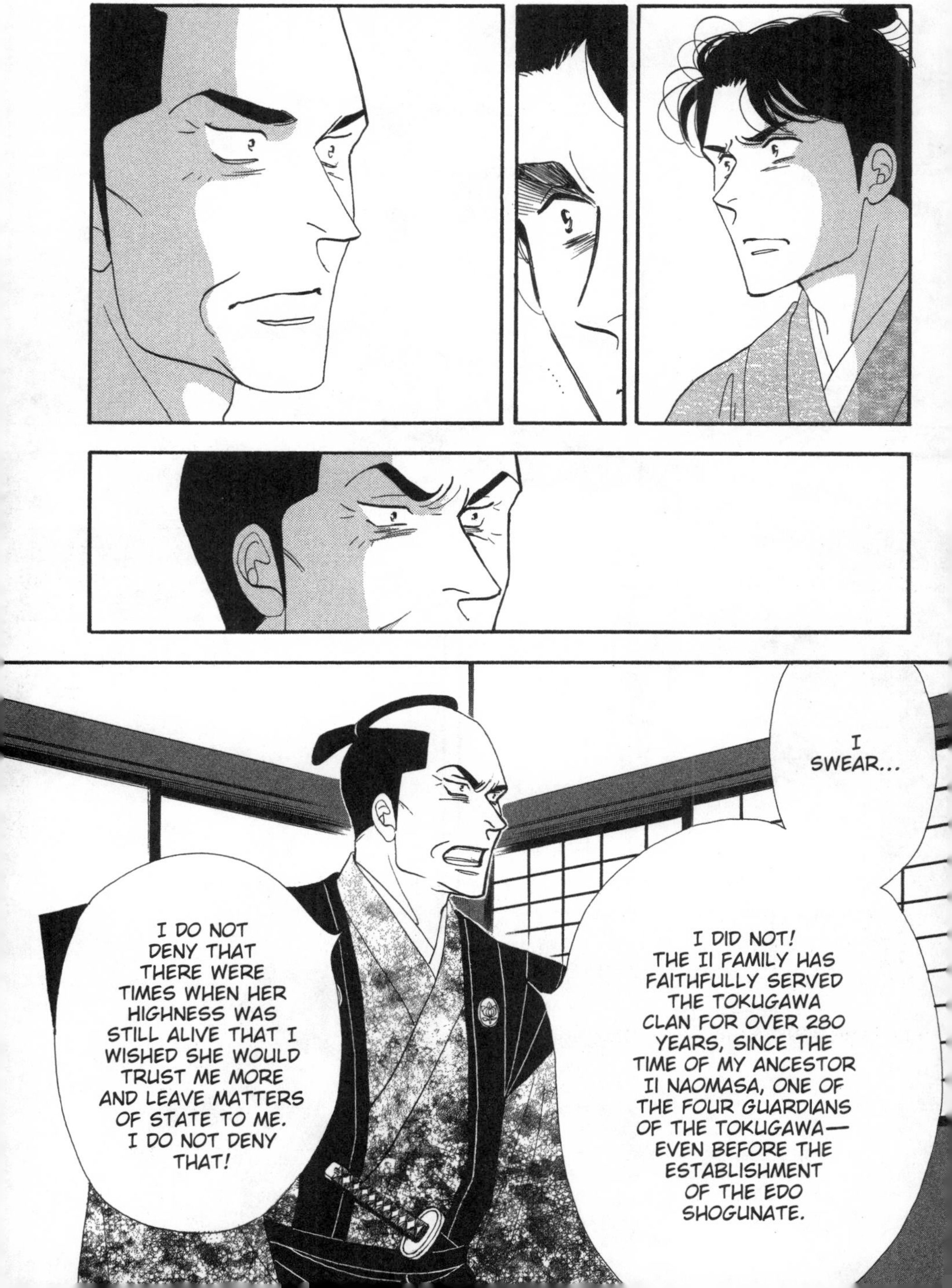
I SWEAR...
I DID NOT! THE II FAMILY HAS FAITHFULLY SERVED THE TOKUGAWA CLAN FOR OVER 280 YEARS, SINCE THE TIME OF MY ANCESTOR II NAOMASA, ONE OF THE FOUR GUARDIANS OF THE TOKUGAWA—EVEN BEFORE THE ESTABLISHMENT OF THE EDO SHOGUNATE.
I DO NOT DENY THAT THERE WERE TIMES WHEN HER HIGHNESS WAS STILL ALIVE THAT I WISHED SHE WOULD TRUST ME MORE AND LEAVE MATTERS OF STATE TO ME. I DO NOT DENY THAT!

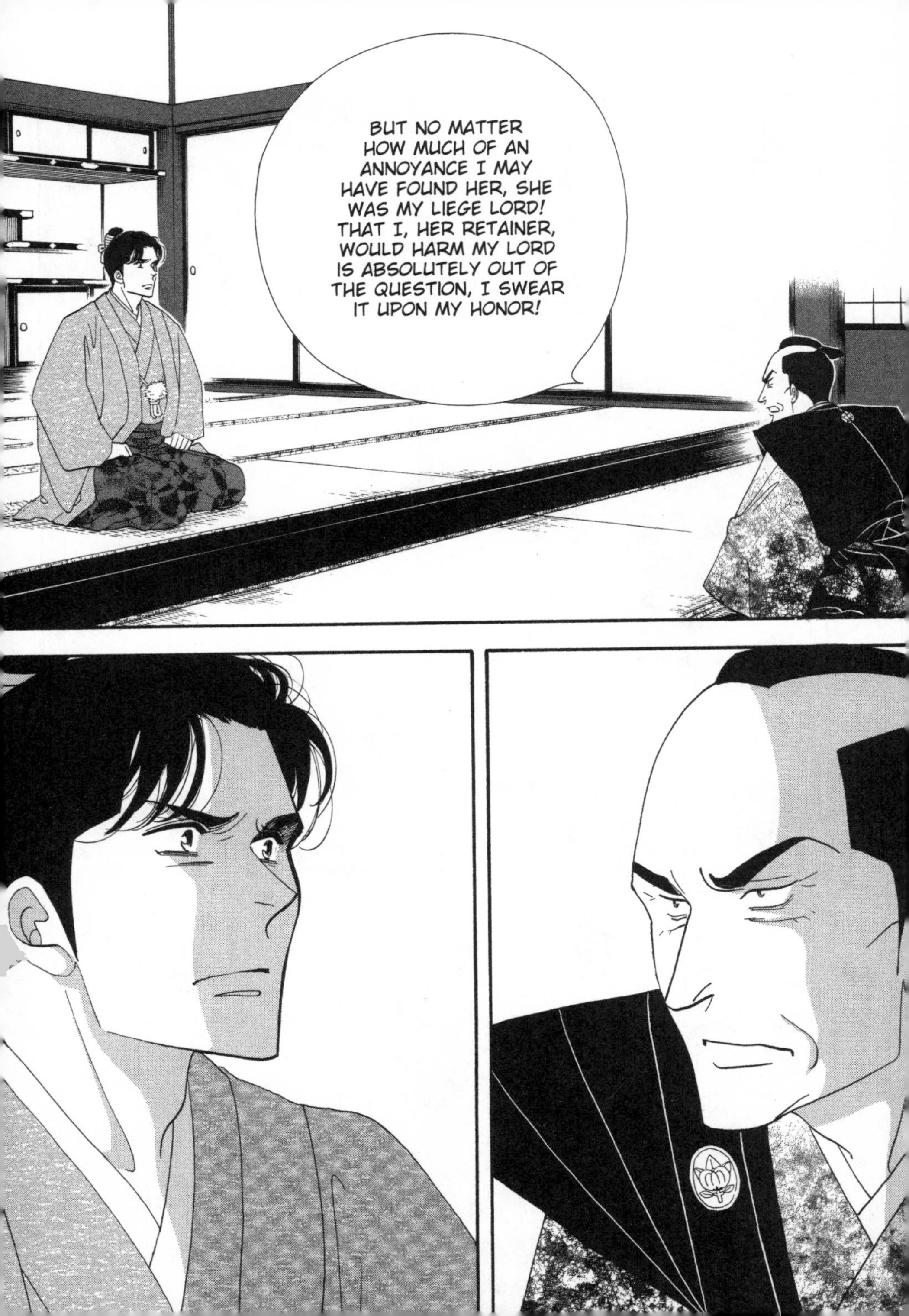
BUT NO MATTER HOW MUCH OF AN ANNOYANCE I MAY HAVE FOUND HER, SHE WAS MY LIEGE LORD! THAT I, HER RETAINER, WOULD HARM MY LORD IS ABSOLUTELY OUT OF THE QUESTION, I SWEAR IT UPON MY HONOR!

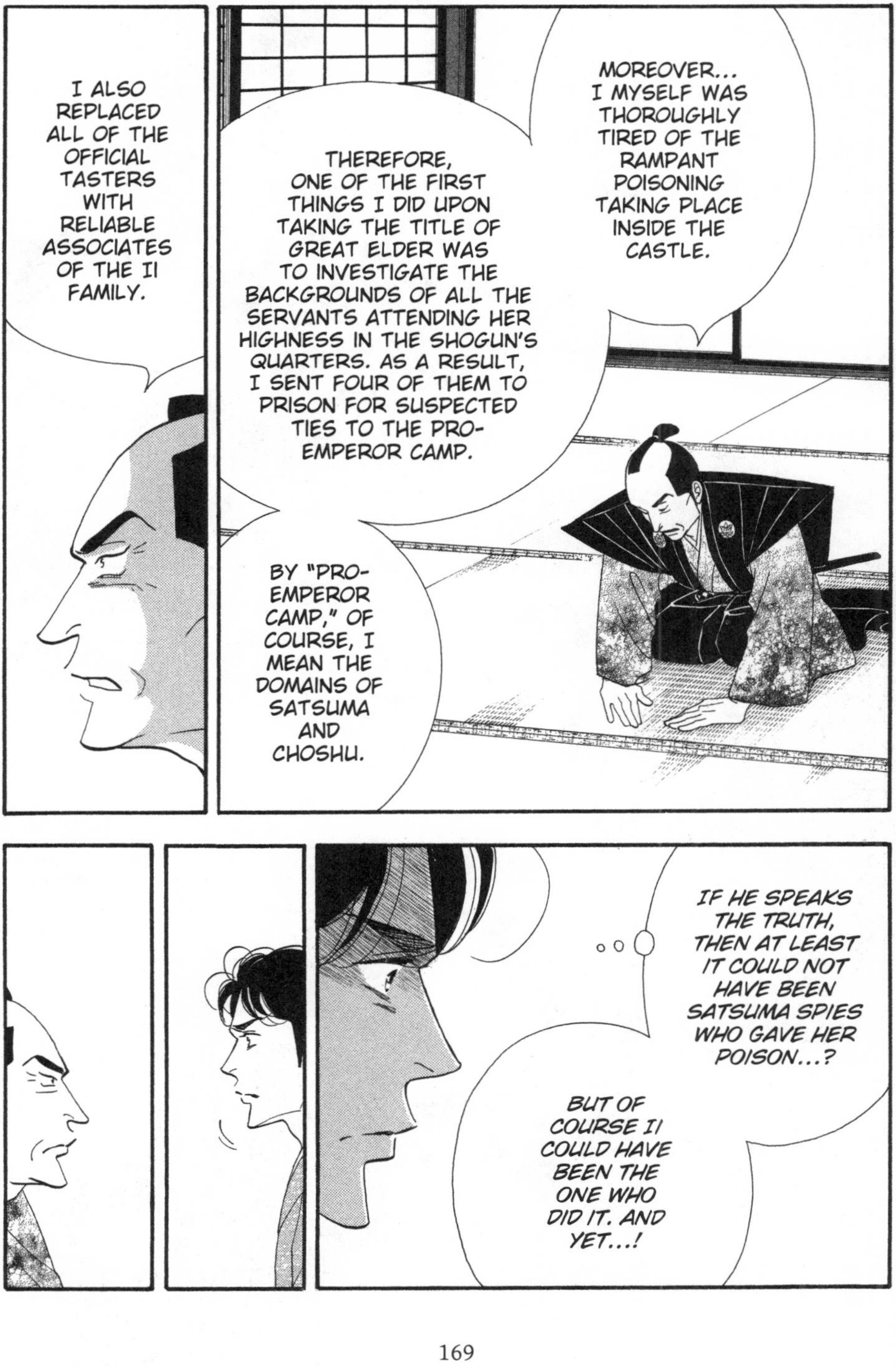
MOREOVER... I MYSELF WAS THOROUGHLY TIRED OF THE RAMPANT POISONING TAKING PLACE INSIDE THE CASTLE.
THEREFORE, ONE OF THE FIRST THINGS I DID UPON TAKING THE TITLE OF GREAT ELDER WAS TO INVESTIGATE THE BACKGROUNDS OF ALL THE SERVANTS ATTENDING HER HIGHNESS IN THE SHOGUN'S QUARTERS. AS A RESULT, I SENT FOUR OF THEM TO PRISON FOR SUSPECTED TIES TO THE PRO-EMPEROR CAMP.
BY "PRO-EMPEROR CAMP," OF COURSE, I MEAN THE DOMAINS OF SATSUMA AND CHOSHU.
I ALSO REPLACED ALL OF THE OFFICIAL TASTERS WITH RELIABLE ASSOCIATES OF THE II FAMILY.
IF HE SPEAKS THE TRUTH, THEN AT LEAST IT COULD NOT HAVE BEEN SATSUMA SPIES WHO GAVE HER POISON...?
BUT OF COURSE II COULD HAVE BEEN THE ONE WHO DID IT. AND YET...!

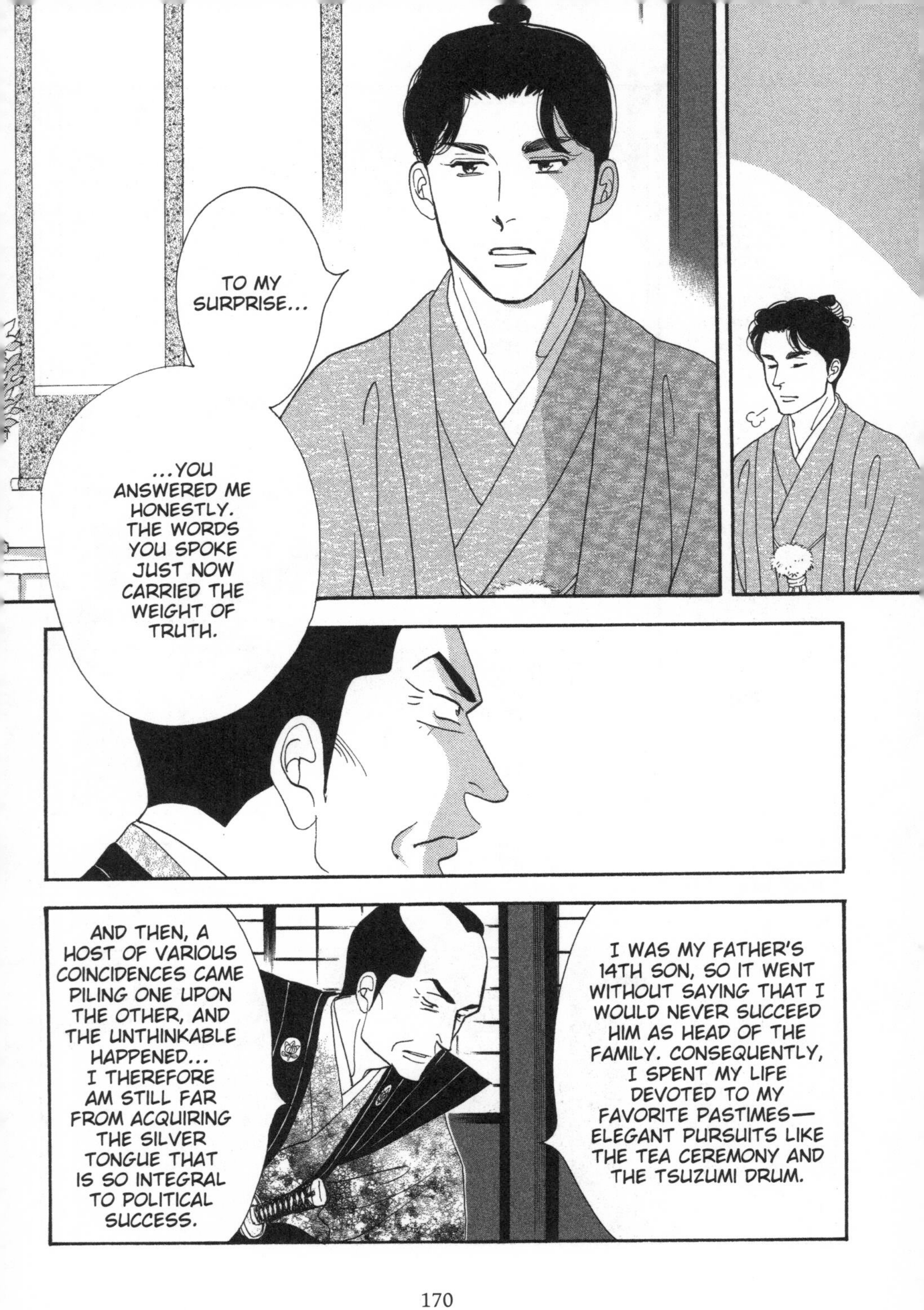
TO MY SURPRISE...
...YOU ANSWERED ME HONESTLY. THE WORDS YOU SPOKE JUST NOW CARRIED THE WEIGHT OF TRUTH.
I WAS MY FATHER'S 14TH SON, SO IT WENT WITHOUT SAYING THAT I WOULD NEVER SUCCEED HIM AS HEAD OF THE FAMILY. CONSEQUENTLY, I SPENT MY LIFE DEVOTED TO MY FAVORITE PASTIMES—ELEGANT PURSUITS LIKE THE TEA CEREMONY AND THE TSUZUMI DRUM.
AND THEN, A HOST OF VARIOUS COINCIDENCES CAME PILING ONE UPON THE OTHER, AND THE UNTHINKABLE HAPPENED... I THEREFORE AM STILL FAR FROM ACQUIRING THE SILVER TONGUE THAT IS SO INTEGRAL TO POLITICAL SUCCESS.

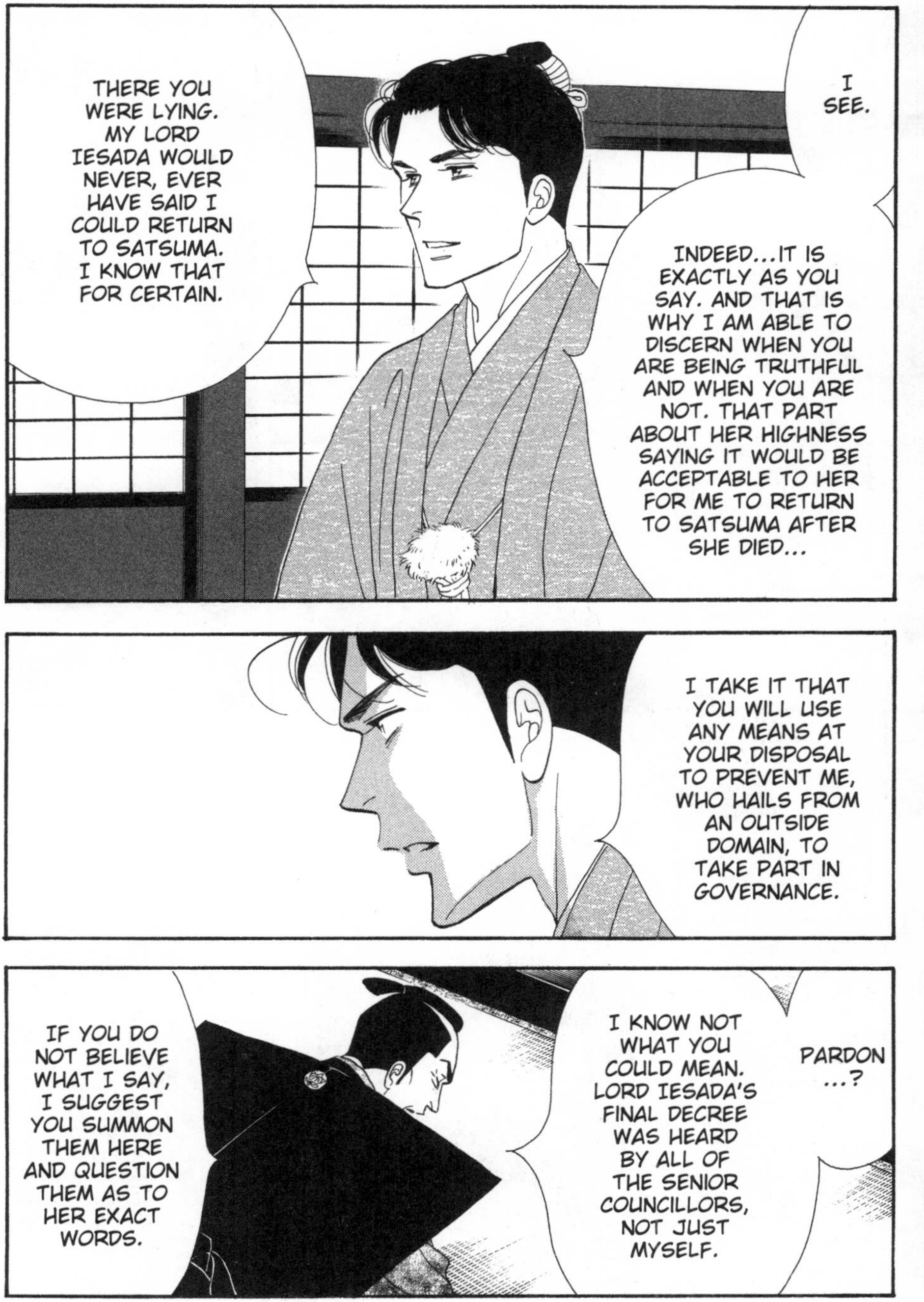
THERE YOU WERE LYING. MY LORD IESADA WOULD NEVER, EVER HAVE SAID I COULD RETURN TO SATSUMA. I KNOW THAT FOR CERTAIN.
I SEE.
INDEED...IT IS EXACTLY AS YOU SAY. AND THAT IS WHY I AM ABLE TO DISCERN WHEN YOU ARE BEING TRUTHFUL AND WHEN YOU ARE NOT. THAT PART ABOUT HER HIGHNESS SAYING IT WOULD BE ACCEPTABLE TO HER FOR ME TO RETURN TO SATSUMA AFTER SHE DIED...
I TAKE IT THAT YOU WILL USE ANY MEANS AT YOUR DISPOSAL TO PREVENT ME, WHO HAILS FROM AN OUTSIDE DOMAIN, TO TAKE PART IN GOVERNANCE.
PARDON ...?
I KNOW NOT WHAT YOU COULD MEAN. LORD IESADA'S FINAL DECREE WAS HEARD BY ALL OF THE SENIOR COUNCILLORS, NOT JUST MYSELF.
IF YOU DO NOT BELIEVE WHAT I SAY, I SUGGEST YOU SUMMON THEM HERE AND QUESTION THEM AS TO HER EXACT WORDS.

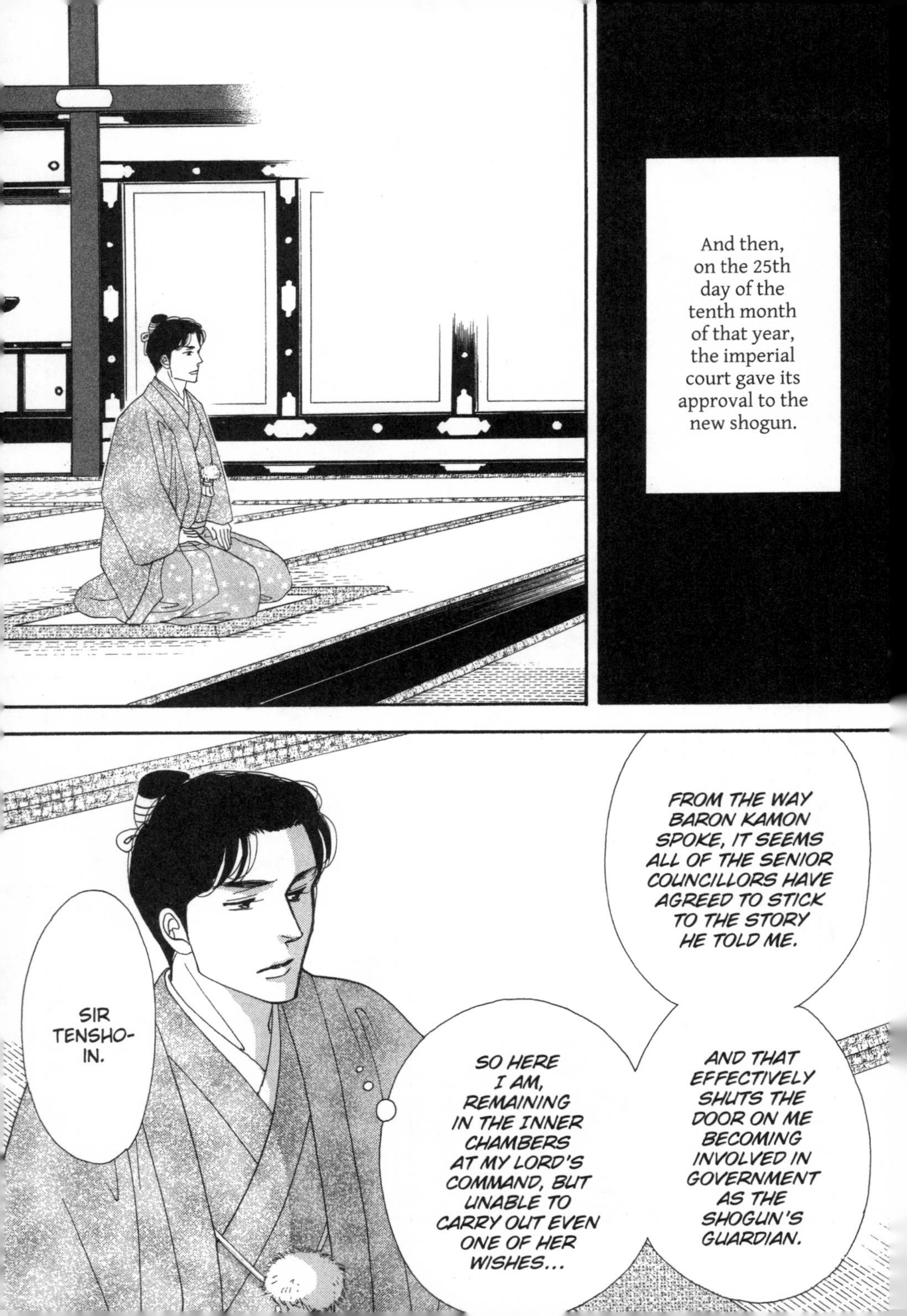
And then, on the 25th day of the tenth month of that year, the imperial court gave its approval to the new shogun.
FROM THE WAY BARON KAMON SPOKE, IT SEEMS ALL OF THE SENIOR COUNCILLORS HAVE AGREED TO STICK TO THE STORY HE TOLD ME.
AND THAT EFFECTIVELY SHUTS THE DOOR ON ME BECOMING INVOLVED IN GOVERNMENT AS THE SHOGUN'S GUARDIAN.
SO HERE I AM, REMAINING IN THE INNER CHAMBERS AT MY LORD'S COMMAND, BUT UNABLE TO CARRY OUT EVEN ONE OF HER WISHES...
SIR TENSHO-IN.

THE 14TH SHOGUN, LORD IEMOCHI, WILL MOMENTARILY ARRIVE TO GREET YOU.

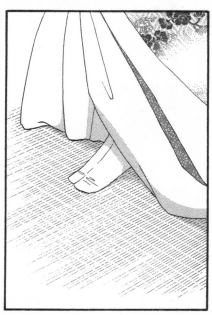

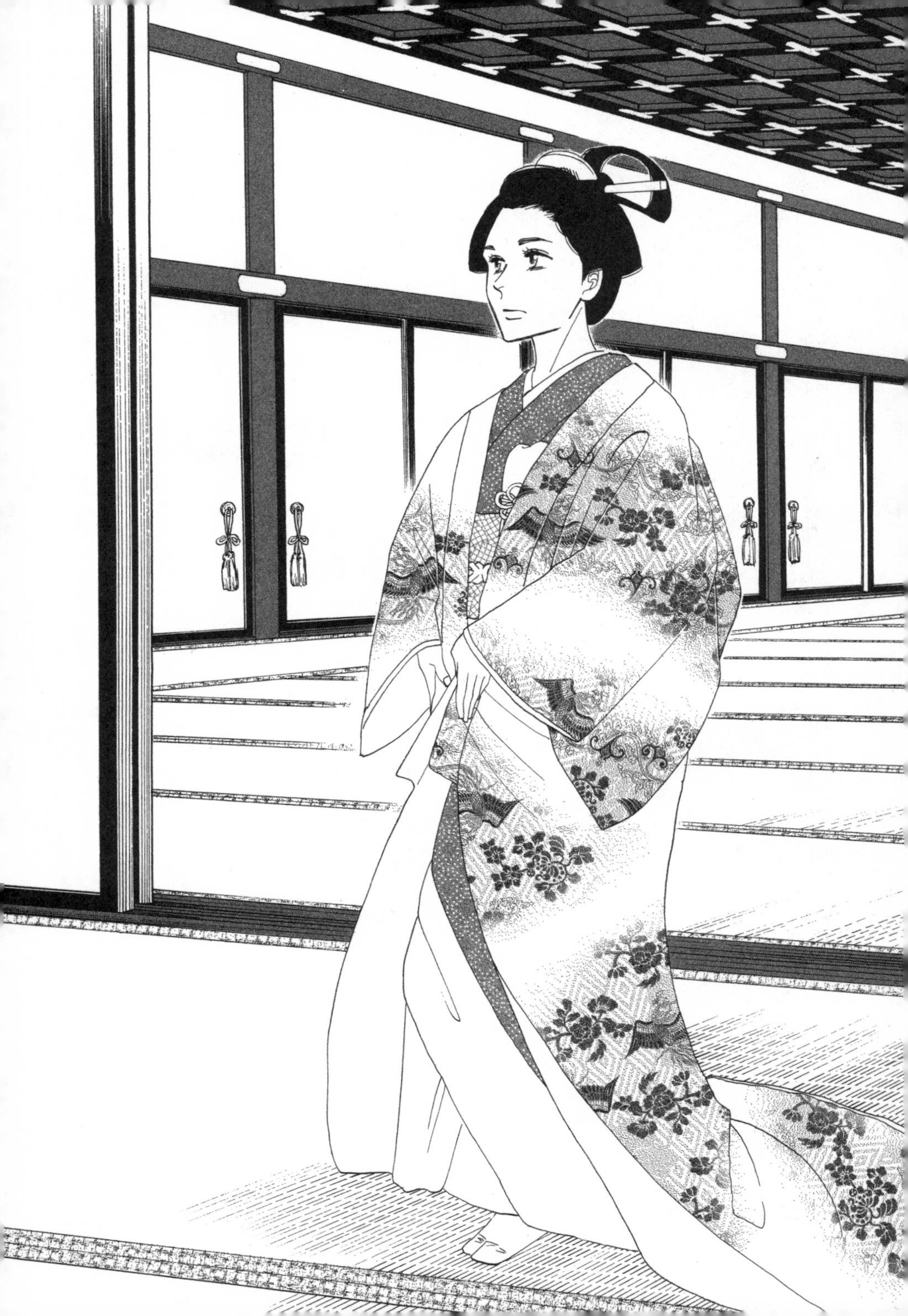

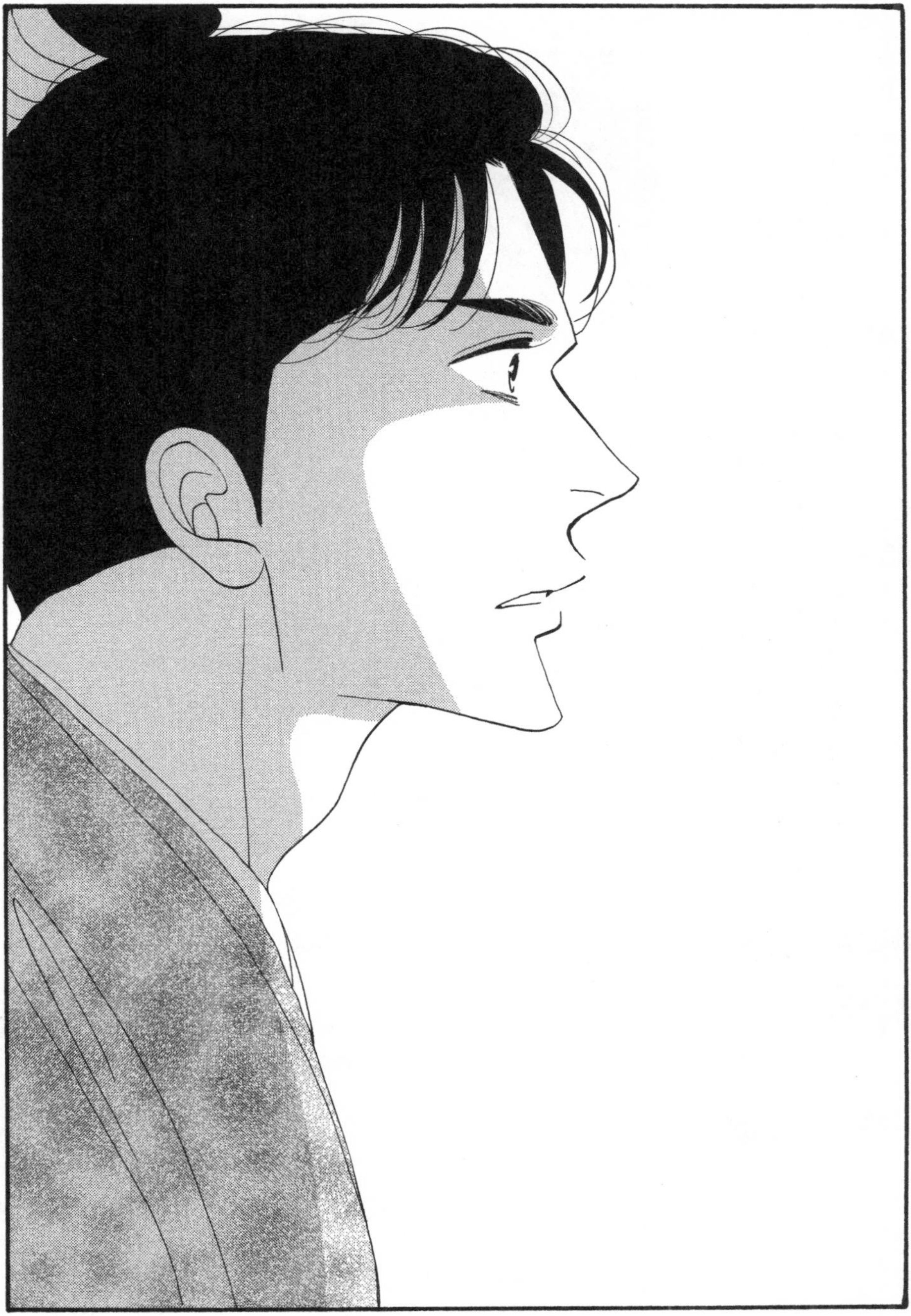

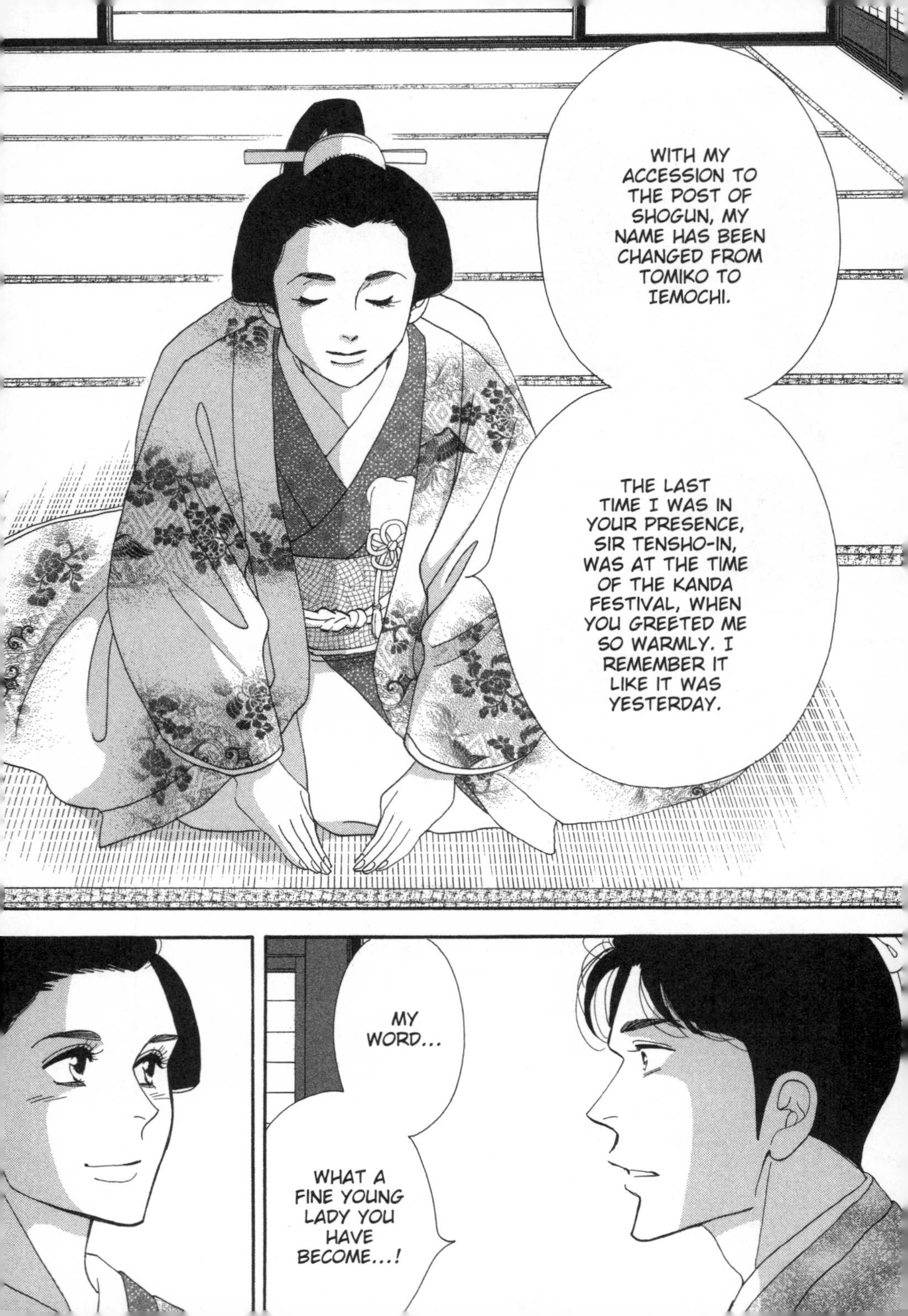
WITH MY ACCESSION TO THE POST OF SHOGUN, MY NAME HAS BEEN CHANGED FROM TOMIKO TO IEMOCHI.
THE LAST TIME I WAS IN YOUR PRESENCE, SIR TENSHO-IN, WAS AT THE TIME OF THE KANDA FESTIVAL, WHEN YOU GREETED ME SO WARMLY. I REMEMBER IT LIKE IT WAS YESTERDAY.
MY WORD...
WHAT A FINE YOUNG LADY YOU HAVE BECOME...!

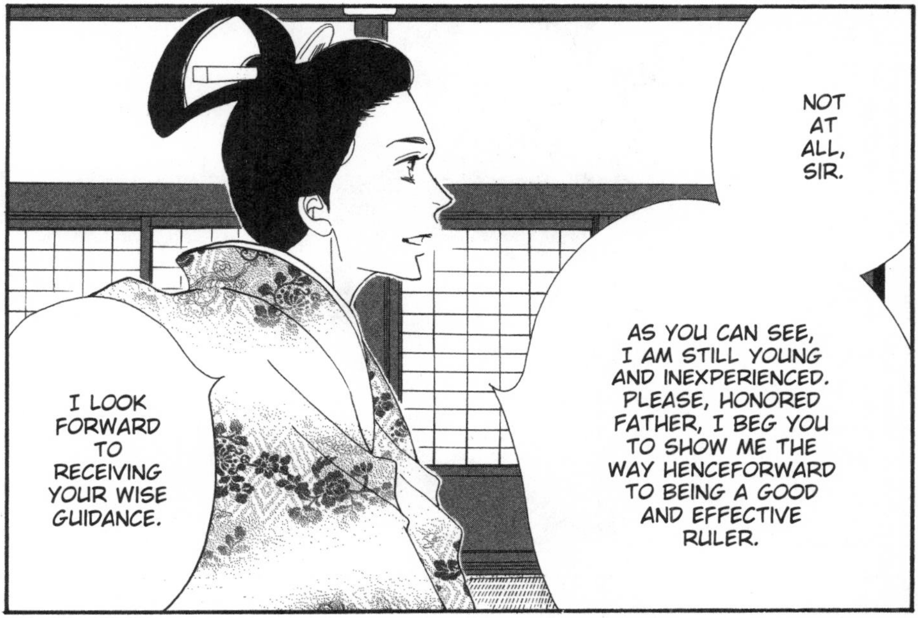
NOT AT ALL, SIR.
AS YOU CAN SEE, I AM STILL YOUNG AND INEXPERIENCED. PLEASE, HONORED FATHER, I BEG YOU TO SHOW ME THE WAY HENCEFORWARD TO BEING A GOOD AND EFFECTIVE RULER.
I LOOK FORWARD TO RECEIVING YOUR WISE GUIDANCE.

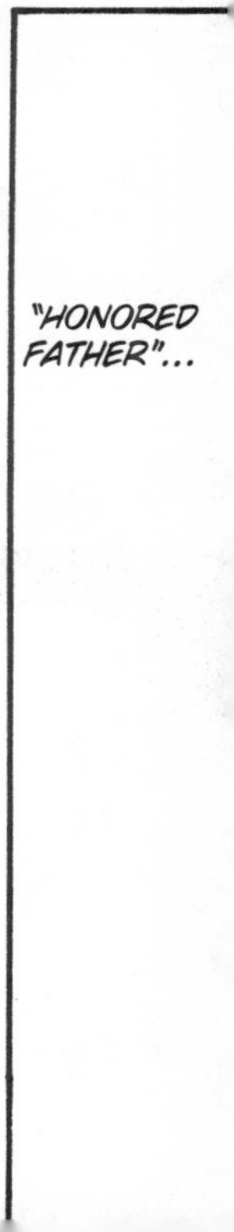
"HONORED FATHER"...

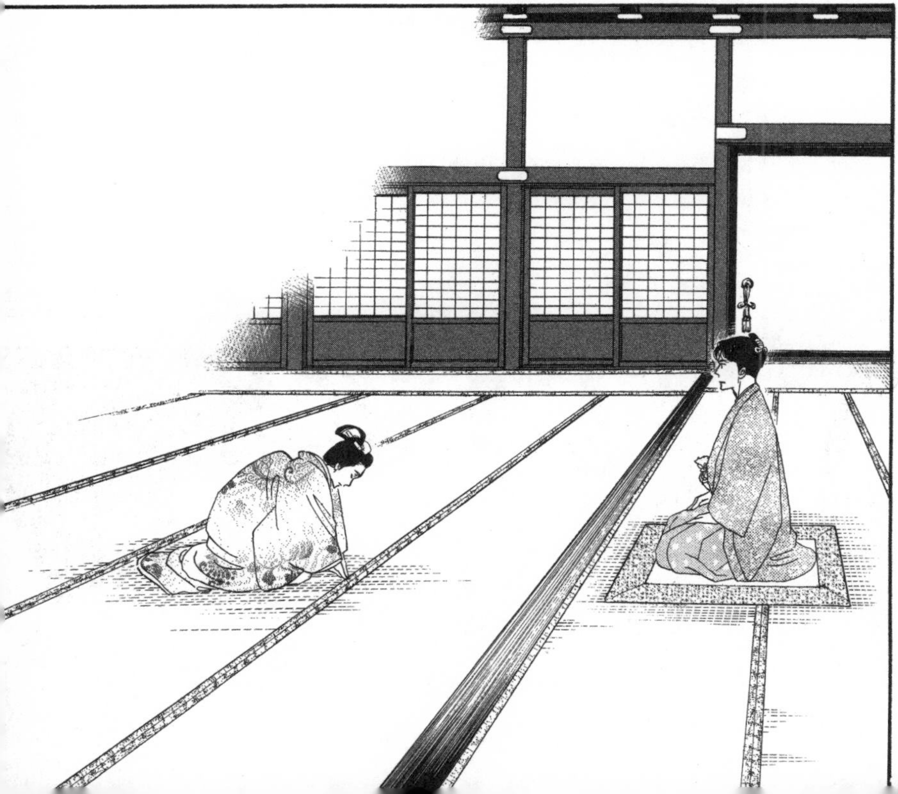

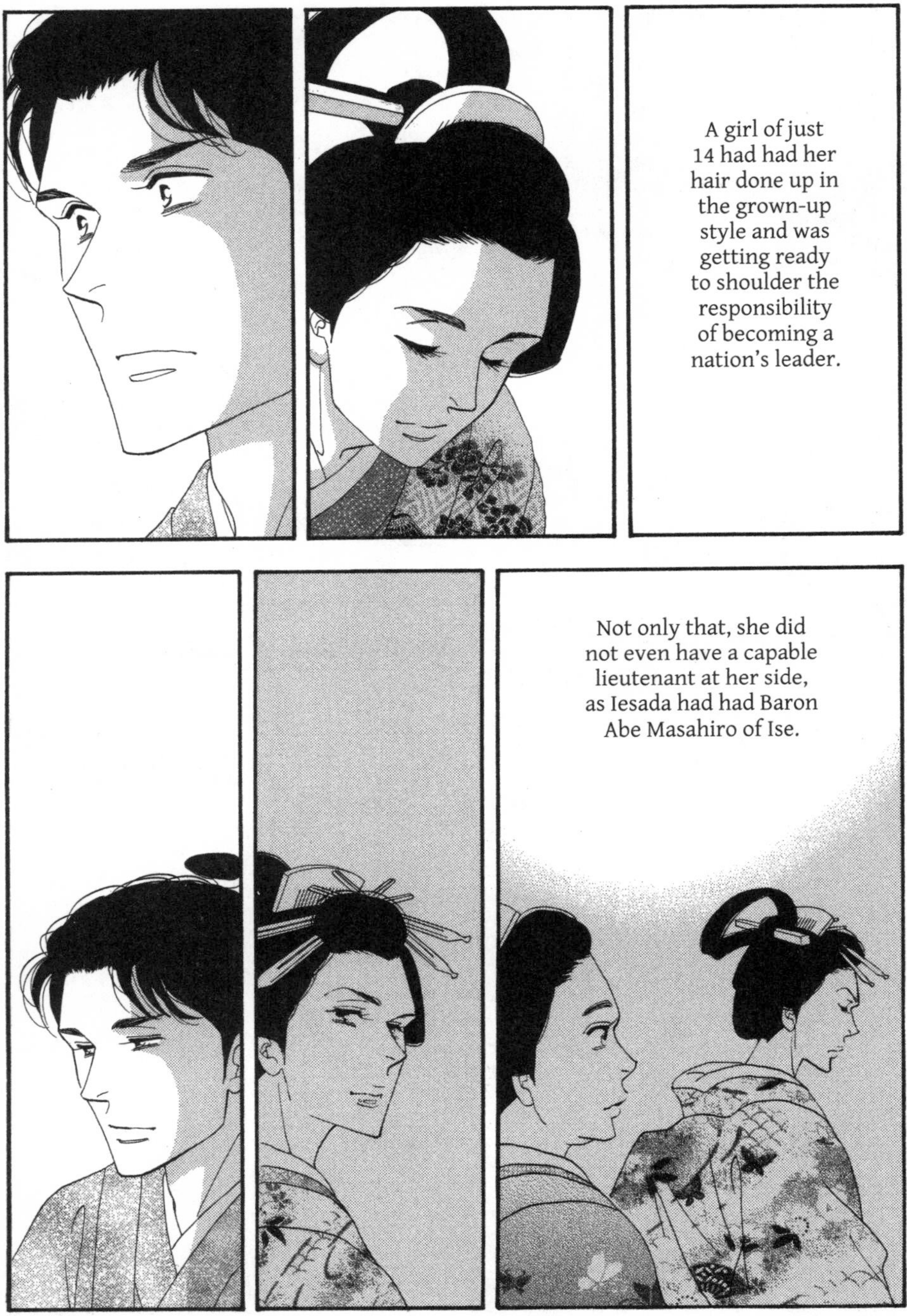
A girl of just 14 had had her hair done up in the grown-up style and was getting ready to shoulder the responsibility of becoming a nation's leader.
Not only that, she did not even have a capable lieutenant at her side, as Iesada had had Baron Abe Masahiro of Ise.

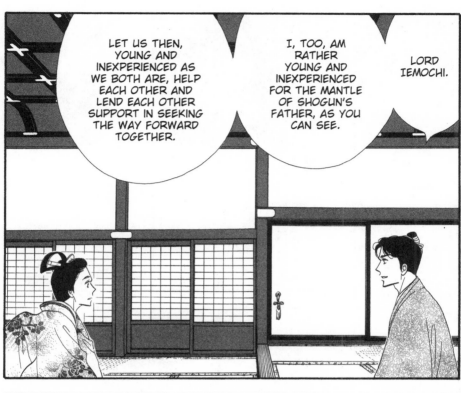

LORD IEMOCHI.
I, TOO, AM RATHER YOUNG AND INEXPERIENCED FOR THE MANTLE OF SHOGUN'S FATHER, AS YOU CAN SEE.
LET US THEN, YOUNG AND INEXPERIENCED AS WE BOTH ARE, HELP EACH OTHER AND LEND EACH OTHER SUPPORT IN SEEKING THE WAY FORWARD TOGETHER.
...
THE TRUTH IS I VERY MUCH WANTED TO SPEND MORE TIME TALKING TO YOU AND TO LORD IESADA THAT DAY OF THE KANDA FESTIVAL.
YES!
ALTHOUGH NOW IT WILL NEVER COME TRUE WITH LORD IESADA, HEARING SUCH KIND WORDS FROM YOU NOW, HONORED FATHER, MAKES ME TRULY HAPPY!

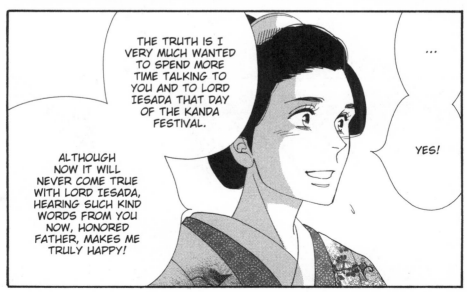

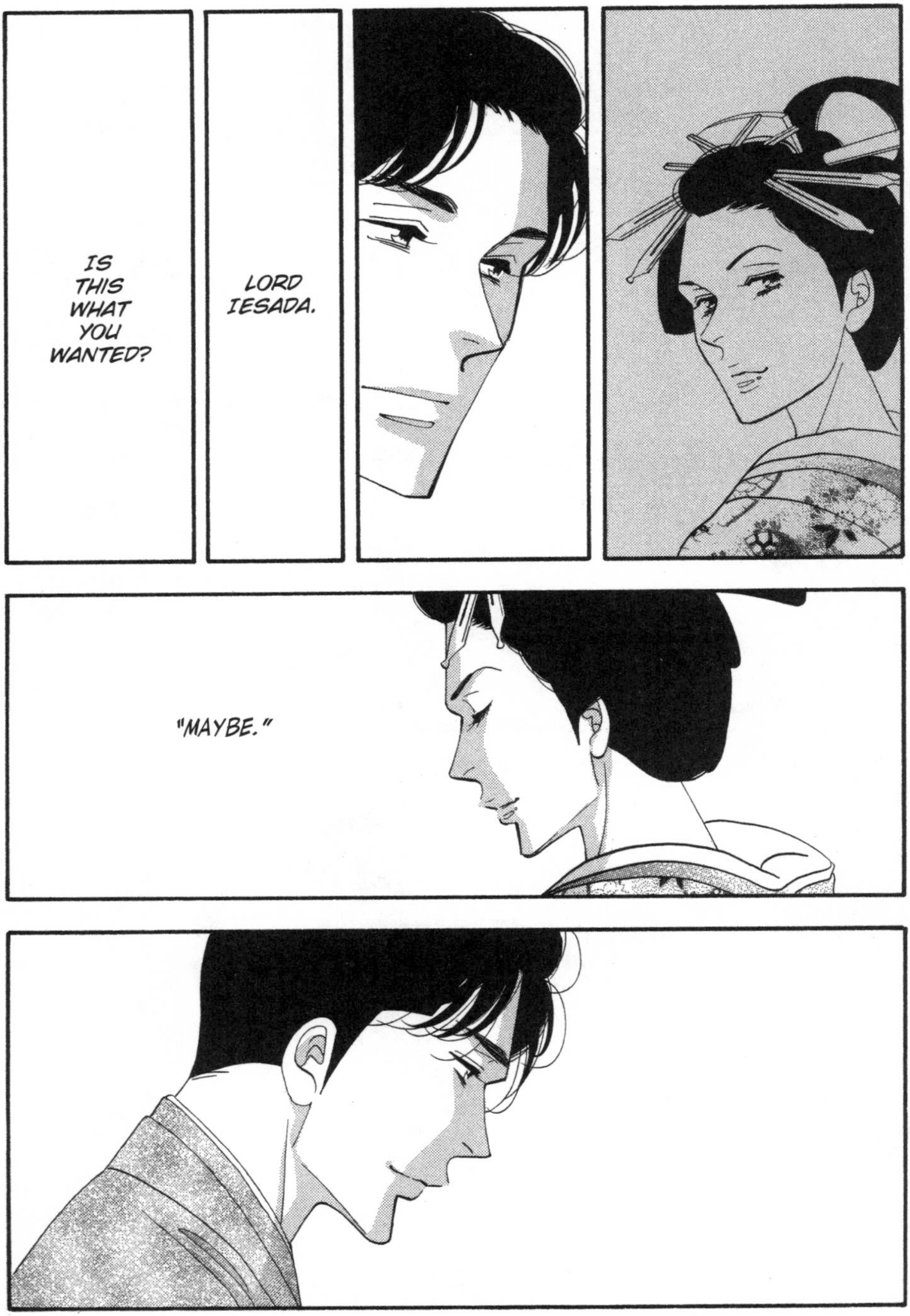
LORD IESADA.
IS THIS WHAT YOU WANTED?
"MAYBE."

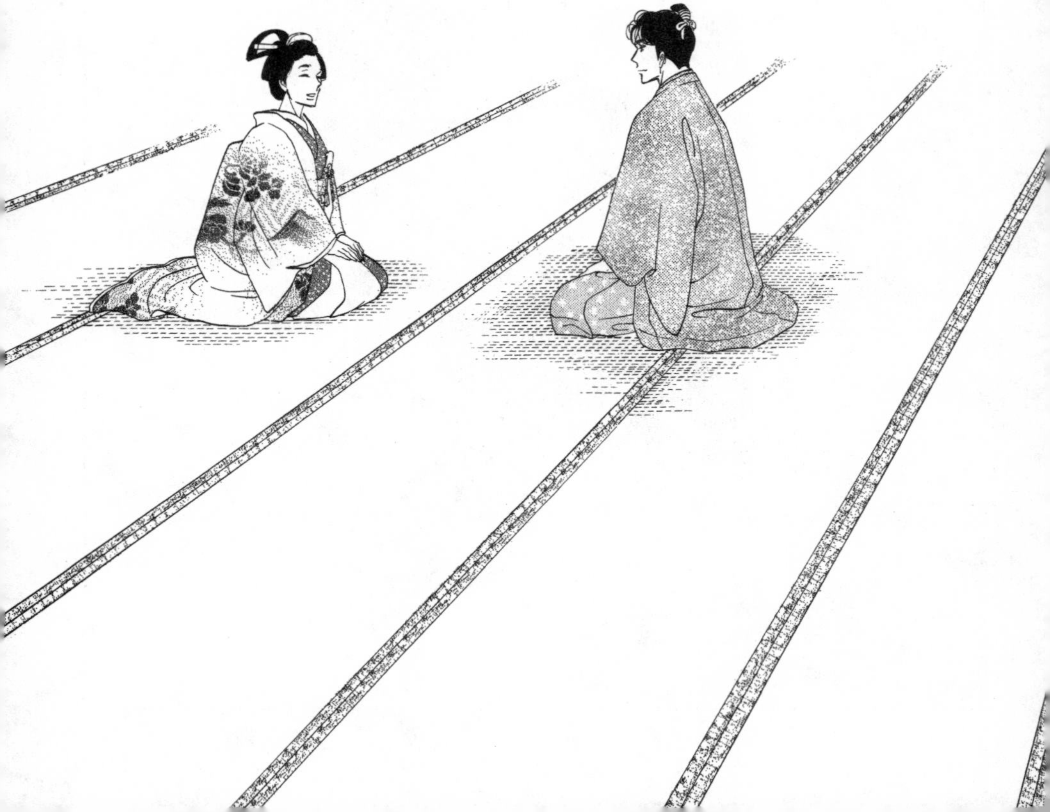

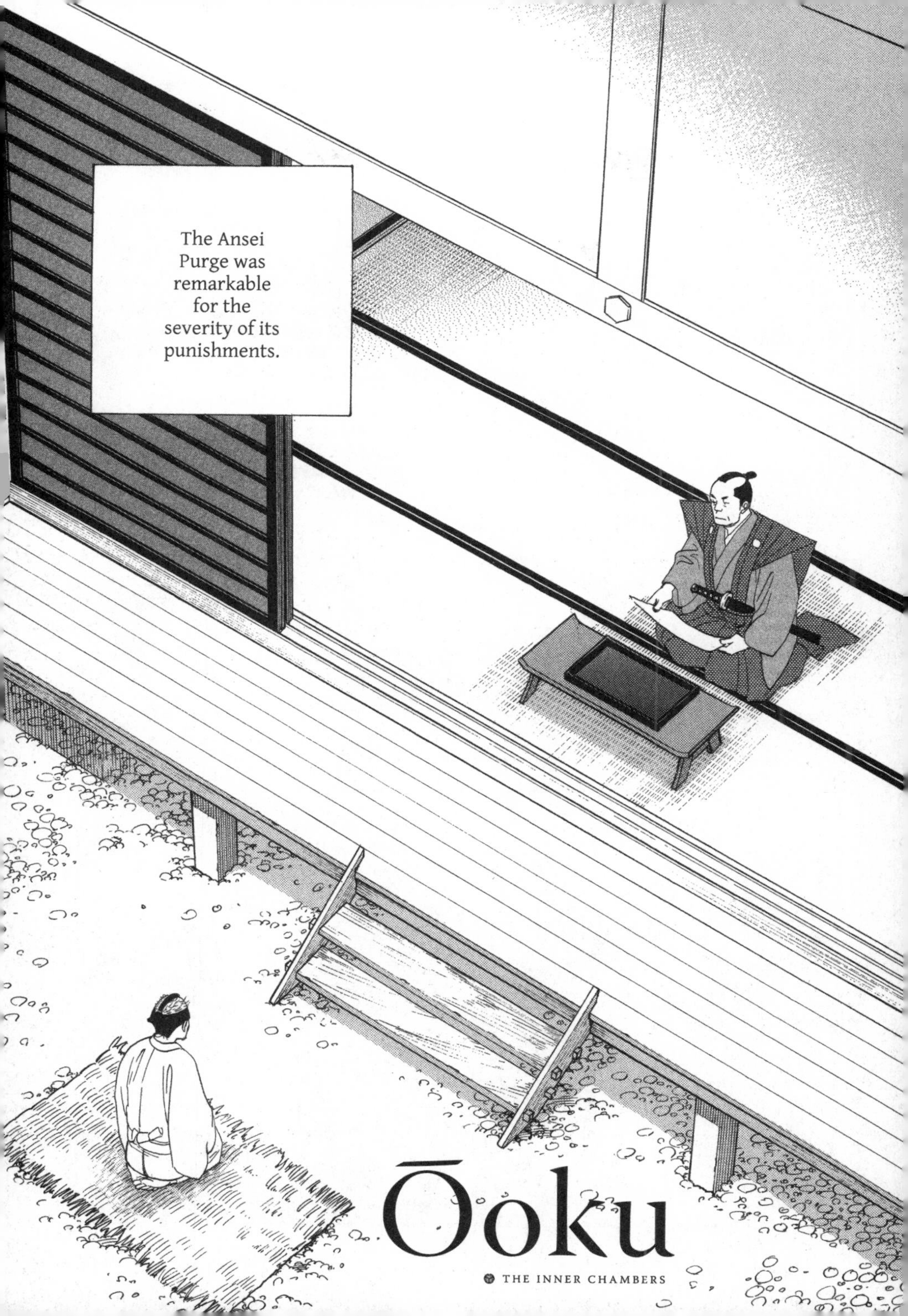
The Ansei Purge was remarkable for the severity of its punishments.
Ōoku
THE INNER CHAMBERS

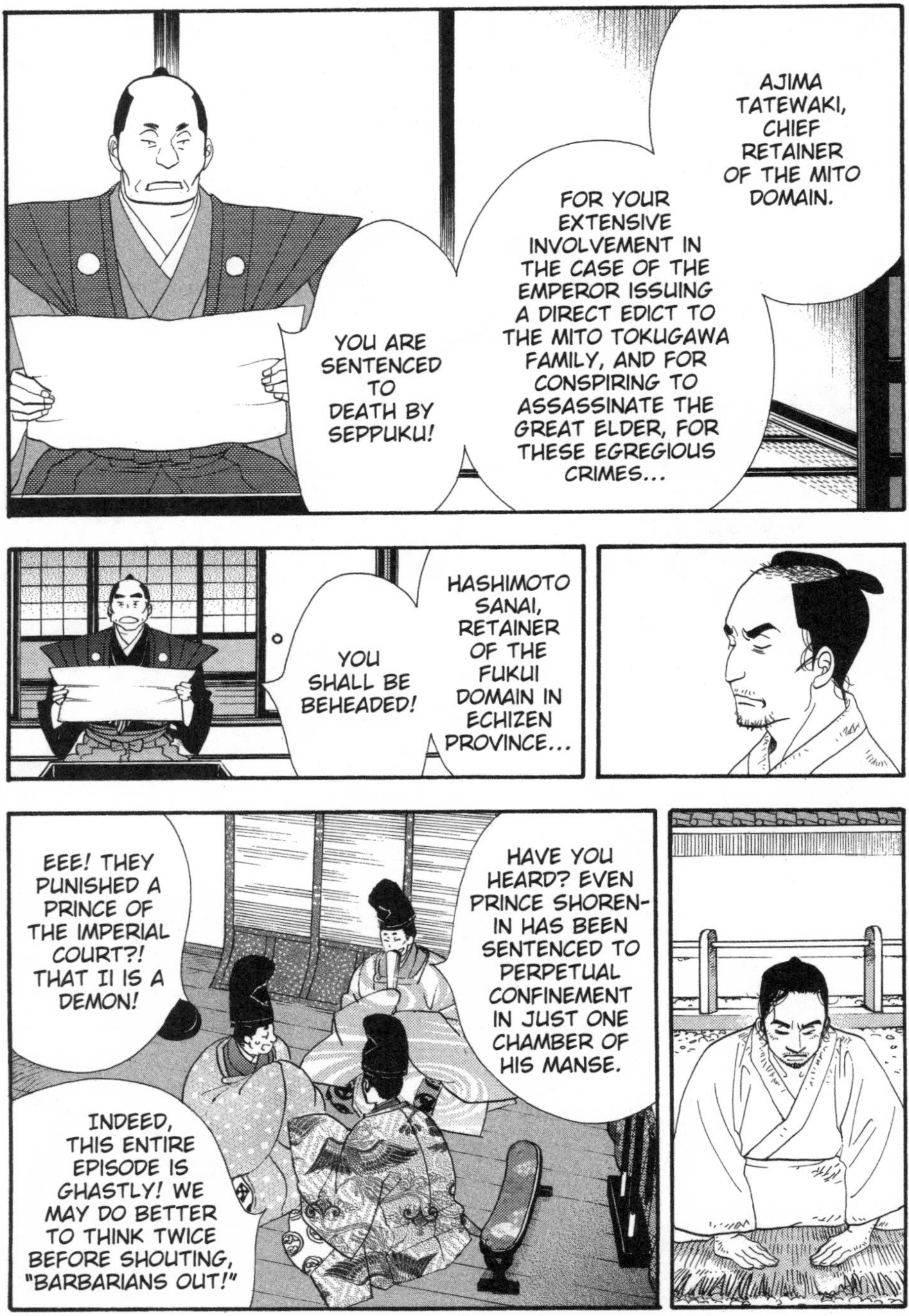
AJIMA TATEWAKI, CHIEF RETAINER OF THE MITO DOMAIN.
FOR YOUR EXTENSIVE INVOLVEMENT IN THE CASE OF THE EMPEROR ISSUING A DIRECT EDICT TO THE MITO TOKUGAWA FAMILY, AND FOR CONSPIRING TO ASSASSINATE THE GREAT ELDER, FOR THESE EGREGIOUS CRIMES...
YOU ARE SENTENCED TO DEATH BY SEPPUKU!
HASHIMOTO SANAI, RETAINER OF THE FUKUI DOMAIN IN ECHIZEN PROVINCE...
YOU SHALL BE BEHEADED!
HAVE YOU HEARD? EVEN PRINCE SHOREN-IN HAS BEEN SENTENCED TO PERPETUAL CONFINEMENT IN JUST ONE CHAMBER OF HIS MANSE.
EEE! THEY PUNISHED A PRINCE OF THE IMPERIAL COURT?! THAT II IS A DEMON!
INDEED, THIS ENTIRE EPISODE IS GHASTLY! WE MAY DO BETTER TO THINK TWICE BEFORE SHOUTING, "BARBARIANS OUT!"

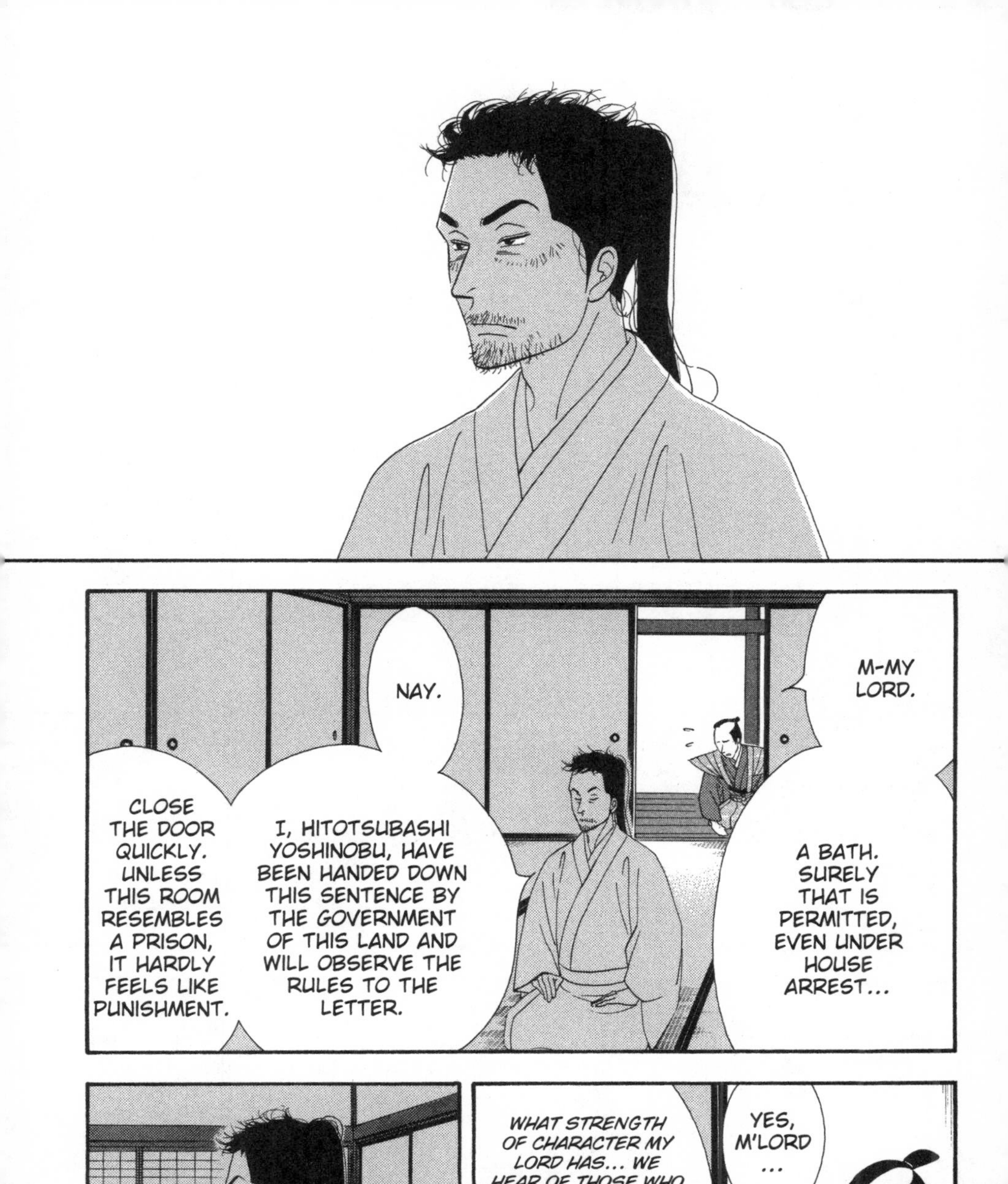
M-MY LORD.
A BATH. SURELY THAT IS PERMITTED, EVEN UNDER HOUSE ARREST...
NAY.
I, HITOTSUBASHI YOSHINOBU, HAVE BEEN HANDED DOWN THIS SENTENCE BY THE GOVERNMENT OF THIS LAND AND WILL OBSERVE THE RULES TO THE LETTER.
CLOSE THE DOOR QUICKLY. UNLESS THIS ROOM RESEMBLES A PRISON, IT HARDLY FEELS LIKE PUNISHMENT.
YES, M'LORD ...
WHAT STRENGTH OF CHARACTER MY LORD HAS... WE HEAR OF THOSE WHO KILL THEMSELVES IN RAGE WHILE UNDER HOUSE ARREST, AND YET HE REMAINS SO CALM, DAY AFTER DAY...!!

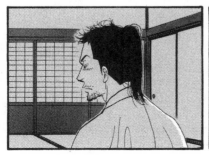

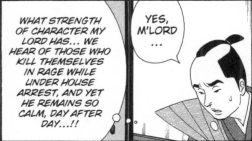

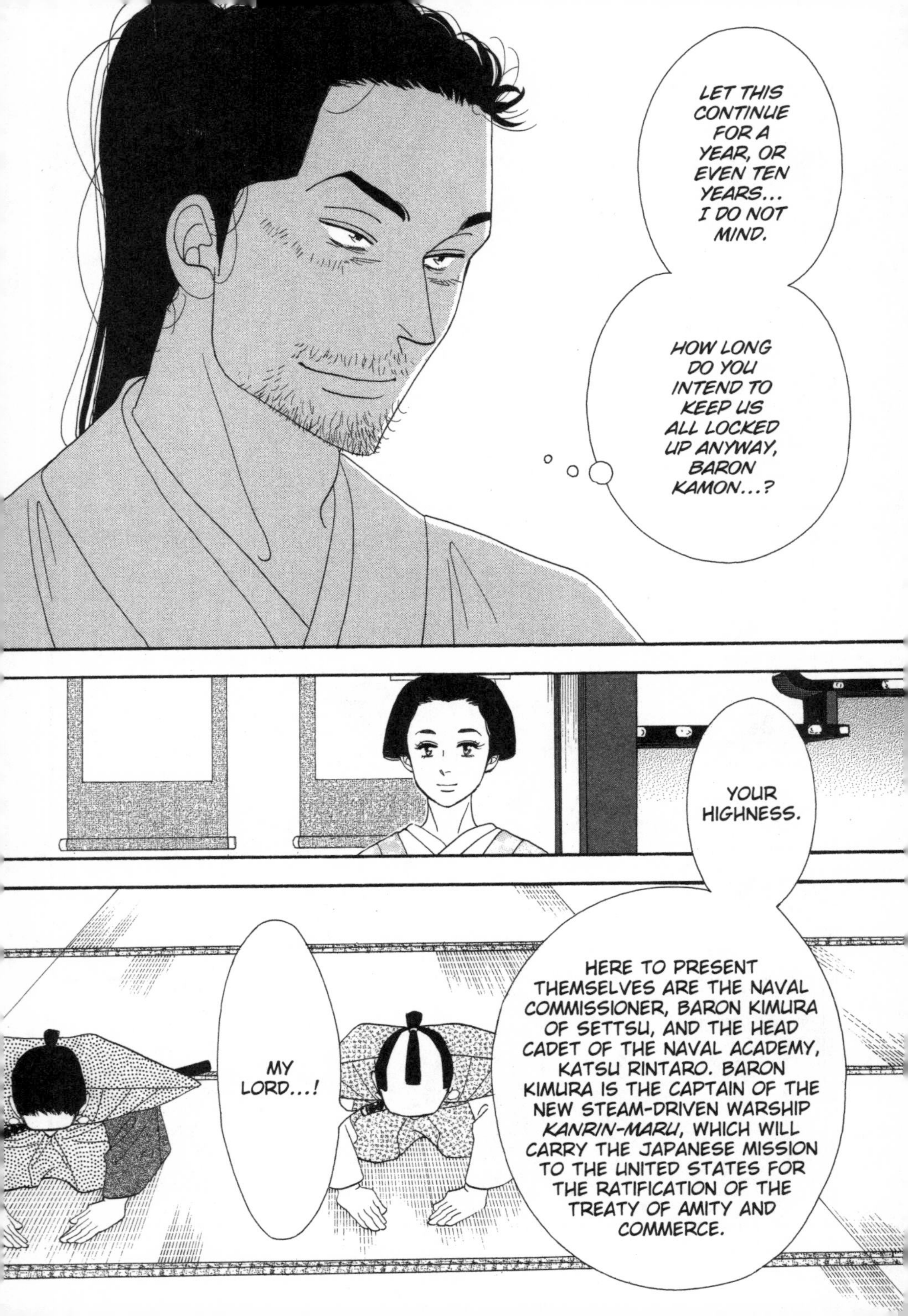
LET THIS CONTINUE FOR A YEAR, OR EVEN TEN YEARS... I DO NOT MIND.
HOW LONG DO YOU INTEND TO KEEP US ALL LOCKED UP ANYWAY, BARON KAMON...?
YOUR HIGHNESS.
HERE TO PRESENT THEMSELVES ARE THE NAVAL COMMISSIONER, BARON KIMURA OF SETTSU, AND THE HEAD CADET OF THE NAVAL ACADEMY, KATSU RINTARO. BARON KIMURA IS THE CAPTAIN OF THE NEW STEAM-DRIVEN WARSHIP *KANRIN-MARU*, WHICH WILL CARRY THE JAPANESE MISSION TO THE UNITED STATES FOR THE RATIFICATION OF THE TREATY OF AMITY AND COMMERCE.
MY LORD...!

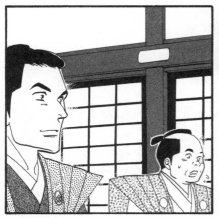

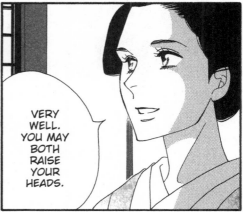

VERY WELL. YOU MAY BOTH RAISE YOUR HEADS.
YOU MUST BE VERY BUSY INDEED WITH MAKING YOUR PREPARATIONS FOR THIS LONG VOYAGE ACROSS THE OCEAN. I AM SORRY TO HAVE INTERRUPTED YOUR ACTIVITIES WITH THIS SUMMONS.
N-NOT AT ALL, MY LORD! IT IS A GREAT HONOR AND PRIVILEGE TO BE GRANTED SO INTIMATE AN AUDIENCE WITH YOUR HIGHNESS. WE ARE MOST GRATIFIED!
GOOD, GOOD. IT WAS MY WISH TO EXAMINE A MODEL OF THE *KANRIN-MARU*, AND THAT IS WHY YOU ARE HERE TODAY. LET US DISPENSE WITH THE FORMALITIES AND BEGIN.

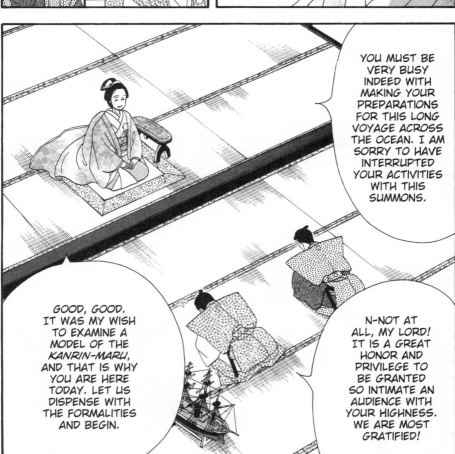

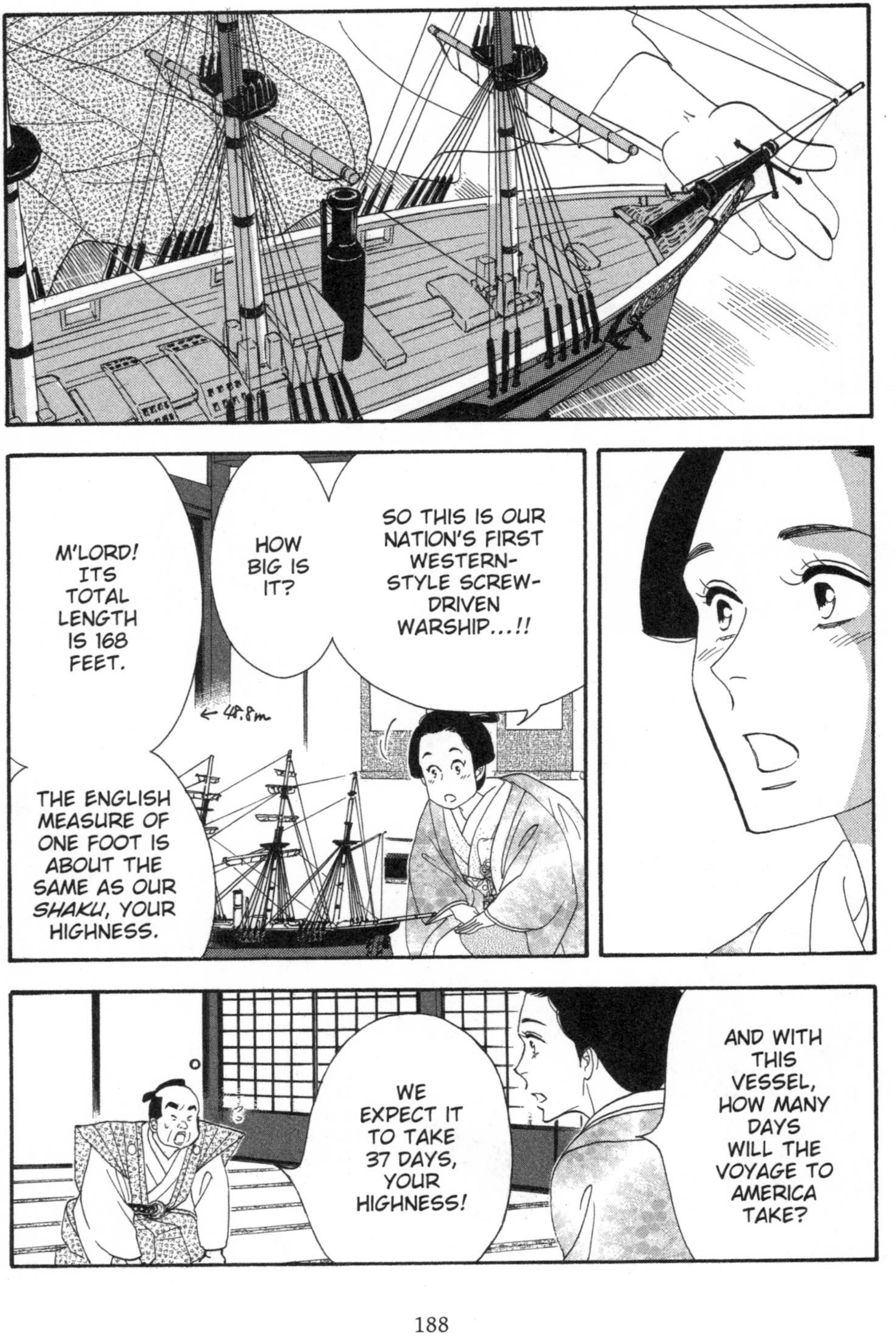
SO THIS IS OUR NATION'S FIRST WESTERN-STYLE SCREW-DRIVEN WARSHIP...!!
HOW BIG IS IT?
M'LORD! ITS TOTAL LENGTH IS 168 FEET.
← 48.8m
THE ENGLISH MEASURE OF ONE FOOT IS ABOUT THE SAME AS OUR *SHAKU*, YOUR HIGHNESS.
AND WITH THIS VESSEL, HOW MANY DAYS WILL THE VOYAGE TO AMERICA TAKE?
WE EXPECT IT TO TAKE 37 DAYS, YOUR HIGHNESS!

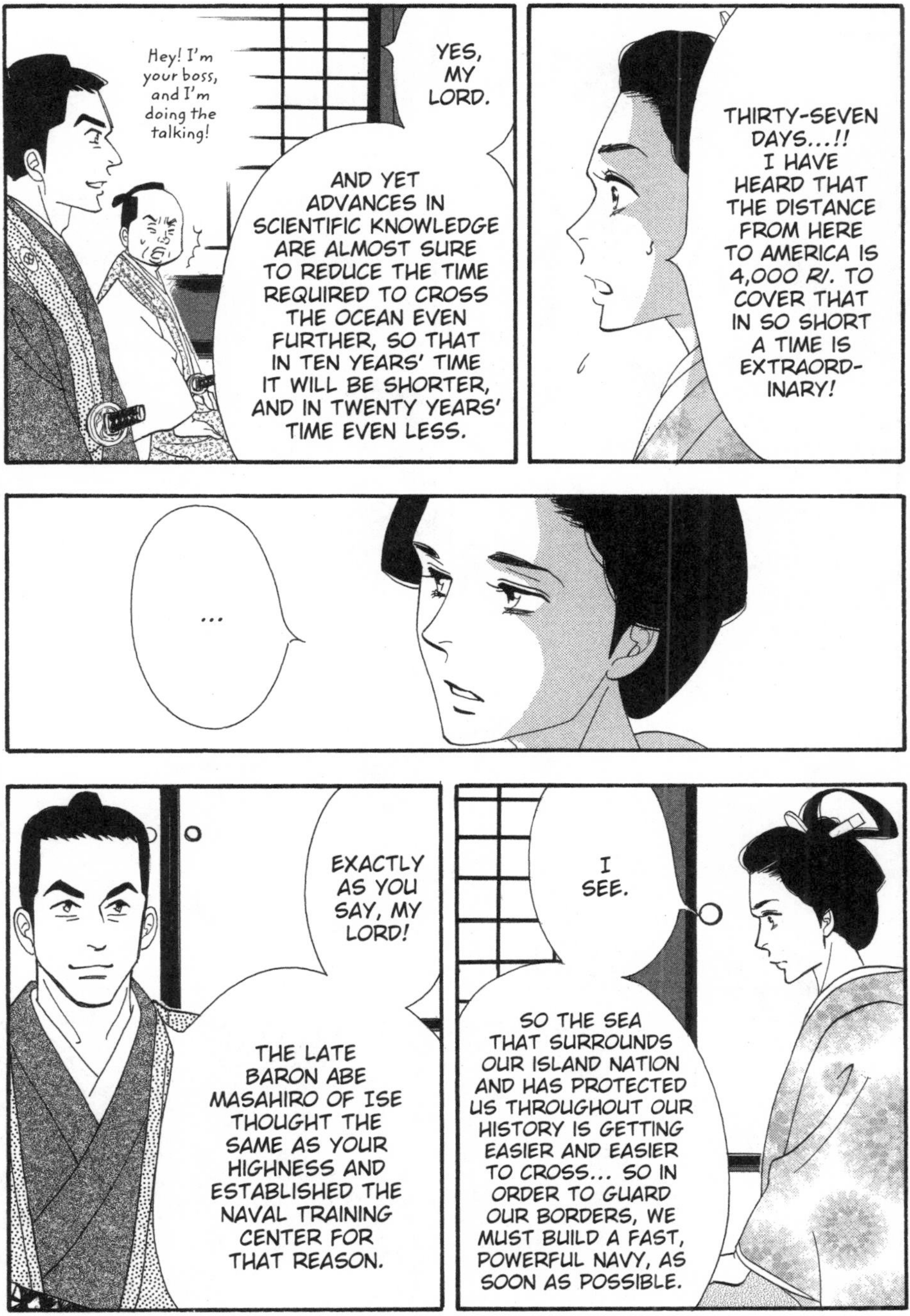
THIRTY-SEVEN DAYS...!! I HAVE HEARD THAT THE DISTANCE FROM HERE TO AMERICA IS 4,000 *RI*. TO COVER THAT IN SO SHORT A TIME IS EXTRAORD-INARY!
YES, MY LORD.
Hey! I'm your boss, and I'm doing the talking!
AND YET ADVANCES IN SCIENTIFIC KNOWLEDGE ARE ALMOST SURE TO REDUCE THE TIME REQUIRED TO CROSS THE OCEAN EVEN FURTHER, SO THAT IN TEN YEARS' TIME IT WILL BE SHORTER, AND IN TWENTY YEARS' TIME EVEN LESS.
...
I SEE.
SO THE SEA THAT SURROUNDS OUR ISLAND NATION AND HAS PROTECTED US THROUGHOUT OUR HISTORY IS GETTING EASIER AND EASIER TO CROSS... SO IN ORDER TO GUARD OUR BORDERS, WE MUST BUILD A FAST, POWERFUL NAVY, AS SOON AS POSSIBLE.
EXACTLY AS YOU SAY, MY LORD!
THE LATE BARON ABE MASAHIRO OF ISE THOUGHT THE SAME AS YOUR HIGHNESS AND ESTABLISHED THE NAVAL TRAINING CENTER FOR THAT REASON.

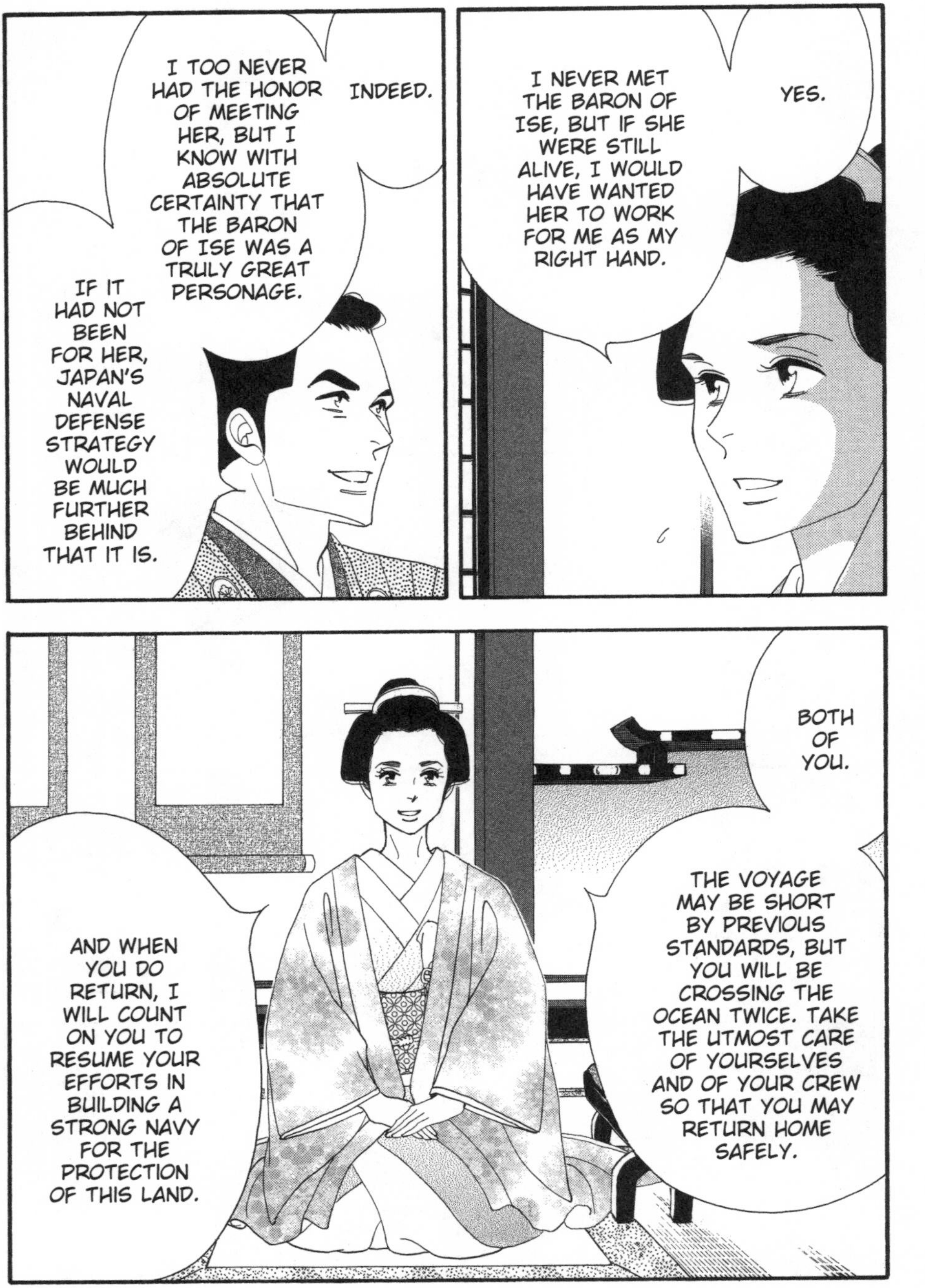
YES.
I NEVER MET THE BARON OF ISE, BUT IF SHE WERE STILL ALIVE, I WOULD HAVE WANTED HER TO WORK FOR ME AS MY RIGHT HAND.
INDEED.
I TOO NEVER HAD THE HONOR OF MEETING HER, BUT I KNOW WITH ABSOLUTE CERTAINTY THAT THE BARON OF ISE WAS A TRULY GREAT PERSONAGE.
IF IT HAD NOT BEEN FOR HER, JAPAN'S NAVAL DEFENSE STRATEGY WOULD BE MUCH FURTHER BEHIND THAT IT IS.
BOTH OF YOU.
THE VOYAGE MAY BE SHORT BY PREVIOUS STANDARDS, BUT YOU WILL BE CROSSING THE OCEAN TWICE. TAKE THE UTMOST CARE OF YOURSELVES AND OF YOUR CREW SO THAT YOU MAY RETURN HOME SAFELY.
AND WHEN YOU DO RETURN, I WILL COUNT ON YOU TO RESUME YOUR EFFORTS IN BUILDING A STRONG NAVY FOR THE PROTECTION OF THIS LAND.

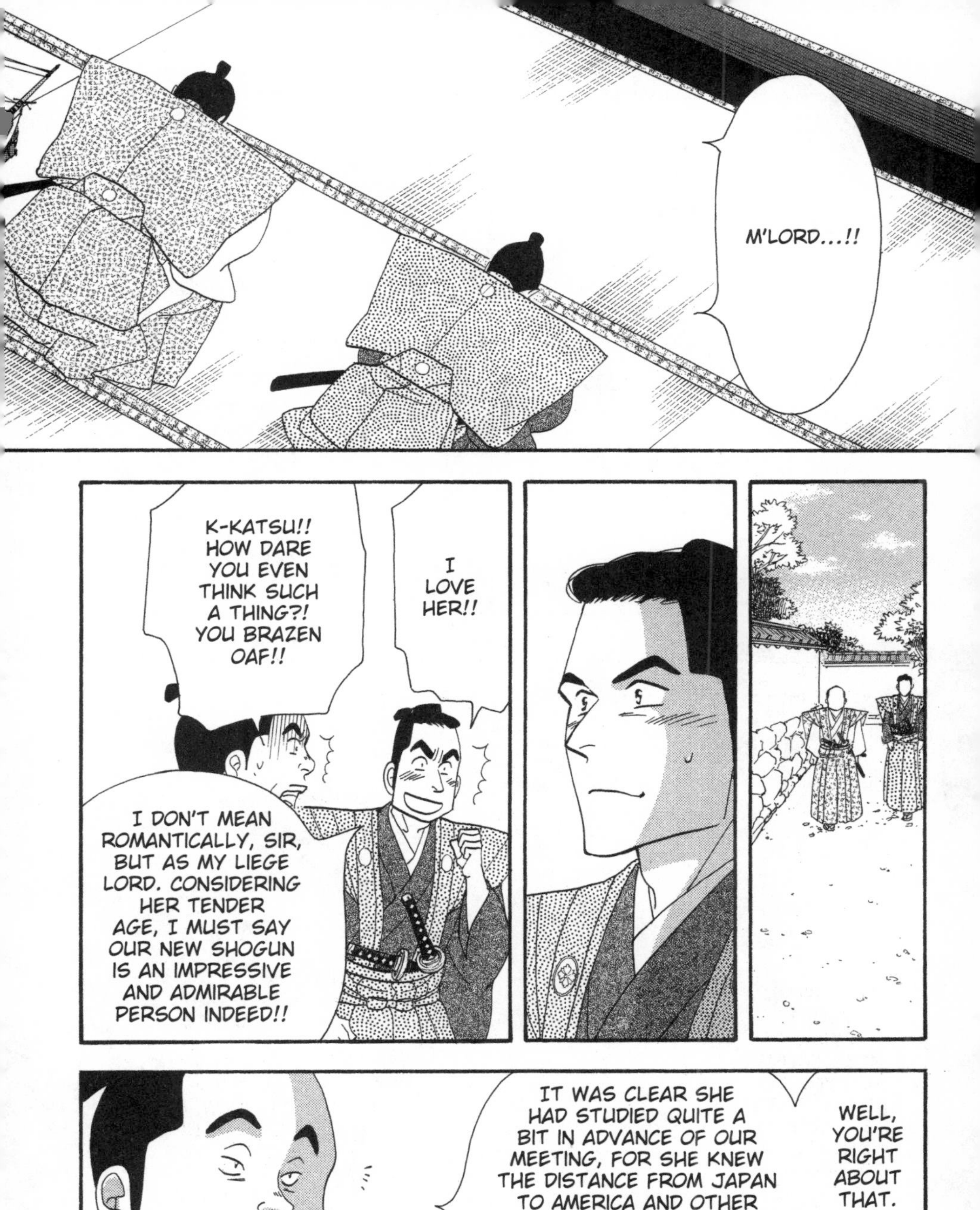
M'LORD...!!
I LOVE HER!!
K-KATSU!! HOW DARE YOU EVEN THINK SUCH A THING?! YOU BRAZEN OAF!!
I DON'T MEAN ROMANTICALLY, SIR, BUT AS MY LIEGE LORD. CONSIDERING HER TENDER AGE, I MUST SAY OUR NEW SHOGUN IS AN IMPRESSIVE AND ADMIRABLE PERSON INDEED!!
WELL, YOU'RE RIGHT ABOUT THAT.
IT WAS CLEAR SHE HAD STUDIED QUITE A BIT IN ADVANCE OF OUR MEETING, FOR SHE KNEW THE DISTANCE FROM JAPAN TO AMERICA AND OTHER THINGS AS WELL. AND HER VIEWS ON MARITIME DEFENSE WERE VERY SENSIBLE INDEED.

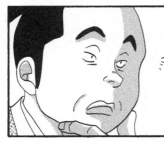

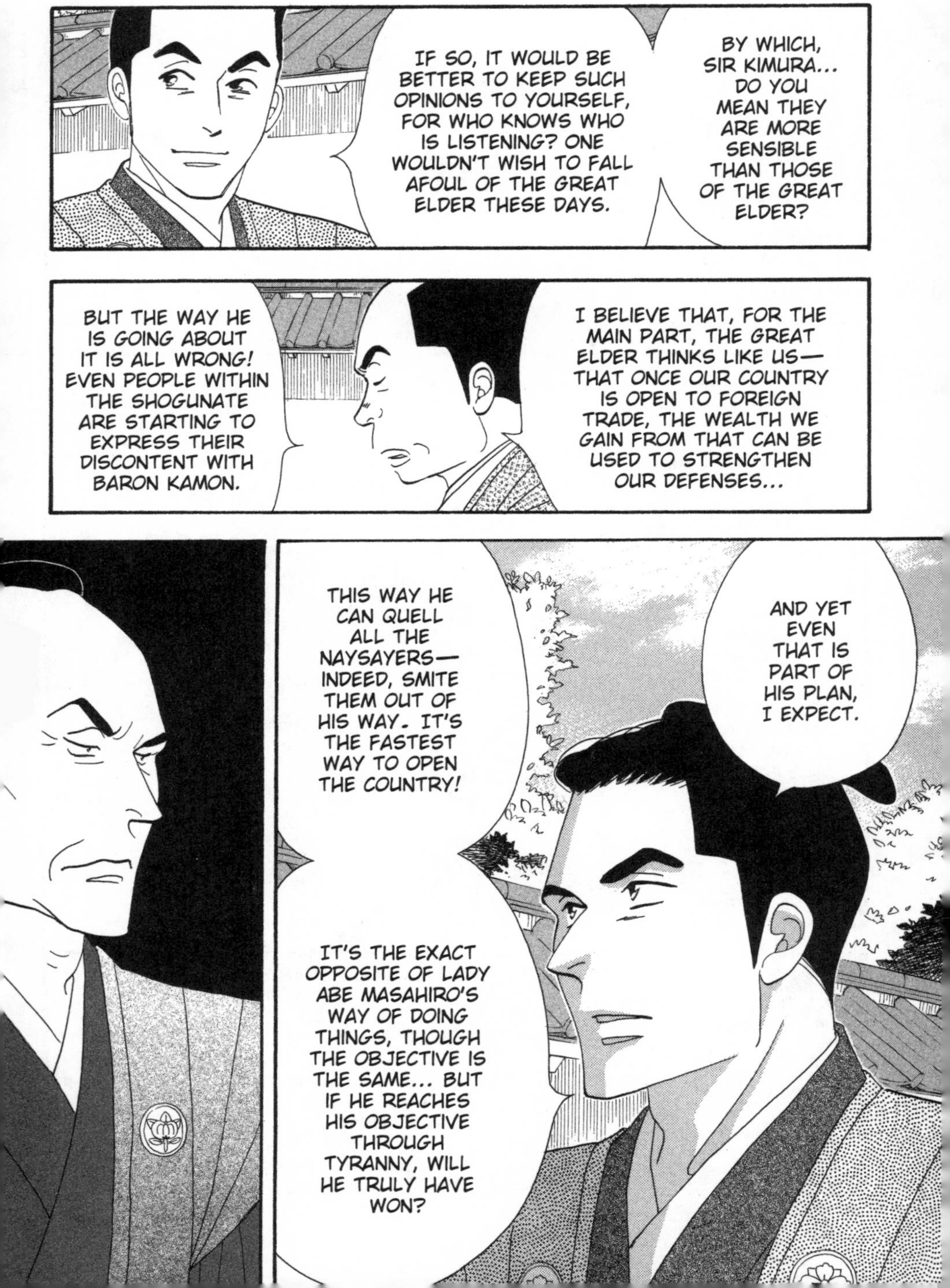
BY WHICH, SIR KIMURA... DO YOU MEAN THEY ARE MORE SENSIBLE THAN THOSE OF THE GREAT ELDER?
IF SO, IT WOULD BE BETTER TO KEEP SUCH OPINIONS TO YOURSELF, FOR WHO KNOWS WHO IS LISTENING? ONE WOULDN'T WISH TO FALL AFOUL OF THE GREAT ELDER THESE DAYS.
I BELIEVE THAT, FOR THE MAIN PART, THE GREAT ELDER THINKS LIKE US—THAT ONCE OUR COUNTRY IS OPEN TO FOREIGN TRADE, THE WEALTH WE GAIN FROM THAT CAN BE USED TO STRENGTHEN OUR DEFENSES...
BUT THE WAY HE IS GOING ABOUT IT IS ALL WRONG! EVEN PEOPLE WITHIN THE SHOGUNATE ARE STARTING TO EXPRESS THEIR DISCONTENT WITH BARON KAMON.
AND YET EVEN THAT IS PART OF HIS PLAN, I EXPECT.
THIS WAY HE CAN QUELL ALL THE NAYSAYERS—INDEED, SMITE THEM OUT OF HIS WAY. IT'S THE FASTEST WAY TO OPEN THE COUNTRY!
IT'S THE EXACT OPPOSITE OF LADY ABE MASAHIRO'S WAY OF DOING THINGS, THOUGH THE OBJECTIVE IS THE SAME... BUT IF HE REACHES HIS OBJECTIVE THROUGH TYRANNY, WILL HE TRULY HAVE WON?

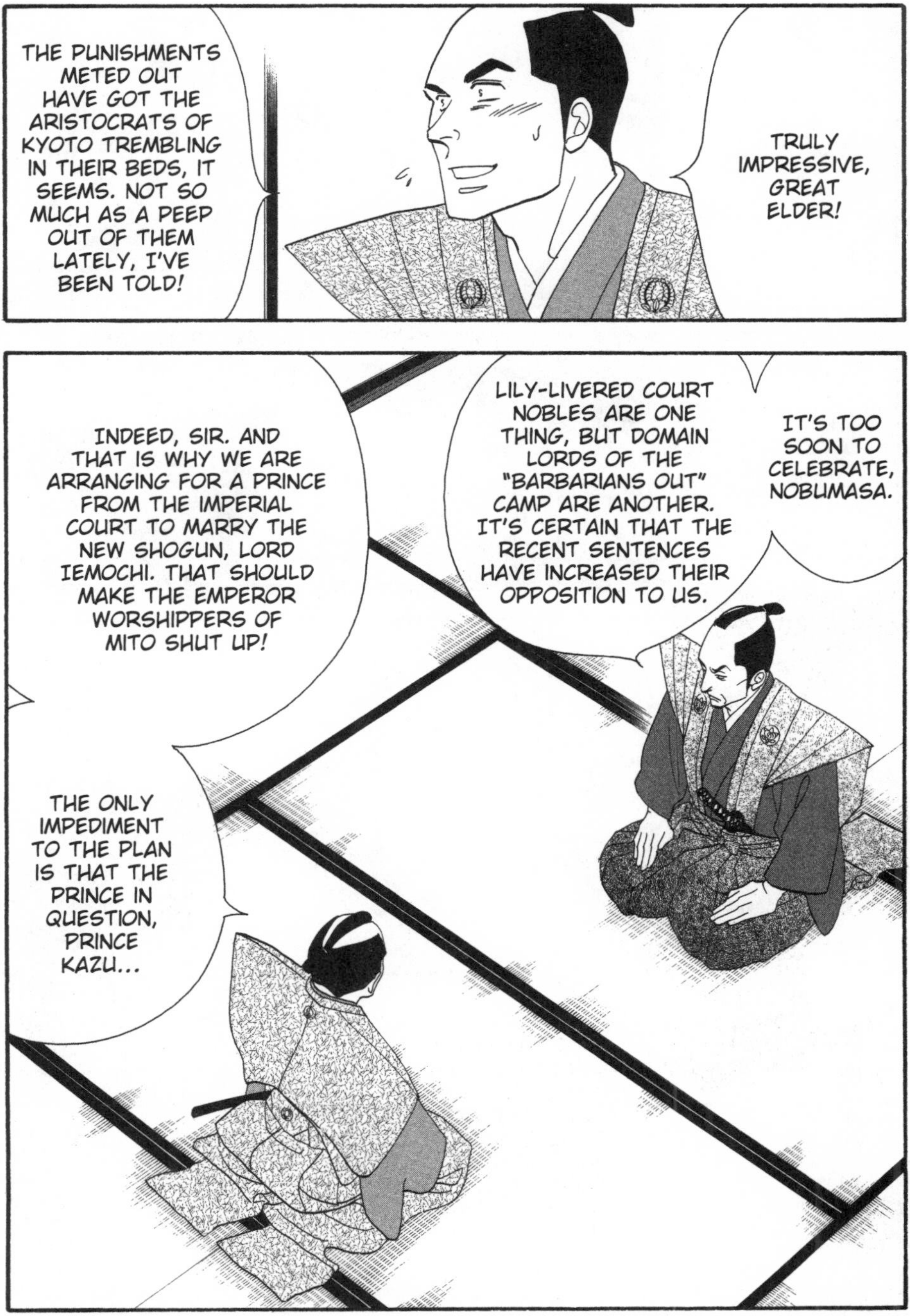
TRULY IMPRESSIVE, GREAT ELDER!
THE PUNISHMENTS METED OUT HAVE GOT THE ARISTOCRATS OF KYOTO TREMBLING IN THEIR BEDS, IT SEEMS. NOT SO MUCH AS A PEEP OUT OF THEM LATELY, I'VE BEEN TOLD!
IT'S TOO SOON TO CELEBRATE, NOBUMASA.
LILY-LIVERED COURT NOBLES ARE ONE THING, BUT DOMAIN LORDS OF THE "BARBARIANS OUT" CAMP ARE ANOTHER. IT'S CERTAIN THAT THE RECENT SENTENCES HAVE INCREASED THEIR OPPOSITION TO US.
INDEED, SIR. AND THAT IS WHY WE ARE ARRANGING FOR A PRINCE FROM THE IMPERIAL COURT TO MARRY THE NEW SHOGUN, LORD IEMOCHI. THAT SHOULD MAKE THE EMPEROR WORSHIPPERS OF MITO SHUT UP!
THE ONLY IMPEDIMENT TO THE PLAN IS THAT THE PRINCE IN QUESTION, PRINCE KAZU...

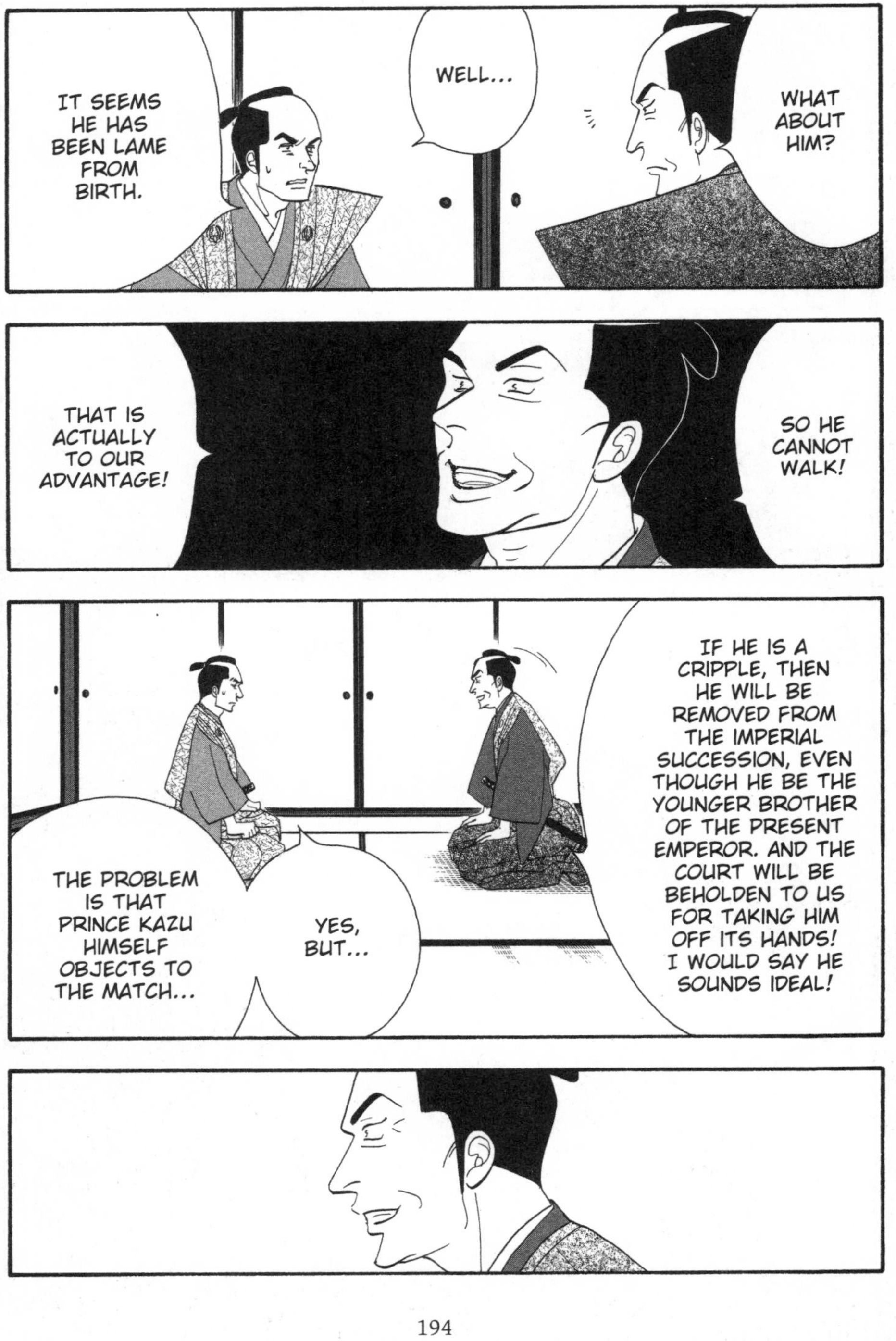
WHAT ABOUT HIM?
WELL...
IT SEEMS HE HAS BEEN LAME FROM BIRTH.
SO HE CANNOT WALK!
THAT IS ACTUALLY TO OUR ADVANTAGE!
IF HE IS A CRIPPLE, THEN HE WILL BE REMOVED FROM THE IMPERIAL SUCCESSION, EVEN THOUGH HE BE THE YOUNGER BROTHER OF THE PRESENT EMPEROR. AND THE COURT WILL BE BEHOLDEN TO US FOR TAKING HIM OFF ITS HANDS! I WOULD SAY HE SOUNDS IDEAL!
YES, BUT...
THE PROBLEM IS THAT PRINCE KAZU HIMSELF OBJECTS TO THE MATCH...

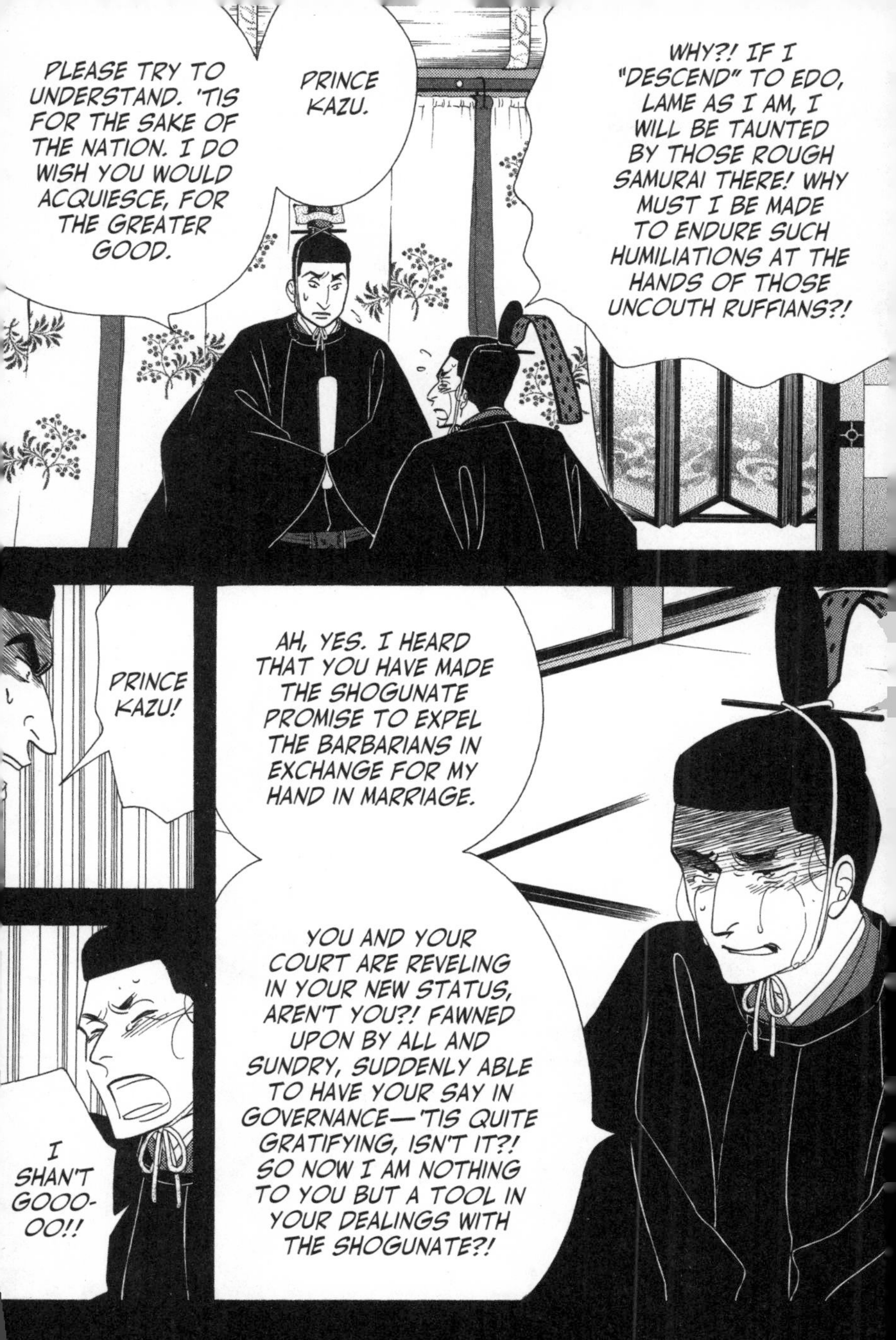
WHY?! IF I "DESCEND" TO EDO, LAME AS I AM, I WILL BE TAUNTED BY THOSE ROUGH SAMURAI THERE! WHY MUST I BE MADE TO ENDURE SUCH HUMILIATIONS AT THE HANDS OF THOSE UNCOUTH RUFFIANS?!
PRINCE KAZU.
PLEASE TRY TO UNDERSTAND. 'TIS FOR THE SAKE OF THE NATION. I DO WISH YOU WOULD ACQUIESCE, FOR THE GREATER GOOD.
AH, YES. I HEARD THAT YOU HAVE MADE THE SHOGUNATE PROMISE TO EXPEL THE BARBARIANS IN EXCHANGE FOR MY HAND IN MARRIAGE.
YOU AND YOUR COURT ARE REVELING IN YOUR NEW STATUS, AREN'T YOU?! FAWNED UPON BY ALL AND SUNDRY, SUDDENLY ABLE TO HAVE YOUR SAY IN GOVERNANCE—'TIS QUITE GRATIFYING, ISN'T IT?! SO NOW I AM NOTHING TO YOU BUT A TOOL IN YOUR DEALINGS WITH THE SHOGUNATE?!
PRINCE KAZU!
I SHAN'T GOOOO-OO!!

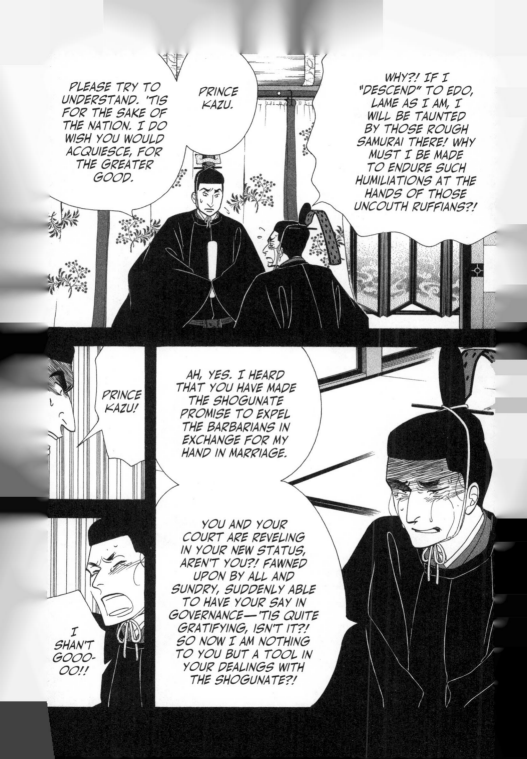

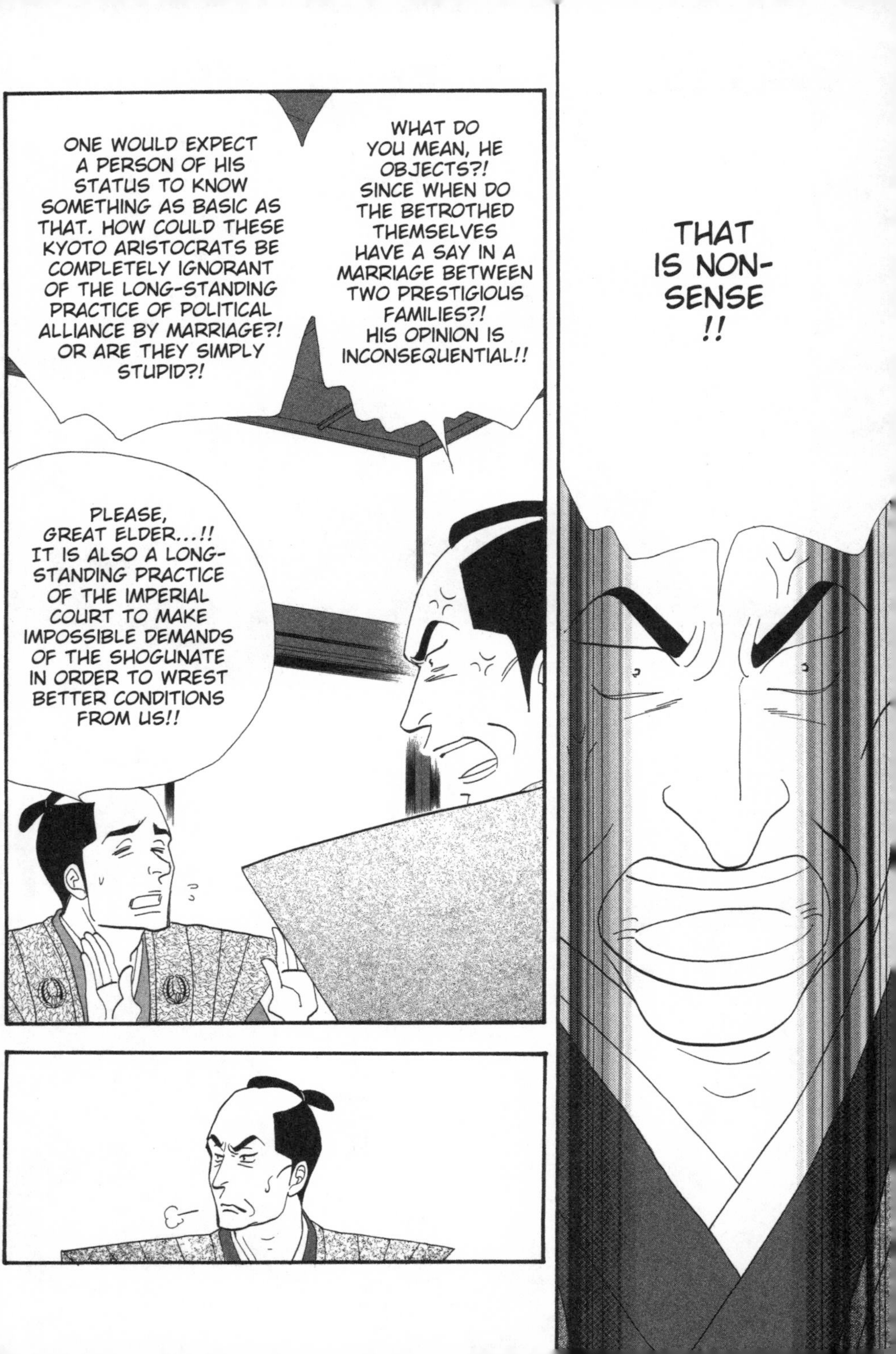
THAT IS NON-SENSE!!
WHAT DO YOU MEAN, HE OBJECTS?! SINCE WHEN DO THE BETROTHED THEMSELVES HAVE A SAY IN A MARRIAGE BETWEEN TWO PRESTIGIOUS FAMILIES?! HIS OPINION IS INCONSEQUENTIAL!!
ONE WOULD EXPECT A PERSON OF HIS STATUS TO KNOW SOMETHING AS BASIC AS THAT. HOW COULD THESE KYOTO ARISTOCRATS BE COMPLETELY IGNORANT OF THE LONG-STANDING PRACTICE OF POLITICAL ALLIANCE BY MARRIAGE?! OR ARE THEY SIMPLY STUPID?!
PLEASE, GREAT ELDER...!! IT IS ALSO A LONG-STANDING PRACTICE OF THE IMPERIAL COURT TO MAKE IMPOSSIBLE DEMANDS OF THE SHOGUNATE IN ORDER TO WREST BETTER CONDITIONS FROM US!!

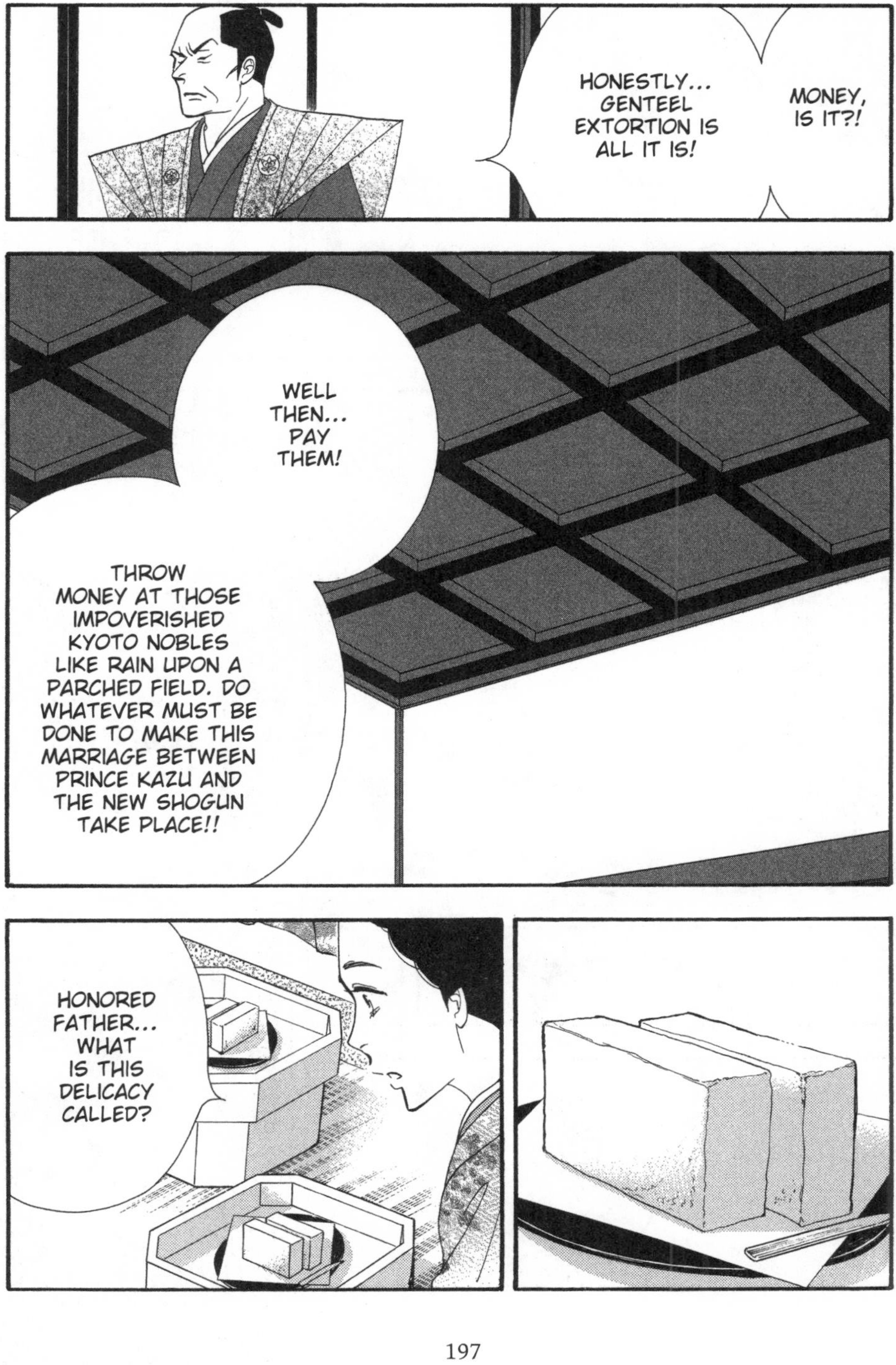
MONEY, IS IT?!
HONESTLY... GENTEEL EXTORTION IS ALL IT IS!
WELL THEN... PAY THEM!
THROW MONEY AT THOSE IMPOVERISHED KYOTO NOBLES LIKE RAIN UPON A PARCHED FIELD. DO WHATEVER MUST BE DONE TO MAKE THIS MARRIAGE BETWEEN PRINCE KAZU AND THE NEW SHOGUN TAKE PLACE!!
HONORED FATHER... WHAT IS THIS DELICACY CALLED?

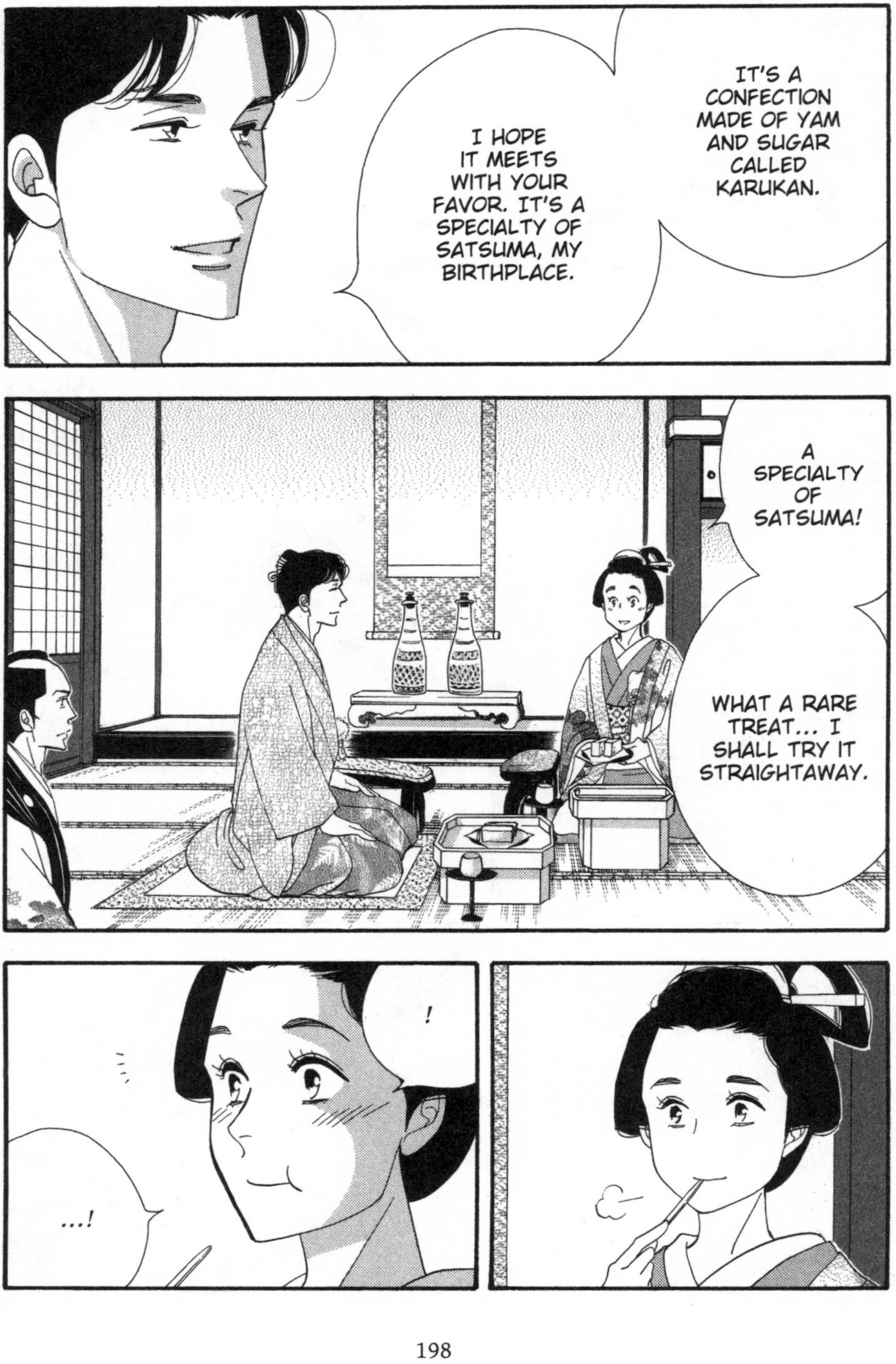
IT'S A CONFECTION MADE OF YAM AND SUGAR CALLED KARUKAN.
I HOPE IT MEETS WITH YOUR FAVOR. IT'S A SPECIALTY OF SATSUMA, MY BIRTHPLACE.
A SPECIALTY OF SATSUMA!
WHAT A RARE TREAT... I SHALL TRY IT STRAIGHTAWAY.
!
...!

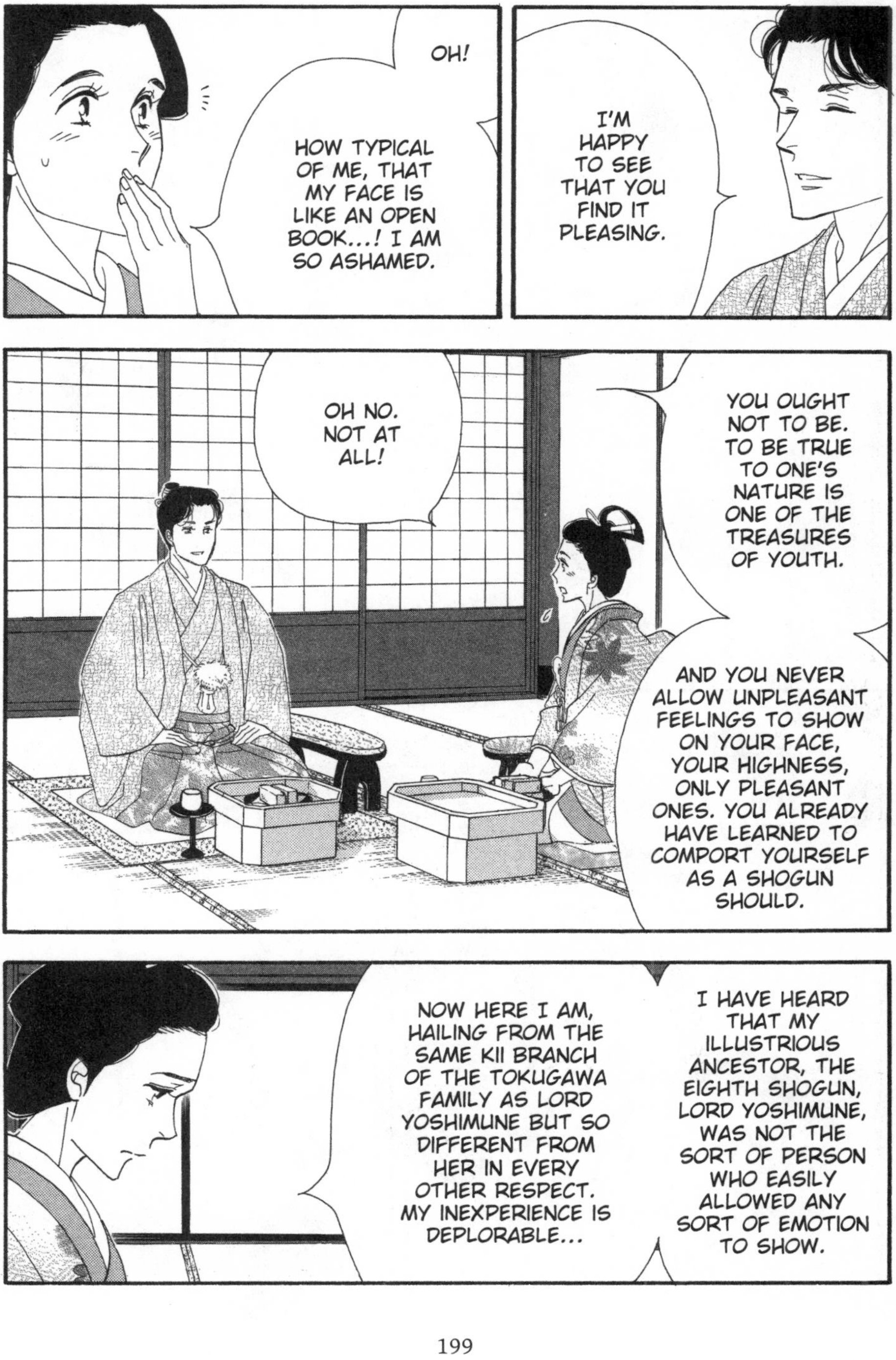
I'M HAPPY TO SEE THAT YOU FIND IT PLEASING.
OH!
HOW TYPICAL OF ME, THAT MY FACE IS LIKE AN OPEN BOOK...! I AM SO ASHAMED.
OH NO. NOT AT ALL!
YOU OUGHT NOT TO BE. TO BE TRUE TO ONE'S NATURE IS ONE OF THE TREASURES OF YOUTH.
AND YOU NEVER ALLOW UNPLEASANT FEELINGS TO SHOW ON YOUR FACE, YOUR HIGHNESS, ONLY PLEASANT ONES. YOU ALREADY HAVE LEARNED TO COMPORT YOURSELF AS A SHOGUN SHOULD.
I HAVE HEARD THAT MY ILLUSTRIOUS ANCESTOR, THE EIGHTH SHOGUN, LORD YOSHIMUNE, WAS NOT THE SORT OF PERSON WHO EASILY ALLOWED ANY SORT OF EMOTION TO SHOW.
NOW HERE I AM, HAILING FROM THE SAME KII BRANCH OF THE TOKUGAWA FAMILY AS LORD YOSHIMUNE BUT SO DIFFERENT FROM HER IN EVERY OTHER RESPECT. MY INEXPERIENCE IS DEPLORABLE...

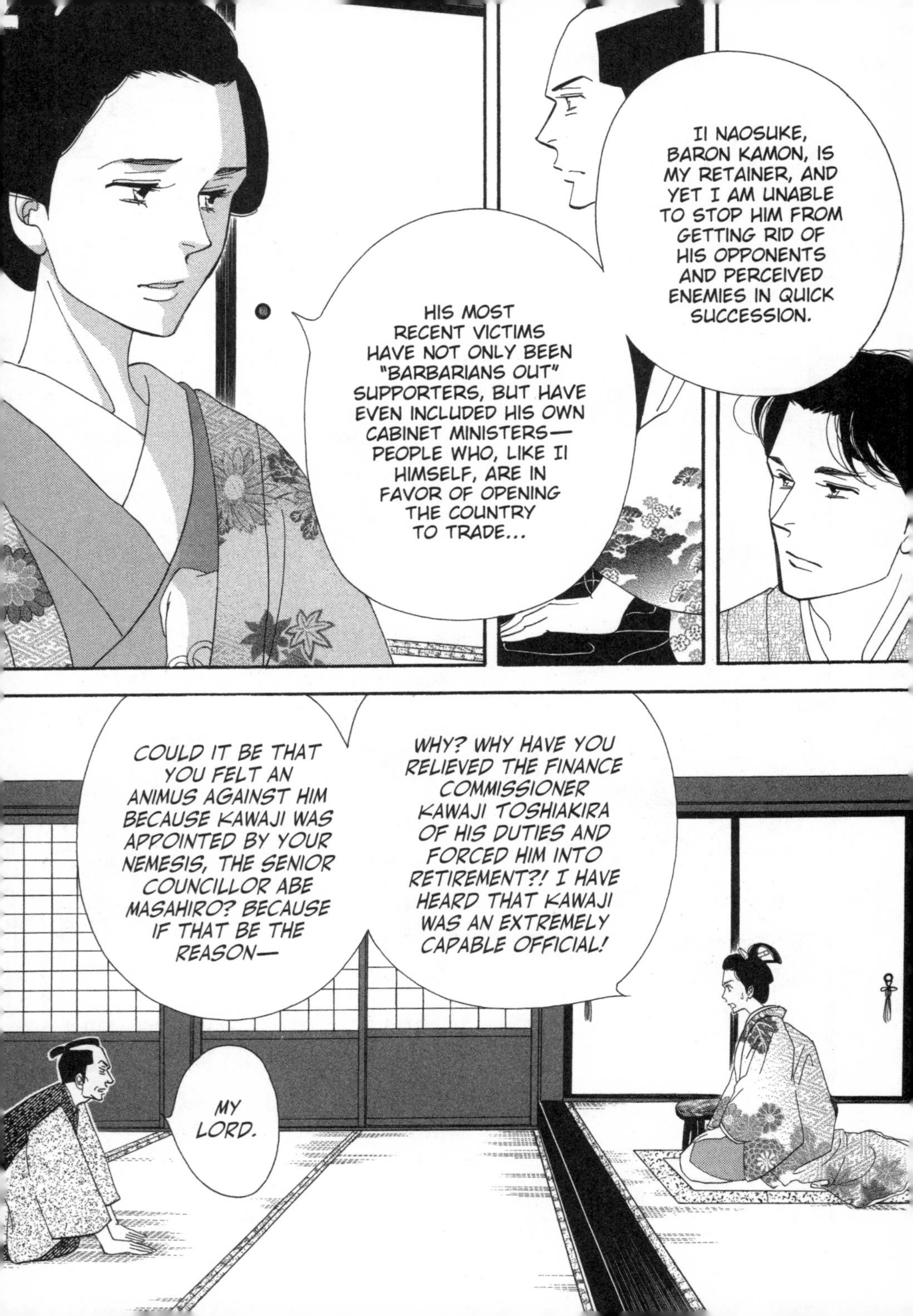
II NAOSUKE, BARON KAMON, IS MY RETAINER, AND YET I AM UNABLE TO STOP HIM FROM GETTING RID OF HIS OPPONENTS AND PERCEIVED ENEMIES IN QUICK SUCCESSION.
HIS MOST RECENT VICTIMS HAVE NOT ONLY BEEN "BARBARIANS OUT" SUPPORTERS, BUT HAVE EVEN INCLUDED HIS OWN CABINET MINISTERS—PEOPLE WHO, LIKE II HIMSELF, ARE IN FAVOR OF OPENING THE COUNTRY TO TRADE...
WHY? WHY HAVE YOU RELIEVED THE FINANCE COMMISSIONER KAWAJI TOSHIAKIRA OF HIS DUTIES AND FORCED HIM INTO RETIREMENT?! I HAVE HEARD THAT KAWAJI WAS AN EXTREMELY CAPABLE OFFICIAL!
COULD IT BE THAT YOU FELT AN ANIMUS AGAINST HIM BECAUSE KAWAJI WAS APPOINTED BY YOUR NEMESIS, THE SENIOR COUNCILLOR ABE MASAHIRO? BECAUSE IF THAT BE THE REASON—
MY LORD.

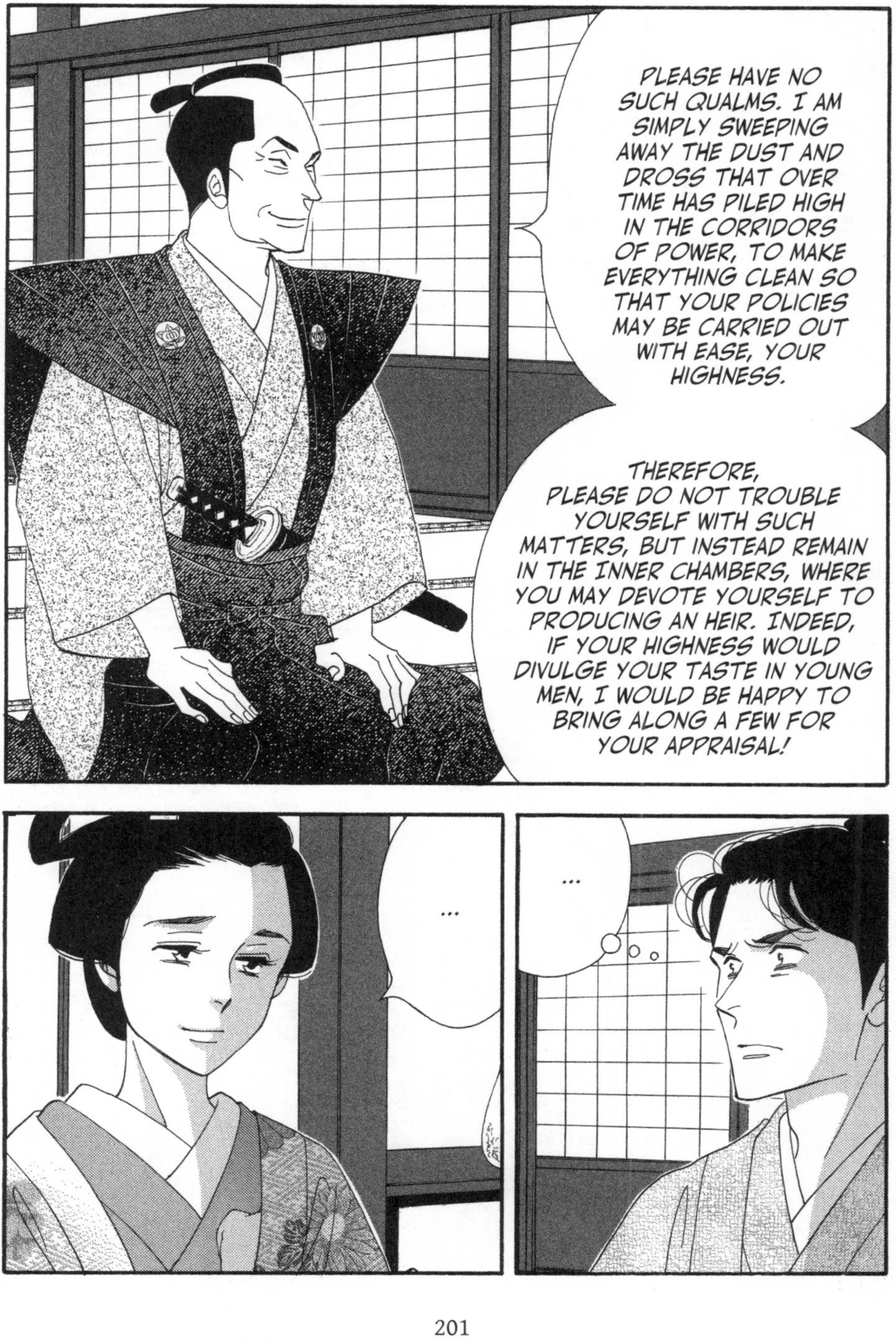
PLEASE HAVE NO SUCH QUALMS. I AM SIMPLY SWEEPING AWAY THE DUST AND DROSS THAT OVER TIME HAS PILED HIGH IN THE CORRIDORS OF POWER, TO MAKE EVERYTHING CLEAN SO THAT YOUR POLICIES MAY BE CARRIED OUT WITH EASE, YOUR HIGHNESS.
THEREFORE, PLEASE DO NOT TROUBLE YOURSELF WITH SUCH MATTERS, BUT INSTEAD REMAIN IN THE INNER CHAMBERS, WHERE YOU MAY DEVOTE YOURSELF TO PRODUCING AN HEIR. INDEED, IF YOUR HIGHNESS WOULD DIVULGE YOUR TASTE IN YOUNG MEN, I WOULD BE HAPPY TO BRING ALONG A FEW FOR YOUR APPRAISAL!
...
...

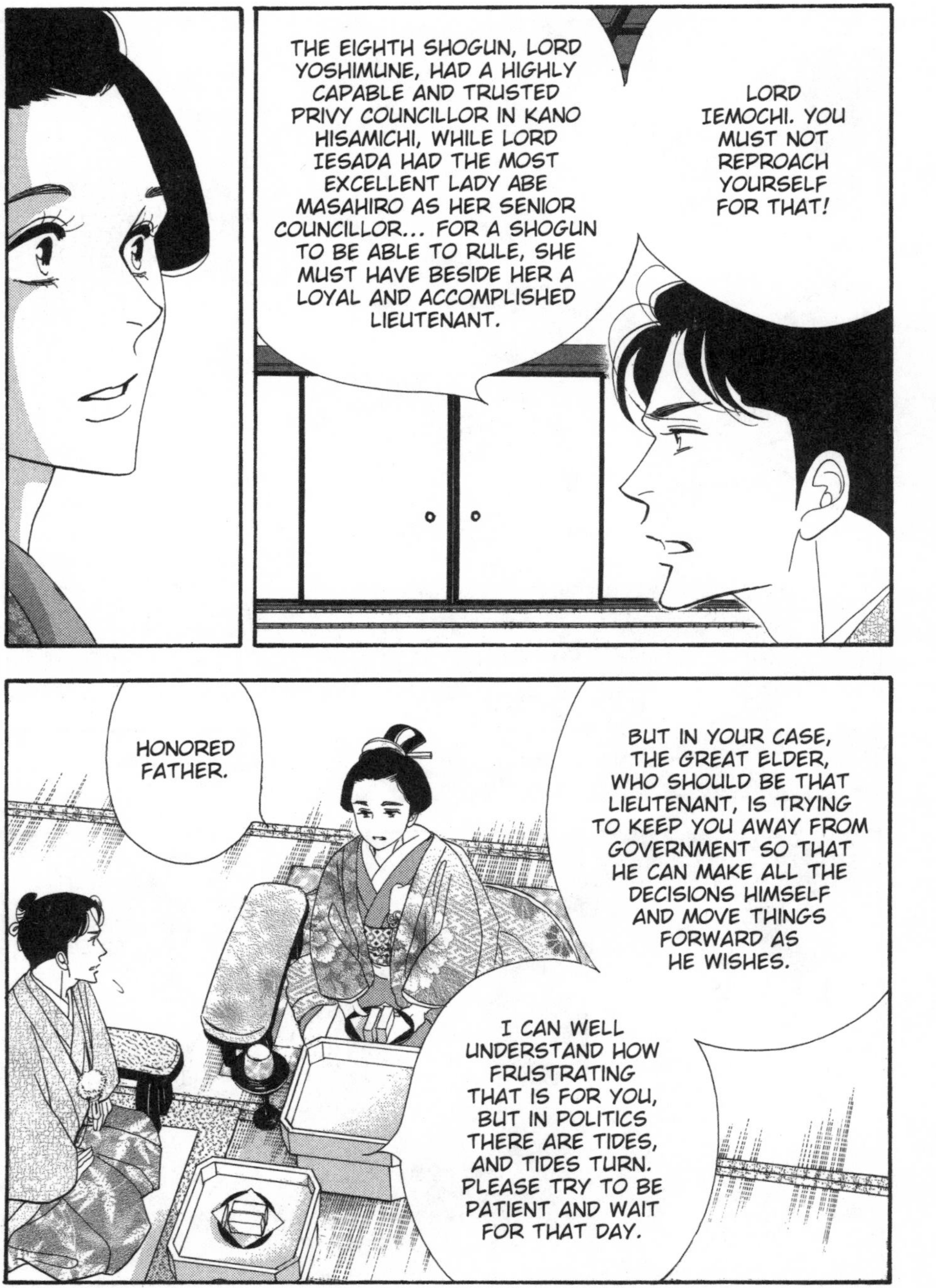
LORD IEMOCHI. YOU MUST NOT REPROACH YOURSELF FOR THAT!
THE EIGHTH SHOGUN, LORD YOSHIMUNE, HAD A HIGHLY CAPABLE AND TRUSTED PRIVY COUNCILLOR IN KANO HISAMICHI, WHILE LORD IESADA HAD THE MOST EXCELLENT LADY ABE MASAHIRO AS HER SENIOR COUNCILLOR... FOR A SHOGUN TO BE ABLE TO RULE, SHE MUST HAVE BESIDE HER A LOYAL AND ACCOMPLISHED LIEUTENANT.
BUT IN YOUR CASE, THE GREAT ELDER, WHO SHOULD BE THAT LIEUTENANT, IS TRYING TO KEEP YOU AWAY FROM GOVERNMENT SO THAT HE CAN MAKE ALL THE DECISIONS HIMSELF AND MOVE THINGS FORWARD AS HE WISHES.
I CAN WELL UNDERSTAND HOW FRUSTRATING THAT IS FOR YOU, BUT IN POLITICS THERE ARE TIDES, AND TIDES TURN. PLEASE TRY TO BE PATIENT AND WAIT FOR THAT DAY.
HONORED FATHER.

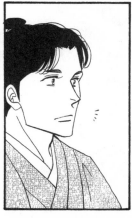

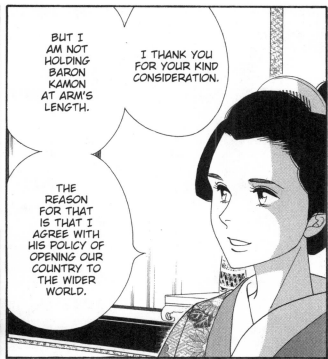

I THANK YOU FOR YOUR KIND CONSIDERATION.
BUT I AM NOT HOLDING BARON KAMON AT ARM'S LENGTH.
THE REASON FOR THAT IS THAT I AGREE WITH HIS POLICY OF OPENING OUR COUNTRY TO THE WIDER WORLD.
MY FEAR IS THAT, IF HE GOES TOO FAR WITH HIS DRACONIAN MEASURES, II WILL EVENTUALLY LOSE THE SUPPORT OF HIS FELLOW CABINET MINISTERS, WHO OUGHT TO BE HIS ALLIES.
JUST AS A SHOGUN CAN DO NOTHING ON HER OWN, I AM AFRAID THAT AN ISOLATED GREAT ELDER WILL FIND IT INCREASINGLY DIFFICULT TO ACHIEVE ANYTHING EITHER...

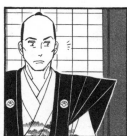

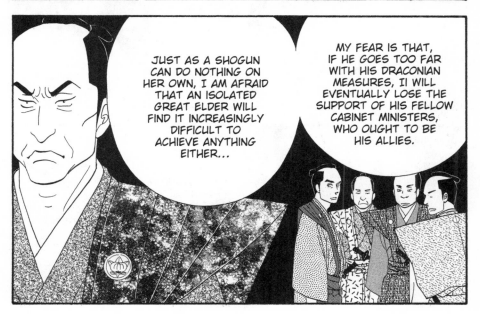

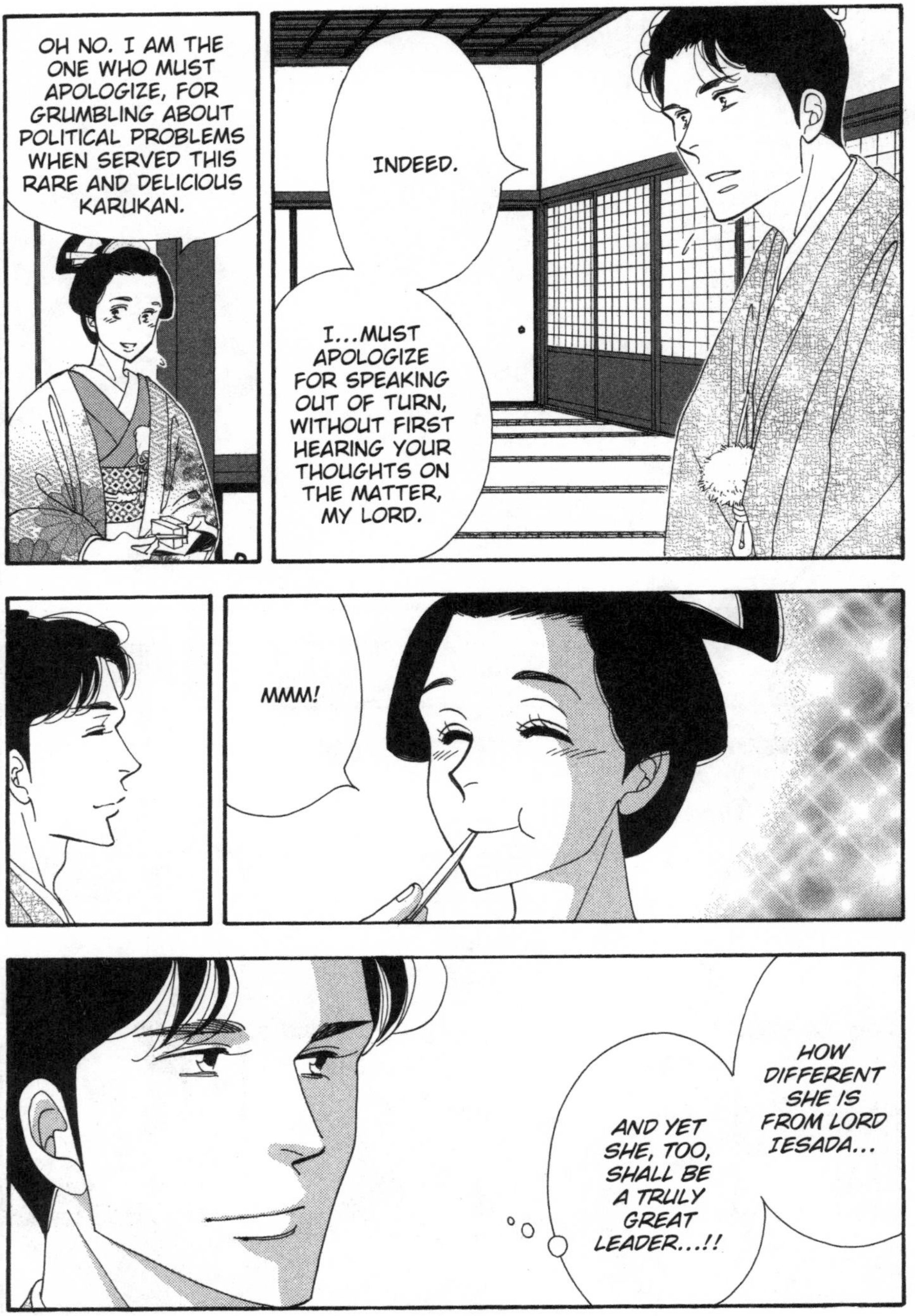
INDEED.
I...MUST APOLOGIZE FOR SPEAKING OUT OF TURN, WITHOUT FIRST HEARING YOUR THOUGHTS ON THE MATTER, MY LORD.
OH NO. I AM THE ONE WHO MUST APOLOGIZE, FOR GRUMBLING ABOUT POLITICAL PROBLEMS WHEN SERVED THIS RARE AND DELICIOUS KARUKAN.
MMM!
HOW DIFFERENT SHE IS FROM LORD IESADA...
AND YET SHE, TOO, SHALL BE A TRULY GREAT LEADER...!!

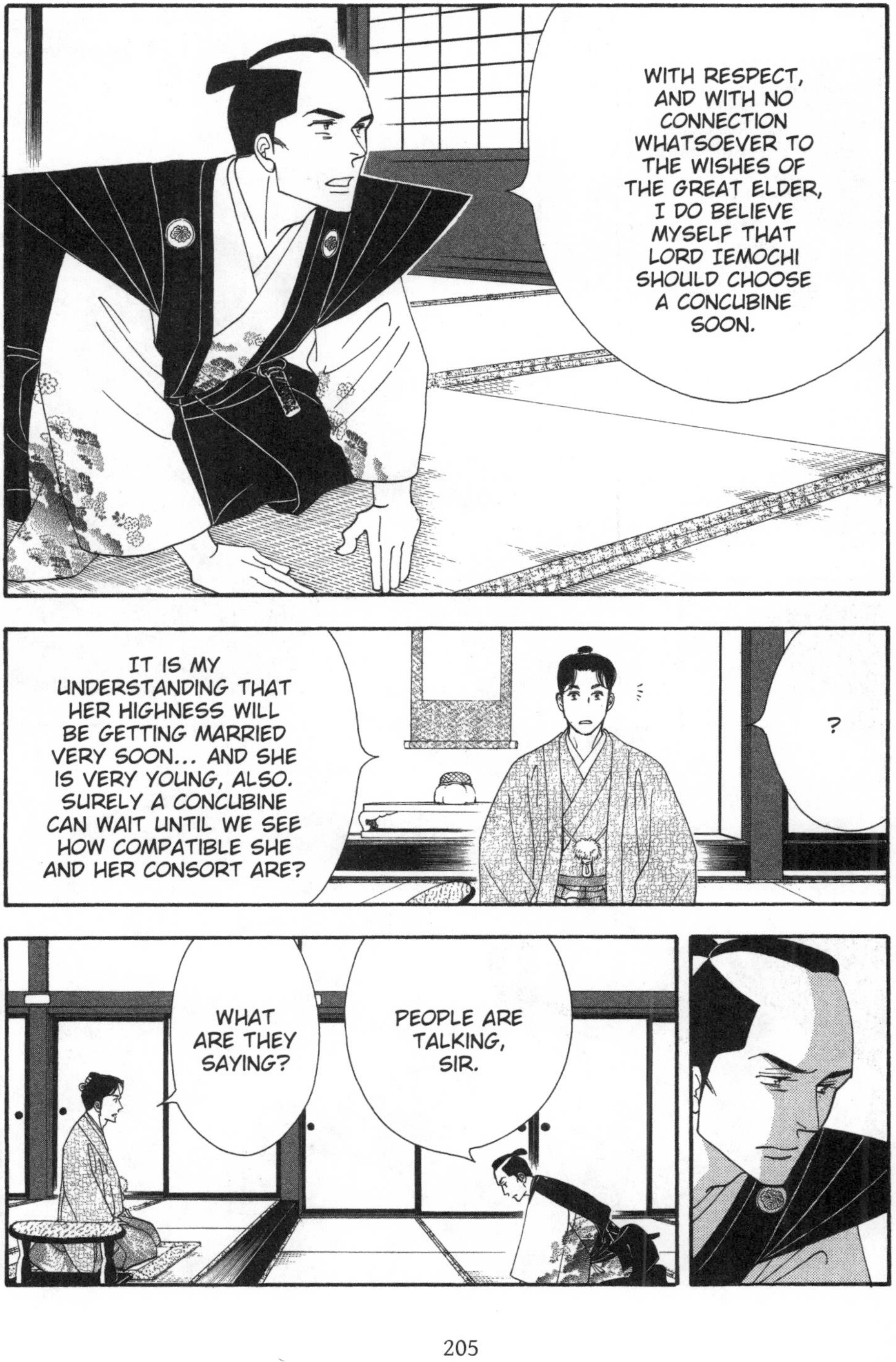
WITH RESPECT, AND WITH NO CONNECTION WHATSOEVER TO THE WISHES OF THE GREAT ELDER, I DO BELIEVE MYSELF THAT LORD IEMOCHI SHOULD CHOOSE A CONCUBINE SOON.
?
IT IS MY UNDERSTANDING THAT HER HIGHNESS WILL BE GETTING MARRIED VERY SOON... AND SHE IS VERY YOUNG, ALSO. SURELY A CONCUBINE CAN WAIT UNTIL WE SEE HOW COMPATIBLE SHE AND HER CONSORT ARE?
PEOPLE ARE TALKING, SIR.
WHAT ARE THEY SAYING?

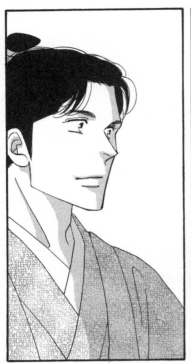

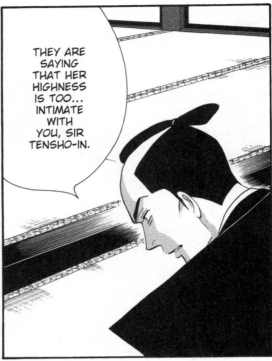

THEY ARE SAYING THAT HER HIGHNESS IS TOO... INTIMATE WITH YOU, SIR TENSHO-IN.
OF COURSE I KNOW BETTER THAN ANYONE ELSE THAT THERE IS NOTHING OF AN AMOROUS NATURE, INDEED NOT EVEN A SUGGESTION OF IT, BETWEEN THE TWO OF YOU! HOWEVER...!
ENOUGH!
I UNDER-STAND! I DON'T NEED TO HEAR ANY MORE!

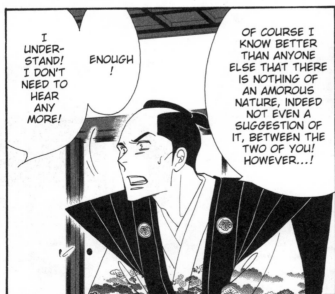

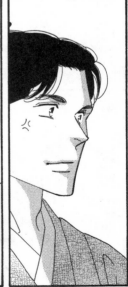

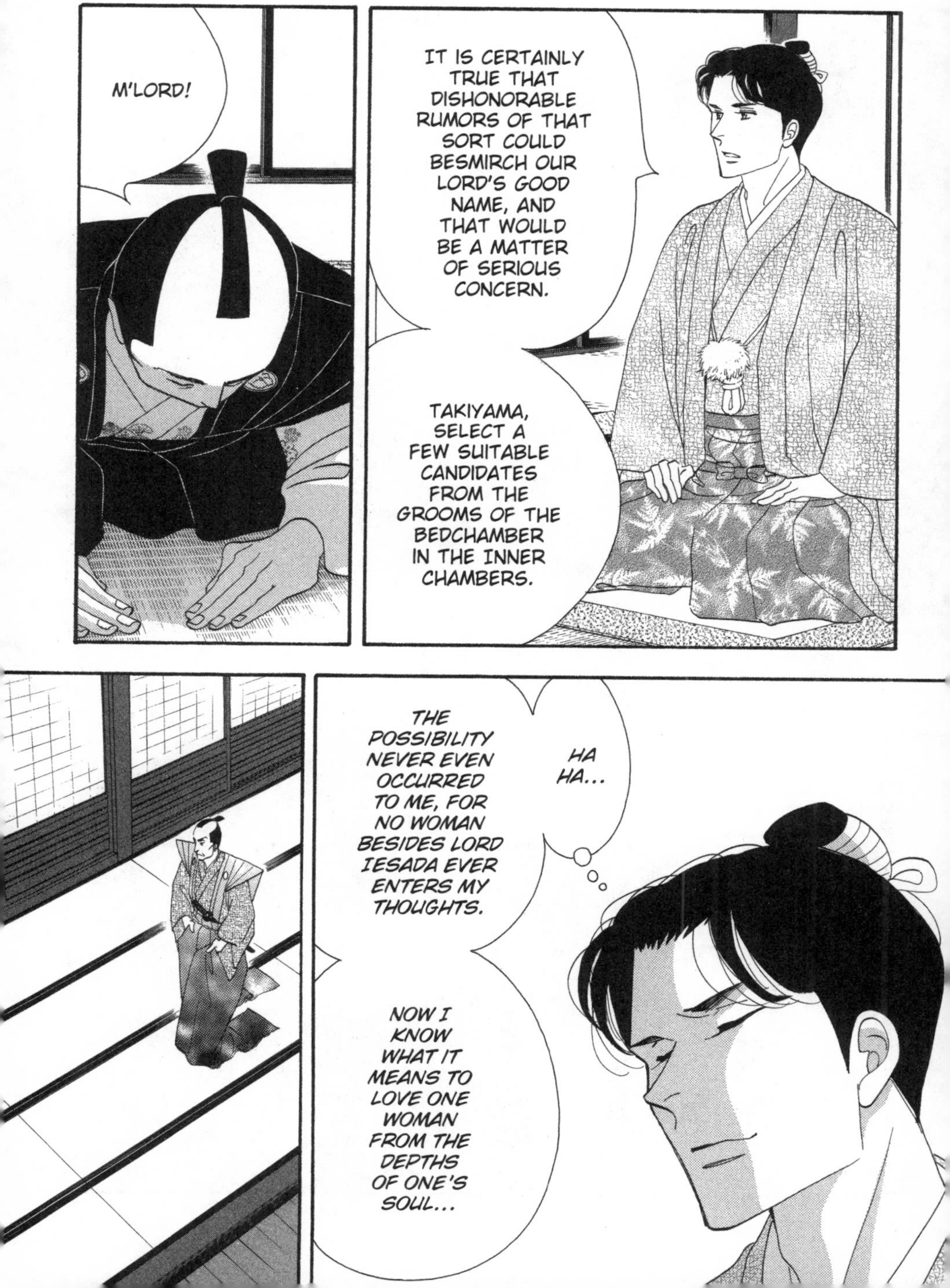
IT IS CERTAINLY TRUE THAT DISHONORABLE RUMORS OF THAT SORT COULD BESMIRCH OUR LORD'S GOOD NAME, AND THAT WOULD BE A MATTER OF SERIOUS CONCERN.
TAKIYAMA, SELECT A FEW SUITABLE CANDIDATES FROM THE GROOMS OF THE BEDCHAMBER IN THE INNER CHAMBERS.
M'LORD!
HA HA...
THE POSSIBILITY NEVER EVEN OCCURRED TO ME, FOR NO WOMAN BESIDES LORD IESADA EVER ENTERS MY THOUGHTS.
NOW I KNOW WHAT IT MEANS TO LOVE ONE WOMAN FROM THE DEPTHS OF ONE'S SOUL...

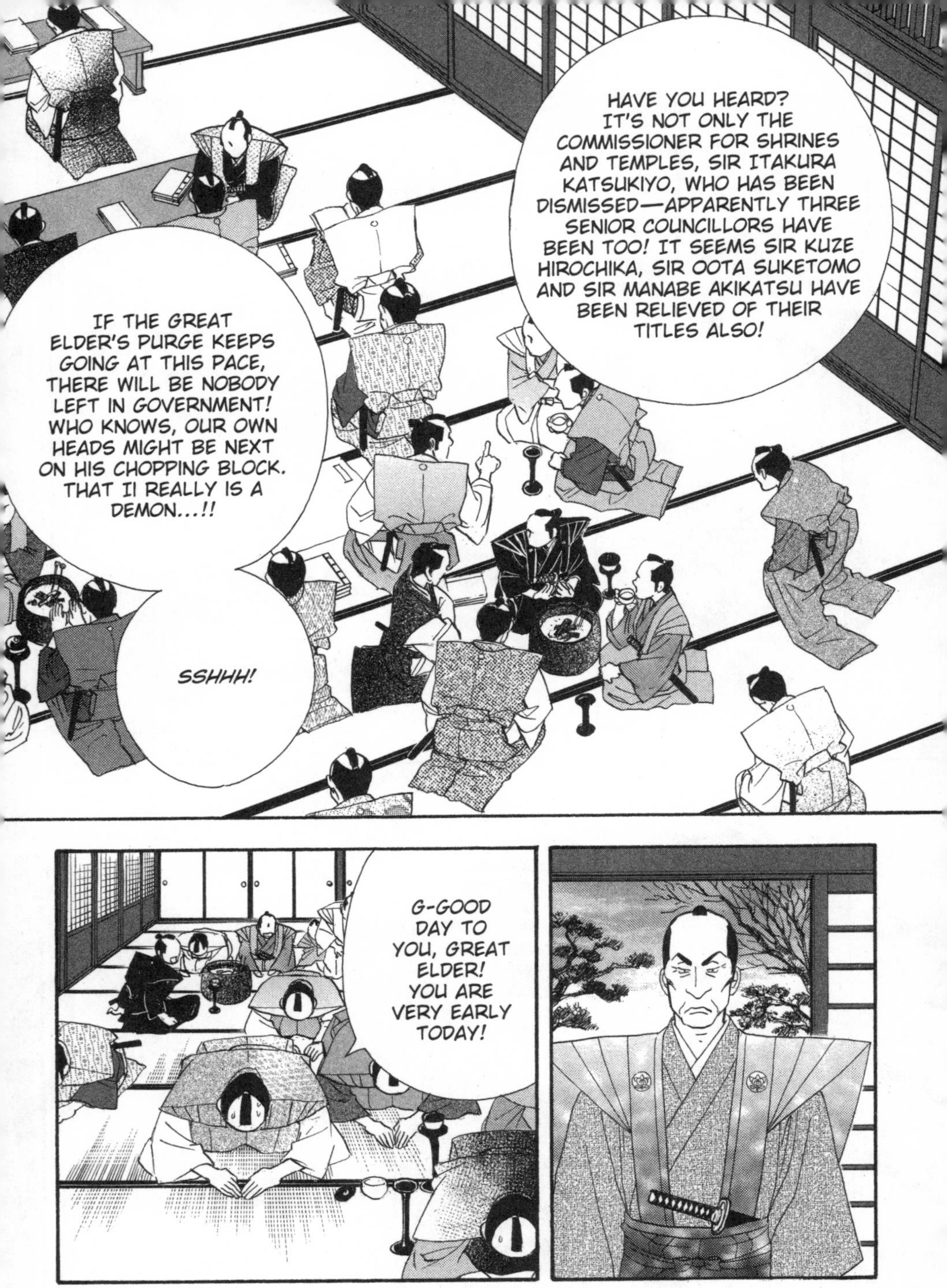
HAVE YOU HEARD? IT'S NOT ONLY THE COMMISSIONER FOR SHRINES AND TEMPLES, SIR ITAKURA KATSUKIYO, WHO HAS BEEN DISMISSED—APPARENTLY THREE SENIOR COUNCILLORS HAVE BEEN TOO! IT SEEMS SIR KUZE HIROCHIKA, SIR OOTA SUKETOMO AND SIR MANABE AKIKATSU HAVE BEEN RELIEVED OF THEIR TITLES ALSO!
IF THE GREAT ELDER'S PURGE KEEPS GOING AT THIS PACE, THERE WILL BE NOBODY LEFT IN GOVERNMENT! WHO KNOWS, OUR OWN HEADS MIGHT BE NEXT ON HIS CHOPPING BLOCK. THAT II REALLY IS A DEMON...!!
SSHHH!
G-GOOD DAY TO YOU, GREAT ELDER! YOU ARE VERY EARLY TODAY!

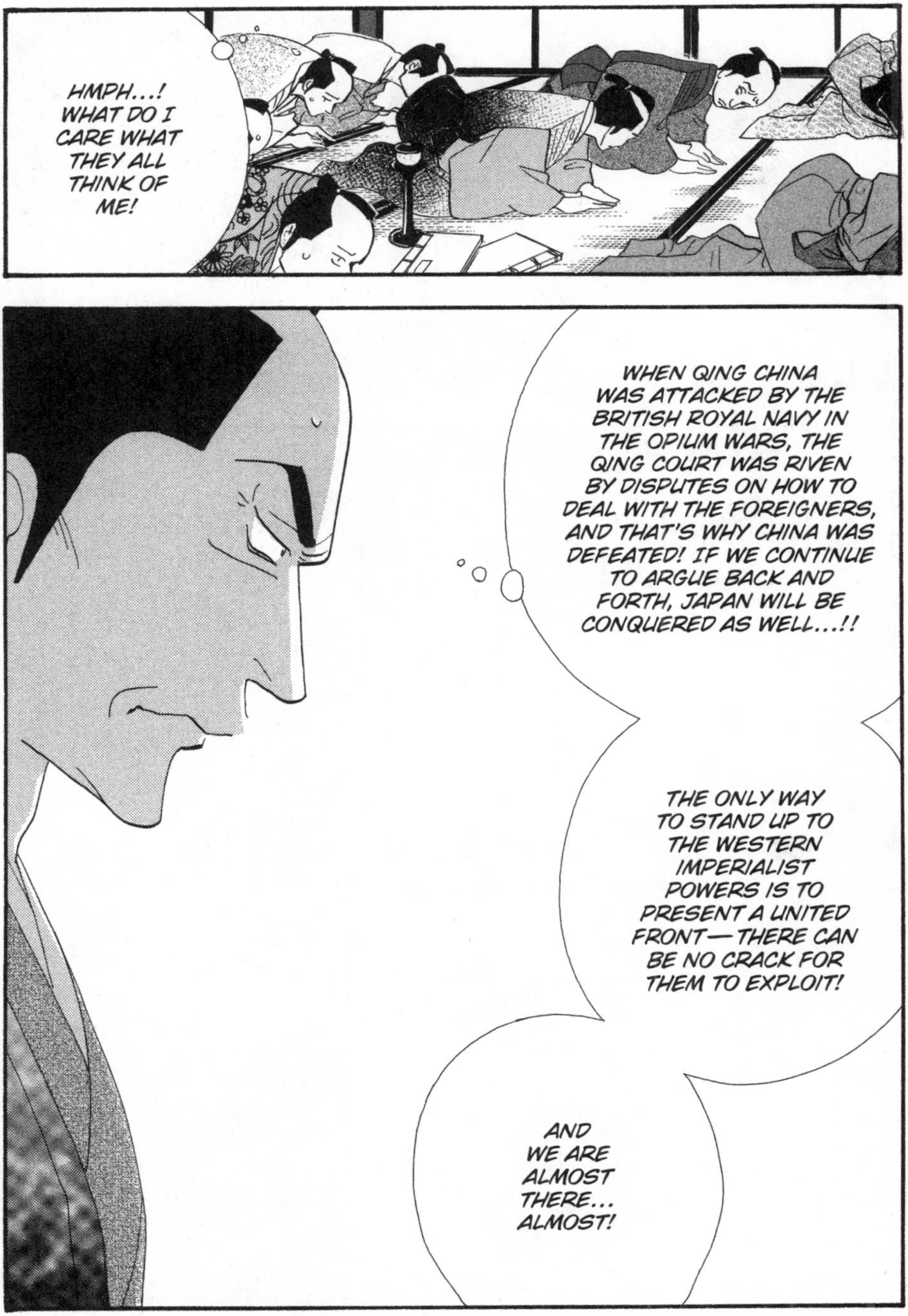
HMPH...! WHAT DO I CARE WHAT THEY ALL THINK OF ME!
WHEN QING CHINA WAS ATTACKED BY THE BRITISH ROYAL NAVY IN THE OPIUM WARS, THE QING COURT WAS RIVEN BY DISPUTES ON HOW TO DEAL WITH THE FOREIGNERS, AND THAT'S WHY CHINA WAS DEFEATED! IF WE CONTINUE TO ARGUE BACK AND FORTH, JAPAN WILL BE CONQUERED AS WELL...!!
THE ONLY WAY TO STAND UP TO THE WESTERN IMPERIALIST POWERS IS TO PRESENT A UNITED FRONT—THERE CAN BE NO CRACK FOR THEM TO EXPLOIT!
AND WE ARE ALMOST THERE... ALMOST!

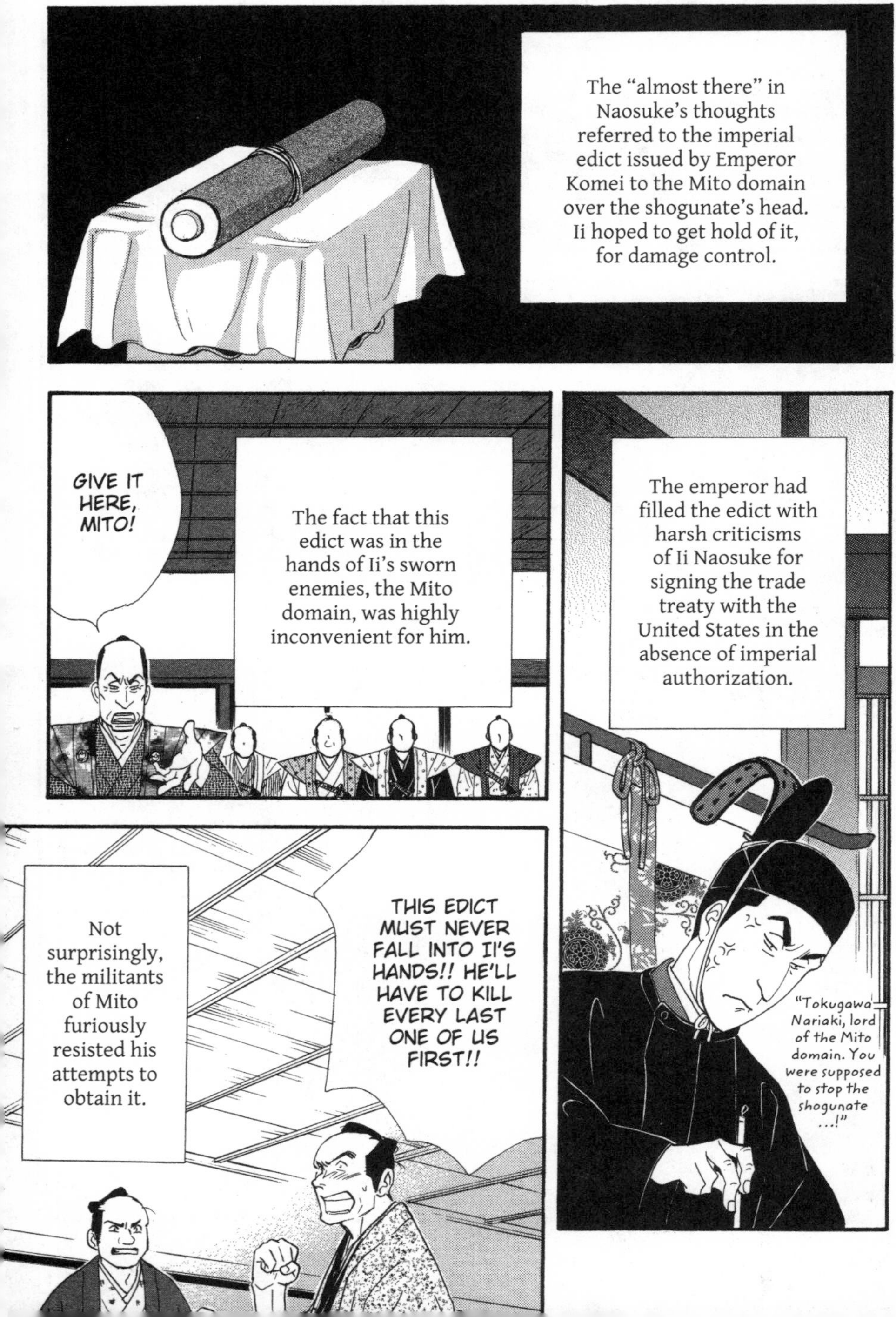
The "almost there" in Naosuke's thoughts referred to the imperial edict issued by Emperor Komei to the Mito domain over the shogunate's head. Ii hoped to get hold of it, for damage control.
The emperor had filled the edict with harsh criticisms of Ii Naosuke for signing the trade treaty with the United States in the absence of imperial authorization.
"Tokugawa Nariaki, lord of the Mito domain. You were supposed to stop the shogunate ...!"
The fact that this edict was in the hands of Ii's sworn enemies, the Mito domain, was highly inconvenient for him.
GIVE IT HERE, MITO!
THIS EDICT MUST NEVER FALL INTO II'S HANDS!! HE'LL HAVE TO KILL EVERY LAST ONE OF US FIRST!!
Not surprisingly, the militants of Mito furiously resisted his attempts to obtain it.

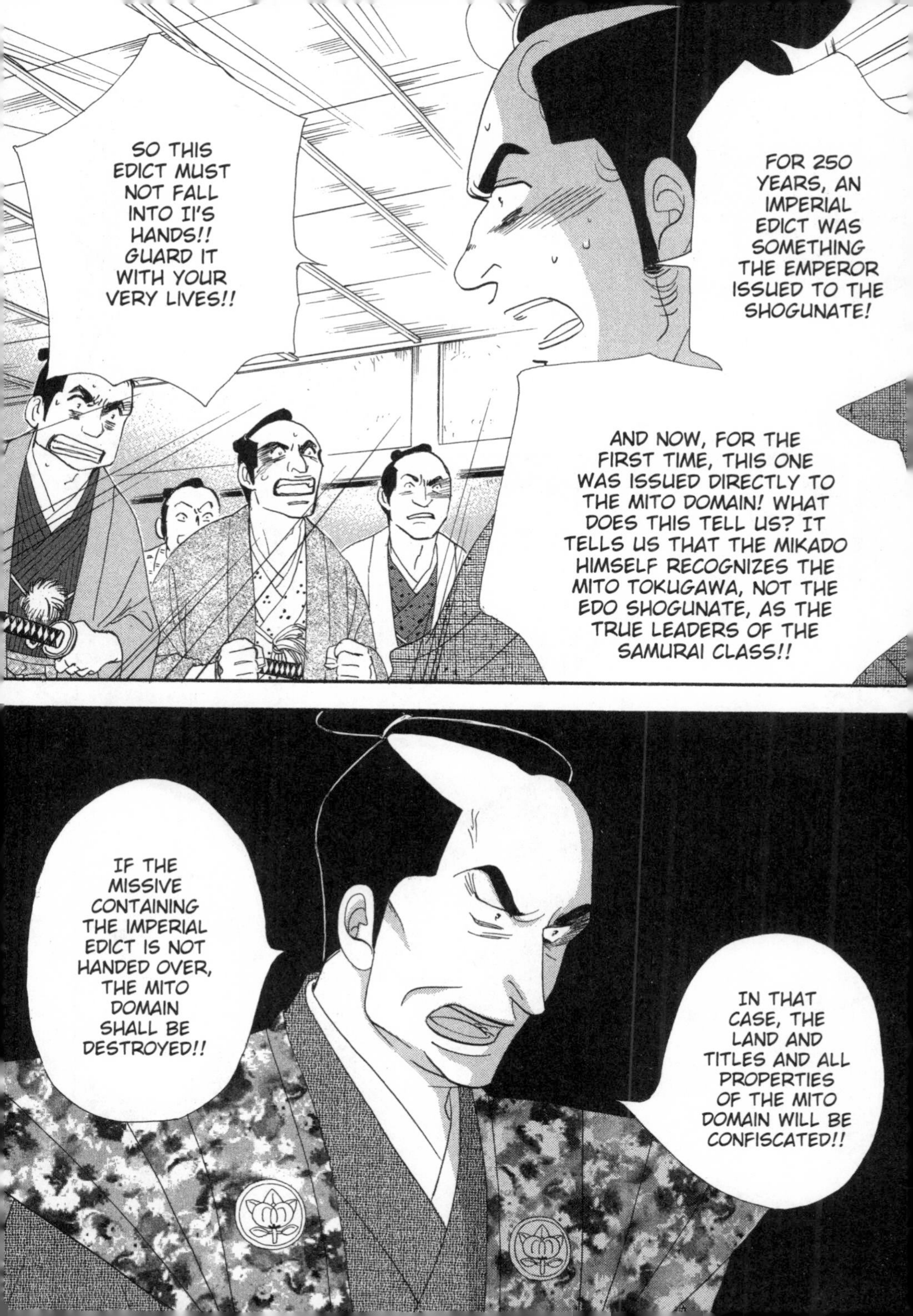
FOR 250 YEARS, AN IMPERIAL EDICT WAS SOMETHING THE EMPEROR ISSUED TO THE SHOGUNATE!
AND NOW, FOR THE FIRST TIME, THIS ONE WAS ISSUED DIRECTLY TO THE MITO DOMAIN! WHAT DOES THIS TELL US? IT TELLS US THAT THE MIKADO HIMSELF RECOGNIZES THE MITO TOKUGAWA, NOT THE EDO SHOGUNATE, AS THE TRUE LEADERS OF THE SAMURAI CLASS!!
SO THIS EDICT MUST NOT FALL INTO II'S HANDS!! GUARD IT WITH YOUR VERY LIVES!!
IF THE MISSIVE CONTAINING THE IMPERIAL EDICT IS NOT HANDED OVER, THE MITO DOMAIN SHALL BE DESTROYED!!
IN THAT CASE, THE LAND AND TITLES AND ALL PROPERTIES OF THE MITO DOMAIN WILL BE CONFISCATED!!

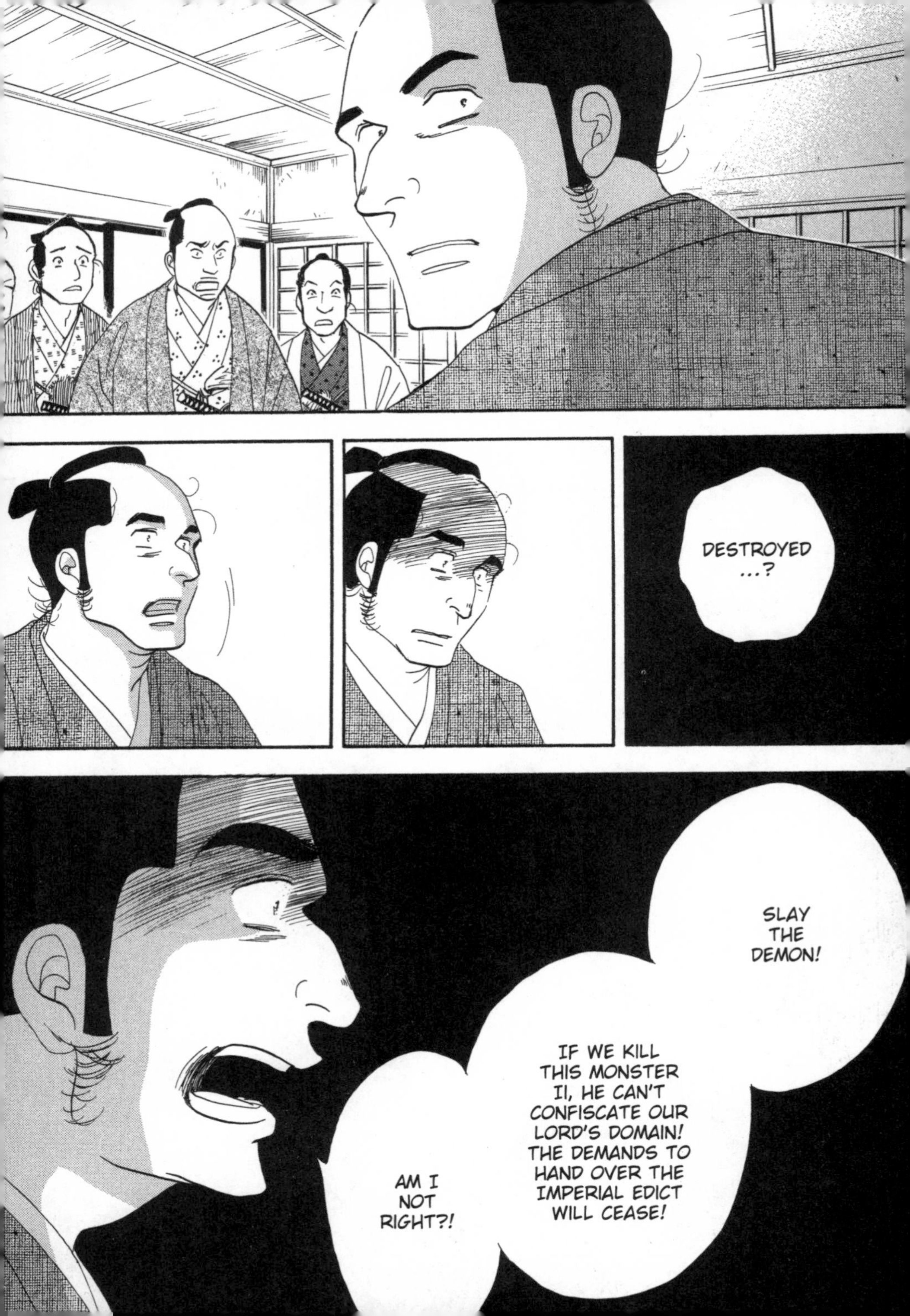
DESTROYED...?
SLAY THE DEMON!
IF WE KILL THIS MONSTER II, HE CAN'T CONFISCATE OUR LORD'S DOMAIN! THE DEMANDS TO HAND OVER THE IMPERIAL EDICT WILL CEASE!
AM I NOT RIGHT?!

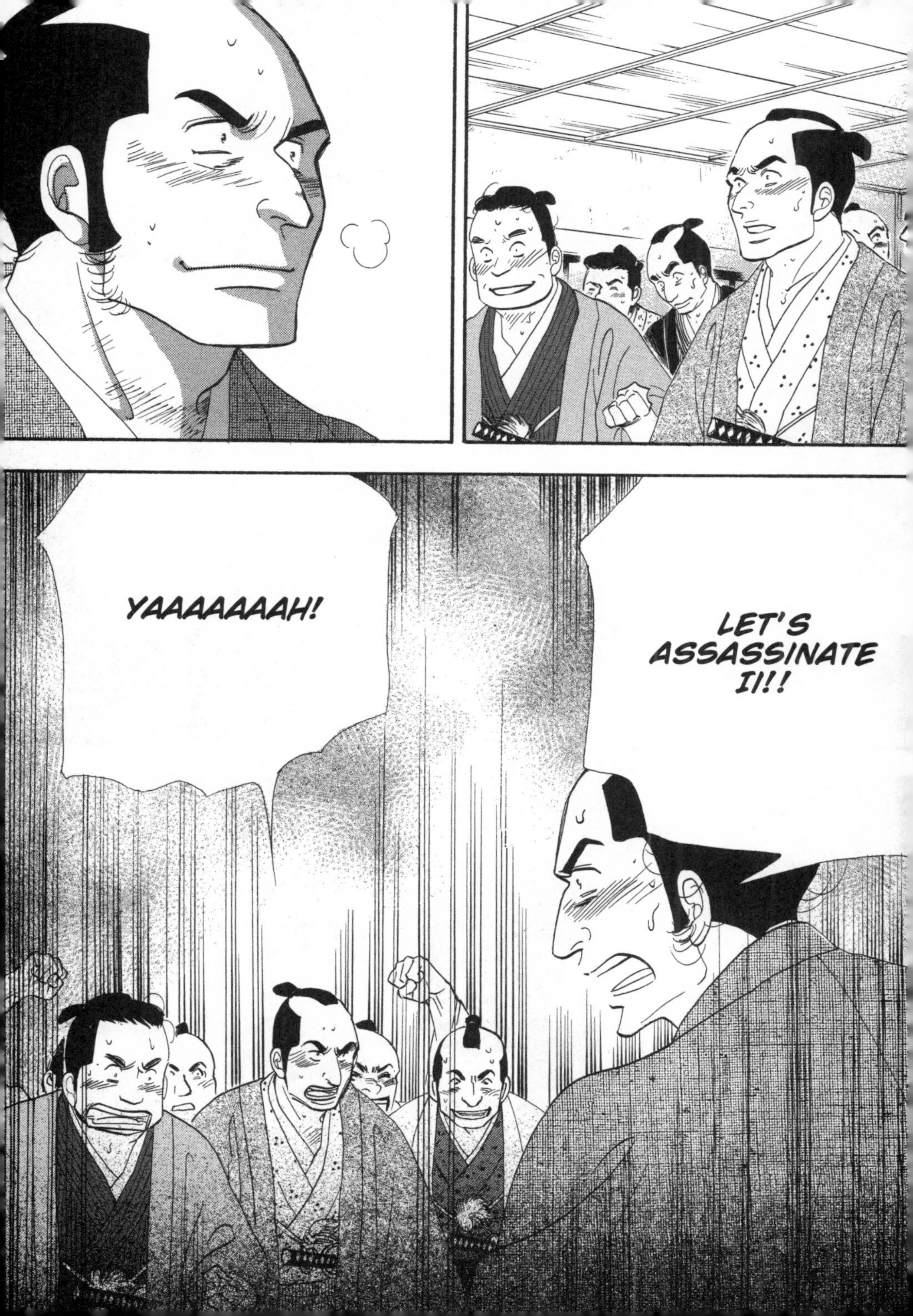
LET'S ASSASSINATE II!!
YAAAAAAAH!

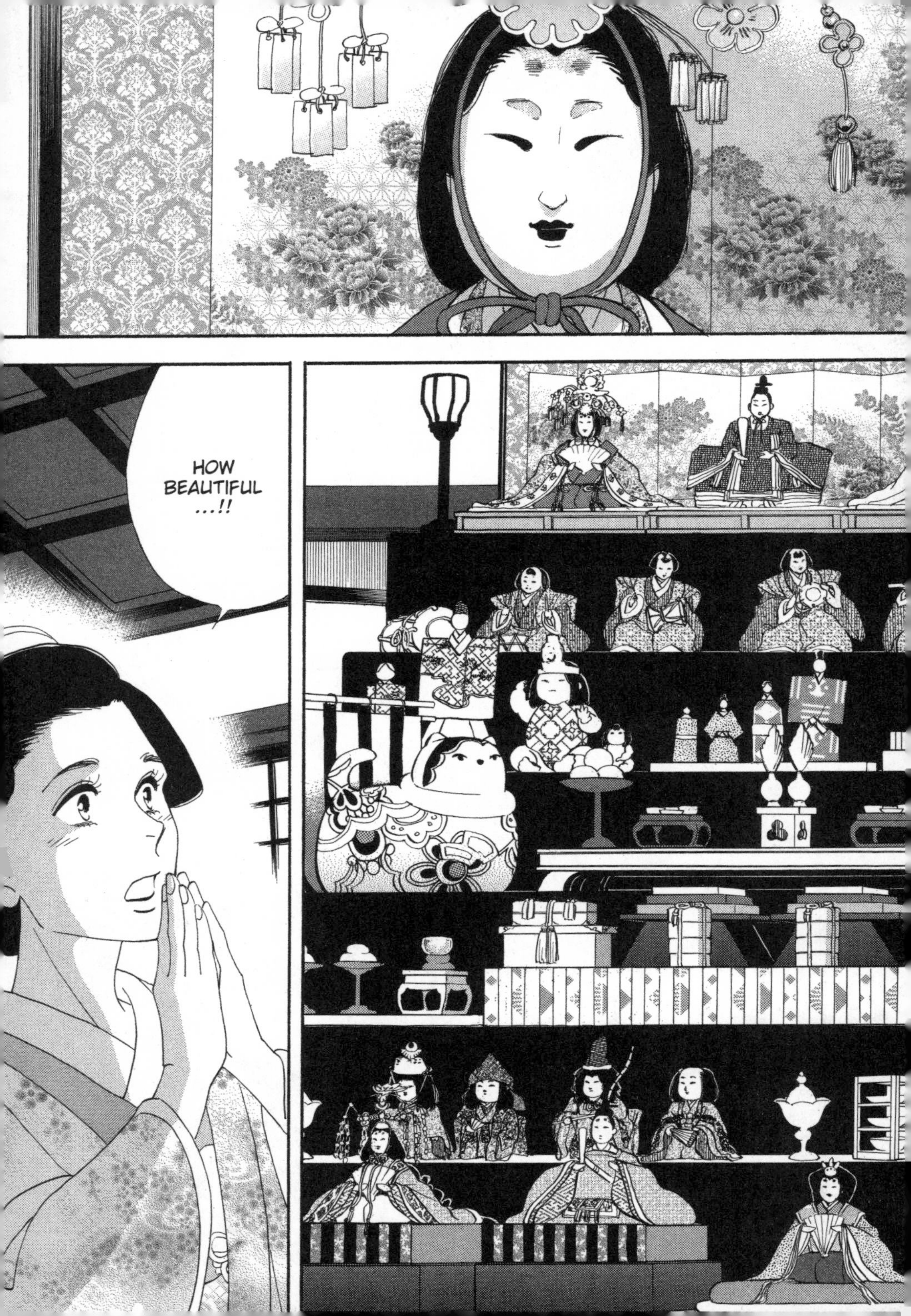
HOW BEAUTIFUL ...!!

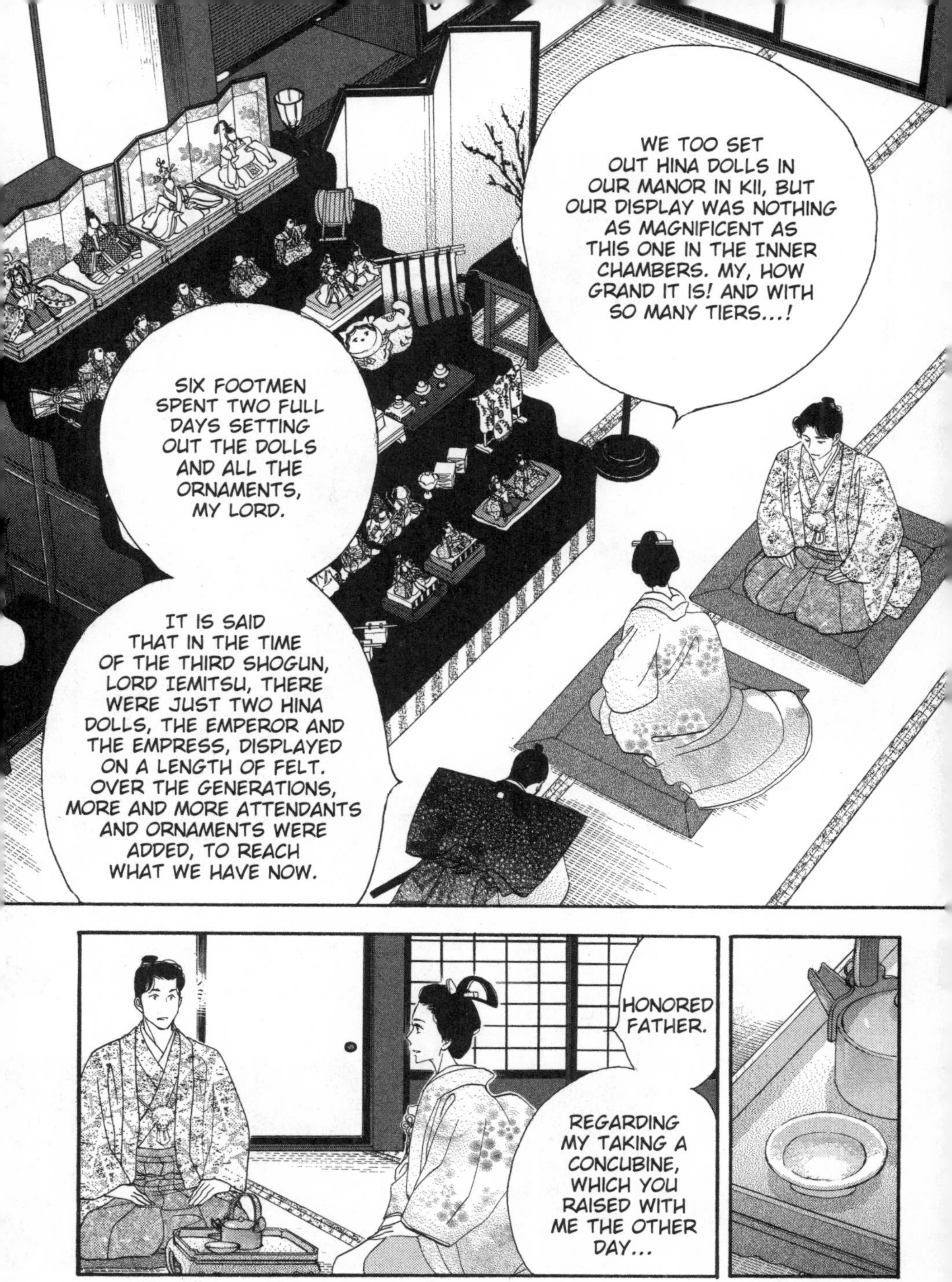
WE TOO SET OUT HINA DOLLS IN OUR MANOR IN KII, BUT OUR DISPLAY WAS NOTHING AS MAGNIFICENT AS THIS ONE IN THE INNER CHAMBERS. MY, HOW GRAND IT IS! AND WITH SO MANY TIERS...!
SIX FOOTMEN SPENT TWO FULL DAYS SETTING OUT THE DOLLS AND ALL THE ORNAMENTS, MY LORD.
IT IS SAID THAT IN THE TIME OF THE THIRD SHOGUN, LORD IEMITSU, THERE WERE JUST TWO HINA DOLLS, THE EMPEROR AND THE EMPRESS, DISPLAYED ON A LENGTH OF FELT. OVER THE GENERATIONS, MORE AND MORE ATTENDANTS AND ORNAMENTS WERE ADDED, TO REACH WHAT WE HAVE NOW.
HONORED FATHER.
REGARDING MY TAKING A CONCUBINE, WHICH YOU RAISED WITH ME THE OTHER DAY...

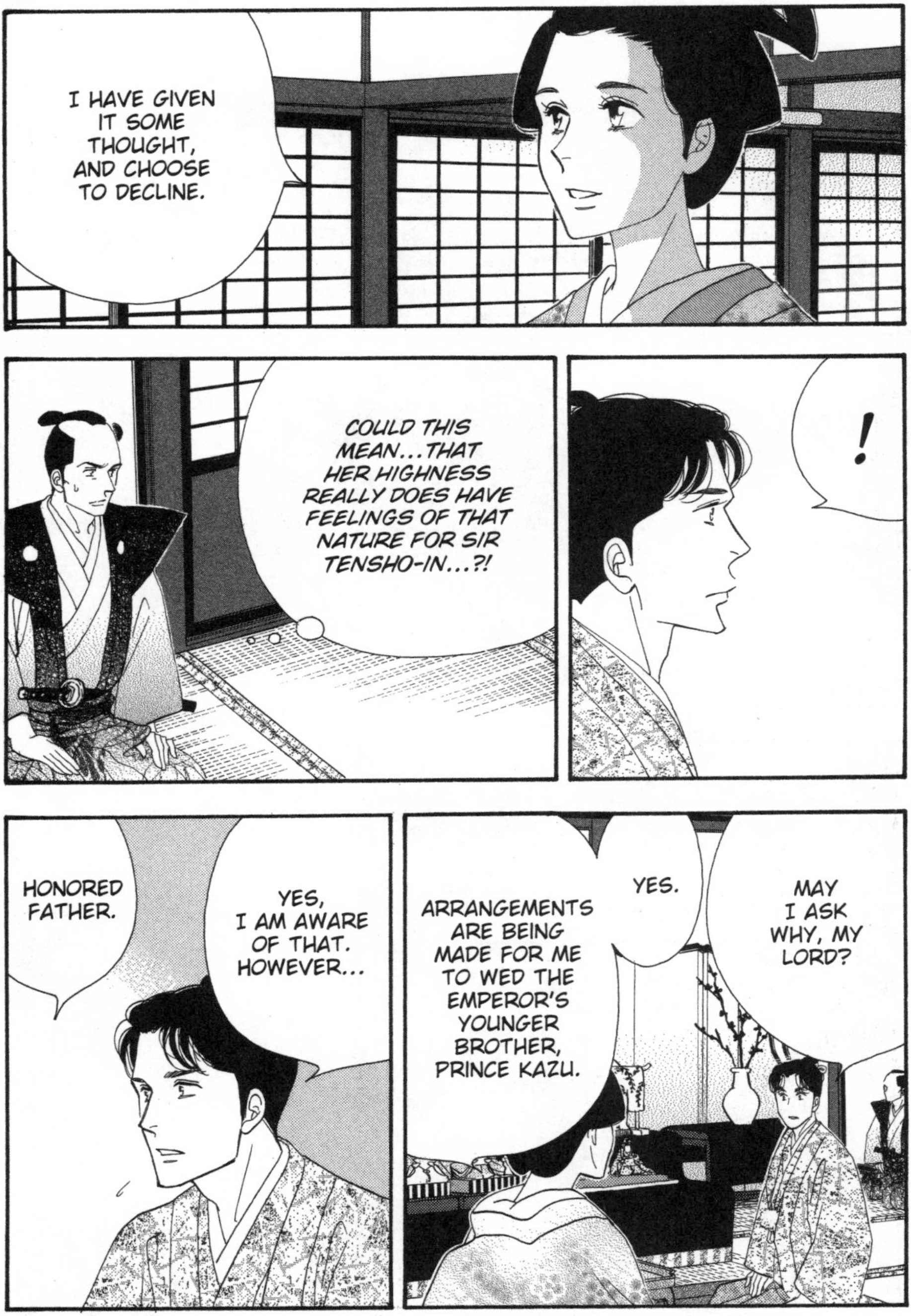
I HAVE GIVEN IT SOME THOUGHT, AND CHOOSE TO DECLINE.
!
COULD THIS MEAN...THAT HER HIGHNESS REALLY DOES HAVE FEELINGS OF THAT NATURE FOR SIR TENSHO-IN...?!
MAY I ASK WHY, MY LORD?
YES.
ARRANGEMENTS ARE BEING MADE FOR ME TO WED THE EMPEROR'S YOUNGER BROTHER, PRINCE KAZU.
YES, I AM AWARE OF THAT. HOWEVER...
HONORED FATHER.

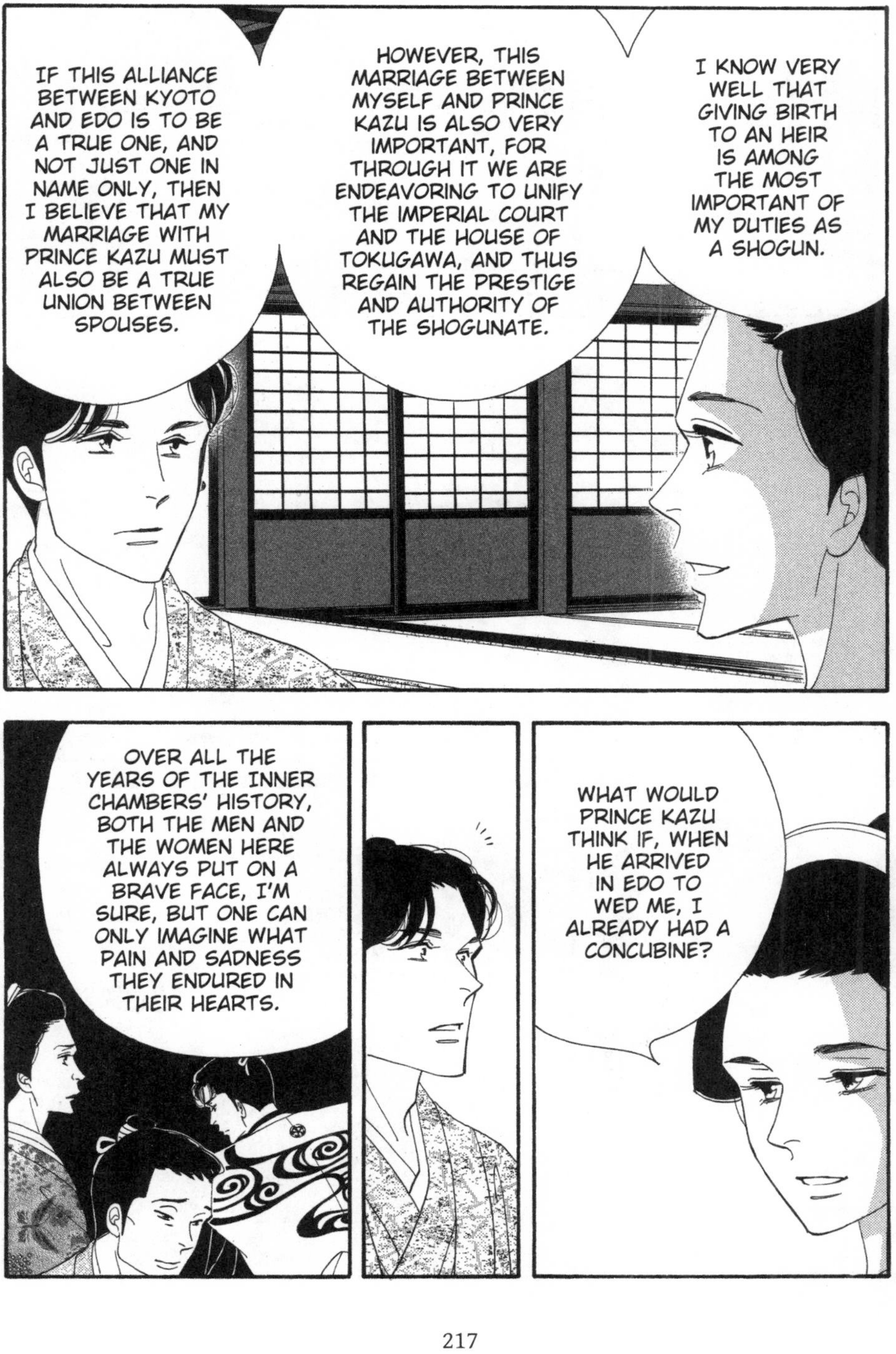
I KNOW VERY WELL THAT GIVING BIRTH TO AN HEIR IS AMONG THE MOST IMPORTANT OF MY DUTIES AS A SHOGUN.
HOWEVER, THIS MARRIAGE BETWEEN MYSELF AND PRINCE KAZU IS ALSO VERY IMPORTANT, FOR THROUGH IT WE ARE ENDEAVORING TO UNIFY THE IMPERIAL COURT AND THE HOUSE OF TOKUGAWA, AND THUS REGAIN THE PRESTIGE AND AUTHORITY OF THE SHOGUNATE.
IF THIS ALLIANCE BETWEEN KYOTO AND EDO IS TO BE A TRUE ONE, AND NOT JUST ONE IN NAME ONLY, THEN I BELIEVE THAT MY MARRIAGE WITH PRINCE KAZU MUST ALSO BE A TRUE UNION BETWEEN SPOUSES.
WHAT WOULD PRINCE KAZU THINK IF, WHEN HE ARRIVED IN EDO TO WED ME, I ALREADY HAD A CONCUBINE?
OVER ALL THE YEARS OF THE INNER CHAMBERS' HISTORY, BOTH THE MEN AND THE WOMEN HERE ALWAYS PUT ON A BRAVE FACE, I'M SURE, BUT ONE CAN ONLY IMAGINE WHAT PAIN AND SADNESS THEY ENDURED IN THEIR HEARTS.

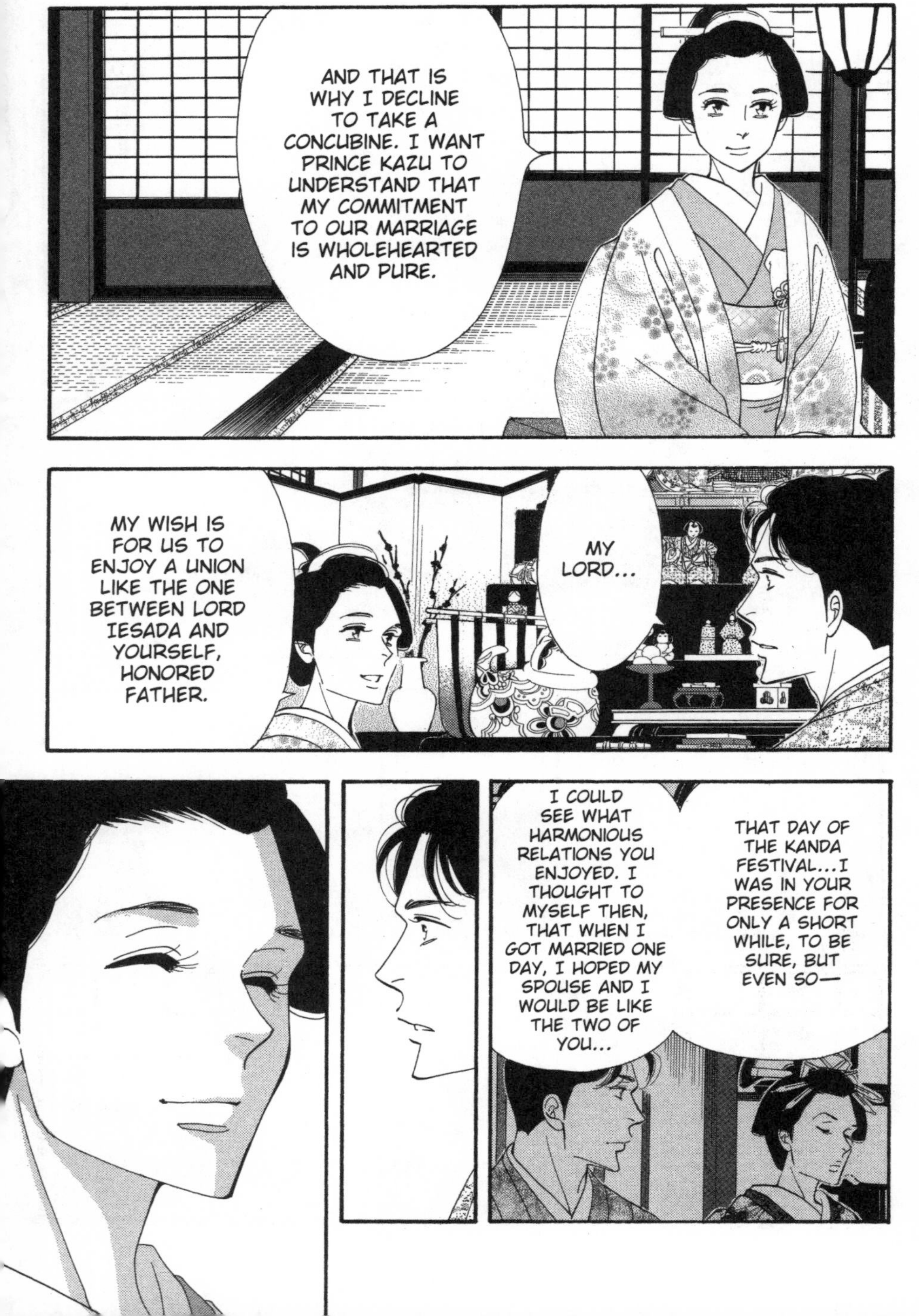
AND THAT IS WHY I DECLINE TO TAKE A CONCUBINE. I WANT PRINCE KAZU TO UNDERSTAND THAT MY COMMITMENT TO OUR MARRIAGE IS WHOLEHEARTED AND PURE.
MY LORD...
MY WISH IS FOR US TO ENJOY A UNION LIKE THE ONE BETWEEN LORD IESADA AND YOURSELF, HONORED FATHER.
THAT DAY OF THE KANDA FESTIVAL...I WAS IN YOUR PRESENCE FOR ONLY A SHORT WHILE, TO BE SURE, BUT EVEN SO—
I COULD SEE WHAT HARMONIOUS RELATIONS YOU ENJOYED. I THOUGHT TO MYSELF THEN, THAT WHEN I GOT MARRIED ONE DAY, I HOPED MY SPOUSE AND I WOULD BE LIKE THE TWO OF YOU...

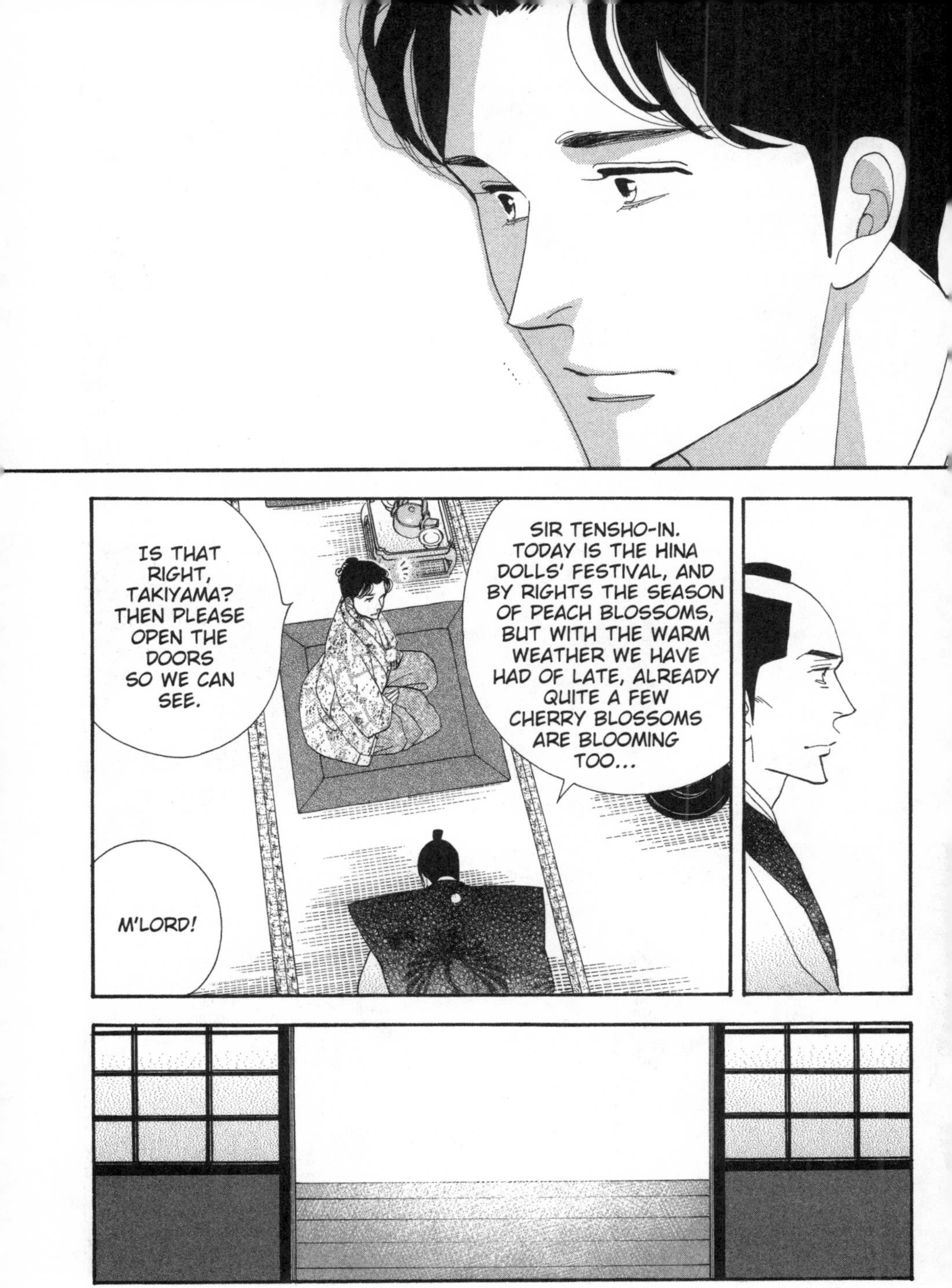
SIR TENSHO-IN. TODAY IS THE HINA DOLLS' FESTIVAL, AND BY RIGHTS THE SEASON OF PEACH BLOSSOMS, BUT WITH THE WARM WEATHER WE HAVE HAD OF LATE, ALREADY QUITE A FEW CHERRY BLOSSOMS ARE BLOOMING TOO...
IS THAT RIGHT, TAKIYAMA? THEN PLEASE OPEN THE DOORS SO WE CAN SEE.
M'LORD!

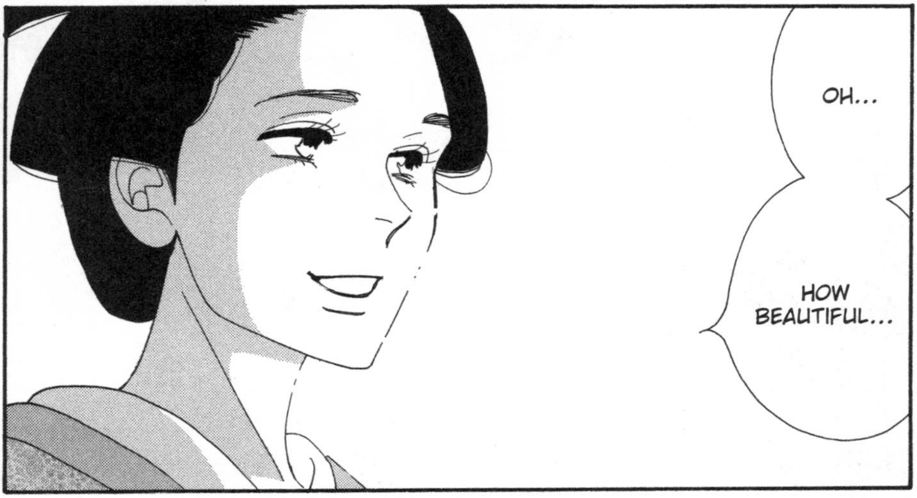
OH...
HOW BEAUTIFUL...

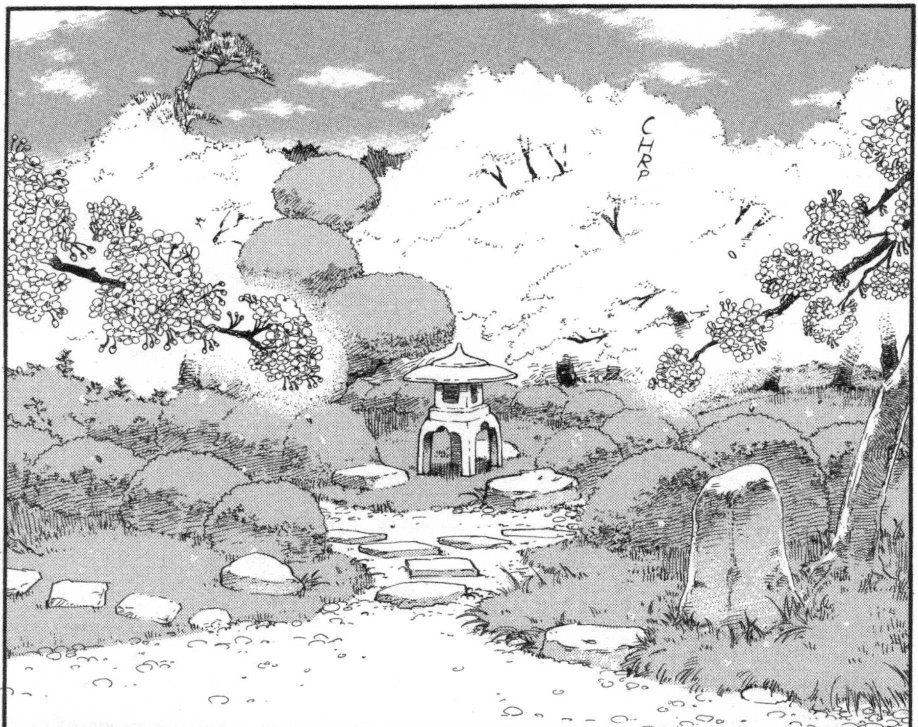
CHRP

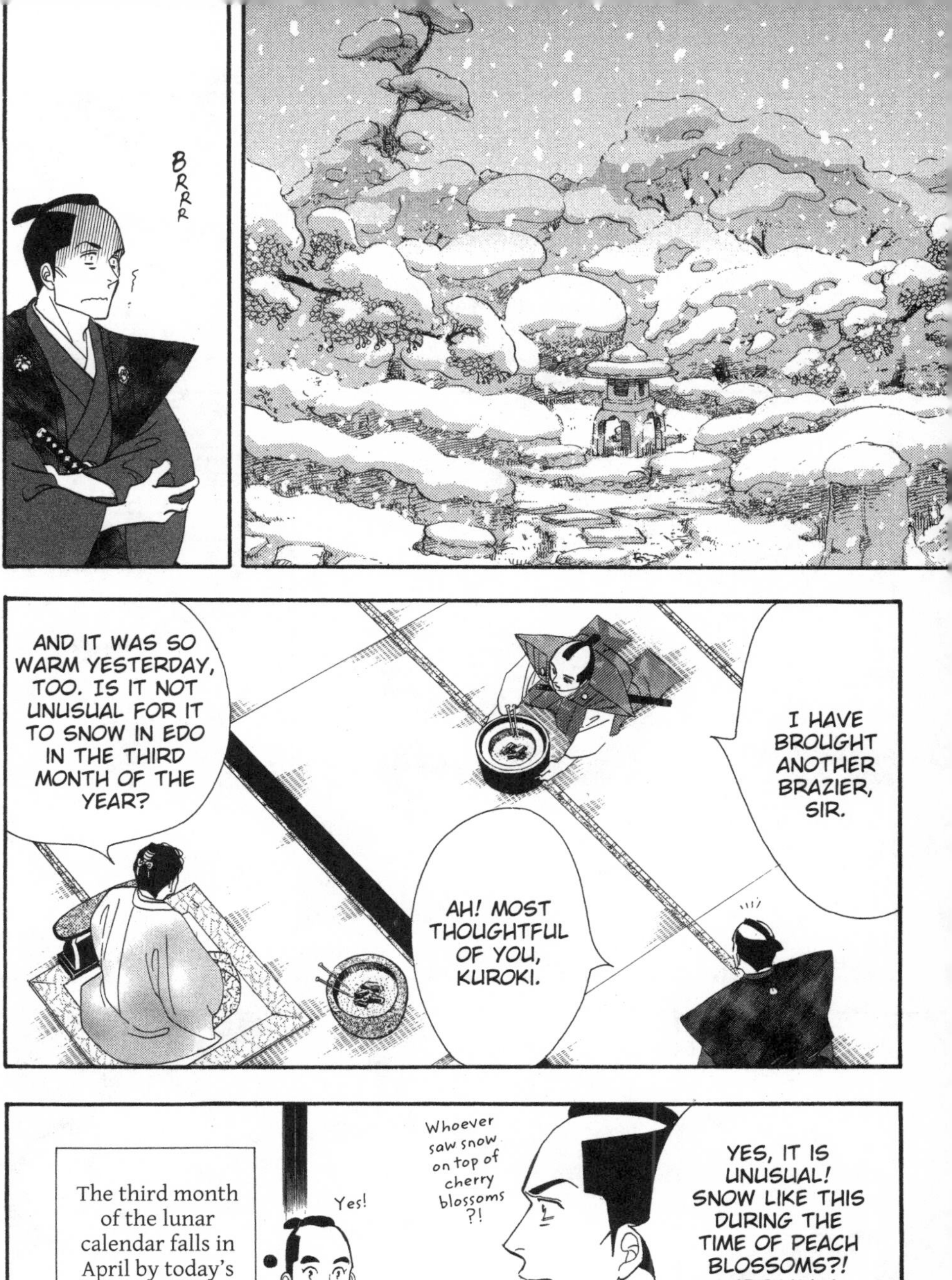
BRRR
I HAVE BROUGHT ANOTHER BRAZIER, SIR.
AH! MOST THOUGHTFUL OF YOU, KUROKI.
AND IT WAS SO WARM YESTERDAY, TOO. IS IT NOT UNUSUAL FOR IT TO SNOW IN EDO IN THE THIRD MONTH OF THE YEAR?
YES, IT IS UNUSUAL! SNOW LIKE THIS DURING THE TIME OF PEACH BLOSSOMS?! VIRTUALLY UNHEARD OF, EH, KUROKI?!
Whoever saw snow on top of cherry blossoms ?!
Yes!
The third month of the lunar calendar falls in April by today's calendar.

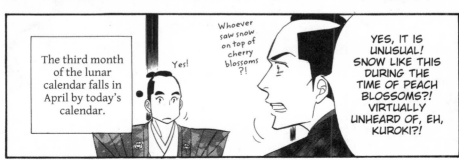

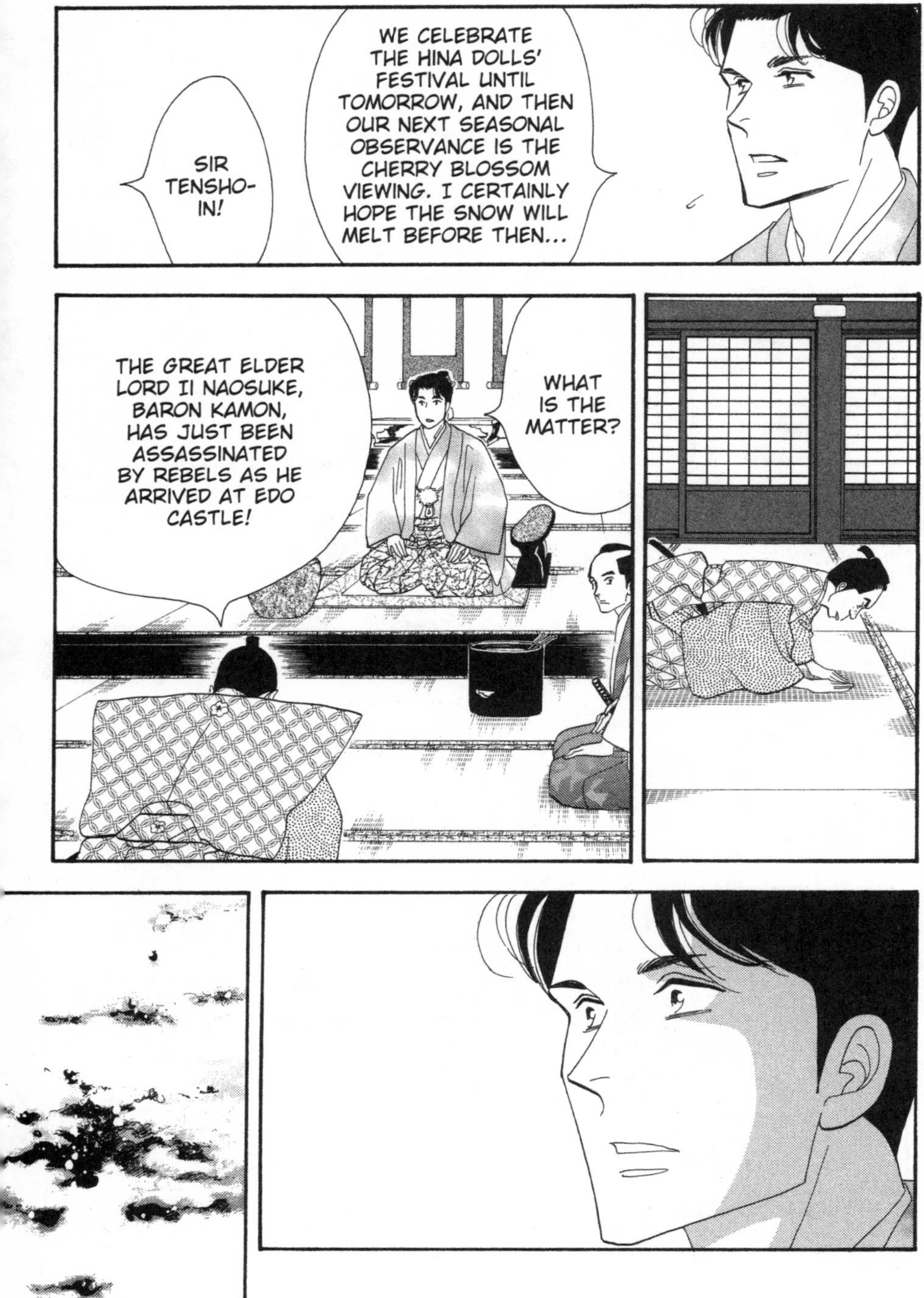
WE CELEBRATE THE HINA DOLLS' FESTIVAL UNTIL TOMORROW, AND THEN OUR NEXT SEASONAL OBSERVANCE IS THE CHERRY BLOSSOM VIEWING. I CERTAINLY HOPE THE SNOW WILL MELT BEFORE THEN...
SIR TENSHO-IN!
WHAT IS THE MATTER?
THE GREAT ELDER LORD II NAOSUKE, BARON KAMON, HAS JUST BEEN ASSASSINATED BY REBELS AS HE ARRIVED AT EDO CASTLE!

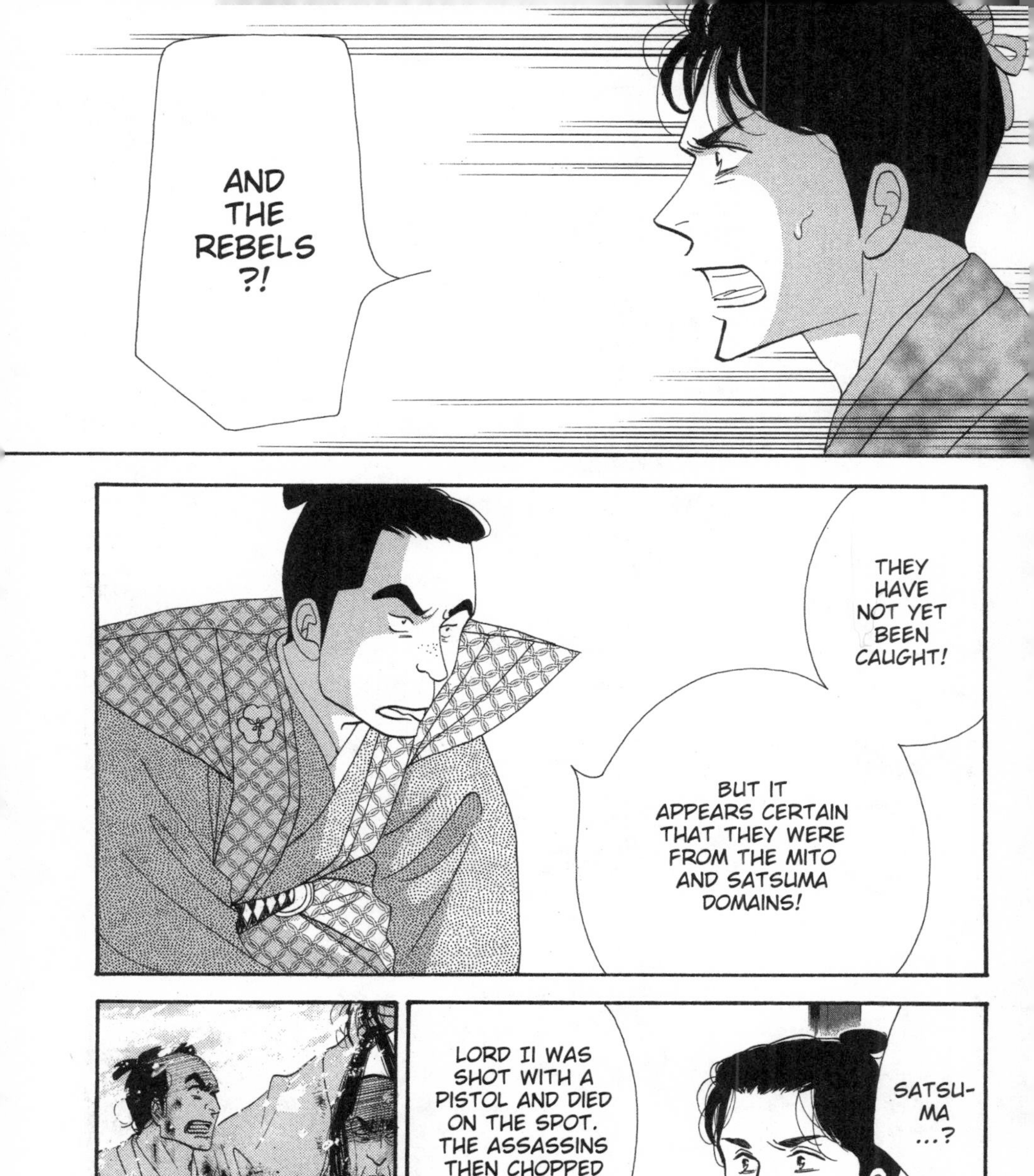
AND THE REBELS ?!
THEY HAVE NOT YET BEEN CAUGHT!
BUT IT APPEARS CERTAIN THAT THEY WERE FROM THE MITO AND SATSUMA DOMAINS!
SATSU-MA ...?
LORD II WAS SHOT WITH A PISTOL AND DIED ON THE SPOT. THE ASSASSINS THEN CHOPPED OFF HIS HEAD AND MADE OFF WITH IT...

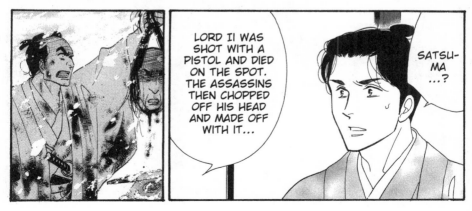

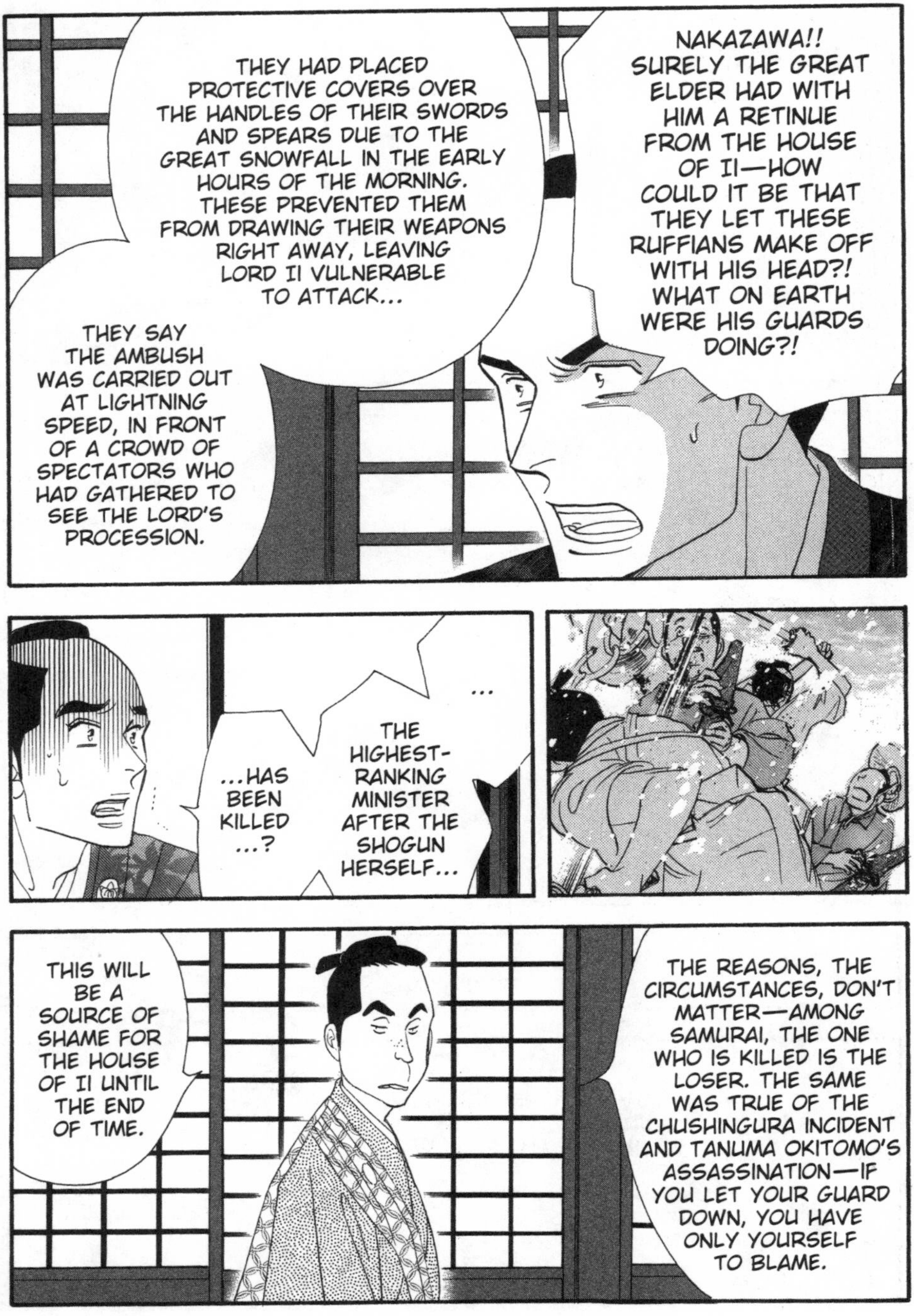
NAKAZAWA!! SURELY THE GREAT ELDER HAD WITH HIM A RETINUE FROM THE HOUSE OF II—HOW COULD IT BE THAT THEY LET THESE RUFFIANS MAKE OFF WITH HIS HEAD?! WHAT ON EARTH WERE HIS GUARDS DOING?!
THEY HAD PLACED PROTECTIVE COVERS OVER THE HANDLES OF THEIR SWORDS AND SPEARS DUE TO THE GREAT SNOWFALL IN THE EARLY HOURS OF THE MORNING. THESE PREVENTED THEM FROM DRAWING THEIR WEAPONS RIGHT AWAY, LEAVING LORD II VULNERABLE TO ATTACK...
THEY SAY THE AMBUSH WAS CARRIED OUT AT LIGHTNING SPEED, IN FRONT OF A CROWD OF SPECTATORS WHO HAD GATHERED TO SEE THE LORD'S PROCESSION.
...
THE HIGHEST-RANKING MINISTER AFTER THE SHOGUN HERSELF...
...HAS BEEN KILLED ...?
THE REASONS, THE CIRCUMSTANCES, DON'T MATTER—AMONG SAMURAI, THE ONE WHO IS KILLED IS THE LOSER. THE SAME WAS TRUE OF THE CHUSHINGURA INCIDENT AND TANUMA OKITOMO'S ASSASSINATION—IF YOU LET YOUR GUARD DOWN, YOU HAVE ONLY YOURSELF TO BLAME.
THIS WILL BE A SOURCE OF SHAME FOR THE HOUSE OF II UNTIL THE END OF TIME.

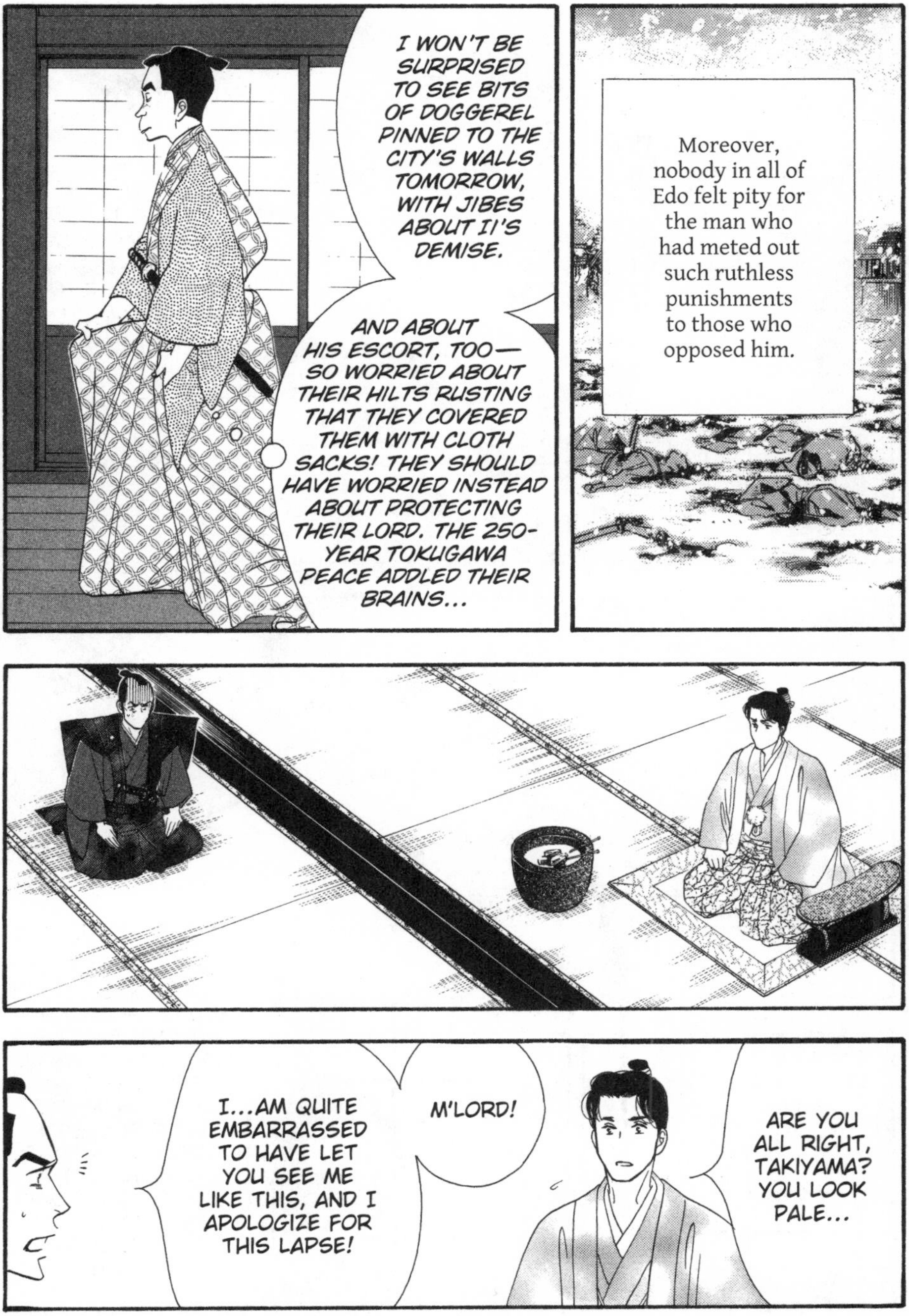
Moreover, nobody in all of Edo felt pity for the man who had meted out such ruthless punishments to those who opposed him.
I WON'T BE SURPRISED TO SEE BITS OF DOGGEREL PINNED TO THE CITY'S WALLS TOMORROW, WITH JIBES ABOUT II'S DEMISE.
AND ABOUT HIS ESCORT, TOO—SO WORRIED ABOUT THEIR HILTS RUSTING THAT THEY COVERED THEM WITH CLOTH SACKS! THEY SHOULD HAVE WORRIED INSTEAD ABOUT PROTECTING THEIR LORD. THE 250-YEAR TOKUGAWA PEACE ADDLED THEIR BRAINS...
ARE YOU ALL RIGHT, TAKIYAMA? YOU LOOK PALE...
M'LORD!
I...AM QUITE EMBARRASSED TO HAVE LET YOU SEE ME LIKE THIS, AND I APOLOGIZE FOR THIS LAPSE!

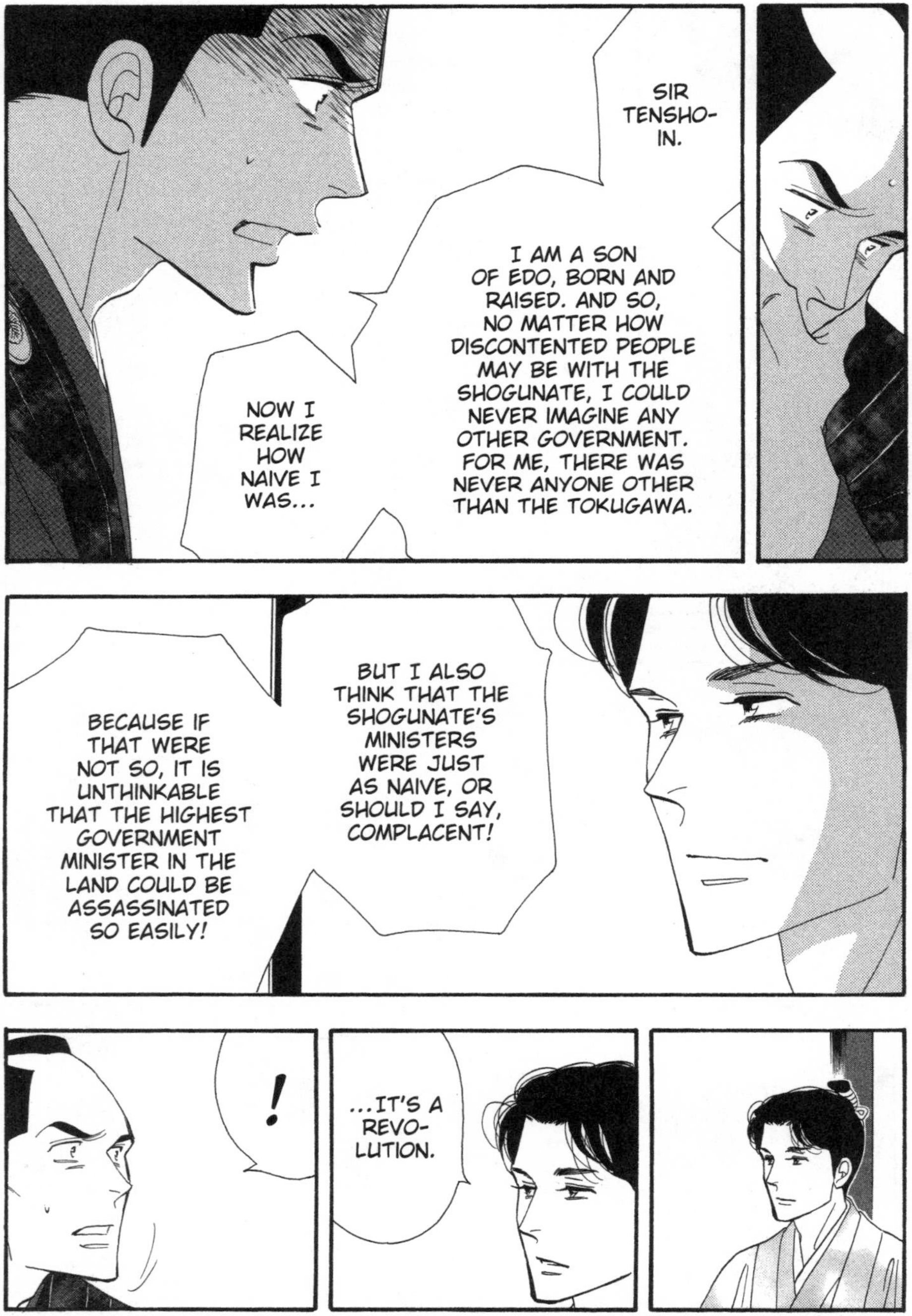
SIR TENSHO-IN.
I AM A SON OF EDO, BORN AND RAISED. AND SO, NO MATTER HOW DISCONTENTED PEOPLE MAY BE WITH THE SHOGUNATE, I COULD NEVER IMAGINE ANY OTHER GOVERNMENT. FOR ME, THERE WAS NEVER ANYONE OTHER THAN THE TOKUGAWA.
NOW I REALIZE HOW NAIVE I WAS…
BUT I ALSO THINK THAT THE SHOGUNATE'S MINISTERS WERE JUST AS NAIVE, OR SHOULD I SAY, COMPLACENT!
BECAUSE IF THAT WERE NOT SO, IT IS UNTHINKABLE THAT THE HIGHEST GOVERNMENT MINISTER IN THE LAND COULD BE ASSASSINATED SO EASILY!
…IT'S A REVO-LUTION.
!

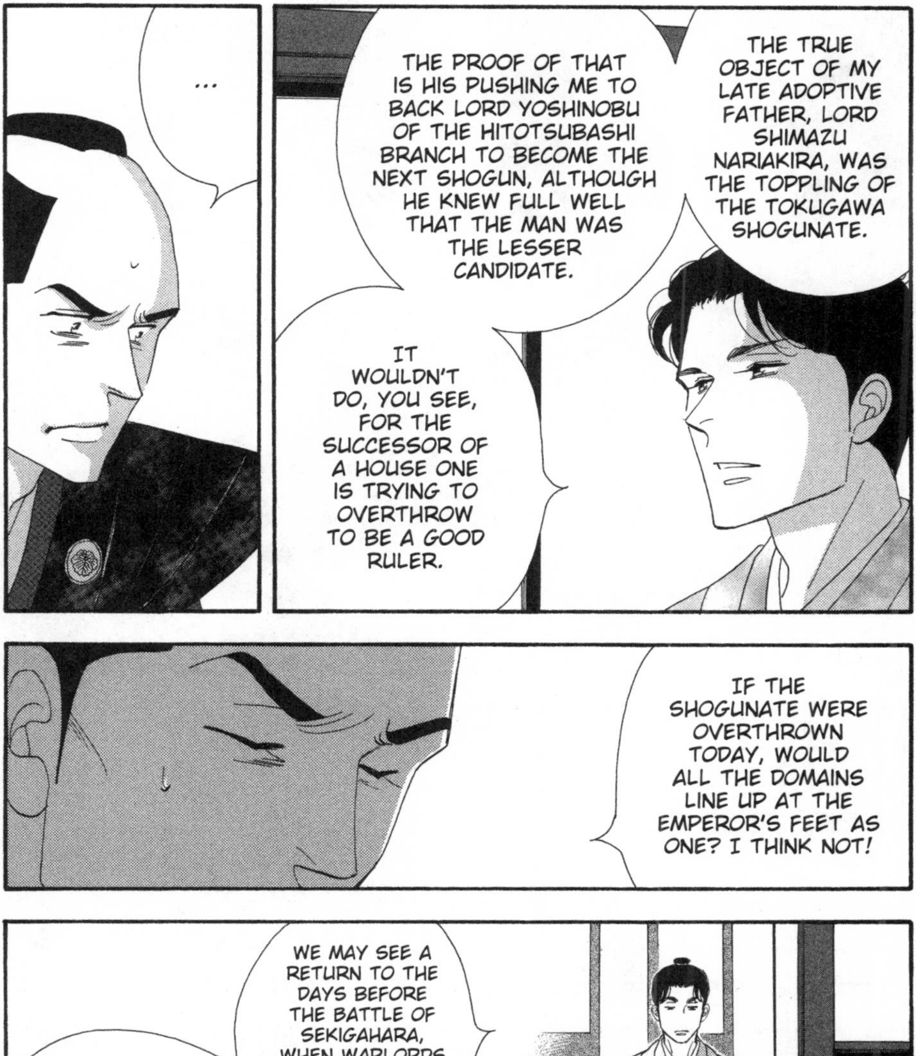
THE TRUE OBJECT OF MY LATE ADOPTIVE FATHER, LORD SHIMAZU NARIAKIRA, WAS THE TOPPLING OF THE TOKUGAWA SHOGUNATE.
THE PROOF OF THAT IS HIS PUSHING ME TO BACK LORD YOSHINOBU OF THE HITOTSUBASHI BRANCH TO BECOME THE NEXT SHOGUN, ALTHOUGH HE KNEW FULL WELL THAT THE MAN WAS THE LESSER CANDIDATE.
IT WOULDN'T DO, YOU SEE, FOR THE SUCCESSOR OF A HOUSE ONE IS TRYING TO OVERTHROW TO BE A GOOD RULER.
...
IF THE SHOGUNATE WERE OVERTHROWN TODAY, WOULD ALL THE DOMAINS LINE UP AT THE EMPEROR'S FEET AS ONE? I THINK NOT!
WE MAY SEE A RETURN TO THE DAYS BEFORE THE BATTLE OF SEKIGAHARA, WHEN WARLORDS CONSTANTLY FOUGHT EACH OTHER FOR DOMINANCE...
OR, BEFORE THAT CAN HAPPEN, JAPAN COULD BECOME A COLONY OF ONE OF THE WESTERN POWERS, IN WHICH CASE OUR NATION WOULD CEASE TO EXIST.

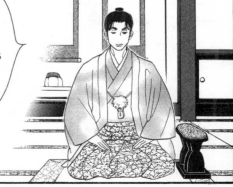

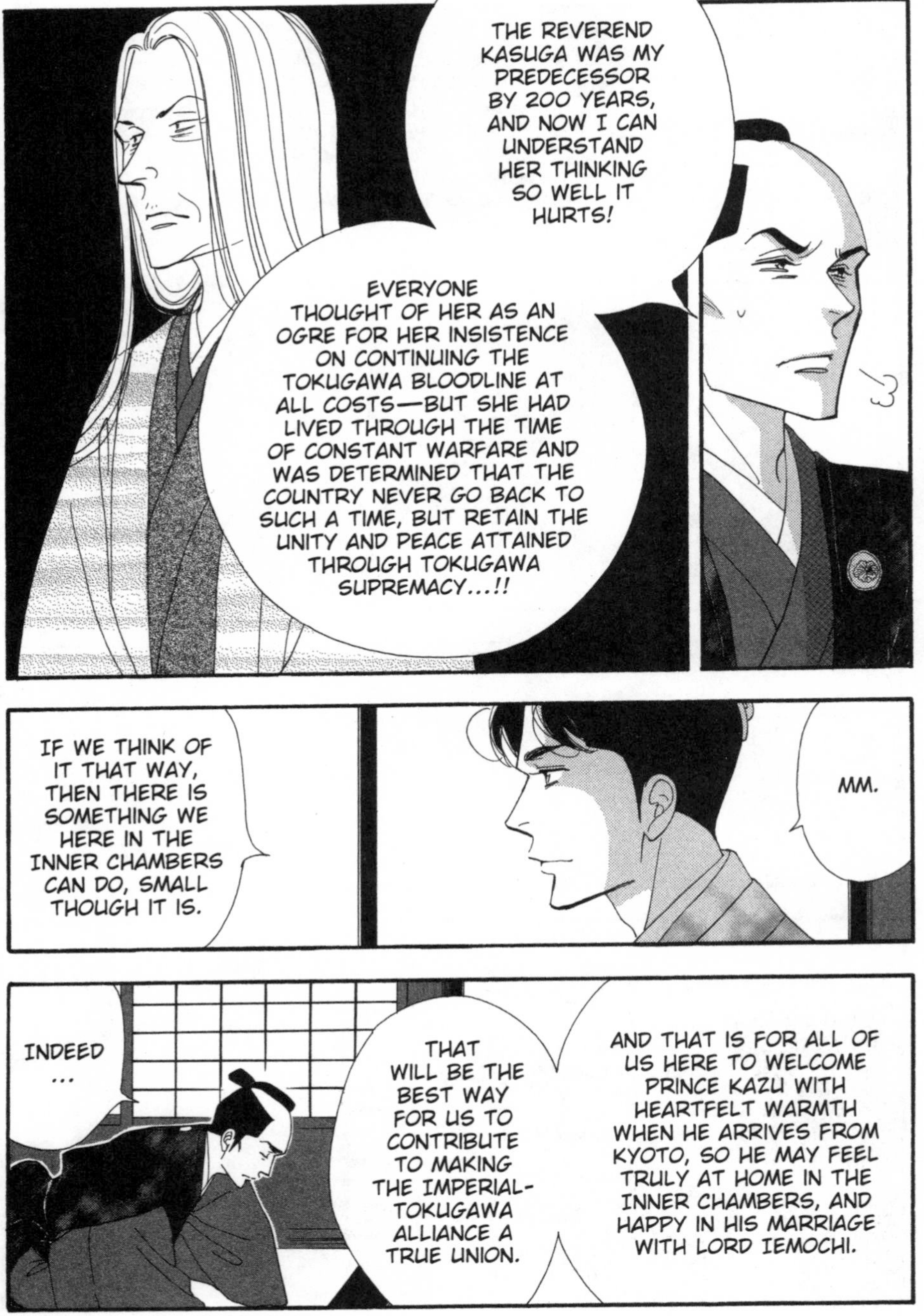
THE REVEREND KASUGA WAS MY PREDECESSOR BY 200 YEARS, AND NOW I CAN UNDERSTAND HER THINKING SO WELL IT HURTS!
EVERYONE THOUGHT OF HER AS AN OGRE FOR HER INSISTENCE ON CONTINUING THE TOKUGAWA BLOODLINE AT ALL COSTS—BUT SHE HAD LIVED THROUGH THE TIME OF CONSTANT WARFARE AND WAS DETERMINED THAT THE COUNTRY NEVER GO BACK TO SUCH A TIME, BUT RETAIN THE UNITY AND PEACE ATTAINED THROUGH TOKUGAWA SUPREMACY...!!
MM.
IF WE THINK OF IT THAT WAY, THEN THERE IS SOMETHING WE HERE IN THE INNER CHAMBERS CAN DO, SMALL THOUGH IT IS.
AND THAT IS FOR ALL OF US HERE TO WELCOME PRINCE KAZU WITH HEARTFELT WARMTH WHEN HE ARRIVES FROM KYOTO, SO HE MAY FEEL TRULY AT HOME IN THE INNER CHAMBERS, AND HAPPY IN HIS MARRIAGE WITH LORD IEMOCHI.
THAT WILL BE THE BEST WAY FOR US TO CONTRIBUTE TO MAKING THE IMPERIAL-TOKUGAWA ALLIANCE A TRUE UNION.
INDEED ...

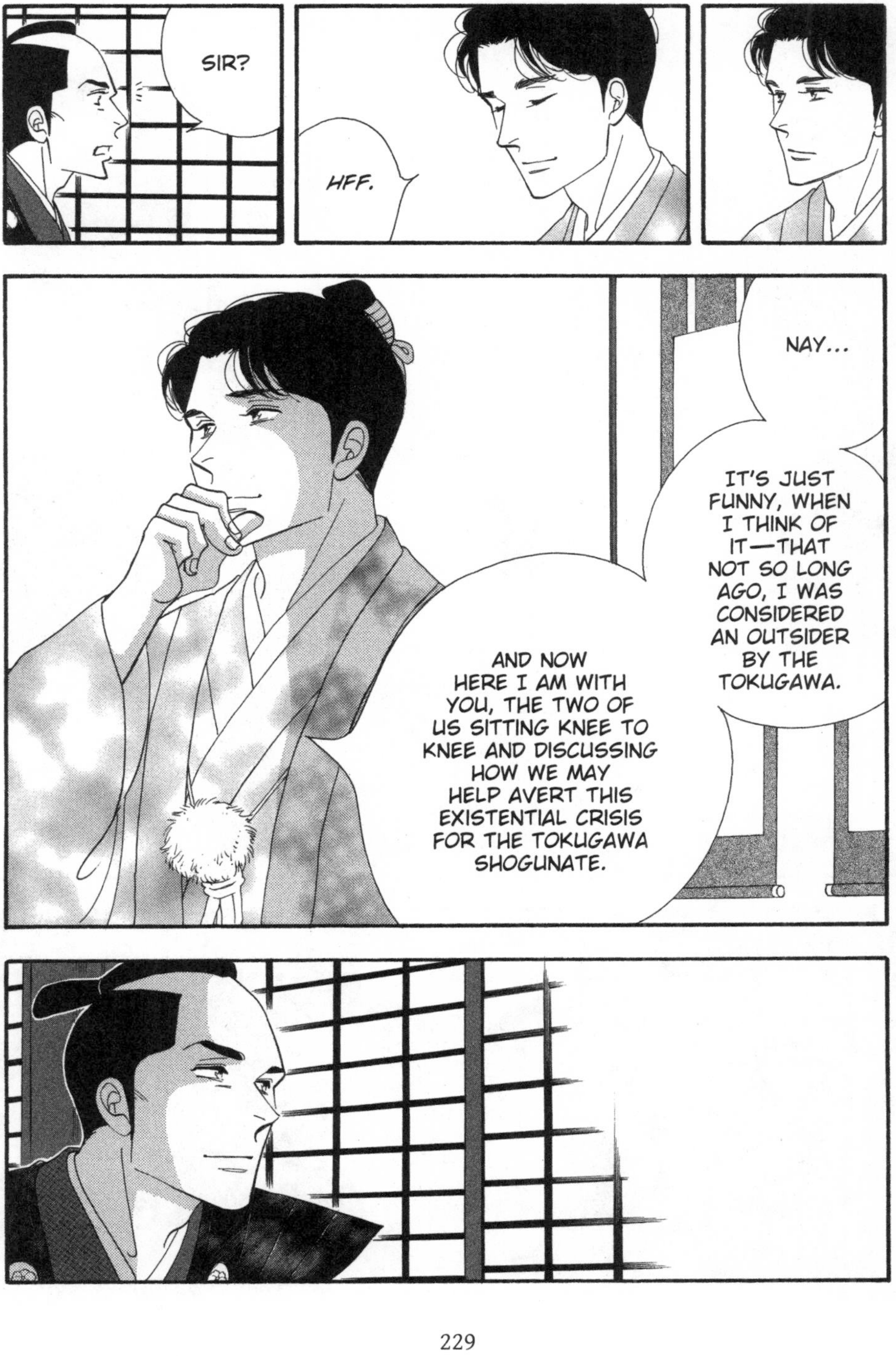
HFF.
SIR?
NAY...
IT'S JUST FUNNY, WHEN I THINK OF IT—THAT NOT SO LONG AGO, I WAS CONSIDERED AN OUTSIDER BY THE TOKUGAWA.
AND NOW HERE I AM WITH YOU, THE TWO OF US SITTING KNEE TO KNEE AND DISCUSSING HOW WE MAY HELP AVERT THIS EXISTENTIAL CRISIS FOR THE TOKUGAWA SHOGUNATE.

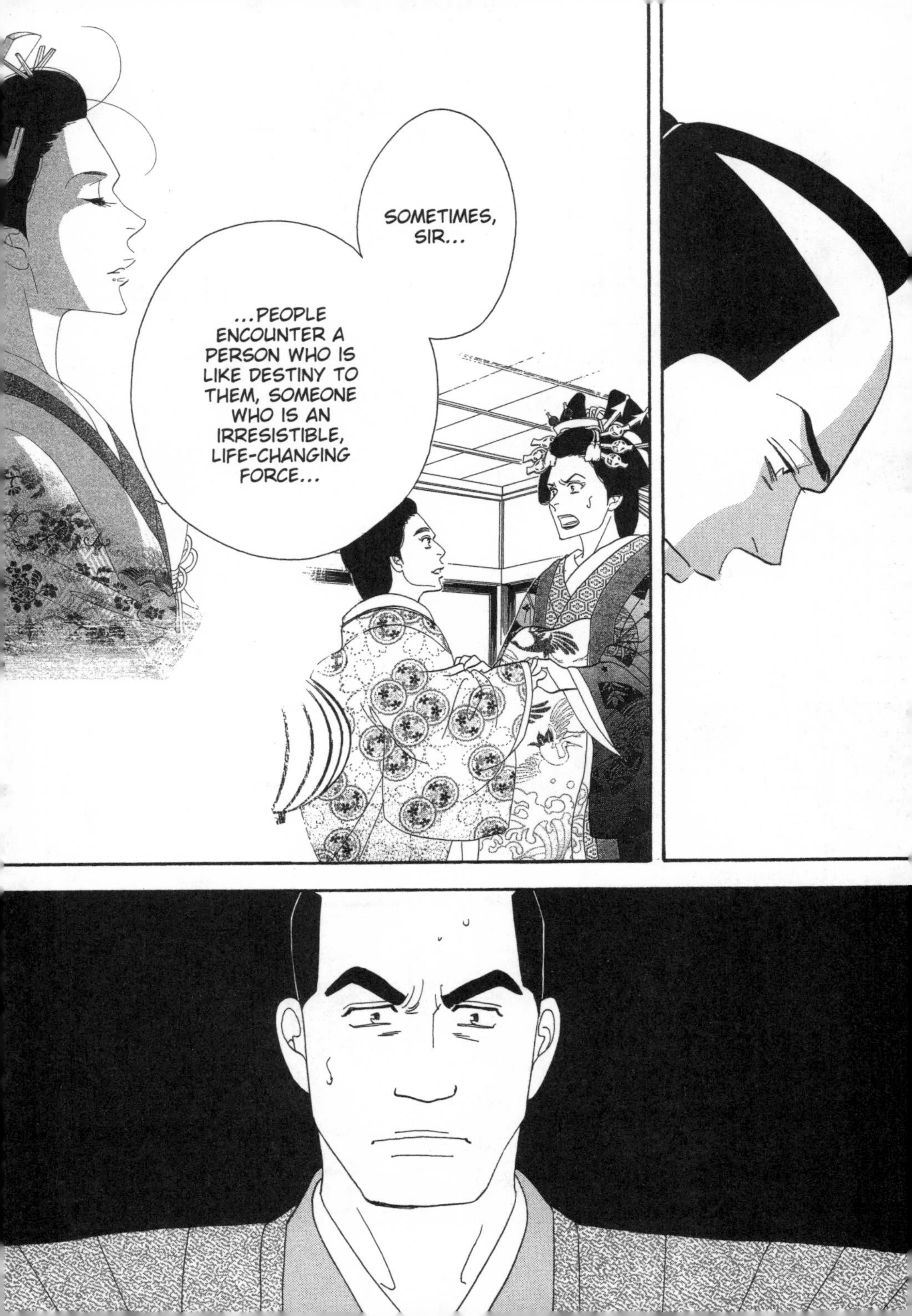
SOMETIMES, SIR...
...PEOPLE ENCOUNTER A PERSON WHO IS LIKE DESTINY TO THEM, SOMEONE WHO IS AN IRRESISTIBLE, LIFE-CHANGING FORCE...

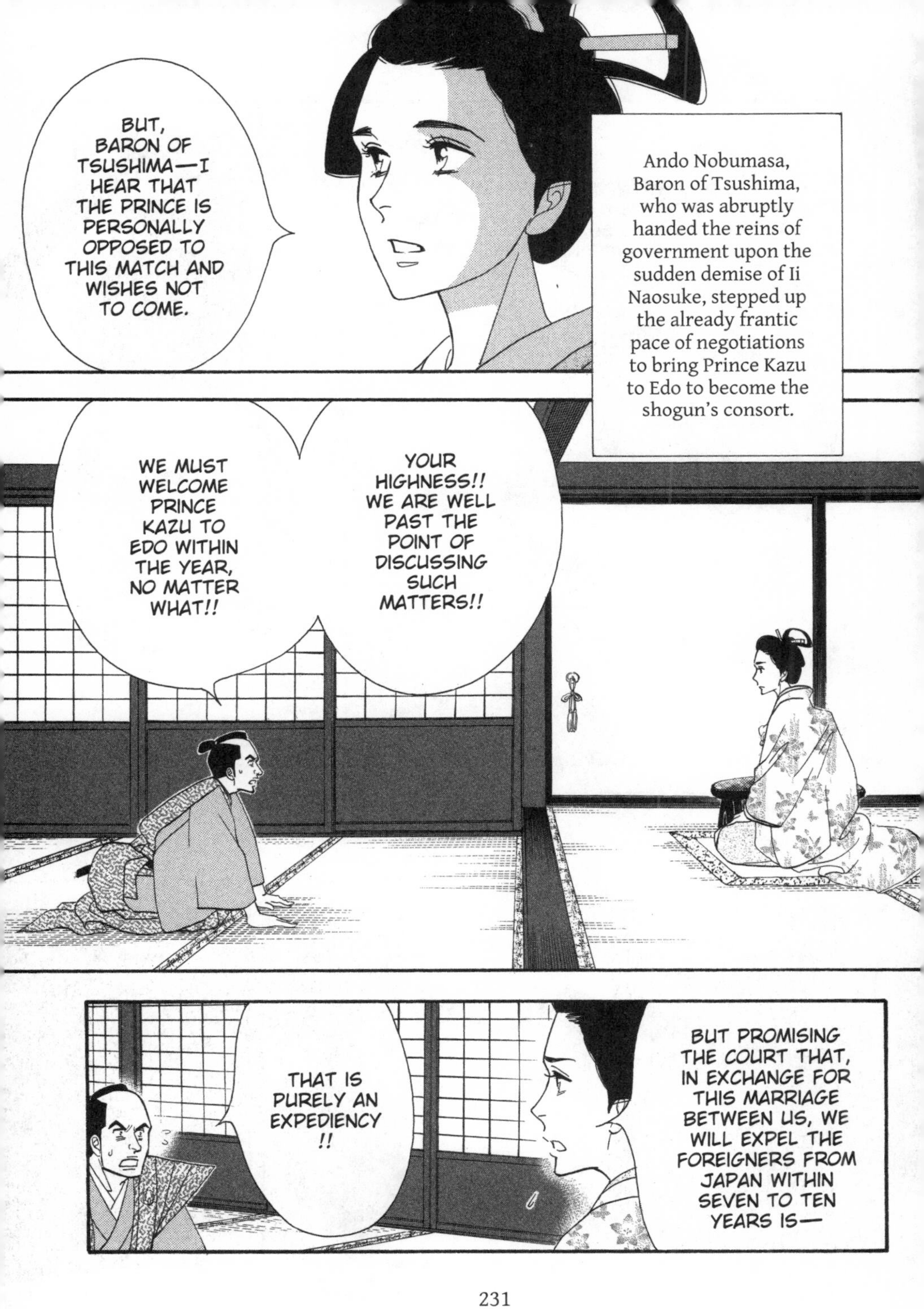
Ando Nobumasa, Baron of Tsushima, who was abruptly handed the reins of government upon the sudden demise of Ii Naosuke, stepped up the already frantic pace of negotiations to bring Prince Kazu to Edo to become the shogun's consort.
BUT, BARON OF TSUSHIMA—I HEAR THAT THE PRINCE IS PERSONALLY OPPOSED TO THIS MATCH AND WISHES NOT TO COME.
YOUR HIGHNESS!! WE ARE WELL PAST THE POINT OF DISCUSSING SUCH MATTERS!!
WE MUST WELCOME PRINCE KAZU TO EDO WITHIN THE YEAR, NO MATTER WHAT!!
BUT PROMISING THE COURT THAT, IN EXCHANGE FOR THIS MARRIAGE BETWEEN US, WE WILL EXPEL THE FOREIGNERS FROM JAPAN WITHIN SEVEN TO TEN YEARS IS—
THAT IS PURELY AN EXPEDIENCY!!

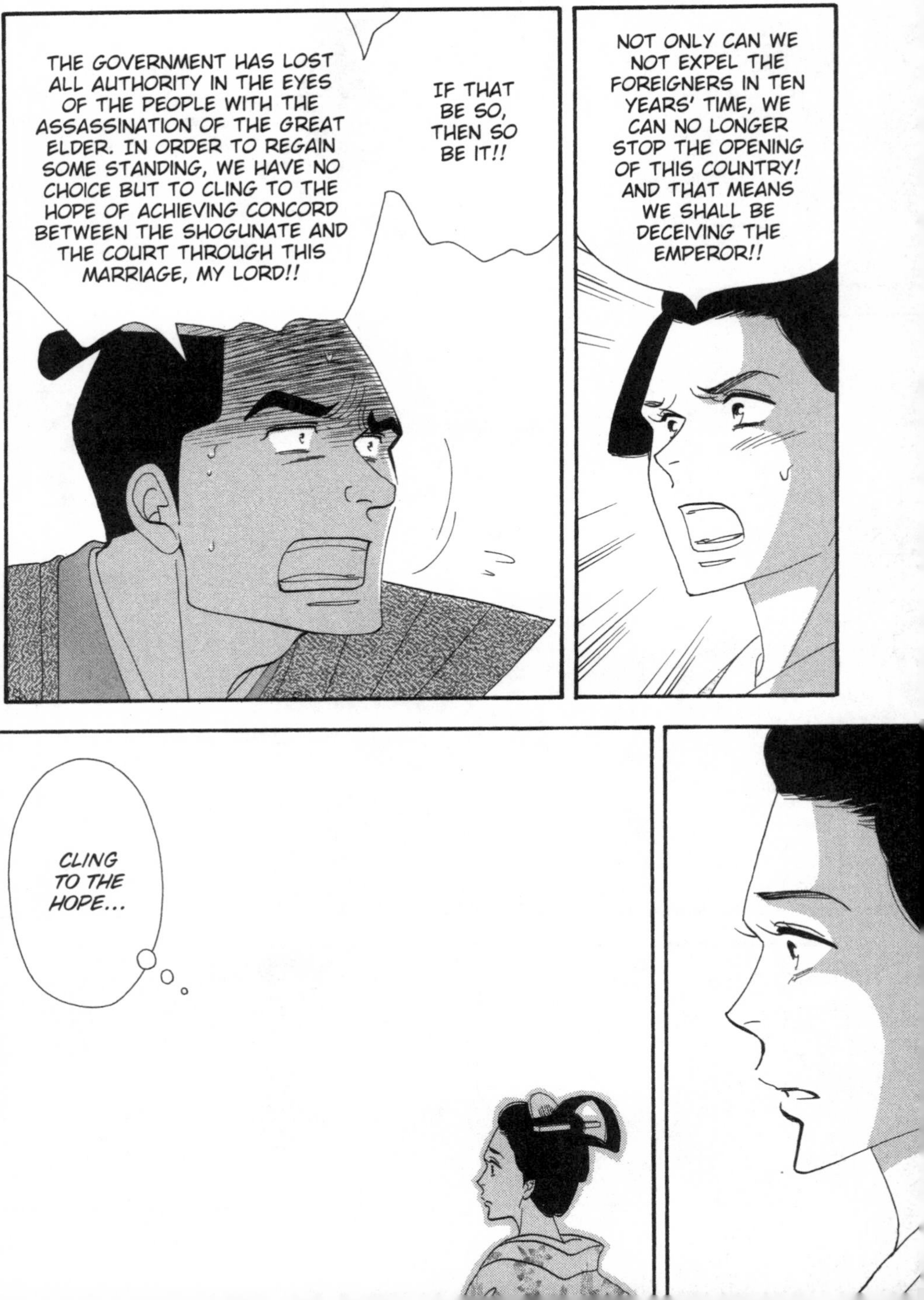
NOT ONLY CAN WE NOT EXPEL THE FOREIGNERS IN TEN YEARS' TIME, WE CAN NO LONGER STOP THE OPENING OF THIS COUNTRY! AND THAT MEANS WE SHALL BE DECEIVING THE EMPEROR!!
IF THAT BE SO, THEN SO BE IT!!
THE GOVERNMENT HAS LOST ALL AUTHORITY IN THE EYES OF THE PEOPLE WITH THE ASSASSINATION OF THE GREAT ELDER. IN ORDER TO REGAIN SOME STANDING, WE HAVE NO CHOICE BUT TO CLING TO THE HOPE OF ACHIEVING CONCORD BETWEEN THE SHOGUNATE AND THE COURT THROUGH THIS MARRIAGE, MY LORD!!
CLING TO THE HOPE...

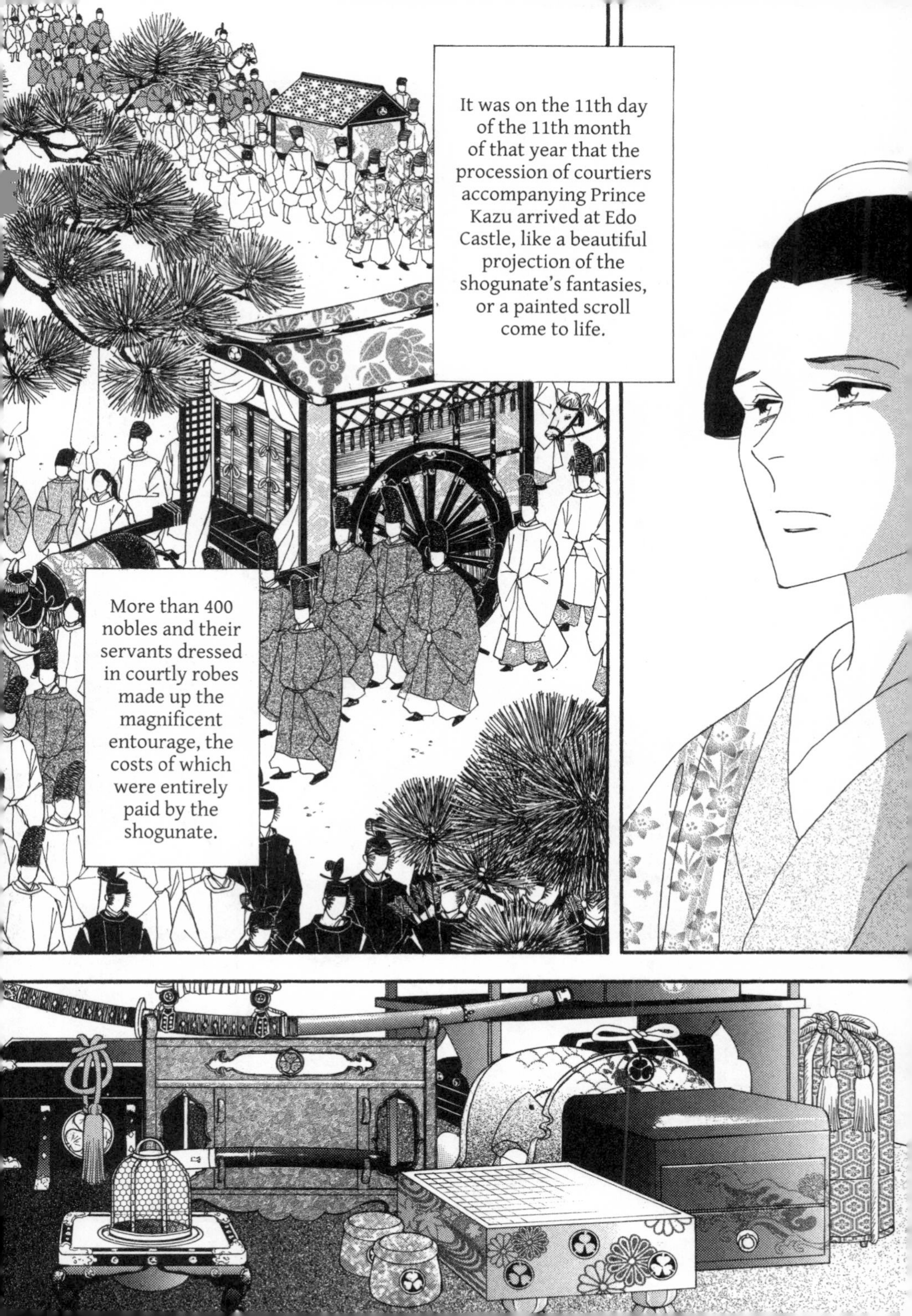
It was on the 11th day of the 11th month of that year that the procession of courtiers accompanying Prince Kazu arrived at Edo Castle, like a beautiful projection of the shogunate's fantasies, or a painted scroll come to life.
More than 400 nobles and their servants dressed in courtly robes made up the magnificent entourage, the costs of which were entirely paid by the shogunate.

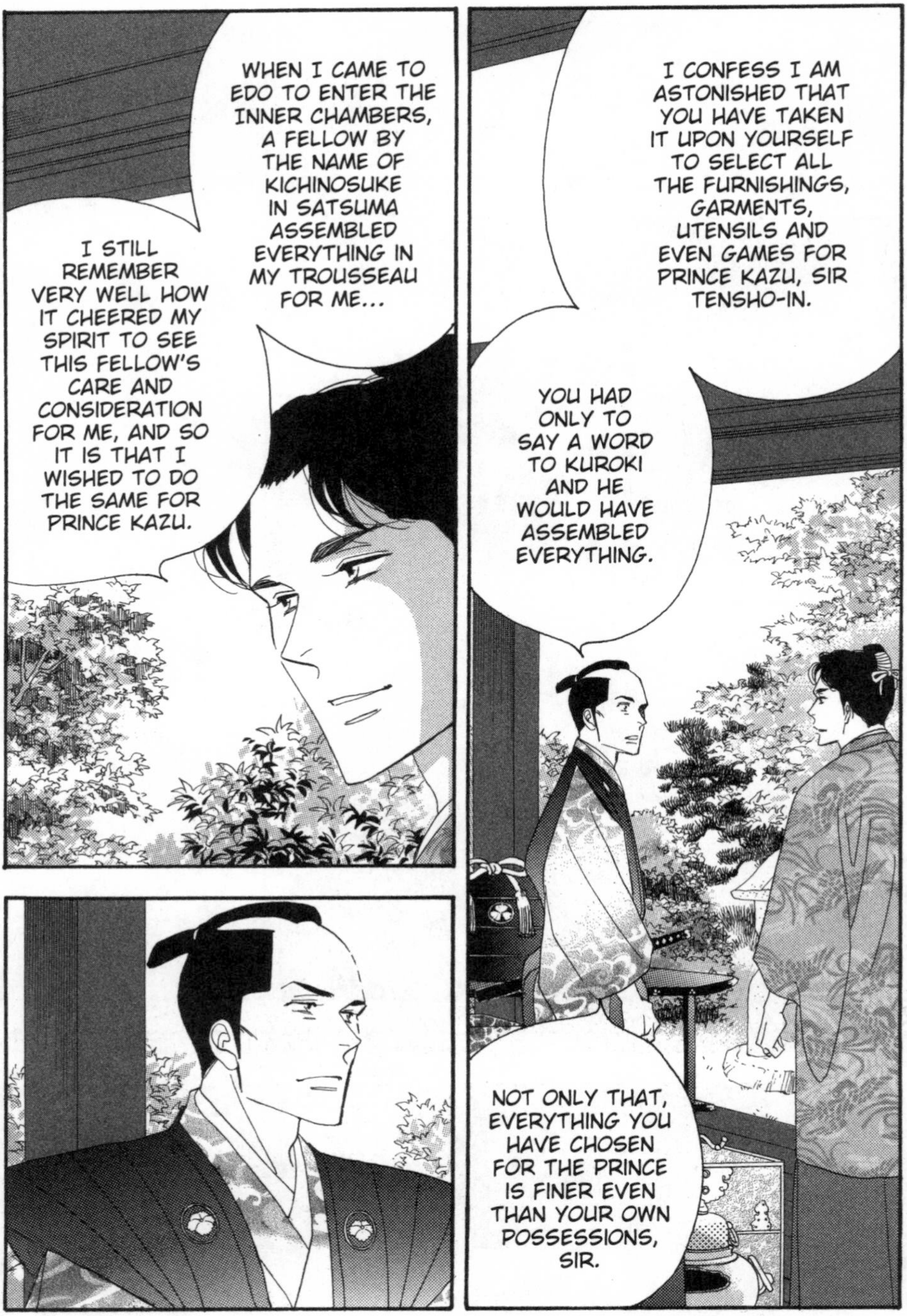
I CONFESS I AM ASTONISHED THAT YOU HAVE TAKEN IT UPON YOURSELF TO SELECT ALL THE FURNISHINGS, GARMENTS, UTENSILS AND EVEN GAMES FOR PRINCE KAZU, SIR TENSHO-IN.
YOU HAD ONLY TO SAY A WORD TO KUROKI AND HE WOULD HAVE ASSEMBLED EVERYTHING.
NOT ONLY THAT, EVERYTHING YOU HAVE CHOSEN FOR THE PRINCE IS FINER EVEN THAN YOUR OWN POSSESSIONS, SIR.
WHEN I CAME TO EDO TO ENTER THE INNER CHAMBERS, A FELLOW BY THE NAME OF KICHINOSUKE IN SATSUMA ASSEMBLED EVERYTHING IN MY TROUSSEAU FOR ME...
I STILL REMEMBER VERY WELL HOW IT CHEERED MY SPIRIT TO SEE THIS FELLOW'S CARE AND CONSIDERATION FOR ME, AND SO IT IS THAT I WISHED TO DO THE SAME FOR PRINCE KAZU.

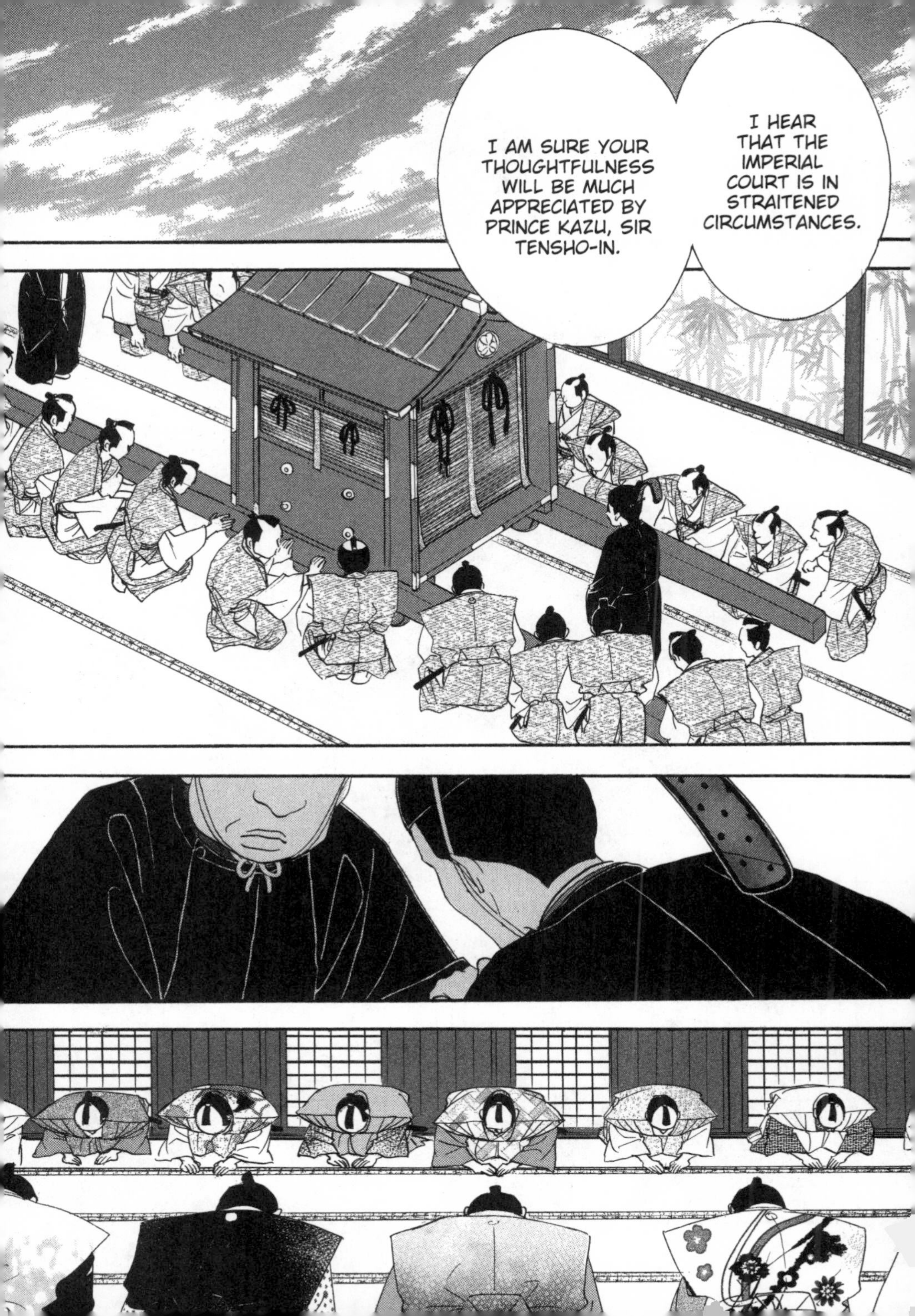
I HEAR THAT THE IMPERIAL COURT IS IN STRAITENED CIRCUMSTANCES.
I AM SURE YOUR THOUGHTFULNESS WILL BE MUCH APPRECIATED BY PRINCE KAZU, SIR TENSHO-IN.

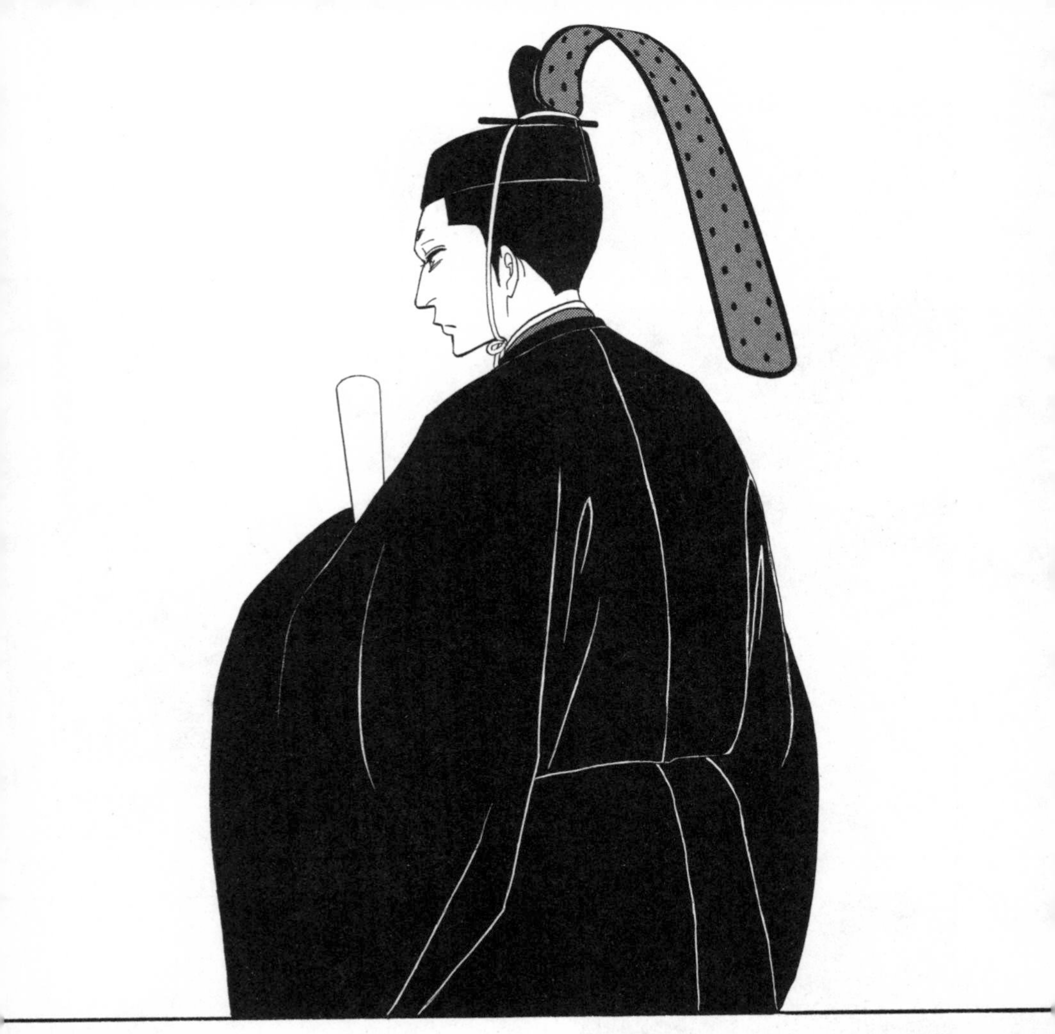

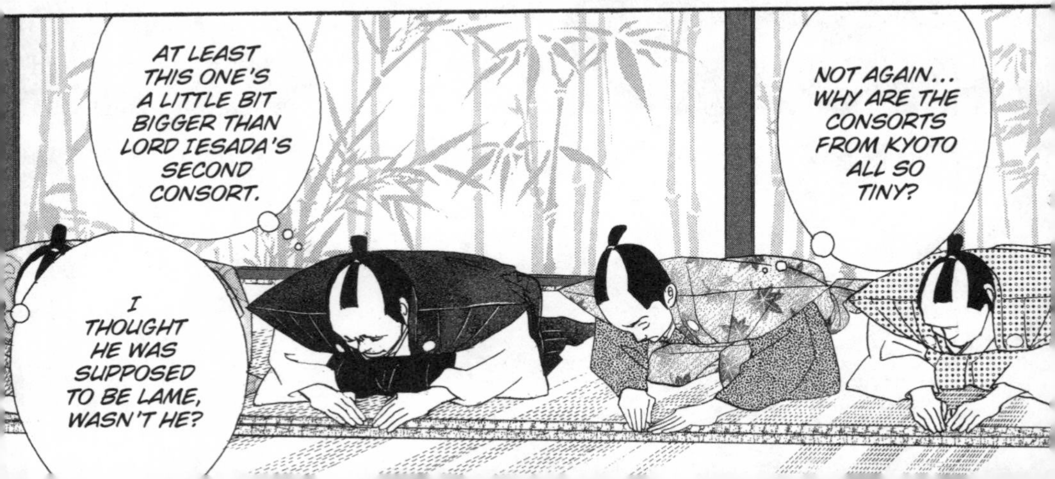
NOT AGAIN... WHY ARE THE CONSORTS FROM KYOTO ALL SO TINY?
AT LEAST THIS ONE'S A LITTLE BIT BIGGER THAN LORD IESADA'S SECOND CONSORT.
I THOUGHT HE WAS SUPPOSED TO BE LAME, WASN'T HE?

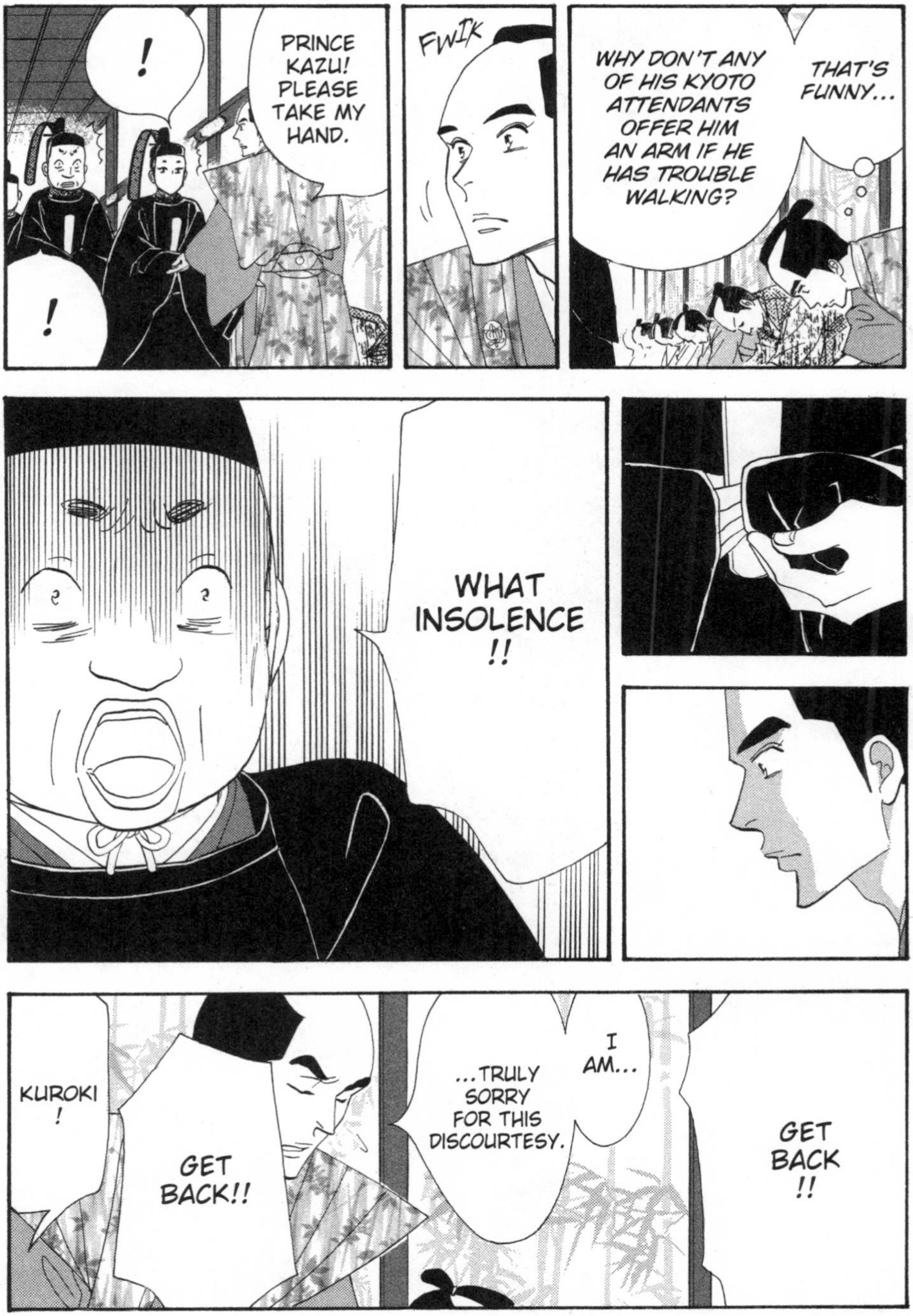
THAT'S FUNNY...
WHY DON'T ANY OF HIS KYOTO ATTENDANTS OFFER HIM AN ARM IF HE HAS TROUBLE WALKING?
FWIK
PRINCE KAZU! PLEASE TAKE MY HAND.
!
!
WHAT INSOLENCE!!
GET BACK!!
I AM...
...TRULY SORRY FOR THIS DISCOURTESY.
GET BACK!!
KUROKI!

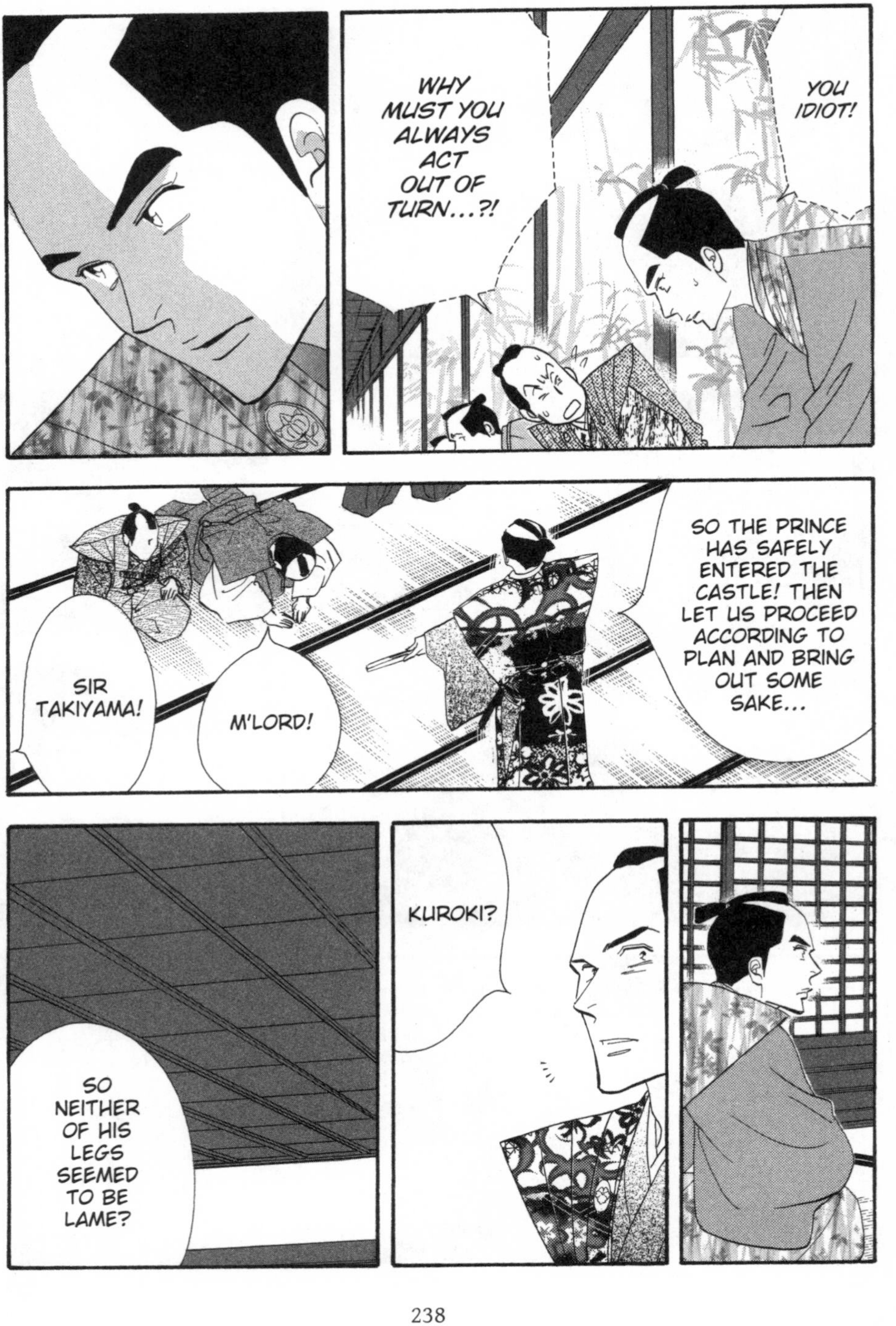
YOU IDIOT!
WHY MUST YOU ALWAYS ACT OUT OF TURN...?!
SO THE PRINCE HAS SAFELY ENTERED THE CASTLE! THEN LET US PROCEED ACCORDING TO PLAN AND BRING OUT SOME SAKE...
M'LORD!
SIR TAKIYAMA!
KUROKI?
SO NEITHER OF HIS LEGS SEEMED TO BE LAME?

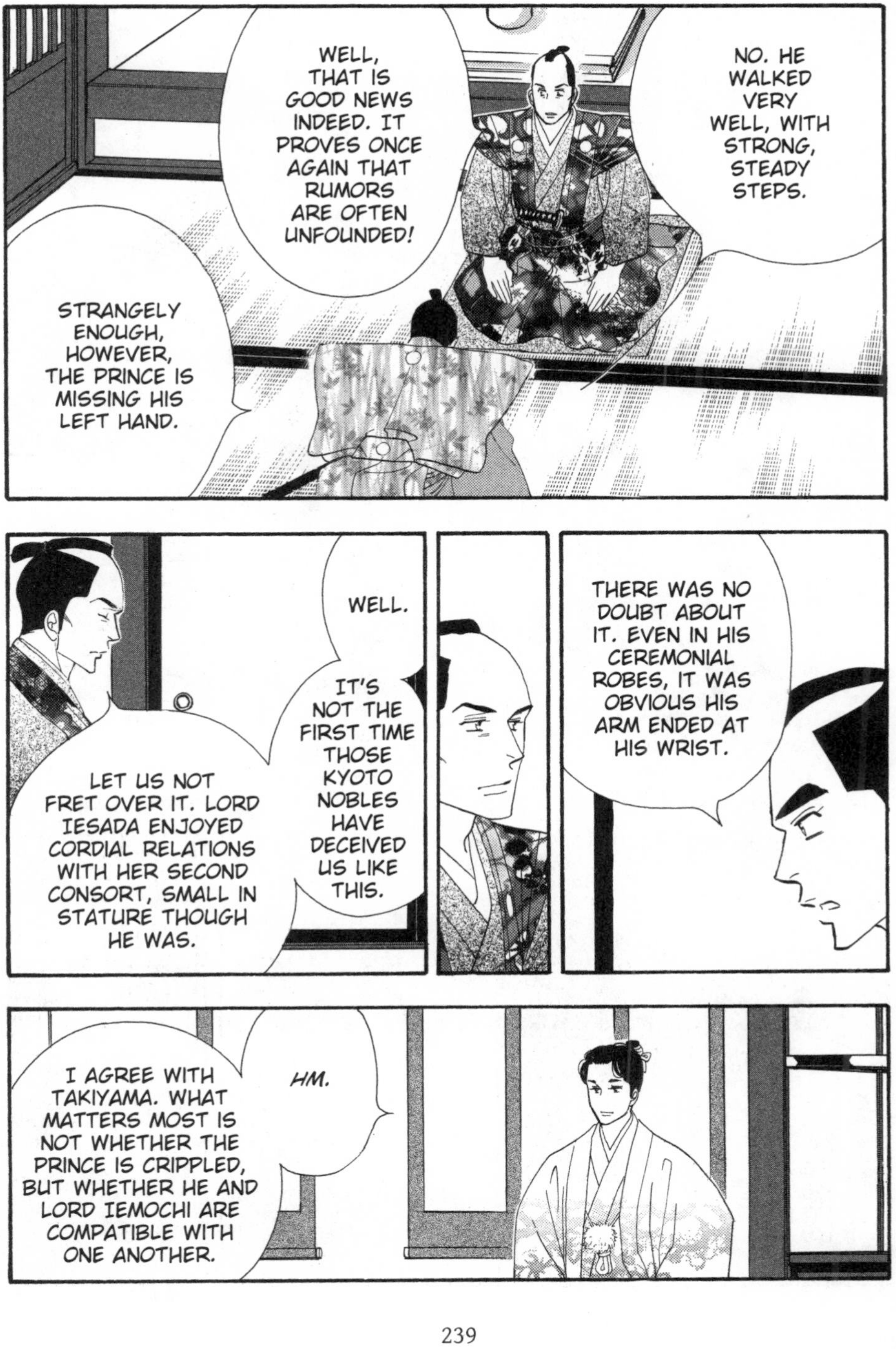
NO. HE WALKED VERY WELL, WITH STRONG, STEADY STEPS.
WELL, THAT IS GOOD NEWS INDEED. IT PROVES ONCE AGAIN THAT RUMORS ARE OFTEN UNFOUNDED!
STRANGELY ENOUGH, HOWEVER, THE PRINCE IS MISSING HIS LEFT HAND.
THERE WAS NO DOUBT ABOUT IT. EVEN IN HIS CEREMONIAL ROBES, IT WAS OBVIOUS HIS ARM ENDED AT HIS WRIST.
WELL.
IT'S NOT THE FIRST TIME THOSE KYOTO NOBLES HAVE DECEIVED US LIKE THIS.
LET US NOT FRET OVER IT. LORD IESADA ENJOYED CORDIAL RELATIONS WITH HER SECOND CONSORT, SMALL IN STATURE THOUGH HE WAS.
HM.
I AGREE WITH TAKIYAMA. WHAT MATTERS MOST IS NOT WHETHER THE PRINCE IS CRIPPLED, BUT WHETHER HE AND LORD IEMOCHI ARE COMPATIBLE WITH ONE ANOTHER.

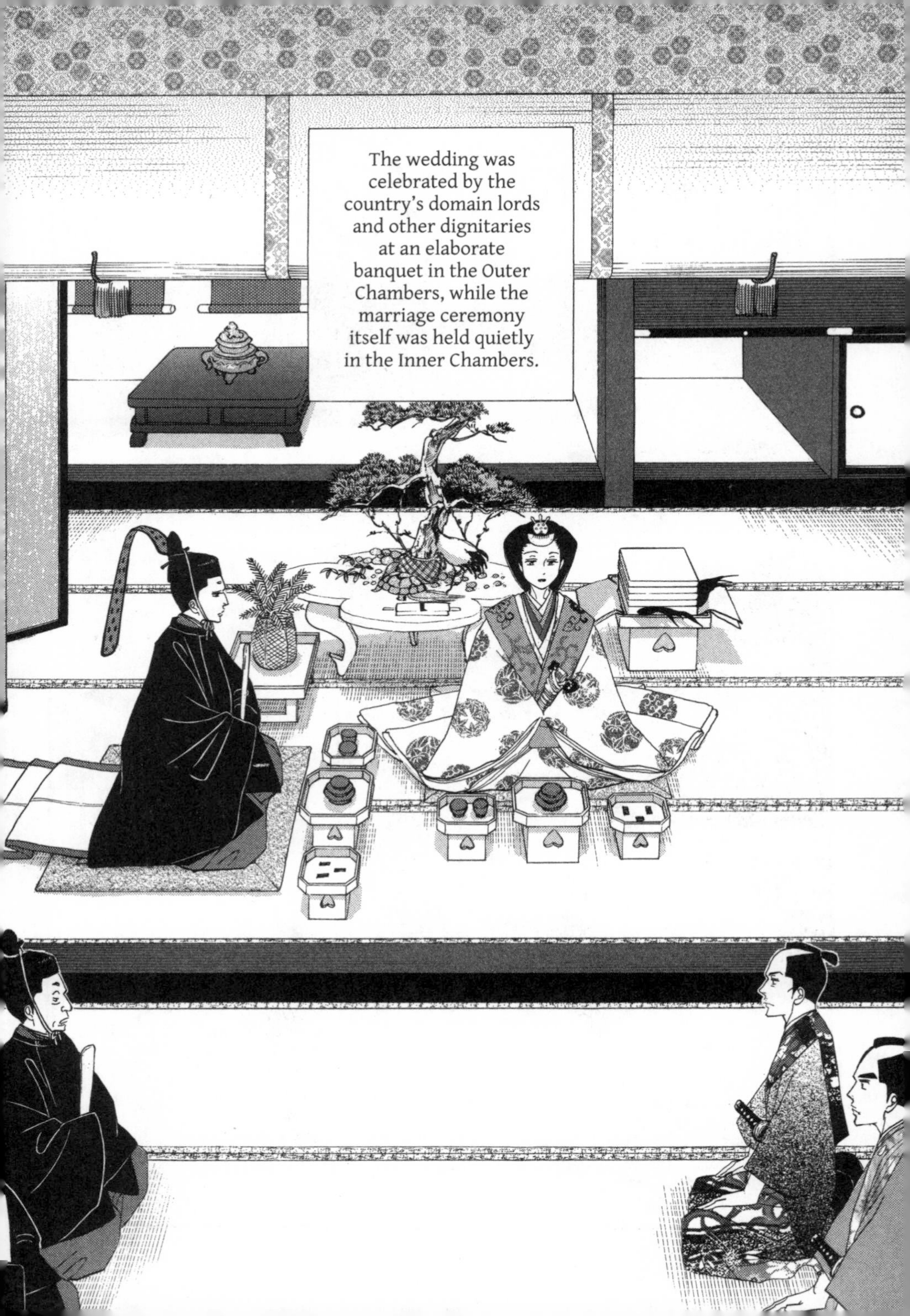
The wedding was celebrated by the country's domain lords and other dignitaries at an elaborate banquet in the Outer Chambers, while the marriage ceremony itself was held quietly in the Inner Chambers.

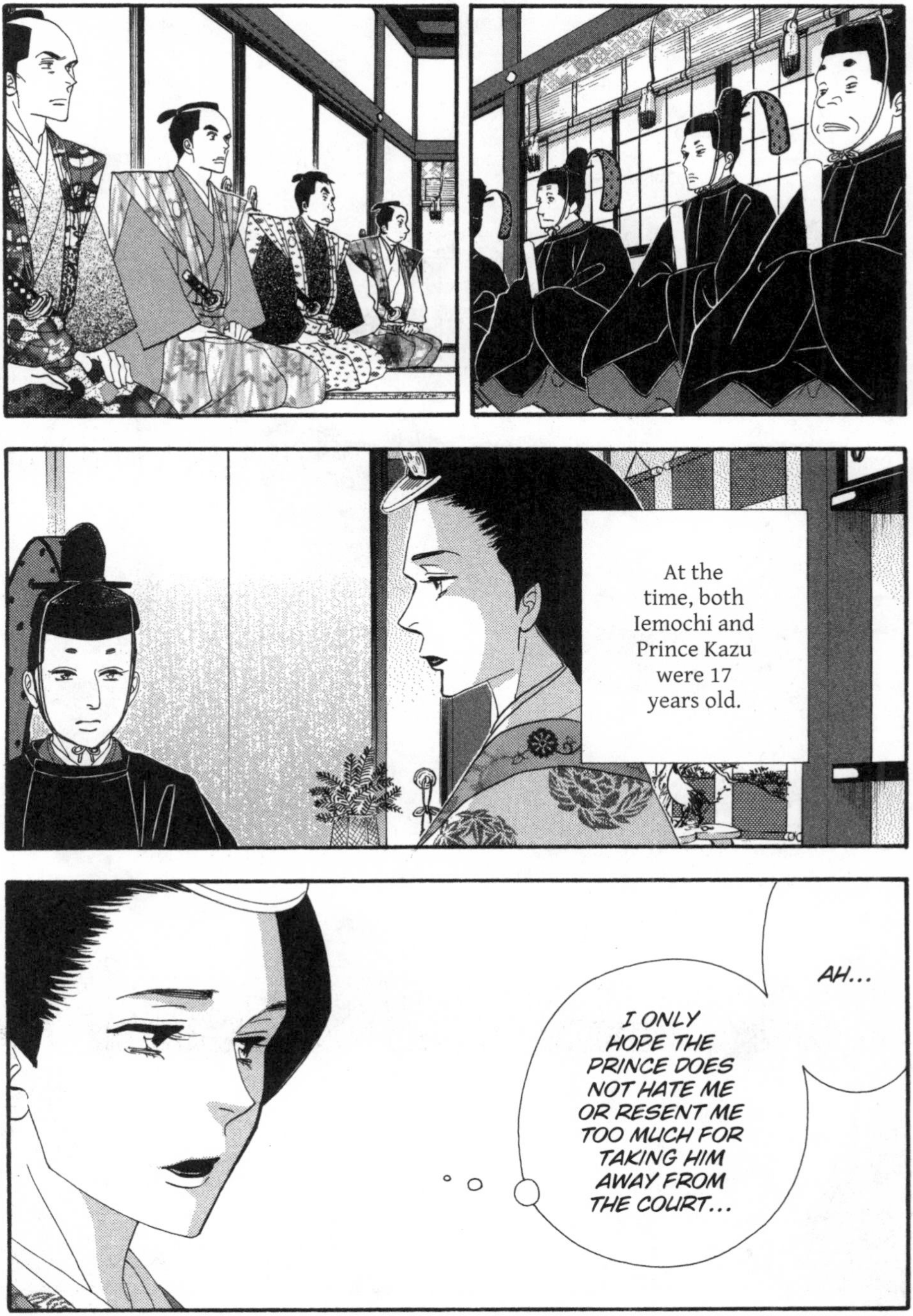
At the time, both Iemochi and Prince Kazu were 17 years old.
AH...
I ONLY HOPE THE PRINCE DOES NOT HATE ME OR RESENT ME TOO MUCH FOR TAKING HIM AWAY FROM THE COURT...

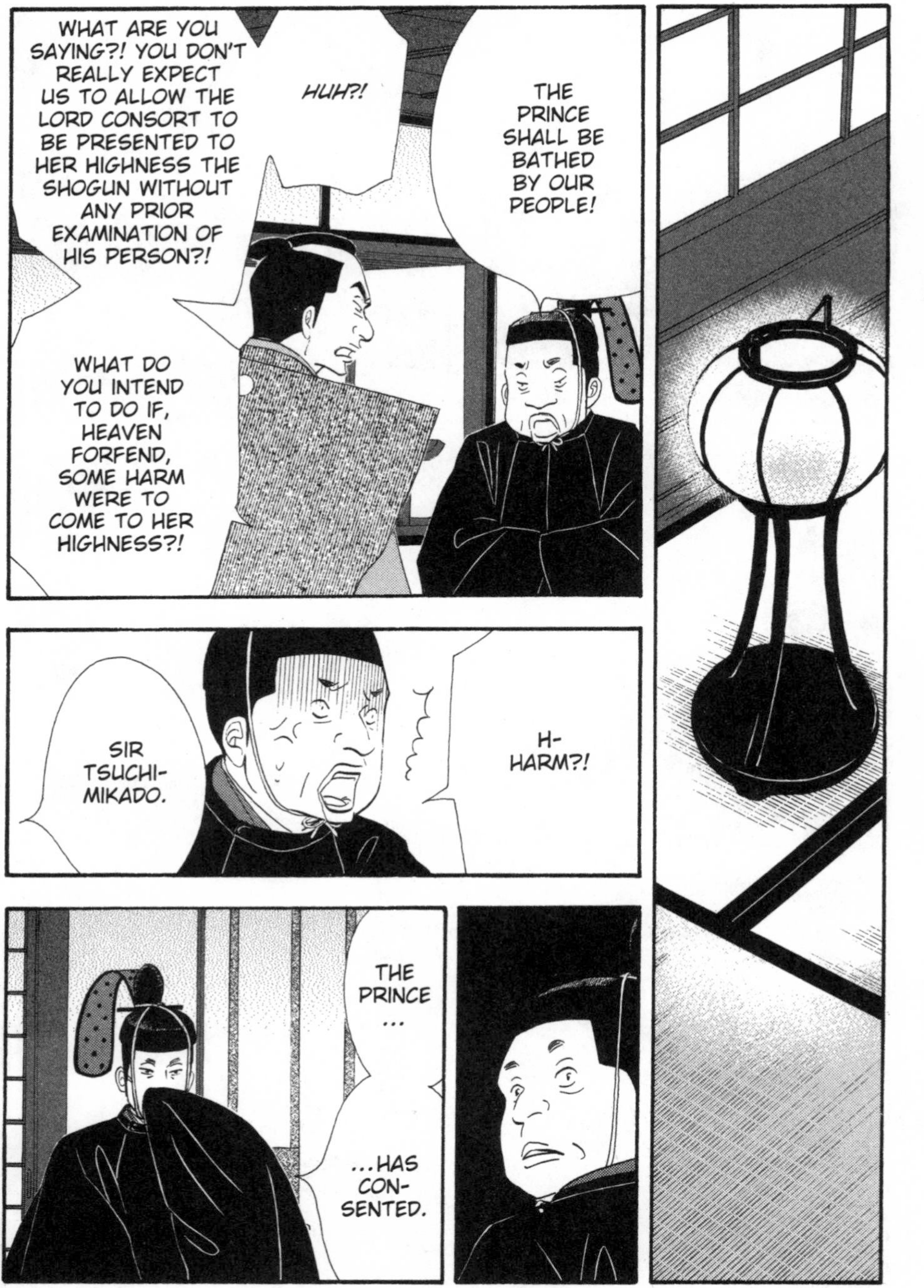
THE PRINCE SHALL BE BATHED BY OUR PEOPLE!
HUH?!
WHAT ARE YOU SAYING?! YOU DON'T REALLY EXPECT US TO ALLOW THE LORD CONSORT TO BE PRESENTED TO HER HIGHNESS THE SHOGUN WITHOUT ANY PRIOR EXAMINATION OF HIS PERSON?!
WHAT DO YOU INTEND TO DO IF, HEAVEN FORFEND, SOME HARM WERE TO COME TO HER HIGHNESS?!
H-HARM?!
SIR TSUCHI-MIKADO.
THE PRINCE ...
...HAS CON-SENTED.

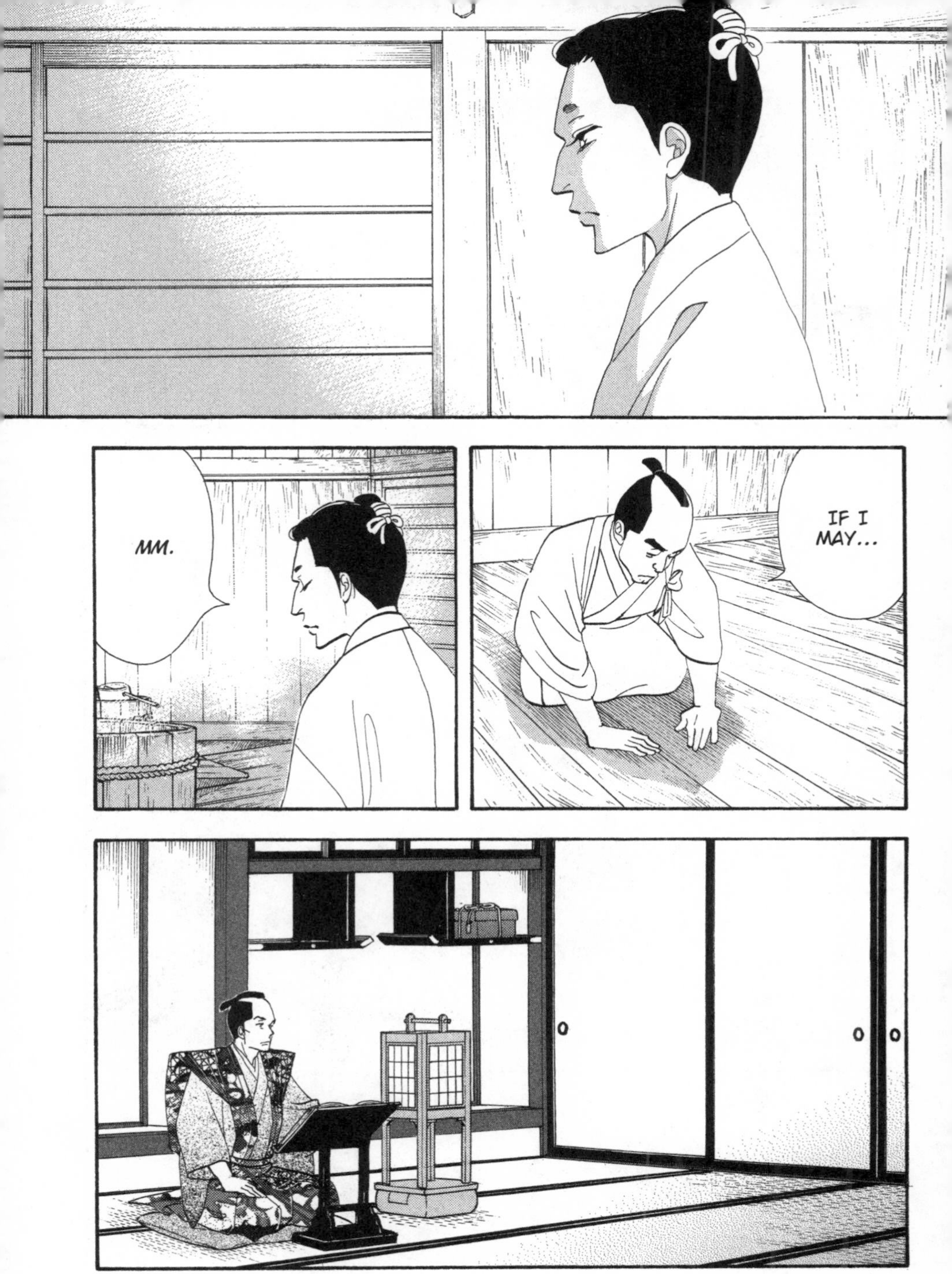
IF I MAY...
MM.

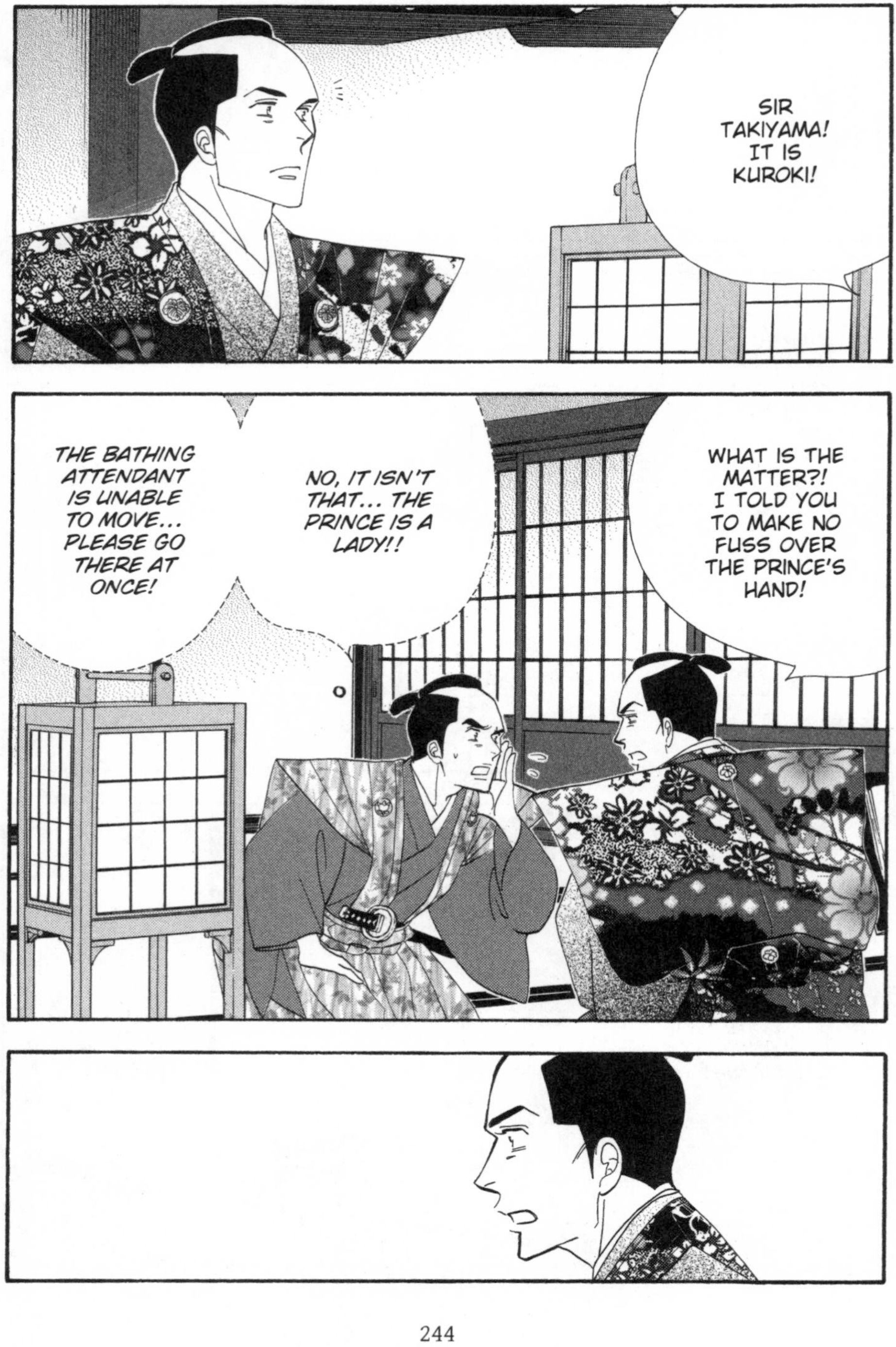
SIR TAKIYAMA! IT IS KUROKI!
WHAT IS THE MATTER?! I TOLD YOU TO MAKE NO FUSS OVER THE PRINCE'S HAND!
NO, IT ISN'T THAT... THE PRINCE IS A LADY!!
THE BATHING ATTENDANT IS UNABLE TO MOVE... PLEASE GO THERE AT ONCE!

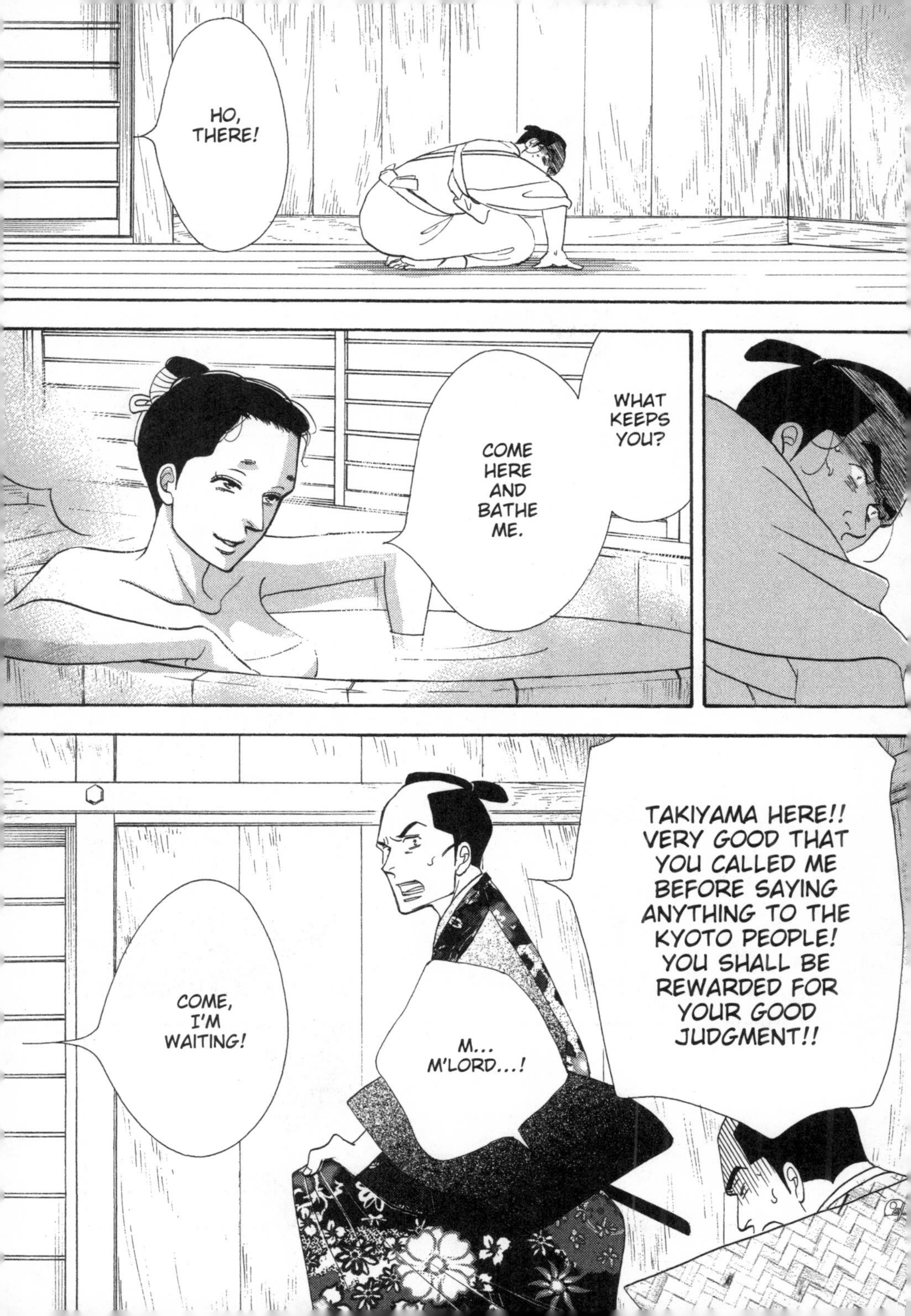
HO, THERE!
WHAT KEEPS YOU?
COME HERE AND BATHE ME.
TAKIYAMA HERE!! VERY GOOD THAT YOU CALLED ME BEFORE SAYING ANYTHING TO THE KYOTO PEOPLE! YOU SHALL BE REWARDED FOR YOUR GOOD JUDGMENT!!
M... M'LORD...!
COME, I'M WAITING!

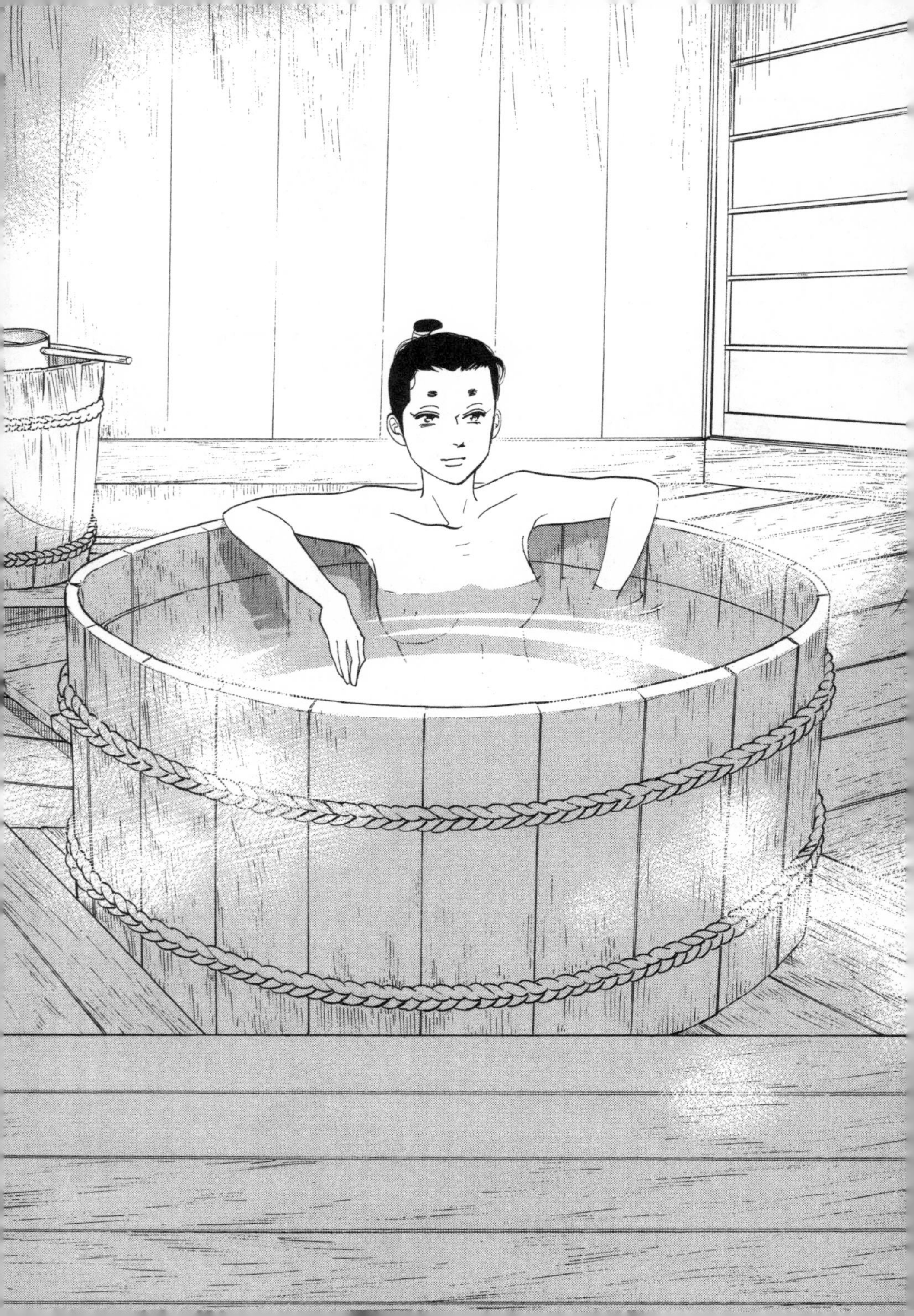

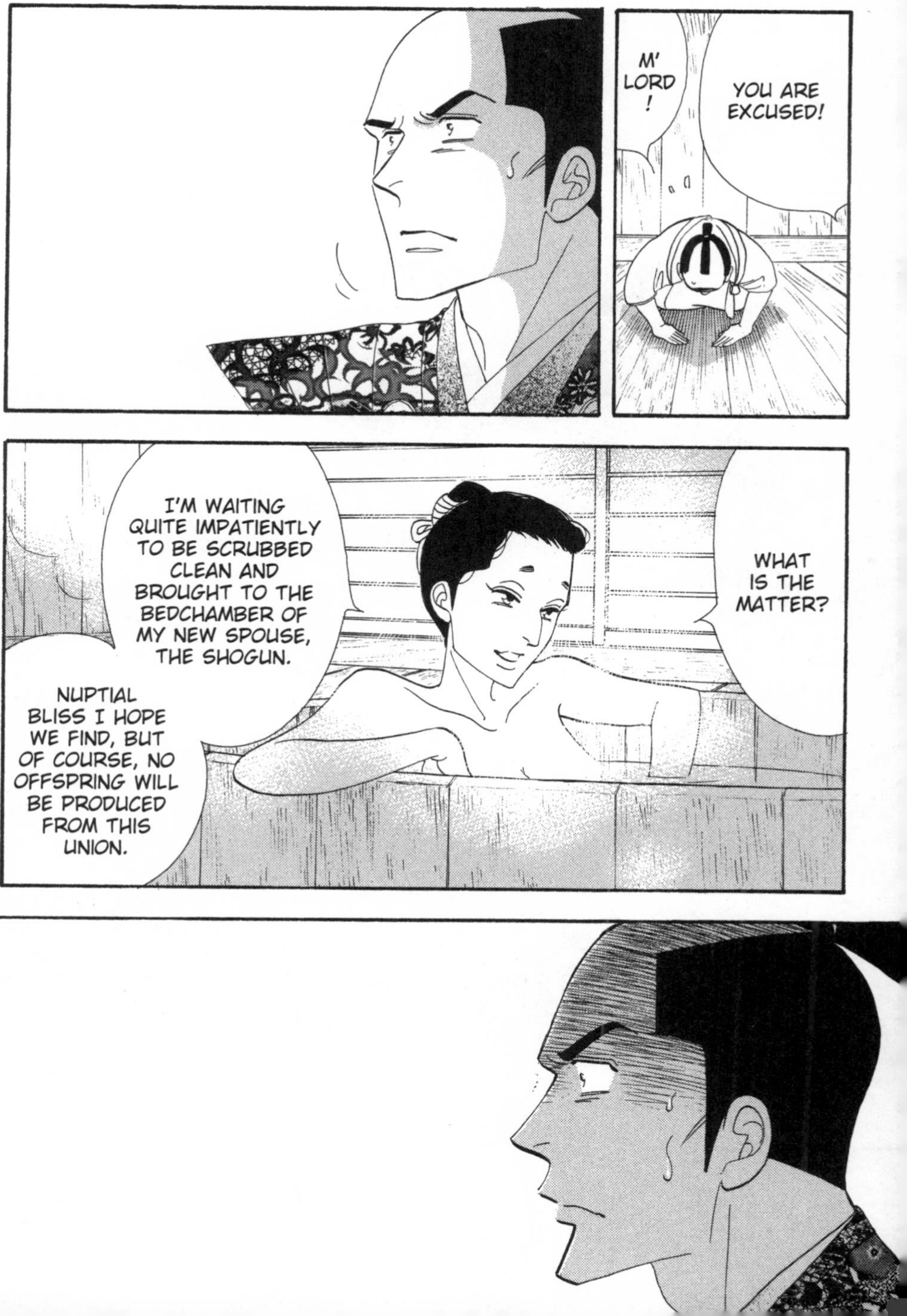
YOU ARE EXCUSED!
M' LORD!
WHAT IS THE MATTER?
I'M WAITING QUITE IMPATIENTLY TO BE SCRUBBED CLEAN AND BROUGHT TO THE BEDCHAMBER OF MY NEW SPOUSE, THE SHOGUN.
NUPTIAL BLISS I HOPE WE FIND, BUT OF COURSE, NO OFFSPRING WILL BE PRODUCED FROM THIS UNION.

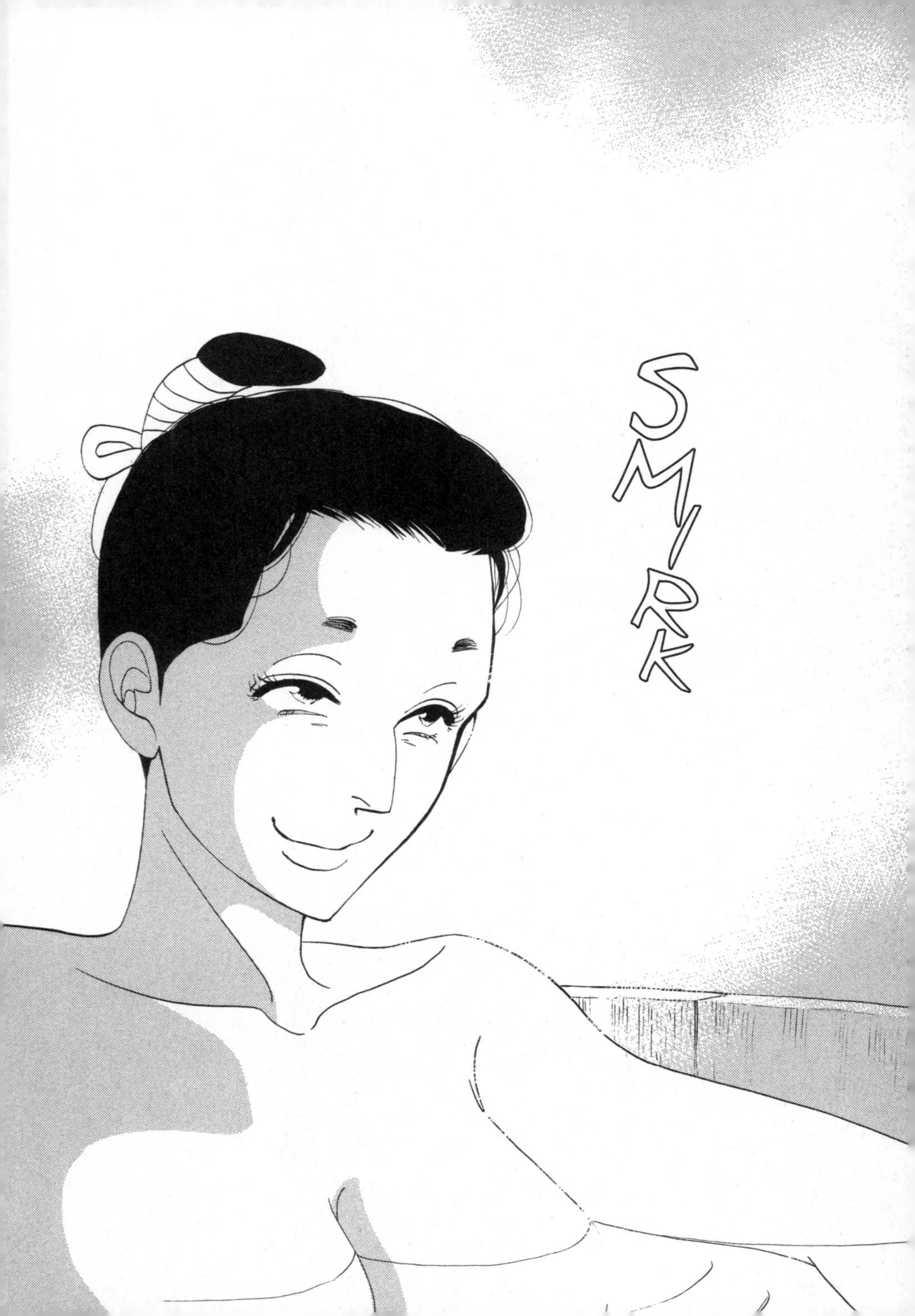
SMIRK

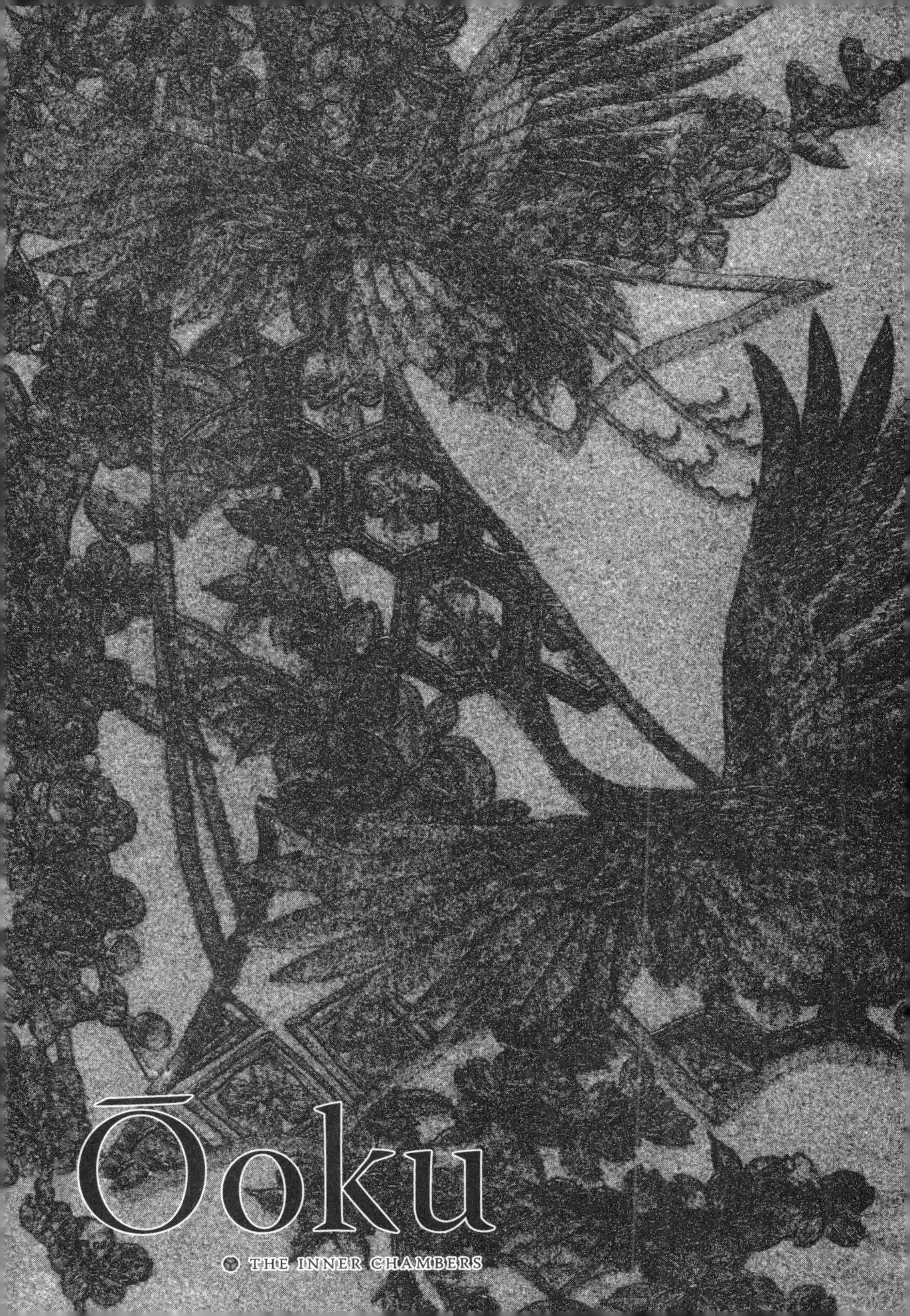
Ōoku
THE INNER CHAMBERS

Ōoku: The Inner Chambers

VOLUME 15 · END NOTES

by Akemi Wegmüller

Page 18, panel 1 · UMEBOSHI

Umeboshi are pickled sour "plums," actually unripe Japanese apricots preserved with salt and red *shiso* leaf. They are said to have antibacterial properties and to aid digestion.

Page 19, panel 4 · CASTELLA

A sponge cake of Portuguese origin, originally brought into Japan through Nagasaki.

PAGE 34, PANEL 3 · KAMISHIMO

A formal suit worn over a kimono, made up of a sleeveless top and *hakama* trousers and worn by samurai during the Edo period.

PAGE 145, PANEL 2 · ANSEI

Ansei was the name of the era that ran from 1854 to 1860.

PAGE 223, PANEL 2 · SATSUMA

Satsuma was the only domain with firearms during this time.

CREATOR BIOGRAPHY

FUMI YOSHINAGA

Fumi Yoshinaga is a Tokyo-born manga creator who de-
buted in 1994 with *Tsuki to Sandaru* (*The Moon and the
Sandals*). Yoshinaga has won numerous awards, includ-
ing the 2009 Osamu Tezuka Cultural Prize for *Ōoku*,
the 2002 Kodansha Manga Award for her series *Antique
Bakery* and the 2006 Japan Media Arts Festival Excel-
lence Award for *Ōoku*. She was also nominated for the
2008 Eisner Award for Best Writer/Artist.

THIS IS THE LAST PAGE.

Ōoku: The Inner Chambers has been printed in the original Japanese format in order to preserve the orientation of the original artwork.

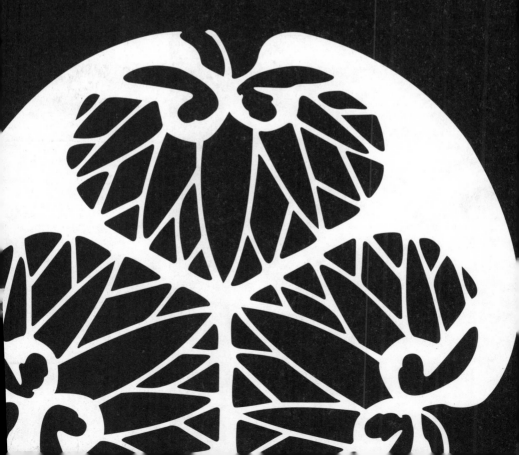

Ōoku

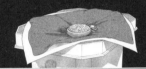

THE INNER CHAMBERS

Ōoku: The Inner Chambers
Vol. 15

VIZ Signature Edition

Story and Art by Fumi Yoshinaga

Translation & Adaptation/Akemi Wegmüller
Touch-up Art & Lettering/Monaliza De Asis
Design/Yukiko Whitley
Editor/Pancha Diaz

Ōoku by Fumi Yoshinaga © Fumi Yoshinaga 2018
All rights reserved. First published in Japan in 2018 by
HAKUSENSHA, Inc., Tokyo. English language translation
rights arranged with HAKUSENSHA, Inc., Tokyo.

Printed in Canada

Published by VIZ Media, LLC
P.O. Box 77010
San Francisco, CA 94107

10 9 8 7 6 5 4 3 2 1
First printing, May 2019

PARENTAL ADVISORY
OOKU: THE INNER CHAMBERS is rated M for
Mature and is recommended for ages 18 and up.
Contains violence and sexual situations.

viz.com

VIZ SIGNATURE
vizsignature.com